Yamaha YZF-R6
Service and Repair Manual

by Phil Mather

Models covered

YZF-R6. 599cc. 1999 to 2002

(3900-256-10AD1)

© Haynes Publishing 2004

A book in the **Haynes Service and Repair Manual Series**

All rights reserved. No part of this book may be reproduced or transmitted in any form or by any means, electronic or mechanical, including photocopying, recording or by any information storage or retrieval system, without permission in writing from the copyright holder.

ISBN **1 85960 900 7**

British Library Cataloguing in Publication Data
A catalogue record for this book is available from the British Library

Library of Congress Catalog Card Number 2001092097

ABCDE
FGHIJ
KLMNO
PQR

Printed in the USA

Haynes Publishing
Sparkford, Yeovil, Somerset BA22 7JJ, England

Haynes North America, Inc
861 Lawrence Drive, Newbury Park, California 91320, USA

Editions Haynes
4, Rue de l'Abreuvoir
92415 COURBEVOIE CEDEX, France

Haynes Publishing Nordiska AB
Box 1504, 751 45 UPPSALA, Sweden

Contents

LIVING WITH YOUR YAMAHA YZF-R6

Introduction
Yamaha – Musical instruments to motorcycles	Page	0•4
Acknowledgements	Page	0•8
About this manual	Page	0•8
Identification numbers	Page	0•9
Buying spare parts	Page	0•9
Performance data and Bike spec	Page	0•10
Safety first!	Page	0•12

Daily (pre-ride checks)
Engine/transmission oil level check	Page	0•13
Brake fluid level checks	Page	0•14
Coolant level check	Page	0•15
Suspension, steering and drive chain checks	Page	0•15
Legal and safety checks	Page	0•15
Tyre checks	Page	0•16

MAINTENANCE

Routine maintenance and servicing
Specifications	Page	1•2
Recommended lubricants and fluids	Page	1•2
Component locations	Page	1•3
Maintenance schedule	Page	1•4
Maintenance procedures	Page	1•6

Contents

REPAIRS AND OVERHAUL

Engine, transmission and associated systems

Engine, clutch and transmission	Page	2•1
Cooling system	Page	3•1
Fuel and exhaust systems	Page	4•1
Ignition system	Page	5•1

Chassis and bodywork components

Frame	Page	6•1
Suspension	Page	6•5
Final drive	Page	6•18
Brakes	Page	7•1
Wheels	Page	7•13
Tyres	Page	7•19
Fairing and bodywork	Page	8•1

Electrical system

Page 9•1

Wiring diagrams

Page 9•22

REFERENCE

Tools and Workshop Tips	Page	REF•2
Security	Page	REF•20
Lubricants and fluids	Page	REF•23
Conversion Factors	Page	REF•26
MOT test checks	Page	REF•27
Storage	Page	REF•32
Fault finding	Page	REF•35
Fault finding equipment	Page	REF•45
Technical terms explained	Page	REF•49

Index

Page REF•53

Introduction

Yamaha
Musical instruments to motorcycles

The FS1E - first bike of many sixteen year olds in the UK

The Yamaha Motor Company

The Yamaha name can be traced back to 1889, when Torakusu Yamaha founded the Yamaha Organ Manufacturing Company. Such was the success of the company, that in 1897 it became Nippon Gakki Limited and manufactured a wide range of reed organs and pianos.

During World War II, Nippon Gakki's manufacturing base was utilised by the Japanese authorities to produce propellers and fuel tanks for their aviation industry. The end of the war brought about a huge public demand for low cost transport and many firms decided to utilise their obsolete aircraft tooling for the production of motorcycles. Nippon Gakki's first motorcycle went on sale in February 1955 and was named the 125 YA-1 Red Dragonfly. This machine was a copy of the German DKW RT125 motorcycle, featuring a single cylinder two-stroke engine with a four-speed gearbox. Due to the outstanding success of this model the motorcycle operation was separated from Nippon Gakki in July 1955 and the Yamaha Motor Company was formed.

The YA-1 also received acclaim by winning two of Japan's biggest road races, the Mount Fuji Climbing race and the Asama Volcano race. The high level of public demand for the YA-1 led to the development of a whole series of two-stroke singles and twins.

Having made a large impact on their home market, Yamahas were exported to the USA in 1958 and to the UK in 1962. In the UK the signing of an Anglo-Japanese trade agreement during 1962 enabled the sale of Japanese lightweight motorcycles and scooters in Britain. At that time, competition between the many motorcycle producers in Japan had reduced numbers significantly and by the end of the sixties, only the big-four which are familiar with today remained.

Yamaha Europe was founded in 1968 and based in Holland. Although originally set up to market marine products, the Dutch base is now the official European Headquarters and distribution centre. Yamaha motorcycles are built at factories in Holland, Denmark, Norway, Italy, France, Spain and Portugal. Yamahas are imported into the UK by Yamaha Motor UK Ltd, formerly Mitsui Machinery Sales (UK) Ltd. Mitsui and Co. were originally a trading house, handling the shipping, distribution and marketing of Japanese products into western countries. Ultimately Mitsui Machinery Sales was formed to handle Yamaha motorcycles and outboard motors.

Based on the technology derived from its motorcycle operation, Yamaha have produced many other products, such as automobile and lightweight aircraft engines, marine engines and boats, generators, pumps, ATVs, snowmobiles, golf cars, industrial robots, lawnmowers, swimming pools and archery equipment.

Two-strokes first

Part of Yamaha's success was a whole string of innovations in the two-stroke world. Autolube engine lubrication, torque induction, multi-ported engines, reed valves and power valves kept their two-strokes at the forefront of technology. Many advances were achieved with the use of racing as a development laboratory. They went to the USA in the late 1950s with an air-cooled 250cc twin but didn't hit the GPs until the early 1960s when Fumio Ito scored a hat-trick of sixth places in the Isle of Man TT, the Dutch TT and the Belgian GP. This experiment gave rise to the idea of the over-the-counter racer, an idea that became reality in the TD1, the first in an unmatched series of two-stroke racers that were the standard issue for privateers at national and international level for years and helped Yamaha develop their road engines. While privateers raced the twins, Yamaha built the outrageously complicated vee-four 250 for Phil Read and followed it with a vee-four 125 that Bill Ivy lapped the Isle of Man on at over 100mph! When the FIM regulations were changed to limit the smaller GP classes to two cylinders, these exotic bikes died but set the scene for an unparalleled dynasty of mass-produced racers based on the same technology as the road bikes.

In the 1960s and 70s the two-stroke engined YAS3 125, YDS1 to YDS7 250 and YR5 350 formed the core of Yamaha's range. By the mid-70s they had been superseded by the RD (Race-Developed) 125, 250, and 350 range of two-stroke twins, featuring improved 7-port engines with reed valve induction. Braking was improved by the use of an hydraulic brake on the front wheel of DX models, instead of the drum arrangement used previously, and cast alloy wheels were available as an option on later RD models. The RD350 was replaced by the RD400 in 1976.

Running parallel with the RD twins was a range of single-cylinder two-strokes. Used in a variety of chassis types, the engine was used in the popular 50 cc FS1-E moped, the V50 to 90 step-thrus, RS100 and 125, YB100 and the DT trail range.

The TD racers got water-cooling in 1973 to become the TZs, the most successful and numerous over-the-counter racers ever built. That same year, Jarno Saarinen became the first rider to win a 500cc GP on a four-cylinder two-stroke on the new in-line four which was effectively a pair of TZs side-by-side. TZs won everywhere – including the Daytona 200 and 500 races when overbored to 351cc. A 700cc TZ also appeared, one year later taken out to 750cc. Steve Baker won the first Formula 750 world title – one of the precursors of Superbike – on one in 1977. The following year Kenny Roberts won Yamaha's first world 500 title and would be succeeded by Wayne Rainey and Eddie Lawson before Mick Doohan and the NSR500 took over.

The air-cooled single and twin cylinder RD road bikes were eventually replaced by the LC series in 1980, featuring liquid-cooled engines, radical new styling, spiral pattern cast wheels and cantilever rear suspension (Yamaha's Monoshock). Of all the LC models, the RD350LC, or RD350R as it was later known, has made the most impact in the market. Later models had YPVS (Yamaha Power Valve System) engines, another first for Yamaha – this was essentially a valve located in the exhaust ports which was electronically operated to alter port timing to achieve maximum power output. The RD500LC was the largest two-stroke made by Yamaha and differed from the other LCs by the use of its vee-four cylinder engine.

With the exception of the RD350R, now manufactured in Brazil, the LC range has been discontinued. Two-stroke engined models have given way to environmental pressure, and thus with a few exceptions, such as the TZR125 and TZR250, are used only in scooters and small capacity bikes.

The distinctive paintwork and trim of the RD models

Introduction

The Four-strokes

Yamaha concentrated solely on two-stroke models until 1970 when the XS1 was produced, their first four-stroke motorcycle. It was perhaps Yamaha's success with two-strokes that postponed an earlier move into the four-stroke motorcycle market, although their work with Toyota during the 1960s had given them a sound base in four-stroke technology.

The XS1 had a 650 cc twin-cylinder SOHC engine and was later to become known as the XS650, appearing also in the popular SE custom form. Yamaha introduced a three cylinder 750 cc engine in 1976, fitted in a sport-tourer frame and called the XS750, TX750 in the USA. The XS750 established itself well in the sport tourer class and remained in production with very few changes until uprated to 850 cc in 1980.

Other four-strokes followed in 1976, with the introduction of the XS250/360/400 series twins. The XS range was strengthened in 1978 by the four-cylinder XS1100.

The 1980s saw a new family of four-strokes, the XJ550, 650, 750 and 900 Fours. Improvements over the XS range amounted to a slimmer DOHC engine unit due to the relocation of the alternator behind the cylinders, electronic ignition and uprated braking and suspension systems. Models were available mainly in standard trim, although custom-styled Maxims were produced especially for the US market. The

The XS650 led the way for Yamaha's four-stroke range

XJ650T was the first model from Yamaha to have a turbo-charged engine. Although these early XJ models have now been discontinued, their roots live on in the XJ600S and XJ900S Diversion (Seca II) models.

The FZR prefix encompasses the pure sports Yamaha models. With the exception of the 16-valve FZR400 and FZR600 models, the FZ/FZR750 and FZR1000 used 20-valve engines, two exhaust valves and three inlet

Yamaha's XS750 was produced from 1976 to 1982 and then uprated to 850 cc

Introduction 0•7

valves per cylinder. This concept was called Genesis and gave improved gas flow to the combustion chambers. Other features of the new engine were the use of down-draught carburetors and the engine's inclined angle in the frame, plus the change to liquid-cooling. Lightweight Deltabox design aluminium frames and uprated suspension improved the bikes's handling. The Genesis engine lives on in the YZF750 and 1000 models.

The Genesis concept was the basis of Yamaha's foray into four-stroke racing, first with a bike known simply as 'The Genesis', an FZ750 motor in a TT Formula 1 bike with which the factory attempted to steal the Honda RVF750's thunder at important events like the Suzuka 8 Hours and the Bol d'Or although they never fielded it for a whole World Championship season. That had to wait for the advent of the World Superbike Championship, although there was no full works team until 1995, instead it was left to individual importers to support teams. It was the Australian Dealer Team Yamaha which scored the factory's first World Superbike win in the series debut year of 1988. The rider? Mick Doohan. Slightly, embarrassingly, it was the steel framed FZ750 rather than the FZR homologation special that won races. The OW01 was a race winner, mainly in the hands of Fabrizio Pirovano, the factory's most successful Superbike racer with ten victories, but national success in the UK, Japan, and in the Daytona 200 has not been translated into World Championships for any of Yamaha's 750s.

The vee-twin engine has been the mainstay of the XV Virago range. Since 1981 XVs have been produced in 535, 700, 750, 920, 1000 and 1100 engine sizes, all using the same basic air-cooled sohc vee-twin engine. Other uses of vee engines have been in the XZ550 of the early 1980s, the XVZ12 Venture and the mighty VMX-12 V-Max.

A new family of four-strokes was released in 1980 with the introduction of the XJ range

Yamaha has always been a sporting-orientated company whose motto could be 'Racing Improves the Breed', so it's no surprise that the latest generation of lightweight sportsters are at the cutting edge of performance on and off the track. The R6 won more races than any other machine in the inaugural year of the World Supersports Championship, the R7 won a race in its debut year in World Superbike in the hands of the mercurial Noriyuki Haga, and the mighty 1000cc R1 ended Honda's domination of the Isle of Man F1 TT when David Jefferies won three races in a week in 1999.

In Grand Prix racing, the factory took several years to get over the shock of Wayne Rainey's crippling accident. and first 500cc win since the American's enforced retirement didn't come until 1998 when Simon Crafar won at Donington Park. For 1999, Yamaha refocussed their ambitions and signed Italian superstar Max Biaggi plus Spanish trier Carlos Checa for the works team, while dashing young Frenchman Regis Laconi and tough little Aussie Gary McCoy rode for the WCM satellite team. Both teams got a win in the '99 season and with a new TZ250 being developed for 2000 it looks as if Yamaha's spirit of competition will go on unabated into the new Millenium.

The XV535 Virago vee-twin

Introduction

Yamaha YZF-R6 – who needs a 750?

Yamaha already had three 600s in the range when they launched the R6 – the Thundercat, the Fazer and the Diversion, so why did they need another one? The answer is simple: to win the World Supersport Championship. The mould-destroying R1 had already firmly planted itself at the top of the Supersports tree when its little brother arrived looking just like, well… a little R1.

The relationship was more than skin-deep, the same philosophy drove the design: high power and light weight. At 169 kg, the R6 was an astonishing 18 kg lighter than the Thundercat and made over 120 hp at the crank (allegedly, Yamaha did honk on a bit about the R6 being the first road bike to make 200 hp/litre). Ultimate top-end power actually only arrived with help from the new ram-air system which was reckoned to boost peak power by around ten per cent; trouble is you have to be travelling at 150 mph to take advantage.

The 600 got the same tarmac-warping four-piston brake calipers as the big bike and the same piggybacked gearbox shafts that keep the engine short and allow a very long swingarm, and the crankcase is cast in one piece for stiffness, again like the R1, to allow the motor to be used as a stressed member of the frame. For efficient combustion at engine speeds up to the 15,500 rpm red line, the R6 got a coil per cylinder and new twin-electrode spark plugs. What's the R1 got that the R6 hasn't? Upside-down front forks, five valves per cylinder and EXUP. Penny-pinching? Not really. Yamaha reckoned upside-down forks were too stiff, and there simply isn't room for five valves in the 600's cylinder head. If one omission had a cost element it's the EXUP, although weight was a consideration here too. But face it, tractability isn't an issue on a bike like the R6. No doubt about it, the R6 is as hard-edged a sportster as you could buy. If you go back a generation of Yamaha sportsters, then the R6 was to the R1 what the FZR600R was to the YZF600R.

No doubt about it, Yamaha were serious about Supersport racing, especially the newly minted World Championship, no fewer than three teams fronted for the inaugural season armed with factory supplied R6s. Everyone else took it seriously too, the other three Japanese factories, plus Ducati and Bimota, entered official teams and while an R6 saw the flag first more than any other bike, therefore winning Yamaha the manufacturers' championship, the number of different riders on them meant the title went to Suzuki. British fans were delighted that Yamaha's first winner was the ever-popular James Whitham, who won the British round at Donington Park in a one-off ride. Other R6 winners were Jorg Teuchert (twice), Wilco Zeelenberg, Piergiorgio Bontempi, and Rueben Xaus.

That changed in 2000 when Yamaha won five of the 11 rounds but took the title thanks to lanky German ex-enduro ace Teuchert. The fact he won it on the last lap of the last round of the year is indicative of how competitive the Supersport class is, not just on the track but off it too.

The 600 cc four-cylinder class is the biggest in terms of world-wide sales volume for the big four Japanese manufacturers. It is big enough to have sub-divisions, niches even, which allow for such single-minded machines as the R6 to be designed and sold alongside much softer but closely related bikes like the Diversion. It is a class in which getting it right means big sales and getting it wrong means wasting a lot of corporate funds and development time. The Yamaha R6 went straight for the extreme end of the 600 cc spectrum as the engine's performance figures tell you: hardly any power or torque below 8000 rpm, peak torque at just over 11,000, peak power at over 12,000, and the ability to rev on to over 15,000 rpm.

Apart from a few minor modifications in 2000, which were impervious to the eye, the R6 did not get an update until 2001 when 1.5 kg was shaved of its weight by the fitting of an aluminium steering stem, plus reduced weight exhaust and electrical components. Twin circular LED tail lights completed the rear bodywork redesign.

Acknowledgements

Our thanks are due to Bransons Motorcycles of Yeovil who supplied the machines featured in the illustrations throughout this manual. We would also like to thank NGK Spark Plugs (UK) Ltd for supplying the colour spark plug condition photographs, the Avon Rubber Company for supplying information on tyre fitting and Draper Tools Ltd for some of the workshop tools shown.

Thanks are also due to Yamaha Motor (UK) Ltd who supplied some of the photographs used on the cover, and to Julian Ryder who wrote the introduction 'Musical Instruments to Motorcycles'.

About this manual

The aim of this manual is to help you get the best value from your motorcycle. It can do so in several ways. It can help you decide what work must be done, even if you choose to have it done by a dealer; it provides information and procedures for routine maintenance and servicing; and it offers diagnostic and repair procedures to follow when trouble occurs.

We hope you use the manual to tackle the work yourself. For many simpler jobs, doing it yourself may be quicker than arranging an appointment to get the motorcycle into a dealer and making the trips to leave it and pick it up. More importantly, a lot of money can be saved by avoiding the expense the shop must pass on to you to cover its labour and overhead costs. An added benefit is the sense of satisfaction and accomplishment that you feel after doing the job yourself.

References to the left or right side of the motorcycle assume you are sitting on the seat, facing forward.

We take great pride in the accuracy of information given in this manual, but motorcycle manufacturers make alterations and design changes during the production run of a particular motorcycle of which they do not inform us. No liability can be accepted by the authors or publishers for loss, damage or injury caused by any errors in, or omissions from, the information given.

The 1999 model in red/white

The revamped 2001 model in blue/white

Identification numbers 0•9

Frame and engine numbers

The frame serial number is stamped into the right-hand side of the steering head. The engine number is stamped into the rear of the crankcase. The model code label is on the top of the sub-frame cross-piece under the passenger seat. These numbers should be recorded and kept in a safe place so they can be furnished to law enforcement officials in the event of a theft. There is also a carburettor identification number on the intake side of each carburettor body.

The frame serial number, engine serial number, carburettor identification number and model code should be recorded and kept in a handy place (such as with your driver's licence) so that they are always available when purchasing or ordering parts for your machine.

The procedures in this manual identify the bikes by year and model (e.g. 1999 YZF-R6). The model codes for all years and models covered are tabled below. Where available, the initial frame and engine numbers are also given.

Buying spare parts

Once you have found all the identification numbers, record them for reference when buying parts. Since the manufacturers change specifications, parts and vendors (companies that manufacture various components on the machine), providing the ID numbers is the only way to be reasonably sure that you are buying the correct parts.

Whenever possible, take the worn part to the dealer so direct comparison with the new component can be made. Along the trail from the manufacturer to the parts shelf, there are numerous places that the part can end up with the wrong number or be listed incorrectly.

The two places to purchase new parts for your motorcycle – the accessory store and the franchised dealer – differ in the type of parts they carry. While dealers can obtain virtually every part for your motorcycle, the accessory dealer is usually limited to normal high wear items such as shock absorbers, tune-up parts, various engine gaskets, cables, chains, brake parts, etc. Rarely will an accessory outlet have major suspension components, cylinders, transmission gears, or cases.

Used parts can be obtained for roughly half the price of new ones, but you can't always be sure of what you're getting. Once again, take your worn part to the breaker's yard for direct comparison.

Whether buying new, used or rebuilt parts, the best course is to deal directly with someone who specialises in parts for your particular make.

UK/Europe models	Code
1999	5EB1 (5EB2 – Austria/Finland/Norway)
2000	5EB5 (5EB6 – Austria/Finland/Norway)
2001	5MT1 (5MT2 – Austria/Finland/Norway)
2002	5MTB (5MTC – Austria/Finland/Norway)

US models	Year	Code
YZF-R6L – 49 State	1999	5GV1
YZF-R6CL – California	1999	5GV2
YZF-R6M – 49-state	2000	5EB1
YZF-R6ML – California	2000	5EB2
YZF-R6N – 49 State	2001	5MT5
YZF-R6NC – California	2001	5MT6
YZF-R6P – 49 State	2002	5MTF
YZF-R6PC – California	2002	5MTG

The model code label is stuck to the rear sub-frame (arrowed)

The frame number is stamped into the right-hand side of the steering head

The engine number is stamped into the rear of the crankcase

0•10 Performance data and Bike spec

Performance data

Maximum power ....101.7 bhp (75.8 kW) @ 12,600 rpm

Maximum torque ....44.8 lbf ft (60.7 Nm) @ 10,800 rpm

Power to weight ratio ....600 bhp per tonne (0.45 kW per kg)

Top speed ....162 mph (261 kmh)

Acceleration
  Time taken to cover a 1/4 mile from a standing start ....11 seconds
  Terminal speed after 1/4 mile ....129 mph (208 kmh)

Average fuel consumption
  Miles per Imp gal, miles per litre,
  litres per 100 km ....34 mpg, 7.5 mpl, 8.3 l/100 km

Fuel tank range ....127 miles (204 km) –
  based on average fuel consumption rate

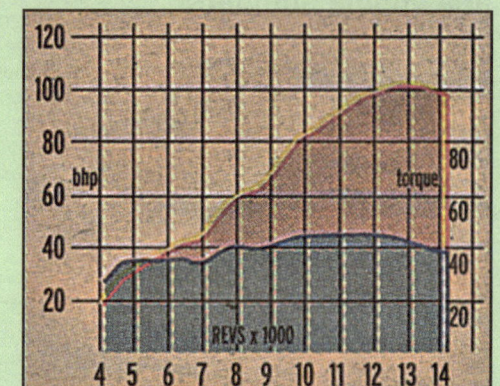

Performance data sourced from Motor Cycle News road test features. See the MCN website for up-to-date biking news.

MCN www.motorcyclenews.com

Bike spec

Dimensions and weights

Overall length ....2025 mm (79.7 in)
Overall width ....690 mm (27.2 in)
Overall height ....1105 mm (43.5 in)
Wheelbase
  California market models ....1385 mm (54.5 in)
  All other market models ....1380 mm (54.3 in)
Seat height ....820 mm (32.3 in)
Ground clearance ....135 mm (5.3 in)

Weight – 1999 and 2000 models
  Dry weight ....169 kg (373 lb)
  Wet weight (with oil and full fuel tank) ....188 kg (415 lb)
Weight – 2001-on models
  Dry weight ....167 kg (368 lb)
  Wet weight (with oil and full fuel tank) ....186 kg (410 lb)
Maximum load
  (rider, passenger, luggage, accessories) ....187 kg (412 lb)

Performance data and bike spec 0•11

Engine
Type	Four-stroke 16V in-line four
Capacity	599 cc
Bore	65.5 mm
Stroke	44.5 mm
Compression ratio	12.4 to 1
Cooling system	Liquid cooled
Clutch	Wet multi-plate
Transmission	Six-speed constant mesh
Final drive	Chain and sprockets
Camshafts	DOHC, chain-driven
Carburettors	4 x 37 mm Keihin CVRD37
Ignition system	Electronic dc CDI

Chassis
Frame type	Twin spar aluminium Deltabox II
Rake and trail	24°, 81 mm
Fuel tank capacity (including reserve)	17 litres (3.74 Imp gal, 4.48 US gal)
Front suspension	
Type	43 mm oil-damped telescopic forks
Travel	130 mm (5.1 in)
Adjustment	Pre-load, compression and rebound damping
Rear suspension	
Type	Single shock absorber, rising rate linkage, box-section aluminium swingarm
Travel	60 mm (2.4 in)
Adjustment	Pre-load, compression and rebound damping
Wheels	17 inch 3-spoke alloys
Tyres	
Front	120/60 x 17 Radial
Rear	180/55 x 17 Radial
Front brake	Twin 295 mm discs with Sumitomo 4-piston opposed calipers
Rear brake	Single 220 mm disc with Sumitomo 2-piston sliding caliper

Model development

1999

The YZF-R6 was launched in December 1998 for the 1999 model year.

The R6 features an extremely lightweight in-line four cylinder engine. Drive to the hollow double overhead camshafts which actuate the four valves per cylinder is by chain from the right-hand end of the crankshaft. The engine is liquid-cooled. The clutch is a conventional wet multi-plate unit and the gearbox is 6-speed. Engine length is kept to a minimum by 'stacking' the transmission shafts, thus enabling a short wheelbase. Drive to the rear wheel is by chain and sprockets.

The engine gets its fuel and air via four 37 mm CV carburettors, and this is ignited by an electronic dc CDI system which uses combined 'stick' style ignition coils and spark plug caps. The exhaust system is a four-into-one design.

The engine sits in a Yamaha's twin spar aluminium Deltabox II style frame which uses the engine as a stressed member. Front suspension is by oil-damped 43 mm forks which have cartridge type dampers. Rear suspension is by a single shock absorber via a rising rate linkage to the truss-type aluminium swingarm.

Braking is via Sumitomo calipers front and rear, with twin 295 mm floating discs at the front and a single 220 mm disc at the rear.

Styling and bodywork are based heavily on its larger stablemate, the YZF-R1. Colours: Bluish White Cocktail 1, Silver Metallic 1 and Deep Purplish Blue Metallic C.

2000

Changes amounted to new pistons with a modified oil ring, minor modifications to the gearchange mechanism, and a revised top mounting for the rear shock absorber.
Bluish White Cocktail 1 and Deep Purplish Blue Metallic C.

2001

The first major change to the R6 came in 2001.

Modifications were made to the piston and connecting rod design, but the engine was otherwise unchanged.

The most noticeable change to the chassis components was the redesigned rear end bodywork and hugger, and to the tail light which featured two circular LED units. A weight saving of 1.5 kg had been achieved by the use of an aluminium steering stem and nut, lighter exhaust header pipes and a more compact battery and ignition control unit.

Rear view visibility was improved by the fitting of longer stem mirrors, a storage space was provided under the seat for a U-lock and fold-away luggage hooks were fitted under the passenger seat. Instrument was improved in line with that fitted to the YZF-R1 and the speedometer featured an R6 decal.

The graphics were revised and colours were Vivid Red Cocktail 1 and Deep Purplish Blue Metallic C.

2002

There were no significant changes for 2002. The only cosmetic change was the black finish of the fairing top section.

Safety First!

Professional mechanics are trained in safe working procedures. However enthusiastic you may be about getting on with the job at hand, take the time to ensure that your safety is not put at risk. A moment's lack of attention can result in an accident, as can failure to observe simple precautions.

There will always be new ways of having accidents, and the following is not a comprehensive list of all dangers; it is intended rather to make you aware of the risks and to encourage a safe approach to all work you carry out on your bike.

Asbestos

● Certain friction, insulating, sealing and other products - such as brake pads, clutch linings, gaskets, etc. - contain asbestos. Extreme care must be taken to avoid inhalation of dust from such products since it is hazardous to health. If in doubt, assume that they do contain asbestos.

Fire

● Remember at all times that petrol is highly flammable. Never smoke or have any kind of naked flame around, when working on the vehicle. But the risk does not end there - a spark caused by an electrical short-circuit, by two metal surfaces contacting each other, by careless use of tools, or even by static electricity built up in your body under certain conditions, can ignite petrol vapour, which in a confined space is highly explosive. Never use petrol as a cleaning solvent. Use an approved safety solvent.

● Always disconnect the battery earth terminal before working on any part of the fuel or electrical system, and never risk spilling fuel on to a hot engine or exhaust.

● It is recommended that a fire extinguisher of a type suitable for fuel and electrical fires is kept handy in the garage or workplace at all times. Never try to extinguish a fuel or electrical fire with water.

Fumes

● Certain fumes are highly toxic and can quickly cause unconsciousness and even death if inhaled to any extent. Petrol vapour comes into this category, as do the vapours from certain solvents such as trichloroethylene. Any draining or pouring of such volatile fluids should be done in a well ventilated area.

● When using cleaning fluids and solvents, read the instructions carefully. Never use materials from unmarked containers - they may give off poisonous vapours.

● Never run the engine of a motor vehicle in an enclosed space such as a garage. Exhaust fumes contain carbon monoxide which is extremely poisonous; if you need to run the engine, always do so in the open air or at least have the rear of the vehicle outside the workplace.

The battery

● Never cause a spark, or allow a naked light near the vehicle's battery. It will normally be giving off a certain amount of hydrogen gas, which is highly explosive.

● Always disconnect the battery ground (earth) terminal before working on the fuel or electrical systems (except where noted).

● If possible, loosen the filler plugs or cover when charging the battery from an external source. Do not charge at an excessive rate or the battery may burst.

● Take care when topping up, cleaning or carrying the battery. The acid electrolyte, evenwhen diluted, is very corrosive and should not be allowed to contact the eyes or skin. Always wear rubber gloves and goggles or a face shield. If you ever need to prepare electrolyte yourself, always add the acid slowly to the water; never add the water to the acid.

Electricity

● When using an electric power tool, inspection light etc., always ensure that the appliance is correctly connected to its plug and that, where necessary, it is properly grounded (earthed). Do not use such appliances in damp conditions and, again, beware of creating a spark or applying excessive heat in the vicinity of fuel or fuel vapour. Also ensure that the appliances meet national safety standards.

● A severe electric shock can result from touching certain parts of the electrical system, such as the spark plug wires (HT leads), when the engine is running or being cranked, particularly if components are damp or the insulation is defective. Where an electronic ignition system is used, the secondary (HT) voltage is much higher and could prove fatal.

Remember...

✗ **Don't** start the engine without first ascertaining that the transmission is in neutral.

✗ **Don't** suddenly remove the pressure cap from a hot cooling system - cover it with a cloth and release the pressure gradually first, or you may get scalded by escaping coolant.

✗ **Don't** attempt to drain oil until you are sure it has cooled sufficiently to avoid scalding you.

✗ **Don't** grasp any part of the engine or exhaust system without first ascertaining that it is cool enough not to burn you.

✗ **Don't** allow brake fluid or antifreeze to contact the machine's paintwork or plastic components.

✗ **Don't** siphon toxic liquids such as fuel, hydraulic fluid or antifreeze by mouth, or allow them to remain on your skin.

✗ **Don't** inhale dust - it may be injurious to health (see Asbestos heading).

✗ **Don't** allow any spilled oil or grease to remain on the floor - wipe it up right away, before someone slips on it.

✗ **Don't** use ill-fitting spanners or other tools which may slip and cause injury.

✗ **Don't** lift a heavy component which may be beyond your capability - get assistance.

✗ **Don't** rush to finish a job or take unverified short cuts.

✗ **Don't** allow children or animals in or around an unattended vehicle.

✗ **Don't** inflate a tyre above the recommended pressure. Apart from over-stressing the carcass, in extreme cases the tyre may blow off forcibly.

✓ **Do** ensure that the machine is supported securely at all times. This is especially important when the machine is blocked up to aid wheel or fork removal.

✓ **Do** take care when attempting to loosen a stubborn nut or bolt. It is generally better to pull on a spanner, rather than push, so that if you slip, you fall away from the machine rather than onto it.

✓ **Do** wear eye protection when using power tools such as drill, sander, bench grinder etc.

✓ **Do** use a barrier cream on your hands prior to undertaking dirty jobs - it will protect your skin from infection as well as making the dirt easier to remove afterwards; but make sure your hands aren't left slippery. Note that long-term contact with used engine oil can be a health hazard.

✓ **Do** keep loose clothing (cuffs, ties etc. and long hair) well out of the way of moving mechanical parts.

✓ **Do** remove rings, wristwatch etc., before working on the vehicle - especially the electrical system.

✓ **Do** keep your work area tidy - it is only too easy to fall over articles left lying around.

✓ **Do** exercise caution when compressing springs for removal or installation. Ensure that the tension is applied and released in a controlled manner, using suitable tools which preclude the possibility of the spring escaping violently.

✓ **Do** ensure that any lifting tackle used has a safe working load rating adequate for the job.

✓ **Do** get someone to check periodically that all is well, when working alone on the vehicle.

✓ **Do** carry out work in a logical sequence and check that everything is correctly assembled and tightened afterwards.

✓ **Do** remember that your vehicle's safety affects that of yourself and others. If in doubt on any point, get professional advice.

● If in spite of following these precautions, you are unfortunate enough to injure yourself, seek medical attention as soon as possible.

Daily or (pre-ride) checks 0•13

Note: *The daily (pre-ride) checks outlined in the owner's manual covers those items which should be inspected on a daily basis.*

Engine/transmission oil level check

Before you start:
✔ Support the motorcycle in an upright position, using an auxiliary stand if required. Make sure it is on level ground.
✔ Start the engine and let it idle for several minutes to allow it to reach normal operating temperature.
Caution: Do not run the engine in an enclosed space such as a garage or workshop.
✔ Leave the motorcycle undisturbed for a few minutes to allow the oil level to stabilise.

Bike care:
● If you have to add oil frequently, you should check whether you have any oil leaks. If there is no sign of oil leakage from the joints and gaskets the engine could be burning oil (see *Fault Finding*).

The correct oil
● Modern, high-revving engines place great demands on their oil. It is very important that the correct oil for your bike is used.
● Always top up with a good quality oil of the specified type and viscosity and do not overfill the engine.
Caution: Do not use chemical additives or oils with a grade of CD or higher, or use oils labelled 'ENERGY CONSERVING II'. Such additives or oils could cause clutch slip.

Oil type	API grade SE, SF or SG
Oil viscosity	SAE 10W30 or 20W40*

*Refer to the viscosity table to select the oil best suited to your conditions.

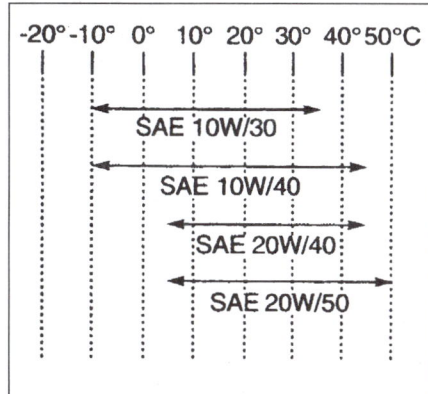

Oil viscosity table; select the oil best suited to the conditions

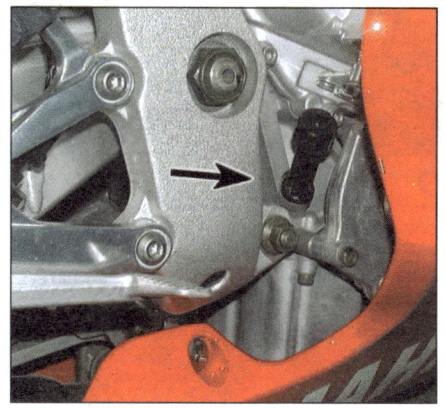

1 Remove the dipstick (arrowed) from the right-hand side of the crankcase and use clean rag or paper towel to wipe off all the oil.

2 Insert the clean dipstick back into the engine, but **do not** screw it in.

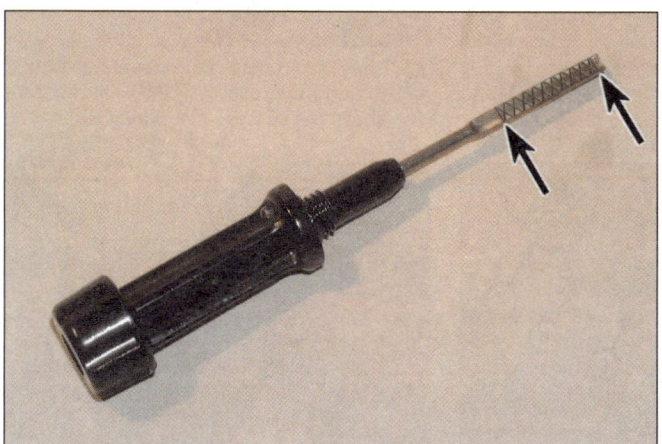

3 Remove the dipstick and observe the level of the oil, which should be somewhere in between the upper and lower level lines (arrowed).

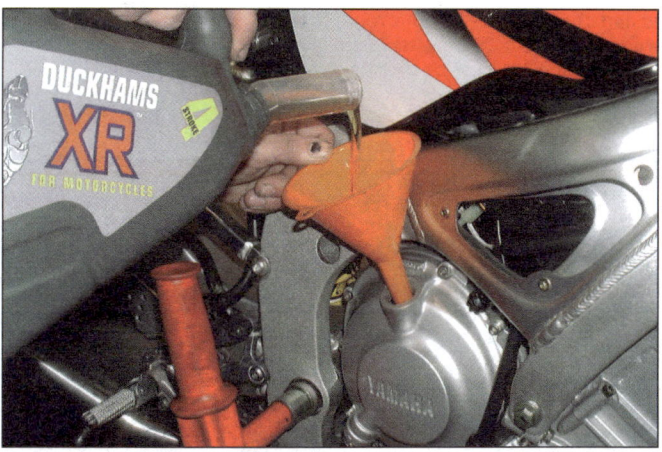

4 If the level is below the lower line, remove the filler cap from the top of the clutch cover and add the recommended grade and type of oil, to bring the level up to the upper line on the dipstick. Do not overfill. Install the filler cap.

Daily (pre-ride) checks

Brake fluid level checks

> **Warning:** Brake hydraulic fluid can harm your eyes and damage painted surfaces, so use extreme caution when handling and pouring it and cover surrounding surfaces with rag. Do not use fluid that has been standing open for some time, as it absorbs moisture from the air which can cause a dangerous loss of braking effectiveness.

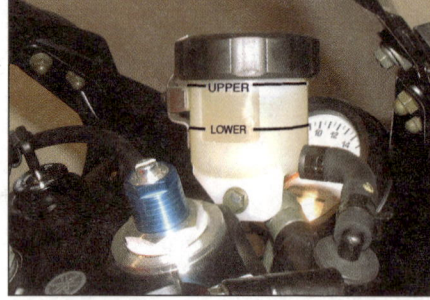

1 The front brake fluid level is visible through the reservoir body – it must be between the UPPER and LOWER level lines.

Before you start:
✔ Support the motorcycle in an upright position, using an auxiliary stand if required. Turn the handlebars until the top of the front master cylinder is as level as possible. The rear master cylinder reservoir is located behind the right-hand side cover.
✔ Make sure you have the correct hydraulic fluid. DOT 4 is recommended.
✔ Wrap a rag around the reservoir being worked on to ensure that any spillage does not come into contact with painted surfaces.

Bike care:
● The fluid in the front and rear brake master cylinder reservoirs will drop slightly as the brake pads wear down.
● If any fluid reservoir requires repeated topping-up this is an indication of an hydraulic leak somewhere in the system, which should be investigated immediately.
● Check for signs of fluid leakage from the hydraulic hoses and brake system components – if found, rectify immediately (see Chapter 7).
● Check the operation of both brakes before taking the machine on the road; if there is evidence of air in the system (spongy feel to lever or pedal), it must be bled as described in Chapter 7.

2 If the level is below the LOWER level line, undo the reservoir cap clamp screw (A) and remove the clamp, then unscrew the cap (B) and remove the diaphragm plate and the diaphragm.

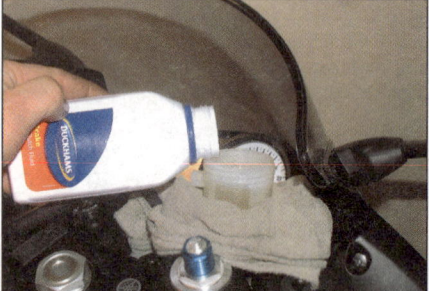

3 Top up with new, clean DOT 4 hydraulic fluid, until the level is above the LOWER level line. Take care to avoid spills (see **Warning** above) and do not overfill.

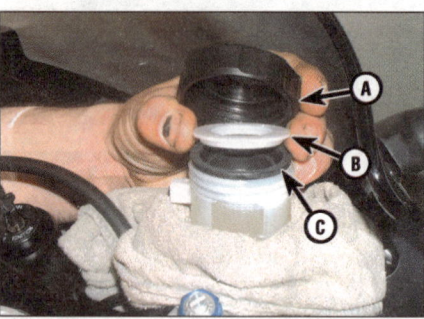

4 Ensure that the diaphragm (C) is correctly seated before installing the plate (B) and cap (A). Secure the cap with its clamp.

5 The rear brake fluid level is visible through the reservoir body – it must be above the LOWER level line.

6 If the level is below the LOWER level line, remove the reservoir mounting screw (arrowed) and displace the reservoir to access the cap.

7 Support the reservoir upright, then unscrew the cap (A) and remove the plate (B) and the diaphragm (C).

8 Top up with new, clean DOT 4 hydraulic fluid, until the level is above the LOWER level line, then refit the diaphragm, plate and cap and secure the reservoir to the frame. Take care to avoid spills (see **Warning** above) and do not overfill.

Daily or (pre-ride) checks 0•15

Coolant level check

> **Warning: DO NOT** remove the cooling system pressure cap to add coolant. Topping up is done via the coolant reservoir tank filler. **DO NOT** leave open containers of coolant about, as it is poisonous.

Before you start:
✔ Make sure you have a supply of coolant available – a mixture of 50% distilled water and 50% corrosion inhibited ethylene glycol anti-freeze is needed. **Note:** *Yamaha specify that soft tap water can be used, but NOT hard water. If in doubt, boil the water first or use only distilled water.*
✔ Always check the coolant level when the engine is cold.
✔ Support the motorcycle in an upright position, using an auxiliary stand if required. Make sure it is on level ground.

Bike care:
● Use only the specified coolant mixture. It is important that anti-freeze is used in the system all year round, and not just in the winter. Do not top the system up using only water, as the system will become too diluted.
● Do not overfill the reservoir. If the coolant is significantly above the FULL level line at any time, the surplus should be siphoned or drained off to prevent the possibility of it being expelled out of the overflow hose.
● If the coolant level falls steadily, check the system for leaks (see Chapter 1). If no leaks are found and the level continues to fall, it is recommended that the machine be taken to a Yamaha dealer for a pressure test.

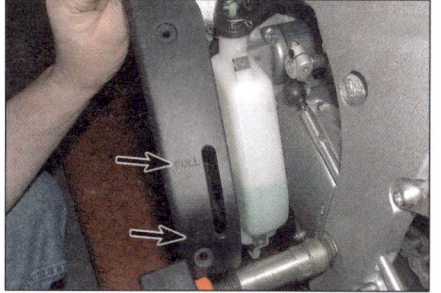

1 The reservoir is mounted on the left-hand side of the motorcycle, inside the fairing. The coolant FULL and LOW level lines (arrowed) are marked on the reservoir.

2 If the coolant level does not lie between the FULL and LOW level lines, remove the reservoir filler cap.

3 Top the coolant level up with the recommended coolant mixture then fit the cap securely.

Suspension, steering and drive chain checks

Suspension and steering:
● Check that the front and rear suspension operates smoothly without binding.
● Check that the suspension is adjusted as required.
● Check that the steering moves smoothly from lock-to-lock.

Final drive:
● Check that the drive chain slack isn't excessive, and adjust it if necessary (see Chapter 1).
● If the chain looks dry, lubricate it (see Chapter 1).

Legal and safety checks

Lighting and signalling:
● Take a minute to check that the headlight, tail light, brake light, instrument lights and turn signals all work correctly.
● Check that the horn sounds when the switch is operated.
● A working speedometer graduated in mph is a statutory requirement in the UK.

Safety:
● Check that the throttle grip rotates smoothly and snaps shut when released, in all steering positions. Also check for the correct amount of freeplay (see Chapter 1).

● Check that the engine shuts off when the kill switch is operated.
● Check that sidestand return spring holds the stand up securely when it is retracted.

Fuel:
● This may seem obvious, but check that you have enough fuel to complete your journey. If you notice signs of fuel leakage – rectify the cause immediately.
● Ensure you use the correct grade fuel – see Chapter 4 Specifications.

Daily or (pre-ride) checks

Tyre checks

Tyre tread depth:
● At the time of writing UK law requires that tread depth must be at least 1 mm over the entire tread breadth all the way around the tyre, with no bald patches. Many riders, however, consider 2 mm tread depth minimum to be a safer limit. Yamaha recommend a minimum of 1.6 mm.
● Many tyres now incorporate wear indicators in the tread. Identify the triangular pointer or TWI mark on the tyre sidewall to locate the indicator bar and renew the tyre if the tread has worn down to the bar.

Loading*/speed	Front	Rear
Up to 90 kg (198 lb) load	36 psi (2.50 Bar)	36 psi (2.50 Bar)
90 kg (198 lb) up to max. load of 187 kg (412 lb)	36 psi (2.50 Bar)	42 psi (2.90 Bar)
High speed riding	36 psi (2.50 Bar)	36 psi (2.50 Bar)

*Load is the total weight of the rider, passenger, luggage and any accessories

The correct pressures:
● The tyres must be checked when **cold**, not immediately after riding. Note that low tyre pressures may cause the tyre to slip on the rim or come off. High tyre pressures will cause abnormal tread wear and unsafe handling.
● Use an accurate pressure gauge. Many garage forecourt gauges are wildly inaccurate. If you buy your own, spend as much as you can justify on a quality gauge.
● Correct air pressure will increase tyre life and provide maximum stability, handling capability and ride comfort.

Tyre care:
● Check the tyres carefully for cuts, tears, embedded nails or other sharp objects and excessive wear. Operation of the motorcycle with excessively worn tyres is extremely hazardous, as traction and handling are directly affected.
● Check the condition of the tyre valve and ensure the dust cap is in place.
● Pick out any stones or nails which may have become embedded in the tyre tread. If left, they will eventually penetrate through the casing and cause a puncture.
● If tyre damage is apparent, or unexplained loss of pressure is experienced, seek the advice of a tyre fitting specialist without delay.

1 Check the tyre pressures when the tyres are **cold** and keep them properly inflated.

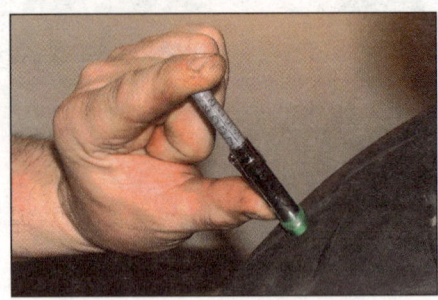

2 Measure tread depth at the centre of the tyre using a tread depth gauge.

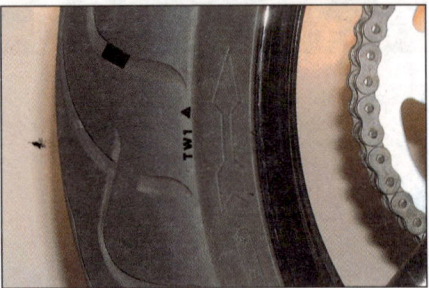

3 Tyre tread wear indicator bar and its location marking (usually either an arrow, a triangle or the letters TWI) on the sidewall.

Chapter 1
Routine maintenance and Servicing

Contents

Air filter – clean and check	3
Battery – charging	see Chapter 9
Battery – check	20
Battery – removal, installation, inspection and maintenance	see Chapter 9
Brake fluid level check	see Daily (pre-ride) checks
Brake hoses – renewal	31
Brake master cylinder and caliper seals – renewal	28
Brake pads – wear check	12
Brake system – check	13
Brakes – fluid change	29
Carburettors – synchronisation	5
Clutch cable – check and adjustment	8
Coolant level check	see Daily (pre-ride) checks
Cooling system – check	10
Cooling system – draining, flushing and refilling	30
Cylinder compression – check	32
Drive chain and sprockets – check, adjustment and lubrication	1
Engine oil pressure – check	33
Engine/transmission – oil and filter change	22
Engine/transmission – oil change	11
Engine/transmission oil level check	see Daily (pre-ride) checks
Front forks – oil change	35
Fuel filter and strainer – cleaning and renewal	23
Fuel hoses – renewal	34
Fuel system and air induction system (AIS) – check	6
Headlight aim – check and adjustment	21
Idle speed – check and adjustment	4
Nuts and bolts – tightness check	19
Sidestand and sidestand switch – check	18
Spark plugs – check and adjustment	2
Stand, lever pivots and cables – lubrication	9
Steering head bearings – freeplay check and adjustment	17
Steering head bearings – re-greasing	25
Suspension – check	16
Suspension linkage bearings – re-greasing	24
Swingarm bearings – re-greasing	27
Throttle and choke cables – check and adjustment	7
Tyre pressure and tread depth	see Daily (pre-ride) checks
Valve clearances – check and adjustment	26
Wheel bearings – check	15
Wheels and tyres – general check	14

Degrees of difficulty

| **Easy,** suitable for novice with little experience | **Fairly easy,** suitable for beginner with some experience | **Fairly difficult,** suitable for competent DIY mechanic | **Difficult,** suitable for experienced DIY mechanic | **Very difficult,** suitable for expert DIY or professional |

1•2 Specifications

Engine
Spark plugs
    Type – California market models . . . . NGK CR9EK
    Type – all other market models . . . . NGK CR10EK
    Electrode gap . . . . 0.6 to 0.7 mm
Engine idle speed . . . . 1250 to 1350 rpm
Cylinder identification . . . . numbered 1 to 4 from left to right
Carburettor synchronisation – intake vacuum at idle . . . . 180.45 mmHg
Carburettor synchronisation – max. difference between carburettors . . 10 mmHg
Valve clearances (COLD engine)
    Intake valves . . . . 0.11 to 0.20 mm
    Exhaust valves . . . . 0.21 to 0.30 mm
Cylinder compression
    Standard . . . . 224.8 psi (15.5 bars)
    Maximum . . . . 232 psi (16.0 bars)
    Minimum . . . . 188.5 psi (13.0 bars)
    Max. difference between cylinders . . . . 14.5 psi (1.0 bar)
Engine oil pressure (at 96°C) . . . . 34.8 psi (2.4 bars) @ 6000 rpm

Cycle parts
Drive chain slack . . . . 40 to 50 mm
Drive chain stretch limit (see text) . . . . 150.1 mm
Brake pad friction material wear limit
    Front calipers . . . . 0.5 mm
    Rear caliper . . . . 0.8 mm
Rear brake pedal height . . . . 4.3 to 9.3 mm
Throttle cable freeplay . . . . 6 to 8 mm
Clutch cable freeplay . . . . 10 to 15 mm
Tyre pressures (cold) . . . . see *Daily (pre-ride) checks*

Recommended lubricants and fluids
Engine/transmission oil type . . . . see *Daily (pre-ride) checks*
Engine/transmission oil capacity
    Oil change . . . . 2.5 litres
    Oil and filter change . . . . 2.7 litres
    Following engine overhaul – dry engine, new filter . . . . 3.5 litres
Coolant type . . . . 50% distilled water, 50% ethylene glycol anti-freeze with corrosion inhibitors for aluminium engines. **Note:** *Yamaha specify that soft tap water can be used, but NOT hard water. If in doubt, boil the water first or use only distilled water.*
Coolant capacity
    Radiator . . . . 2.15 litres
    Reservoir . . . . 0.44 litres
Brake fluid . . . . DOT 4
Drive chain . . . . Engine oil or chain lubricant suitable for O-ring chains
Steering head bearings . . . . Lithium-based multi-purpose grease
Swingarm pivot and bearings . . . . Lithium-based multi-purpose grease
Suspension linkage bearings . . . . Lithium-based multi-purpose grease
Bearing seals . . . . Lithium-based multi-purpose grease
Gearchange lever, clutch lever, front brake lever,
    rear brake pedal, sidestand pivots . . . . Lithium-based multi-purpose grease
Cables . . . . 10W30 motor oil or Yamaha cable lubricant
Throttle twistgrip . . . . Multi-purpose grease or dry film lubricant

Torque wrench settings
Rear axle nut . . . . 150 Nm
Rear brake caliper anchor bolt . . . . 40 Nm
Spark plugs . . . . 13 Nm
Oil drain plug . . . . 43 Nm
Oil filter . . . . 17 Nm
Steering stem nut . . . . 115 Nm
Fork clamp bolts (top yoke) . . . . 23 Nm
Handlebar positioning bolts . . . . 13 Nm
Handlebar clamp bolts . . . . 13 Nm
Ignition rotor/pick-up coil cover bolts . . . . 12 Nm
Cooling system drain plug . . . . 7 Nm
Oil gallery bolt . . . . 20 Nm

Component locations

Component locations on right-hand side

1 Rear brake fluid reservoir
2 Engine oil filler cap
3 Idle speed adjuster
4 Front brake fluid reservoir
5 Radiator pressure cap
6 Coolant drain bolt
7 Clutch cable lower adjuster
8 Engine oil level dipstick
9 Rear brake light switch
10 Drive chain adjuster

Component locations on left-hand side

1 Clutch cable upper adjuster
2 Steering head bearing adjuster
3 Air filter
4 Coolant reservoir
5 Fuel filter
6 Battery
7 Drive chain adjuster
8 Engine oil drain bolt
9 Engine oil filter

Maintenance schedule – 1999 and 2000 models

Note: *The Daily (pre-ride) checks outlined in the owner's manual covers those items which should be inspected on a daily basis. Always perform the pre-ride inspection at every maintenance interval (in addition to the procedures listed). The intervals listed below are the intervals recommended by the manufacturer for each particular operation during the model years covered in this manual. Your owner's manual may have different intervals for your model.*

Daily (pre-ride)
- [ ] See *Daily (pre-ride) checks* at the beginning of this manual.

After the initial 1000 km (600 miles)
Note: *This check is usually performed by a Yamaha dealer after the first 1000 km (600 miles) from new. Thereafter, maintenance is carried out according to the following intervals of the schedule.*

Every 1000 km (600 miles)
- [ ] Check, adjust and lubricate the drive chain (Section 1)

Every 6000 km (3700 miles)
- [ ] Check and adjust the spark plugs (Section 2)
- [ ] Clean and check the air filter element (Section 3)
- [ ] Check and adjust the idle speed (Section 4)
- [ ] Check/adjust the carburettor synchronisation (Section 5)
- [ ] Check the fuel hoses and air induction system (AIS) (Section 6)
- [ ] Check and adjust the throttle and choke cables (Section 7)
- [ ] Check and adjust the clutch and clutch cable (Section 8)
- [ ] Lubricate the clutch/gearchange/brake lever/brake pedal/sidestand pivots and the throttle/choke cables (Section 9)
- [ ] Check the cooling system (Section 10)
- [ ] Change the engine/transmission oil (Section 11)
- [ ] Check the brake pads (Section 12)
- [ ] Check the brake system and brake light switch operation (Section 13)
- [ ] Check the condition of the wheels and tyres (Section 14)
- [ ] Check the wheel bearings (Section 15)
- [ ] Check the suspension (Section 16)
- [ ] Check and adjust the steering head bearings (Section 17)
- [ ] Check the sidestand and sidestand switch (Section 18)
- [ ] Check the tightness of all nuts, bolts and fasteners (Section 19)
- [ ] Check the battery (Section 20)
- [ ] Check and adjust the headlight aim (Section 21)

Every 12,000 km (7500 miles)
Carry out all the items under the previous interval, plus the following:
- [ ] Renew the spark plugs (see Section 2)
- [ ] Renew the air filter element (see Section 3)
- [ ] Renew the engine/transmission oil filter (Section 22)
- [ ] Renew the fuel filter, and if necessary, clean the fuel strainer (Section 23)

Every 24,000 km (15,000 miles)
- [ ] Re-grease the suspension linkage bearings (Section 24)
- [ ] Re-grease the steering head bearings (Section 25)
- [ ] Re-grease the swingarm bearings (Section 27)
- [ ] Change the coolant (Section 30)

Every 42,000 km (26,000 miles)
- [ ] Check and adjust the valve clearances (Section 26)

Every two years
- [ ] Renew the seals in the brake master cylinders and calipers (Section 28)
- [ ] Change the brake fluid (Section 29)

Every four years
- [ ] Renew the brake hoses (Section 31)

Non-scheduled maintenance
- [ ] Check the cylinder compression (Section 32)
- [ ] Check the engine oil pressure (Section 33)
- [ ] Renew the fuel hoses (Section 34)
- [ ] Change the front fork oil (Section 35)

Maintenance schedule – 2001-on models

Note: *The Daily (pre-ride) checks outlined in the owner's manual covers those items which should be inspected on a daily basis. Always perform the pre-ride inspection at every maintenance interval (in addition to the procedures listed). The intervals listed below are the intervals recommended by the manufacturer for each particular operation during the model years covered in this manual. Your owner's manual may have different intervals for your model.*

Daily (pre-ride)
- [ ] See *Daily (pre-ride) checks* at the beginning of this manual.

After the initial 1000 km (600 miles)
Note: *This check is usually performed by a Yamaha dealer after the first 1000 km (600 miles) from new. Thereafter, maintenance is carried out according to the following intervals of the schedule.*

Every 1000 km (600 miles)
- [ ] Check, adjust and lubricate the drive chain (Section 1)

Every 10,000 km (6000 miles)
- [ ] Check and adjust the spark plugs (Section 2)
- [ ] Clean and check the air filter element (Section 3)
- [ ] Check and adjust the idle speed (Section 4)
- [ ] Check/adjust the carburettor synchronisation (Section 5)
- [ ] Check the fuel hoses and air induction system (AIS) (Section 6)
- [ ] Check and adjust the throttle and choke cables (Section 7)
- [ ] Check and adjust the clutch and clutch cable (Section 8)
- [ ] Lubricate the clutch/gearchange/brake lever/brake pedal/sidestand pivots and the throttle/choke cables (Section 9)
- [ ] Check the cooling system (Section 10)
- [ ] Change the engine/transmission oil (Section 11)
- [ ] Check the brake pads (Section 12)
- [ ] Check the brake system and brake light switch operation (Section 13)
- [ ] Check the condition of the wheels and tyres (Section 14)
- [ ] Check the wheel bearings (Section 15)
- [ ] Check the suspension (Section 16)
- [ ] Check and adjust the steering head bearings (Section 17)
- [ ] Check the sidestand and sidestand switch (Section 18)
- [ ] Check the tightness of all nuts, bolts and fasteners (Section 19)
- [ ] Check the battery (Section 20)
- [ ] Check and adjust the headlight aim (Section 21)

Every 20,000 km (12,000 miles)
Carry out all the items under the previous interval, plus the following:
- [ ] Renew the spark plugs (see Section 2)
- [ ] Renew the air filter element (see Section 3)
- [ ] Renew the engine/transmission oil filter (Section 22)
- [ ] Renew the fuel filter, and if necessary, clean the fuel strainer (Section 23)
- [ ] Re-grease the suspension linkage bearings (Section 24)
- [ ] Re-grease the steering head bearings (Section 25)

Every 40,000 km (24,000 miles)
- [ ] Check and adjust the valve clearances (Section 26)

Every 50,000 km (31,000 miles)
- [ ] Re-grease the swingarm bearings (Section 27)

Every two years
- [ ] Renew the seals in the brake master cylinders and calipers (Section 28)
- [ ] Change the brake fluid (Section 29)

Every three years
- [ ] Change the coolant (Section 30)

Every four years
- [ ] Renew the brake hoses (Section 31)

Non-scheduled maintenance
- [ ] Check the cylinder compression (Section 32)
- [ ] Check the engine oil pressure (Section 33)
- [ ] Renew the fuel hoses (Section 34)
- [ ] Change the front fork oil (Section 35)

1•6 Introduction

1 This Chapter is designed to help the home mechanic maintain his/her motorcycle for safety, economy, long life and peak performance.
2 Deciding where to start or plug into the routine maintenance schedule depends on several factors. If the warranty period on your motorcycle has just expired, and if it has been maintained according to the warranty standards, you may want to pick up routine maintenance as it coincides with the next mileage or calendar interval. If you have owned the machine for some time but have never performed any maintenance on it, then you may want to start at the beginning and include all frequent procedures to ensure that nothing important is overlooked. If you have just had a major engine overhaul, then you should start the engine maintenance routines from the beginning. If you have a used machine and have no knowledge of its history or maintenance record, you should combine all the checks into one large initial service and then settle into the maintenance schedule prescribed.
3 Before beginning any maintenance or repair, the machine should be cleaned thoroughly, especially around the oil filter, spark plugs, valve cover, side panels, carburettors, etc. Cleaning will help ensure that dirt does not contaminate the engine and will allow you to detect wear and damage that could otherwise easily go unnoticed.
4 Certain maintenance information is sometimes printed on decals attached to the motorcycle. If any information on the decals differs from that included here, use the information on the decal.

 Warning: Read the Safety first! section of this manual carefully before starting work.

Maintenance procedures

1 Drive chain and sprockets – check, adjustment and lubrication

Interval:
All models – every 1000 km (600 miles)

Check

1 As the chain stretches with wear, adjustment will periodically be necessary. A neglected drive chain won't last long and can quickly damage the sprockets. Routine chain adjustment and lubrication isn't difficult and will ensure maximum chain and sprocket life.
2 To check the chain tension, support the bike upright, but do not have someone sit on it to do this, and shift the transmission into neutral.
3 Push up on the bottom run of the chain and measure the slack midway between the two sprockets **(see illustration)**, then compare your measurement to that listed in this Chapter's Specifications. Since the chain will rarely wear evenly, rotate the rear wheel so that another section of chain can be checked; do this several times to check the entire length of the chain. Any adjustment should be based upon the measurement taken at the tightest point.
4 If the chain has reached the end of its adjustment, it has probably stretched beyond its service limit. This can be checked by measuring a section of the chain with the chain held taut, and then measuring the same section of the chain with the links compressed. Compare the difference between the two measurements (the stretch) to the limit in the Specifications **(see illustration)**. To take the measurement, first remove the chainguard, then take the measurement on the chain's top run, midway between the sprockets. Take three measurements in different places on the chain. If the chain has stretched beyond the limit, replace it with a new one (see Chapter 6).
5 In some cases where lubrication has been neglected, corrosion and galling may cause the links to bind and kink, which effectively shortens the chain's length. Any such links should be thoroughly cleaned and worked free. If the chain is tight between the sprockets, rusty or kinked, it is time to replace it with a new one. If you find a tight area, mark it with felt pen or paint, and repeat the measurement after the bike has been ridden. If the chain is still tight in the same area, it may be damaged or worn. Because a tight or kinked chain can damage the transmission output shaft bearing, it is a good idea to replace it with a new one (see Chapter 6).
6 Check the entire length of the chain for damaged or missing rollers, loose links and pins, and missing O-rings and replace with a new one it if damage is found. **Note:** *Never install a new chain on old sprockets, and never use the old chain if you install new sprockets – renew the chain and sprockets as a set.*
7 Remove the front sprocket cover (see Chapter 6). Check the teeth on the engine sprocket and the rear wheel sprocket for wear **(see illustration)**.
8 Inspect the drive chain slider on the swingarm for excessive wear and renew it if worn (see Chapter 6, Section 13).

Adjustment

9 Rotate the rear wheel until the chain is positioned with the tightest point at the centre

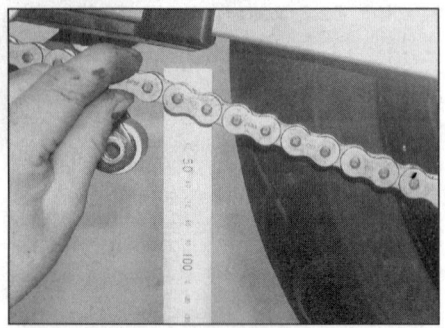
1.3 Push up on the chain and measure the slack

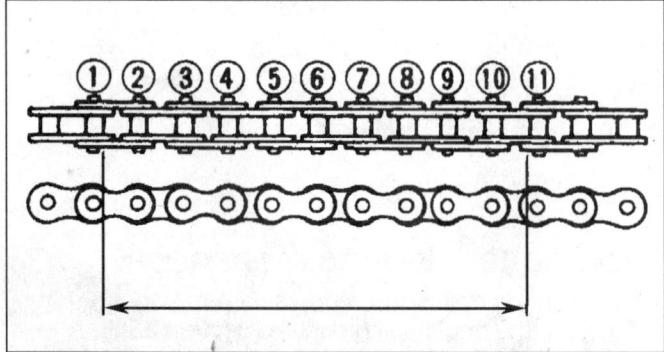
1.4 Check the amount of stretch by measuring as shown

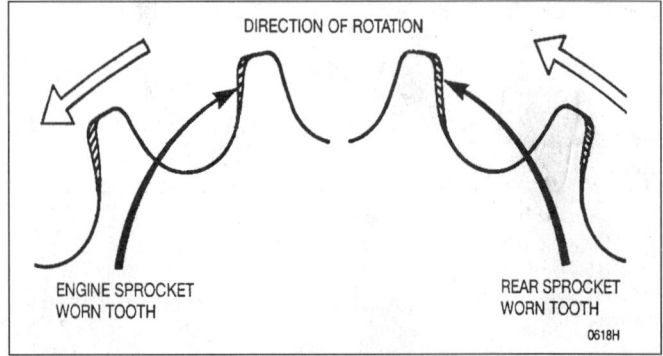
1.7 Check the sprockets in the areas indicated to see if they are worn excessively

Routine maintenance and servicing 1•7

1.10a Loosen the rear axle nut...

1.10b ...and the brake caliper anchor bolt

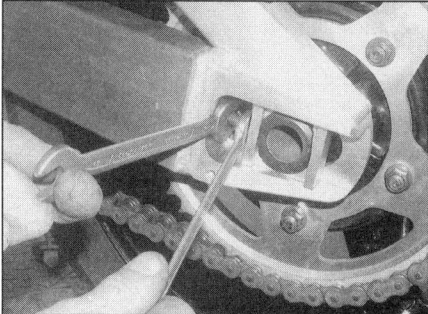

1.11a Loosen the adjuster locknuts...

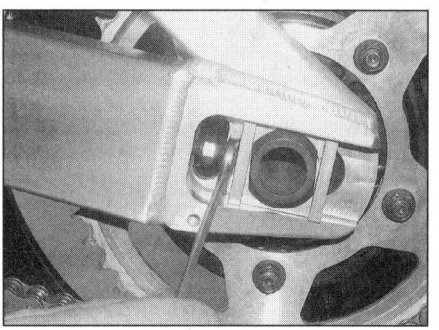

1.11b ...and turn the adjusters evenly

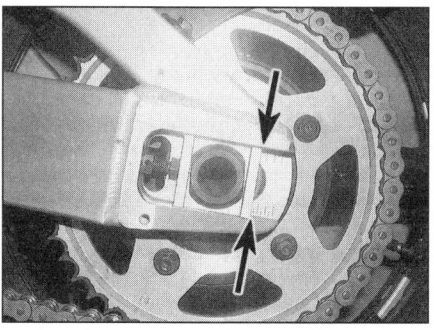

1.11c Check the position of the adjuster plate (arrowed) with the marks on the swingarm

1.15 Apply lubricant to the overlap between the chain sideplates

of its bottom run. Support the bike upright (but not by having someone sit on it).

10 Loosen the axle nut and the brake caliper bracket anchor bolt (see illustrations).

11 Loosen the adjuster locknut on each side of the swingarm, then turn the adjusters evenly, a small amount at a time, until the specified chain tension is obtained (see illustrations). Following chain adjustment, check that the back edge of each adjuster plate is in the same position in relation to the marks on each side of the swingarm (see illustration). It is important that each plate aligns with the same mark; if not, the rear wheel will be out of alignment with the front.

 **Refer to Chapter 7 for information on checking wheel alignment.**

12 If there is a discrepancy in the position of the plates, correct it with the adjusters and then check the chain tension as described above. Also check that there is no clearance between the adjuster and the front of the adjuster plate – push the wheel forwards to eliminate any clearance.

13 Tighten the axle nut and the caliper anchor bolt to the torque settings specified at the beginning of this Chapter, then tighten the adjuster locknuts securely. Recheck the adjustment.

Lubrication

14 If required, wash the chain in paraffin (kerosene), then wipe it off and allow it to dry,

using compressed air if available. If the chain is excessively dirty, remove the rear wheel (see Chapter 7) and soak the chain in paraffin. *Caution: Don't use petrol (gasoline), solvent or other cleaning fluids which might damage the internal sealing properties of the chain. Don't use high-pressure water. The entire process shouldn't take longer than five to six minutes – if it does, the O-rings in the chain rollers could be damaged.*

15 For routine lubrication, the best time to lubricate the chain is after the motorcycle has been ridden. When the chain is warm, the lubricant will penetrate the joints between the side plates better than when cold. **Note:** *Yamaha specifies engine oil or chain lube that is specifically for O-ring chains; do not use chain lube that is not specifically for O-ring chains, as it may contain solvents that could*

2.3 Unscrewing the spark plug using the Yamaha tool

damage the O-rings. Apply the lubricant to the area where the side plates overlap – not the middle of the rollers and protect the tyre from overspray with a rag (see illustration).

 Apply the lubricant to the top of the lower chain run, so centrifugal force will work it into the chain when the bike is moving. After applying the lubricant, let it soak in a few minutes before wiping off any excess.

2 Spark plugs – check and adjustment

Interval:
   1999 and 2000 models –
      every 6000 km (3700 miles)
   2001-on models –
      every 10,000 km (6000 miles)

1 Make sure your spark plug socket is the correct size (16 mm) before attempting to remove the plugs – a special plug spanner is supplied in the motorcycle's tool kit which is stored under the passenger seat.

2 Remove the fairing side panels (see Chapter 8), the air filter housing (see Chapter 4) and the ignition coils (see Chapter 5).

3 Using either a plug spanner or a deep socket type wrench, unscrew the plugs from the cylinder head (see illustration). Lay each

1•8 Routine maintenance and servicing

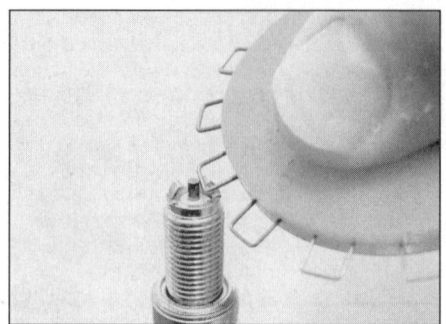

2.7a Using a wire gauge to measure the spark plug electrode gap

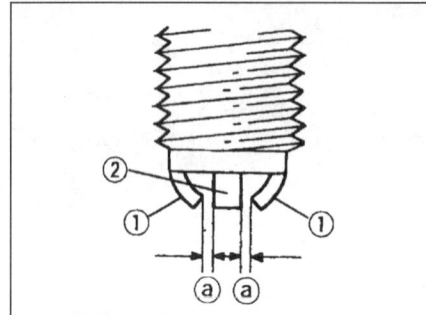

2.7b The gaps (a) between the two earth electrodes (1) and the centre electrode (2) must be equal and as specified

2.7c Adjust the electrode gap by bending the side electrodes only

plug out in relation to its cylinder so that, if any plug shows up a problem, it will be easy to identify the troublesome cylinder.

4 Inspect the electrodes for wear. Both the centre and side electrodes should have square edges and the side electrodes should be of uniform thickness. Look for excessive deposits and evidence of a cracked or chipped insulator around the centre electrode. Compare your spark plugs to the colour spark plug reading chart at the end of this manual. Check the threads, the washer and the ceramic insulator body for cracks and other damage.

5 If the electrodes are not excessively worn, and if the deposits can be easily removed with a wire brush, and there are no cracks or chips visible in the insulator, the plugs can be re-gapped and re-used. If in doubt concerning the condition of the plugs, replace them with new ones, as the expense is minimal. Note that the spark plugs should be renewed at every second service interval, i.e. every 12,000 miles (20,000 km).

6 Cleaning spark plugs by sandblasting is permitted, provided you clean the plugs with a high flash-point solvent afterwards.

7 Before installing the plugs, make sure they are the correct type and heat range and check the gap between the side (earth) electrodes and the centre electrode **(see illustrations)**. Compare the gap to that specified and adjust as necessary. If the gap must be adjusted, bend the side electrodes only and be very careful not to chip or crack the insulator nose **(see**

illustration). Make sure the sealing washer is in place on the plug before installing it.

8 Since the cylinder head is made of aluminium, which is soft and easily damaged, thread the plugs into the head and turn the tool by hand **(see illustration)**. Once the plugs are finger-tight, the job can be finished with a spanner on the tool supplied or a socket drive. If a torque wrench is available, tighten the spark plugs to the torque setting specified at the beginning of this Chapter. Otherwise tighten them by 1/4 to 1/2 turn after they have been fully hand tightened and have seated. Do not over-tighten them.

 *As the plugs are quite recessed, you can slip a short length of hose over the end of the plug to use as a tool to thread it into place. The hose will grip the plug well enough to turn it, but will start to slip if the plug begins to cross-thread in the hole – this will prevent damaged threads.*

9 Install the ignition coils, the air filter housing (see Chapter 4) and the fairing side panels (see Chapter 8).

 Stripped plug threads in the cylinder head can be repaired with a thread insert – see Section 2 of 'Tools and Workshop Tips' in the Reference section.

3 Air filter – clean and check

Interval:
1999 and 2000 models – every 6000 km (3700 miles)
2001-on models – every 10,000 km (6000 miles)

Note: If the machine is continually ridden in dusty conditions, the filter should be cleaned more frequently than specified.

1 Remove the fuel tank (see Chapter 4).
2 Remove the screws securing the air filter housing cover, then remove the cover, the filter element and the seal **(see illustrations)**.
Note: A modification was made to the filter element assembly in December 1999. On early models the filter element is held in a clip-together frame; unclip the frame and remove the filter element. On later models the filter element and frame area one-piece unit.
3 Check the element for signs of damage. If the element is torn or is obviously beyond further use, replace it with a new one.
4 If the element is undamaged but dirty, wash it in warm soapy water then rinse it thoroughly in clean water and dry it.
5 Soak the element in clean engine oil, then squeeze out any excess oil. Install the removable filter element in its frame.
6 Install the seal and the filter element and fit the cover, making sure the components

2.8 Thread the plug as far as possible turning the tool by hand

3.2a Remove the air filter housing cover . . .

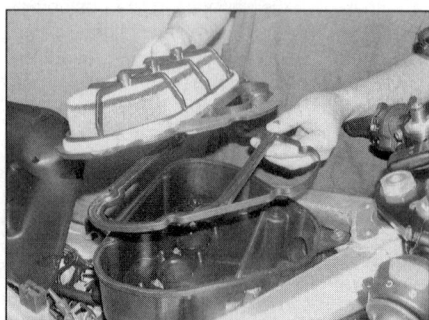

3.2b . . . and remove the filter element and seal

Routine maintenance and servicing 1•9

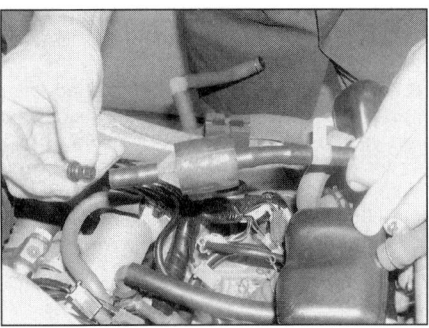

3.7 Drain the air filter housing vent hose

locate correctly in the rim of the housing **(see illustrations 3.2b and a)**.

7 Remove the plug from the end of the air filter housing vent hose and drain the collector **(see illustration)**. Check that the collector is not blocked.

8 Check the carburettor vent hose collector. Disconnect the clips securing the vent hoses to the collector and remove the collector for cleaning, then install the collector and secure the hoses with the clips.

9 Check the air filter housing vent hose, the carburettor vent hose and the crankcase breather hose between the engine and the rear of the air filter housing for loose connections, cracks and deterioration, and renew components where necessary.

10 Install the fuel tank (see Chapter 4).

4 Idle speed – check and adjustment

Interval:
  1999 and 2000 models –
    every 6000 km (3700 miles)
  2001-on models –
    every 10,000 km (6000 miles)

1 The idle speed should be checked and adjusted before and after the carburettors are synchronised (balanced), and when it is obviously too high or too low. Before adjusting the idle speed, make sure the valve clearances and spark plug gaps are correct,

and the air filter is clean. Also, turn the handlebars back-and-forth and see if the idle speed changes as this is done. If it does, the throttle cables may not be adjusted or routed correctly, or may be worn out. This is a dangerous condition that can cause loss of control of the bike. Be sure to correct this problem before proceeding.

2 The engine should be at normal operating temperature, which is usually reached after 10 to 15 minutes of stop-and-go riding. Make sure the transmission is in neutral, and place the motorcycle on its stand.

3 The idle speed adjuster is located on the right-hand side of the motorcycle under the frame beam **(see illustration)**. With the engine idling, turn the adjuster until the speed listed in this Chapter's Specifications is obtained. Turn the knob clockwise to increase idle speed, and anti-clockwise to decrease it.

4 Snap the throttle open and shut a few times, then recheck the idle speed. If necessary, repeat the adjustment procedure.

5 If a smooth, steady idle cannot be achieved, the fuel/air mixture may be incorrect (check the pilot screw settings – see Chapter 4) or the carburettors may need synchronising (see Section 5). Also check the intake manifold rubbers for cracks which will cause an air leak, resulting in a weak mixture.

5 Carburettors – synchronisation

Interval:
  1999 and 2000 models –
    every 6000 km (3700 miles)
  2001-on models –
    every 10,000 km (6000 miles)

⚠ **Warning: Petrol (gasoline) is extremely flammable, so take extra precautions when you work on any part of the fuel system. Don't smoke or allow open flames or bare light bulbs near the work area, and don't work in a garage where a natural gas-type appliance is present. If you spill any fuel on your skin, rinse it off immediately with soap and water. When you perform any kind of work on the fuel system, wear safety glasses and have a fire extinguisher suitable for a Class B type fire (flammable liquids) on hand.**

⚠ **Warning: Take great care not to burn your hand on the hot engine unit when accessing the gauge take-off points on the intake manifolds. Do not allow exhaust gases to build up in the work area; either perform the check outside or use an exhaust gas extraction system.**

1 Carburettor synchronisation is simply the process of adjusting the carburettors so that they pass the same amount of fuel/air mixture to each cylinder. This is done by measuring the vacuum produced in each cylinder. Carburettors that are out of synchronisation will result in decreased fuel mileage, increased engine temperature, less than ideal throttle response and higher vibration levels. Before synchronising the carburettors, make sure that the valve clearances and idle speed are properly adjusted and that the ignition timing has been checked.

2 To synchronise the carburettors you will need a set of vacuum gauges or a manometer. These instruments measure engine vacuum, and can be obtained from motorcycle dealers or mail order parts suppliers. The equipment used should be suitable for a four cylinder engine and come complete with the necessary adapters and hoses to fit the take-off points. **Note:** *Because of the nature of the synchronisation procedure and the need for special instruments, most owners leave the task to a Yamaha dealer.*

3 Start the engine and let it run until it reaches normal operating temperature, then shut it off. Remove the fuel tank (see Chapter 4).

4 Locate the balance hoses between the intake manifolds for Nos. 1 and 3 cylinders. Release the clips that secure the joining plug midway between the hoses and remove the plug. Fit suitable adapters to the hose ends and connect them to the appropriate vacuum gauge or manometer hoses **(see illustrations)**. Make sure the No. 1 gauge is attached to the hose from the No. 1 (left-hand) intake manifold, and so on. Now locate the balance hoses for Nos. 2 and 4 cylinders and connect them to the vacuum gauge or manometer hoses.

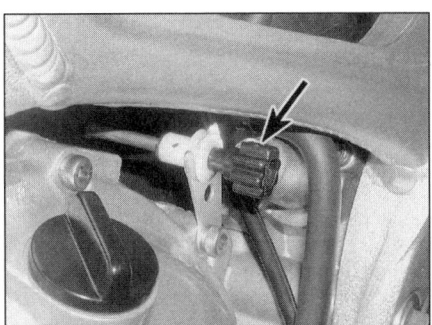

4.3 Turn the adjuster (arrowed) clockwise to increase idle speed, anticlockwise to decrease it

5.4a Remove the balance hose joining plugs (arrowed) . . .

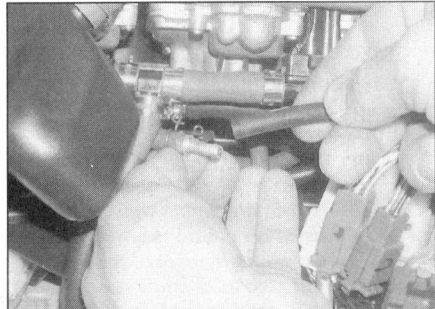

5.4b . . . and connect the vacuum gauge to the hoses

1•10 Routine maintenance and servicing

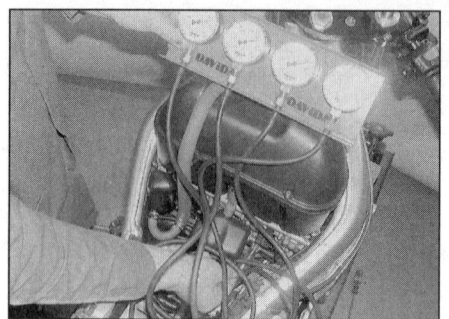

5.6 Carburettor synchronisation set-up

5.8 The synchronisation screws are located in the linkage between the carburettors

5 Arrange a temporary fuel supply using an auxiliary tank and some hosing.
6 Start the engine and let it idle. If the gauges are fitted with damping adjustment, set this so that the needle flutter is just eliminated but so that they can still respond to small changes in pressure (see illustration).
7 The vacuum readings for all cylinders should be the same. If the vacuum readings differ, proceed as follows.
8 The carburettors are balanced by turning the synchronising screws situated in between each carburettor, in the throttle linkage (see illustration). Note: *Do not press on the screws whilst adjusting them, otherwise a false reading will be obtained.* First synchronise No. 1 carburettor to No. 2 using the left-hand synchronising screw until the gauge readings are the same. Then synchronise No. 3 carburettor to No. 4 using the right-hand screw. Finally synchronise Nos. 1 and 2 carburettors to Nos. 3 and 4 using the centre screw.
9 When all the carburettors are synchronised, open and close the throttle quickly to settle the linkage, and recheck the gauge readings, readjusting if necessary.
10 When the adjustment is complete, adjust the idle speed (see Section 4), and check the throttle cable freeplay (see Section 7). Remove the gauges and refit the joining plugs and the hose clips (see illustration 5.4a). Detach the temporary fuel supply and install the fuel tank (see Chapter 4).

6 Fuel system and air induction system (AIS) – check

Interval:
1999 and 2000 models –
every 6000 km (3700 miles)
2001-on models –
every 10,000 km (6000 miles)

⚠ *Warning: Petrol (gasoline) is extremely flammable, so take extra precautions when you work on any part of the fuel system. Don't smoke or allow open flames or bare light bulbs near the work area, and don't work in a garage where a natural gas-type appliance is present. If you spill any fuel on your skin, rinse it off*

immediately with soap and water. When you perform any kind of work on the fuel system, wear safety glasses and have a fire extinguisher suitable for a Class B type fire (flammable liquids) on hand.

Fuel system – check

1 Remove the fuel tank (see Chapter 4) and check the tank, fuel tap and fuel hoses, and the filter and fuel pump, for signs of leakage, deterioration or damage; in particular check that there is no leakage from the fuel hoses. Renew any hoses which are cracked or have deteriorated (see Section 34).
2 If the tap has been leaking from the face, tightening the assembly screws on the face may help. Slacken the screws a little first, then tighten them evenly and a little at a time to ensure the cover seats properly on the tap body. If leakage persists, remove the screws on the face of the tap and disassemble it, noting how the components fit. Inspect all components for wear or damage, and renew the O-ring. None of the other components are available individually, so if they are worn fit a new tap. If the tap has been leaking from the base, tightening the mounting screws may help. Otherwise, remove the tap and fit a new O-ring (see Chapter 4). Remove any corrosion or paint bubbles before installing the tap.
3 If the carburettor gaskets are leaking, the carburettors should be disassembled and rebuilt using new gaskets and seals (see Chapter 4).

Air induction system (AIS) – check (California models)

4 If the valves clearances are all correct and the carburettors have been synchronised and have no other faults, but the idle speed cannot be set properly, it is possible that the AIS is faulty. Information on the function of the system is in Chapter 4.
5 Remove the fairing side panels (see Chapter 8). Check the air cut-off valve and the reed valve assembly on the front of the engine for signs of physical damage and replace it with a new one if necessary (see Chapter 4).
6 Check the AIS hoses and pipes for signs of deterioration or damage, and check that they are all securely connected with the hoses clamped at each end. Replace any hoses which are cracked or deteriorated with new ones (see Chapter 4).

7 Remove the reed valve assembly and disassemble it for inspection and cleaning (see Chapter 4).
8 Any further testing of the air induction system requires the use of an exhaust gas analyser and temperature sensors. If the system is thought to be faulty, take the bike to a Yamaha dealer for assessment. Make sure that the idle speed, valve clearances and carburettor synchronisation have all been checked before assuming that the AIS is faulty.

7 Throttle and choke cables – check and adjustment

Interval:
1999 and 2000 models –
every 6000 km (3700 miles)
2001-on models –
every 10,000 km (6000 miles)

Throttle cables

1 Make sure the throttle twistgrip rotates easily from fully closed to fully open with the front wheel turned at various angles. The twistgrip should return automatically from fully open to fully closed when released.
2 If the throttle sticks, this is probably due to a cable fault. Remove the cables (see Chapter 4) and lubricate them (see Section 9). If the inner cables still do not run smoothly in the outer cables, renew the cables.
3 With the cables removed, check that the twistgrip turns smoothly around the handlebar – dirt combined with a lack of lubrication can cause the action to be stiff. Clean and lightly grease the twistgrip pulley and the inside of the twistgrip housing. Install the lubricated or new cables, making sure they are correctly routed (see Chapter 4). If this fails to improve the operation of the throttle, the fault could lie in the carburettors. Remove them and check the action of the throttle linkage and butterflies (see Chapter 4).
4 With the throttle operating smoothly, check for a small amount of freeplay in the cables, measured in terms of the amount of twistgrip rotation before the throttle opens, and compare the amount to that listed in this Chapter's Specifications (see illustration). If it is incorrect, adjust the cables.

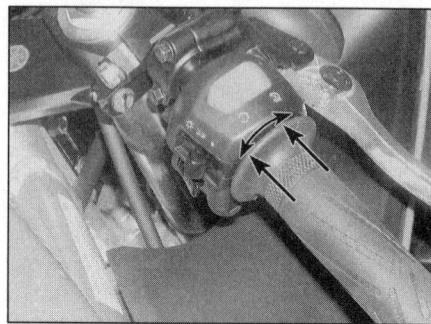

7.4 Measure the amount of freeplay in the throttle as shown

Routine maintenance and servicing 1•11

7.5 Accelerator cable lock ring (arrowed)

7.7 Accelerator cable adjuster (arrowed) at carburettor end

7.13 Choke cable clamp (arrowed) at carburettor end

5 Adjustment can be made at the twistgrip end of the accelerator cable. Loosen the lock ring and turn the adjuster until the specified amount of freeplay is obtained, then retighten the lock ring **(see illustration)**. Turn the adjuster in to increase freeplay and out to reduce it.

6 If the adjuster has reached its limit of adjustment, reset it so that the freeplay is at a maximum, then adjust the cable at the carburettor end as follows. Remove the fuel tank and air filter housing (see Chapter 4) and the frame left-hand side panel (see Chapter 8).

7 Loosen the lock nut on the accelerator cable adjuster and turn the adjuster nut until the specified amount of freeplay is obtained, then tighten the lock nut **(see illustration)**. Further adjustments can now be made at the twistgrip (see Step 5). If the cable cannot be adjusted as specified, renew the cable (see Chapter 4).

⚠️ **Warning: Turn the handlebars all the way through their travel with the engine idling. Idle speed should not change. If it does, the cables may be routed incorrectly. Correct this condition before riding the motorcycle.**

8 Check that the throttle twistgrip operates smoothly and snaps shut quickly when released.

Choke cable

9 If the choke does not operate smoothly this is probably due to a cable fault. Remove the cable (see Chapter 4) and lubricate it (see Section 9). If the inner cable still does not run smoothly in the outer cable, renew the cable.

10 With the cable removed, check that the choke lever turns smoothly around the handlebar – dirt combined with a lack of lubrication can cause the action to be stiff. Clean and lightly grease the lever pulley and the inside of the pulley housing. Install the lubricated or new cable, making sure it is correctly routed (see Chapter 4).

11 If this fails to improve the operation of the choke, the fault could lie in the carburettors, necessitating their removal and inspection of the choke plungers (see Chapter 4).

12 Make sure there is a small amount of freeplay in the cable before the plungers move. If there isn't, check that the cable is correctly installed at both ends.

13 Remove the fuel tank and the air filter housing (see Chapter 4) to access the carburettor end of the cable. You can create some freeplay in the cable by slackening the outer cable clamp screw on the carburettor and sliding the cable further into the clamp **(see illustration)**. Otherwise, renew the cable.

8 Clutch cable – and adjustment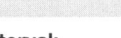

Interval:
1999 and 2000 models –
every 6000 km (3700 miles)
2001-on models –
every 10,000 km (6000 miles)

1 Check that the clutch lever operates smoothly and easily.

2 If the lever action is heavy or stiff, remove the cable (see Chapter 2) and lubricate it (see Section 9). If the inner cable still does not run smoothly in the outer cable, replace the cable with a new one. Install the lubricated or new cable (see Chapter 2).

3 If the lever itself is stiff, remove the lever from its bracket (see Chapter 6) and check for damage or distortion, or any other cause, and remedy as necessary. Clean and lubricate the pivot and contact areas (see Section 9).

4 If the lever and cable are good, refer to Chapter 2 and check the release mechanism in the clutch cover and the clutch itself.

5 With the clutch operating smoothly, check that the clutch lever is correctly adjusted. Periodic adjustment is necessary to compensate for wear in the clutch plates and stretch of the cable. Check that the amount of freeplay at the clutch lever end is within the specifications listed at the beginning of this Chapter **(see illustration)**.

6 If adjustment is required, loosen the locking ring and turn the adjuster in or out until the required amount of freeplay is obtained **(see illustration)**. To increase freeplay, turn the adjuster clockwise (into the lever bracket). To reduce freeplay, turn the adjuster anti-clockwise (out of the lever bracket). Tighten the locking ring securely.

7 If all the adjustment has been taken up at the lever, reset the adjuster to give the maximum amount of freeplay, then set the correct amount of freeplay using the adjuster on the lower end of the cable in the bracket on the right-hand side of the engine.

8 Remove the lower fairing (see Chapter 8). Slacken the rear adjuster nut, then turn the front nut as required to obtain the correct freeplay **(see illustration)**. To increase

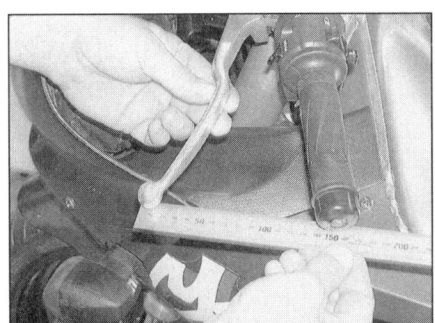

8.5 Check the amount of freeplay in the cable as shown

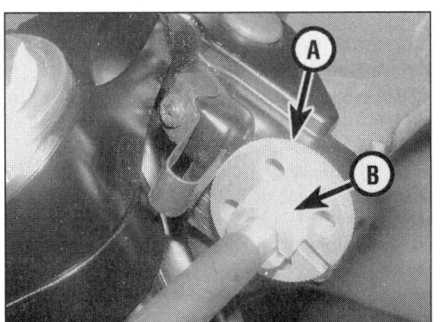

8.6 Loosen lockring (A) and turn adjuster (B)

8.8 Adjuster (arrowed) on lower end of clutch cable

1•12 Routine maintenance and servicing

freeplay, thread the front nut along the threaded section towards the front of the motorcycle. To reduce freeplay, thread the front nut along the threaded section towards the back of the motorcycle. When the correct amount of freeplay has been achieved, locate the front nut against the bracket, then tighten the rear nut against the bracket.
9 Subsequent adjustments can now be made using the clutch lever adjuster only.

9 Stand, lever pivots and cables – lubrication

Interval:
  1999 and 2000 models –
    every 6000 km (3700 miles)
  2001-on models –
    every 10,000 km (6000 miles)

1 Since the controls, cables and various other components of a motorcycle are exposed to the elements, they should be lubricated periodically to ensure safe and trouble-free operation.
2 The footrest pivots, clutch and brake levers, brake pedal and gearchange lever pivots and linkage and sidestand pivot should be lubricated frequently. In order that the lubricant is applied where it will do the most good, the component should be disassembled. However, if chain and cable lubricant is being used, it can be applied to the pivot joint gaps and will usually work its way into the areas where friction occurs. If motor oil or light grease is being used, apply it sparingly as it may attract dirt (which could cause the controls to bind or wear at an accelerated rate). **Note:** *One of the best lubricants for the control lever pivots is a dry-film lubricant (available from many sources by different names).*
3 To lubricate the throttle and choke cables, disconnect the relevant cable at its upper end, then lubricate the cable with a pressure adapter **(see illustration)** or, if one is not available, using the set-up shown **(see illustration)**. See Chapter 4 for the throttle and choke cable removal procedures, and Chapter 2 for the clutch cable.

10 Cooling system – check

Interval:
  1999 and 2000 models –
    every 6000 km (3700 miles)
  2001-on models –
    every 10,000 km (6000 miles)

⚠ **Warning:** *The engine must be cool before beginning this procedure.*

1 Check the coolant level (see *Daily (pre-ride) checks*).
2 The entire cooling system should be checked for evidence of leakage. Remove the lower fairing and the fairing side panels (see

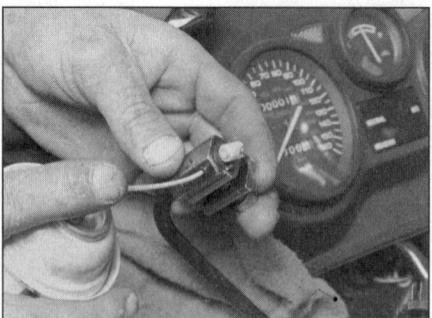

9.3a Lubricating a cable with a pressure adapter

Chapter 8). Examine each coolant hose along its entire length. Look for splits, abrasions and other signs of deterioration. Squeeze each hose at various points. They should feel firm, yet pliable, and return to their original shape when released. If they are cracked or hard, replace them with new ones.
3 Check for evidence of leaks at each cooling system joint. If necessary, tighten the hose clips carefully to prevent future leaks.
4 Examine the oil cooler inlet and outlet hoses for damage and signs of deterioration. Ensure that the hose clips are secure and that there is no sign of leakage at the oil cooler to crankcase joint.
5 To prevent leakage of water from the cooling system to the lubrication system and vice versa, two seals are fitted on the water pump shaft. If either seal fails, a drain hole in the underside of the pump body allows the coolant or oil to escape and prevents them mixing **(see illustration)**. Look for telltale signs of leakage where the water pump body enters the crankcase.
6 The water seal on the pump shaft is of the mechanical type and bears on the inner face of the pump body and the rear face of the pump impeller. The oil seal, which is mounted in the pump body, is of the normal feathered lip type. If there are signs of coolant leakage, remove the pump and replace the mechanical seal with a new one. If it is oil that is leaking, or if the leakage is white and with the texture of emulsion, replace both seals with new ones (the mechanical seal has to be removed in order to remove the oil seal, and it cannot be reused). Refer to Chapter 3 for seal renewal.

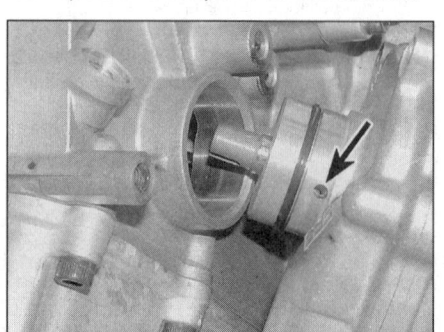

10.5 Water pump drain hole (arrowed)

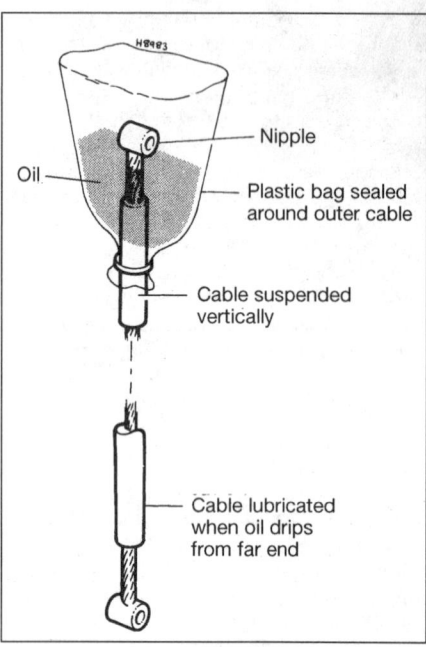

9.3b Lubricating a cable with a makeshift funnel and motor oil

7 Check the radiator for leaks and other damage. Leaks in the radiator leave tell-tale scale deposits or coolant stains on the outside of the core below the leak. If leaks are noted, remove the radiator (see Chapter 3) and have it repaired by a specialist.
Caution: *Do not use a liquid leak stopping compound to try to repair leaks.*
8 Check the radiator fins for mud, dirt and insects, which may impede the flow of air through the radiator. If the fins are dirty, remove the radiator (see Chapter 3) and clean it, using water or low pressure compressed air directed through the fins from the back. If the fins are bent or distorted, straighten them carefully with a screwdriver. Bent or damaged fins will restrict the air flow and impair the efficiency of the radiator causing the engine to overheat. Where there is substantial damage to the radiator's surface area, renew the radiator.
9 Remove the pressure cap from the radiator filler neck by turning it anti-clockwise until it reaches a stop. If you hear a hissing sound

10.9 Remove the pressure cap as described

Routine maintenance and servicing 1•13

(indicating that there is still pressure in the system), wait until it stops. Now press down on the cap and continue turning until it can be removed **(see illustration)**.

10 Check the condition of the coolant in the system. If it is rust-coloured or if accumulations of scale are visible, drain, flush and refill the system with new coolant (see Section 30). Check the cap seal for cracks and other damage. If in doubt about the pressure cap's condition, have it tested by a Yamaha dealer or replace it with a new one.

11 Check the antifreeze content of the coolant with an antifreeze hydrometer (see Specifications). A mixture with less than 40% antifreeze (40/60 antifreeze to distilled water) will not provide proper corrosion protection. Sometimes coolant looks like it's in good condition, but might be too weak to offer adequate protection. If the hydrometer indicates a weak mixture, drain, flush and refill the system (see Section 30). A higher than specified concentration of antifreeze decreases the performance of the cooling system and should only be used when additional protection against freezing is needed.

12 Install the cap by turning it clockwise until it reaches the first stop then push down on the cap and continue turning until it will turn no further.

13 Start the engine and let it reach normal operating temperature, then check for leaks again. As the coolant temperature increases beyond normal, the fan should come on automatically and the temperature should begin to drop. If it does not, refer to Chapter 3 and check the fan switch, fan motor and fan circuit carefully.

14 If the coolant level is consistently low, and no evidence of leaks can be found, have the entire system pressure-checked by a Yamaha dealer.

11 Engine/transmission oil – change

Interval:
  1999 and 2000 models –
    every 6000 km (3700 miles)
  2001-on models –
    every 10,000 km (6000 miles)

Warning: Be careful when draining the oil, as the exhaust pipes, the engine, and the oil itself can cause severe burns.

1 Regular oil and filter changes are the single most important maintenance procedure you can perform on a motorcycle. The oil not only lubricates the internal parts of the engine, transmission and clutch, but it also acts as a coolant, a cleaner, a sealant, and a protector. Because of these demands, the oil takes a terrific amount of abuse and should be drained and the engine/transmission refilled with new oil of the recommended grade and type. Saving a little money on the difference in cost between a good oil and a cheap oil won't pay off if the engine is damaged. The oil filter

11.3 Remove the oil filler cap from the top of the clutch cover

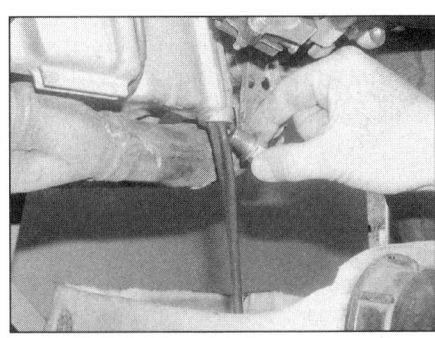
11.4b . . . and allow the oil to drain completely

should be changed with every second oil change (see Section 22).

2 Before changing the oil, warm up the engine so the oil will drain easily. Remove the lower fairing (see Chapter 8).

3 Position a clean drain tray below the engine. Unscrew the oil filler cap from the clutch cover to vent the engine unit and to act as a reminder that there is no oil in the engine **(see illustration)**.

4 Unscrew the oil drain plug from the underside of the engine and allow the oil to flow into the drain tray **(see illustrations)**. Check the condition of the sealing washer on the drain plug and discard it if it is damaged or worn **(see illustration)**. It is always advisable to use a new washer even if the old one looks all right **(see illustration)**.

5 When the oil has completely drained, fit the plug with its washer into the crankcase and tighten it to the torque setting specified at the beginning of this Chapter. Avoid overtightening, as you will damage the sump.

6 Refill the engine to the proper level using the recommended type and amount of oil (see *Daily (pre-ride) checks*). With the motorcycle vertical, the oil level should lie between the maximum and minimum level lines on the dipstick (see *Daily (pre-ride) checks*). Install the filler cap **(see illustration 11.3)**. Start the engine and let it run for two or three minutes. Stop the engine, wait a few minutes, then check the oil level. If necessary, add more oil to bring the level up to the maximum level line on the dipstick. Check that there are no leaks around the drain plug.

7 Every so often, and especially as Yamaha do not fit an oil pressure switch and warning

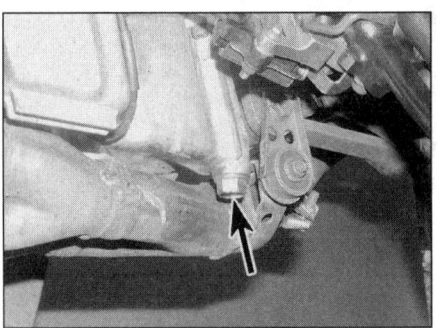
11.4a Unscrew the oil drain plug . . .

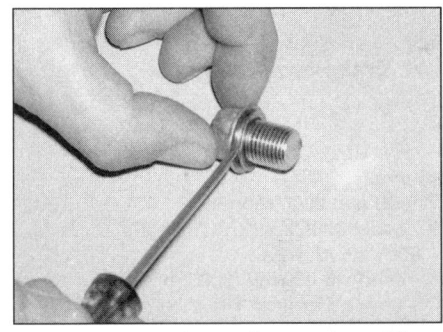
11.4c Replace the sealing washer with a new one if necessary

light (the system fitted uses an oil level sensor), it is advisable to perform an oil pressure check (see Section 33).

8 The old oil drained from the engine cannot be re-used and should be disposed of properly. Check with your local refuse disposal company, disposal facility or environmental agency to see whether they will accept the used oil for recycling. Don't pour used oil into drains or onto the ground.

9 Install the lower fairing (see Chapter 8).

> **HAYNES HiNT** Check the old oil carefully – if it is very metallic coloured, then the engine is experiencing wear from break-in (new engine) or from insufficient lubrication. If there are flakes or chips of metal in the oil, then something is drastically wrong internally and the engine will have to be disassembled for inspection and repair. If there are pieces of fibre-like material in the oil, the clutch is experiencing excessive wear and should be checked.

Note: It is antisocial and illegal to dump oil down the drain. To find the location of your local oil recycling bank in the UK, call this number free. In the USA, note that any oil supplier must accept used oil for recycling.

0800 66 33 66
www.oilbankline.org.uk

1•14 Routine maintenance and servicing

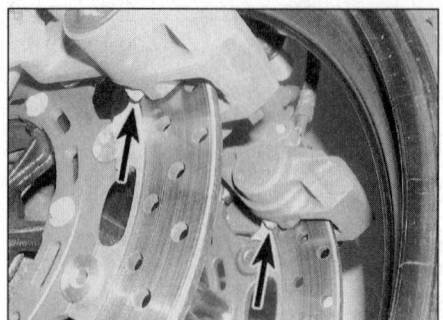

12.2 Check front brake pad wear from the underside of the caliper

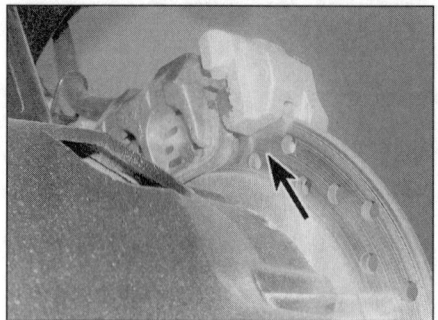

12.3 Check rear brake pad wear from the underside of the caliper

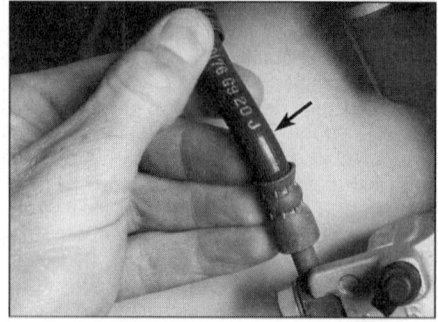

13.3 Inspect the brake hoses for cracks, bulges and leaking fluid

12 Brake pads – wear check

Interval:
  1999 and 2000 models –
    every 6000 km (3700 miles)
  2001-on models –
    every 10,000 km (6000 miles)

Warning: *The dust created by the brake system may contain asbestos, which is harmful to your health. Never blow it out with compressed air and don't inhale any of it. An approved filtering mask should be worn when working on the brakes.*

1 Each brake pad has wear indicators that can be viewed without removing the pads from the caliper.
2 On the front brake pads the turned-in corners of the pad backing material indicate the wear limit – when the corners are almost contacting the disc the pads must be renewed. The indicators are visible by looking up at the bottom corner of the pads **(see illustration)**.
Caution: *Do not allow the pads to wear to the extent that the indicators contact the disc itself, as the disc will be damaged.*
3 On the rear brake pads a groove cut in the friction material indicates the wear limit. Renew the pads when they are worn to the bottom of the groove. The grooves are visible by looking up at the bottom edge of the pads **(see illustration)**.
Note: *Some after-market pads may use different wear indicators; always check with your supplier before fitting.*
4 If the pads are worn to the limit, new ones must be installed. If the pads are dirty or if you are in doubt as to the amount of friction material remaining, remove them for inspection (see Chapter 7). If required, measure the amount of friction material remaining – the minimum is 0.5 mm (front) or 0.8 mm (rear).
Note: *It is not possible to degrease the friction material; if the pads are contaminated in any way they must be renewed.*
5 Refer to Chapter 7 for details of pad renewal.

13 Brake system – check

Interval:
  1999 and 2000 models –
    every 6000 km (3700 miles)
  2001-on models –
    every 10,000 km (6000 miles)

1 A routine general check of the brake system will ensure that any problems are discovered and remedied before the rider's safety is jeopardised.
2 Check the brake lever and pedal for looseness, improper or rough action, excessive play, bends, and other damage. Replace any damaged parts with new ones (see Chapter 7). Clean and lubricate the lever and pedal pivots if their action is stiff or rough (see Section 9).
3 Make sure all brake fasteners are tight. Check the brake pads for wear (see Section 12) and make sure the fluid level in the reservoirs is correct (see *Daily (pre-ride) checks*). Look for leaks at the hose connections and check for cracks in the hoses themselves **(see illustration)**. If the lever or pedal is spongy, bleed the brakes (see Chapter 7). The brake fluid should be changed every two years (see Section 29) and the hoses renewed if they deteriorate, or every four years irrespective of their condition (see Section 31). The master cylinder and caliper seals should be renewed every two years, or if leakage from them is evident (see Section 28).
4 Make sure the brake light operates when the front brake lever is pulled in. The front brake light switch, mounted on the underside of the master cylinder, is not adjustable. If it fails to operate properly, check it (see Chapter 9).
5 Make sure the brake light is activated just before the rear brake takes effect. If adjustment is necessary, hold the switch and turn the adjuster nut on the switch body until the brake light is activated when required **(see illustration)**. If the brake light comes on too late, turn the nut clockwise. If the brake light comes on too soon or is permanently on, turn the nut anti-clockwise. If the switch doesn't operate the brake light, check it (see Chapter 9).
6 The front brake lever has a span adjuster which alters the distance of the lever from the handlebar. Each setting is identified by a number on the adjuster which aligns with the arrow on the lever bracket. Pull the lever away from the handlebar and turn the adjuster ring until the setting which best suits the rider is obtained **(see illustration)**. There are four settings – setting 1 gives the largest span, and setting 4 the smallest. When making adjustment ensure that the pin set in the lever bracket is engaged in its detent in the adjuster.
7 Check the position of the brake pedal (brake pedal height). Yamaha recommend the distance between the front edge of the brake

13.5 Adjust the rear brake light switch with the nut (arrowed)

13.6 Front brake lever span adjuster (arrowed)

Routine maintenance and servicing 1•15

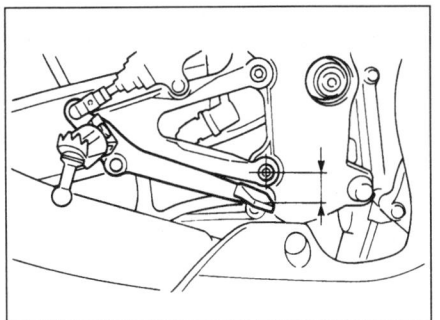

13.7 Measure the brake pedal height between the two points (arrowed)

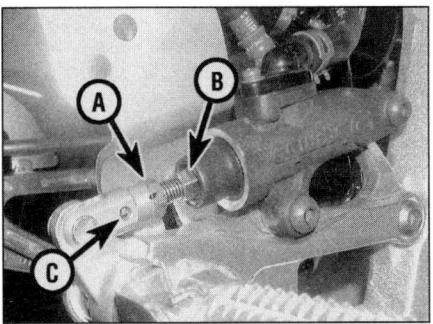

13.8 Loosen locknut (A) and adjust pushrod at hex (B), making sure rod end is still visible in hole (C)

14.3 Check the security of the wheel balance weights (arrowed)

pedal and the centre line of the lower footrest bracket bolt should be as specified at the beginning of this Chapter **(see illustration)**.

8 If the pedal height is incorrect, or if the rider's preference is different, loosen the locknut on the master cylinder pushrod, then turn the pushrod using a spanner on the hex at the top of the rod until the pedal is at the correct or desired height. After adjustment check that the pushrod end is still visible in the hole in the clevis **(see illustration)**. On completion tighten the locknut securely. Adjust the rear brake light switch after adjusting the pedal height (see Step 5).

14 Wheels and tyres – general check
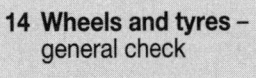

Interval:
1999 and 2000 models –
every 6000 km (3700 miles)
2001-on models –
every 10,000 km (6000 miles)

Tyres

1 Check the tyre condition and tread depth thoroughly – see *Daily (pre-ride) checks*.

Wheels

2 Cast wheels are virtually maintenance free, but they should be kept clean and checked periodically for cracks and other damage. Also check the wheel runout and alignment

(see Chapter 7). Never attempt to repair damaged cast wheels; they must be replaced with new ones.

3 Check the tyre valve rubber for signs of damage or deterioration and have it renewed if necessary. Also, make sure the valve cap is in place and tight. Check that the wheel balance weights are fixed firmly to the wheel rim **(see illustration)**. If the weights have fallen off, have the wheel rebalanced by a motorcycle tyre specialist.

15 Wheel bearings – check

Interval:
1999 and 2000 models –
every 6000 km (3700 miles)
2001-on models –
every 10,000 km (6000 miles)

1 Wheel bearings will wear over a period of time and result in handling problems.
2 Support the motorcycle upright using an auxiliary stand. Check for any play in the bearings by pushing and pulling the wheel against the hub **(see illustration)**. Also rotate the wheel and check that it rotates smoothly.
3 If any play is detected in the hub, or if the wheel does not rotate smoothly (and this is not due to brake or transmission drag), the wheel bearings must be removed and inspected for wear or damage (see Chapter 7).

15.2 Checking for play in the wheel bearings

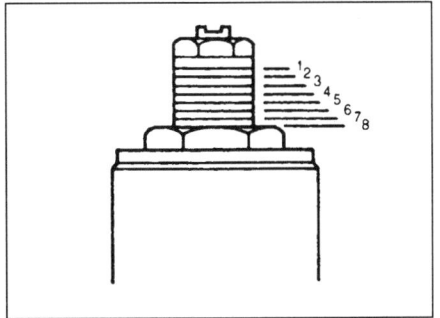

16.4 Check spring pre-load by counting the number of grooves visible

16 Suspension – check

Interval:
1999 and 2000 models –
every 6000 km (3700 miles)
2001-on models –
every 10,000 km (6000 miles)

1 The suspension components must be maintained in top operating condition to ensure rider safety. Loose, worn or damaged suspension parts decrease the motorcycle's stability and control.

Front suspension

2 While standing alongside the motorcycle, apply the front brake and push on the handlebars to compress the forks several times. Check that they move up and down smoothly without binding. If binding is felt, the forks should be disassembled and inspected (see Chapter 6).
3 Inspect the fork tubes for signs of scratches, corrosion and pitting, and oil leakage. Displace the stoneguard from the top of the fork slider, then carefully lever up the dust seals using a flat-bladed screwdriver and inspect the area around the fork seals (see Chapter 6). Any scratches, corrosion and pitting will cause premature seal failure. If the damage is excessive, new tubes should be installed (see Chapter 6). If oil leakage is evident, new seals must be fitted (see Chapter 6).
4 The forks are adjustable for spring pre-load, rebound damping and compression damping and it is essential that both fork legs are adjusted equally. The spring pre-load setting can be checked by counting the number of grooves visible below the adjuster bolt **(see illustration)** (see Chapter 6). Rebound damping and compression damping require the adjusters to be screwed fully in to check the current setting and then screwed out to reset as required (see Chapter 6).
5 Check the tightness of all suspension nuts and bolts to be sure none have worked loose, referring to the torque settings specified at the beginning of Chapter 6.

1•16 Routine maintenance and servicing

16.8a Checking for play in the swingarm bearings

16.8b Checking for play in the suspension linkage bearings

16.9 Checking the swingarm bearings with the wheel removed

Rear suspension

6 Inspect the rear shock for fluid leakage and tightness of its mountings. If leakage is found, a new shock should be installed (see Chapter 6).

7 With the aid of an assistant to support the bike, compress the rear suspension several times. It should move up and down freely without binding. If any binding is felt, the worn or faulty component must be identified and renewed. The problem could be due to either the shock absorber, the suspension linkage components or the swingarm components.

8 Support the motorcycle using an auxiliary stand so that the rear wheel is off the ground. Grab the swingarm and rock it from side to side – there should be no discernible movement at the ends of the swingarm (Yamaha specify a maximum of 1 mm sideplay) **(see illustration)**. If there is a little movement or a slight clicking can be heard, inspect the tightness of all the rear suspension mounting bolts and nuts, referring to the torque settings specified at the beginning of Chapter 6, and re-check for movement. Next, grasp the top of the rear wheel and pull it upwards – there should be no discernible freeplay before the shock absorber begins to compress **(see illustration)**. Any freeplay felt in either check indicates worn bearings in the suspension linkage or swingarm, or worn shock absorber mountings. The worn components must be renewed (see Chapter 6).

9 To make an accurate assessment of the swingarm bearings it is necessary to remove the rear wheel (see Chapter 7) and the bolt securing the suspension linkage plates to the swingarm (see Chapter 6). Grasp the rear of the swingarm with one hand and place your other hand at the junction of the swingarm and the frame. Try to move the rear of the swingarm from side to side. Any wear (play) in the bearings should be felt as movement between the swingarm and the frame at the front **(see illustration)**. If there is any play, the swingarm will be felt to move forward and backward at the front (not from side-to-side). Next, move the swingarm up and down through its full travel. It should move freely, without any binding or rough spots. If any play in the swingarm is noted or if the swingarm does not move freely, the bearings must be removed for inspection or renewal (see Chapter 6).

10 The rear shock is adjustable for spring pre-load, rebound damping and compression damping. Ensure that the spring seat is correctly located on the pre-load adjustment stopper **(see illustration)**. See Chapter 6 for shock adjustment.

17 Steering head bearings – freeplay check and adjustment

Interval:
 1999 and 2000 models –
  every 6000 km (3700 miles)
 2001-on models –
  every 10,000 km (6000 miles)

1 This motorcycle is equipped with caged ball steering head bearings which can become dented, rough or loose during normal use of the machine. In extreme cases, worn or loose steering head bearings can cause steering wobble – a condition that is potentially dangerous.

Check

2 Support the motorcycle in an upright position using an auxiliary stand. Raise the front wheel off the ground either by having an assistant push down on the rear, or by placing a support under the engine, in which case remove the lower fairing first (see Chapter 8).

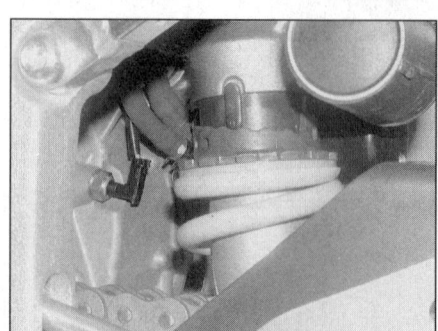

16.10 Ensure rear shock spring seat is correctly located on adjustment stopper (arrowed)

3 Point the front wheel straight ahead, and slowly turn the handlebars from side to side. Any dents or roughness in the bearing races will be felt and if the bearings are too tight the bars will not move smoothly and freely. If the bearings are damaged or the action is rough, they should be renewed (see Chapter 6). If the bearings are too tight they should be adjusted as described below.

4 Next, grasp the fork sliders and try to pull and push them forwards and backwards **(see illustration)**. Any looseness in the steering head bearings will be felt as front-to-rear movement of the forks. If play is felt in the bearings, adjust them as follows.

> **HAYNES HINT** *Freeplay in the fork due to worn fork bushes can be misinterpreted as steering head bearing play – do not confuse the two.*

Adjustment

5 Position the motorcycle in an upright position using an auxiliary stand. Remove the fuel tank (see Chapter 4) and the fairing (see Chapter 8). **Note:** *Although it is not strictly necessary to remove the fuel tank and fairing, doing so will prevent the possibility of damage, should a tool slip.*

6 Displace the handlebars and slacken the fork clamp bolts in the upper yoke (see Chapter 6).

7 Unscrew the steering stem nut and remove

17.4 Checking for play in the steering head bearings

Routine maintenance and servicing 1•17

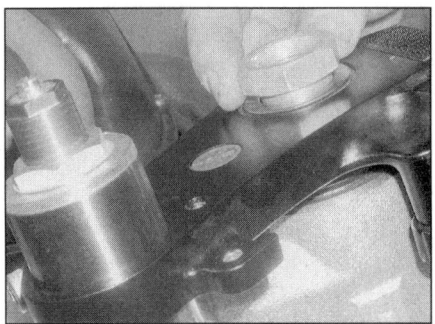

17.7 Unscrew the steering stem nut and remove the washer

17.8a Remove the tabbed lockwasher...

17.8b ... and the locknut...

it along with its washer **(see illustration)**, then ease the top yoke upwards off the fork tubes.
8 Remove the tabbed lockwasher, noting how it fits, then unscrew and remove the locknut, using either a C-spanner, a peg spanner or a drift located in one of the notches – though it should only be finger-tight **(see illustrations)**. Remove the rubber washer **(see illustration)**.
9 To adjust the bearings as specified by Yamaha, a special service tool (Pt. No. 90890-01403 for Europe, or YU-33975 for USA) and a torque wrench are required. If the tool is available, first slacken the adjuster nut slightly to take pressure off the bearing, then tighten the nut to the initial torque setting specified at the beginning of this Chapter. Make sure the torque wrench handle is at right-angles (90°) to the centre line between the adjuster nut and the service tool wrench socket **(see illustration)**. Now slacken the nut, then tighten it to the final torque setting specified.
10 If the Yamaha tool is not available, using either a C-spanner, a peg spanner or a drift located in one of the notches, slacken the adjuster nut slightly to take pressure off the bearing then tighten the nut until all freeplay is removed. Now tighten the nut a little more to pre-load the bearings. Now slacken the nut and retighten it, setting it so that all freeplay is just removed from the bearings, yet the steering is able to move freely from side to

17.8c ... and the rubber washer

side. Tighten the nut only a little at a time, and after each adjustment repeat the checks outlined in Steps 3 and 4.
11 Turn the steering from lock to lock five times to settle the bearings, then recheck the adjustment or the torque setting depending on your method used. The object is to set the adjuster nut so that the bearings are under a very light loading, just enough to remove any freeplay.
Caution: Take great care not to apply excessive pressure because this will cause premature failure of the bearings.
12 With the bearings correctly adjusted, install the rubber washer and the locknut **(see illustrations 17.8c and b)**. Tighten the locknut finger-tight, then tighten it further until

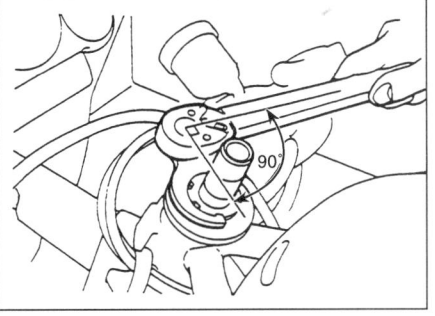

17.9 Make sure the torque wrench arm is at right-angles (90°) to the service tool

its notches align with those in the adjuster nut, making sure the adjuster nut does not turn as well. Install the tabbed lockwasher so that the tabs fit into the notches in both the locknut and adjuster nut **(see illustration 17.8a)**. Recheck the bearing adjustment as described in Steps 3 and 4 to ensure the adjuster nut hasn't moved.
13 Fit the top yoke onto the steering stem and the fork legs. Install the washer and steering stem nut and tighten it and the fork clamp bolts to the torque settings specified at the beginning of this Chapter.
14 Install the handlebars (see Chapter 6).
15 Recheck the bearing adjustment as described in Steps 3 and 4 and re-adjust if necessary.

17.10a Alternately loosen ...

17.10b ... and then tighten the adjuster nut to remove bearing freeplay

1•18 Routine maintenance and servicing

18.1 Check the sidestand return spring for wear and sagging

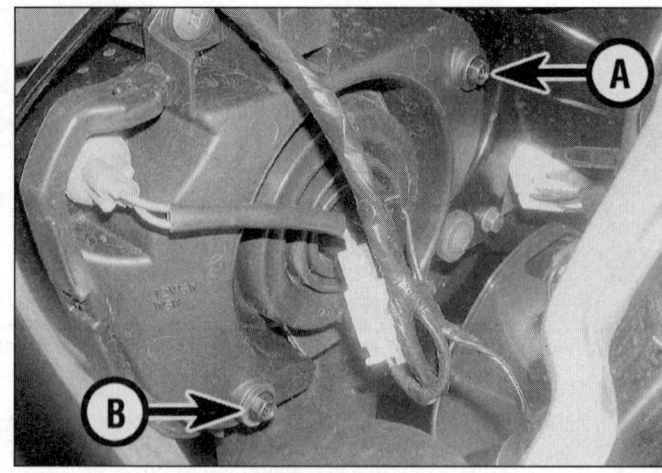

21.2 Vertical adjuster (A), horizontal adjuster (B) on the left-hand headlight

18 Sidestand and sidestand switch – check

Interval:
1999 and 2000 models –
every 6000 km (3700 miles)
2001-on models –
every 10,000 km (6000 miles)

1 The stand return spring must be capable of retracting the stand fully and holding it retracted when the motorcycle is in use. If a spring has sagged or broken, it must be replaced with a new one **(see illustration)**.
2 Lubricate the stand pivot regularly (see Section 9).
3 The sidestand switch prevents the motorcycle being started if the transmission is in gear and the stand is down, and cuts the engine if the stand is put down while the engine is running and in gear.
4 Check the operation of the switch by shifting the transmission into neutral, retracting the stand and starting the engine. Pull in the clutch lever and select a gear. Extend the sidestand. The engine should stop as the sidestand is extended. If the sidestand switch does not operate as described, check its circuit (see Chapter 9).

19 Nuts and bolts – tightness check

Interval:
1999 and 2000 models –
every 6000 km (3700 miles)
2001-on models –
every 10,000 km (6000 miles)

1 Since vibration of the machine tends to loosen fasteners, all nuts, bolts, screws, etc. should be periodically checked for proper tightness.

2 Pay particular attention to the following:
Spark plugs
Engine oil drain plug
Gearchange lever, brake and clutch lever, and brake pedal mounting bolts
Footrest and stand bolts
Engine mounting bolts
Shock absorber and suspension linkage bolts and swingarm pivot bolts
Handlebar clamp bolts
Front wheel axle and axle clamp bolt
Front fork clamp bolts (top and bottom yoke)
Rear wheel axle nut
Brake caliper mounting bolts
Brake hose banjo bolts and caliper bleed valves
Brake disc bolts
Exhaust system bolts/nuts

3 If a torque wrench is available, use it along with the torque specifications at the beginning of this and other Chapters.

20 Battery – check

Interval:
1999 and 2000 models –
every 6000 km (3700 miles)
2001-on models –
every 10,000 km (6000 miles)

1 All models are fitted with a sealed, gel-type maintenance-free battery. **Note:** *Do not attempt to open the battery as resulting damage will mean it will be unfit for further use.*
2 All that should be done is to check that the terminals are clean and tight and that the casing is not damaged or leaking. See Chapter 9 for further details.
Caution: Be extremely careful when handling or working around the battery. The electrolyte gel is very caustic and an explosive gas (hydrogen) is given off when the battery is charging.
3 If the machine is not in regular use, disconnect the battery and give it a refresher charge every month to six weeks (see Chapter 9, Section 4).

21 Headlight aim – check and adjustment

Interval:
1999 and 2000 models –
every 6000 km (3700 miles)
2001-on models –
every 10,000 km (6000 miles)

Note: *An improperly adjusted headlight may cause problems for oncoming traffic or provide poor, unsafe illumination of the road ahead. Before adjusting the headlight aim, be sure to consult with local traffic laws and regulations – for UK models refer to MOT Test Checks in the Reference section.*

1 The headlight beam can be adjusted both horizontally and vertically. Before making any adjustment, check that the tyre pressures are correct and the suspension is adjusted as required. Make any adjustments to the headlight aim with the machine on level ground, with the fuel tank half full and with an assistant sitting on the seat. If the bike is usually ridden with a passenger on the back, have a second assistant to do this.
2 Remove the fairing inner trim panels (see Chapter 8). Vertical adjustment is made by turning the adjuster screw on the bottom outer corner of each headlight unit **(see illustration)**. Turn anti-clockwise to raise the beam, and clockwise to lower it.
3 Horizontal adjustment is made by turning the adjuster screw on the top inner corner of each headlight unit **(see illustration 21.2)**. For the left-hand beam, turn it anti-clockwise to move the beam to the right, and clockwise to move it to the left. For the right-hand beam, turn it clockwise to move the beam to the right, and anti-clockwise to move it to the left.
4 Check the operation of the headlights and replace the inner trim panels.

Routine maintenance and servicing 1•19

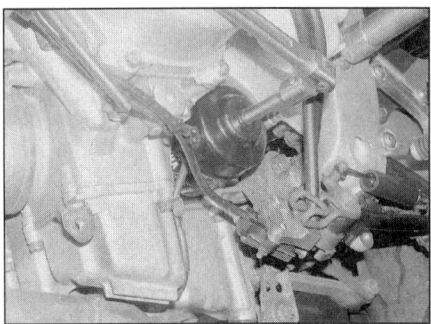
22.2 Unscrew the oil filter and drain any residual oil

22.3a Ensure the sealing surface is clean . . .

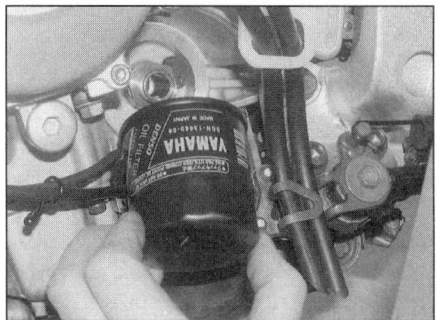
22.3b . . . then lubricate the filter seal and install the filter

22.3c Tighten the filter as specified

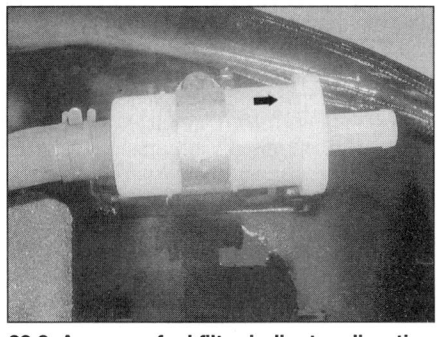
23.2 Arrow on fuel filter indicates direction of fuel flow

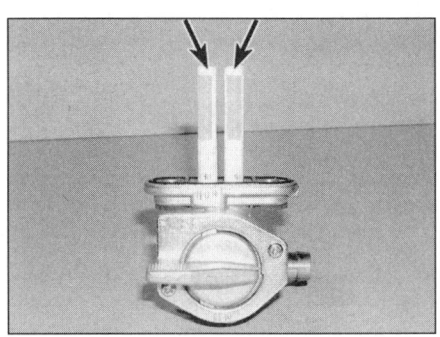
23.5 Fuel strainers (arrowed) cover each fuel pipe

22 Engine/transmission – oil and filter change

Interval:
1999 and 2000 models –
every 12,000 km (7500 miles)
2001-on models –
every 20,000 km (12,000 miles)

Warning: Be careful when draining the oil, as the exhaust pipes, the engine, and the oil itself can cause severe burns.

1 Drain the engine oil as described in Section 11, Steps 2 to 5.
2 Now place the drain tray below the oil filter, which is on the lower, left-hand side of the engine unit. Clean the crankcase around the filter, then unscrew the filter using an adapter tool, or a strap wrench and tip any residual oil into the drain tray **(see illustration)**.
3 Clean the sealing surface on the crankcase with a suitable solvent, then smear clean engine oil onto the rubber seal on the new filter, and screw the filter onto the engine until the seal just seats **(see illustrations)**. If a filter adapter tool is available, tighten the filter to the torque setting specified at the beginning of this Chapter **(see illustration)**. Otherwise, tighten the filter as tight as possible by hand, or by the number of turns specified on the filter or its packaging. **Note:** *Do not use a strap or chain wrench to tighten the filter as you may damage it.*
4 Refill the engine to the proper level as described in Section 11, Step 6.

5 Note the advice in Section 11 for disposing of used oil. Remember to drain all the old oil from the filter (you can punch a hole in the filter to ensure it drains fully) into the drain pan. Note that the old filter should be taken to the oil disposal facility rather than disposed of with the household rubbish.

23 Fuel filter and strainer – cleaning and renewal

Interval:
1999 and 2000 models –
every 12,000 km (7500 miles)
2001-on models –
every 20,000 km (12,000 miles)

Warning: Petrol (gasoline) is extremely flammable, so take extra precautions when you work on any part of the fuel system. Don't smoke or allow open flames or bare light bulbs near the work area, and don't work in a garage where a natural gas-type appliance is present. If you spill any fuel on your skin, rinse it off immediately with soap and water. When you perform any kind of work on the fuel system, wear safety glasses and have a fire extinguisher suitable for a Class B type fire (flammable liquids) on hand.

Fuel filter

1 An in-line fuel filter is fitted next to the fuel tap on the underside of the tank. At the service interval, or if the filter is dirty or clogged, replace it with a new one – this type of filter cannot be cleaned.
2 Have a rag ready to soak up any residual fuel, then release the clip and disconnect the tap hose from the filter. Slacken the screw that retains the filter clamp and remove the filter and discard it. Install the new filter so that its arrow points in the direction of fuel flow (i.e. away from the tap) **(see illustration)**. Fit the hose onto the filter union and secure it with the clamp.
3 Install the fuel tank and start the engine to check that there are no leaks.

Fuel strainer

4 A fuel strainer is mounted in the tank and is integral with the fuel tap. Cleaning the strainer is not strictly required at this maintenance interval, but is advised after a high mileage has been covered or if fuel starvation is suspected. Remove the fuel tank and the fuel tap (see Chapter 4).
5 Once the strainer is dry, clean the gauze with a soft brush or low pressure compressed air to remove all traces of dirt and fuel sediment. Check the gauze for holes. If any are found, a new tap should be fitted – the strainer is not available separately **(see illustration)**. If the strainer is dirty, check the condition of the inside of the tank – if there is evidence of rust, drain and clean the tank (see Chapter 4).
6 Check the condition of the tap O-ring and renew it if it is in any way damaged or deteriorated. It is advisable to renew it as a matter of course.

1•20 Routine maintenance and servicing

24 Suspension linkage bearings – re-greasing

Interval:
1999 and 2000 models –
every 24,000 km (15,000 miles)
2001-on models –
every 20,000 km (12,000 miles)

1 Over a period of time the grease will harden and dirt will penetrate the bearings.
2 The rear suspension components are not equipped with grease nipples. Remove the suspension linkage to grease the bearings (see Chapter 6).

25 Steering head bearings – re-greasing

Interval:
1999 and 2000 models –
every 24,000 km (15,000 miles)
2001-on models –
every 20,000 km (12,000 miles)

1 Over a period of time the grease will harden or may be washed out of the bearings by incorrect use of jet washes.
2 Disassemble the steering head to grease the bearings (see Chapter 6).

26 Valve clearances – check and adjustment

Interval:
1999 and 2000 models –
every 42,000 km (26,000 miles)
2001-on models –
every 40,000 km (24,000 miles)

1 The engine must be completely cool for this maintenance procedure, so let the machine sit overnight before beginning.
2 Remove the lower fairing and the fairing side panels (see Chapter 8) and the radiator (see Chapter 3).
3 Remove the valve cover (see Chapter 2). Each cylinder is referred to by a number. They are numbered 1 to 4 from left to right, viewed as normally seated on the bike.
4 Make a chart or sketch of all valve positions so that a note of each clearance can be made against the relevant valve.
5 Unscrew the bolts securing the ignition rotor cover on the right-hand side of the engine and remove the cover, noting the clamp for the coolant hose and the bracket for the clutch cable **(see illustration)**. Discard the gasket, as a new one must be used and remove the dowels from either the crankcase or the cover if they are loose. To turn the engine in a clockwise direction only, use a spanner on the ignition rotor bolt. Alternatively, to turn the engine in either direction, place the motorcycle on an auxiliary

26.5 Remove the ignition rotor cover, noting the coolant hose clamp (A) and clutch cable bracket (B)

stand so that the rear wheel is off the ground, select a high gear and rotate the rear wheel by hand.
6 Turn the engine clockwise until the 'T' mark on the ignition rotor faces to the rear and aligns with the crankcase mating surfaces **(see illustration)** and the camshaft lobes for the No. 1 (left-hand) cylinder face away from each other. If the cam lobes are facing towards each other, rotate the engine clockwise 360° (one full turn) so that the 'T' mark again aligns with the crankcase mating surfaces. The camshaft lobes will now be facing away from each other and the No. 1 cylinder will be at TDC (top dead centre) on the compression stroke.
7 Check the clearances on the four No. 1 cylinder intake and exhaust valves. Insert a feeler gauge of the same thickness as the correct valve clearance (see Specifications) between the camshaft lobe and follower of each valve and check that it is a firm sliding fit – you should feel a slight drag when the you pull the gauge out **(see illustrations)**. If not, use the feeler gauges to measure the exact clearance. Record the measured clearance on your chart.
8 Now turn the engine clockwise 180° (half a turn) so that the 'T' mark faces forward and aligns with the crankcase mating surfaces and the camshaft lobes for the No. 2 cylinder are

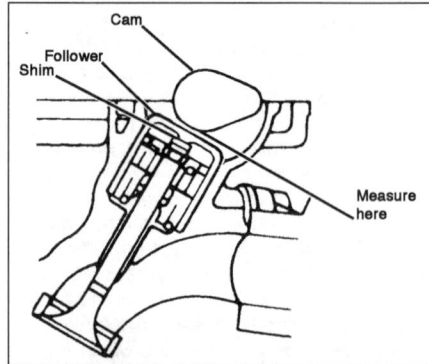

26.7a Ensure the cam lobes are facing away from each other and are not depressing the valves, then insert the feeler gauge between the cam and follower

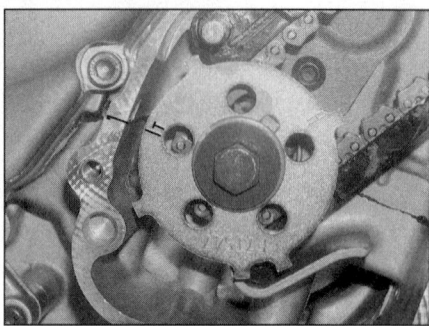

26.6 Align the 'T' mark with the rear facing crankcase mating surfaces

facing away from each other. The No. 2 cylinder is now at TDC on the compression stroke. Measure the clearances of the No. 2 cylinder valves using the method described in Step 7.
9 Now turn the engine clockwise 180° (half a turn) so that the 'T' mark faces to the rear and aligns with the crankcase mating surfaces and the camshaft lobes for the No. 4 cylinder are facing away from each other. The No. 4 cylinder is now at TDC on the compression stroke. Measure the clearances of the No. 4 cylinder valves using the method described in Step 7.
10 Now turn the engine clockwise 180° (half a turn) so that the 'T' mark faces forward and aligns with the crankcase mating surfaces and the camshaft lobes for the No. 3 cylinder are facing away from each other. The No. 3 cylinder is now at TDC on the compression stroke. Measure the clearances of the No. 3 cylinder valves using the method described in Step 7.
11 When all clearances have been measured and recorded, identify whether the clearance on any valve falls outside that specified. If it does, the shim between the cam follower and the valve must be replaced with one of a thickness which will restore the correct clearance.
12 Shim replacement requires removal of the camshafts (see Chapter 2). There is no need to remove both camshafts if shims from only one need replacing. Place rags over the spark plug holes and the cam chain tunnel to prevent a shim from dropping into the engine on removal.

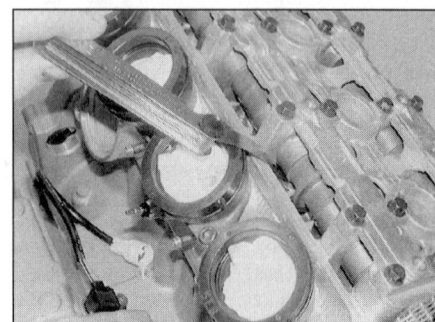

26.7b Measuring the valve clearance using a feeler gauge

Routine maintenance and servicing 1•21

26.13a Remove the cam follower...

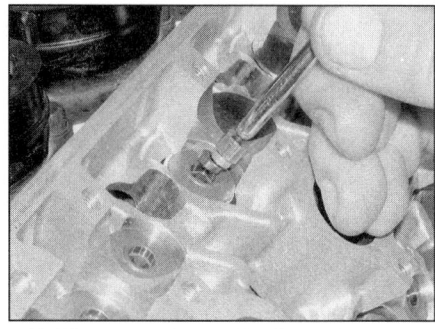

26.13b ...and the shim from the top of the valve

26.14a Each shim has its size marked on the upper face

26.14b Measure the shim with a micrometer

13 With the camshaft removed, remove the cam follower of the valve in question, then retrieve the shim from inside the follower **(see illustrations)**. If it is not in the follower, pick it out of the top of the valve using either a magnet, a small screwdriver with a dab of grease on it (the shim will stick to the grease), or a screwdriver and a pair of pliers. Do not allow the shim to fall into the engine.

14 A size should be marked on the upper face of the shim – a shim marked 175 is 1.75 mm thick. If the mark is not visible, the shim thickness will have to be measured. It is recommended that the shim is measured anyway, to check that it has not worn **(see illustrations)**.

15 Using the appropriate shim selection chart, find where the measured valve clearance and existing shim thickness values intersect and read off the shim size required **(see illustrations)**. Note: *If the existing shim is marked with a number not ending in 0 or 5, round it up or down as appropriate to the nearest number ending in 0 or 5, so that the chart can be used.* Shims are available in 0.05 mm increments from 1.20 mm to 2.40 mm. Note: *If the required replacement shim is greater than 2.40 mm (the largest available), the valve is probably not seating correctly due to a build-up of carbon deposits and should be checked and cleaned or resurfaced as required (see Chapter 2).*

16 Obtain the replacement shim, then lubricate it with molybdenum disulphide grease and fit it into its recess in the top of the

Example:
Valve Clearance (cold)
  0.11 ~ 0.20 mm
  Rounded value 150
    Measured valve clearance is 0.24 mm
Replace pad 150 with pad 160

26.15a Shim selection chart – intake camshaft

Example:
Valve Clearance (cold)
  0.21 ~ 0.30 mm
  Rounded value 175
    Measured valve clearance is 0.35 mm
Replace pad 150 with pad 185

26.15b Shim selection chart – exhaust camshaft

1•22 Routine maintenance and servicing

26.18 Install a new gasket on the cover dowels

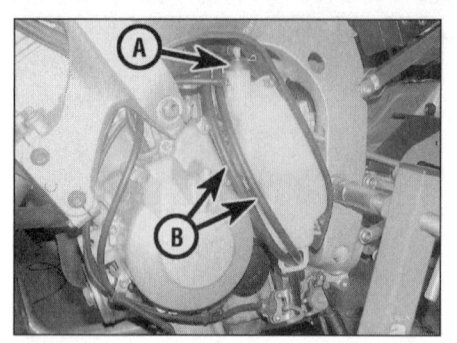

30.2 Release the reservoir cap (A) and fuel tank breather hoses (B)

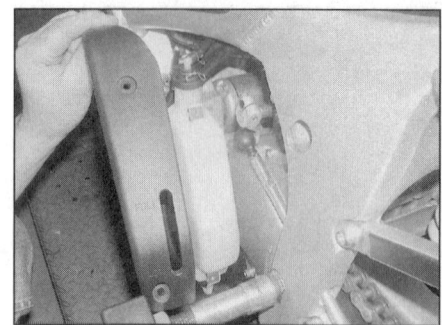

30.3 Remove the fluid level indicator panel

valve, with the size marking facing up **(see illustration 26.14a)**. Check that the shim is correctly seated, then lubricate the follower with molybdenum disulphide oil (a 50/50 mixture of molybdenum disulphide grease and engine oil) and install it onto the valve **(see illustration 26.13a)**. Repeat the process for any other valves until the clearances are correct, then install the camshafts (see Chapter 2).

17 Rotate the crankshaft several turns to seat the new shim(s), then check the clearances again.

18 Install all disturbed components in a reverse of the removal sequence using new gaskets for the valve cover and the ignition rotor cover **(see illustration)**. Ensure the dowels for the rotor cover are in place and that the cam chain tensioner blade pivot pin locates in the hole in the cover. Install the cover bolts, the clamp for the coolant hose and the bracket for the clutch cable and tighten the bolts to the torque setting specified at the beginning of this Chapter **(see illustration 26.5)**.

27 Swingarm bearings – re-greasing

Interval:
  1999 and 2000 models –
   every 24,000 km (15,000 miles)
  2001-on models –
   every 50,000 km (31,000 miles)

1 Over a period of time the grease will harden and dirt will penetrate the bearings.
2 The rear suspension components are not equipped with grease nipples. Remove the swingarm to grease the bearings (see Chapter 6).

28 Brake master cylinder and caliper seals – renewal

Interval:
  All models – every two years

1 The seals will deteriorate over a period of time and lose their effectiveness, leading to sticky operation or fluid loss, or the ingress of air and dirt. Disassemble the master cylinders and calipers for seal renewal (see Chapter 7).

29 Brakes – fluid change

Interval: All models – every two years
1 The brake fluid should be changed at this interval or whenever a master cylinder or caliper overhaul is carried out. Refer to the brake bleeding section in Chapter 7, noting that all old fluid must be pumped from the fluid reservoir and hydraulic line before filling with new fluid.

> **HAYNES HINT** Old brake fluid is invariably much darker in colour than new fluid, making it easy to see when all old fluid has been expelled from the system.

30 Cooling system – draining, flushing and refilling

Interval:
  1999 and 2000 models –
   every 24,000 km (15,000 miles)
  2001-on models – every three years

⚠️ *Warning: Allow the engine to cool completely before performing this maintenance operation. Also, don't allow antifreeze to come into contact with your skin or the painted surfaces of the motorcycle. Rinse off spills immediately with plenty of water. Antifreeze is highly toxic if ingested. Never leave antifreeze lying around in an open container or in puddles on the floor; children and pets are attracted by its sweet smell and may drink it. Check with local authorities (councils) about disposing of antifreeze. Many communities have collection centres where antifreeze can be disposed of safely. Antifreeze is also combustible, so don't store it near open flames.*

Draining

1 Secure the motorcycle upright on a level surface using an auxiliary stand. Remove the lower fairing and the left and right-hand fairing side panels (see Chapter 8).
2 Pull the two fuel tank breather hoses out of the retaining loop on the bottom of the coolant reservoir and remove the reservoir cap and integral radiator overflow hose. Note the routing of the hoses **(see illustration)**.
3 Remove the two screws securing the fluid level indicator panel to the reservoir and remove the panel **(see illustration)**.
4 Unscrew the bolts that retain the reservoir and lift it away from the motorcycle; note the routing of the breather hose attached to the reservoir neck. Empty the contents of the reservoir into a suitable container, rinse the inside with clean water and refit it to the motorcycle temporarily **(see illustrations)**.
5 Remove the pressure cap from the radiator

30.4a Unscrew the bolts that retain the reservoir . . .

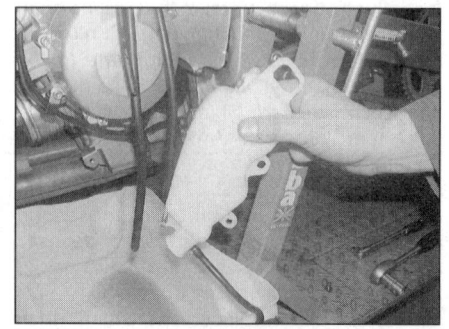

30.4b . . . and empty the contents into a suitable container

Routine maintenance and servicing 1•23

30.5 Remove the radiator pressure cap

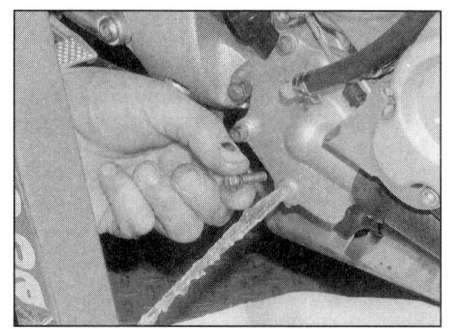

30.6 Remove the drain plug on the water pump and empty the system completely

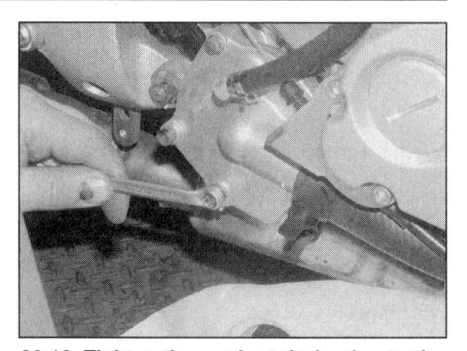

30.13 Tighten the coolant drain plug to the specified torque

filler neck by turning it anti-clockwise until it reaches a stop **(see illustration)**. If you hear a hissing sound (indicating there is still pressure in the system), wait until it stops. Now press down on the cap and continue turning until it can be removed.

6 Position a suitable container beneath the drain plug on the water pump, remove the plug and allow the coolant to completely drain from the system **(see illustration)**. Retain the old sealing washer for use during flushing.

Flushing

7 Flush the system with clean tap water by inserting a garden hose in the radiator filler neck. Allow the water to run through the system until it is clear when it flows out of the drain hole. If there is a lot of rust in the water, remove the radiator (see Chapter 3) and have it professionally cleaned. If the drain hole appears to be clogged with sediment, remove the water pump cover and clean the inside of the pump (see Chapter 3).

8 Install the drain plug using the old sealing washer. Fill the system via the radiator with clean water mixed with a flushing compound. Make sure the flushing compound is compatible with aluminium components, and follow the manufacturer's instructions carefully. Install the pressure cap. Fill the coolant reservoir to the FULL mark with clean water.

9 Start the engine and allow it to reach normal operating temperature. Let it run for about ten minutes.

10 Stop the engine. Let it cool for a while, then cover the pressure cap with a heavy rag and turn it anti-clockwise to the first stop, releasing any pressure that may be present in the system. Once the hissing stops, push down on the cap and remove it completely. Drain the system once again.

11 Fill the system with clean water and repeat the procedure in Steps 8 to 10.

12 Empty the coolant reservoir and refit it to the motorcycle. Tighten the mounting bolts securely and clip the overflow hose to the frame. Install the coolant level indicator panel.

Refilling

13 Fit a new sealing washer onto the drain plug and tighten it to the torque setting specified at the beginning of this Chapter **(see illustration)**.

14 Fill the system via the radiator with the proper coolant mixture (see this Chapter's Specifications) **(see illustration)**. **Note:** *Pour the coolant in slowly to minimise the amount of air entering the system.* When the system appears full, move the bike off its stand and shake it slightly to dissipate the coolant, then place the bike back on the auxiliary stand and top the system up.

15 When the system is full (all the way up to the top of the radiator filler neck), install the pressure cap. Now fill the coolant reservoir to the FULL mark and fit the cap (see *Daily (pre-ride) checks*).

16 Start the engine and allow it to run for several minutes. Flick the throttle open 3 or 4 times, so that the engine speed rises to approximately 4000 – 5000 rpm, then stop the engine. Any air trapped in the system should bleed back to the top of the radiator via the small-bore air bleed hoses.

17 Wait a few minutes for the coolant to settle, then check the coolant level in the coolant reservoir. If the level has fallen, add the specified mixture until it reaches the FULL mark.

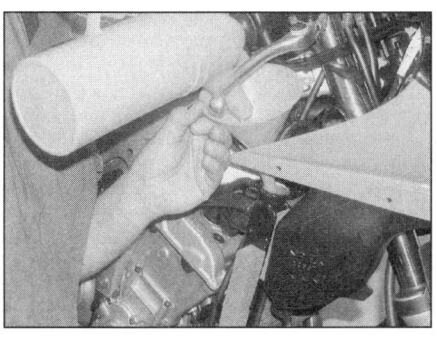

30.14 Fill the system with the correct coolant mixture

18 Check the system for leaks.

19 Do not dispose of the old coolant by pouring it down the drain. Instead pour it into a heavy plastic container, cap it tightly and take it into an authorised disposal site or service station – see **Warning** at the beginning of this Section.

20 Install the fairing panels (see Chapter 8).

31 Brake hoses – renewal

Interval:
All models – every four years

1 The hoses will deteriorate with age and should be replaced with new ones every four years regardless of their apparent condition (see Chapter 7).

2 Always replace the banjo union sealing washers with new ones and bleed the hydraulic system after fitting the new hoses.

Non-scheduled maintenance

32 Cylinder compression – check

1 Among other things, poor engine performance may be caused by leaking valves, incorrect valve clearances, a leaking head gasket, or worn pistons, rings and/or cylinder walls. A compression check will help pinpoint these conditions and can also indicate the presence of excessive carbon deposits in the combustion chambers.

2 The only tools required are a compression gauge (with a threaded end to match the spark plug hole size) and a spark plug wrench.

Depending on the outcome of the initial test, a squirt-type oil can may also be needed.

3 Make sure the valve clearances are correctly set (see Section 26) and that the cylinder head bolts are tightened to the correct torque setting (see Chapter 2).

4 Refer to *Fault Finding Equipment* in the *Reference* section for details of the

33 Engine oil pressure – check

1 This engine is fitted with an oil level sensor and warning light. The function of the circuit is described in Chapter 9.
2 If there is any doubt about the performance of the engine lubrication system an oil pressure check must be carried out. The check provides useful information about the condition of the engine's lubrication system.
3 To check the oil pressure, a suitable pressure gauge (which screws into the crankcase) will be needed. Yamaha provide a gauge (part no. 90890-03153) and gauge adapter (part no. 90890-03139) for this purpose.
4 Warm the engine up to normal operating temperature then stop it. Check the engine oil level and top up if necessary (see *Daily (pre-ride) checks*).
5 Unscrew the oil gallery bolt in the left-hand side of the crankcase below the generator cover **(see illustration)** and quickly screw the adapter into the crankcase threads. Connect the pressure gauge to the adapter.

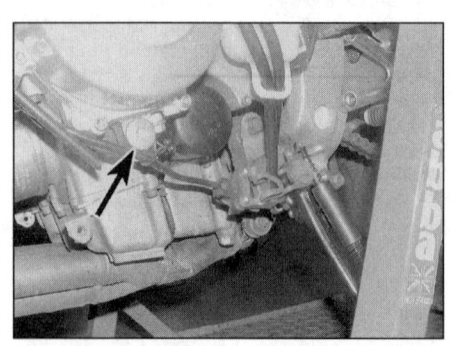

compression test. Refer to the specifications at the beginning of this Chapter for compression figures.

Warning: Take great care not to burn your hand on the hot engine unit, exhaust pipe or with engine oil when accessing the gauge take-off point on the crankcase. Do not allow exhaust gases to build up in the work area; either perform the check outside or use an exhaust gas extraction system.

Discard the oil gallery bolt O-ring as a new one must be fitted on reassembly.
6 Start the engine and increase the engine speed to 6000 rpm whilst watching the pressure gauge reading. The oil pressure should be similar to that given in the Specifications at the beginning of this Chapter.
7 If the pressure is significantly lower than the standard, either the pressure relief valve is stuck open, the oil pump is faulty, the oil strainer or filter is blocked, or there is considerable engine wear. Begin diagnosis by checking the oil filter, strainer and relief valve, then the oil pump (see Chapter 2). If those items check out okay, the engine bearing oil clearances are likely to be excessive and the engine needs to be overhauled.
8 If the pressure is too high, either an oil passage is clogged, the relief valve is stuck closed or the wrong grade of oil is being used.
9 Stop the engine and unscrew the gauge and adapter from the crankcase.
10 Lubricate the oil gallery bolt O-ring with clean engine oil and install the bolt. Tighten the bolt to the specified torque setting, then check the oil level (see *Daily (pre-ride) checks*).
11 Refer to Chapter 2 and rectify any problems before running the engine again.

34 Fuel hoses – renewal

Warning: Petrol (gasoline) is extremely flammable, so take extra precautions when you work on any part of the fuel system. Don't smoke or allow open flames or bare light bulbs near the work area, and don't work in a garage where a natural gas-type appliance is present. If you spill any fuel on your skin, rinse it off immediately with soap and water. When you perform any kind of work on the fuel system, wear safety glasses and have a fire extinguisher suitable for a Class B type fire (flammable liquids) on hand.

1 The fuel delivery hoses should be renewed after a few years, regardless of their condition.
2 Remove the fuel tank (see Chapter 4). Disconnect the fuel hoses from the fuel tap, filter, fuel pump and from the carburettors, noting the routing of each hose and where it connects (see Chapter 4 if required). It is advisable to make a sketch of the various hoses before removing them, to ensure they are correctly installed.
3 Secure each new hose to its unions using new clamps. Run the engine and check that there are no leaks before taking the machine out on the road.

35 Front forks – oil change

1 Fork oil degrades over a period of time and loses its damping qualities. Refer to the following sections of Chapter 6 for changing the oil. Note that the forks do not need to be completely disassembled.
2 Remove the fork legs from the yokes as described in Chapter 6, Section 6. Follow the procedure in Section 7 (Steps 3 to 6) to remove the fork top bolt, spacer, spring seat, spring and damper adjuster rod, then invert the fork leg over a suitable container and pump the damper rod to expel as much oil as possible.
3 Refill the fork with new oil as described in Steps 27 to 32 of the same section. Refit the forks as described in Section 6.

33.5 Remove oil gallery bolt (arrowed) to fit a pressure gauge

Chapter 2
Engine, clutch and transmission

Contents

Alternator – check, removal and installation . . . . .see Chapter 9	Neutral switch – check, removal and installation . . . . . . .see Chapter 9
Cam chain tensioner – removal, inspection and installation 8	Oil and filter – change . . . . .see Chapter 1
Cam chain, tensioner blade and guides	Oil cooler – removal and installation 18
– removal, inspection and installation 10	Oil level – check . . . . .see Daily (pre-ride) checks
Camshafts and followers – removal, inspection and installation 9	Oil pressure – check . . . . .see Chapter 1
Clutch – check . . . . see Chapter 1	Oil pump – removal, inspection and installation 20
Clutch – removal, inspection and installation 15	Oil sump, oil strainer and pressure relief valve
Clutch cable – removal and installation 14	– removal, inspection and installation 19
Connecting rods – removal, inspection and installation 23	Operations possible with the engine in the frame 2
Crankcase halves – separation and reassembly 21	Operations requiring engine removal 3
Crankcase halves and cylinder bores – inspection and servicing . . . 30	Pick-up coil assembly – removal and installation . . . . . .see Chapter 5
Crankshaft and main bearings –	Piston rings – inspection and installation 25
removal, inspection and installation 26	Pistons – removal, inspection and installation 24
Cylinder head – removal and installation 11	Running-in procedure 32
Cylinder head and valves – disassembly, inspection	Selector drum and forks – removal, inspection and installation 29
and reassembly 13	Spark plug gap – check and adjustment . . . . .see Chapter 1
Engine – cylinder compression check . . . . .see Chapter 1	Starter clutch and idler gear
Engine – removal and installation 5	– check, removal, inspection and installation 16
Engine disassembly and reassembly – general information 6	Starter motor – removal and installation . . . . .see Chapter 9
Gearchange mechanism – removal, inspection and installation 17	Transmission shafts – disassembly, inspection and reassembly . . . 28
General information 1	Transmission shafts – removal and installation 27
Idle speed – check and adjustment . . . . see Chapter 1	Valve clearances – check and adjustment . . . . .see Chapter 1
Initial start-up after overhaul 31	Valve cover – removal and installation 7
Main and connecting rod bearings – general information 22	Valves/valve seats/valve guides – servicing 12
Major engine repair – general information 4	Water pump – removal and installation . . . . .see Chapter 3

Degrees of difficulty

Easy, suitable for novice with little experience	Fairly easy, suitable for beginner with some experience	Fairly difficult, suitable for competent DIY mechanic	Difficult, suitable for experienced DIY mechanic	Very difficult, suitable for expert DIY or professional

Specifications

General
Type	Four-stroke in-line four
Capacity	599 cc
Bore	65.5 mm
Stroke	44.5 mm
Compression ratio	12.4 to 1
Cylinder numbering	1 to 4 from left to right
Cooling system	Liquid cooled
Clutch	Wet multi-plate
Transmission	Six-speed constant mesh
Final drive	Chain

Cylinder head
Warpage (max)	0.05 mm

2•2 Engine, clutch and transmission

Camshafts
Intake lobe height
  Standard .... 33.05 to 33.15 mm
  Service limit (min) .... 33.0 mm
Exhaust lobe height
  Standard .... 32.55 to 32.65 mm
  Service limit (min) .... 32.50 mm
Journal diameter .... 22.967 to 22.980 mm
Holder diameter .... 23.000 to 23.021 mm
Journal oil clearance
  1999 and 2000 models .... 0.020 to 0.054 mm
  2001-on models .... 0.028 to 0.064 mm
  Service limit (all models) .... 0.080 mm
Runout (max) .... 0.06 mm

Valves, guides and springs
Valve clearances .... see Chapter 1
Intake valve
  Stem diameter
    Standard .... 3.975 to 3.990 mm
    Service limit .... 3.950 mm
  Guide bore diameter
    Standard .... 4.000 to 4.012 mm
    Service limit .... 4.042 mm
  Stem-to-guide clearance
    Standard .... 0.010 to 0.037 mm
    Service limit .... 0.08 mm
  Head diameter .... 24.9 to 25.1 mm
  Face width .... 1.14 to 1.98 mm
  Seat width .... 0.9 to 1.1 mm
    Service limit .... 1.6 mm
  Margin thickness .... 0.6 to 0.8 mm
    Service limit .... 0.5 mm
  Valve lift .... 7.81 to 8.01 mm
Exhaust valve
  Stem diameter
    Standard .... 3.960 to 3.975 mm
    Service limit .... 3.935 mm
  Guide bore diameter
    Standard .... 4.000 to 4.012 mm
    Service limit .... 4.042 mm
  Stem-to-guide clearance
    Standard .... 0.025 to 0.052 mm
    Service limit .... 0.10 mm
  Head diameter .... 21.9 to 22.1 mm
  Face width .... 1.14 to 1.98 mm
  Seat width .... 0.9 to 1.1 mm
    Service limit .... 1.6 mm
  Margin thickness .... 0.6 to 0.8 mm
    Service limit .... 0.5 mm
  Valve lift .... 7.38 to 7.58 mm
Valve stem runout .... 0.04 mm
Valve spring free length
  Intake (inner) .... 37.0 mm
    Service limit .... 35.0 mm
  Intake (outer) .... 38.4 mm
    Service limit .... 36.5 mm
  Exhaust .... 41.7 mm
    Service limit .... 39.5 mm
Valve spring bend (max)
  Intake (inner) .... 1.6 mm
  Intake (outer) .... 1.7 mm
  Exhaust .... 1.8 mm

Lubrication system
Oil pressure .... see Chapter 1
Relief valve opening pressure .... 65.25 to 79.75 psi (4.5 to 5.5 bars)
Oil pump
  Inner rotor tip-to-outer rotor clearance .... 0.03 to 0.09 mm
  Outer rotor-to-body clearance .... 0.03 to 0.08 mm

Cylinder bores
Bore .... 65.50 to 65.51 mm
Ovality (max) .... 0.05 mm
Taper (max) .... 0.05 mm
Cylinder compression .... see Chapter 1

Crankshaft and bearings
Main bearing oil clearance
  1999 models .... 0.034 to 0.058 mm
  2000-on models .... 0.028 to 0.052 mm
Runout (max) .... 0.03 mm

Connecting rods
Big-end side clearance .... 0.160 to 0.262 mm
Big-end oil clearance .... 0.028 to 0.052 mm

Pistons
Piston diameter (measured 4 mm up from skirt, at 90° to piston
  pin axis) .... 65.460 to 65.475 mm
Piston-to-bore clearance
  Standard .... 0.025 to 0.050 mm
  Service limit .... 0.07 mm
Piston pin diameter .... 15.991 to 16.000 mm
Piston pin bore diameter in piston .... 16.002 to 16.013 mm
Piston pin-to-piston pin bore clearance
  Standard .... 0.002 to 0.022 mm
  Service limit .... 0.072 mm

Piston rings
Top compression ring
  Type .... Barrel
  Ring width .... 2.45 mm
  Ring thickness .... 0.80 mm
  Ring end gap (installed) .... 0.15 to 0.25 mm
    Service limit .... 0.50 mm
  Piston ring-to-groove clearance .... 0.030 to 0.065 mm
    Service limit .... 0.115 mm
2nd compression ring
  Type .... Taper
  Ring width .... 2.5 mm
  Ring thickness .... 0.8 mm
  Ring end gap (installed) .... 0.40 to 0.50 mm
    Service limit .... 0.85 mm
  Piston ring-to-groove clearance .... 0.020 to 0.055 mm
    Service limit .... 0.115 mm
Oil ring
  Ring width
    1999 model .... 2.3 mm
    2000-on models .... 2.0 mm
  Ring thickness .... 1.5 mm
  Side-rail end gap (installed) .... 0.10 to 0.35 mm

Clutch
Friction plate
  Quantity 8
  Thickness
    Standard .... 2.9 to 3.1 mm
    Service limit .... 2.8 mm
Plain plate
  Standard
    Quantity 7
    Thickness .... 1.9 to 2.1 mm
    Warpage (max) .... 0.1 mm
  Inner plate
    Quantity 1
    Thickness .... 2.2 to 2.4 mm
    Warpage (max) .... 0.1 mm
Clutch springs
  Free length .... 55 mm
  Service limit .... 54 mm

Transmission
Gear ratios (no. of teeth)
- Primary reduction .... 1.955 to 1 (86/44T)
- Final reduction .... 3.000 to 1 (48/16T)
- 1st gear .... 2.846 to 1 (37/13T)
- 2nd gear .... 1.947 to 1 (37/19T)
- 3rd gear .... 1.555 to 1 (28/18T)
- 4th gear .... 1.333 to 1 (32/24T)
- 5th gear .... 1.190 to 1 (25/21T)
- 6th gear .... 1.083 to 1 (26/24T)

Shaft runout (max) .... 0.02 mm

Selector drum and forks
Selector fork shaft runout (max) .... 0.05 mm
Gearchange rod installed length .... 242 mm

Torque wrench settings
- Alternator cover bolts .... 12 Nm
- Alternator rotor bolt .... 65 Nm
- Cam chain tensioner centre bolt
  - 1999 and 2000 models .... 10 Nm
  - 2001-on models .... 7 Nm
- Cam chain tensioner mounting bolts .... 12 Nm
- Camshaft holder bolts .... 10 Nm
- Camshaft sprocket bolts .... 24 Nm
- Clutch centre nut .... 70 Nm
- Clutch cover bolts .... 12 Nm
- Clutch pressure plate bolts .... 8 Nm
- Connecting rod cap nuts
  - Initial setting .... 15 Nm
  - Final setting (see Section 23) .... + 90°
- Crankcase 6 mm bolts (Nos. 13 and 14) .... 14 Nm
- Crankcase 6 mm bolts (all other bolts) .... 12 Nm
- Crankcase 8 mm bolts .... 24 Nm
- Cylinder head bolts
  - 10 mm (stage 1) .... 25 Nm
  - 10 mm (stage 2) .... 51 Nm
  - 6 mm .... 10 Nm
- Engine mounting adjuster bolts .... 7 Nm
- Engine mounting bolts
  - Rear mounting bolt nuts .... 45 Nm
  - Front mounting bolts .... 55 Nm
  - Mounting bolt lug pinch bolts .... 24 Nm
  - Left-hand front button-head mounting bolts .... 38 Nm
  - Button-head bolt lug pinch bolts .... 13 Nm
- Front sprocket cover bolts .... 10 Nm
- Gearchange shaft centralising spring locating pin .... 22 Nm
- Ignition rotor bolt .... 35 Nm
- Ignition rotor/pick-up coil cover bolts .... 12 Nm
- Oil baffle plate bolts .... 12 Nm
- Oil cooler bolt .... 63 Nm
- Oil level switch bolts .... 10 Nm
- Oil passageway plug .... 80 Nm
- Oil pump drive chain guide bolts .... 12 Nm
- Oil pump housing bolts .... 12 Nm
- Oil pump mounting/drive chain guard bolts .... 10 Nm
- Oil sump bolts .... 12 Nm
- Selector drum retaining plate bolts .... 10 Nm
- Transmission input shaft bearing housing Torx screws .... 12 Nm
- Valve cover bolts .... 10 Nm
- Water pump mounting bolts .... 12 Nm
- Water pump cover bolts .... 10 Nm

Engine, clutch and transmission 2•5

1 General information

The engine/transmission unit is a liquid-cooled in-line four, with four valves per cylinder. The valves are operated by double overhead camshafts which are chain driven off the right-hand end of the crankshaft. The engine/transmission assembly is constructed from aluminium alloy. The crankcase is divided horizontally.

The crankcase incorporates a wet sump, pressure-fed lubrication system which uses a chain-driven, dual-rotor oil pump, an oil filter, a relief valve and an oil level sensor. The pump is chain driven from the back of the clutch housing. The oil is circulated through a cooler which is located on the front of the crankcases.

The alternator is on the left-hand end of the crankshaft, and the starter clutch is on the back of the alternator.

Power from the crankshaft is routed to the transmission via the clutch. The clutch is of the wet, multi-plate type and is gear-driven off the crankshaft. The transmission is a six-speed constant-mesh unit. Final drive to the rear wheel is by chain and sprockets.

Read the *Safety first!* section of this manual carefully before starting work.

2 Operations possible with the engine in the frame

The components and assemblies listed below can be removed without having to remove the engine/transmission assembly from the frame. If however, a number of areas require attention at the same time, removal of the engine is recommended.

Valve cover
Camshafts
Cam chain
Water pump and thermostat
Clutch and starter clutch
Gearchange mechanism
Alternator
Starter motor
Pick-up coil assembly
Oil filter and cooler
Oil sump, oil strainer and oil pressure relief valve
Oil pump

3 Operations requiring engine removal

It is necessary to remove the engine/transmission assembly from the frame to gain access to the following components.
Cylinder head
Crankshaft and bearings
Connecting rods and bearings
Cylinder bores, pistons and piston rings
Transmission shafts
Selector drum and forks

4 Major engine repair – general information

1 It is not always easy to determine when, or if, an engine should be completely overhauled, as a number of factors must be considered.
2 High mileage is not necessarily an indication that an overhaul is needed, while low mileage, on the other hand, does not preclude the need for an overhaul. Frequency of servicing is probably the single most important consideration. An engine that has regular and frequent oil and filter changes, as well as other required maintenance, will most likely give many miles of reliable service. Conversely, a neglected engine, or one that has not been run-in properly, may require an overhaul very early in its life.
3 Exhaust smoke and excessive oil consumption are both indications that piston rings and/or valve guides are in need of attention, although make sure that the fault is not due to oil leakage.
4 If the engine is making obvious knocking or rumbling noises, the connecting rod bearings and/or main bearings are probably the cause.
5 Loss of power, rough running, excessive valve train noise and high fuel consumption rates may also point to the need for an overhaul, especially if they are all present at the same time. If a complete tune-up does not remedy the situation, major mechanical work is the only solution.
6 An engine overhaul generally involves restoring the internal parts to the specifications of a new engine. During a major overhaul, the piston rings and main and connecting rod bearings are usually replaced with new ones and the cylinder walls honed. Generally, the valve seats are re-ground, since they are usually in less than perfect condition at this point. The end result should be a like-new engine that will give as many trouble-free miles as the original.
7 Before beginning the engine overhaul, read through the related procedures to familiarise yourself with the scope and requirements of the job. Overhauling an engine is not all that difficult, but it is time-consuming. Plan on the motorcycle being tied up for a minimum of two weeks. Check on the availability of parts and make sure that any necessary special tools, equipment and materials are obtained in advance.
8 Most work can be done with typical workshop hand tools, although a number of precision measuring tools are required for inspecting parts to determine if they must be renewed. Often a dealer will handle the inspection of parts and offer advice concerning reconditioning and replacement. As a general rule, time is the primary cost of an overhaul so it does not pay to install worn or substandard parts.
9 As a final note, to ensure maximum life and minimum trouble from a rebuilt engine, everything must be assembled with care in a spotlessly clean environment.

5 Engine – removal and installation

Caution: The engine is very heavy. Engine removal and installation should be carried out with the aid of at least one assistant. Personal injury or damage could occur if the engine falls or is dropped. An hydraulic or mechanical floor jack should be used to support and lower or raise the engine, if possible.

Removal

1 If the engine is dirty, particularly around its mountings, wash it thoroughly before starting any major dismantling work. This will make work much easier and rule out the possibility of dirt falling inside.
2 Support the motorcycle securely in an upright position using an auxiliary stand. Work can be made easier by raising the machine to a suitable working height on an hydraulic ramp or a suitable platform. Make sure the motorcycle is secure and will not topple over (see Section 1 of *Tools and Workshop Tips* in the *Reference* section). When disconnecting any wiring, cables and hoses, it is advisable to mark or tag them as a reminder of where they connect.
3 Remove the seats (see Chapter 8) and disconnect the negative (–ve) lead from the battery, then disconnect the positive (+ve) lead (see Chapter 9).
4 Remove the lower fairing, fairing side panels, top fairing, seat cowling and the frame side covers (see Chapter 8). **Note:** *The top fairing and seat cowling can stay on the bike, though it is wise to remove them as they could be damaged accidentally.*
5 Drain the engine oil and the coolant and remove the coolant reservoir (see Chapter 1).
6 Remove the fuel tank, the air filter housing, the carburettor breather catch tank and drain hose, and the crankcase breather catch tank (see Chapter 4).
7 Remove the radiator, the radiator cover and the coolant hoses to the engine, water pump and oil cooler (see Chapter 3).

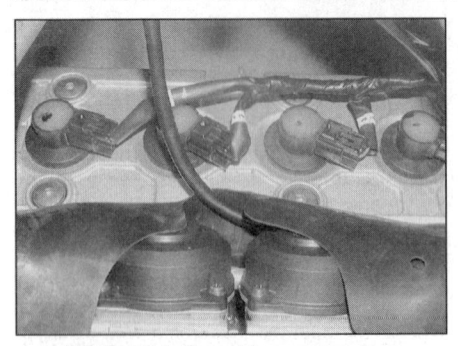

2•6 Engine, clutch and transmission

5.8 Detach the wiring connectors to the ignition coils

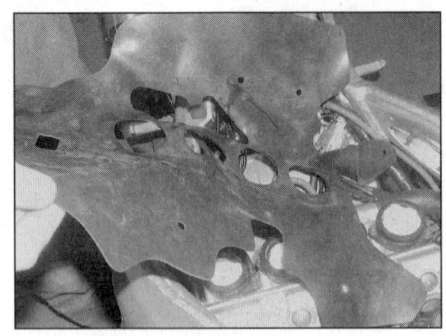

5.10 Remove the heat protector

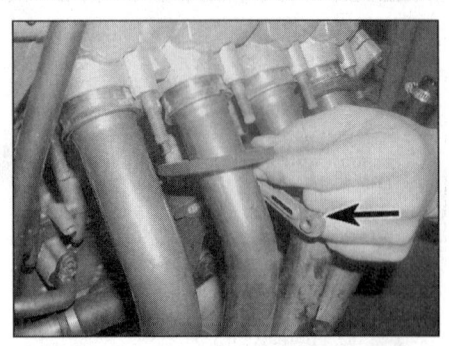

5.11 Remove the exhaust system and the radiator mounting bracket (arrowed)

8 Detach the wiring connectors to the ignition coils **(see illustration)**.
9 Remove the carburettors (see Chapter 4). Plug the intake manifolds with clean rag.

10 Remove the trim clips that retain the heat protector and remove the heat protector, noting how it fits **(see illustration)**.
11 Remove the exhaust system (see Chapter 4), then unscrew the bolt securing the radiator mounting bracket to the front of the engine and remove it, noting how it fits **(see illustration)**.
12 Detach the clutch cable from the release mechanism arm (see Section 14). Unscrew the bolts securing the clutch cable adjuster bracket to the ignition rotor cover, remove the bracket and secure the cable clear of the engine **(see illustration)**.
13 Trace the oil level sensor wire from underneath the engine and disconnect it at the single connector, then trace the side stand switch wiring from the switch to the dark blue connector and disconnect it **(see illustrations)**. Release the wires from any ties and coil them so that they do not impede engine removal **(see illustration)**.
14 Trace the alternator wiring from the top of the alternator cover on the left-hand side of the engine and disconnect it at the white, three-pin connector **(see illustration)**. Coil the wiring so that it does not impede engine removal.
15 Trace the speed sensor wiring from the sensor on the top of the transmission case and disconnect it at the solid white connector **(see illustration)**.
16 Trace the earth wire from the thermostat housing and the wire from the coolant temperature sender and disconnect them at the white, two-pin connector **(see illustration)**.
17 Peel back the boot on the starter motor terminal, then unscrew the starter motor

5.12 Detach the clutch cable adjuster bracket

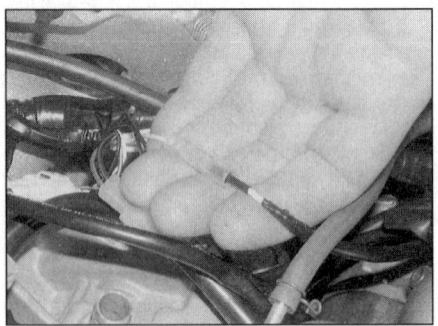

5.13a Disconnect the oil level sensor wire ...

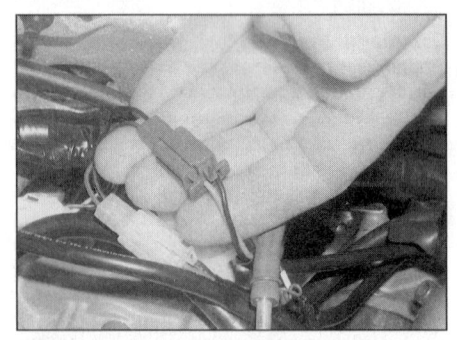

5.13b ... and the side stand switch wiring connector

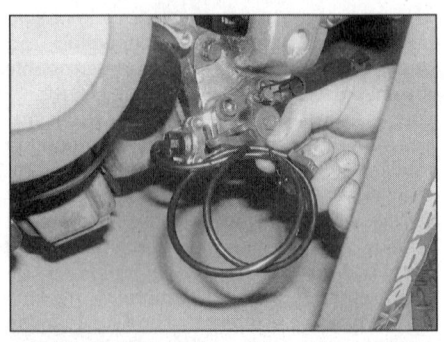

5.13c Coil the wires clear of the engine unit

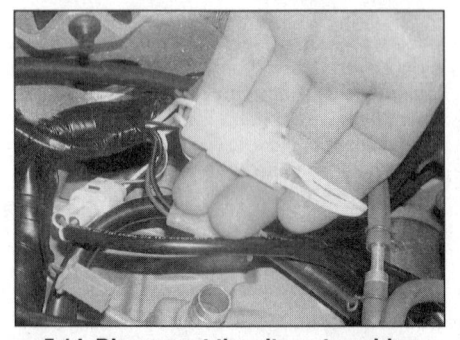

5.14 Disconnect the alternator wiring connector ...

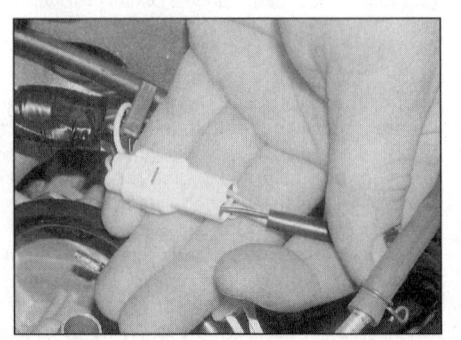

5.15 ... the speed sensor wiring connector ...

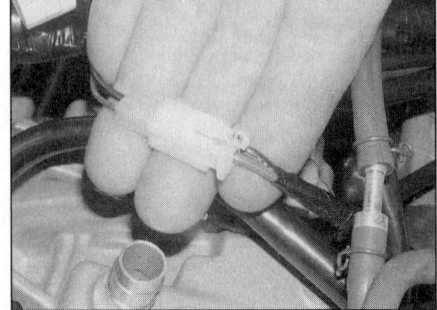

5.16 ... and the coolant temperature sensor/thermostat housing earth wiring connector

Engine, clutch and transmission 2•7

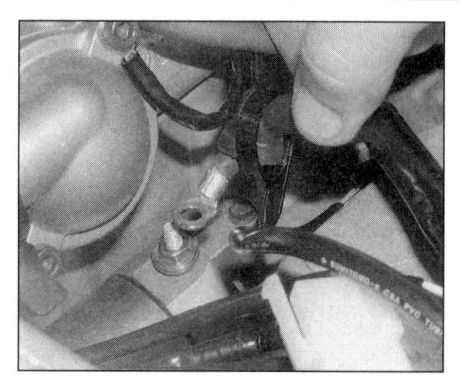

5.17 Disconnect the starter motor terminal lead

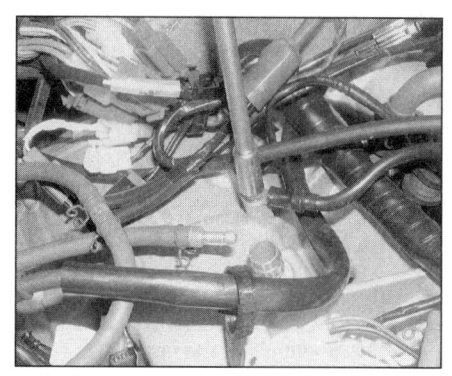

5.18 Detach the crankcase earth lead

5.19 Disconnect the ignition coil pick-up wiring and feed it clear of the frame

terminal nut and detach the lead **(see illustration)**.

18 Unscrew the bolt retaining the crankcase earth (ground) lead and detach the lead **(see illustration)**. Secure the lead clear of the engine.

19 Trace the ignition pick-up coil wiring from the ignition rotor cover on the right-hand side of the engine and disconnect it at the white, two-pin connector. Coil the wiring so that it does not impede engine removal **(see illustration)**.

20 Trace the neutral switch wiring from the back of the engine and disconnect it at the single connector. Coil the wiring so that it does not impede engine removal.

21 Make sure the transmission is in neutral. Loosen the gearchange linkage rod locknuts, then unscrew the rod and separate it from the lever and the arm (see Section 17). Withdraw the rod from the frame **(see illustration)**.

22 Remove the front sprocket and disengage the chain from the gearbox output shaft (see Chapter 6). Note the position of the chain adjuster plates for reassembly (see Chapter 1, Section 1).

23 At this point, position an hydraulic or mechanical jack under the engine with a block

5.21 Withdraw the gearchange linkage rod from the frame

5.23 Support the engine unit with a jack

of wood between the jack head and crankcase **(see illustration)**. Make sure the jack is centrally positioned so the engine will not topple in any direction when the last mounting bolt is removed and the engine is supported only by the jack. Take the weight of the engine on the jack. It is also advisable to place a block of wood between the rear wheel and the ground in case the bike tilts back onto the rear wheel when the engine is removed.

24 Check around the engine and frame to

make sure that all the necessary wiring, cables and hoses have been disconnected, and that any that remain connected to the engine are not retained by any clips, guides or brackets on the frame.

25 Slacken the pinch bolts on the mounting lugs for the left and right-hand front engine mounting bolts and the left-hand front button-head mounting bolts **(see illustration)**.

26 Unscrew and remove the button-head bolts and their collars **(see illustration)**.

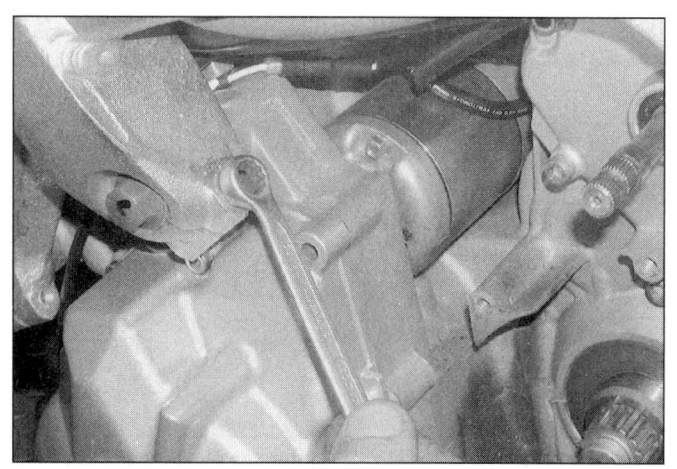

5.25 Slacken the pinch bolts on the engine mounting lugs

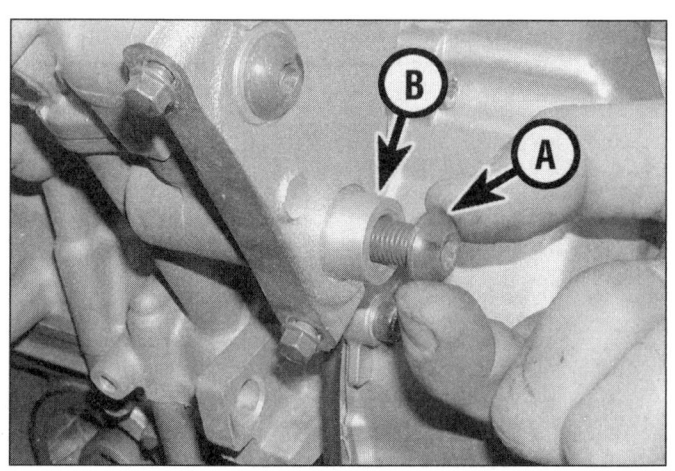

5.26 Remove the button-head bolts (A) and collars (B)

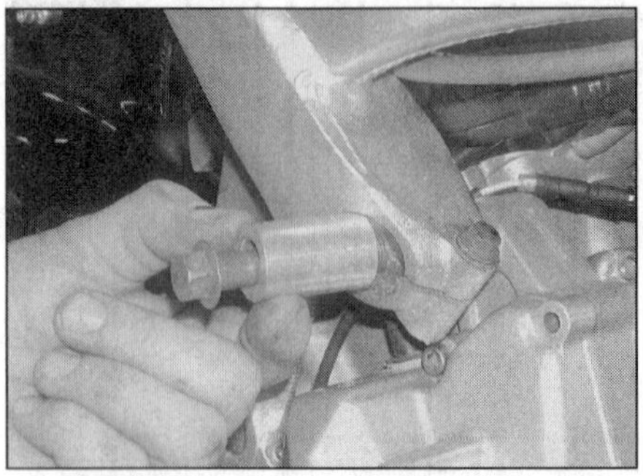

2•8 Engine, clutch and transmission

5.27 Remove the engine front mounting bolts and collars

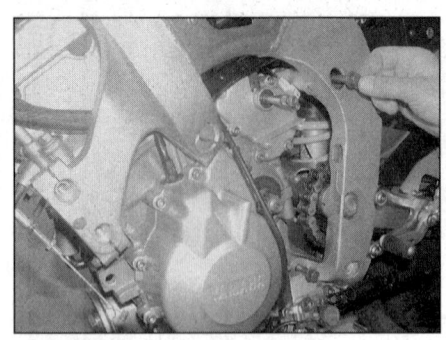

5.28a Withdraw the upper . . .

5.28b . . . and lower rear mounting bolts

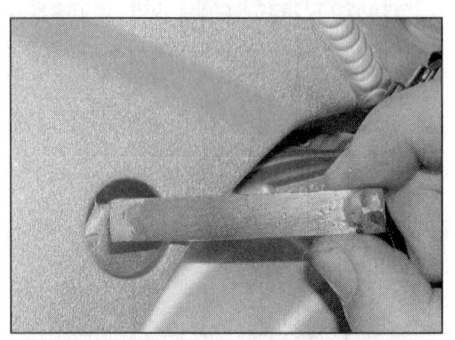

5.29 Unscrew the engine mounting adjusters with the special tool described

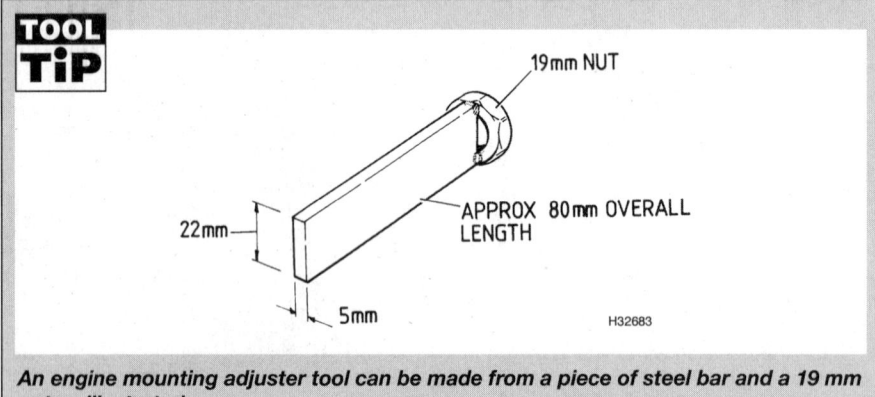

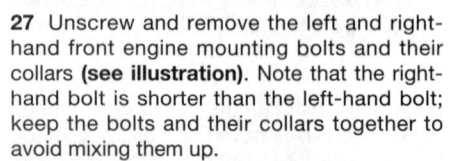

An engine mounting adjuster tool can be made from a piece of steel bar and a 19 mm nut as illustrated.

27 Unscrew and remove the left and right-hand front engine mounting bolts and their collars **(see illustration)**. Note that the right-hand bolt is shorter than the left-hand bolt; keep the bolts and their collars together to avoid mixing them up.

28 Unscrew the nuts on the upper and lower rear mounting bolts, but do not withdraw the bolts. Make sure the engine is properly supported on the jack, and have an assistant support it as well, then withdraw the mounting bolts **(see illustrations)**. Note that the upper bolt is shorter than the lower bolt. Carefully lower the engine and bring it forward, then manoeuvre it out of the frame from the right-hand side.

29 Unscrew the engine rear mounting adjusters **(see illustration)**. Yamaha provide a shaft wrench for this purpose (part No. 90890-01471) but because the adjusters have a specified torque setting, a suitable tool for use with a torque wrench can be made **(see Tool Tip)**.

Installation

30 Installation is the reverse of removal, noting the following points:
● Before lifting the engine into position, screw the engine rear mounting adjusters finger-tight, all the way into the right-hand side of the frame to ease engine installation.
● With the aid of an assistant, place the engine unit onto the jack and block of wood and carefully raise it into position so that the mounting bolt holes align. Make sure no wires, cables or hoses become trapped between the engine and the frame.

● Lubricate the threads of the upper and lower rear mounting bolts with lithium-based grease and apply a suitable thread locking compound to the right-hand front mounting bolt **(see illustration)**. Locate all the mounting bolts, not forgetting the collars and pinch bolts (if removed) for the front mounting bolts. The engine mounting bolts are of different sizes and lengths. Make sure the correct bolt is installed in its correct location.
● Tighten the front mounting bolts finger-tight. Displace first the upper and then the lower rear engine mounting bolts sufficiently enough to use the engine mounting adjuster tool to tighten the adjusters to the torque setting specified at the beginning of this Chapter **(see illustration)**. Install the upper

5.30a Apply a suitable thread locking compound to the right-hand front mounting bolt

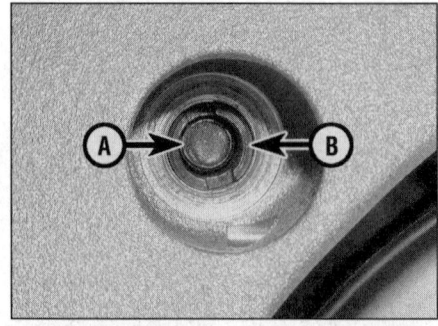

5.30b Displace the engine bolt (A) and tighten the adjuster (B) as specified

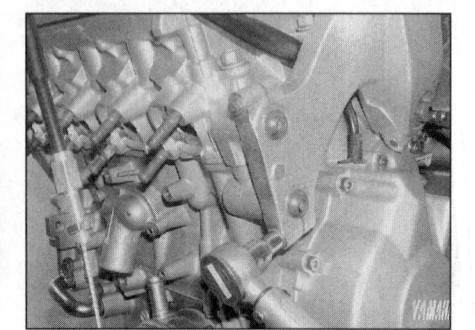

5.30c Tighten the pinch bolts to the specified settings last

Engine, clutch and transmission 2•9

bolt fully and tighten its nut finger-tight before setting the lower adjuster.
● Tighten the bolts in the following order to the specified torque settings. First tighten the upper and lower rear mounting bolt nuts, then the front mounting bolts and then the button-head bolts. Then tighten the pinch bolts for the front mounting bolts and the button-head bolts **(see illustration)**.
● Make sure all wires, cables and hoses are correctly routed and connected, and secured by any clips or ties.
● Refill the engine with oil and coolant to the correct levels (see Chapter 1).
● Check the throttle and clutch cable freeplay (see Chapter 4).
● Adjust the drive chain tension (see Chapter 1).
● Tighten all nuts and bolts to the specified torque settings.
● Start the engine and check for any oil or coolant leaks before installing the fairing panels.
● Adjust the engine idle speed (see Chapter 1).

6 Engine disassembly and reassembly – general information

Disassembly

1 Before disassembling the engine, the external surfaces of the unit should be thoroughly cleaned and degreased. This will prevent contamination of the engine internals, and will also make working a lot easier and cleaner. A high flash-point solvent, such as paraffin (kerosene) can be used, or better still, a proprietary engine degreaser such as Gunk. Use old paintbrushes and toothbrushes to work the solvent into the various recesses of the engine casings. Take care to exclude solvent or water from the electrical components and from the inlet and exhaust ports.

⚠ **Warning: The use of petrol (gasoline) as a cleaning agent should be avoided because of the risk of fire.**

2 When clean and dry, arrange the unit on the workbench, leaving a suitable clear area for working. Gather a selection of small containers and plastic bags so that parts can be grouped together in an easily identifiable manner. Some paper and a pen should be on hand so that notes can be made and labels attached where necessary. A supply of clean rag is also required.

3 Before commencing work, read through the appropriate section so that some idea of the necessary procedure can be gained. When removing components it should be noted that great force is seldom required, unless specified. In many cases, a component's reluctance to be removed is indicative of an incorrect approach or removal method – if in any doubt, re-check with the text.

4 When disassembling the engine, keep 'mated' parts together (e.g. valve assemblies,

> **HAYNES HiNT** *A useful engine support stand can be made from short lengths of 2 x 4 inch wood screwed together into a rectangle. The stand should be just big enough to accommodate the sump within it, so that the engine rests on its crankcase.*

pistons and connecting rods, clutch plates etc. that have been in contact with each other during engine operation). These 'mated' parts must be reused or renewed as assemblies.

5 A complete engine/transmission disassembly should be done in the following general order with reference to the appropriate Sections (or Chapters, where indicated).

Remove the valve cover
Remove the cam chain tensioner
Remove the camshafts
Remove the cylinder head
Remove the clutch
Remove the pick-up coil assembly (see Chapter 5)
Remove the alternator and starter clutch
Remove the starter motor (see Chapter 9)
Remove the gearchange mechanism
Remove the water pump (see Chapter 3)
Remove the oil cooler
Remove the oil sump
Remove the oil pump
Separate the crankcase halves

Remove the crankshaft
Remove the connecting rods and pistons
Remove the transmission output shaft
Remove the selector drum and forks
Remove the transmission input shaft

Reassembly

6 Reassembly is accomplished by reversing the general disassembly sequence.

7 Valve cover – removal and installation

Note: *This procedure can be carried out with the engine in the frame. If the engine has been removed, ignore the steps that do not apply.*

Removal

1 Remove the carburettors (see Chapter 4), and the radiator (see Chapter 3). Disconnect the ignition coil wiring connectors, noting which fits where, and remove the coils.
2 Unscrew the bolts securing the valve cover and remove them with their sealing washers **(see illustration)**. Lift the cover off the cylinder head; if the cover is stuck, break the gasket seal by tapping gently around the edge with a soft-faced hammer or block of wood. Do not lever the cover off as this will damage the sealing surface.
3 Remove the main gasket and circular seals. If it is loose, remove the cam chain top guide from inside the valve cover **(see illustration)**.

Installation

4 Examine the valve cover gasket and seals for signs of damage or deterioration and fit new ones, if necessary. Similarly check the sealing washers on the cover bolts for cracks, hardening and deterioration and renew them if necessary.
5 Clean the mating surfaces of the cylinder head and the valve cover with a suitable solvent.
6 Apply a smear of a suitable sealant to the valve cover and into the cutouts in the cylinder head. Fit the gasket and seals onto the valve cover, making sure they locate correctly. If removed, fit the cam chain top guide into the valve cover.
7 Position the valve cover on the cylinder head, making sure the gaskets stay in place **(see illustration)**. Fit the sealing washers into

7.2 Remove the cover bolts and sealing washers

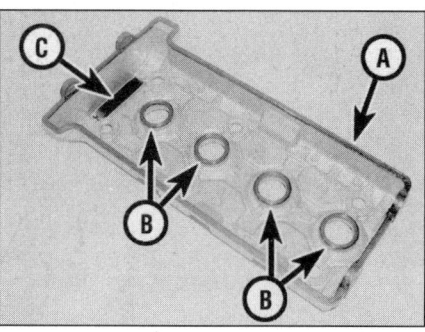

7.3 Remove the main gasket (A), seals (B) and, if loose, the cam chain top guide (C)

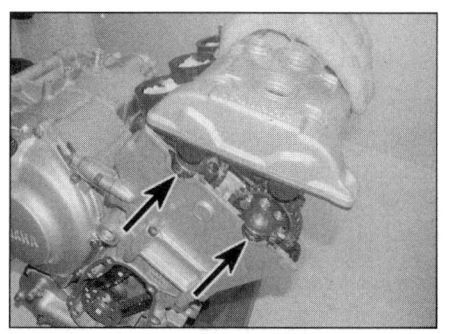

7.7 Refit the valve cover; note sealant in cut-outs (arrowed)

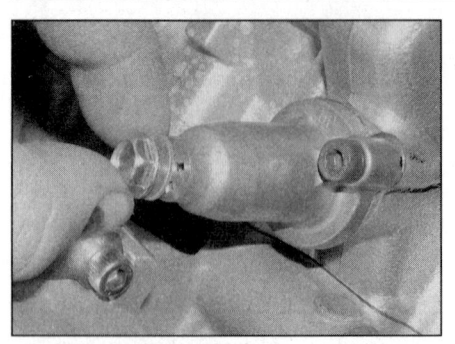

2•10 Engine, clutch and transmission

8.3a Remove the centre bolt and sealing washer

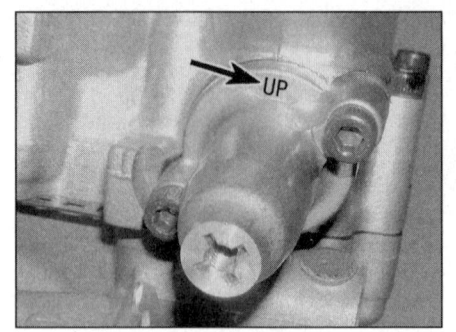

8.3b Note the 'UP' mark (arrowed)

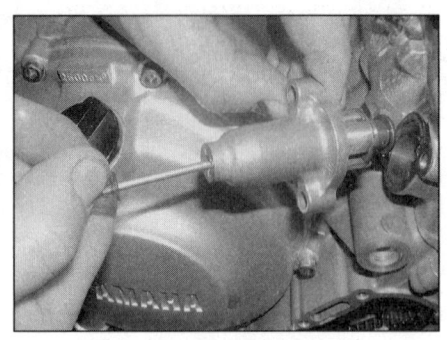

8.4 Hold the tensioner plunger retracted while the tensioner is removed

the cover, install the cover bolts and tighten them to the torque setting specified at the beginning of this Chapter.

8 Install the remaining components in the reverse order of removal.

8 Cam chain tensioner – removal, inspection and installation

Note: *This procedure can be carried out with the engine in the frame. If the engine has been removed, ignore the steps that do not apply.*

Removal

1 Remove the lower fairing, right-hand fairing side panel and right-hand frame side cover (see Chapter 8).
2 Remove the carburettors (see Chapter 4) and the heat protector (see Section 5, Step 10).
3 Unscrew the tensioner centre bolt and remove the bolt and the sealing washer. Note the 'UP' mark on the tensioner body **(see illustrations)**.
4 Slacken the tensioner mounting bolts slightly. Insert a small flat-bladed screwdriver into the tensioner so that it engages the slotted plunger. Turn the screwdriver clockwise until the plunger is fully retracted and hold it in this position while unscrewing the tensioner mounting bolts and removing the tensioner **(see illustration)**.
5 Release the screwdriver – the plunger will spring back out once the screwdriver is removed, but can be easily reset on installation.

6 Discard the gasket, as a new one must be used on reassembly. Do not dismantle the tensioner.

Inspection

7 Apply hand pressure to the end of the tensioner plunger and wind it into the tensioner body by turning the screwdriver. Hold the plunger under pressure and remove the screwdriver, then slowly release the plunger. Check that the plunger moves smoothly and springs out freely when released.
8 If the tensioner is worn or damaged, or if the plunger does not run smoothly in the body, the tensioner must be replaced with a new one – individual internal components are not available.

Installation

9 Ensure the tensioner and cylinder block surfaces are clean and dry. Lightly smear the new gasket with grease and position it on the cylinder block **(see illustration)**.
10 Insert a small flat-bladed screwdriver into the tensioner so that it engages the slotted plunger, then turn it clockwise until the plunger is fully retracted. Make sure the 'UP' mark is facing up **(see illustration 8.3b)**. Hold the screwdriver so the plunger remains retracted while the tensioner is installed in the cylinder block and its bolts are tightened to the torque setting specified at the beginning of this Chapter **(see illustration)**.
11 Release the tension on the screwdriver and remove it. Install the tensioner centre bolt with a new sealing washer and tighten it to the specified torque.

12 Install the remaining components in the reverse order of removal.

9 Camshafts and followers – removal, inspection and installation

Note: *This procedure can be carried out with the engine in the frame. If the engine has been removed, ignore the steps that do not apply.*

Removal

1 Remove the valve cover (see Section 7). Place rags in the spark plug holes and the cam chain tunnel to prevent components dropping into the engine.
2 Unscrew the bolts securing the ignition rotor cover on the right-hand side of the engine and remove the cover, noting the guide for the coolant hose and the clutch cable adjuster bracket. Discard the gasket, as a new one must be used. Remove the dowels from either the crankcase or the cover, if they are loose.
3 The engine can be turned in a clockwise direction using the ignition rotor bolt. Alternatively, to turn the engine in either direction, place the motorcycle on an auxiliary stand so that the rear wheel is off the ground, select a high gear and rotate the rear wheel by hand.
4 Turn the engine clockwise until the 'T' mark on the ignition rotor faces to the rear and aligns with the crankcase mating surfaces **(see illustration)**. The camshaft lobes for the No. 1 (left-hand) cylinder should face away

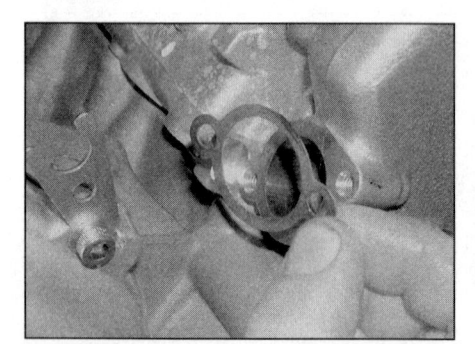

8.9 Install the tensioner with a new gasket

8.10 Hold the tensioner retracted while tightening the bolts to the specified torque

9.4 Align the 'T' mark with the rear facing crankcase mating surfaces

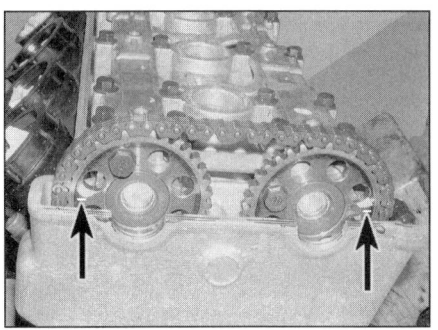

Engine, clutch and transmission 2•11

9.5 Check the position of the camshaft sprocket marks (arrowed)

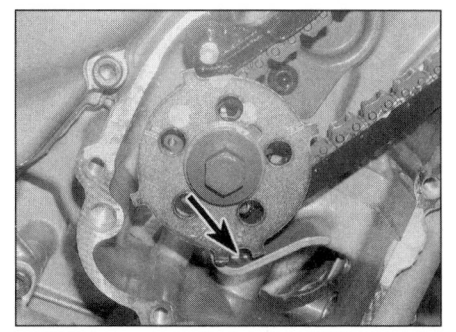

9.7 Note location of cam chain front guide (arrowed)

9.9 Remove the camshaft holder and discard the seals

from each other: if the cam lobes are facing towards each other, rotate the engine clockwise 360° (one full turn) so that the 'T' mark again faces to the rear and aligns with the crankcase mating surfaces. The camshaft lobes will now be facing away from each other and the No. 1 cylinder will be at TDC (top dead centre) on the compression stroke.

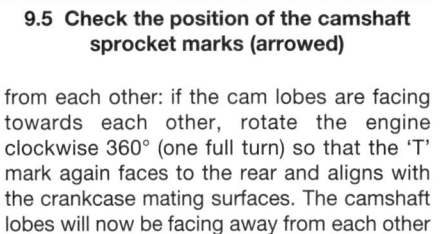

5 Before disturbing the camshafts, ensure that the timing marks on the camshaft sprockets face away from each other and align with the cylinder head mating surface **(see illustration)**. If you are in any doubt as to the alignment of the markings, or if they are not visible, make your own alignment marks between all components, and also between a tooth on each sprocket (including the timing sprocket) and its corresponding link on the chain, before disturbing them. These markings ensure that the valve timing can be correctly set up on assembly. As it is easy to be a tooth out on installation, marking between a tooth on each sprocket and its link in the chain is especially useful.

6 Remove the cam chain tensioner (see Section 8).

7 Lift the cam chain front guide out of the front of the cam chain tunnel, noting which way round it fits and how it locates **(see illustration)**.

8 Unscrew the camshaft holder bolts evenly and a little at a time in a criss-cross pattern, starting from the outside and working towards the centre. Slacken the bolts above any cam lobes that are pressing onto a valve last in the sequence so that the pressure from the open valves cannot cause the camshaft to bend.

Caution: If the bolts are loosened carelessly and the holder does not come away from the head squarely, the holder is likely to break. If this happens the complete cylinder head assembly must be renewed as the holder is matched to the cylinder head and cannot be renewed separately. Also, the camshaft could be damaged if the holder bolts are not slackened evenly and the pressure from a depressed valve causes a shaft to bend.

9 Remove the bolts, then lift off the camshaft holder. Retrieve the dowels from either the holder or the cylinder head, if they are loose. Remove the camshaft holder seals and discard them as new ones must be fitted on reassembly **(see illustration)**.

10 Note the identification mark on the camshaft sprockets; the intake camshaft sprocket is marked 'I', the exhaust sprocket is marked 'E' **(see illustration)**. Disengage each camshaft sprocket from the cam chain and lift each camshaft out of the head. Secure the cam chain with a length of wire to prevent it dropping into the crankcase and avoid rotating the crankshaft in case the chain jams between the timing sprocket and the case. Also note the camshaft identification markings – the intake camshaft has a plain centre rim whereas the centre rim of the exhaust camshaft is grooved.

11 If the followers and shims are being removed from the cylinder head, obtain a container which is divided into sixteen compartments, and label each compartment with the location of its corresponding valve in the cylinder head **(see illustration)**. If a container is not available, use labelled plastic bags (egg cartons also work very well). Remove the cam follower of the valve in question, then retrieve the shim from the inside of the follower. If it is not in the follower, pick it out of the top of the valve using either a magnet, a small screwdriver with a dab of grease on it (the shim will stick to the grease), or a screwdriver and a pair of pliers **(see illustration)**. Do not allow the shim to fall into the engine.

Inspection

12 Inspect the bearing surfaces of the cylinder head and camshaft holder and the corresponding journals on the camshaft **(see illustration)**. Look for score marks, deep

9.10 Note the camshaft sprocket identification marks (arrowed)

9.11a Keep the shims and followers in separate containers

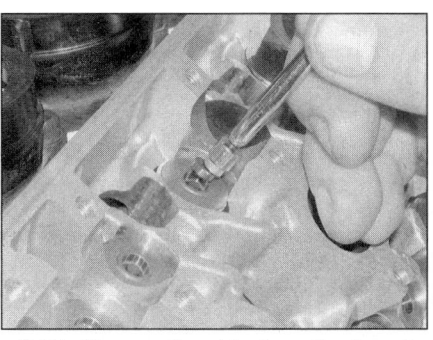

9.11b Remove the shim from the top of the valve carefully

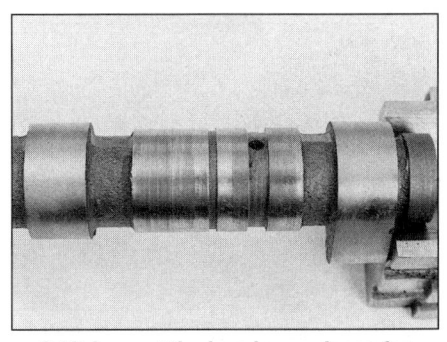

9.12 Inspect the bearing surfaces for score marks and wear

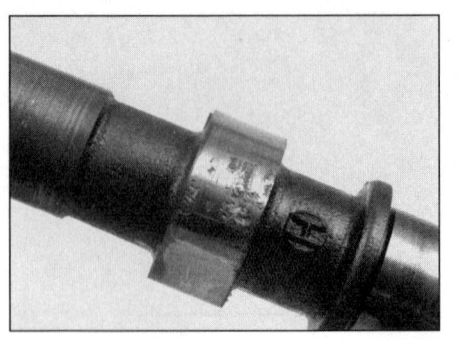

2•12 Engine, clutch and transmission

9.13a Inspect the camshaft lobes carefully – damage as shown will require repair or a new component

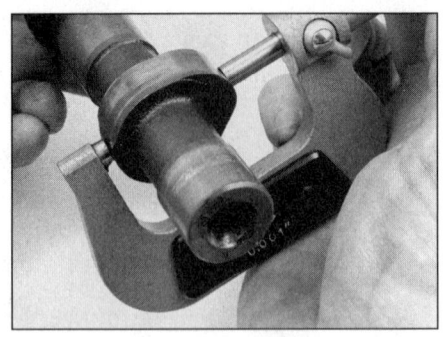

9.13b Measuring the height of the camshaft lobes with a micrometer

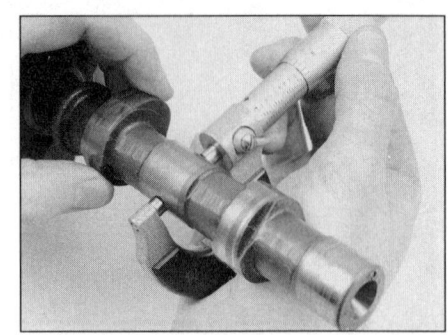

9.17 Measuring the camshaft journals with a micrometer

scratches and evidence of spalling (a pitted appearance). If damage is noted or wear is excessive, the relevant parts must be renewed. The cylinder head and holder must be replaced as a matched set – individual parts are not available.

13 Check the camshaft lobes for heat discolouration (blue appearance), score marks, chipped areas, flat spots and spalling **(see illustration)**. Measure the height of each lobe with a micrometer **(see illustration)** and compare the results to the minimum lobe height listed in this Chapter's Specifications. If damage is noted or wear is excessive, the camshaft must be replaced with a new one. Also check the condition of the cam followers.

14 Check the amount of camshaft runout by supporting each end of the camshaft on V-blocks, and measuring any runout at the journals using a dial gauge. If the runout exceeds the specified limit the camshaft must be replaced with a new one.

> **HAYNES HiNT** *Refer to Tools and Workshop Tips (Section 3) in the Reference section for details of how to read a micrometer and dial gauge.*

15 The camshaft journal oil clearance should now be checked. There are two possible ways of doing this, either by direct measurement (see Steps 16 to 19) or by the use of a product known as Plastigauge (see Steps 20 to 25).

16 If the direct measurement method is to be used, make sure the camshaft holder dowels are in position then install the holder. Lubricate the threads of the holder bolts with clean engine oil, then tighten the bolts evenly and a little at a time in a criss-cross pattern to the torque setting specified at the beginning of this Chapter. Using telescoping gauges and a micrometer (see *Tools and Workshop Tips*), measure the inside diameter of the holder journals.

17 Now measure the diameter of the corresponding camshaft journals with a micrometer **(see illustration)**. To determine the journal oil clearance, subtract the journal diameter from the holder diameter and compare the result to the clearance specified. If any clearance is greater than specified, it is an indication of wear on the camshaft, the holder, or both.

18 First check to see if the camshaft journals are worn below the service limit. If they are, a new camshaft must be fitted. However, since it is likely that the holder is also worn, ensure that the specified journal diameter for a new camshaft will restore the oil clearance to within specification before buying a new camshaft.

19 If the camshaft journals are good, or if fitting a new camshaft will not restore the oil clearance to within specification, the holder and cylinder head will have to be renewed as a matched set.

20 If the Plastigauge method is to be used, clean the camshafts, the bearing surfaces in the cylinder head and camshaft holder with a suitable solvent and a clean, lint-free cloth, then lay the camshafts in place in the cylinder head.

21 Cut some strips of Plastigauge and lay one piece on each journal, parallel with the camshaft centreline **(see illustration)**. Make sure the camshaft holder dowels are installed and lay the holder in place. Lubricate the threads of the holder bolts with clean engine oil, then tighten the bolts evenly and a little at a time in a criss-cross pattern to the torque setting specified at the beginning of this Chapter. Work from the centre of the camshafts outwards (i.e. starting with the bolts that are above valves that will be opened when the camshafts are tightened down). Whilst tightening the bolts, make sure the holder is being pulled down squarely and is not binding on the dowels. Whilst doing this, don't let the camshaft rotate.

22 Now unscrew the bolts evenly and a little at a time in a criss-cross pattern, starting from the outside and working towards the centre, and carefully lift off the camshaft holder.

23 To determine the oil clearance, compare the crushed Plastigauge (at its widest point) on each journal to the scale printed on the Plastigauge container **(see illustration)**. Compare the results to this Chapter's Specifications. Carefully clean away all traces of Plastigauge using a fingernail or other object which will not score the bearing surfaces. If any clearance is greater than specified, it is an indication of wear on the camshaft, the holder, or both.

24 First check to see if the camshaft journals are worn below the service limit by measuring them with a micrometer **(see illustration 9.17)**. If they are, a new camshaft must be fitted. However, since it is likely that the holder is also worn, ensure that the specified journal diameter for a new camshaft will restore the oil clearance to within specification before buying a new camshaft.

25 If the camshaft journals are good, or if fitting a new camshaft will not restore the oil clearance to within specification, the holder and cylinder head will have to be renewed as a matched set.

9.21 Lay a strip of Plastigauge across each bearing journal, parallel with the camshaft centreline

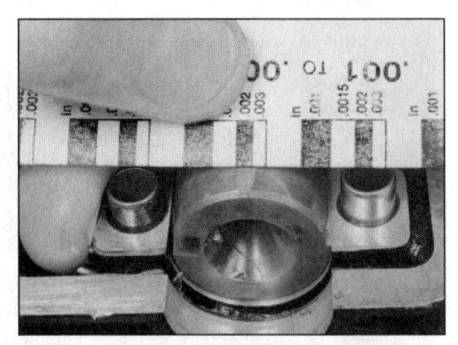

9.23 Compare the width of the crushed Plastigauge with the scale printed on the container

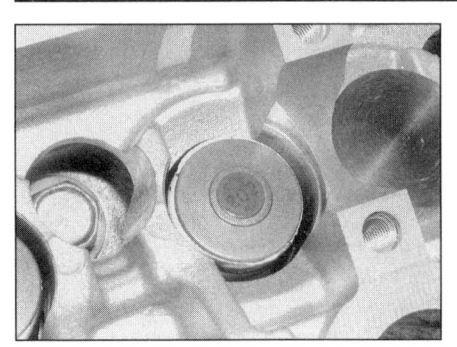

9.29 Shim size should face up on installation

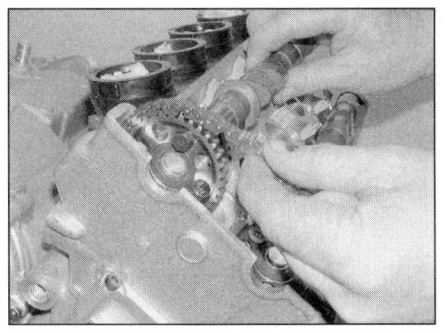

9.33 Install the camshaft and align the timing mark as described

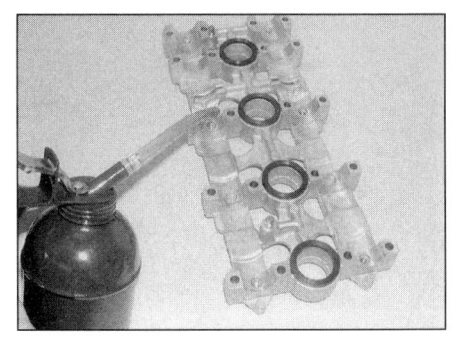

9.34 Lubricate the camshaft holder journals before installation

> **HAYNES HiNT** *Before renewing the camshafts, cylinder head or holders because of damage, check with local machine shops specialising in motorcycle engine work. In the case of the camshafts, it may be possible for cam lobes to be welded, reground and hardened, at a cost far lower than that of a new camshaft. If the bearing surfaces in the head or holders are damaged, it may be possible for them to be bored out to accept bearing inserts. Due to the cost of new components it is recommended that all options are explored!*

26 Inspect the cam chain guide blade, tensioner blade and cam chain (see Section 10).

27 Inspect the camshaft sprockets; if they show signs of wear, cracks or other damage, renew them and the cam chain as a set. The camshaft sprockets are retained by two bolts; unscrew the bolts and remove the sprockets, noting how they fit. The intake camshaft sprocket is marked with an 'I', the exhaust camshaft sprocket is marked with an 'E' **(see illustration 9.10)**. Install the new sprockets on their respective camshafts with the marks facing out, and tighten the bolts to the specified torque setting.

28 Inspect the outer surfaces of the cam followers for evidence of wear, scoring or other damage. If the side of a follower is in poor condition, it is probable that the bore in which it works is also damaged. Check for clearance between the followers and their bores. Whilst no specifications are given, if slack is excessive, renew the followers. If the bores are seriously out-of-round or tapered, then renew the cylinder head and followers.

Installation

29 If removed, lubricate each valve shim and follower with molybdenum disulphide oil (a 50/50 mixture of molybdenum disulphide grease and engine oil) and fit each shim into its recess on the top of the valve, with the size marking on the shim facing up **(see illustration)**. Make sure the shim is correctly seated, then install the follower, making sure it fits squarely in its bore. **Note:** *It is most important that the shims and followers are returned to their original valves, otherwise the valve clearances will be inaccurate.*

30 Make sure the camshaft journals and the bearing surfaces in the cylinder head are clean, then apply molybdenum disulphide oil to them and to the camshaft lobes.

31 Ensure that the 'T' mark on the ignition rotor still aligns with the crankcase mating surfaces (see Step 4) and, if removed, install the cam chain tensioner blade (see Section 10).

32 Fit the exhaust camshaft, making sure the timing mark on the sprocket faces forward and aligns with the cylinder head mating surface **(see illustration 9.5)**. If alignment marks were made prior to disassembly (see Step 5), check that the marks on the cam chain and sprocket align, then fit the chain around the camshaft sprocket, again aligning the marks between the sprocket and chain. When fitting the chain, pull up on the front run to remove all slack.

33 Now fit the intake camshaft **(see illustration)**, making sure the timing mark on the sprocket faces to the rear and aligns with the cylinder head mating surface. Fit the cam chain around the sprocket, aligning the marks (if made) between sprocket and chain. When fitting the chain, pull it tight to make sure there is no slack between the two camshaft sprockets – any slack in the chain must lie in the rear run, so that it is taken up by the tensioner.

34 Fit the camshaft holder dowels into the holder or cylinder head and install new seals in the holder. Make sure the bearing surfaces in the holder are clean, then lubricate them with molybdenum disulphide oil and install the holder on the head **(see illustration)**.

35 Lubricate the threads of the holder bolts with clean engine oil, and install the bolts **(see illustration)**. Ensure that the holder locates correctly over the rims on the camshafts **(see illustration)**, then tighten the bolts evenly and a little at a time in a criss-cross pattern to the torque setting specified at the beginning of this Chapter **(see illustration)**. Work from the centre of the holder outwards (i.e. starting with the bolts that are above valves that will be opened when the camshafts are tightened

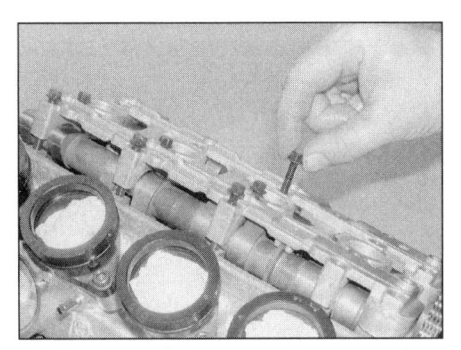

9.35a Lubricate the threads of the bolts with clean engine oil

9.35b Ensure that the holder locates correctly over the rims on the camshafts (arrowed)

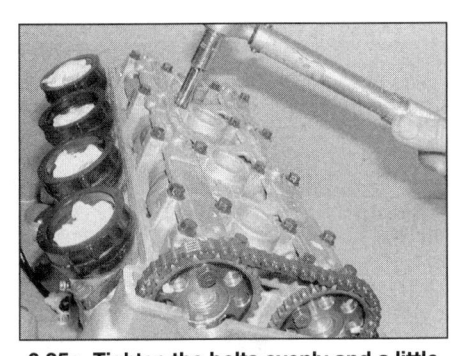

9.35c Tighten the bolts evenly and a little at a time

2•14 Engine, clutch and transmission

9.40a Install the new gasket on the dowels (arrowed)

9.40b Tensioner blade pivot pin locates inside the cover (arrowed)

down). Whilst tightening the bolts, make sure the holder is being pulled down squarely and is not binding on the dowels.
Caution: The camshaft holder is likely to break if it is not tightened down evenly and squarely and the camshaft is likely to bend if it is tightened down onto the closed valves before the open ones.

36 Install the cam chain front guide then, using a piece of wooden dowel, press on the back of the cam chain tensioner blade via the tensioner bore in the crankcase to take up any slack in the cam chain. Check that all the timing marks are still in **exact** alignment as described in Steps 4 and 5. If it is necessary to turn the engine slightly to align the marks with the engine mating surfaces, keep the wooden dowel pressed onto the tensioner blade as without the tensioner in place, the chain may slip on the sprockets. Note that it is easy to be slightly out (by one tooth on a sprocket) without the marks appearing drastically out of alignment.

37 If the camshaft marks are out, release the tension on the chain and remove the cam chain front guide, slip the chain around the relevant sprocket to correct the alignment, install the guide and recheck the timing marks.
Caution: If the marks are not aligned exactly as described, the valve timing will be incorrect and the valves may strike the pistons, causing extensive damage to the engine.

38 With everything correctly aligned, install the cam chain tensioner (see Section 8). Turn the engine clockwise through two full turns and check again that all the timing marks still align (see Steps 4 and 5).

39 Check the valve clearances and adjust them if necessary (see Chapter 1).

40 Ensure the dowels for the ignition rotor cover are in place and install the cover using a new gasket, making sure the cam chain tensioner blade pivot pin locates in the hole in the cover **(see illustrations)**. Install the guide for the coolant hose and the clutch cable adjuster bracket and tighten the cover bolts to the torque setting specified at the beginning of this Chapter.

41 Install the valve cover (see Section 7).

10 Cam chain, tensioner blade and guides – removal, inspection and installation

Note: This procedure can be carried out with the engine in the frame. If the engine has been removed, ignore the steps that do not apply.

Tensioner blade and guides

Removal

1 Remove the valve cover (see Section 7), the ignition rotor cover (see Section 9) and the cam chain tensioner (see Section 8). The cam chain top guide is located in the valve cover.

2 To remove the cam chain front guide, lift it out of the front of the cam chain tunnel, noting which way round it fits and how it locates **(see illustration 9.7)**.

3 To remove the cam chain tensioner blade, first remove the intake camshaft (see Section 9). Withdraw the tensioner blade pivot pin, then draw the blade out of the top of the engine, noting which way round it fits **(see illustration)**.

Inspection

4 Check the sliding surfaces of the tensioner blade and guides for excessive wear, deep grooves, cracking and other obvious damage, and renew them if necessary.

Installation

5 Install the top guide in the valve cover.

6 Apply some clean engine oil to the tensioner blade pivot pin, then install the tensioner blade and insert the pin **(see illustration 10.3)**. Install the intake camshaft (see Section 9).

7 Slide the front guide into the front of the cam chain tunnel, making sure it locates correctly onto its seat at its lower end and its lugs at the top locate in their cut-outs.

8 Install the cam chain tensioner and the valve and ignition rotor covers.

Cam chain

Removal

9 Remove the camshafts (see Section 9).

10 Unscrew the bolt securing the ignition rotor. To prevent the crankshaft turning, either select a gear and apply the rear brake (if the engine is in the frame), or remove the alternator cover (see Chapter 9) and use a rotor holding strap to counter-hold the crankshaft. Remove the bolt, washer and the rotor, noting how it fits **(see illustrations)**.

11 Lift the cam chain off the crankshaft sprocket and out of the engine. The sprocket is an integral part of the crankshaft.

Inspection

12 Except in cases of oil starvation, the cam chain wears very little. If the chain is stiff or the links are binding, or if the links are loose, discard the chain. A chain in poor condition will wear the sprocket teeth and ideally a chain and sprockets should be replaced as a set. The camshaft sprockets are easily renewed, but if the crankshaft sprocket is unfit for further use the crankshaft will have to be renewed.

Installation

13 Installation of the chain is the reverse of

10.3 Withdraw the tensioner blade pivot pin to release the blade

10.10a Remove the bolt and washer, then . . .

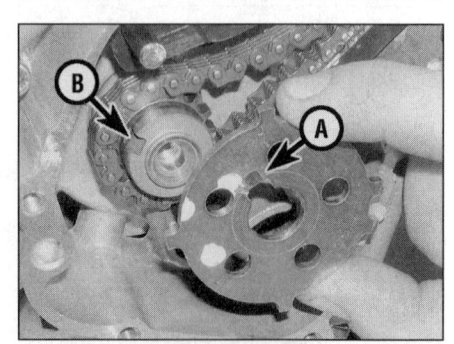

10.10b . . . remove the rotor, noting how the key (A) locates in the keyway (B)

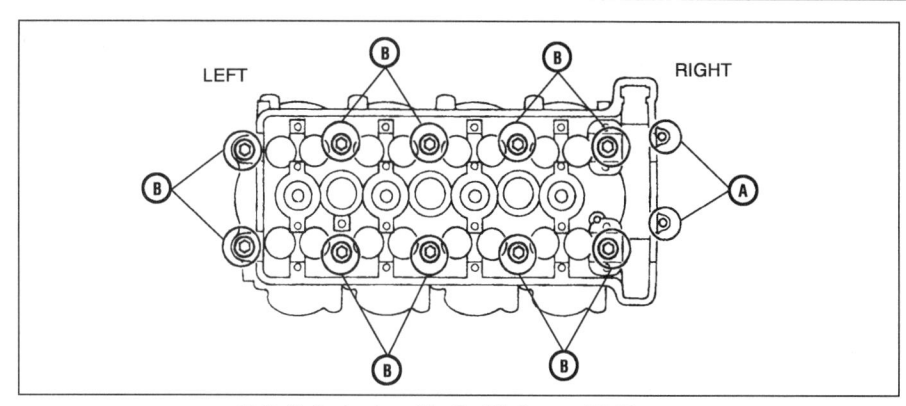

Engine, clutch and transmission 2•15

11.3 Cylinder head bolts (A) 6 mm, (B) 10 mm

11.9 Lay the new gasket over the dowels (arrowed)

removal. Make sure the marked side of the ignition rotor faces out and that the key on the rotor locates in the keyway on the crankshaft. Tighten the rotor bolt to the torque setting specified at the beginning of this Chapter, counter-holding the crankshaft as on removal.

11 Cylinder head – removal and installation

Note: *To remove the cylinder head the engine must be removed from the frame.*

Removal

1 Remove the engine from the frame (see Section 5).
2 Remove the valve cover (see Section 7) and the camshafts and followers (see Section 9). On models fitted with the air induction system (AIS), remove the system components (see Chapter 4).
3 The cylinder head is secured by twelve bolts **(see illustration)**. First unscrew and remove the 6 mm bolts on the right-hand end of the head. Now unscrew the 10 mm bolts evenly and no more than a half turn at a time in a criss-cross pattern, starting from the outside and working inwards (see *Tools and Workshop Tips* (Section 4) in the *Reference* section). When all the bolts are loose, remove them.
4 Pull the cylinder head up off the cylinder block. If it is stuck, tap around the joint faces of the head with a soft-faced hammer or block of wood to free it. Do not attempt to free the head by inserting a lever between it and the cylinder block – you will damage the sealing surfaces.
5 If they are loose, remove the dowels from the cylinder block **(see illustration 11.9)**. If they appear to be missing they are probably stuck in the underside of the cylinder head.
6 Check the cylinder head gasket and the mating surfaces on the cylinder head and block for signs of leakage from the cylinders, the oil or coolant passages, which could indicate that the head is warped. Refer to Section 13 and check the flatness of the cylinder head.
7 Remove the old cylinder head gasket and discard it, as a new one must be fitted on reassembly.

Installation

8 Clean all traces of old gasket material from the cylinder head and block with a suitable solvent. If you need to use a scraper, take care not to scratch or gouge the soft aluminium. Be careful not to let any of the gasket material fall into the crankcase, the cylinder bores or the oil or coolant passages.

HAYNES HiNT *Refer to Tools and Workshop Tips (Section 7) for details of gasket removal methods.*

9 Lubricate the cylinder bores with clean engine oil. If removed, fit the dowels into the crankcase, then lay the new head gasket in place, making sure it locates correctly over the dowels, and all the holes are correctly aligned **(see illustration)**.
10 Carefully fit the cylinder head onto the crankcase, making sure it locates correctly onto the dowels **(see illustration)**.
11 Lubricate the threads and seating surfaces of the 10 mm cylinder head bolts with clean engine oil. Install the bolts and tighten them finger-tight **(see illustrations 11.3)**. Now tighten the bolts evenly and in two stages, working in a criss-cross pattern starting from the centre and moving outwards (see *Tools and Workshop Tips* (Section 4) in the *Reference* section), to the torque setting specified at the beginning of this Chapter **(see illustration)**.
12 Install the 6 mm bolts and tighten them to the specified torque setting **(see illustration)**.
13 Install the remaining components in the reverse order of removal.

12 Valves/valve seats/valve guides – servicing

1 Because of the complex nature of this job and the special tools and equipment required, most owners leave servicing of the valves, valve seats and valve guides to a professional. However, you can make an initial assessment of whether the valves are seating, and

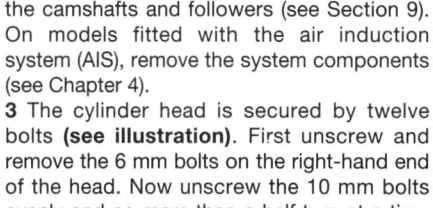

11.10 Fit the cylinder head, ensuring it locates on the dowels

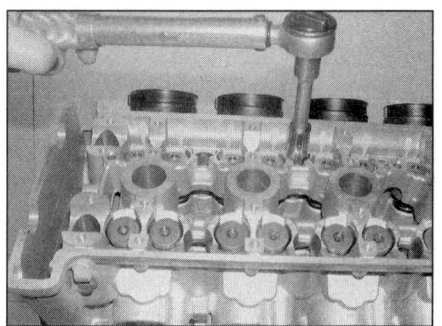

11.11 Tighten the head bolts evenly, working from the centre out

11.12 Tighten the 6 mm bolts (arrowed) to the specified torque

2•16 Engine, clutch and transmission

therefore sealing, correctly by pouring a small amount of solvent into each of the valve ports. If the solvent leaks past any valve into the combustion chamber the valve is not seating and sealing correctly.

2 You can also remove the valves from the cylinder head, clean the components, check them for wear to assess the extent of the work needed and, unless a valve service is required, grind in the valves (see Section 13). The head can then be reassembled.

3 The dealer service department will remove the valves and springs, renew the valves and guides, recut the valve seats, check and renew the valve springs, spring retainers and collets (as necessary), replace the valve seals with new ones and reassemble the valve components.

4 After the valve service has been performed, the head will be in like-new condition. When the head is returned, be sure to clean it again very thoroughly before installation on the engine, to remove any metal particles or abrasive grit that may still be present from the valve service operations. Use compressed air, if available, to blow out all the holes and passages.

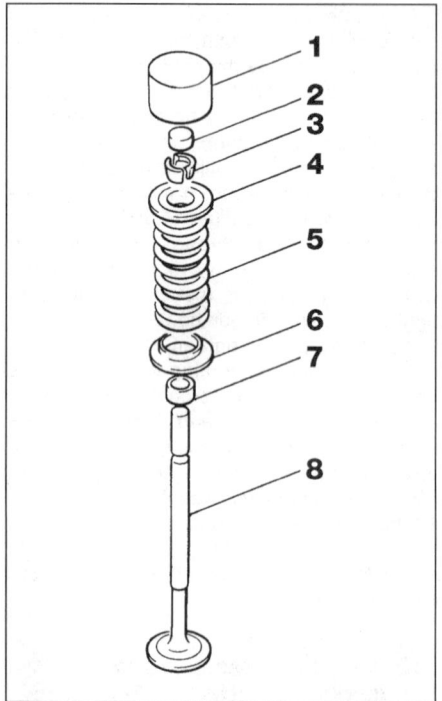

13 Cylinder head and valves – disassembly, inspection and reassembly

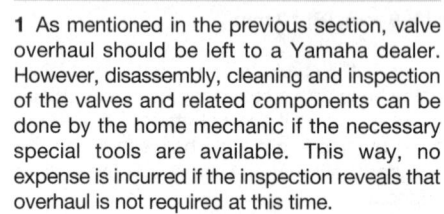

1 As mentioned in the previous section, valve overhaul should be left to a Yamaha dealer. However, disassembly, cleaning and inspection of the valves and related components can be done by the home mechanic if the necessary special tools are available. This way, no expense is incurred if the inspection reveals that overhaul is not required at this time.

2 To disassemble the valve components without the risk of damaging them, a valve spring compressor is absolutely essential. Make sure it is suitable for motorcycle work.

Disassembly

3 Before proceeding, arrange to label and store the valves along with their related components in such a way that they can be returned to their original locations without getting mixed up (see illustration). Either use the same container as the valve shims and followers are stored in (see Section 9), or obtain a separate container which is divided into sixteen compartments, and label each compartment with the identity of the valve which will be stored in it. Alternatively, labelled plastic bags will do just as well.

4 Clean all traces of old gasket material from the cylinder head with a suitable solvent. If you need to use a scraper, take care not to scratch or gouge the soft aluminium.

> **HAYNES HINT** *Refer to Tools and Workshop Tips (Section 7) in the Reference section for details of gasket removal methods.*

5 Compress the valve spring on the first valve with a spring compressor, making sure it is correctly located onto each end of the valve assembly. On the underside of the head, make sure the plate on the compressor only contacts the valve and not the soft aluminium of the head – if the plate is too big for the valve, use a spacer between them (see illustrations). Do not compress the springs any more than is absolutely necessary.

6 Remove the collets, using either needle-nose pliers, tweezers, a magnet or a screwdriver with a dab of grease on it (see illustration). Carefully release the valve spring compressor and remove the spring retainer, noting which way up it fits, the spring and the valve (see illustration 13.3). If the valve binds in the guide (won't pull through), push it back into the head and deburr the area around the collet groove with a very fine file or whetstone (see illustration). Note: *There are two springs*

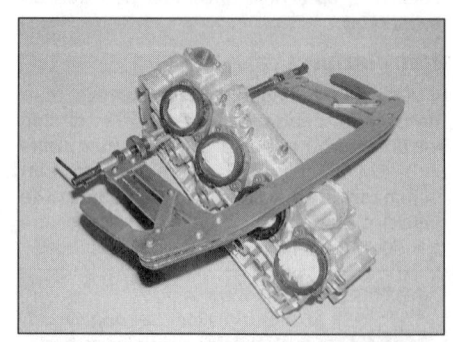

13.3 Valve components – exhaust valve shown

1 Follower
2 Shim
3 Collets
4 Spring retainer
5 Valve spring
6 Spring seat – (intake spring seat differs)
7 Valve stem oil seal
8 Valve

13.5a Compressing the valve springs using a valve spring compressor

13.5b Make sure the compressor is a good fit on the top . . .

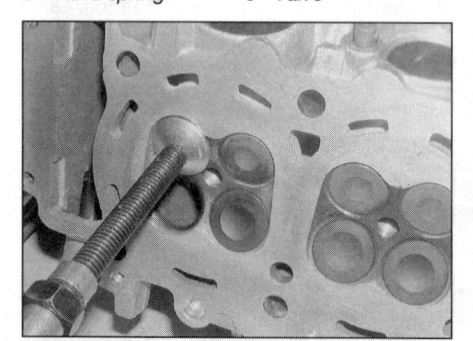

13.5c . . . and the bottom of the valve

13.6a Remove the collets taking care not to drop them into the engine

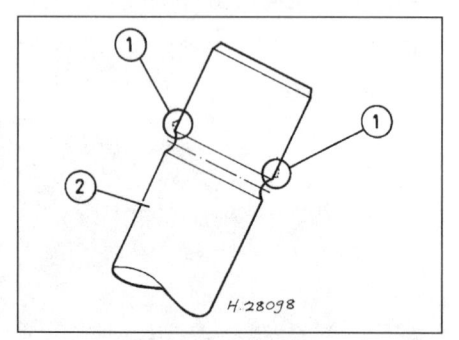

13.6b If the valve stem (2) won't pull through the guide, deburr the area above the collet groove (1)

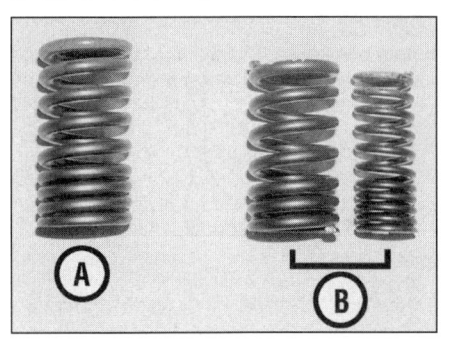

Engine, clutch and transmission 2•17

13.6c Exhaust (A) and intake (B) valve springs differ in length. Springs are fitted with the closer wound coils into the head

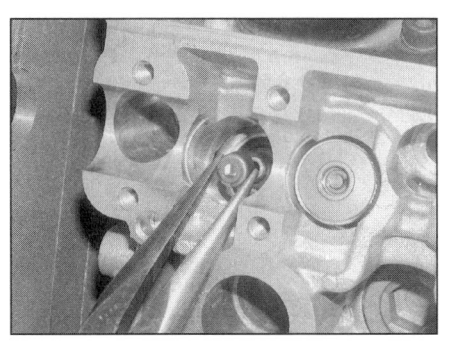

13.7 Pull the stem seal off with long nosed pliers

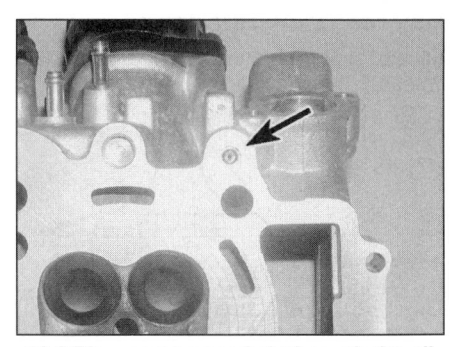

13.9 Blow compressed air through the oil nozzle (arrowed) to ensure it is clear

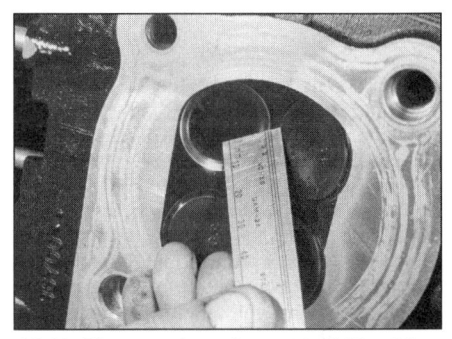

fitted to each intake valve. Note the difference in length between the exhaust and intake valve springs – do not mix them up **(see illustration)**.
7 Pull the valve stem seal off the top of the valve guide with pliers and discard it (the old seals should never be reused) **(see illustration)**. Remove the spring seat, noting which way up it fits – using a magnet is the easiest way to lift the seat off the head.
8 Repeat the procedure for the remaining valves. Remember to keep the parts for each valve together and labelled so they can be reinstalled in the correct location.
9 Next, clean the cylinder head with solvent and dry it thoroughly. Compressed air will speed the drying process and ensure that all holes and recessed areas are clean. Check that the oil nozzle on the right-hand underside of the head is clear **(see illustration)**.
10 Clean all the valve springs, collets, retainers and spring seats with solvent and dry them thoroughly. Clean the parts from one valve at a time so that no mixing of parts between valves occurs. Scrape off any deposits that may have formed on the valves, then use a motorised wire brush to remove deposits from the valve heads and stems. Again, make sure the valves do not get mixed up.

Inspection

11 Inspect the head very carefully for cracks

13.12 Checking the head for warpage with a straight-edge

and other damage. If cracks are found, a new head will be required. Check the cam bearing surfaces for wear and evidence of seizure. Check the camshafts for wear as well (see Section 9).
12 Using a precision straight-edge and a feeler gauge, check the head gasket mating surface for warpage **(see illustration)**. Refer to *Tools and Workshop Tips* (Section 3) in the *Reference* section for details of how to use the straight-edge. If the head is warped beyond the limit specified at the beginning of this Chapter, consult your Yamaha dealer or take it to an engineer for rectification.
13 Examine the valve seats in the combustion chamber. If they are pitted, cracked or burned, the head will require work beyond the scope of the home mechanic.

13.13 Measure the valve seat width with a ruler (or for greater accuracy use a vernier caliper)

Measure the valve seat width and compare it to this Chapter's Specifications **(see illustration)**. If it exceeds the service limit, or if it varies around its circumference, consult your Yamaha dealer or take the head to an engineer for rectification.
14 Examine each valve face for cracks, pits and burned spots **(see illustration)**. **Note:** *Slight imperfections between the valve face and seat may be overcome by grinding the valve (see Steps 22 to 26).*
15 Rotate the valve and check for any obvious indication that it is bent. Using V-blocks and a dial gauge if available, measure the valve stem runout and compare the results to the specifications at the beginning of this Chapter **(see illustration)**. If the

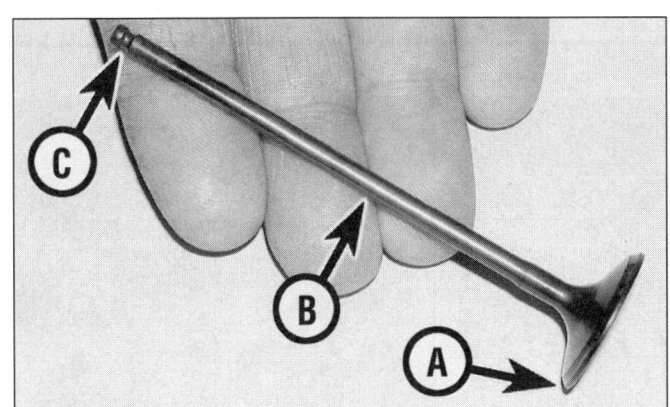

13.14 Check the valve face (A), stem (B) and collet groove (C) for wear and damage

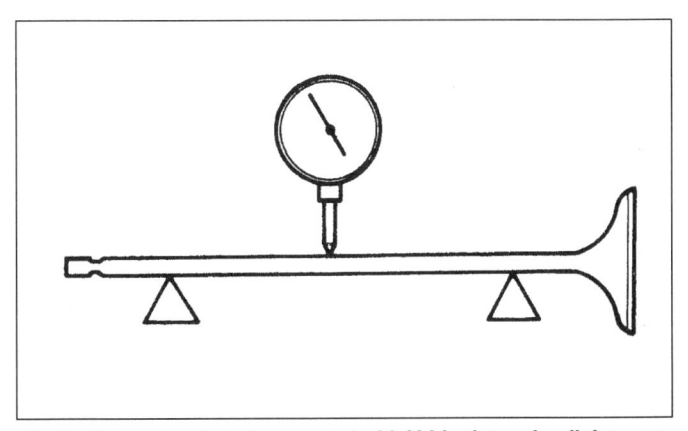

13.15 Measure valve stem runout with V-blocks and a dial gauge

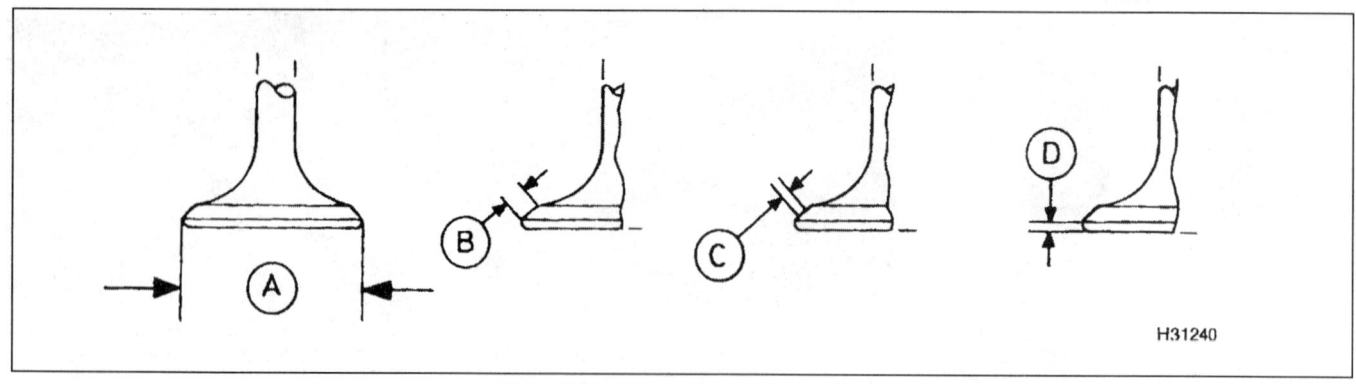

2•18 Engine, clutch and transmission

13.16 Valve head measurement points

A Head diameter   B Face width   C Seat width   D Margin thickness

measurement exceeds the service limit specified, the valve must be replaced with a new one. Note that a slightly bent valve stem will prevent the valve from seating properly in the head.

16 Measure the various aspects of the valve head and compare them with the listed specifications **(see illustration)**. If the valve is worn it should be replaced with a new one.

17 Measure the valve stem diameter **(see illustration)**. Clean the valve guides to remove any carbon build-up, then measure the inside diameters of the guides (at both ends and the centre of the guide) with a small hole gauge and micrometer (see *Tools and Workshop Tips* (Section 3) in the *Reference* section). The guides are measured at the ends and at the centre to determine if they are worn in a bell-mouth pattern (more wear at the ends). Subtract the stem diameter from the valve guide diameter to obtain the valve stem-to-guide clearance. If the stem-to-guide clearance is greater than listed in this Chapter's Specifications, renew whichever components are worn beyond their specified limits. If the valve guide is within specifications, but is worn unevenly, it should be renewed.

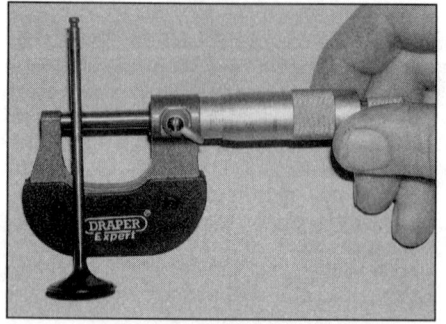

18 Inspect the valve stem and collet groove area for scuffing and cracks **(see illustration 13.14)**. Check the end of the stem for pitting and wear. The presence of any of the above conditions indicates the need for fitting new valves.

19 Check the end of each valve spring for wear. Measure the spring free length and compare it to that listed in the specifications **(see illustration)**. If any spring is shorter than specified it has sagged and must be replaced with a new one. Also place the spring upright on a flat surface and check it for bend by placing a ruler or engineer's square against it. If the bend in any spring exceeds the specified limit, it must be replaced with a new one.

20 Check the spring retainers and collets for obvious wear and cracks. Any questionable parts should not be reused, as extensive damage will occur in the event of failure during engine operation.

21 If the inspection indicates that no overhaul work is required, the valve components can be reinstalled in the head.

Reassembly

22 Unless a valve service has been performed, before installing the valves in the head they should be ground in (lapped) to ensure a positive seal between the valves and seats. This procedure requires coarse and fine valve grinding compound and a valve grinding tool. If a grinding tool is not available, a piece of rubber or plastic hose can be slipped over the valve stem (after the valve has been installed in the guide) and used to turn the valve.

23 Apply a small amount of coarse grinding compound to the valve face **(see illustration)**. Lubricate the valve stem with some molybdenum disulphide oil (a 50/50 mixture of molybdenum disulphide grease and engine oil), then slip the valve into the guide. **Note:** *Make sure each valve is installed in its correct guide and be careful not to get any grinding compound on the valve stem.*

24 Attach the grinding tool (or hose) to the valve and rotate the tool between the palms of your hands. Use a back-and-forth motion (as though rubbing your hands together) rather than a circular motion so that the valve rotates alternately clockwise and anti-clockwise on its seat **(see illustration)**. Lift the valve off the seat and turn it at regular intervals to distribute the grinding compound evenly. Continue the grinding procedure until the

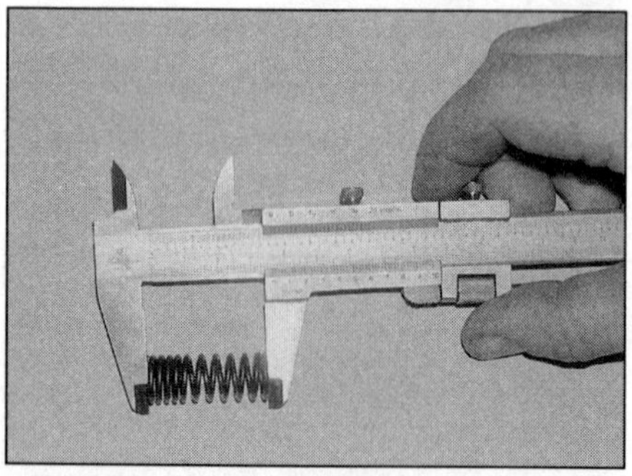

13.17 Measuring valve stem diameter with a micrometer

13.19 Measuring spring free length with a vernier caliper

13.23 Apply small dabs of grinding compound to the valve face only

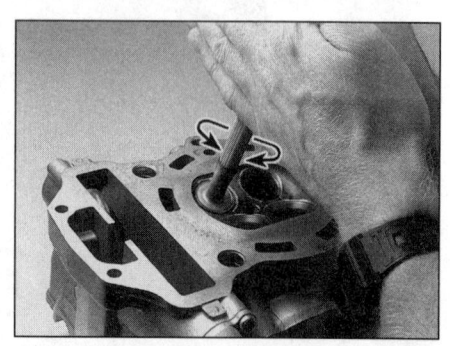

13.24a Rotate the valve grinding tool back and forth between the palms of your hands

Engine, clutch and transmission 2•19

13.24b The valve face (arrowed) and seat should appear as a uniform, unbroken ring . . .

13.24c . . . and the seat (arrowed) should be the specified width all the way round

13.27a Install the valve spring seat

13.27b Press the new stem seal into place with a suitable deep socket

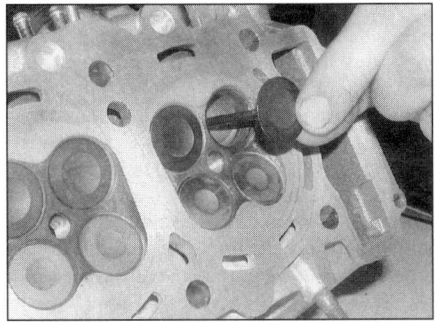

13.28a Lubricate the valve stem then install the valve

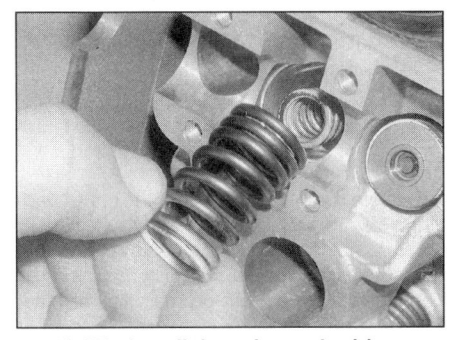

13.28b Install the valve spring(s) . . .

valve face and seat contact areas are of uniform and correct width and unbroken around their entire circumference **(see illustrations)**.

25 Carefully remove the valve from the guide and wipe off all traces of grinding compound. Use solvent to clean the valve and wipe the seat area thoroughly with a solvent soaked cloth.

26 Repeat the procedure with fine valve grinding compound, then repeat the entire procedure for the remaining valves.

27 Working on one valve at a time, lay the spring seat in place in the cylinder head so that its shouldered side faces upwards **(see illustration)**. Fit a new valve stem seal onto the guide and use an appropriate size deep socket to press the seal over the end of the valve guide until it is felt to clip into place **(see illustration)**. Don't twist or cock the seal, or it will not seal properly against the valve stem.

Also, don't remove it again or it will be damaged.

28 Coat the valve stem with molybdenum disulphide oil, then install it into its guide, rotating it slowly to avoid damaging the seal **(see illustration)**. Check that the valve moves up and down freely in the guide. Next, install the spring (two springs on the intake valves), with its closer-wound coils facing down into the cylinder head, followed by the spring retainer, with its shouldered side facing down so that it fits into the top of the spring **(see illustrations)**.

29 Apply a small amount of grease to the inside of the collets – this will help to help hold them in place when fitting them on the valve stem **(see illustration)**. Compress the spring with the valve spring compressor and install the collets **(see illustration 13.6a)**. When compressing the spring, do so only as far as is necessary to slip the collets into place. Make

certain that the collets are securely located in the collet groove and release the spring compressor.

30 Repeat the procedure for the remaining valves. Remember to keep the parts for each valve together and separate from the other valves so they can be reinstalled in their original locations.

31 Support the cylinder head on blocks so the valves can't contact the workbench top, then very gently tap the top of each valve stem to seat the collets in the groove **(see illustration)**.

> **HAYNES HiNT** *Check for proper sealing of the valves by pouring a small amount of solvent into each of the valve ports. If the solvent leaks past any valve into the combustion chamber the valve grinding operation on that valve should be repeated.*

13.28c . . . and the spring retainer

13.29 A small dab of grease will help to keep the collets in place on the valve while the spring is released

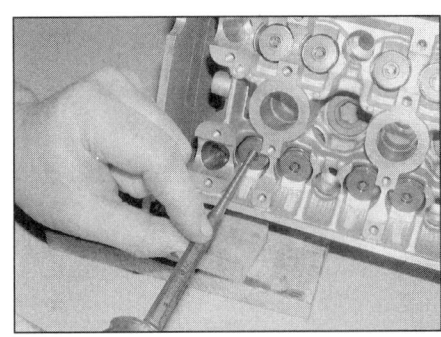

13.31 Tap the valve stem gently to seat the collets in the groove

2•20 Engine, clutch and transmission

14.2a Bend back the tab (arrowed) in the cable retainer . . .

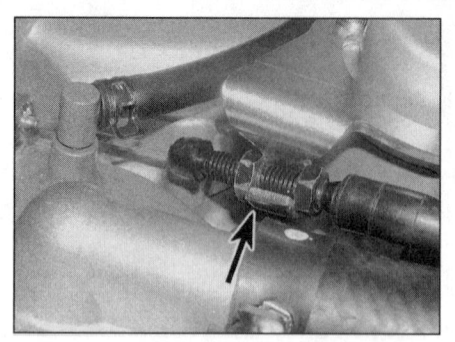

14.2b . . . then loosen the adjuster nut (arrowed)

14.3 Release the clutch cable end from the retainer

14 Clutch cable – removal and installation

Removal

1 Remove the lower fairing and the right-hand fairing side panel (see Chapter 8).
2 Bend back the tab in the cable retainer on the end of the clutch release mechanism arm, then loosen the rear nut on the adjuster **(see illustrations)**.
3 Slip the adjuster out of the bracket on the engine cover and release the cable end from the retainer, noting how it fits **(see illustration)**.
4 Screw the adjuster at the handlebar end of the cable fully into the lever bracket and align the slot in the adjuster with that in the lever bracket **(see illustration)**. Pull the outer cable end from the socket in the adjuster and release the inner cable nipple from the lever **(see illustration)**.
5 Release the cable tie that holds the clutch cable to the radiator lower hose and release the clip on the back of the radiator **(see illustrations)**. Feed the cable through the guides on the right-hand side of the frame and the top yoke, then remove the cable from the machine, noting its routing **(see illustrations)**.

Installation

6 Installation is the reverse of removal. Apply grease to the cable ends and make sure the cable is correctly routed and clipped into place. With the cable installed, turn the adjuster on the lever bracket so that the slots are not aligned **(see illustration 14.4a)** and bend the retainer on the release mechanism arm to secure the cable end **(see illustration 14.2a)**. Check the clutch release mechanism for smooth operation and any signs of wear or damage. Remove it for cleaning and re-greasing if required (see Section 15).

> **HAYNES HINT** *When fitting a new cable, tape the lower end of the new cable to the upper end of the old cable before removing it from the motorcycle. Slowly pull the lower end of the old cable out, guiding the new cable down into position. Using this method will ensure the cable is routed correctly.*

14.4a Align the slots in the adjuster and the handlebar bracket . . .

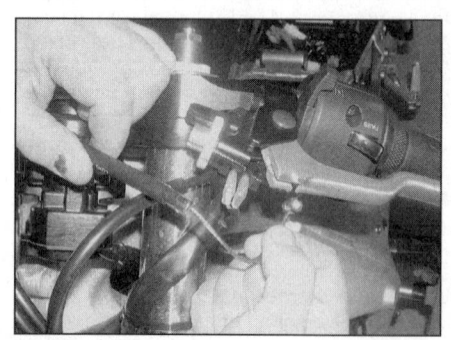

14.4b . . . and release the inner cable from the lever

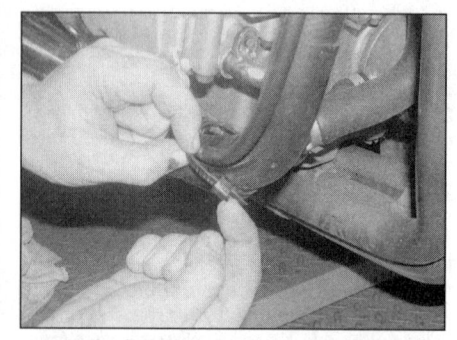

14.5a Release the tie on the clutch cable . . .

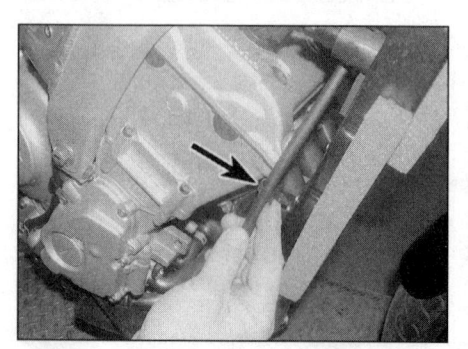

14.5b . . . and the clip on the back of the radiator

14.5c Clutch cable passes through guides on the frame (arrowed) . . .

14.5d . . . and the top yoke (arrowed)

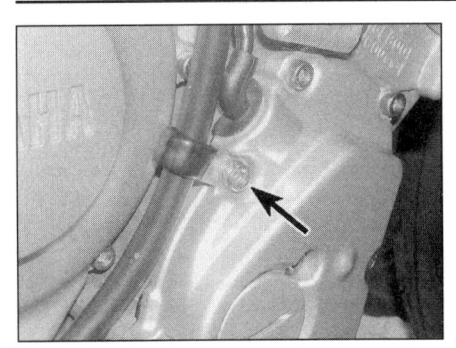

Engine, clutch and transmission 2•21

15.2 Displace the coolant hose guide before removing the clutch cover

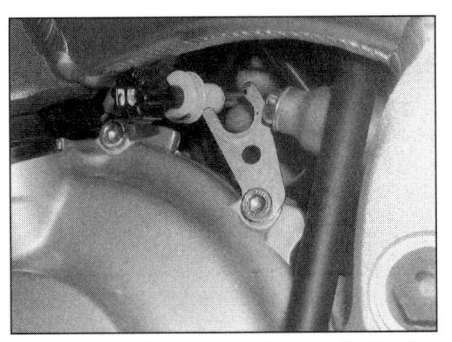

15.4a Press the engine idle speed adjuster out of its bracket

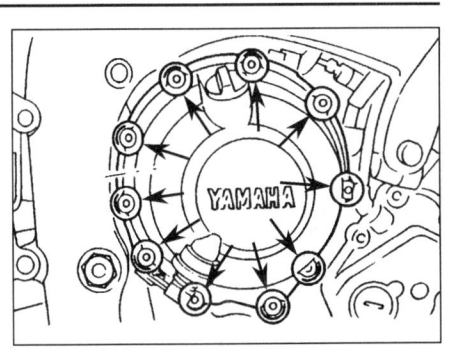

15.4b Unscrew the bolts (arrowed) and remove the cover

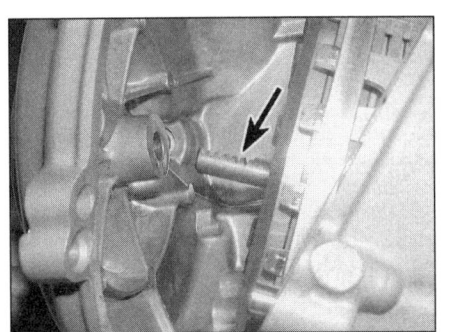

15.4c Note how the pull rod (arrowed) engages the actuating shaft

15.6a Remove the clutch bolts and springs . . .

15.6b . . . and the pressure plate, noting the reference marks (arrowed)

7 Adjust the clutch lever freeplay (see Chapter 1). Install the lower fairing and fairing side panel (see Chapter 8).

15 Clutch – removal, inspection and installation

Note: *This procedure can be carried out with the engine in the frame. If the engine has been removed, ignore the steps that do not apply.*

Removal

1 Remove the lower fairing and the right-hand fairing side panel (see Chapter 8). Drain the engine oil (see Chapter 1).
2 To allow clearance for removing the clutch cover, unscrew the bolt on the ignition rotor cover that retains the coolant hose guide and release the guide **(see illustration)**.
3 Detach the clutch cable from the release mechanism arm (see Section 14).
4 Detach the engine idle speed adjuster from its bracket **(see illustration)**. Working evenly in a criss-cross pattern, unscrew the clutch cover bolts and remove the cover and the idle adjuster bracket, being prepared to catch any residual oil **(see illustration)**. If the cover will not lift away easily, break the gasket seal by tapping gently around the edge with a soft-faced hammer or block of wood. Note how the teeth on the clutch pull rod engage on the actuating shaft in the clutch cover **(see illustration)**.
5 Remove the cover gasket and discard it as a new one must be fitted on reassembly. Note the position of the two locating dowels and

remove them for safe-keeping if they are loose – they could be in either the cover or the crankcase.
6 Select a gear and apply the rear brake (if the engine is in the frame), or remove the alternator cover (see Chapter 9) and use a rotor holding strap to counter-hold the clutch. Working in a criss-cross pattern, gradually slacken the clutch spring bolts until the spring pressure is released. Remove the bolts,

springs and clutch pressure plate, noting the reference marks on the clutch pressure plate and the clutch centre **(see illustrations)**. Remove the pull-rod from the pressure plate, noting the bearing.
7 Grasp the complete set of clutch plates and remove them as a pack. Unless the plates are being replaced with new ones, keep them in their original order. Note that the innermost plain plate is thicker than the rest **(see illustration)**.

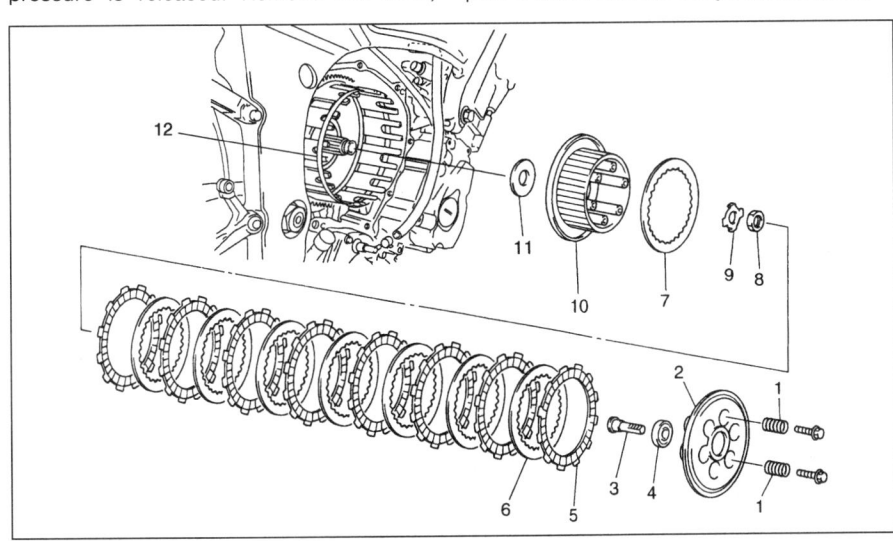

15.7 Clutch components

1 Compression spring
2 Pressure plate
3 Pull rod
4 Bearing
5 Friction plate
6 Plain plate
7 Inner plain plate
8 Clutch centre nut
9 Lock washer
10 Clutch centre
11 Thrust washer
12 Clutch housing

2•22 Engine, clutch and transmission

15.8a Bend back the lockwasher tabs

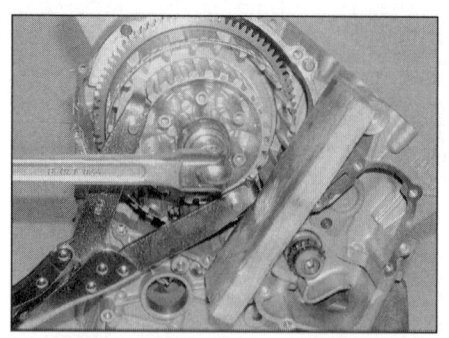

15.8b Remove the clutch nut as described

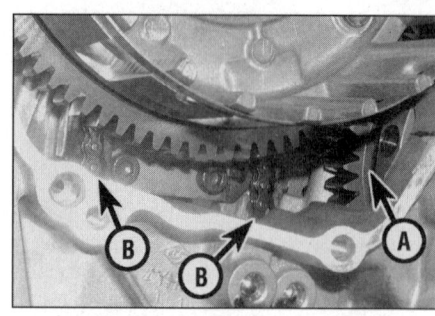

15.11 Note the primary drive gear engagement (A) and the position of the oil pump drive chain (B)

TOOL TiP

A clutch centre holding tool can easily be made using two strips of steel with the ends bent over, and bolted together in the middle

(Dimensions shown: 2.5 IN. APPROX.; APPROX. 2FT. OVERALL; FILE EDGE OF JAW TO CORRESPOND WITH PROFILE OF CLUTCH CENTRE SPLINES)

H16190

8 Bend back the tabs on the clutch centre nut lockwasher **(see illustration)**. To remove the clutch centre nut, the transmission input shaft must be locked. This can be done in several ways. If the engine is in the frame, engage 1st gear and have an assistant hold the rear brake on hard with the rear tyre in firm contact with the ground. Alternatively, the Yamaha service tool – Pt. No. 90890-04086 (European models) or YM-91042 (USA models) – or a similar commercially available or home-made tool **(see Tool tip)**, can be used to stop the clutch centre from turning while the nut is loosened. Protect the engine casing with a piece of wood if the clutch holding tool bears against it **(see illustration)**.

9 Unscrew the nut and remove the lockwasher from the transmission input shaft, noting how it fits. Discard the lockwasher, as a new one must be fitted on reassembly.

10 Slide the clutch centre and the thrust washer off the input shaft.

11 Note how the primary driven gear on the clutch housing engages with the primary drive gear on the crankshaft. Note also the position of the oil pump drive chain which engages on a sprocket on the back of the clutch housing **(see illustration)**.

12 Support the clutch housing and use a small punch or rod to pull the clutch bearing centre out of the clutch housing, then pull the bearing centre and the needle roller bearing cage off the shaft **(see illustrations)**.

13 There is now enough clearance to pull the clutch housing out along the input shaft and expose the oil pump drive chain behind it **(see illustration)**. Disengage the chain from the drive sprocket and remove the clutch housing, the thrust washer and spacer. **Note:** *It may be necessary to rotate the crankshaft to obtain clearance between the primary driven gear and the connecting rod of No. 4 cylinder or the right-hand web on the crankshaft (see illustration). Unscrew the inspection plug in the ignition rotor cover and turn the rotor bolt*

15.12a Use a tool to dislodge the bearing centre from the clutch housing . . .

15.12b . . . then remove the bearing centre . . .

15.12c . . . and the needle roller cage

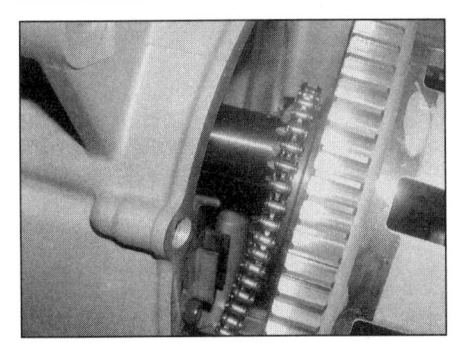

Engine, clutch and transmission 2•23

15.13a Withdraw the clutch housing to expose the oil pump drive chain

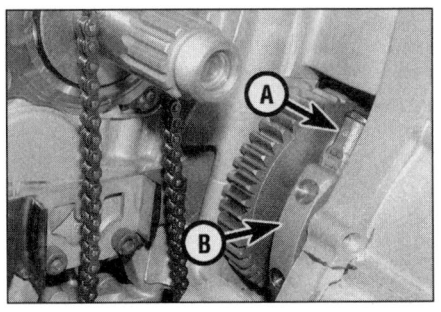

15.13b Rotate the crankshaft to obtain clearance from the connecting rod (A) and crankshaft web (B)

15.14 Remove the oil pump drive chain guide if required

on the end of the crankshaft in a clockwise direction only.

14 If required, unscrew the bolts that retain the oil pump drive chain guide to the crankcase and remove the guide **(see illustration)**.

Inspection

15 After an extended period of service the clutch friction plates will wear and promote clutch slip. Measure the thickness of each friction plate using a vernier caliper **(see illustration)**. If any plate has worn to or beyond the service limit given in the Specifications at the beginning of this Chapter, the friction plates must be renewed as a set. Also, if any of the plates smell burnt or are glazed, they must be renewed as a set.

16 The plain plates should not show any signs of excess heating (bluing). Check for warpage using a flat surface and feeler gauges **(see illustration)**. If any plate exceeds the maximum permissible amount of warpage, or shows signs of bluing, all the plain plates must be renewed as a set.

17 Measure the free length of each clutch spring **(see illustration)**. If any spring is below the service limit specified, renew all the springs as a set.

18 Inspect the clutch assembly for burrs and indentations on the edges of the protruding tangs of the friction plates and/or slots in the edge of the housing with which they engage. Similarly check for wear between the inner teeth of the plain plates and the slots in the clutch centre. Wear will cause clutch drag and slow disengagement during gear changes, as the plates will snag when the pressure plate is

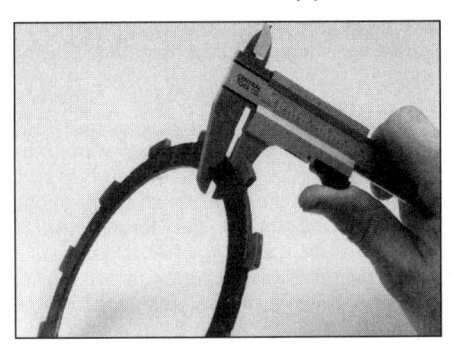

15.15 Measuring clutch friction plate thickness

lifted. With care, a small amount of wear can be corrected by dressing with a fine file, but if it is excessive the worn components should be renewed.

19 Inspect the needle roller bearing in conjunction with the internal bearing surface of the clutch housing and the bearing centre. If there are any signs of wear, pitting or other damage the affected parts must be renewed.

20 Check the teeth of the primary driven gear on the clutch housing and the corresponding teeth of the primary drive gear on the end of the crankshaft. Renew the clutch housing if any teeth are worn or chipped. The primary drive gear is an integral part of the crankshaft (see Section 26 for removal of the crankshaft).

21 Check the teeth of the oil pump drive sprocket on the back of the clutch housing. If any are worn or chipped, renew the housing and remove the oil pump and chain for inspection (see Section 20).

15.16 Checking the plain plates for warpage

22 The clutch housing incorporates a cush-drive mechanism; check that the springs are not loose and that there is no backlash between the centre of the housing and the primary driven gear, otherwise renew the housing.

23 Check the pressure plate and its bearing for signs of wear or damage and roughness. Check the pull-rod for signs of wear or damage. Replace any parts, as necessary, with new ones.

24 Check the clutch actuating shaft pinion and pull-rod teeth for signs of damage. Check that the clutch actuating shaft turns smoothly in the clutch cover. If necessary, remove the E-clip and washer securing the actuating shaft in the cover, and withdraw the shaft **(see illustration)**. Note the position of the shaft return spring and the alignment marks on the clutch cover and clutch arm **(see illustration)**.

25 Check the condition of the actuating

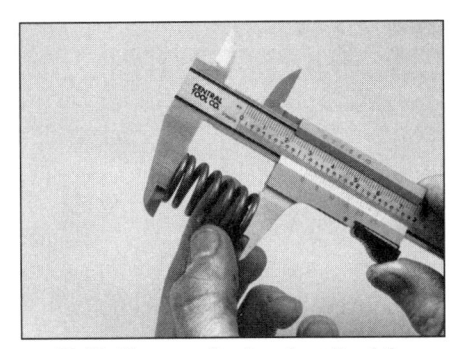

15.17 Measure the free length of the clutch springs as shown

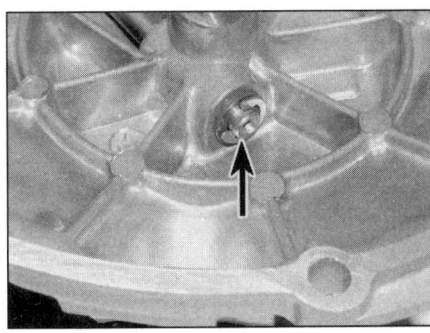

15.24a Remove the E-clip (arrowed) and washer securing the clutch actuating shaft

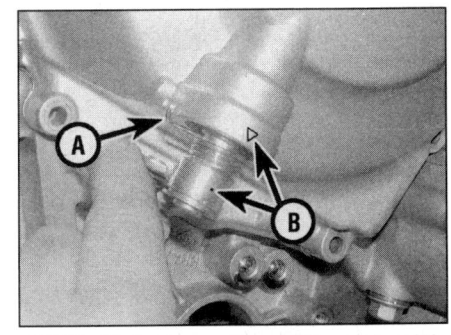

15.24b Note the position of the spring (A) and the alignment marks (B)

2•24 Engine, clutch and transmission

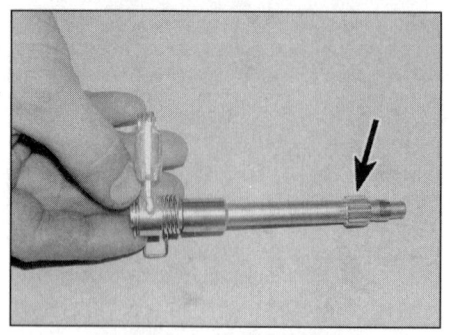

15.25a Examine the actuating shaft pinion (arrowed) and bearing surfaces

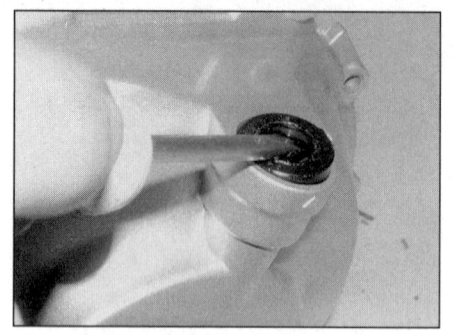

15.25b Lever the oil seal out . . .

15.25c . . . before removing the actuating shaft bearing

shaft, oil seal and two bearings, and fit new parts if necessary **(see illustration)**. If the bearings need to be renewed, first remove the oil seal **(see illustrations)**, then heat the cover in very hot water to ease removal and drift the bearings out (see *Tools and Workshop Tips* (Sections 5 and 6) in the *Reference* section). Discard the oil seal as a new one must be fitted on reassembly.

26 If required, remove the E-clip and washer securing the arm on the end of the shaft. Note the position of the arm and return spring, then press the arm off the shaft and remove the spring.

27 Clean all components and lubricate the seal and bearings with grease. Installation is the reverse of removal. Before installing the arm on the actuating shaft, install the spring and ensure that the 'UP' mark on the arm is facing up when the shaft is installed in the cover.

Installation

28 Remove all traces of old gasket from the crankcase and clutch cover surfaces. If removed, install the oil pump chain guide and tighten the bolts to the torque setting specified at the beginning of this Chapter.

29 Install the spacer and the thrust washer on the transmission input shaft **(see illustration)**. Slide the clutch housing along the shaft to a position where the oil pump drive chain can be located onto the drive sprocket on the back of the clutch housing. Slowly rotate the housing and feed the chain onto the sprocket **(see illustration)**. Ensure that the chain is correctly routed between the guides on the inside of the crankcase.

30 Lubricate the needle roller bearing with clean engine oil. Support the clutch housing and engage the primary driven and drive gears, then slide the bearing and the bearing centre into place on the input shaft **(see illustrations 15.12c and 12b)**.

31 Lubricate the thrust washer with clean engine oil and fit it onto the shaft **(see illustration)**.

32 Slide the clutch centre onto the shaft splines, then fit the new lockwasher. Note how two of the lockwasher tabs locate on flats on the clutch centre boss **(see illustrations)**. Install the clutch centre nut with the shouldered side on the inside, and tighten the nut to the torque setting specified at the beginning of this Chapter using the method employed on removal to lock the input shaft (see Step 8) **(see illustration)**. **Note:** *Check*

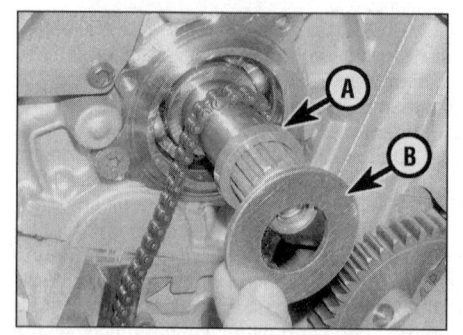

15.29a Install the spacer (A) and thrust washer (B)

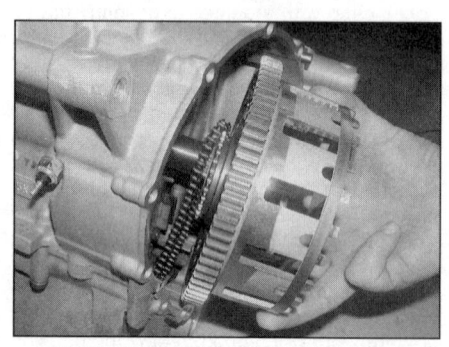

15.29b Rotate the clutch housing to engage the oil pump drive chain

15.31 Install the thrust washer . . .

15.32a . . . and the clutch centre

15.32b Align the new lockwasher tabs with the flats on the clutch centre boss

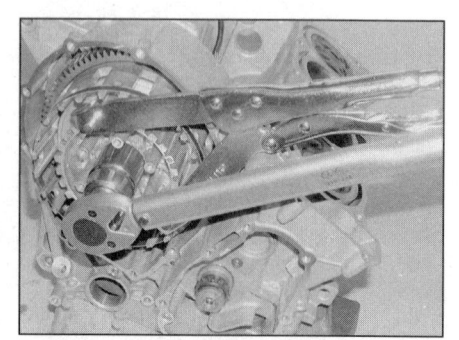

15.32c Tighten the clutch nut to the specified torque . . .

Engine, clutch and transmission 2•25

15.32d ... and secure it with the lockwasher tabs

15.33a First install the thick plain plate ...

15.33b ... then a friction plate, and so on

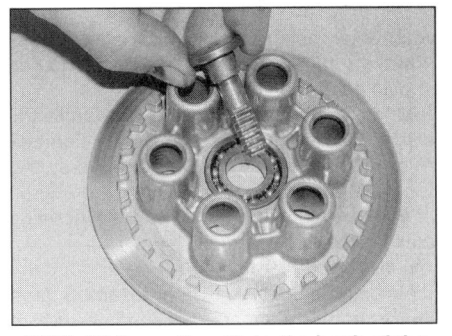

15.34 Fit the pull-rod into the back of the pressure plate

15.36 Tighten the bolts in a criss-cross sequence to the specified torque

15.37 Fit a new gasket onto the dowels (arrowed)

that the clutch centre rotates freely after tightening. Bend up the tabs of the lockwasher to secure the nut **(see illustration)**.

33 Coat each clutch plate with clean engine oil prior to installation. Build up the plates as follows: first fit the thick plain plate, then a friction plate, then alternate plain and friction plates until all the plates are installed **(see illustrations)**.

34 Lubricate the bearing in the pressure plate with clean engine oil. Fit the pull-rod into the back of the pressure plate **(see illustration)**.

35 Align the reference marks on the clutch pressure plate and the clutch centre and fit the pressure plate, making sure the castellations in its rim locate into the slots in the clutch centre **(see illustration 15.6b)**.

36 Install the clutch springs and bolts and tighten the bolts evenly and a little at a time in a criss-cross sequence to the specified torque setting **(see illustration)**. Counter-hold the clutch housing to prevent it turning when tightening the spring bolts. Set the pull-rod so that its teeth point towards the rear and are angled up slightly.

37 If removed, insert the dowels in the crankcase and fit the new gasket onto them **(see illustration)**. When installing the clutch cover, getting the actuating shaft to engage correctly with the pull-rod teeth can be tricky. Set the release arm so that it is pointing to the rear, then as the cover is installed and the teeth engage, the arm should turn in. With the cover fully installed, the alignment marks on the cover and the clutch arm should be in line when any backlash in the mechanism is taken up by light finger pressure **(see illustration 15.24b)**; if they are not, pull the cover off, reposition the clutch arm and refit the cover.

38 Check that both ends of the return spring are correctly located, then install the cover bolts and the idle speed adjuster bracket and tighten the bolts evenly in a criss-cross sequence to the specified torque setting.

39 Install the idle speed adjuster and the coolant hose guide.

40 Fit the clutch cable onto the release arm and adjust the cable as necessary (see Section 14).

41 Refill the engine with oil to the correct level (see Chapter 1).

42 Install the fairing side panel and the lower fairing (see Chapter 8).

16 Starter clutch and idler gear – check, removal, inspection and installation

Note: *This procedure can be carried out with the engine in the frame. If the engine has been removed, ignore the steps which do not apply.*

1 Remove the lower fairing and the left-hand fairing side panel (see Chapter 8). Remove the coolant reservoir (see Chapter 3). Remove the fuel tank (see Chapter 4).

2 Trace the alternator wiring from the top of the alternator cover on the left-hand side of the engine and disconnect it at the white, three-pin connector (see Section 5). Feed the wiring through to the left-hand engine cover, noting its routing.

3 Unscrew the bolts securing the alternator cover and remove the bolts, the wiring guide and the mounting bracket for the coolant reservoir. Remove the cover, being prepared to catch any residual oil **(see illustration)**. If the cover will not lift away easily, break the gasket seal by tapping gently around the edge with a soft-faced hammer or block of wood. Discard the gasket as a new one must be used. Remove the dowels from either the cover or the crankcase if they are loose.

Check

4 The operation of the starter clutch can be checked while it is in place. Check that the idler gear is able to rotate freely anti-clockwise as you look at it from the left-hand side of the bike, but locks when rotated

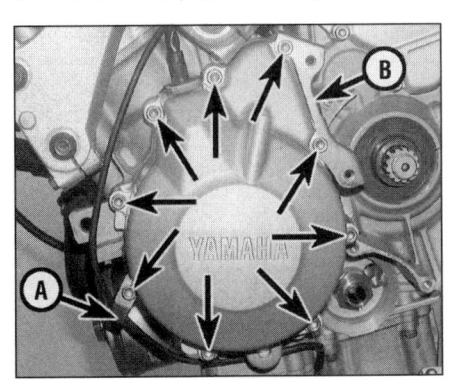

16.3 Unscrew the bolts (arrowed) and remove the wiring guide (A) and coolant reservoir bracket (B)

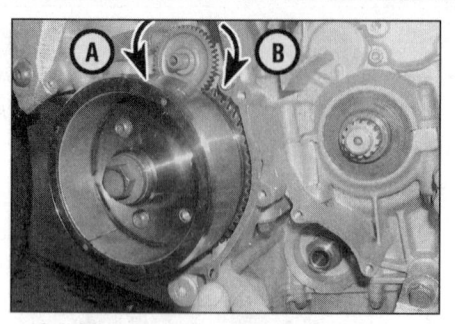

2•26 Engine, clutch and transmission

16.4 Idler gear should rotate freely anti-clockwise (A), and lock when turned clockwise (B)

16.5a Withdraw the shaft and the idler gear

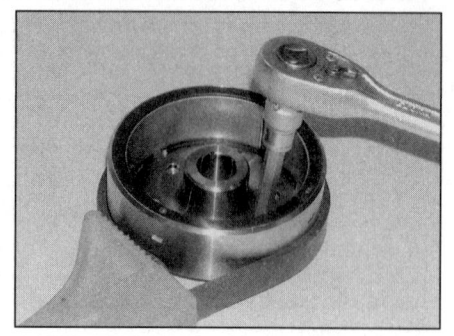

16.5b Remove the bolts to separate the starter clutch from the alternator rotor

clockwise **(see illustration)**. If not, the starter clutch is faulty and should be removed for inspection.

Removal

5 Withdraw the idler gear shaft from the crankcase and remove the gear **(see illustration)**. Remove the alternator rotor – the starter clutch is mounted on the back of it (see Chapter 9). **Note:** *Before removing the alternator rotor, slacken the three starter clutch bolts while holding the rotor centre bolt. If the rotor has already been removed from the bike, hold the rotor with a strap wrench to slacken the bolts* **(see illustration)**.
6 Lay the alternator rotor face down on the work surface and withdraw the starter driven gear from the starter clutch. If the gear appears stuck, rotate it anti-clockwise as you withdraw it to free it from the starter clutch. If the starter driven gear does not come away with the alternator rotor, slide it off the crankshaft.

Inspection

7 Inspect the teeth on the idler gear and replace it if any are chipped or worn **(see illustration)**. Check the idler shaft and bearing surfaces for signs of wear or damage, and renew if necessary.
8 Fit the starter driven gear into the starter clutch, rotating it anti-clockwise to spread the sprags and allow the gear hub to enter. With the alternator rotor face down, check that the starter driven gear rotates freely in an anti-clockwise direction and locks against the rotor in a clockwise direction **(see illustration)**. If it doesn't, the starter clutch should be dismantled.
9 Unscrew the three bolts and remove the clutch housing from the back of the alternator rotor **(see illustration)**. Depress the spring lock on the outside edge of the clutch assembly and withdraw it from the housing **(see illustration)**.
10 Inspect the condition of the sprags and their cage inside the clutch assembly **(see illustration)**. If they are damaged or worn at any point, the starter clutch should be renewed.
11 Inspect the driven gear bearing surfaces for signs of wear and scoring. If the bearing surfaces show signs of excessive wear, replace the gear with a new one and inspect the surface of the crankshaft for damage. Inspect the teeth of the driven gear and renew the gear if they are worn or damaged.

Installation

12 Clean the starter clutch bolts and apply a drop of locking compound to their threads. Press the clutch assembly into its housing and ensure that the spring lock engages. Install the housing into the back of the alternator rotor, then install the bolts and tighten them securely **(see illustration)**. **Note**: *If a strap wrench is not available to hold the alternator rotor, final tightening of the bolts can take place once the rotor has been fitted to the crankshaft.*

16.7 Examine the idler gear teeth for wear and damage

16.8 Check that the driven gear turns freely anti-clockwise

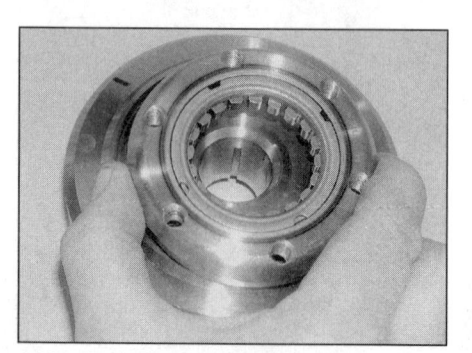

16.9a Remove the clutch housing from the back of the rotor

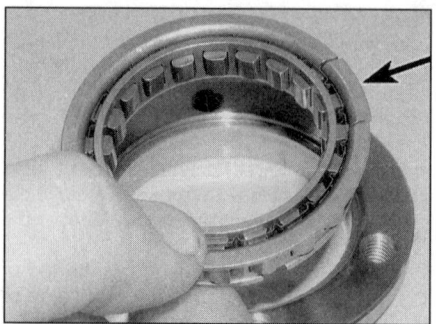

16.9b Depress the spring lock (arrowed) to release the clutch assembly from its housing

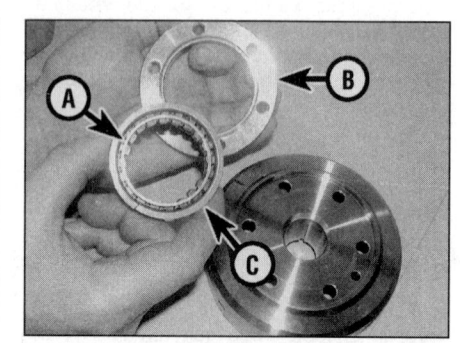

16.10 Inspect the starter clutch sprags (A), cage (B) and housing (C)

Engine, clutch and transmission 2•27

16.12 Apply locking compound to the starter clutch bolts and tighten them securely

16.16 Install a new gasket for the alternator cover

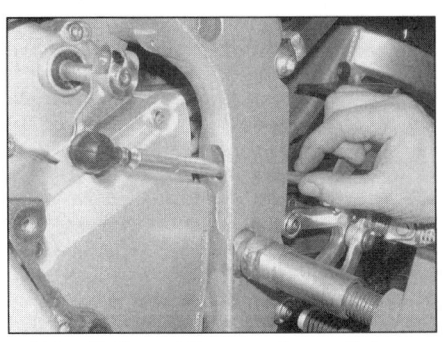

17.2a Unthread the gearchange linkage rod . . .

13 Lubricate the starter driven gear hub with clean engine oil, then fit it into the starter clutch, rotating it anti-clockwise to spread the sprags and allow the hub to enter **(see illustration 16.8)**. Check the operation of the starter clutch as described in Step 8.

14 Install the alternator (see Chapter 9).

15 Lubricate the idler gear shaft with clean engine oil. Slide the gear onto the shaft, making sure the smaller pinion faces inwards, and the teeth of the larger pinion mesh with the teeth of the starter motor shaft.

16 If removed, insert the dowels in the crankcase, then install the alternator cover using a new gasket, making sure the cover locates correctly onto the dowels and the idle gear shaft **(see illustration)**. Install the cover bolts, the wiring guide and the mounting bracket for the coolant reservoir, and tighten the bolts evenly in a criss-cross sequence to the torque setting specified at the beginning of this Chapter **(see illustration 16.3)**.

17 Install the remaining components in the reverse order of removal.

18 Top-up the engine with oil (see *Daily (pre-ride) checks*).

17 Gearchange mechanism – removal, inspection and installation

Note: *This procedure can be carried out with the engine in the frame. If the engine has been removed, ignore the steps which do not apply.*

Removal

1 Remove the lower fairing and the left-hand fairing side panel (see Chapter 8). Remove the coolant reservoir (see Chapter 3)

2 Make sure the transmission is in neutral. Loosen the gearchange linkage rod locknuts, then unscrew the rod and separate it from the lever and the arm (the rod is reverse-threaded on the lever end, so will unscrew from both lever and arm simultaneously when turned in the one direction) **(see illustration)**. Note how far the rod is threaded into the lever and arm, as this determines the height of the lever relative to the footrest. Withdraw the rod from the frame **(see illustration)**.

3 Unscrew the pinch bolt on the gearchange shaft arm and slide the arm off the shaft, noting how the punch mark on the shaft aligns with the slot in the arm **(see illustration)**. If no mark is visible, make your own before removing the arm so that it can be correctly aligned with the shaft on installation.

4 Unscrew the bolts securing the coolant reservoir bracket and remove the bracket, then unscrew the bolts securing the front sprocket cover and remove it **(see illustrations)**.

5 Unscrew the bolts securing the gearchange mechanism cover and remove it **(see illustration)**. Discard the gasket, as a new one must be used. Remove the dowels from either the cover or the crankcase if they are loose.

6 Note how the gearchange shaft centralising spring ends fit on each side of the locating pin in the crankcase, and where the stopper arm spring locates. Note how the pawls on the selector arm locate onto the pins on the end

17.2b . . . and withdraw it from the frame

17.3 Note the alignment of the punch mark (arrowed) with the slot before removing the arm

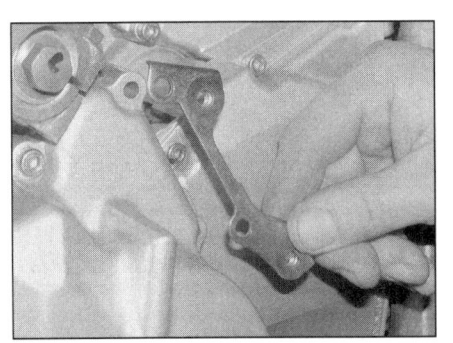

17.4a Remove the coolant reservoir bracket . . .

17.4b . . . and the front sprocket cover

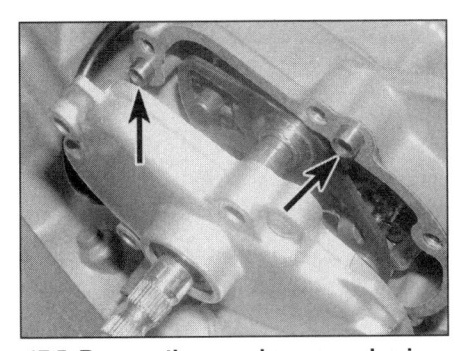

17.5 Remove the gearchange mechanism cover, noting the position of the dowels

2•28 Engine, clutch and transmission

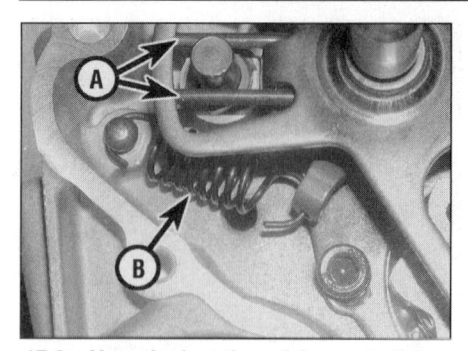

17.6a Note the location of the centralising spring ends (A) and the stopper arm spring (B)

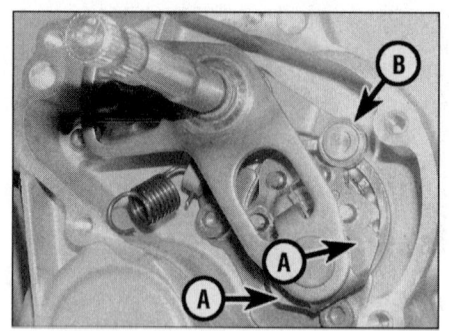

17.6b Note the position of the selector arm pawls (A) and the stopper arm roller (B)

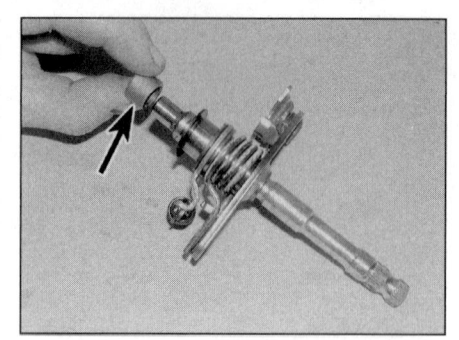

17.7 Remove the complete gearchange shaft assembly and collar (arrowed)

of the selector drum and how the roller on the stopper arm locates in the neutral detent on the selector drum **(see illustrations)**.

7 Unhook the stopper arm spring from its anchor pin, then withdraw the gearchange shaft assembly **(see illustration)**. Ensure the collar is on the inner end of the shaft or retrieve it from the shaft bore in the crankcase.

8 Slide the collar, the washer, the circlip, the second washer and stopper arm off the gearchange shaft **(see illustrations)**.

Inspection

9 Inspect the splines on the gearchange shaft; if they are worn or damaged, or if the shaft is bent, renew the shaft. Check the shaft selector arm for cracks, distortion and wear of its pawls, and check for any corresponding wear on the selector pins on the selector drum **(see illustration)**.

10 Check the stopper arm roller and the detents in the selector drum for any wear or damage, and make sure the roller turns freely. Replace any components that are worn or damaged with new ones.

11 If necessary, slide the stopper arm collar, centralising spring and spring collar off the shaft, noting how the ends of the spring locate each side of the tab on the selector arm. Inspect the centralising spring, the pawl spring and the stopper arm return spring for fatigue, wear or damage. If any faults are found, renew the components.

12 Check that the centralising spring locating pin in the crankcase is securely tightened. If it is loose, remove it and apply a non-permanent thread locking compound to its threads, then tighten it to the torque setting specified at the beginning of this Chapter.

13 Check the condition of the gearchange shaft oil seal and bearing in the cover. If the oil seal is damaged, deteriorated or shows signs of leakage it must be replaced with a new one. Lever out the old seal with a flat-bladed screwdriver. If the bearing is damaged or does not run smoothly and freely, it must be replaced with a new one (see Section 5 of *Tools and Workshop Tips* in the *Reference* section) **(see illustration)**. Drive the new seal squarely into place, with its lip facing inward, using a seal driver or suitable socket.

Installation

14 Lubricate the gearchange shaft with clean engine oil. If removed, slide the centralising spring collar and centralising spring onto the

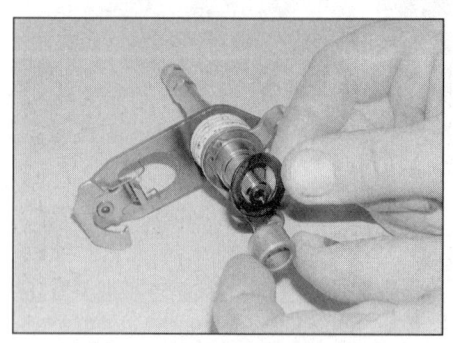

17.8a Slide the collar and the washer . . .

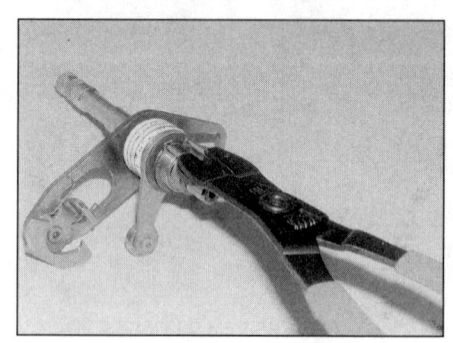

17.8b . . . then the circlip . . .

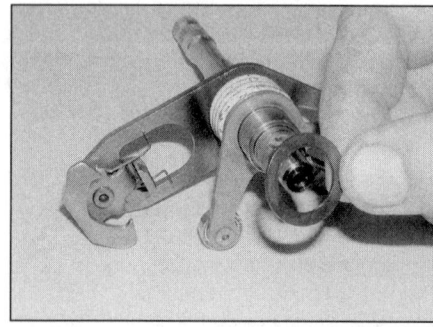

17.8c . . . and the second washer . . .

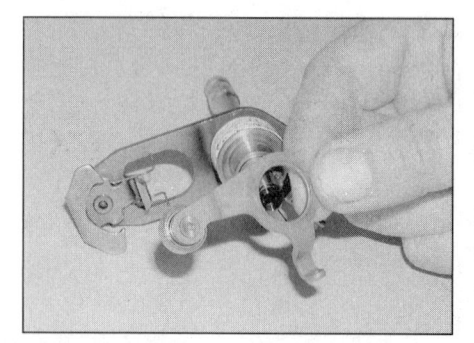

17.8d . . . and the stopper arm off the shaft

17.9 Check the selector pins for wear

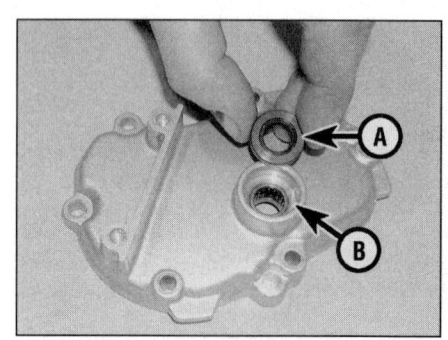

17.13 Examine the oil seal (A) and bearing (B) for wear and damage

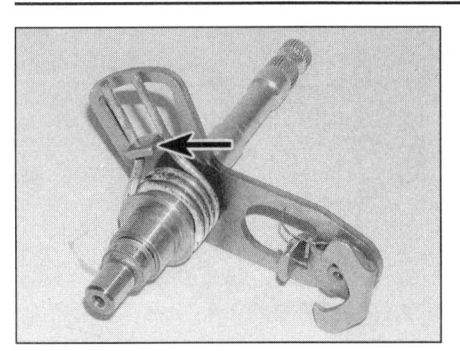

Engine, clutch and transmission 2•29

17.14 Centralising spring ends locate on each side of tab (arrowed)

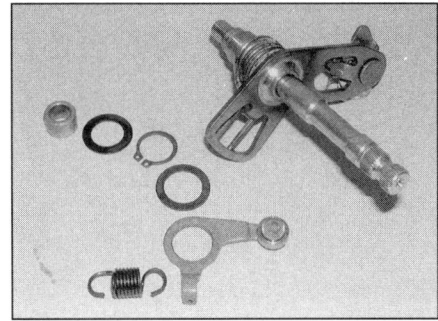

17.15 Gearchange shaft stopper arm components

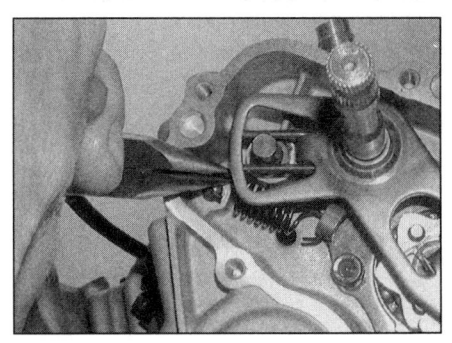

17.18 Hook the stopper arm spring over its anchor pin

gearchange shaft. Make sure the centralising spring ends are correctly positioned each side of the selector arm tab **(see illustration)**.

15 Assemble the gearchange shaft assembly **(see illustration)**. First slide the stopper arm collar onto the gearchange shaft and slide the stopper arm onto the collar, making sure it is the correct way round, then fit the washer and the circlip.

16 Fit the washer onto the end of the stopper arm collar, the small collar onto the end of the gearchange shaft, and the stopper arm spring onto the stopper arm, then install the gearchange shaft assembly into the crankcase.

17 Ensure that the centralising spring ends fit on each side of the locating pin and that the selector arm pawls engage the pins on the selector drum. Locate the stopper arm roller onto the neutral detent on the selector drum **(see illustration 17.6)**.

18 Hook the stopper arm spring over its anchor pin **(see illustration)**.

19 If removed, fit the dowels into the crankcase and lubricate the gearchange shaft oil seal with grease. Install the gearchange mechanism cover using a new gasket, ensuring the gasket and cover locate correctly onto the dowels, and tighten the cover bolts securely **(see illustration 17.5)**.

20 Install the remaining components in the reverse order of removal. **Note:** *To adjust the gearchange lever position, first loosen both locknuts on the linkage rod. Rotate the rod in one direction or the other to either raise or lower the lever height. Make sure the linkage rod length is within specification, then tighten both locknuts securely.*

21 Check the engine oil level and top up if necessary (see *Daily (pre-ride) checks*).

18 Oil cooler – removal and installation

Note: *This procedure can be carried out with the engine in the frame. If the engine has been removed, ignore the steps that do not apply.*

⚠️ **Warning: Allow the engine to cool completely before starting work.**

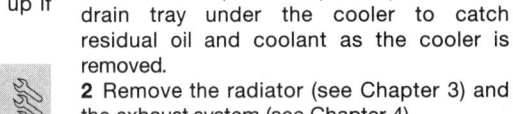

Removal

1 The cooler is located on the front of the engine. Drain the engine oil and the coolant (see Chapter 1). Leave a drain tray under the cooler to catch residual oil and coolant as the cooler is removed.

2 Remove the radiator (see Chapter 3) and the exhaust system (see Chapter 4).

3 Loosen the clips securing the water pump outlet hose and the water jacket hose to the front of the cylinder block, and detach the hoses **(see illustrations)**. Loosen the clips securing the inlet and outlet water hoses to the oil cooler and detach the hoses **(see illustrations)**.

4 Unscrew the oil cooler centre bolt and remove the bolt, washer and oil cooler. Note how the tab on the cooler body locates

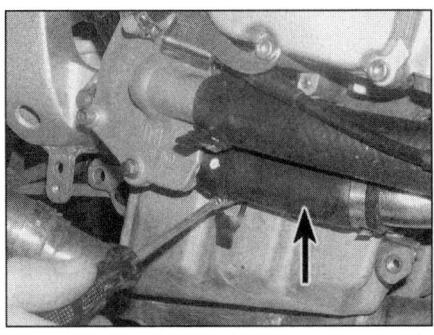

18.3a Loosen the clips on the water pump outlet hose (arrowed) . . .

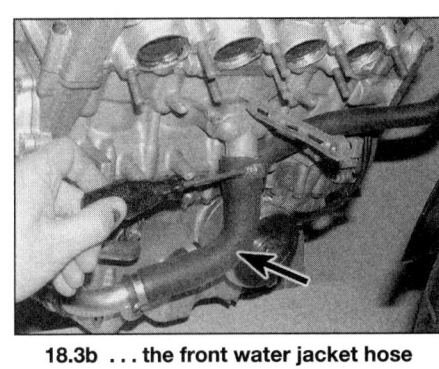

18.3b . . . the front water jacket hose (arrowed) . . .

18.3c . . . the oil cooler inlet hose . . .

18.3d . . . and the oil cooler outlet hose . . .

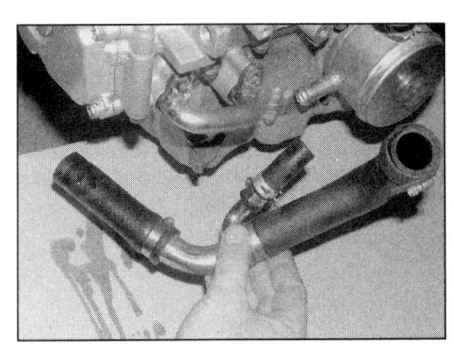

18.3e . . . and detach the hoses

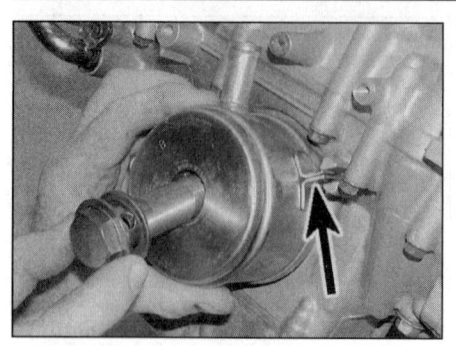

2•30 Engine, clutch and transmission

18.4 Remove the oil cooler, noting how the tab (arrowed) locates against the crankcase

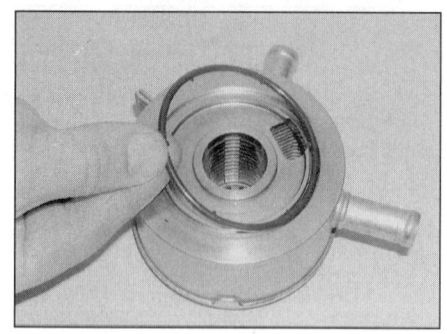

18.7 Use a new O-ring on the oil cooler body

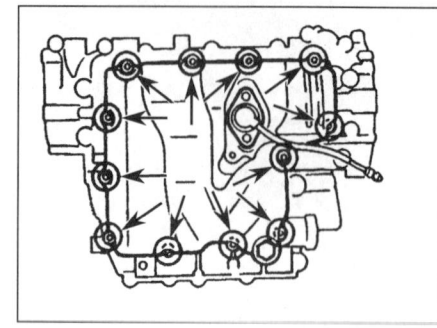

19.3a Unscrew the bolts (arrowed) and remove the sump

between the lugs on the crankcase (see illustration).
5 Discard the washer and the O-ring from the cooler body as new ones must be fitted on reassembly.
6 Check the cooler body for cracks and dents and any evidence of coolant leakage and replace it with a new one if necessary. Also check the hoses for splits, cracks, hardening and deterioration and fit new ones if required.

Installation

7 Installation is the reverse of removal, noting the following:
● Clean the mating surfaces of the crankcase and the cooler with a rag and solvent.
● Before reassembly, lubricate the new O-ring with clean engine oil and ensure it

seats correctly on the cooler body (see illustration).
● Locate the tab on the cooler body between the lugs on the crankcase (see illustration 18.4).
● Use a new washer on the centre bolt and tighten it to the torque setting specified at the beginning of this Chapter.
● Make sure the coolant hoses are pressed fully onto their unions and tighten the clips securely.
● Refill the engine with oil and refill the cooling system (see Chapter 1).
● Start the engine and check that there are no leaks before taking the machine on the road.

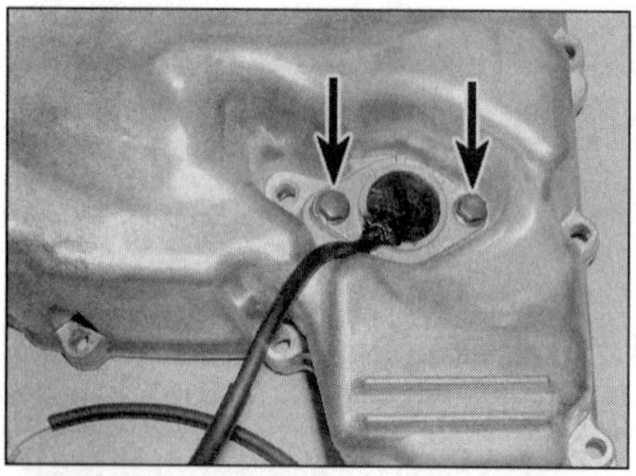

19 Oil sump, oil strainer and pressure relief valve – removal, inspection and installation

Note: *This procedure can be carried out with the engine in the frame. If the engine has been removed, ignore the steps which do not apply.*

⚠️ **Warning: Allow the engine to cool completely before starting work.**

Removal

1 Remove the fuel tank and the exhaust system (see Chapter 4).
2 Drain the engine oil (see Chapter 1). Trace the wire from the oil level sensor underneath

the sump and disconnect it at the connector (see illustration 5.13a). Feed the wire through to the underside of the engine, noting its routing.
3 Unscrew the sump bolts, slackening them evenly in a criss-cross sequence to prevent distortion, and remove the sump (see illustration). **Note:** *Do not unscrew the two bolts retaining the oil level sensor* (see illustration). If necessary, break the gasket seal by tapping gently around the edge of the sump with a soft-faced hammer or block of wood; do not lever the sump off as this will damage the sealing surface. Note the position of the oil level sensor wiring clamp and the two lower fairing fixing brackets (see illustration). Discard the gasket, as a new one must be used. Note the positions of the dowels and remove them if they are loose.
4 Pull the oil strainer out of its socket in the oil pump, noting how the tab on the strainer locates between the lugs on the crankcase. Remove the seal and discard it as a new one must be fitted on reassembly (see illustration).
5 Pull the pressure relief valve out of the crankcase (see illustration). Discard the O-ring, as a new one must be fitted on reassembly.

Inspection

6 Remove all traces of gasket from the sump and crankcase mating surfaces, and clean the inside of the sump with a suitable solvent (see

19.3b Do not unscrew the oil level sensor bolts (arrowed) when removing the sump

19.3c Note the position of the wiring clamp (A) and lower fairing brackets (B)

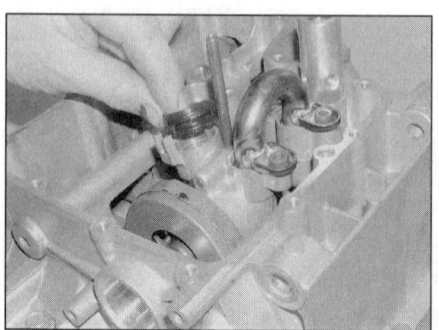

19.4 Pull out the old seal and discard it

19.5 Pull the pressure relief valve out of its socket

Engine, clutch and transmission 2•31

19.6 Clean the inside of the sump thoroughly

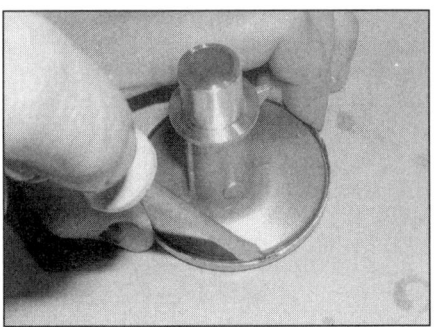

19.7a Lever off the oil strainer mesh

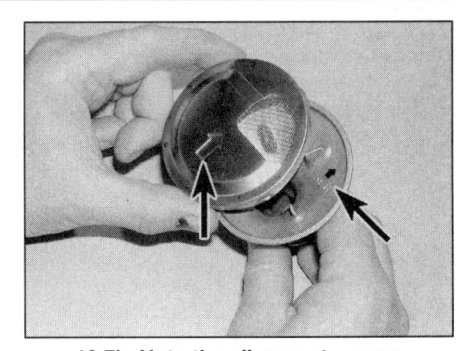

19.7b Note the alignment arrows (arrowed)

illustration). Do not remove the oil level sensor unless it is necessary for testing the unit (see Chapter 9).

7 Lever the oil strainer mesh off the strainer body and note the alignment arrows on the mesh and the body **(see illustrations)**. Clean the components in solvent and remove any debris caught in the strainer mesh. Inspect the mesh for any signs of wear or damage and replace it with a new one if necessary.

8 Push the relief valve plunger into the valve body and check that it moves smoothly and freely against spring pressure. If not, remove the circlip, noting that it is under spring pressure, and remove the spring seat, spring and plunger **(see illustrations)**. Clean all the components in solvent and check them for scoring, wear or damage. If any is found, replace the relief valve with a new one – individual components are not available. Otherwise, coat the inside of the valve body and the plunger with clean engine oil, then insert the plunger, spring and spring seat and secure them with the circlip. Check the action of the valve plunger again – if it is still suspect, replace the valve with a new one.

Installation

9 Fit a new O-ring onto the relief valve and smear it with grease. Push the valve into its socket in the crankcase **(see illustration 19.5)**.

10 Lubricate the new seal for the oil strainer with grease and fit it to the strainer, then install the strainer, making sure the tab locates between the lugs on the crankcase

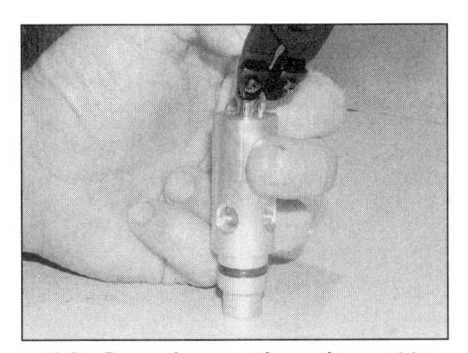

19.8a Press down on the spring seat to remove the circlip

and the arrow points to the front of the engine **(see illustration)**.

11 If removed, fit the sump dowels into the crankcase. Lay a new gasket onto the sump (if the engine is in the frame) or onto the crankcase (if the engine has been removed and is upside down on the work surface) **(see illustration)**. Make sure the holes in the gasket align correctly with the bolt holes.

12 Position the sump on the crankcase, then install the bolts, the oil level sensor wiring clamp and the lower fairing fixing brackets **(see illustration)**. Tighten the bolts evenly and a little at a time in a criss-cross pattern to the specified torque setting.

13 Connect the oil level sensor wire at the connector.

14 Fill the engine with the correct type and quantity of oil (see Chapter 1).

15 Install the exhaust system and the fuel

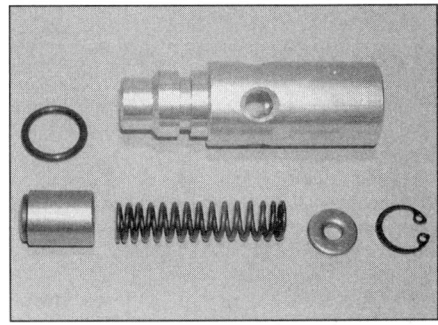

19.8b Disassemble the relief valve and examine the components

tank (see Chapter 4). Start the engine and check that there are no leaks around the sump before taking the machine on the road.

20 Oil pump – removal, inspection and installation

Note: *This procedure can be carried out with the engine in the frame. If the engine has been removed, ignore the steps which do not apply.*

⚠ **Warning: Allow the engine to cool completely before starting work.**

Removal

1 Remove the water pump (see Chapter 3).
2 Remove the sump and the oil strainer (see Section 19).

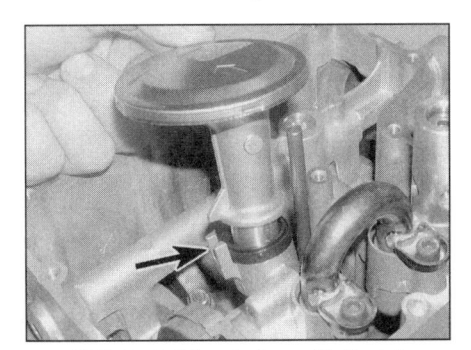

19.10 Install the strainer with the tab between the lugs (arrowed) on the crankcase

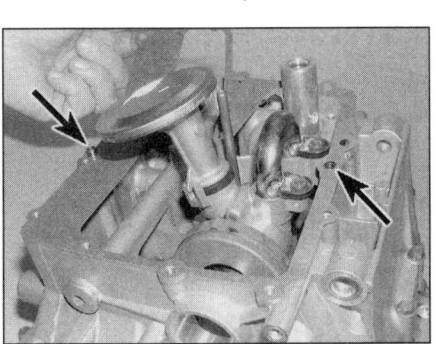

19.11 Ensure the new gasket aligns with the dowels (arrowed) and sump bolt holes

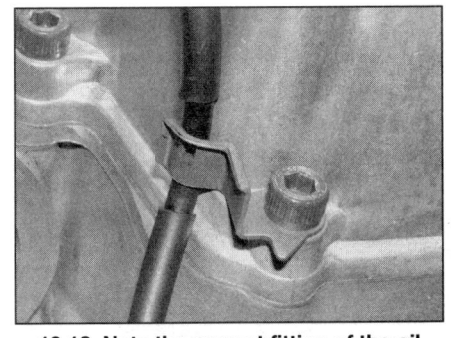

19.12 Note the correct fitting of the oil level sensor wiring clamp

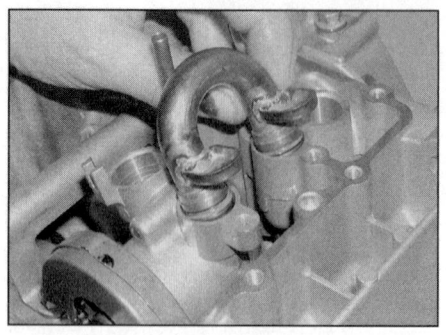

2•32 Engine, clutch and transmission

20.3 Remove the U-shaped oil pipe ...

20.4 ... and the oil return pipe

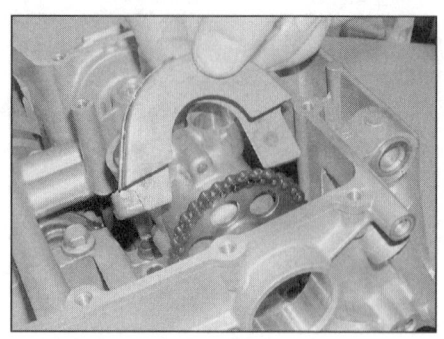

20.5 Remove the oil pump sprocket cover ...

20.6 ... then disengage the chain and remove the pump

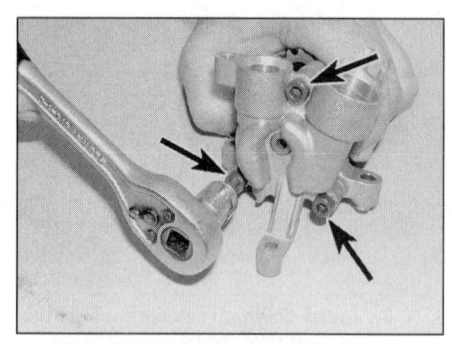

20.7a Unscrew the pump body bolts (arrowed) ...

3 Unscrew the U-shaped oil pipe retaining bolts and pull the pipe out of its sockets in the crankcase (see illustration). Discard the O-rings as new ones must be fitted on reassembly.

4 Unscrew the bolt retaining the oil return pipe and pull out the pipe (see illustration).

5 Unscrew the bolts securing the oil pump driven sprocket cover and remove the cover, noting how it fits (see illustration).

6 Tilt the pump to disengage the driven pump sprocket from the drive chain, then remove the pump from the engine (see illustration). If the engine is upside down on the work surface, secure the chain with a length of wire to prevent it dropping into the crankcase. Note the dowels in the pump mounting lugs and remove them if they are loose.

Inspection

7 Unscrew the bolts securing the two halves of the oil pump body, then separate the body halves and remove the dowels (see illustrations).

8 Slide the outer and inner pump rotors off the pump shaft, noting how they fit (see illustrations). The outer rotor is not marked but it should be installed in the pump the same way round on reassembly.

9 Withdraw the drive pin from the shaft, noting how it locates in the slots in the inner rotor, then slide the washer off the shaft and pull the shaft out of the pump body (see illustrations).

20.7b ... and separate the body halves. Remove the dowels (arrowed)

20.8a First slide the outer ...

20.8b ... and then the inner rotor off the pump shaft

20.9a Withdraw the drive pin ...

20.9b ... and then remove the washer ...

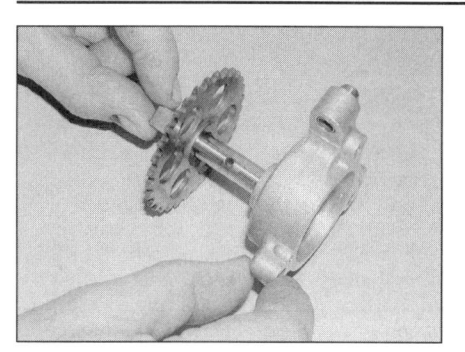

Engine, clutch and transmission 2•33

20.9c ... and pull the shaft out of the pump body

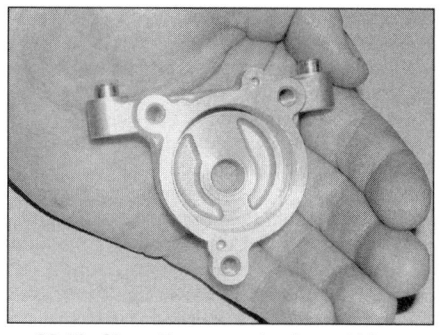

20.10 Clean the pump body and blow through the oil ways with compressed air

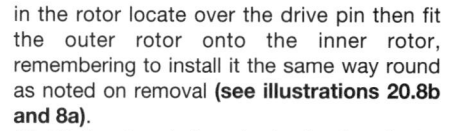

20.12 Measure the outer rotor to body clearance as shown

10 Clean all components in solvent. Check that the oil ways in the body are clear by blowing them through with compressed air **(see illustration)**.

11 Inspect the components for scoring and wear. If any damage, scoring or uneven or excessive wear is evident, renew the pump (individual components are not available).

12 Reassemble the pump components and measure the clearance between the outer rotor and the pump body with a feeler gauge and compare it to the maximum clearance listed in the specifications at the beginning of this Chapter **(see illustration)**. If the clearance measured is greater than the maximum listed, renew the pump.

13 Measure the clearance between the inner rotor tip and the outer rotor with a feeler gauge and compare it to the maximum clearance listed in the specifications at the beginning of the Chapter **(see illustration)**. If the clearance measured is greater than the maximum listed, renew the pump.

14 Check the pump driven sprocket and the chain for wear or damage, and replace them with new ones if necessary. **Note:** *When replacing the chain and driven sprocket, also check the condition of the drive sprocket on the back of the clutch housing (see Section 15).*

15 If the pump is good, make sure all the components are clean, then lubricate them with clean engine oil. Fit the pump shaft through the pump body and install the washer and drive pin **(see illustration 20.9a)**. Slide the inner rotor onto the shaft so that the slots in the rotor locate over the drive pin then fit the outer rotor onto the inner rotor, remembering to install it the same way round as noted on removal **(see illustrations 20.8b and 8a)**.

16 Fit the dowels into the body, then fit the other half of the pump body over the rotors and the shaft **(see illustration)**.

17 Install the bolts and tighten them to the torque setting specified at the beginning of this Chapter. Rotate the pump shaft by hand and check that the rotors turn freely. If not, strip and reassemble the pump.

Installation

18 Before installing the pump, prime it with clean engine oil and ensure that the dowels are in place on the mounting lugs.

19 Install the pump, tilting it to engage the driven sprocket on the drive chain. Ensure the chain is correctly routed between the guides on the inside of the crankcase (see Section 15).

20 Apply a suitable non-permanent thread locking compound to the sprocket cover bolts, install the sprocket cover and the bolts, then tighten the bolts to the torque setting specified at this beginning of this Chapter **(see illustration)**.

21 Smear the new O-rings for the U-shaped oil pipe with grease and install them on the pipe. Install the U-shaped pipe and the oil return pipe and tighten their retaining bolts securely **(see illustration)**.

22 Install the oil strainer and the sump (see Section 19), then the water pump (see Chapter 3).

20.13 Measure the inner rotor tip to outer rotor clearance as shown

23 Fill the engine with the specified quantity and type of new engine oil and coolant (see Chapter 1).

21 Crankcase halves – separation and reassembly

Note: *To separate the crankcase halves, the engine must be removed from the frame.*

Separation

1 To gain access to the connecting rods, pistons and rings, crankshaft, bearings, transmission shafts and selector drum and forks, the crankcase must be split into two parts.

2 Remove the engine from the frame (see Section 5).

20.16 Don't forget to fit the dowels before joining the pump halves

20.20 Tighten the sprocket cover bolts to the specified torque setting

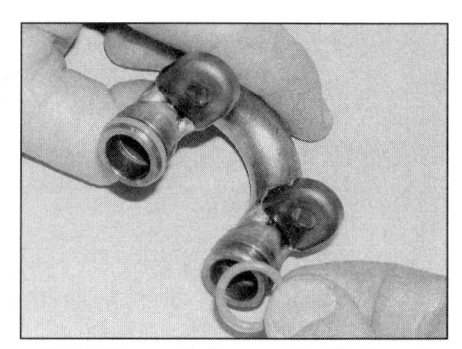

20.21 Fit new O-rings on the U-shaped pipe before reassembly

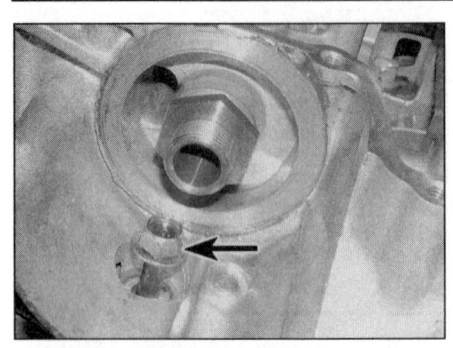

2•34 Engine, clutch and transmission

21.4 Remove the oil filter and fitting to access crankcase bolt No. 12 (arrowed)

3 Before the crankcases can be separated the following components must be removed:
  Camshafts and cam chain tensioner (Sections 8 and 9).
  Cylinder head (Section 11).
  Alternator rotor (Chapter 9).
  Thermostat (Chapter 3).
  Starter motor (Chapter 9).
  Ignition rotor (Chapter 5).
  Cam chain (Section 10).
  Clutch (Section 15).
  Gearchange mechanism (Section 17).
  Oil cooler (Section 18).
  Water pump (Chapter 3)
  Oil sump, strainer and pressure relief valve (Section 19).
  Oil pump assembly and drive chain (Section 20).
  Oil filter fitting (see below)

4 If not already done, remove the oil filter and unscrew the filter fitting from the crankcase to gain access to crankcase bolt No. 12 **(see illustration)**.

5 Turn the engine upside down. The crankcases are joined by twelve 8 mm bolts (Nos. 1 to 12) and fifteen 6 mm bolts (Nos. 13 to 27). Unscrew the bolts a $1/4$ turn at a time in a **reverse** of the numerical sequence shown and as marked on the crankcase (the number of each bolt is cast into the crankcase), until they are finger-tight, then remove them **(see illustrations)**. Note the washers fitted to bolts Nos. 1 to 10. Discard the copper washer on bolt No. 21 as a new one must be fitted on reassembly.

6 Carefully lift the lower crankcase half off the upper half, using a soft-faced hammer or block of wood to tap around the joint to initially separate the halves, if necessary **(see illustration)**. **Note:** *If the halves do not separate easily, make sure all fasteners have*

HAYNES HiNT *Make a cardboard template of the crankcase and punch a hole for each bolt location. Number the holes. As each bolt is removed, store it in its relative position, with its washer where applicable, in the template. This will ensure all bolts are installed correctly on reassembly – this is important, as many bolts differ slightly in length.*

been removed. Do not try and separate the halves by levering between the sealing surfaces as they are easily damaged and will leak oil on reassembly.

7 Remove the three locating dowels from the crankcase (they could be in either half) **(see illustration)**.

8 Refer to Sections 22 to 30 for the removal and installation of the components housed within the crankcases.

Reassembly

9 Remove all traces of sealant from the crankcase mating surfaces.

10 Ensure that all components and their bearings are in place in the upper and lower crankcase halves. If the transmission shafts have not been removed, check the condition of the oil seal on the left-hand end of the output shaft and replace it with a new one if it is damaged, deformed or deteriorated **(see illustration)**. It is sound practice to renew this seal anyway. Apply some grease to the inside of the new seal on installation. Check that the selector drum is in the neutral position.

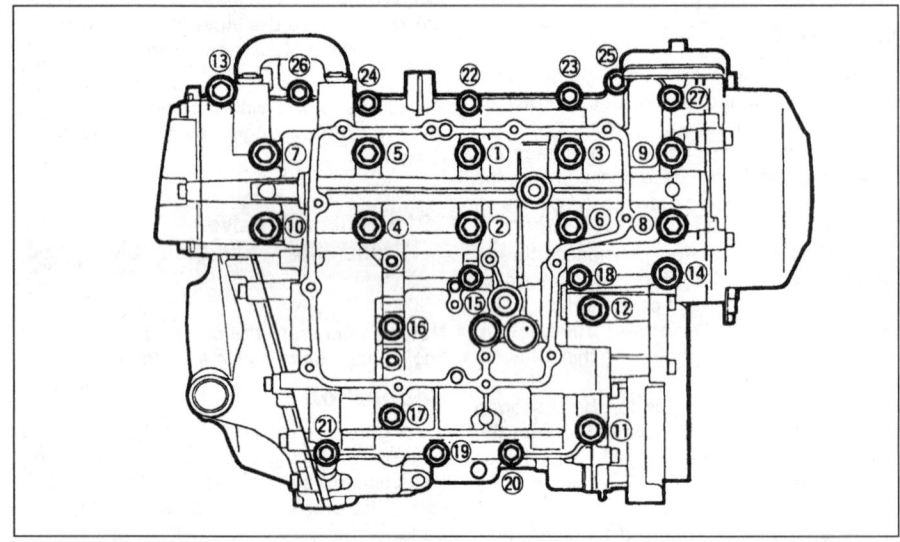

21.5a Crankcase bolt location and TIGHTENING sequence. Loosen bolts in REVERSE order

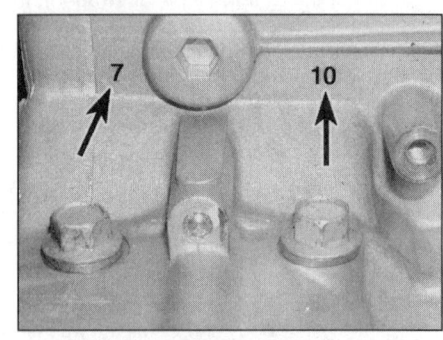

21.5b Bolt numbers (arrowed) are cast into the crankcase

21.6 Lift the lower half of the crankcase off the upper half

21.7 Remove the three locating dowels (arrowed) shown in the upper crankcase

21.10 Check the condition of the output shaft oil seal before reassembly

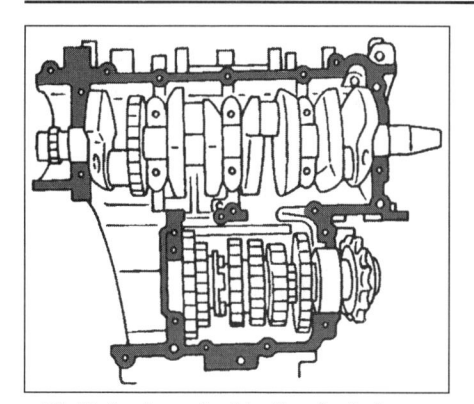

Engine, clutch and transmission 2•35

21.12 Apply sealant to the shaded area

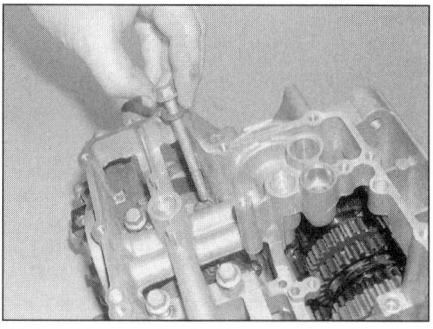

21.17a Ensure the bolts are refitted in their correct locations, with washers as required . . .

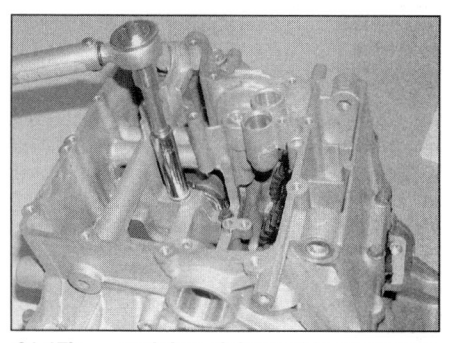

21.17b . . . and then tightened in sequence to the specified torques

11 Generously lubricate the crankshaft, transmission shafts and selector drum and forks, particularly around the bearings, with clean engine oil, then use a rag soaked in high flash-point solvent to wipe over the mating surfaces of both crankcase halves to remove all traces of oil.

12 Apply a small amount of suitable sealant (such as Yamaha Bond 1215) to the mating surface of one crankcase half as shown **(see illustration)**.

Caution: Do not apply an excessive amount of sealant as it will ooze out when the case halves are assembled and may obstruct oil passages. Do not apply the sealant on or too close (within 2 to 3 mm) to any of the bearing inserts or surfaces.

13 If removed, fit the three locating dowels into the crankcase **(see illustration 21.7)**.

14 Check again that all components are in position, particularly that the bearing shells are located in their seats in the lower crankcase half, then fit the lower crankcase half onto the upper crankcase half, making sure the dowels locate correctly.

15 Check that the lower crankcase half is seated correctly. *Note: The crankcase halves should fit together without being forced. If the casings are not correctly seated, remove the lower crankcase half and investigate the problem. Do not attempt to pull them together using the crankcase bolts as the casing will crack and be ruined.* Rotate the transmission selector drum to ensure that the gears select correctly and investigate any problems before bolting the crankcase halves together.

16 Clean the threads of the crankcase bolts and lubricate the threads of all except bolt Nos. 12 and 18 **(see illustration 21.5a)** with clean engine oil. Lubricate the underside of the heads and washers of bolt Nos. 1 to 10. Install a new copper washer on bolt No. 21 and apply a suitable thread locking compound to the threads of bolt No. 18.

17 Install the bolts in their correct locations and secure them finger-tight. Now tighten the bolts, evenly and a little at a time, in the numerical sequence as marked on the crankcase to the torque settings specified at the beginning of this Chapter **(see illustrations)**.

18 With all crankcase bolts tightened, check that the crankshaft and transmission shafts rotate smoothly and easily. Check that all gears can be selected and that the shafts rotate freely in every gear. If there are any signs of undue stiffness, rough spots, or of any other problem, the fault must be rectified before proceeding further.

19 Install all the removed assemblies in the reverse order of removal, according to your procedure (see Steps 2 and 3).

22 Main and connecting rod bearings – general information

1 Even though main and connecting rod bearings are generally replaced with new ones during an engine overhaul, the old bearings should be carefully examined as they can reveal valuable information about the condition of the engine.

2 Bearing failure occurs mainly because of lack of lubrication, the presence of dirt or other foreign particles, overloading the engine and/or corrosion. Regardless of the cause of bearing failure, it must be corrected before the engine is reassembled to prevent it from happening again.

3 When examining the bearings, match them with their corresponding journal on the crankshaft to help identify the cause of any problem.

4 Dirt and other foreign particles get into the engine in a variety of ways. They may be left in the engine during assembly or they may pass through filters or breathers, then get into the oil and from there into the bearings. Metal chips from machining operations and normal engine wear are often present. Abrasives are sometimes left in engine components after reconditioning operations, especially when parts are not thoroughly cleaned using the proper cleaning methods. Whatever the source, foreign objects often end up imbedded in the soft bearing material and are easily recognised. Large particles will not imbed in the bearing and will score or gouge the bearing and journal. The best prevention for this type of bearing failure is to clean all parts thoroughly and keep everything spotlessly clean during engine reassembly. Regular oil and filter changes are also essential.

5 Lack of lubrication or lubrication breakdown have a number of interrelated causes. Excessive heat (which thins the oil), overloading (which squeezes the oil from the bearing face) and oil leakage or throw off (from excessive bearing clearances, a worn oil pump or high engine speeds) all contribute to a breakdown of the protective lubricating film. Blocked oil passages will starve a bearing of lubrication and destroy it. When lack of lubrication is the cause of bearing failure, the bearing material is wiped or extruded from the steel backing of the bearing. Temperatures may increase to the point where the steel backing and the journal turn blue from overheating.

> **HAYNES HINT** *Refer to Tools and Workshop Tips (Section 5) in the Reference section for bearing fault finding.*

6 Riding habits can have a definite effect on bearing life. Full throttle, low speed operation, or labouring the engine, puts very high loads on bearings, which tend to squeeze out the oil film. These loads cause the bearings to flex, which produces fine cracks in the bearing face (fatigue failure). Eventually the bearing material will loosen in pieces and tear away from the steel backing. Short trip riding leads to corrosion of bearings, as insufficient engine heat is produced to drive off the condensed water and corrosive gases produced. These products collect in the engine oil, forming acid and sludge. As the oil is carried to the engine bearings, the acid attacks and corrodes the bearing material.

7 Incorrect bearing installation during engine assembly will lead to bearing failure as well. Tight fitting bearings which leave insufficient bearing oil clearances result in oil starvation. Dirt or foreign particles trapped behind a bearing insert result in high spots on the bearing which lead to failure.

8 To avoid bearing problems, clean all parts

2•36 Engine, clutch and transmission

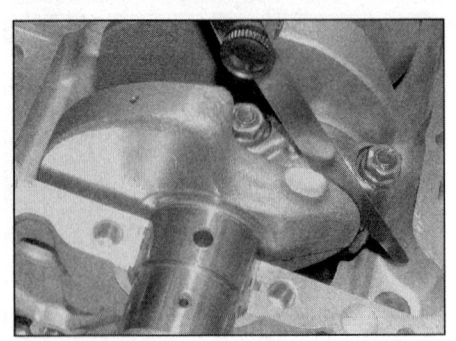

23.2 Measuring the connecting rod side clearance with a feeler gauge

23.4a Unscrew the nuts (arrowed) . . .

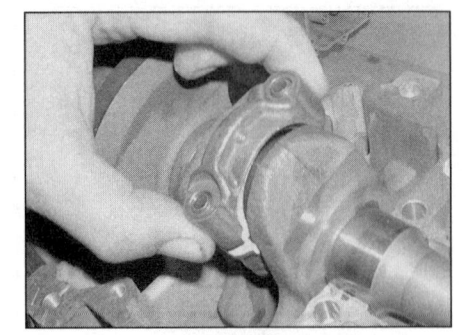

23.4b . . . and pull the cap off the connecting rod

thoroughly before reassembly, double check all bearing clearance measurements and lubricate the new bearings with clean engine oil during installation.

23 Connecting rods – removal, inspection and installation

Note: *To remove the connecting rods the engine must be removed from the frame.*

Removal

1 Remove the engine from the frame (see Section 5) and separate the crankcase halves (see Section 21).
2 Before separating the rods from the crankshaft, measure the side clearance on each rod with a feeler gauge **(see illustration)**. If the clearance on any rod is greater than the service limit listed in this Chapter's Specifications, replace that rod with a new one.
3 Using paint or a marker pen, mark the cylinder identity on the top of each piston and on each connecting rod and cap. Cylinders are numbered 1 to 4 from the left-hand side of the motorcycle. Note that the number and letter already written on the rod and cap are the rod size code and weight grade respectively, not the cylinder number.
4 Unscrew the connecting rod cap nuts and separate the caps, complete with the lower bearing shells from the crankpins **(see illustrations)**. If a cap appears stuck, tap it on one end with a hammer while pulling it.
5 Detach the connecting rods, complete with the upper bearing shells, from the crankpins, then lift the crankshaft out of the upper crankcase half, taking care not to dislodge the main bearing shells **(see illustration 26.2)**. If required, remove the main bearing shells from the crankcase halves by pushing their centres to the side, then lifting them out **(see illustration 26.3)** – it is imperative that the shells are kept in order so that they can be returned to their original locations.
6 Push each piston/connecting rod assembly to the top end of the cylinder bore and remove it, making sure the connecting rod does not mark the bore walls **(see illustration)**. Note the 'Y' mark on each connecting rod that must face to the left-hand side of the engine **(see illustration 23.27)**, and the arrow on the top of each piston which points to the front of the engine **(see illustration 24.2)**. If this is not visible, mark the piston accordingly so that it can be installed the correct way round.

HAYNES HiNT *To ease removal of the pistons, carefully remove any ridge of carbon built up on the top of each cylinder bore using a scraper. If there is a pronounced wear ridge, remove it using a ridge reamer.*

Caution: *Do not try to remove the piston/connecting rod from the bottom of the cylinder bore. The piston will not pass the crankcase main bearing webs. If the piston is pulled right to the bottom of the bore the oil control ring will expand and lock the piston in position. If this happens it is likely the ring will be broken.*

7 Fit the related bearing shells (if removed), bearing cap, and bolts on each piston/connecting rod assembly so that they are all kept together as a matched set. **Note:** *New big-end bolts must be used on final assembly. Use the old bolts for the oil clearance check, then discard them.*
8 Separate the pistons from the connecting rods (see Section 24).

Inspection

9 Check the connecting rods for cracks and other obvious damage.

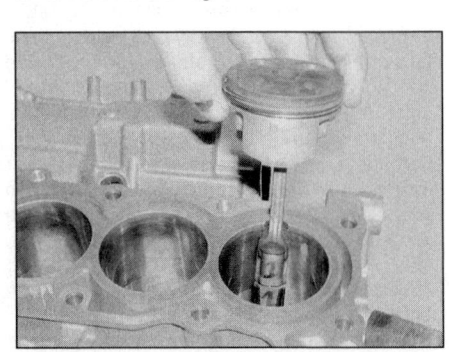

23.6 Remove each piston and connecting rod from the top of its bore

10 Apply clean engine oil to the piston pin, insert it into its connecting rod small-end and check for any freeplay between the two **(see illustration)**. If freeplay is excessive, measure the pin external diameter **(see illustration 24.12b)**. Compare the result to the specifications at the beginning of this Chapter. Replace the pin with a new one if it is worn beyond its specified limits. If the pin diameter is within specifications, replace the connecting rod with a new one. Repeat the measurements for all the rods.
11 Refer to Section 22 and examine the connecting rod bearing shells. If they are scored, badly scuffed or appear to have seized, new shells must be installed. Always renew the shells in the connecting rods as a set. If they are badly damaged, check the corresponding crankpin. Evidence of extreme heat, such as bluing, indicates that lubrication failure has occurred. Be sure to thoroughly check the oil pump and pressure relief valve as well as all oil holes and passages before reassembling the engine.
12 Have the rods checked by a Yamaha dealer if you are in doubt about their straightness.

Oil clearance check

13 Whether new bearing shells are being fitted or the original ones are being re-used, the connecting rod big-end bearing oil clearance should be checked prior to reassembly. Bearing oil clearance is measured with a product known as Plastigauge.

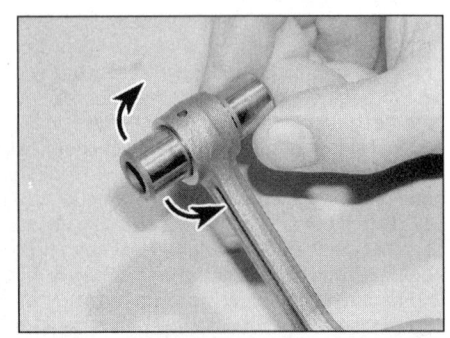

23.10 Rock the piston pin back and forth in the small-end to check for looseness

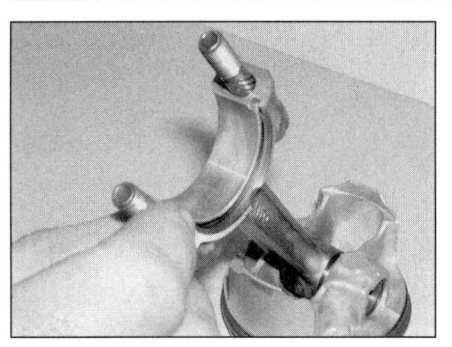

Engine, clutch and transmission 2•37

23.14 To remove a big end-end bearing shell, push it sideways and then lift it out

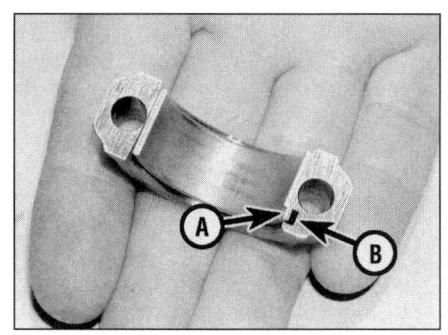

23.15 Ensure tab (A) locates in notch (B)

14 Remove the bearing shells from the rods and caps, keeping them in order **(see illustration)**. Clean the backs of the shells, the bearing locations in both the connecting rod and cap, and the crankpin journal with a suitable solvent.
15 Press the bearing shells into their locations, ensuring that the tab on each shell engages the notch in the connecting rod or cap **(see illustration)**. Make sure the bearings are fitted in the correct locations and take care not to touch any shell's bearing surface with your fingers.
16 Cut an appropriate size length of Plastigauge (it should be slightly shorter than the width of the crankpin) and place it on the crankpin journal to be checked **(see illustration 26.12)**. Do not place Plastigauge over the oil holes in the journal.
17 Apply molybdenum disulphide grease to the bolt shanks and threads and to the seats of the nuts. Fit the connecting rod and cap onto the crankpin **(see illustrations 23.34)**. Make sure the cap is fitted the correct way around so the previously made markings align (see Step 3), and that the 'Y' mark on the rod is facing the right way (see Step 6). Fit the nuts and tighten them finger-tight. **Note:** It is essential that, throughout this procedure, the connecting rod does not rotate on the crankshaft.
18 Tighten the cap nuts to the initial torque setting specified at the beginning of this Chapter with a torque wrench **(see illustration 23.36a)**. Now tighten each nut in turn and in one continuous movement to the final torque setting specified using a torque

angle gauge **(see illustration 23.36b)**. If tightening is paused between the initial and final settings, slacken the nut to below the initial setting and repeat the procedure. **Note:** If a torque angle gauge is not available, paint a small reference mark on the top of each nut after tightening them to the initial torque setting. Then, using a ring spanner so that you can see the mark, tighten the nuts to the final setting **(see illustrations 23.36c and 36d)**.
19 Slacken the cap nuts and remove the cap and rod from the crankshaft.
20 Compare the width of the crushed Plastigauge on the crankpin to the scale printed on the Plastigauge envelope to obtain the connecting rod bearing oil clearance **(see illustration 26.16)**. Compare the reading to the specifications at the beginning of this Chapter. If the clearance is within the range specified and the bearings are in perfect condition, they can be reused.
21 Carefully clean away all traces of the Plastigauge from the crankpin journal and bearing shells using a fingernail or other object which will not score the bearing surfaces.
22 If the clearance is beyond the service limit, replace the bearing shells with new ones (see Steps 25 and 26) and check the oil clearance once again. Always renew all of the shells at the same time.
23 If the clearance is still greater than the service limit listed in this Chapter's Specifications, the big-end bearing journal is worn and the crankshaft should be replaced with a new one.
24 Repeat the procedure for the remaining

connecting rods, then discard the old big-end bolts

Bearing shell selection

25 Replacement bearing shells for the big-end bearings are supplied on a selected fit basis. Code numbers for the crankshaft journals are stamped on the outside of the crankshaft web on the left-hand end of the crankshaft **(see illustration)**. The right-hand block of four numbers is the size codes for the big-end bearing journals (the left-hand block of five numbers is the size codes for the main bearing journals). The first number of the block is for the left-hand (No. 1 cylinder) journal, and so on. Each connecting rod size code number is marked in ink on the flat face of the connecting rod and cap **(see illustration)**.
26 A range of bearing shells are available. To select the correct shells for a particular journal, subtract the big-end bearing journal number from the connecting rod number and compare the result with the table below to find the colour coding of the replacement shells, e.g. connecting rod number 4 minus journal number 2 = 2; No. 2 bearing shells are colour coded black. The colour code is marked on the side of each bearing shell.

Number	Colour
1	blue
2	black
3	brown
4	green

Installation

27 New big-end bolts must be used on final assembly. Note the alignment of the bolt head with the recess in the connecting rod, then press the old bolt out of the rod. Align the head of the new bolt with the recess in the rod and press the bolt into place **(see illustration)**.
28 Fit the pistons onto the connecting rods (see Section 24).
29 Ensure that the backs of the bearing shells, the bearing seats in the caps and rods and the crankpin journals are clean. If new shells are being fitted, ensure that all traces of protective grease are removed using paraffin (kerosene). Dry the shells, caps, rods and journals with a clean, lint-free cloth. Install the shells, making sure the tab on each shell

23.25a Main bearing journal numbers (A) and big-end bearing journal numbers (B)

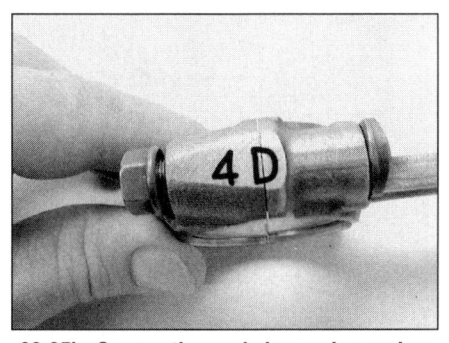

23.25b Connecting rod size code number

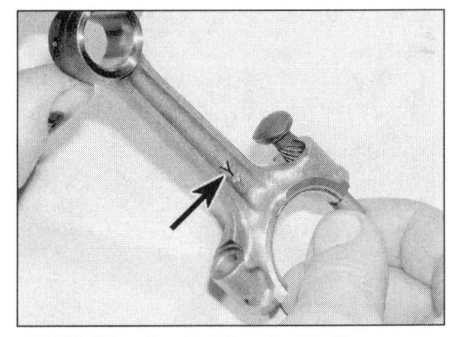

23.27 Align the bolt head with the recess in the rod. Note the 'Y' mark (arrowed)

2•38 Engine, clutch and transmission

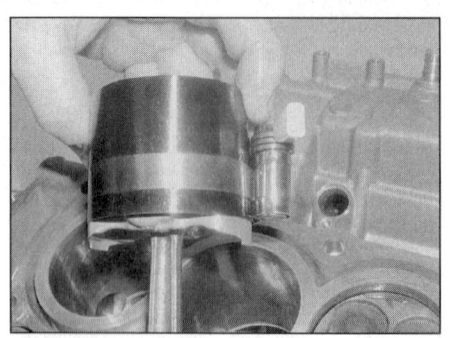

23.32a With the ring ends staggered, fit the ring compressor over the piston . . .

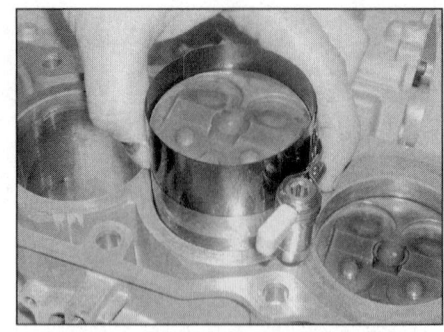

23.32b . . . then insert the rod assembly into the top of the bore . . .

23.32c . . . and carefully press the piston into the bore

engages the notch in the cap or rod **(see illustration 23.15)**.

30 Make sure the bearings are fitted in their correct locations and take care not to touch any bearing surfaces with your fingers. Lubricate the shells with clean engine oil.

31 Lubricate the pistons, rings and cylinder bore with clean engine oil. Insert the piston/connecting rod assembly into the top of its bore, taking care not to allow the connecting rod to mark the bore. Make sure the arrow on the top of the piston points to the front and the 'Y' mark on the rod faces the left-hand side of the engine (see Step 6).

32 Stagger the piston ring end gaps (see Section 25) and carefully compress and feed each piston ring into the bore until the piston crown is flush with the top of the bore. If available, a piston ring compressor makes installation a lot easier **(see illustrations)**.

33 Lower the crankshaft into position in the upper crankcase, making sure all the main bearing shells are in place (see Section 26).

34 Working on one connecting rod at a time, lubricate the crankpin and the shells in the connecting rod and cap with clean engine oil. Apply molybdenum disulphide grease to the shanks and threads of the new big-end bolts. Pull the rod onto the crankpin and fit the cap onto the rod **(see illustration)**. Make sure the cap is fitted the correct way around so the previously made markings align (see Step 3).

35 Apply molybdenum disulphide grease to the seats of the cap nuts, then fit the nuts and tighten them finger-tight **(see illustration)**. Check that all components have been returned to their original locations using the marks made on disassembly.

36 Tighten the cap nuts to the initial torque setting specified at the beginning of this Chapter with a torque wrench **(see illustration)**. Now tighten each nut in turn and in one continuous movement to the final torque setting specified using a torque angle gauge **(see illustration)**. If tightening is paused between the initial and final settings, slacken the nut to below the initial setting and repeat the procedure. Fit the remaining rods onto the crankshaft in the same way. **Note:** *If a torque angle gauge is not available, paint a small reference mark on the top of each nut after tightening them to the initial torque setting. Then, using a ring spanner so that you can see the mark, tighten the nuts to the final setting* **(see illustrations)**.

37 Lubricate the bores liberally with clean engine oil and check that the crankshaft rotates smoothly and freely. If there are any signs of roughness or tightness, detach the rods and recheck the assembly. Sometimes

23.34 Align the markings and fit the big-end cap onto the rod . . .

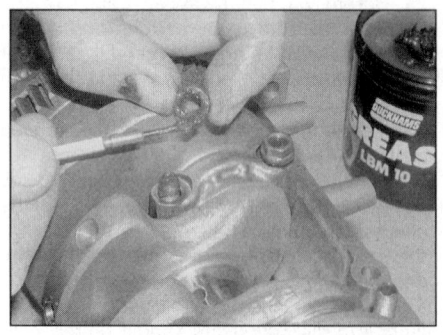

23.35 . . . then install the cap nuts finger-tight

23.36a Tighten the nuts to the initial torque setting with a torque wrench . . .

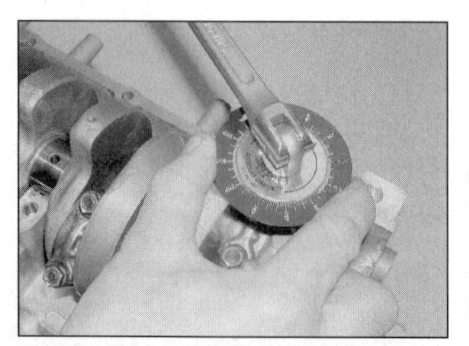

23.36b . . . and then to the final setting with a torque angle gauge

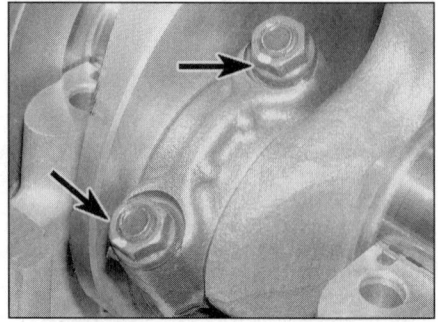

23.36c Alternatively, paint reference marks (arrowed) on the cap nuts . . .

23.36d . . . and tighten them finally with a ring spanner as described

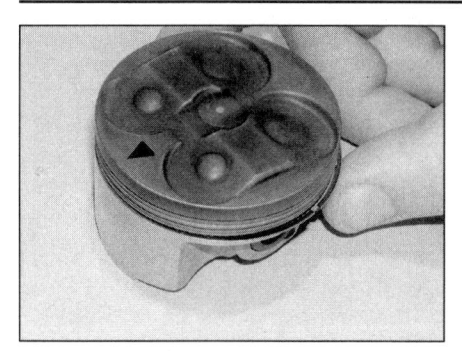

Engine, clutch and transmission 2•39

24.2 Note the arrow that points to the front of the engine

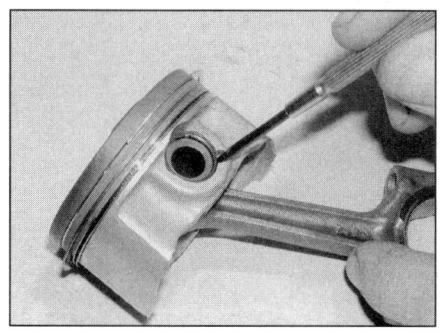

24.3a Prise out the circlip . . .

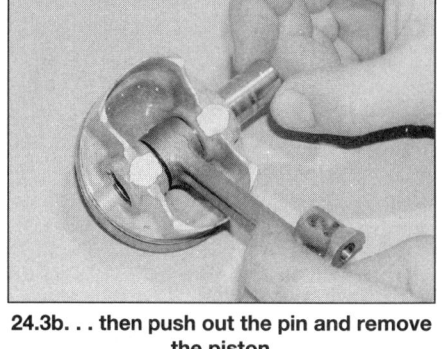

24.3b . . . then push out the pin and remove the piston

tapping the bottom of the connecting rod cap will relieve tightness.
38 Reassemble the crankcase halves (see Section 21).

24 Pistons – removal, inspection and installation

Note: *To remove the pistons the engine must be removed from the frame.*

Removal

1 Remove the engine from the frame (see Section 5), separate the crankcase halves (see Section 21) and remove the piston/connecting rod assemblies (see Section 23).
2 Before removing the piston from the connecting rod, ensure it is marked with its cylinder identity. If the piston is going to be cleaned, scratch the identity lightly on the inside of the piston skirt. Each piston must be installed in its original cylinder on reassembly. Note the arrow on the top of each piston that points to the front of the engine **(see illustration)**. If this is not visible, mark the piston accordingly so that it can be installed the correct way round.
3 Carefully prise out the circlips on each side of the piston pin using needle-nose pliers or a small flat-bladed screwdriver inserted into the notch **(see illustration)**. Check for burring around the circlip grooves and remove any with a very fine file or knife blade, then push the piston pin out to free the piston from the connecting rod **(see illustration)**. Discard the circlips as new ones must be used on reassembly. When the piston has been removed from the rod, keep the piston and its pin together so that related parts do not get mixed up.

> **HAYNES HiNT** *If a piston pin is a tight fit in the piston, soak a rag in boiling water then wring it out and wrap it around the piston – this will expand the alloy piston sufficiently to release its grip on the pin. If the piston pin is particularly stubborn, extract it using a drawbolt tool, but be careful to protect the piston's working surfaces.*

4 Using your thumbs or a piston ring removal and installation tool, carefully remove the rings from the pistons, working on one piston at a time **(see illustration)**. Do not nick or gouge the pistons in the process. Note which way up each ring fits and in which groove, as they must be installed in their original positions if being re-used. The upper surface of the two top rings (compression rings) should have a manufacturer's mark or letter at one end – if the mark on each ring is different, note which mark is for the top ring and which is for the second **(see illustration)**.
5 Scrape all traces of carbon from the tops of the pistons. A hand-held wire brush or a piece of fine emery cloth can be used once most of the deposits have been scraped away. Do not, under any circumstances, use a wire brush mounted in a drill motor; the piston material is soft and is easily damaged.
6 Use a piston ring groove cleaning tool to remove any carbon deposits from the ring grooves. If a tool is not available, a piece broken off an old ring will do the job. Be very careful to remove only the carbon deposits. Do not remove any metal and do not nick or gouge the sides of the ring grooves.
7 Once the carbon has been removed, clean the pistons with a suitable solvent and dry them thoroughly. Make sure the oil return holes at the back of the oil ring groove are clear **(see illustration)**. If the identification mark previously applied to the piston is cleaned off, be sure to re-mark it correctly **(see illustration)**.

24.4a Removing the piston rings using a ring removal and installation tool

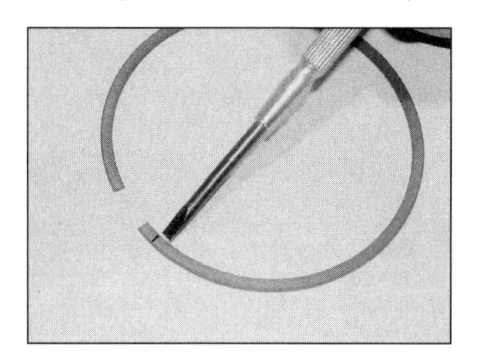

24.4b Note the mark on the end of the two top rings (compression)

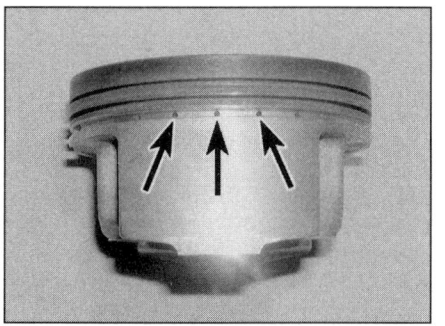

24.7a Ensure that the oil return holes (arrowed) are clear . . .

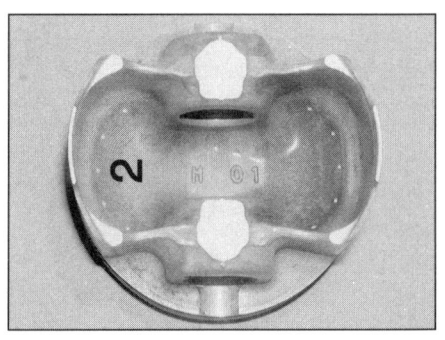

24.7b . . . and that the piston is still clearly marked

2•40 Engine, clutch and transmission

24.10 Measuring the piston diameter with a micrometer

24.11 Measuring the piston ring-to-groove clearance with a feeler gauge

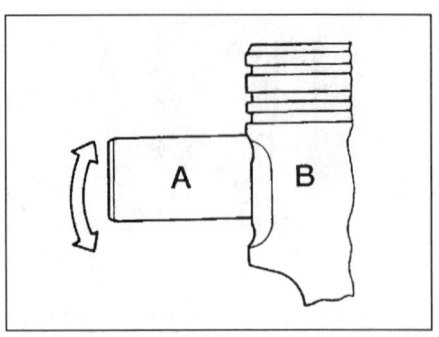

24.12a Insert the pin (A) into the piston (B) and try to rock it back and forth. If the pin is loose . . .

Inspection

8 Inspect each piston for cracks around the skirt, at the pin bosses and at the ring lands. Normal piston wear appears as even, vertical wear on the thrust surfaces of the piston and slight looseness of the top ring in its groove. If the skirt is scored or scuffed, the engine may have been suffering from overheating and/or abnormal combustion, resulting in excessively high operating temperatures.

9 A hole in the top of the piston (only likely in extreme circumstances), or burned areas around the edge of the piston crown, indicate that pre-ignition or knocking under load have occurred. If you find evidence of any problems the cause must be corrected or the damage will occur again (see *Fault Finding* in the *Reference* section).

10 Check the piston-to-bore clearance by measuring the bore (see Section 30) and the piston diameter. Make sure each piston is matched to its correct cylinder. Measure the piston 4 mm up from the bottom of the skirt and at 90° to the piston pin axis **(see illustration)**. Subtract the piston diameter from the bore diameter to obtain the clearance. If it is greater than the figure specified at the beginning of this Chapter, check whether it is the bore or piston that is worn beyond its service limit. If the bores are good, install new pistons and rings and have the bores honed (see Section 30). If the bores are worn, replace the crankcases, pistons and rings.

11 Measure the piston ring-to-groove clearance by laying each compression ring in its groove and slipping a feeler gauge in beside it **(see illustration)**. Make sure you have the correct ring for the groove (see Step 4). Check the clearance at three or four locations around the groove. If the clearance is greater than specified, renew both the piston and rings as a set. If new rings are being used, measure the clearance using the new rings. If the clearance is greater than that specified, the piston is worn and must be renewed.

12 Apply clean engine oil to the piston pin, insert it part way into the piston and check for any freeplay between the two **(see illustration)**. Measure the pin external diameter, and the pin bore in the piston **(see illustrations)**. Subtract the pin diameter from the bore diameter to obtain the clearance. If it is greater than the specified figure, check whether it is the bore or pin that is worn beyond its service limit and renew them as required. Repeat the checks between the pin and the connecting rod small-end (see Section 23).

Installation

13 Inspect and install the piston rings (see Section 25).

14 Install a **new** circlip into one side of the piston (never re-use old circlips), then lubricate the piston pin, the piston pin bore and the connecting rod small-end bore with clean engine oil.

15 Line up the piston on its connecting rod so that the arrow on the top of the piston will point to the front and the 'Y' mark on the rod will face the left-hand side of the engine when they are installed. Insert the piston pin from the side without the circlip **(see illustration 24.3b)**. Secure the pin with the other **new** circlip. When installing the circlips, compress them only just enough to fit them in the piston, and make sure they are properly seated in their grooves with the open end away from the removal notch **(see illustration)**.

16 Install the connecting rods (see Section 23).

25 Piston rings – inspection and installation

1 It is good practice to renew the piston rings when an engine is being overhauled. Before installing the rings on the pistons, the ring end gaps must be checked with the rings installed in the cylinder.

Inspection

2 Lay out each piston with its new ring set so the rings will be matched with the same piston and cylinder during the measurement procedure and engine reassembly. The upper surface of the two top rings (compression rings) should have a manufacturer's mark or letter at one end – if the mark on each ring is

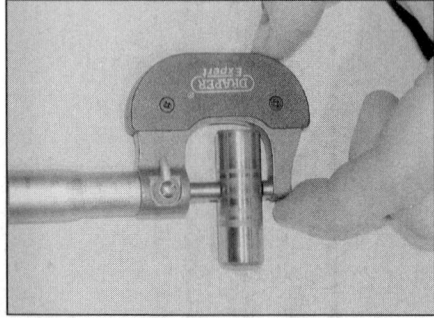

24.12b . . . measure the pin external diameter . . .

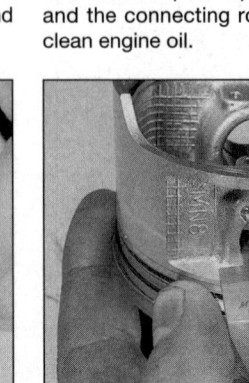

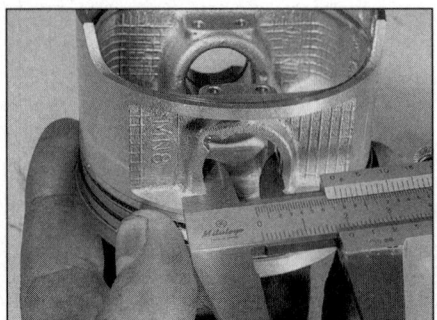

24.12c . . . and the pin bore in the piston

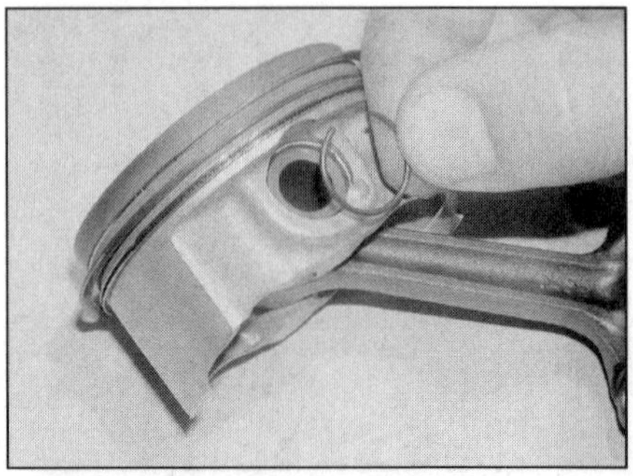

24.15 Fit the circlip with the open end away from the removal notch

Engine, clutch and transmission 2•41

25.3 Measuring piston ring end gap

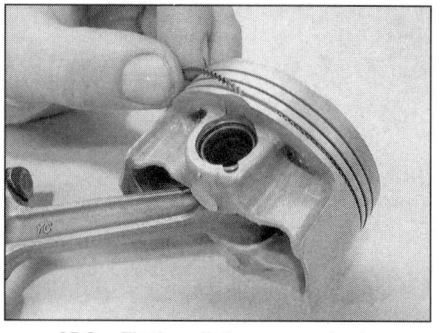

25.8a Fit the oil ring expander in its groove . . .

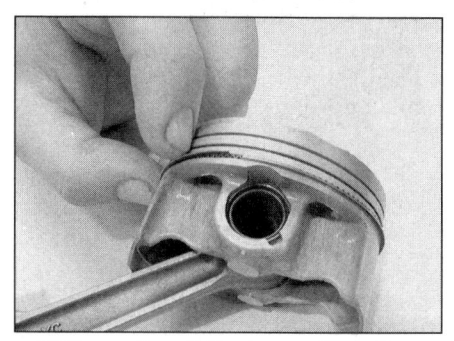

25.8b . . . then fit the lower side rail . . .

different, note which mark is for the top ring and which is for the second **(see illustration 24.4b)**.

3 To measure the ring end gap, insert the ring into the top of the cylinder and square it up with the cylinder walls by pushing it in with the top of the piston. The ring should be about 5 mm below the top edge of the cylinder. Slip a feeler gauge between the ends of the ring and compare the measurement to the specifications at the beginning of this Chapter **(see illustration)**.

4 If the gap is larger or smaller than specified, double check to make sure that you have the correct rings before proceeding.

5 Excess end gap is not critical unless it exceeds the service limit. Check that the bore is not worn (see Section 30).

6 Repeat the procedure for each ring and each cylinder in turn. Note that the end gaps differ between the top, second and oil ring. When checking the oil ring, only the side-rails can be checked as the ends of the expander ring should contact each other. Remember to keep the rings together with their matched pistons and cylinders.

Installation

7 Once the ring end gaps have been checked and corrected as necessary, the rings can be installed on the pistons.

8 The oil control ring (lowest on the piston) is installed first. It is composed of three separate components, namely the expander and the upper and lower side rails. Slip the expander into the ring groove, then install the lower side rail **(see illustrations)**. Do not use a piston ring installation tool on the oil ring side rails as they may be damaged. Instead, place one end of the side rail into the groove between the expander and the ring land. Hold it firmly in place and slide a finger around the piston while pushing the rail into the groove. Next, install the upper side rail in the same manner **(see illustration)**. Make sure the ends of the expander touch but do not overlap.

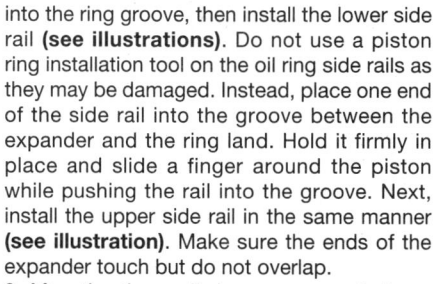

9 After the three oil ring components have been installed, check to make sure that both the upper and lower side rails can be turned smoothly in the ring groove.

10 The upper surface of each compression ring should have a mark or letter at one end which must face up when the ring is installed on the piston (see Step 2). Fit the second ring into the middle groove in the piston. Do not expand the ring any more than is necessary to slide it into place **(see illustration)**. To avoid breaking the ring, use a piston ring installation tool **(see illustration 24.4a)**, or pieces of old feeler gauge blades **(see illustration)**.

11 Finally, install the top ring in the same manner into the top groove in the piston **(see illustration)**.

12 Once the rings are correctly installed, check they move freely without snagging and stagger their end gaps as shown **(see illustration)**.

26 Crankshaft and main bearings – removal, inspection and installation

Note: *To remove the crankshaft the engine must be removed from the frame.*

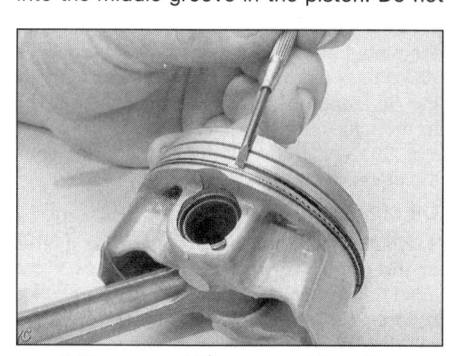

25.8c . . . and the upper side rail as described

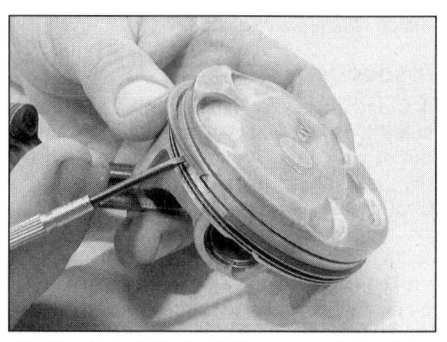

25.10a Carefully feed the second ring into its groove

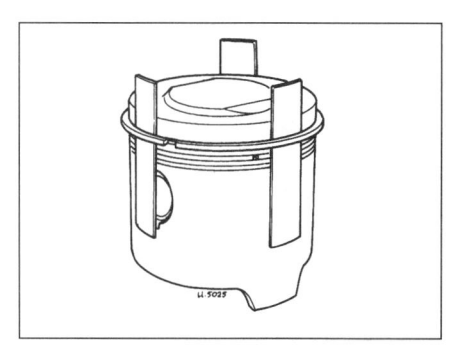

25.10b Old pieces of feeler gauge blade can be used to guide the ring over the piston

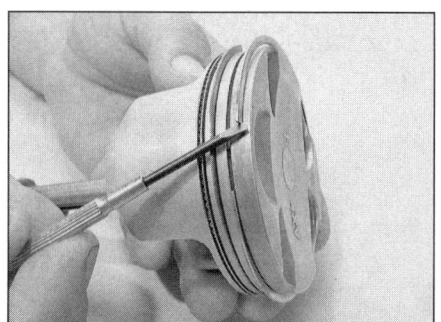

25.11 Finally, install the top ring . . .

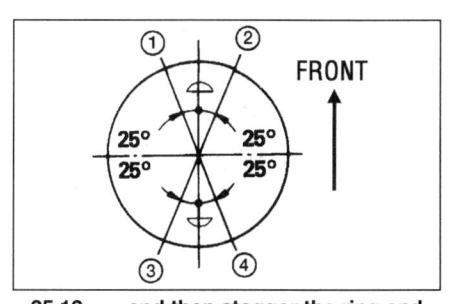

25.12 . . . and then stagger the ring end gaps as shown – top ring (1), oil ring lower side rail (2), oil ring upper slide ring (3), second ring (4)

26.2 Lift the crankshaft out of the crankcase carefully

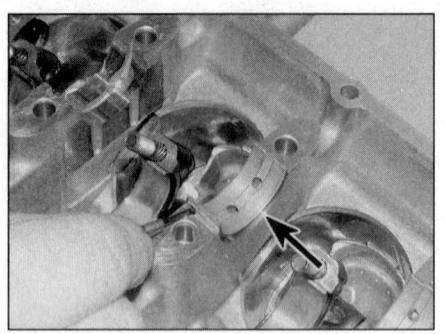

26.3 To remove a main bearing shell, push it sideways and lift it out

Removal

1 Remove the engine from the frame (see Section 5), separate the crankcase halves (see Section 21) and disconnect the piston/connecting rod assemblies from the crankshaft (see Section 23). There is no need to remove the piston/connecting rod assemblies from the cylinders; push them up the bores so that the connecting rod ends are clear of the crankshaft and wrap clean rag around the rod ends to prevent damage to the bores. **Note:** *New big-end bolts must be used on reassembly.*

2 Lift the crankshaft out of the upper crankcase half, taking care not to dislodge the main bearing shells **(see illustration)**.

3 If required, remove the bearing shells from the crankcase halves by pushing their centres to the side, then lifting them out **(see illustration)**. Keep the shells in order so that they can be fitted in their original locations for the oil clearance check.

Inspection

4 Clean the crankshaft with a suitable solvent, paying particular attention to flush out the oil passages. If available, blow the crank dry with compressed air, and also blow through the oil passages. Check the primary drive gear for wear or damage. If any of the teeth are excessively worn, chipped or broken, the crankshaft must be replaced with a new one. Check the primary driven gear on the clutch housing for corresponding wear or damage. Also check the cam chain sprocket, the sprockets on the camshafts and the cam chain itself and replace them with new ones, if necessary.

5 Refer to Section 22 and examine the main bearing shells. If they are scored, badly scuffed or appear to have seized, new bearings must be installed. Always renew the main bearings as a set. If they are badly damaged, check the corresponding crankshaft journals. Evidence of extreme heat, such as bluing, indicates that lubrication failure has occurred. Be sure to thoroughly check the oil pump and pressure relief valve as well as all oil holes and passages before reassembling the engine.

6 Give the crankshaft journals a close visual examination, paying particular attention where damaged bearings have been discovered. If the journals are scored or pitted in any way, a new crankshaft will be required. Note that undersized bearing shells are not available, precluding the option of re-grinding the crankshaft.

7 Place the crankshaft on V-blocks and check the runout at the main bearing journals using a dial gauge (see *Tools and Workshop Tips* in the *Reference* section). Compare the reading to the maximum specified at the beginning of this Chapter. If the runout exceeds the limit, the crankshaft must be renewed.

Oil clearance check

8 Whether new bearing shells are being fitted or the original ones are being re-used, the main bearing oil clearance should be checked before the engine is reassembled. Main bearing oil clearance is measured with a product known as Plastigauge.

9 If not already done, remove the bearing shells from the crankcase halves (see Step 3). Clean the backs of the shells and the bearing seats in both crankcase halves, and the main bearing journals on the crankshaft.

10 Press the bearing shells into their seats, ensuring that the tab on each shell engages in the notch in the crankcase **(see illustration)**. Make sure the bearings are fitted in the correct locations and take care not to touch the bearing surfaces with your fingers.

11 Ensure the shells and crankshaft are clean and dry. Lay the crankshaft in position in the upper crankcase.

12 Cut five appropriate size lengths of Plastigauge (they should be slightly shorter than the width of the crankshaft journals). Place a strand of Plastigauge on each journal **(see illustration)**. Do not place Plastigauge over the oil holes in the crankshaft. Make sure the crankshaft is not rotated.

13 If removed, fit the dowels into the crankcase **(see illustration 21.7)**. Carefully fit the lower crankcase half onto the upper half, making sure the dowels locate correctly and the Plastigauge is not disturbed. Check that the lower crankcase half is correctly seated. **Note:** *Do not tighten the crankcase bolts if the casing is not correctly seated.*

14 Clean the threads of the crankcase bolts and lubricate all except bolt Nos. 12 and 18 with clean engine oil. Insert the bolts with their washers in their original locations and secure them finger-tight. Now tighten the bolts, evenly and a little at a time, in the numerical sequence as marked on the crankcase to the torque settings specified at the beginning of this Chapter (see Section 21).

15 Unscrew the bolts a $1/4$ turn at a time in a **reverse** of the numerical sequence shown in illustration 21.5a and as marked on the crankcase, until they are loose, then remove them. **Note:** *As each bolt is removed, store it in its relative position, with its washer where applicable, in the cardboard template of the crankcase halves.* Carefully lift off the lower crankcase half, making sure the Plastigauge is not disturbed.

16 Compare the width of the crushed Plastigauge on each crankshaft journal to the scale printed on the Plastigauge envelope to obtain the main bearing oil clearance **(see illustration)**. Compare the reading to the

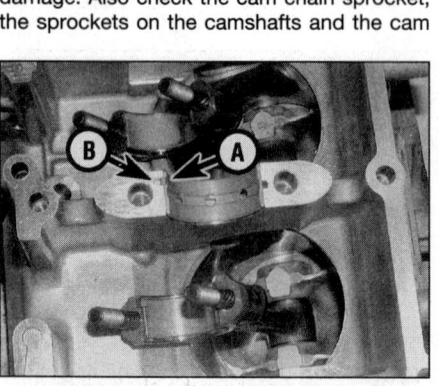

26.10 Ensure tab (A) locates in notch (B)

26.12 Place a strip of Plastigauge on each bearing journal

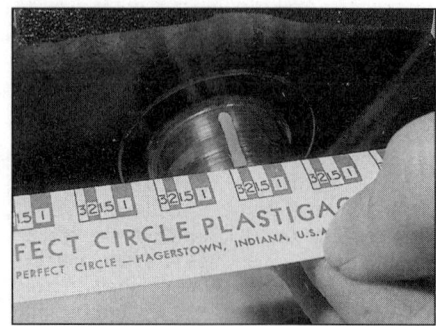

26.16 Measure the crushed Plastigauge using the scale on the pack

Engine, clutch and transmission 2•43

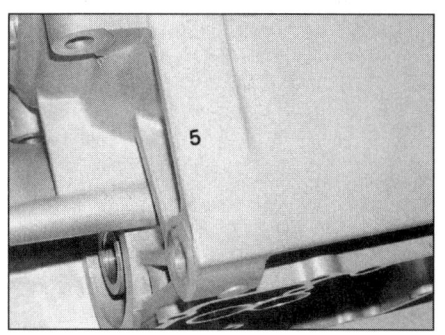

26.21 Main bearing size code(s) (arrowed)

27.2a Note the locating pin (arrowed) on the output shaft bearing

27.2b Lift the output shaft out of the crankcase

specifications at the beginning of this Chapter. If the clearance is within the range specified and the bearings are in perfect condition, they can be reused.

17 Carefully clean away all traces of the Plastigauge from the journals and bearing shells using a fingernail or other object which will not score the bearing surfaces.

18 If the clearance is beyond the service limit, replace the bearing shells with new ones (see Steps 20 to 22) and check the oil clearance once again. Always renew all of the shells at the same time.

19 If the clearance is still greater than the service limit listed in this Chapter's Specifications, the crankshaft journal is worn and the crankshaft should be renewed.

Bearing shell selection

20 Replacement bearing shells for the main bearings are supplied on a selected fit basis. Code numbers for the crankshaft journals are stamped on the outside of the crankshaft web on the left-hand end of the crankshaft **(see illustration 23.25a)**. The left-hand block of five numbers are the size codes for the main bearing journals (the right-hand block of four numbers are the size codes for the big-end bearing journals). The first number of the block is for the left-hand (No. 1) journal, and so on.

21 The main bearing size codes are stamped into the back of the lower crankcase half **(see illustration)**. The first number of the five is for the left-hand (No. 1) bearing, and so on. **Note:** *If there is only one number stamped into the crankcase, it means that all the bearings are the same number.*

22 A range of bearing shells are available. To select the correct shells for a particular journal, subtract the crankshaft journal number from the crankcase number, and then subtract 1. Compare the result with the table below to find the colour coding of the replacement shells, e.g. crankcase number 5 minus crankshaft journal number 2 minus 1 = 2; No. 2 bearing shells are colour coded black. The colour code is marked on the side of each bearing shell.

Number	Colour
0	white
1	blue
2	black
3	brown
4	green

Installation

23 Ensure the backs of the bearing shells, the bearing seats in both crankcase halves, and the main bearing journals on the crankshaft are clean. If new shells are being fitted, ensure that all traces of the protective grease are cleaned off using paraffin (kerosene). Wipe the shells and crankcase halves dry with a lint-free cloth. Make sure all the oil passages and holes are clear, and blow them through with compressed air if it is available.

24 Press the bearing shells into their seats. Make sure the tab on each shell engages in the notch in the casing **(see illustration 26.10)**. Make sure the bearings are fitted in the correct locations and take care not to touch any bearing surfaces with your fingers. Lubricate the shells with clean engine oil.

25 Lower the crankshaft into position in the upper crankcase, making sure all bearing shells remain in place.

26 Refer to Section 23, Steps 33 to 37, and fit the connecting rods onto the crankshaft using new big-end bolts.

27 Reassemble the crankcase halves (see Section 21).

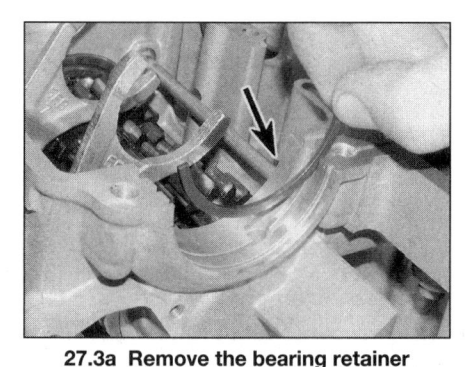

27 Transmission shafts – removal and installation

Note: *To remove the transmission shafts the engine must be removed from the frame.*

Removal

1 Position the transmission in neutral, then remove the engine from the frame (see Section 5). Remove the gearchange mechanism (see Section 17) and separate the crankcase halves (see Section 21).

2 Note how the pin on the output shaft bearing locates in the upper crankcase half **(see illustration)**. Lift the output shaft out of the crankcase **(see illustration)**; if it is stuck, use a soft-faced hammer and gently tap on the ends of the shaft to free it.

3 Remove the bearing half-ring retainer from the crankcase or bearing, noting how it fits **(see illustration)**. Discard the oil seal from the left-hand end of the shaft as a new seal must be fitted on reassembly **(see illustration)**.

4 Remove the selector drum and forks (see Section 29).

5 Undo the Torx screws securing the input shaft bearing housing. Discard the screws as new ones must be fitted on reassembly. Obtain two 6 mm bolts, 30 mm long excluding the bolt head, and with a 1 mm thread pitch, and screw them into the two holes in the

27.3a Remove the bearing retainer (arrowed) ...

27.3b ... and discard the shaft oil seal

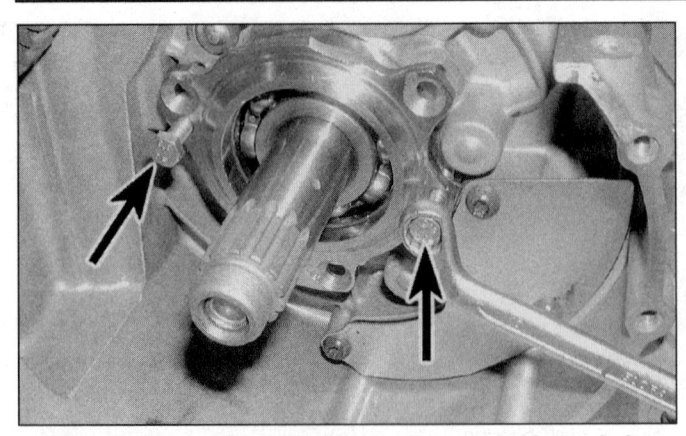

2•44 Engine, clutch and transmission

27.5a Displace the bearing housing by screwing in two bolts (arrowed) ...

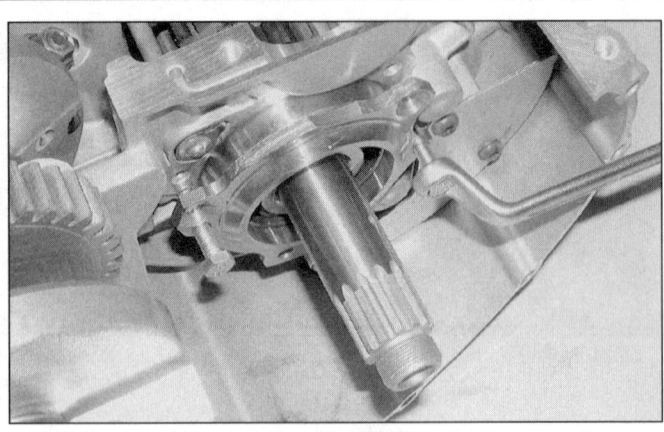

27.5b ... and turning them against the crankcase surface

bearing housing as shown **(see illustration)**. Tighten the bolts until they contact the surface of the crankcase, then continue tightening them evenly and a little at a time until the bearing housing is displaced **(see illustration)**. Withdraw the input shaft from the crankcase.

6 To remove the inner input shaft bearing see *Tools and Workshop Tips* in the *Reference* section.

Installation

7 Slide the input shaft into the crankcase far enough for the left-hand end of the shaft to locate in its bearing **(see illustration)**. Obtain three 6 mm bolts, 25 mm long excluding the bolt head, and three flat washers. Insert the bolts and washers through the bearing housing screw holes and screw them into the crankcase. Tighten the bolts evenly and a little at a time to draw the bearing housing into its location in the crankcase **(see illustrations)**. When the housing is fully installed, unscrew the bolts.

8 Apply a suitable thread locking compound to the new Torx screws and tighten them to the torque setting specified at the beginning of this Chapter. Stake the edge of each screw into the indent in the housing using a suitable punch **(see illustration)**.

9 Install the selector drum and forks (see Section 29).

10 Fit the output shaft bearing half-ring retainer into its slot in the upper crankcase **(see illustration 27.3a)**. Smear the inside of the new output shaft seal with grease. Slide the seal onto the left-hand end of the shaft.

11 Lower the output shaft into position in the upper crankcase, making sure the groove in the bearing engages correctly with the half-ring retainer and the pin on the bearing locates correctly in the crankcase **(see illustration 27.2a)**.

Caution: If the half-ring retainer is not correctly engaged, the crankcase halves will not seat correctly.

12 Make sure output shaft is correctly seated and that the selector forks are located in the grooves in the appropriate gear pinions (see Sections 28 and 29).

13 Position the gears in the neutral position and check the shafts are free to rotate easily and independently (i.e. the input shaft can turn whilst the output shaft is held stationary) before proceeding further.

14 Reassemble the crankcase halves (see Section 21).

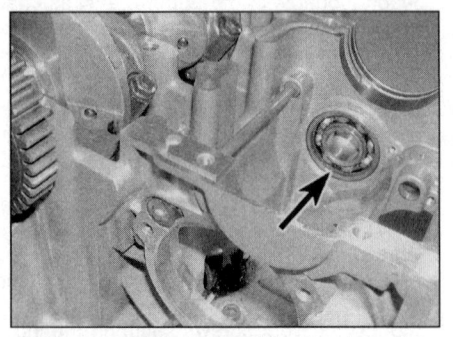

27.7a Locate the end of the input shaft in the bearing (arrowed)

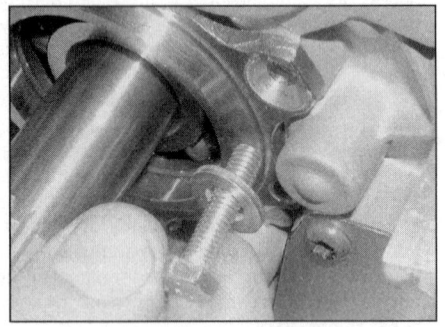

27.7b Using bolts and washers ...

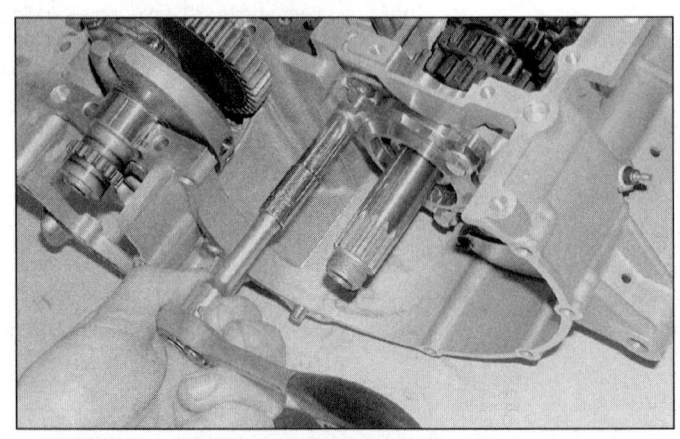

27.7c ... draw the bearing housing into the crankcase

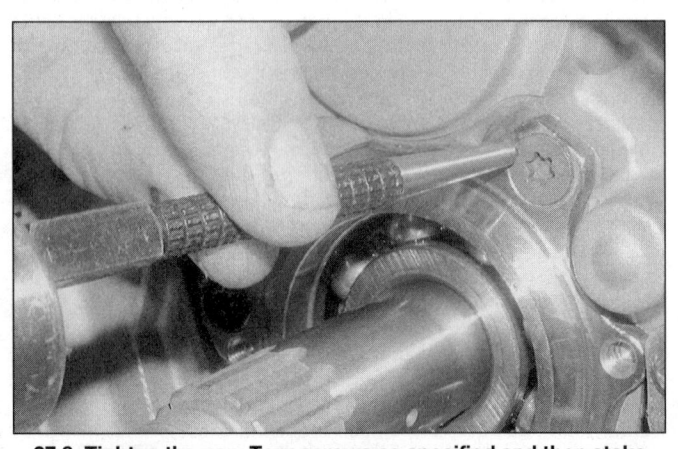

27.8 Tighten the new Torx screws as specified and then stake them in place

Engine, clutch and transmission 2•45

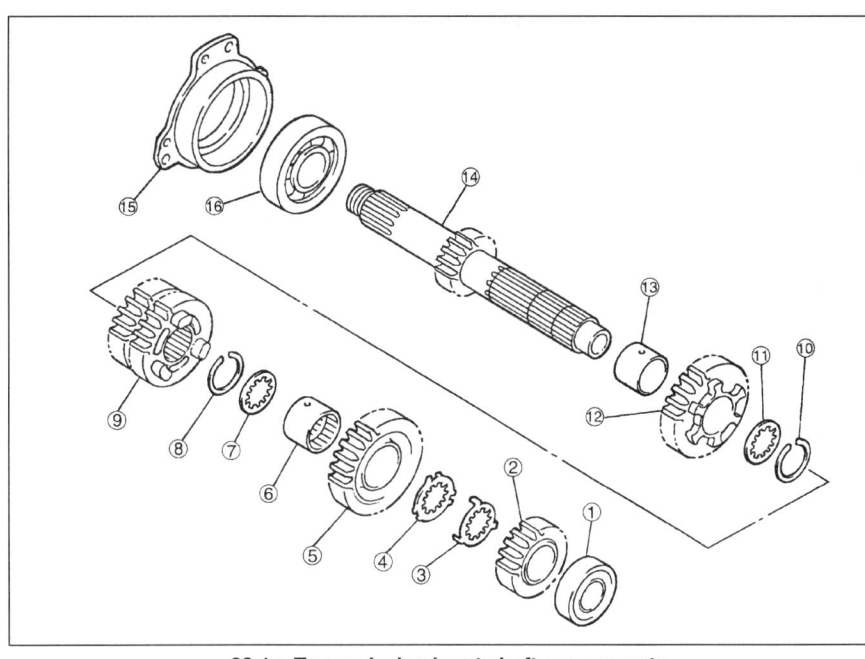

28.1a Transmission input shaft components

1 Bearing
2 2nd gear pinion
3 Tabbed lockwasher
4 Slotted splined washer
5 6th gear pinion
6 6th gear pinion bush
7 Splined washer
8 Circlip
9 3rd gear pinion
10 Circlip
11 Splined washer
12 5th gear pinion
13 5th gear pinion bush
14 Input shaft
15 Bearing
16 Bearing housing

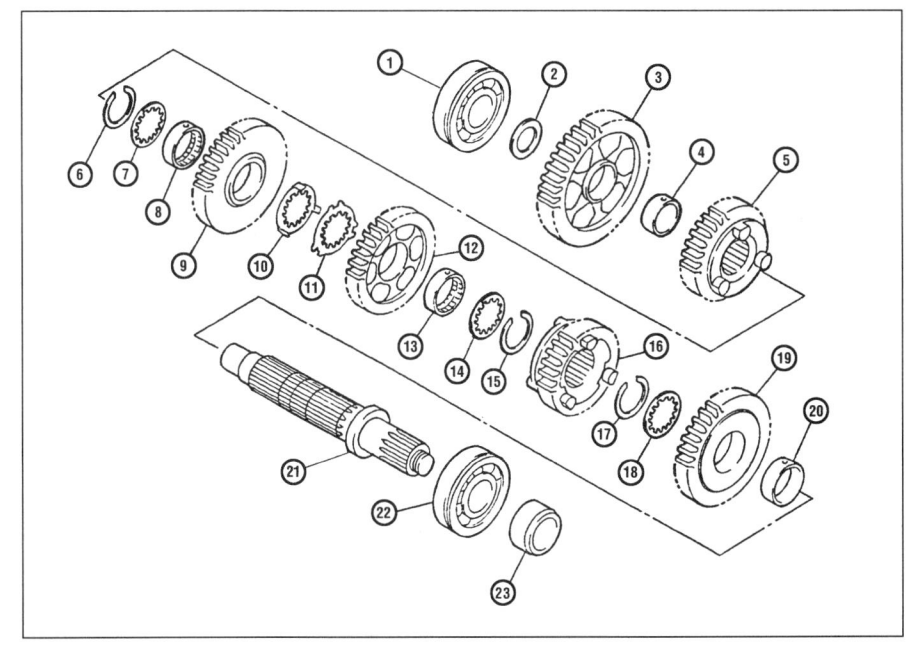

28.1b Transmission output shaft components

1 Bearing
2 Thrust washer
3 1st gear pinion
4 1st gear pinion bush
5 5th gear pinion
6 Circlip
7 Splined washer
8 3rd gear pinion bush
9 3rd gear pinion
10 Tabbed lockwasher
11 Slotted splined washer
12 4th gear pinion
13 4th gear pinion bush
14 Splined washer
15 Circlip
16 6th gear pinion
17 Circlip
18 Splined washer
19 2nd gear pinion
20 2nd gear pinion bush
21 Input shaft
22 Bearing
23 Collar

28 Transmission shafts – disassembly, inspection and reassembly

1 Remove the transmission shafts from the crankcase (see Section 27). Always disassemble the transmission shafts separately to avoid mixing up the components **(see illustrations)**.

Input shaft disassembly

HAYNES HiNT: *When disassembling the transmission shafts, place the parts on a long rod or thread a wire through them to keep them in order and facing the proper direction.*

2 Slide the 2nd gear pinion off the left-hand end of the shaft, noting which way around it is fitted – mark its outer face with a marker pen as an aid to reassembly **(see illustration 28.26)**.
3 Note how the tabs on the lock washer fit into the slotted splined washer and remove the lockwasher **(see illustration 28.25)**.
4 Turn the slotted splined washer to align it with the splines on the shaft and slide it off the shaft **(see illustration 28.24)**.
5 Slide the 6th gear pinion and its splined bush off the shaft, followed by the splined washer **(see illustrations 28.23c, b and a)**.
6 Remove the circlip securing the combined 3rd/4th gear pinion, then slide the pinion off the shaft noting which way round it fits **(see illustrations 28.22b and a)**. Discard the circlip as a new one must be fitted on reassembly.
7 Remove the circlip securing the 5th gear pinion, then slide the splined washer, the pinion and its bush off the shaft **(see illustrations 28.21b and a and 28.20b and a)**. Discard the circlip as a new one must be fitted on reassembly.
8 The 1st gear pinion is integral with the shaft **(see illustration)**.
9 If required, remove the bearing and its housing from the right-hand end of the shaft, referring to *Tools and Workshop Tips*

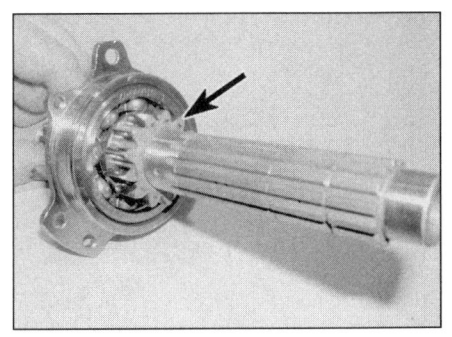

28.8 The 1st gear pinion (arrowed) is integral with the shaft

2•46 Engine, clutch and transmission

28.9 Remove the bearing and housing if required

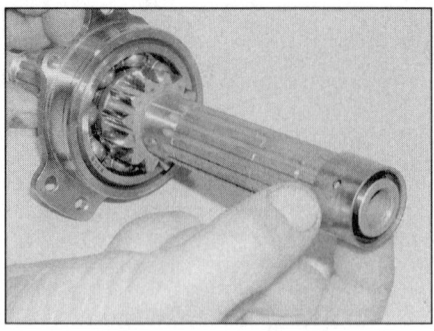

28.20a Slide the 5th gear pinion bush . . .

28.20b . . . the 5th gear pinion . . .

(Section 5) in the *Reference* section **(see illustration)**.

Input shaft inspection

10 Wash all the components in solvent and dry them off.
11 Check the gear teeth for cracking, chipping, pitting and other obvious wear or damage. Any pinion that is damaged must be renewed.
12 Inspect the dogs and the dog holes in the gears for cracks, chips, and excessive wear especially in the form of rounded edges. Make sure mating gears engage properly. Renew mating gears as a set if necessary.
13 Check for signs of scoring or bluing on the pinions, bushes and shaft. This could be caused by overheating due to inadequate lubrication. Check that all the oil holes and passages are clear. Replace any worn or damaged parts with new ones.
14 Check that each pinion moves freely on the shaft or bush but without undue freeplay. Check that each bush moves freely on the shaft but without undue freeplay.
15 The shaft is unlikely to sustain damage unless the engine has seized, placing an unusually high loading on the transmission, or the machine has covered a very high mileage. Check the surface of the shaft, especially where a pinion turns on it, and replace the shaft with a new one if it has scored or picked up, or if there are any cracks. Check the shaft runout using V-blocks and a dial gauge and replace the shaft with a new one if the runout exceeds the limit specified at the beginning of this Chapter.
16 Check the washers and renew any that are bent or worn.
17 Check the bearings referring to *Tools and Workshop Tips* (Section 5) in the *Reference* section. Do not forget the input shaft left-hand bearing, which is housed in the crankcase.

Input shaft reassembly

18 During reassembly, apply clean engine oil or molybdenum disulphide oil (a 50/50 mixture of molybdenum disulphide grease and engine oil) to the mating surfaces of the shaft, pinions and bushes. Use new circlips and do not expand their ends any further than is necessary to slide them along the shaft. Install them so that their chamfered side faces the pinion they secure (see *Correct fitting of a stamped circlip* illustration in *Tools and Workshop Tips* (Section 2) in the *Reference* section). Also refer to the exploded view of the input shaft in illustration 28.1a.
19 If removed, fit the bearing and its housing onto the right-hand end of the shaft, referring to *Tools and Workshop Tips* (Section 5) in the *Reference* section **(see illustration 28.9)**.
20 Slide the 5th gear pinion bush onto the left-hand end of the shaft then fit the 5th gear pinion with its dog holes facing away from the integral 1st gear **(see illustrations)**.
21 Slide the splined washer onto the shaft, then fit the new circlip, making sure that it locates correctly in the groove in the shaft **(see illustrations)**.
22 Slide the combined 3rd/4th gear pinion onto the shaft with the smaller 3rd gear pinion facing the 5th gear pinion. Ensure the oil hole in the pinion aligns with the oil holes in the shaft. Fit the new circlip, making sure it locates correctly in its groove in the shaft **(see illustrations)**.
23 Slide the splined washer onto the shaft, followed by the splined 6th gear pinion bush, aligning the oil hole in the bush with the hole in the shaft. Fit the 6th gear pinion, making sure its dog holes face the 3rd/4th gear pinion **(see illustrations)**.
24 Slide the slotted splined washer onto the shaft and locate it in its groove, then turn it in the groove, so that the splines on the washer locate against the splines on the

28.21a . . . and the splined washer onto the shaft . . .

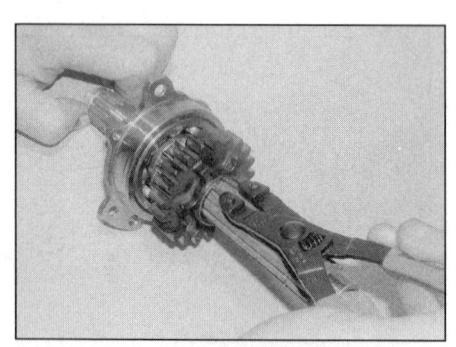

28.21b . . . and secure them with the circlip

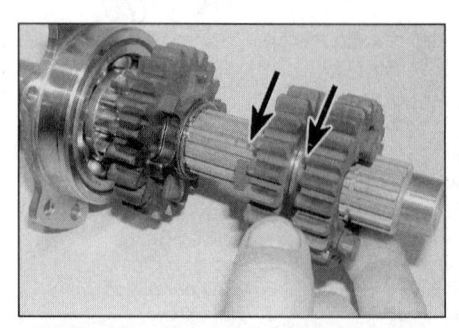

28.22a Align the oil holes (arrowed), then slide the 3rd/4th gear pinion onto the shaft . . .

28.22b . . . and secure it with the circlip

Engine, clutch and transmission 2•47

28.23a Install the splined washer . . .

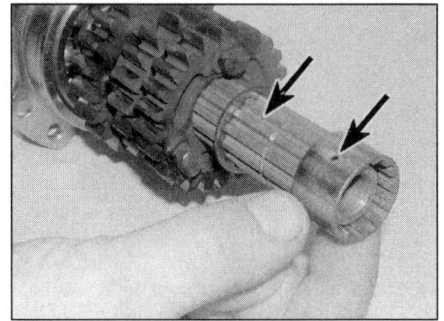

28.23b . . . align the oil holes (arrowed) and fit the 6th gear pinion bush . . .

28.23c . . . and slide on the 6th gear pinion

shaft and secure the washer in the groove **(see illustration)**.

25 Slide the lockwasher onto the shaft, so that the tabs on the lockwasher locate in the slots on the outside edge of the splined washer **(see illustration)**.

26 Slide the 2nd gear pinion onto the shaft, the correct way around as noted on removal **(see illustration)**.

27 Check that all components have been correctly installed **(see illustration 28.1a)**. The assembled shaft should look as shown **(see illustration)**.

Output shaft disassembly

28 Slide the bearing off the right-hand end of the shaft **(see illustration 28.49)**.

29 Slide the thrust washer off the shaft, followed by the 1st gear pinion and its bush **(see illustrations 28.48c, b and a)**.

30 Slide the 5th gear pinion off the shaft **(see illustration 28.47)**.

31 Remove the circlip securing the 3rd gear pinion, then slide the splined washer, the pinion and its splined bush off the shaft **(see illustrations 28.46d, c, b and a)**. Discard the circlip as a new one must be fitted on reassembly.

32 Note how the tabs on the lock washer fit into the slotted splined washer and remove the lockwasher **(see illustration 28.45)**.

33 Turn the slotted splined washer to align it with the splines on the shaft and slide it off the shaft **(see illustrations 28.44)**.

34 Slide the 4th gear pinion and its splined bush, followed by the splined washer, off the shaft **(see illustrations 28.43c, b and a)**.

35 Remove the circlip securing the 6th gear pinion, then slide the pinion off the shaft **(see illustrations 28.42b and a)**. Discard the circlip as a new one must be fitted on reassembly.

36 Remove the circlip securing the 2nd gear pinion, then slide the splined washer, the pinion and its bush off the shaft **(see illustrations 28.41d, c, b and a)**.

37 If required, remove the collar and bearing from the left-hand end of the shaft, referring to *Tools and Workshop Tips* (Section 5) in the *Reference* section **(see illustration)**.

Output shaft inspection

38 Refer to Steps 10 to 17 above.

28.24 Install the slotted splined washer as described . . .

Output shaft reassembly

39 During reassembly, apply engine oil or molybdenum disulphide oil (a 50/50 mixture of molybdenum disulphide grease and engine oil) to the mating surfaces of the shaft, pinions and bushes. When installing the new circlips, do not expand their ends any further than is necessary to slide them along the shaft. Install them so that their chamfered side faces the pinion they secure (see *Correct fitting of a stamped circlip* illustration in *Tools and Workshop Tips* (Section 2) in the *Reference* section). Also refer to the exploded view of the input shaft in illustration 28.1b.

40 If removed, fit the bearing and collar onto the left-hand end of the shaft, referring to *Tools and Workshop Tips* (Section 5) in the *Reference* section.

28.25 . . . then slide on the tabbed lockwasher . . .

28.26 . . . and the 2nd gear pinion

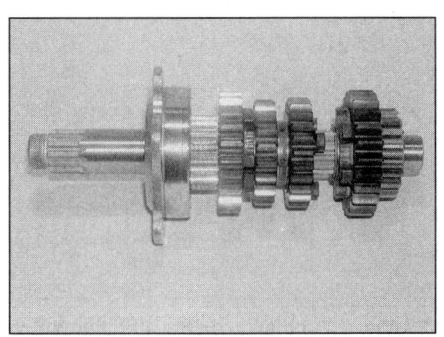

28.27 The assembled gearbox input shaft

28.37 Remove the collar (A) and bearing (B) if required

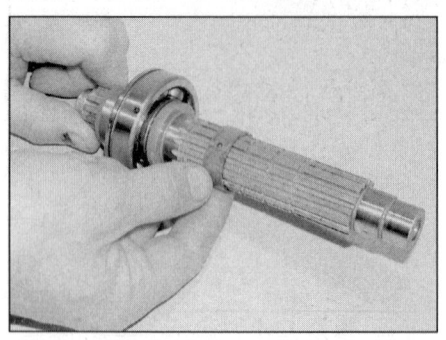

2•48 Engine, clutch and transmission

28.41a Slide the 2nd gear pinion bush ...

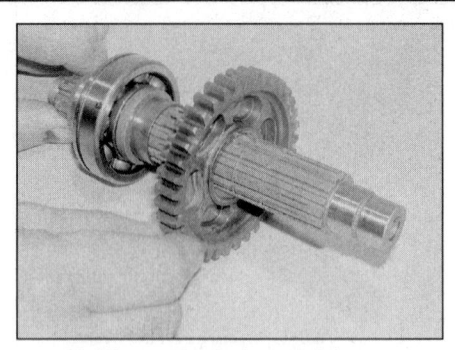

28.41b ... the 2nd gear pinion ...

28.41c ... and the splined washer onto the shaft ...

28.41d ... and secure them with the circlip

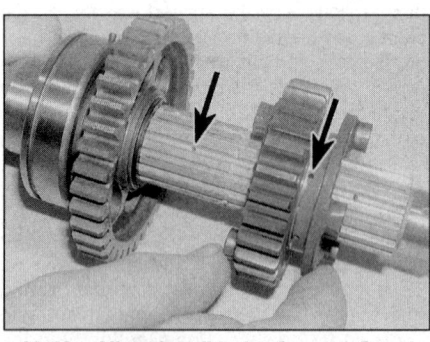

28.42a Align the oil holes (arrowed) and slide the 6th gear pinion onto the shaft ...

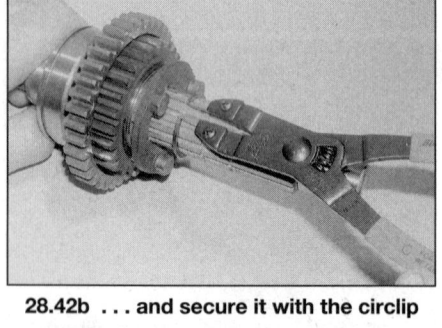

28.42b ... and secure it with the circlip

28.43a Install the splined washer ...

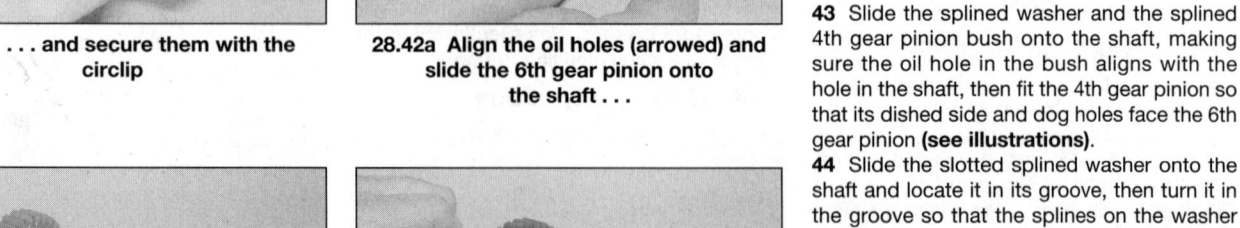

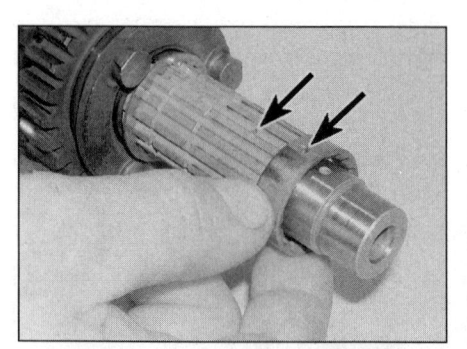

28.43b ... then align the oil holes (arrowed) and fit the 4th gear pinion bush ...

28.43c ... and slide on the 4th gear pinion

28.44 Install the slotted splined washer as described ...

41 Slide the 2nd gear pinion bush onto the shaft, then slide on the 2nd gear pinion (dog holes facing away from the bearing) and the splined washer. Fit the new circlip, making sure it is locates correctly in its groove on the shaft **(see illustrations)**.

42 Align the oil holes in the shaft and the 6th gear pinion, and slide the pinion onto the shaft with its selector fork groove facing away from the 2nd gear pinion, then fit the new circlip, making sure it locates correctly in its groove on the shaft **(see illustrations)**.

43 Slide the splined washer and the splined 4th gear pinion bush onto the shaft, making sure the oil hole in the bush aligns with the hole in the shaft, then fit the 4th gear pinion so that its dished side and dog holes face the 6th gear pinion **(see illustrations)**.

44 Slide the slotted splined washer onto the shaft and locate it in its groove, then turn it in the groove so that the splines on the washer align against the splines on the shaft and secure the washer in the groove **(see illustration)**.

45 Slide the lockwasher onto the shaft, so that the tabs on the lockwasher locate into the slots in the outer rim of the splined washer **(see illustration)**.

46 Slide the splined 3rd gear pinion bush onto the shaft, making sure the oil hole in the bush aligns with the hole in the shaft, then fit the 3rd gear pinion (dished side and dog holes facing away from the 4th gear pinion) and the splined washer. Fit the new circlip, making

Engine, clutch and transmission 2•49

28.45 ... then slide on the tabbed lockwasher

28.46a Align the oil holes (arrowed) and fit the 3rd gear pinion bush ...

28.46b ... then slide on the 3rd gear pinion ...

sure it locates correctly in its groove in the shaft **(see illustrations)**.

47 Align the oil holes in the shaft and the 5th gear pinion, and slide the pinion onto the shaft with its selector fork groove facing the 3rd gear pinion **(see illustration)**.

48 Slide the 1st gear pinion bush onto the shaft, followed by the 1st gear pinion (dished side facing the 5th gear pinion) and the thrust washer **(see illustrations)**.

49 Fit the bearing onto the end of the shaft with its open side facing the 1st gear pinion **(see illustration)**.

50 Check that all components have been correctly installed **(see illustration 28.1b)**. The assembled shaft should look as shown **(see illustration)**.

28.46c ... and the splined washer ...

28.46d ... and secure them with the circlip

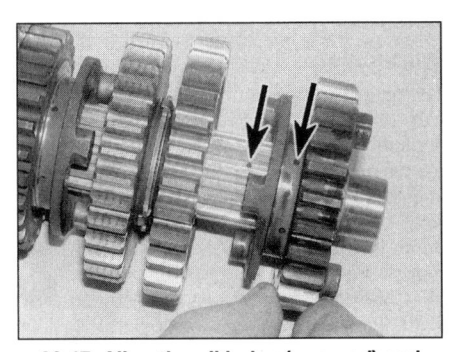

28.47 Align the oil holes (arrowed) and slide the 5th gear pinion onto the shaft

28.48a Install the 1st gear pinion bush ...

28.48b ... then slide the 1st gear pinion ...

28.48c ... and the thrust washer onto the shaft ...

28.49 ... and fit the bearing

28.50 The assembled gearbox output shaft

2•50 Engine, clutch and transmission

29.3 Note the position of the neutral detent (arrowed) on the end of the selector drum

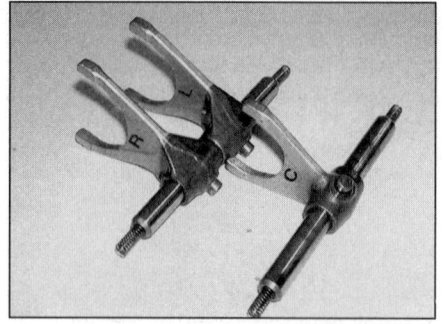

29.4 Note the letter on each fork denoting its position

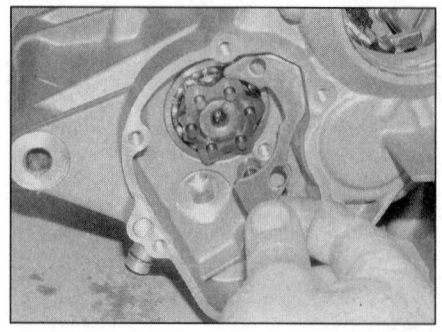

29.6a Remove the selector drum retainer plate . . .

29 Selector drum and forks – removal, inspection and installation

Note: *To remove the selector drum and forks the engine must be removed from the frame.*

Removal

1 Position the transmission in neutral. Remove the engine from the frame (see Section 5) and remove the gearchange mechanism (see Section 17), then separate the crankcase halves (see Section 21).
2 Note how the output shaft selector forks locate in the grooves on the 5th and 6th gear pinions and how the guide pins on the forks locate in the grooves in the selector drum, then remove the output shaft (see Section 27).
3 Note the position of the selector drum as an aid for installation; note the position of the neutral detent on the left-hand end of the selector drum **(see illustration)**.
4 Note that each selector fork is lettered for identification. The right-hand fork has an 'R', the centre fork a 'C', and the left-hand fork an 'L' **(see illustration)**. These letters face the right-hand side (clutch side) of the engine. If no letters are visible, mark the forks yourself using a felt pen before removing the forks.
5 Note how the input shaft selector fork locates in the groove on the 3rd/4th gear pinion and how the guide pin on the fork locates in the groove in the selector drum.
6 Unscrew the bolts securing the selector drum retainer plate and remove the plate, noting how it fits **(see illustration)**. Support the output shaft selector forks ('L' and 'R') and withdraw the fork shaft from the crankcase **(see illustration)**. Note the springs in the ends of the shaft and remove them for safekeeping, if loose.
7 Remove the selector forks and slide them back onto the shaft in the correct order and the right way round **(see illustration)**.
8 Support the input shaft selector fork ('C') and withdraw the fork shaft from the crankcase **(see illustration)**. Remove the springs from the ends of the shaft for safekeeping, if loose. Move the fork guide pin out of its track in the selector drum, then withdraw the selector drum from the left-hand side of the casing **(see illustration)**.
9 Move the selector fork round in its groove in the 3rd/4th gear pinion and remove it **(see illustration)**. Slide the fork back onto the shaft.

Inspection

10 Inspect the selector forks for any signs of wear or damage, especially around the fork ends where they engage with the grooves in the pinions. Check that each fork fits correctly in its pinion groove. Check closely to see if the forks are bent. If the forks are in any way damaged they must be replaced with new ones.
11 Check that the forks fit correctly on their shaft. They should move freely with a light fit but no appreciable freeplay. Check that the fork shaft holes in the casing are not worn or damaged.
12 Check the selector fork shaft runout using

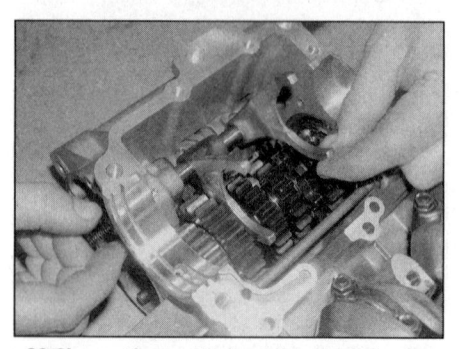

29.6b . . . then withdraw the shaft for the output shaft selector forks

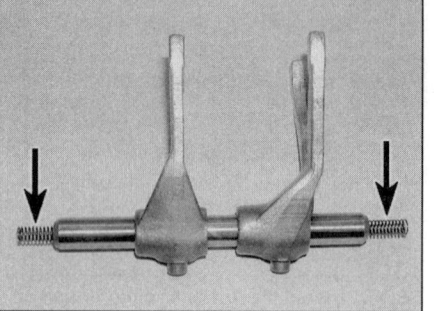

29.7 Install the forks on the shaft for safekeeping. Note the springs (arrowed)

29.8a Withdraw the shaft for the input shaft selector fork . . .

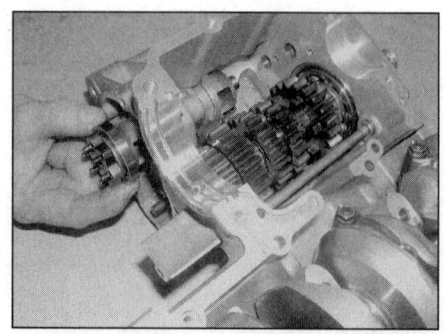

29.8b . . . then disengage the fork guide pin and withdraw the selector drum . . .

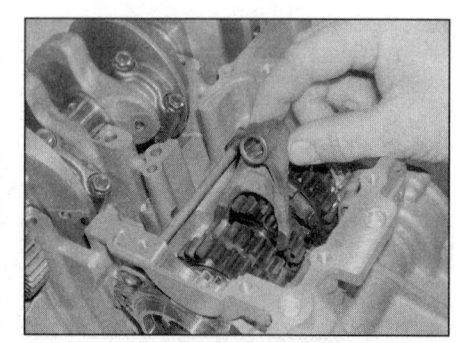

29.9 . . . and the fork

Engine, clutch and transmission 2•51

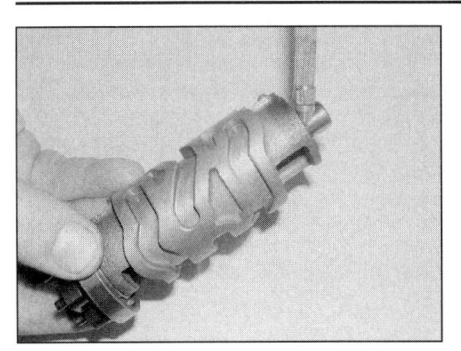

29.16a Lubricate the end of the selector drum before assembly

29.16b Neutral contact on the drum (arrowed) should align with the neutral switch

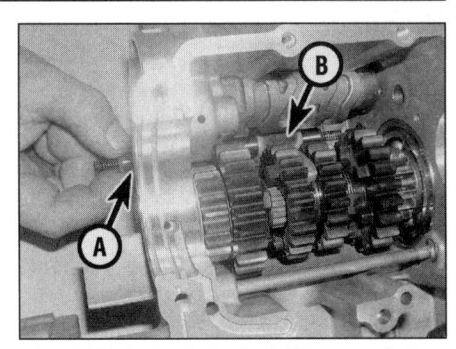

29.18 Slide the fork shaft (A) through the fork (B)

V-blocks and a dial gauge and renew the shaft if the runout exceeds the limit specified at the beginning of this Chapter. A bent shaft will cause difficulty in selecting gears and make the gearchange action heavy and should be replaced with a new one.

13 Inspect the selector drum grooves and selector fork guide pins for signs of wear or damage. If either show signs of wear or damage they must be replaced with new ones.

14 Check the selector drum bearing referring to *Tools and Workshop Tips* (Section 5) in the *Reference* section. If the bearing is worn a new selector drum will have to be fitted as the bearing is not available separately. Also check that the neutral switch contact on the right-hand end of the drum is not damaged or worn away. If required, remove the contact and replace it with a new one.

Installation

15 Locate the input shaft selector fork ('C') in its groove in the 3rd/4th gear pinion, making sure the letter faces the right-hand (clutch) side of the engine, then slide the fork round and below the input shaft so that it does not get in the way when installing the selector drum.

16 Lubricate the end of the selector drum with clean engine oil, then align the selector drum so that the neutral detent points to the upper rear engine mounting and slide the drum into the crankcase **(see illustration)**. Make sure the drum end locates in its bore in the crankcase, and that the neutral contact on the drum locates against the neutral switch contact on the inside back of the crankcase **(see illustration)**.

17 If removed, fit the springs into the ends of the selector fork shafts and lubricate the shafts with clean engine oil.

18 Move the input shaft selector fork round in its groove and locate the fork guide pin into its track in the selector drum, then slide the fork shaft into the crankcase and through the fork **(see illustration)**.

19 Position the output shaft forks ('R' and 'L') in the crankcase, making sure the letters face the right-hand (clutch) side of the engine and the fork guide pins locate in their tracks in the drum. Slide the fork shaft into the crankcase and through the forks **(see illustration 29.6b)**.

20 Apply a suitable non-permanent thread locking compound to the selector drum retainer plate bolts. Install the plate and tighten the bolts to the torque setting specified at the beginning of this Chapter.

21 Lower the transmission output shaft into the crankcase. Ensure that the fork marked 'R' locates in the groove in the 5th gear pinion, and that the fork marked 'L' locates in the groove in the 6th gear pinion (see Step 2).

22 Check that the output shaft is correctly seated and that the transmission shafts rotate easily and independently (see Section 27).

30 Crankcase halves and cylinder bores – inspection and servicing

Crankcase halves

1 After the crankcases have been separated, remove the crankshaft, connecting rods and pistons, bearings, transmission shafts, selector drum and forks, and any other components or assemblies, referring to the relevant Sections of this and other Chapters (see Step 3 of Section 21).

2 Withdraw the oil feed pipe from the upper crankcase – it is a push-fit **(see illustration)**. Check the condition of the pipe O-rings and replace them with new ones if they are in any way damaged, deformed or deteriorated **(see illustration)**.

3 Unscrew the bolts retaining the external U-shaped oil pipe on the front of the lower crankcase and pull the pipe out of its sockets **(see illustration)**. Discard the O-rings as new ones must be fitted on reassembly.

4 Unscrew the oil passageway plug from the right-hand side of the lower crankcase and

30.2a Withdraw the oil feed pipe (arrowed) from the crankcase . . .

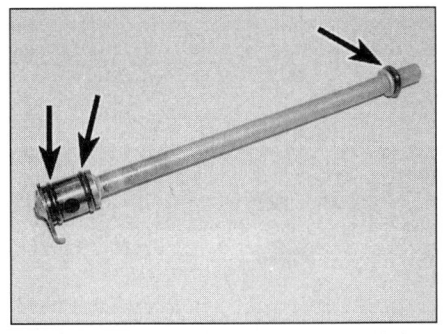

30.2b . . . and check the condition of the O-rings (arrowed)

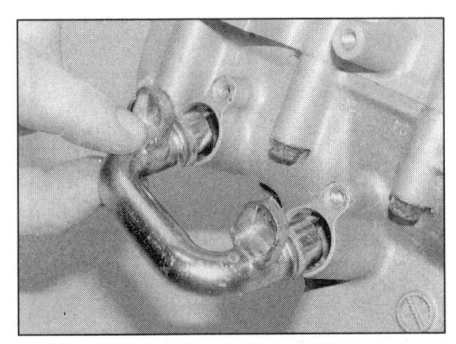

30.3 Remove the external oil pipe . . .

2•52 Engine, clutch and transmission

30.4 ... and the oil passageway plug and discard the O-rings

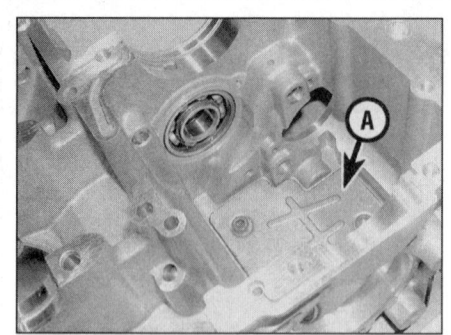

30.5a Oil baffle plates are located above the transmission shafts (A) ...

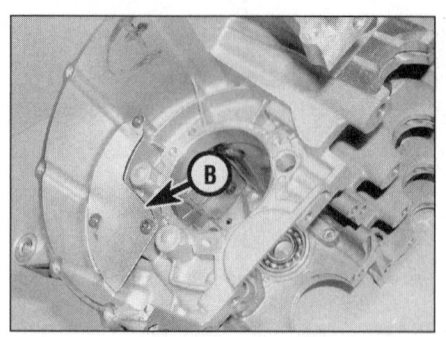

30.5b ... and in the back of the clutch housing (B)

discard the O-ring as a new one must be fitted on reassembly **(see illustration)**.

5 If required, unscrew the bolts securing the two oil baffle plates in the upper crankcase half and remove them, noting how they fit **(see illustrations)**. **Note:** *It is usually only necessary to remove the baffle plates if there is a danger that metal swarf from a damaged engine component is lodged behind them. The baffle plates prevent engine oil being blown out through the crankcase breather by crankcase pressure.*

6 Clean the crankcases thoroughly with solvent and dry them with compressed air. Blow out all oil passages and pipes with compressed air **(see illustrations)**.

7 Remove all traces of old gasket sealant from the mating surfaces. Minor damage to the surfaces can be cleaned up with careful use of a fine sharpening stone.

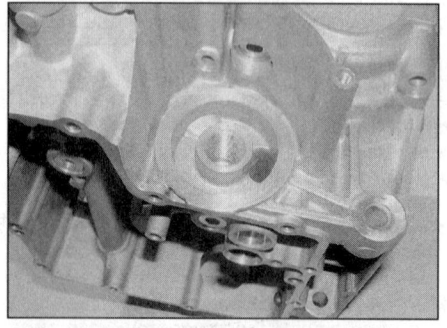

Caution: Be very careful not to nick or gouge the crankcase mating surfaces, or oil leaks will result. Check both crankcase halves very carefully for cracks and other damage.

8 Before proceeding further, check the cylinder bores (see Steps 18 to 21).

9 Inspect the bearing seats for signs of damage, especially if an engine or transmission bearing has overheated or seized (see Section 22) **(see illustration)**. If bearing shells or a ball bearing cage are not a precise fit in their seats, ask your Yamaha dealer for a suitable bearing locking compound which will overcome small amounts of wear. Otherwise the crankcase halves will have to be renewed as a set.

10 Small cracks or holes in aluminium castings can be repaired with an epoxy resin adhesive as a temporary measure. Permanent repairs can only be effected by argon-arc welding, and only a specialist in this process is in a position to advise on the economy or practical aspect of such a repair. Note that low temperature aluminium welding kits are available for minor repairs. If any damage is found that can't be repaired, renew the crankcase halves as a set.

11 Damaged threads can be economically reclaimed by using a diamond section wire insert, of the Heli-Coil type, which is easily fitted after drilling and re-tapping the affected thread.

12 Sheared studs or screws can usually be removed with stud or screw extractors; if you are in any doubt consult your Yamaha dealer or specialist motorcycle engineer.

HAYNES HiNT *Refer to Tools and Workshop Tips (Section 2) in the Reference section for details of installing a thread insert and using screw extractors.*

13 If removed, install the oil baffle plates, then apply a suitable non-permanent thread locking compound to the threads of the bolts and tighten them to the torque setting specified at the beginning of this Chapter. Apply a suitable sealant (such as Yamaha Bond 1215) to the top baffle plate in the area shown **(see illustration)**.

14 Lightly grease the O-ring for the oil passageway plug and install the plug, tightening it to the specified torque setting.

15 Lightly grease the O-rings for the external U-shaped oil pipe and install the pipe, then tighten the retaining bolts securely.

16 Lightly grease the O-rings on the oil feed pipe and install the pipe, locating the tab on the outer end in the cut-out in the crankcase. Ensure the outer end of the pipe is a flush fit with the crankcase; the pipe is retained by the lip of the input shaft bearing housing.

17 Install the remaining components in the reverse order of removal (see Step 1).

30.6a Clean the crankcases thoroughly ...

30.6b ... and blow through the oil passageways with compressed air

30.9 Inspect the bearing seats and oilways (arrowed)

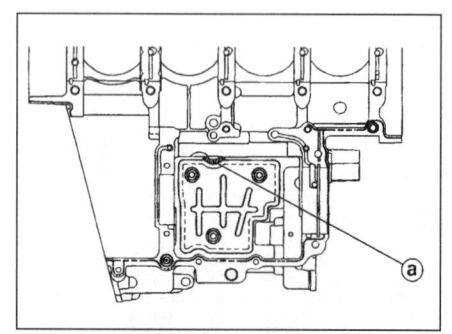

30.13 Apply sealant to the shaded area (a) of the top baffle plate

Engine, clutch and transmission 2•53

30.18 Examine the cylinder walls carefully

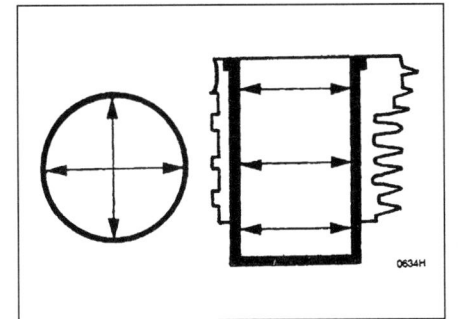

30.19 Measure the cylinder bore in the directions shown with a telescoping gauge

Cylinder bores

Caution: Do not attempt to separate the liners from the cylinder block.

18 Check the cylinder walls carefully for scratches and score marks **(see illustration)**.

19 Using telescoping gauges and a micrometer (see *Tools and Workshop Tips*), check the dimensions of each cylinder to assess the amount of wear, taper and ovality. Measure near the top (but below the level of the top piston ring at TDC), the centre and bottom (but above the level of the oil ring at BDC) of the bore. Measure both parallel to and across the crankshaft axis in each case and calculate the average cylinder dimension at each point **(see illustration)**. Compare the results to the specifications at the beginning of this Chapter.

20 If the precision measuring tools are not available, take the crankcase to a Yamaha dealer or specialist motorcycle engineer for assessment and advice.

21 If the cylinders are worn beyond the service limit, or badly scratched, scuffed or scored, renew the crankcases as a set. The cylinders cannot be rebored as Yamaha do not supply an oversize piston and ring set. If new crankcases are fitted, new pistons and rings must be used.

22 If the cylinders are in good condition and the piston-to-bore clearance is within specifications (see Section 24), the cylinders should be honed (de-glazed). To perform this operation you will need the proper size flexible hone with fine stones (see *Specialist Tools* in *Tools and Workshop Tips* in the *Reference* section), or a bottle-brush type hone, plenty of light oil or honing oil, some clean rags and an electric drill motor.

23 Clamp the cylinder block securely so that the bores are horizontal rather than vertical. Mount the hone in the drill motor, compress the stones and insert the hone into the cylinder. Thoroughly lubricate the cylinder, then turn on the drill and move the hone up and down in the cylinder at a pace which produces a fine cross-hatch pattern on the cylinder wall with the lines intersecting at an angle of approximately 60°.

24 Be sure to use plenty of lubricant and do not take off any more material than is necessary to produce the desired effect. Do not withdraw the hone from the cylinder while it is still turning. Switch off the drill and continue to move it up and down in the cylinder until it has stopped turning, then compress the stones and withdraw the hone. Wipe the oil from the cylinder and repeat the procedure on the other cylinders. Remember, do not take too much material from the cylinder wall.

25 Wash the cylinders thoroughly with warm soapy water to remove all traces of the abrasive grit produced during the honing operation. After rinsing, dry the cylinders thoroughly and clear the oil and coolant passages with compressed air. Apply a thin coat of light, rust-preventative oil to all machined surfaces.

26 If you do not have the equipment or desire to perform the honing operation, take the crankcase to a Yamaha dealer or specialist motorcycle engineer.

31 Initial start-up after overhaul

1 Make sure the engine oil and coolant levels are correct (see *Daily (pre-ride) checks*).

2 Make sure there is fuel in the tank, then turn the fuel tap to the 'ON' position, and set the choke.

3 Turn the ignition 'ON' and check that the oil level/coolant temperature warning light and the fuel indicator light come on for a few seconds and then go off. Ensure that the transmission is in neutral and that the neutral light is illuminated.

4 Start the engine, then allow it to run at a moderately fast idle until it reaches normal operating temperature.

5 As no oil pressure warning light is fitted, an oil pressure check must be carried out (see Chapter 1).

6 Check carefully that there are no oil or coolant leaks and make sure the transmission and controls, especially the brakes and clutch, work properly before road testing the machine. Refer to Section 32 for the recommended running-in procedure.

7 Upon completion of the road test, and after the engine has cooled down completely, recheck the valve clearances (see Chapter 1) and check the engine oil and coolant levels (see *Daily (pre-ride) checks*).

32 Running-in procedure

1 Treat the machine gently for the first few miles to allow the oil to circulate throughout the engine and any new parts installed to seat.

2 Great care is necessary if the engine has been extensively overhauled – the bike will have to be run in as when new. This means more use of the transmission and a restraining hand on the throttle until at least 600 miles (1000 km) have been covered. There is no point in keeping to any set road speed – the main idea is to keep from labouring the engine and to gradually increase performance up to the 1000 mile (1600 km) mark. These recommendations apply less when only a partial overhaul has been done, though it does depend on the nature of the work carried out and which components have been renewed. Experience is the best guide, since it is easy to tell when an engine is running freely. If in any doubt, consult a Yamaha dealer. The following maximum engine speed limitations, which Yamaha provide for new motorcycles, can be used as a guide.

3 If a lubrication failure is suspected, stop the engine immediately and try to find the cause. If an engine is run without oil, even for a short period of time, severe damage will occur. After running the rebuilt engine for 1000 miles (1600 km), change the engine oil and filter (see Chapter 1).

Up to 600 miles (1000 km)	Do not exceed 5000 rpm
600 to 1000 miles (1000 to 1600 km)	Vary throttle position/speed. Do not exceed 6000 rpm for long periods
Over 1000 miles (1600 km)	Normal riding. Do not exceed tachometer red line

Notes

Chapter 3
Cooling system

Contents

Coolant hoses, pipes and unions – removal and installation 9
Coolant level check ....see *Daily (pre-ride) checks*
Coolant reservoir – removal and installation 3
Coolant temperature display, warning light and sender –
  check and renewal 5
Cooling fan and cooling fan switch – check and renewal 4
Cooling system checks ....see Chapter 1
Cooling system draining, flushing and refilling ....see Chapter 1
General information 1
Oil cooler – removal and installation ....see Chapter 2
Radiator – removal and installation 7
Radiator pressure cap – check 2
Thermostat – removal, check and installation 6
Water pump – check and overhaul 8

Degrees of difficulty

Easy, suitable for novice with little experience	Fairly easy, suitable for beginner with some experience	Fairly difficult, suitable for competent DIY mechanic	Difficult, suitable for experienced DIY mechanic	Very difficult, suitable for expert DIY or professional

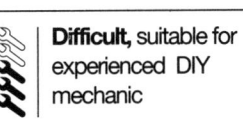

Specifications

Coolant
Mixture type and capacity .... see Chapter 1

Radiator
Cap valve opening pressure .... 15.9 to 20.3 psi (1.1 to 1.4 bars)

Cooling fan switch
Cooling fan cut-in temperature .... 102 to 108°C
Cooling fan cut-out temperature .... 97 to 103°C

Coolant temperature sender
Resistance @ 80°C .... 5.06 to 6.42 K-ohms
Resistance @ 120°C .... 1.61 to 1.73 K-ohms

Thermostat
Opening temperature .... 71 to 84°C
Valve lift .... 8 mm @ 84°C

Water pump
Impeller shaft tilt (max.) .... 0.15 mm

Torque wrench settings
Radiator mounting bolts .... 7 Nm
Cooling fan bolts .... 9 Nm
Cooling fan switch .... 28 Nm
Temperature sender .... 15 Nm
Thermostat housing bolts .... 10 Nm
Water pump mounting bolts .... 12 Nm
Water pump cover bolts .... 10 Nm

3•2 Cooling system

1 General information

The cooling system uses a water/antifreeze mixture to carry excess heat away from the engine. The cylinders are surrounded by a water jacket, through which the coolant is circulated by thermo-syphonic action in conjunction with a water pump. The water pump drives off the oil pump which is driven by chain and sprockets off the back of the clutch.

Heated coolant rises through the system to a thermostat and then to the radiator. It flows across the radiator, where it is cooled by the air flow, then down to the water pump and back into the engine, where the cycle is repeated. The thermostat is fitted in the system to prevent the coolant flowing through the radiator when the engine is cold, therefore accelerating the speed at which the engine reaches normal operating temperature.

A coolant temperature sender is fitted into the back of the cylinder head and transmits coolant temperature to the display on the instrument panel.

A thermostatically-controlled cooling fan is fitted behind the radiator, to aid cooling in extreme conditions. The fan switch is mounted in the back of the radiator on the right-hand side.

In certain countries a carburettor warmer system is fitted to prevent carburettor icing. Coolant is routed through the carburettor bodies and controlled by a thermostatic valve.

The complete cooling system is partially sealed and pressurised, the pressure being controlled by a spring-loaded valve contained in the radiator cap. By pressurising the coolant the boiling point is raised, preventing premature boiling in adverse conditions. The overflow hose from the system is connected to a reservoir mounted inside the left-hand fairing side panel, into which excess coolant is expelled under pressure. The discharged coolant automatically returns to the radiator when the engine cools.

⚠ **Warning: Do not remove the pressure cap from the radiator when the engine is hot. Scalding hot coolant and steam may be blown out under pressure and could cause serious injury. When the engine has cooled, place a thick rag such as a towel over the pressure cap; slowly rotate the cap anti-clockwise to the first stop. This procedure allows any residual pressure to escape. When the pressure has stopped escaping, press down on the cap while turning it anti-clockwise, and remove it.**

Do not allow antifreeze to come into contact with your skin, or painted surfaces of the motorcycle. Rinse off any spills immediately with plenty of water. Antifreeze is highly toxic if ingested. Never leave antifreeze lying around in an open container or in puddles on the floor; children and pets are attracted by its sweet smell and may drink it. Check with the local authorities about disposing of used antifreeze. Many communities will have collection centres which will see that antifreeze is disposed of safely.

Caution: At all times use the specified type of antifreeze, and always mix it with distilled water in the correct proportion. The antifreeze contains corrosion inhibitors which are essential to avoid damage to the cooling system. A lack of these inhibitors could lead to a build-up of corrosion which will block the coolant passages inside the engine, resulting in overheating and severe engine damage. Distilled water must be used as opposed to tap water to avoid a build-up of scale which would also block the passages.

Read the *Safety first!* section of this manual carefully before starting work.

2 Radiator pressure cap – check

1 If problems such as overheating or loss of coolant occur, check the entire system as described in Chapter 1. The radiator cap opening pressure should be checked by a Yamaha dealer with the special tester required for the job. If the cap is defective, replace it with a new one.

3 Coolant reservoir – removal and installation

Removal

1 Remove the lower fairing and the left-hand fairing side panel (see Chapter 8).
2 Remove the reservoir cap and pull out the radiator overflow hose **(see illustration)**.
3 Unscrew the reservoir mounting bolts and lift the reservoir off the motorcycle, carefully threading the breather hose attached to the filler neck out of its guides **(see illustration)**. Tip the coolant out of the reservoir into a suitable container.

Installation

4 Installation is the reverse of removal, noting the following:
● Ensure the breather hose is correctly routed and secured.
● Fill the reservoir with coolant up to the correct level (see Daily (pre-ride) checks).

4 Cooling fan and cooling fan switch – check and renewal

Cooling fan

Check

1 If the engine is overheating and the coolant temperature warning light is on, yet the cooling fan isn't cutting in, first check the fan fuse (see Chapter 9).
2 If the fuse is good and voltage is present at the brown wire to the fan switch when the ignition is ON, the fault lies in either the cooling fan motor or the fan switch.
3 To test the cooling fan motor, remove the left and right-hand fairing side panels (see Chapter 8). Trace the wiring from the fan motor and disconnect it at the connector **(see illustration)**. Using a 12 volt battery and two jumper wires, connect the positive (+ve) battery lead to the blue wire terminal on the

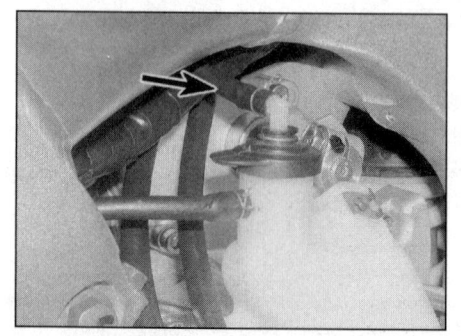

3.2 Remove the reservoir cap and overflow pipe (arrowed)

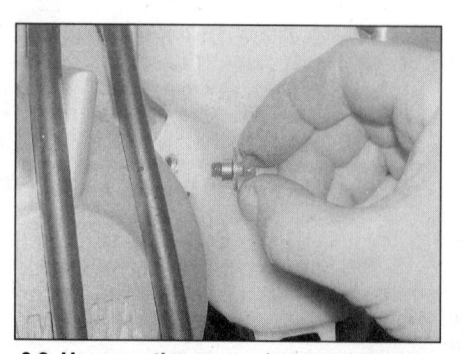

3.3 Unscrew the reservoir mounting bolts

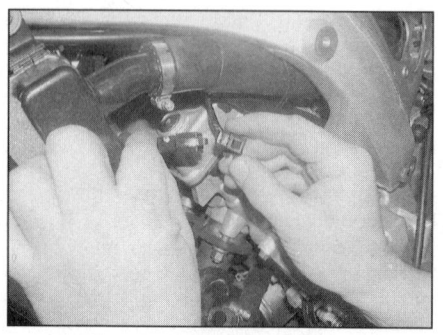

4.3 Disconnect the fan motor wiring connector

Cooling system 3•3

4.5 Fan assembly mounting bolts (arrowed)

4.8 Disconnect the wiring connector from the fan switch

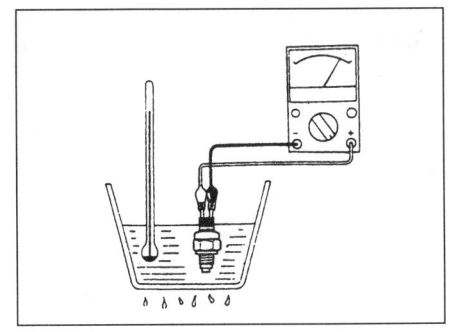

4.11 Arrangement for testing the fan switch

fan side of the wiring connector and the negative (–ve) lead to the black wire terminal. Once connected, the fan should operate. If it does not, and the wiring is all good, then the fan motor is faulty. Replace the fan assembly with a new one – individual components are not available.

Renewal

> **Warning:** *The engine must be completely cool before carrying out this procedure.*

4 Remove the radiator (see Section 7).
5 Unscrew the three bolts securing the fan assembly to the radiator and remove it **(see illustration)**.
6 Installation is the reverse of removal. Tighten the bolts to the torque setting specified at the beginning of this Chapter.

Cooling fan switch

Check

7 If the engine is overheating and the cooling fan isn't coming on, first check the fan fuse (see Chapter 9). If the fuse is blown, check the fan circuit for a short to earth (ground) (see *Wiring Diagrams* at the end of this book). If the fuse is good and voltage is present at the brown wire to the fan switch when the ignition is ON, the fault lies in either the cooling fan motor or the fan switch.
8 The fan switch is mounted on the back of the radiator on the right-hand side. To test the switch, first disconnect the switch wiring connector **(see illustration)**. Using a jumper wire, connect between the terminals in the wiring connector, then turn the ignition ON. The fan should come on. If it does, the fan switch is defective and must be replaced with a new one. If the fan does not come on, test the fan motor (see Step 3).
9 If the fan stays on all the time the switch is defective and must be replaced with a new one.
10 If the fan works but is suspected of cutting in at the wrong temperature, test the switch as follows.
11 Remove the switch (see below). Fill a small heatproof container with coolant (see Chapter 1 Specifications) and place it on a stove. Connect the probes of an ohmmeter to the terminals of the switch and, using some wire or other support, suspend the switch in the coolant so that just the sensing portion and the threads are submerged **(see illustration)**. Place a thermometer capable of reading temperatures up to 120°C in the coolant so that its bulb is close to the switch. **Note:** *None of the components should be allowed to directly touch the container.*
12 Initially the ohmmeter should show infinite (very high) resistance indicating that the switch is open (OFF). Heat the coolant, stirring it gently. When the temperature reaches between 102 to 108°C the meter reading should drop to around zero ohms, indicating that the switch has closed (ON). Now turn the heat off. As the temperature falls between 97 and 103°C the meter reading should show infinite (very high) resistance, indicating that the switch has opened (OFF). If the meter readings obtained are widely different, or they are obtained at different temperatures, then the switch is faulty and must be replaced with a new one.

> **Warning:** *This must be done very carefully to avoid the risk of personal injury.*

Renewal

> **Warning:** *The engine must be completely cool before carrying out this procedure.*

13 Partially drain the cooling system to a level sufficient to avoid spilling coolant when the fan switch is removed from the radiator (see Chapter 1).
14 Disconnect the wiring connector from the fan switch **(see illustration 4.8)**. Unscrew the switch and remove it from the radiator.
15 Apply a suitable sealant (Yamaha advise Three Bond Sealock 10) to the switch threads, then install the switch and tighten it to the torque setting specified at the beginning of this Chapter. Take care not to over-tighten the switch as it or the radiator could be damaged.
16 Reconnect the switch wiring and top-up the cooling system (see Chapter 1).

5 Coolant temperature display, warning light and sender – check and renewal

Temperature display and warning light

Check

1 The circuit consists of the sender mounted in the back of the cylinder head and the display and warning light mounted in the instrument cluster.
2 The temperature display should function as follows:

0 to 40°C	LO
41 to 117°C	Actual temperature of coolant
118 to 140°C	Actual temperature of coolant, temperature symbol flashing and warning light on
Above 141°C	HI, temperature symbol flashing and warning light on

3 If the system malfunctions, first check the signal fuse and the sender wiring and connections (see Chapter 9). Check for battery voltage at the brown wire to the instruments with the ignition ON. Next check the temperature sender as described below.
4 If no problems are found, take the instrument cluster to a Yamaha dealer for further assessment – Yamaha provide no specific test data for the instruments themselves. If there are any faults, even if just the warning light LED is faulty, a new cluster will have to be fitted, as no individual components are available.

Renewal

5 See Chapter 9.

Temperature sender

Check

6 Remove the carburettors and the heat protector (see Chapter 4).
7 Check for continuity between the sender body and earth (ground). There should be continuity. If there is no continuity, check that

3•4 Cooling system

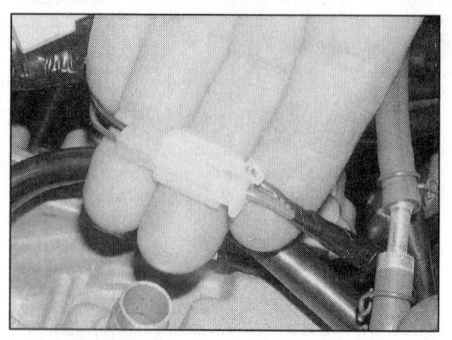

5.8 Disconnect the sender/thermostat earth wiring connector

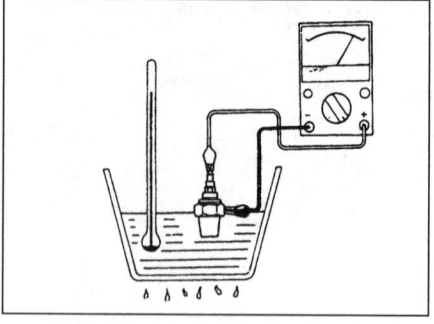

5.10 Arrangement for testing the temperature sender

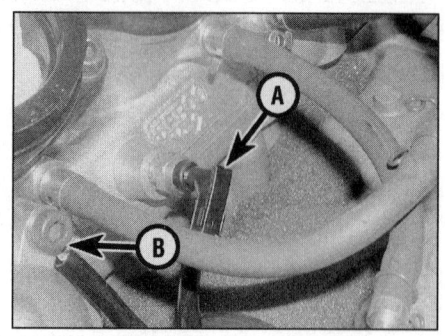

5.12 Temperature sender wiring connector (A) and thermostat earth (B)

the sender is tight in the cylinder head (see Specifications at the beginning of this Chapter) and that the earth wire on the thermostat housing mounting bolt is secure, and that the earth terminal is clean.

8 Disconnect the sender/thermostat earth wiring connector **(see illustration)**. Using a jumper wire, connect between the terminals on the wiring harness side of the connector, then turn the ignition ON. The temperature display and warning light should come on. If they don't, check the wiring between the connector and the instrument cluster (see the wiring diagrams at the end of this manual). If the wiring is good, refer to Step 4 above.

9 If the display and warning light do come on, it is likely that the sender is faulty, although check first that the green/red wire between the connector and sender is undamaged.

10 To check the operation of the sender, remove it from the engine as described below, then fill a small heatproof container with coolant (see Chapter 1 Specifications) and place it on a stove. Using an ohmmeter, connect its positive (+ve) probe to the terminal on the sender, and its negative (–ve) probe to the body of the sender. Suspend the sender in the coolant so that just the sensing portion and the threads are submerged. Also place a thermometer capable of reading temperatures of up to 125°C in the water so that its bulb is close to the sender **(see illustration)**. **Note:** *None of the components should be allowed to directly touch the container.* Heat the coolant, stirring it gently.

⚠ **Warning: This must be done very carefully to avoid the risk of personal injury.**

When the temperature reaches around 80°C the meter reading should be as specified at the beginning of this Chapter. When the temperature reaches around 120°C the meter should again be as specified. If the meter readings obtained are widely different, or they are obtained at different temperatures, then the sender is faulty and must be renewed.

Renewal

⚠ **Warning: The engine must be completely cool before carrying out this procedure.**

11 Remove the carburettors and heat protector (see Chapter 4), and the right-hand fairing side panel (see Chapter 8). Partially drain the cooling system sufficient to avoid spilling coolant when the sender is removed from the cylinder head (see Chapter 1).

12 Disconnect the sender wiring connector **(see illustration)**. Unscrew the sender and remove it from the head.

13 On reassembly, apply a suitable sealant (Yamaha advise Three Bond Sealock 10) to the sender threads, then install the sender and tighten it to the torque setting specified at the beginning of this Chapter. Connect the sender wiring.

14 Top-up the cooling system (see Chapter 1 and *Daily (pre-ride) checks*) and install the remaining components in the reverse order of removal.

6 Thermostat – removal, check and installation

⚠ **Warning: The engine must be completely cool before carrying out this procedure.**

1 The thermostat is automatic in operation and should give many years' service without requiring attention. In the event of a failure, the valve will probably jam open, in which case the engine will take much longer than normal to warm up. Conversely, if the valve jams shut, the coolant will be unable to circulate and the engine will overheat. Neither

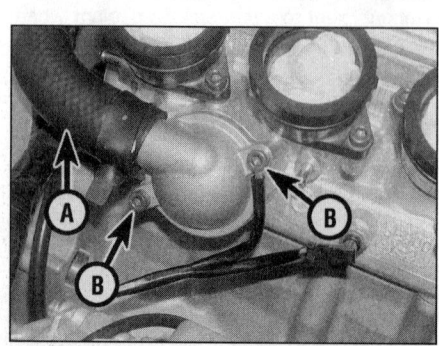

6.3 Disconnect the hose (A) and unscrew the thermostat housing bolts (B)

condition is acceptable, and the fault must be investigated promptly.

Removal

2 Remove the carburettors and heat protector (see Chapter 4), and the right-hand fairing side panel (see Chapter 8). Partially drain the cooling system to a sufficient level to avoid spilling coolant when the thermostat housing is removed from the cylinder head (see Chapter 1).

3 Loosen the clip securing the radiator inlet hose to the thermostat housing and detach the hose **(see illustration)**. Unscrew the bolts securing the housing to the cylinder head, noting the earth (ground) terminal retained by the upper bolt, and remove the housing, being prepared to catch any residual coolant.

4 Lift the thermostat out of its recess in the cylinder head, noting how it fits **(see illustration)**.

5 Inspect the housing for cracks and corrosion, especially around the hose unions. Clean off any corrosion with a wire brush or steel wool. Check the condition of the housing O-ring and renew it if necessary.

Check

6 Examine the thermostat visually before carrying out the test. If it remains in the open position at room temperature, it should be replaced with a new one.

7 To check the operation of the thermostat, suspend it in a container of cold water. Place a thermometer capable of reading

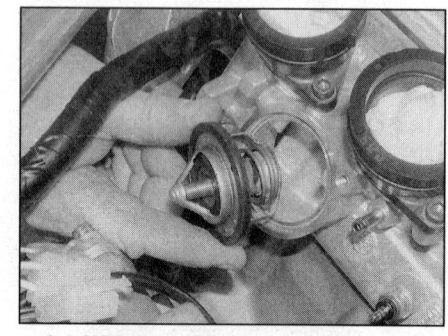

6.4 Withdraw the thermostat from the back of the cylinder head

Cooling system 3•5

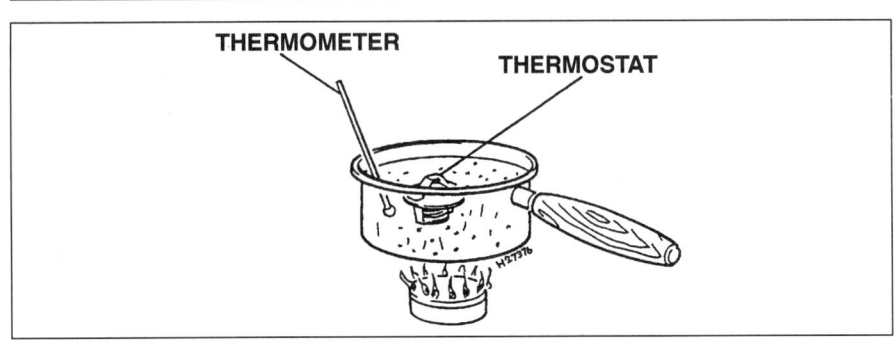

6.7 Arrangement for testing the thermostat

6.9 Install thermostat with breather hole (arrowed) at top

temperatures up to 100°C in the water so that the bulb is close to the thermostat **(see illustration)**. Heat the water whilst stirring it gently, noting the temperature when the thermostat opens, and compare the result with the specifications given at the beginning of this Chapter. Also check the amount the valve opens after it has been heated at 84°C for a few minutes and compare the measurement to the specifications. If the readings obtained differ from those given, the thermostat is faulty and must be replaced with a new one.

8 In the event of the thermostat jamming closed, *as an emergency measure only*, it can be removed and the machine used without it. **Note:** *Take care when starting the engine from cold, as it will take much longer than usual to warm up. Ensure that a new unit is installed as soon as possible.*

Installation

9 Fit the thermostat into the cylinder head, making sure that it seats correctly and that the breather hole is at the top **(see illustration)**.
10 Smear the O-ring lightly with lithium-based grease and install the housing, the earth (ground) wire and the fixing bolts, then tighten the bolts to the specified torque setting. Make sure the radiator inlet hose is pushed fully onto its union and tighten the clip securely **(see illustration 6.3)**.
11 Top-up the cooling system (see Chapter 1 and *Daily (pre-ride) checks*) and install the remaining components in the reverse order of removal.

7 Radiator – removal and installation

Removal

⚠ **Warning:** *The engine must be completely cool before carrying out this procedure.*

1 Remove the lower fairing and fairing side panels (see Chapter 8). Remove the air filter housing (see Chapter 4).
2 Drain the cooling system (see Chapter 1).
3 Disconnect the cooling fan switch wiring from the switch on the back of the radiator on the right-hand side **(see illustration 4.8)**.

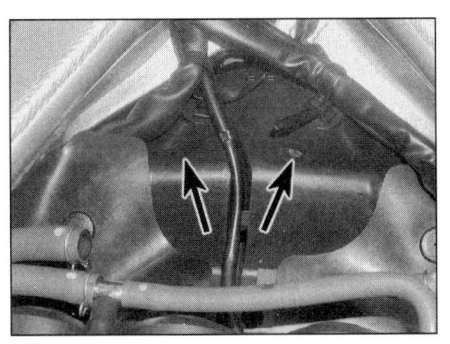

7.5 Remove the radiator housing trim clips

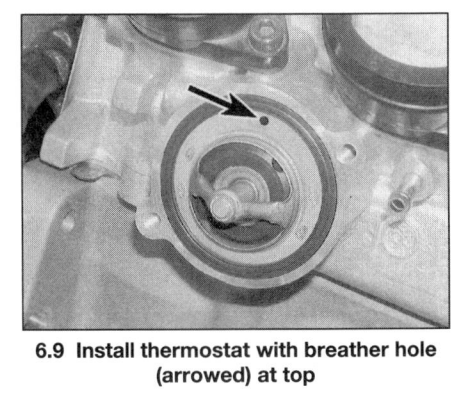

Disconnect the cooling fan motor wiring at the connector **(see illustration 4.3)**.
4 Unfasten the clutch cable guide from the right-hand side of the radiator.
5 Remove the trim clips that secure the radiator cover to the cooling fan housing **(see illustration)**. To remove a trim clip, first press the centre down with a small screwdriver, then pull the clip out. The clips can be re-used.
6 Unscrew the radiator lower mounting bolt and remove the bolt and washer **(see illustration)**. Note the spacer that fits in the bush in the radiator mounting tab and remove it if it is loose.
7 Loosen the clips securing the radiator inlet and outlet hoses, the overflow hose and the oil cooler outlet hose, and detach them from the radiator, noting which fits where **(see illustrations)**. **Note:** *Loosen the upper (left-*

7.6 Unscrew the radiator lower mounting bolt

7.7a Detach the three (two on models without carb warmer system) small-bore hoses from the upper right-hand side ...

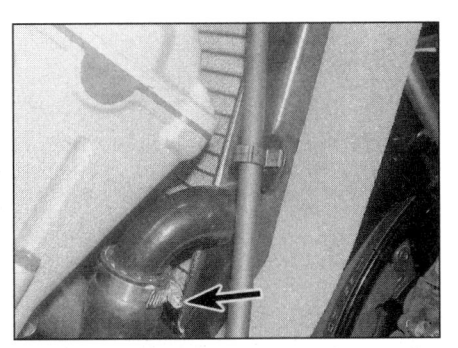

7.7b ... the large-bore hoses (arrowed) from the lower right-hand side ...

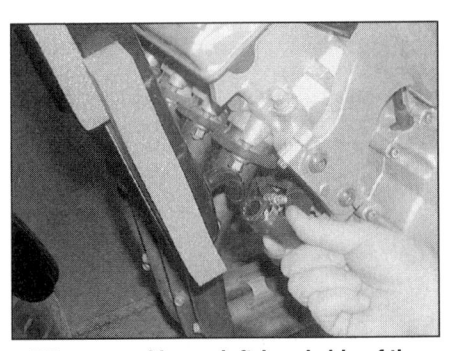

7.7c ... and lower left-hand side of the radiator

3•6 Cooling system

7.7d Loosen the left-hand mounting bolt and swing the radiator forward . . .

7.7e . . . to disconnect the upper left-hand large-bore hose

7.8 Free the radiator from the right-hand mounting

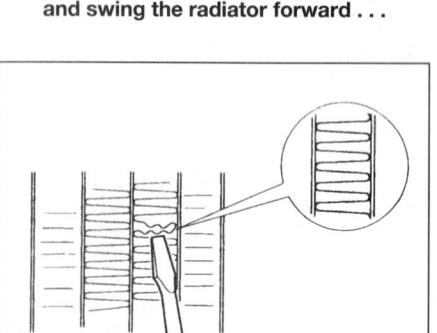

7.10 Damaged radiator fins can be straightened with a flat-bladed screwdriver

hand) radiator mounting bolt and swing the radiator forward to facilitate removal of the left-hand inlet hose **(see illustrations)**.

8 Unscrew the upper (left-hand) mounting bolt and remove the bolt and washer. Note the spacer that fits in the bush in the radiator mounting tab and remove it if it is loose.

Carefully manoeuvre the radiator to the right-hand side to free the upper right-hand radiator mounting tab from the frame lug, then remove the radiator **(see illustration)**.

9 If necessary, separate the cooling fan from the radiator (see Section 4).

10 Check the radiator for signs of damage and clear any dirt or debris that might obstruct air flow and inhibit cooling. Radiator fins can be straightened carefully with a flat bladed screwdriver, but if the fins are badly damaged or broken the radiator must be renewed **(see illustration)**. Also check the mounting bushes, and replace them with new ones if necessary.

Installation

11 Installation is the reverse of removal, noting the following.
● Make sure the spacers, bushes and washers are correctly installed with the mounting bolts. Tighten the bolts to the torque setting specified at the beginning of this Chapter.

● Make sure that the wiring connectors are a good fit.
● Ensure the coolant hoses are in good condition (see Chapter 1), and are securely retained by their clips, using new ones if necessary.
● Refill the cooling system as described in Chapter 1.

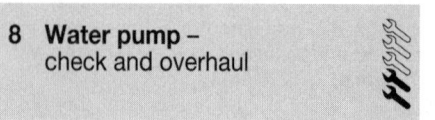

8 Water pump – check and overhaul

Check

1 Remove the lower fairing and right-hand fairing side panel (see Chapter 8).
2 The water pump is located on the right-hand side of the engine and is driven by the oil pump. The pump impeller bearing is located in the pump body **(see illustration)**.
3 To prevent leakage of water from the cooling system to the lubrication system and vice versa, two seals are fitted on the pump shaft. The seal inside the water pump is of the mechanical type which bears on the rear face of the impeller. The other seal, which is located in the pump housing, is of the normal feathered lip type. If either seal fails, a drain hole in the pump body allows the coolant or oil to escape and prevents them mixing **(see illustration)**. If on inspection there are signs of leakage, the pump must be removed and new seals installed (see Steps 14 to 19). If you are not sure about the condition of the seals, remove the pump and check them visually.

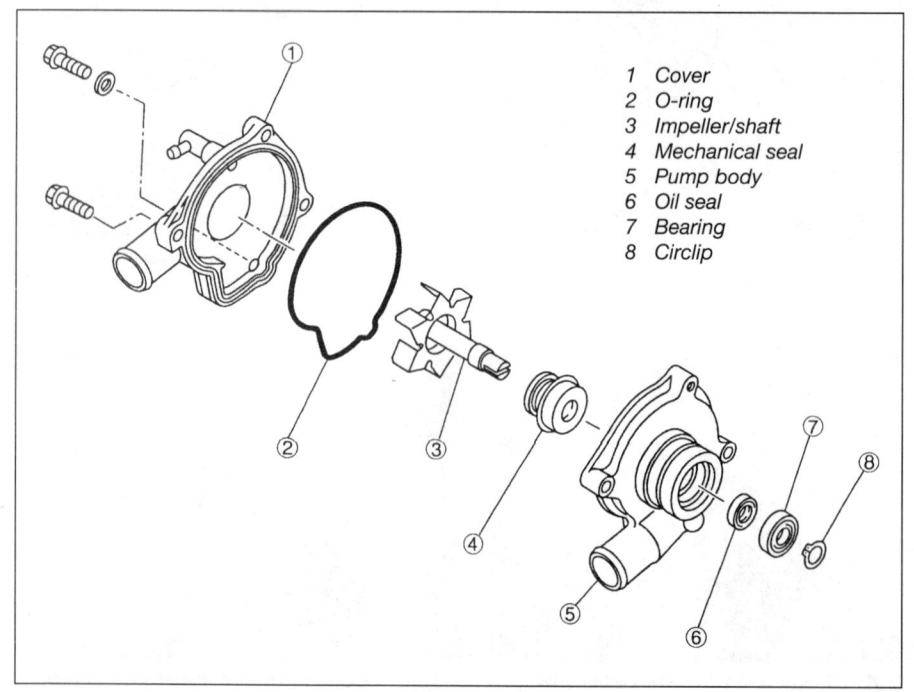

1 Cover
2 O-ring
3 Impeller/shaft
4 Mechanical seal
5 Pump body
6 Oil seal
7 Bearing
8 Circlip

8.2 Water pump components

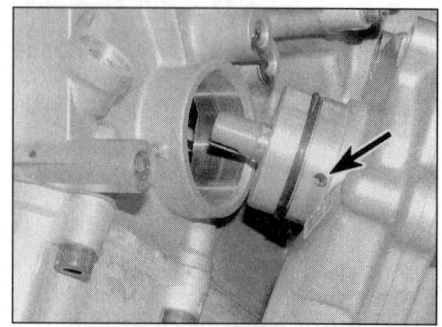

8.3 Water pump drain hole (arrowed)

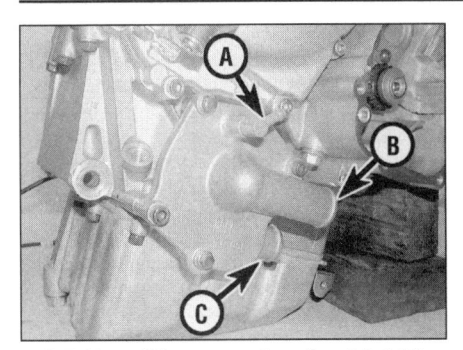

Cooling system 3•7

8.5 Hose (A) to rear of engine, inlet (B) from radiator, and outlet (C) to engine and oil cooler

8.7a Unscrew the pump mounting bolts (arrowed) . . .

8.7b . . . and withdraw the pump. Discard the O-ring (arrowed)

Removal

4 Drain the coolant (see Chapter 1).
5 Slacken the clips securing the hoses onto the pump cover and detach the hoses, noting which fits where **(see illustration)**.
6 Detach the clutch cable from the release mechanism arm then unscrew the bolts securing the clutch cable adjuster bracket to the ignition rotor cover and secure the cable clear of the engine (see Chapter 2).
7 Unscrew the pump mounting bolts and draw the pump out of the crankcase. Discard the O-ring on the back of the pump body as a new one must be fitted on reassembly **(see illustrations)**.
8 Unscrew the pump cover bolts and lift off the pump cover; discard the O-ring as a new one must be fitted on reassembly **(see illustration)**.
9 Withdraw the impeller from the pump body, noting how the mechanical seal fits on the impeller shaft **(see illustration)**.

Inspection

10 To check the pump impeller bearing, wiggle the impeller back-and-forth and spin it by hand. If there is excessive movement, or the bearing is noisy or rough when turned, the bearing must be renewed. Also check the bearing referring to *Tools and Workshop Tips* (Section 5) in the *Reference* section.
11 Withdraw the impeller from the pump body to check the condition of the impeller shaft. If there are signs of wear or other damage, the impeller must be renewed.

Check that the shaft is straight – if it tilts by more than the specified limit, replace it with a new one.
12 Check the condition of the rubber damper and its holder on the rear face of the impeller. Do not remove them from the shaft unnecessarily, as they cannot be reused. If they are damaged or deteriorated, fit a new impeller – Yamaha do not list the damper and holder as being available separately, though it is worth checking first. If they are available, lever off the old ones with a flat-bladed screwdriver. Apply coolant to the new ones and press them squarely down the shaft on to the back of the impeller.
13 Inspect the pump body for corrosion or a build-up of scale and clean with steel wool as necessary, then rinse the pump body in running clean water.

Seal and bearing renewal

14 To remove the mechanical seal, tap it out towards the inside of the pump body from the outside using a suitable punch, noting which way round it fits **(see illustration)**. Discard it, as a new one must be fitted.
15 To remove the oil seal, first remove the mechanical seal (see Step 14) then remove the circlip retaining the bearing in the pump body **(see illustration)**. Tap the oil seal and bearing out from the inside of the body using a suitable sized bearing driver or socket **(see illustration 8.14)**. Note which way round the seal fits. Discard it, as a new one must be fitted.
16 Clean any traces of sealant from around the mechanical seal seat with a suitable solvent.
17 Press or drive the bearing into the pump body until it is properly seated, then install the circlip **(see illustration 8.14)**.
18 Apply a smear of coolant to the outside of the new oil seal. Press or drive the seal into the body from the inside until it fits against the bearing. The marked side of the seal should be facing the bearing.
19 Smear Yamaha Bond 1215 or a suitable equivalent to the mechanical seal seat. Press or carefully drive the new mechanical seal into the pump body using a suitable sized socket or seal driver which bears only on the outer rim of the seal and not on the centre. Yamaha produce a special tool, Part No. 90890-04078 (European models) or YM-33221 (US models), for installing the seal if required.

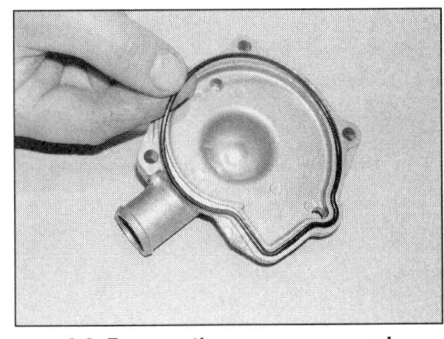

8.8 Remove the pump cover and O-ring . . .

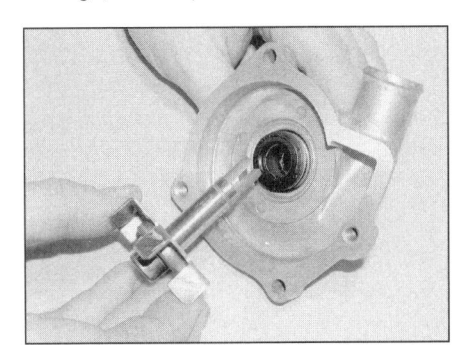

8.9 . . . and pull the impeller out of the seal

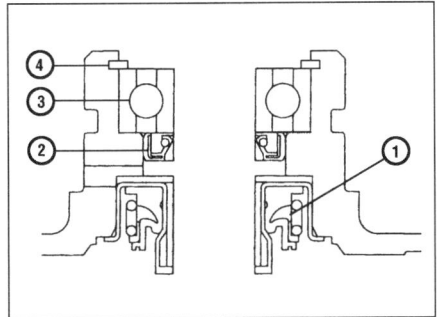

8.14 Mechanical seal (1), oil seal (2), bearing (3) and circlip (4)

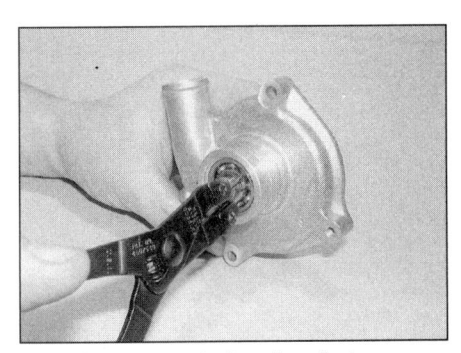

8.15 To remove the bearing, first remove the circlip

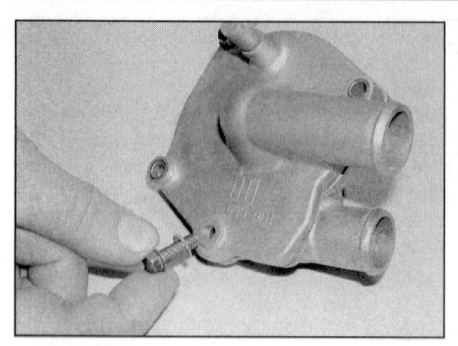

3•8 Cooling system

8.21 Fit a new washer to the drain bolt . . .

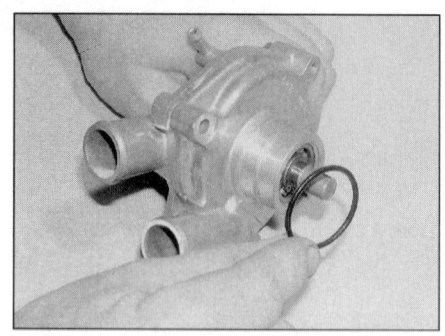

8.22 . . . and a new O-ring to the pump body

Installation

20 Lubricate the impeller shaft with coolant and slide it into the pump body.
21 Fit the new cover O-ring into its groove then fit the cover and install the cover bolts. Remember to fit a new sealing washer to the drain bolt and tighten the bolts to the specified torque setting **(see illustration)**.
22 Fit a new pump body O-ring and smear it lightly with grease **(see illustration)**. Install the pump in the crankcase, ensuring that the impeller shaft engages the drive peg on the oil pump spindle.
23 Install the remaining components in the reverse order of removal

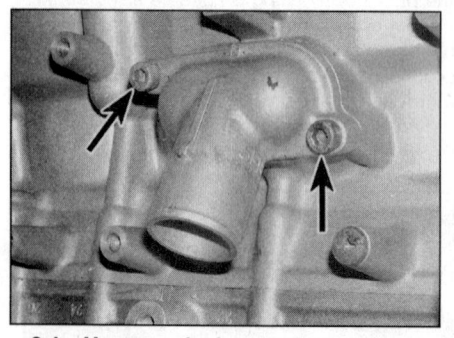

9 Coolant hoses, pipes and unions – removal and installation

Removal

1 Before removing a hose, pipe or union, drain the coolant (see Chapter 1). **Note:** *When removing components of the cooling system, be prepared to catch any residual fluids.*
2 Use a screwdriver to slacken the larger-bore hose clips, then slide them back along the hose and clear of the union spigot. The smaller-bore hoses are secured by spring clips which can be expanded by squeezing their ears together with pliers.
Caution: The radiator unions are fragile. Do not use excessive force when attempting to remove the hoses.
3 If a hose proves stubborn, release it by rotating it on its union before working it off. If all else fails, cut the hose with a sharp knife then slit it at each union so that it can be peeled off in two pieces. Whilst this means renewing the hose, it is preferable to buying a new radiator.
4 Remove the union on the engine by detaching the hose (see above), then unscrewing the union retaining bolts. Discard the O-ring, as a new one must be fitted on reassembly **(see illustrations)**.

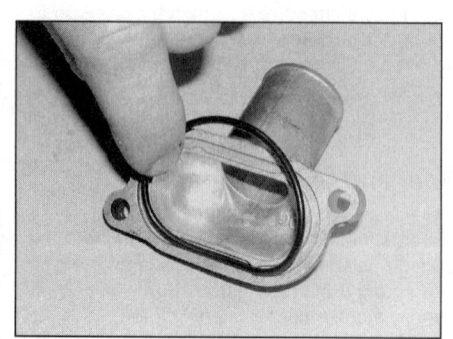

Installation

5 Slide the clip onto the hose and then work the hose onto its union.
6 Rotate the hose on its union to settle it in position before sliding the clip into place and tightening it securely.
7 If the union on the engine has been removed, fit a new O-ring and smear it with grease, then install the union and tighten the mounting securely.

9.4a Unscrew the hose union retaining bolts (arrowed) . . .

9.4b . . . and renew the O-ring on reassembly

> **HAYNES HiNT**
> *If the hose is difficult to push onto its union, it can be softened by soaking it in very hot water, or alternatively a little soapy water can be used as a lubricant.*

Chapter 4
Fuel and exhaust systems

Contents

Air filter – cleaning and renewal .see Chapter 1	Fuel hoses – renewal . . . . .see Chapter 1
Air filter housing – removal and installation 4	Fuel pump and relay – check, removal and installation 14
Air induction system (AIS) – function, disassembly and reassembly 16	Fuel system – check . . . . .see Chapter 1
Air/fuel mixture adjustment – general information 5	Fuel tank – cleaning and repair 3
Carburettor overhaul – general information 6	Fuel tank, tap and filter – removal and installation 2
Carburettor synchronisation . . . . .see Chapter 1	Fuel warning light and sender – check and renewal 15
Carburettors – disassembly, cleaning and inspection 8	General information and precautions 1
Carburettors – reassembly and fuel level check 9	Idle speed – check . . . . .see Chapter 1
Carburettors – removal and installation 7	Throttle and choke cables – check and adjustment . . . .see Chapter 1
Carburettors – separation and joining 10	Throttle cables – removal and installation 11
Choke cable – removal and installation 12	Throttle position sensor – check and adjustment . . . . . .see Chapter 5
Exhaust system – removal and installation 13	

Degrees of difficulty

Easy, suitable for novice with little experience	**Fairly easy,** suitable for beginner with some experience	**Fairly difficult,** suitable for competent DIY mechanic	**Difficult,** suitable for experienced DIY mechanic	**Very difficult,** suitable for expert DIY or professional

Specifications

Fuel
Grade	Unleaded, minimum 91 RON (Research Octane Number)
Fuel tank capacity (including reserve)	17 litres
Reserve	approx. 3.5 litres

Carburettors – European models
Type	4 x Keihin CVRD37
Fuel level	to 18.5 mm below line on float chamber
Idle speed	see Chapter 1
Pilot screw setting (no. of turns out)	
1998 and 1999 models	2
2000-on models	$1\frac{1}{2}$ to 2
Main jet	
Cylinders 1 and 4	152
Cylinders 2 and 3	148
Main air jet	110
Jet needle	
1998 and 1999 models	N7RA
2000 models	
Cylinders 1 and 4	N7RA
Cylinders 2 and 3	N7SA
Needle jet	2.6
Pilot air jet	110
Pilot outlet	0.9
Pilot jet	38
Starter jet 1	50
Starter jet 2	0.6
Butterfly valve size	110

Carburettors – US models

Type	4 x Keihin CVRD37
Fuel level	17.5 to 18.5 mm below line on float chamber
Idle speed	see Chapter 1
Pilot screw setting (no. of turns out)	fixed
Main jet	
Cylinders 1 and 4	152 (148 California models)
Cylinders 2 and 3	148 (all models)
Main air jet	110
Jet needle	
Cylinders 1 and 4	N7SB (N7SD California models)
Cylinders 2 and 3	N7SA (N7SE California models)
Needle jet	2.6
Pilot air jet	
Cylinders 1 and 4	105
Cylinders 2 and 3	110
Pilot outlet	0.9
Pilot jet	38 (35 California models)
Starter jet 1	50
Starter jet 2	0.6
Butterfly valve size	110

Throttle position sensor

Resistance	4.0 to 6.0 K-ohms @ 20°C

Fuel pump

Output pressure	15 to 20kPa (2.2 to 2.9 psi)
Resistance	4 to 30 ohms @ 20°C

Torque wrench settings

Fuel tank mountings	
Front mounting bolts	10 Nm
Rear mounting bolt	10 Nm
Fuel tap screws	7 Nm
Fuel level sender screws	7 Nm
Carburettor through-bolt nuts	7 Nm
Exhaust downpipe nuts	20 Nm
Exhaust system mounting bolt	20 Nm
Silencer clamp bolt	20 Nm
Silencer mounting bolt	38 Nm

1 General information and precautions

General information

The fuel system consists of the fuel tank with internal level sender, the fuel tap, fuel filter, fuel pump, fuel hoses, carburettors and control cables. The fuel tap has an integral strainer and the in-line fuel filter is mounted on the underside of the tank. The fuel pump is mounted to the right-hand side of the frame behind the engine unit.

The carburettors used are semi-flat slide CV types, one for each cylinder. For cold starting, a handlebar mounted choke lever is connected to the carburettors by a cable. In certain countries a carburettor warmer system is fitted to prevent carburettor icing; a thermostatic valve controls the flow of engine coolant through the carburettor bodies.

Air is drawn into the carburettors through an air filter, which is housed under the fuel tank. Air is ducted to the filter housing from the front of the fairing.

The exhaust system is a four-into-one design. Certain models have an integral air induction system (AIS) to reduce harmful emissions.

Many of the fuel system service procedures are considered routine maintenance items and for that reason are included in Chapter 1.

Precautions

Warning: Petrol (gasoline) is extremely flammable, so take extra precautions when you work on any part of the fuel system. Don't smoke or allow open flames or bare light bulbs near the work area, and don't work in a garage where a natural gas-type appliance is present. If you spill any fuel on your skin, wash it off immediately with soap and water. When you perform any kind of work on the fuel system, wear safety glasses and have a fire extinguisher suitable for a class B type fire (flammable liquids) on hand.

Always perform service procedures in a well-ventilated area to prevent a build-up of fumes.

Never work in a building containing a gas appliance with a pilot light, or any other form of naked flame. Ensure that there are no naked light bulbs or any sources of flame or sparks nearby.

Do not smoke (or allow anyone else to smoke) while in the vicinity of petrol (gasoline), or of components containing petrol. Remember the possible presence of vapour from these sources and move well clear before smoking.

Check all electrical equipment belonging to the house, garage or workshop where work is being undertaken (see the *Safety First!* section of this manual). Remember that certain electrical appliances such as drills, cutters etc. create sparks in the normal course of operation and must not be used near petrol (gasoline) or any component containing it. Again, remember the possible presence of fumes before using electrical equipment.

Always mop up any spilt fuel and safely dispose of the rag used.

Any stored fuel that is drained off during servicing work must be kept in sealed containers that are suitable for holding petrol (gasoline), and clearly marked as such; the containers themselves should be kept in a safe place. Note that this last point applies equally to the fuel tank if it is removed from the machine; also remember to keep its filler cap closed at all times.

Read the *Safety first!* section of this manual carefully before starting work.

2 Fuel tank, tap and filter – removal and installation

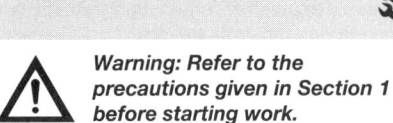

Warning: *Refer to the precautions given in Section 1 before starting work.*

Fuel tank

Removal

1 Make sure the fuel filler cap is secure. Remove the rider's seat (see Chapter 8).

2 Loosen the bolt securing the rear of the tank but do not remove it **(see illustration)**. Unscrew the bolts securing the front of the tank and remove the bolts **(see illustration)**.

3 Raise the tank at the front and support it using a length of wood **(see illustration)**.

4 Turn the fuel tap OFF – it is located on the base of the tank **(see illustration)**. Have a rag ready to catch any residual fuel from the hose and the fuel filter, then release the clip securing the fuel hose to the filter and detach the hose **(see illustration)**.

5 Release the clips securing the overflow hose and the breather hose to their unions and detach the hoses, noting which fits where **(see illustration)**.

6 Disconnect the fuel level sender green wiring connector **(see illustration)**.

7 Remove the support and lower the tank. Unscrew the bolt securing the rear of the tank, then carefully lift the tank off the frame and remove it **(see illustration)**.

8 Inspect the tank mounting rubbers for signs of damage or deterioration and replace them with new ones, if necessary **(see illustration)**.

2.2a Loosen the rear bolt . . .

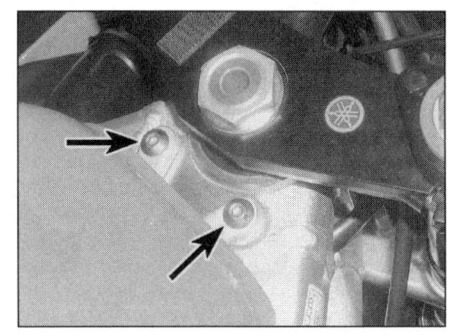

2.2b . . . and remove the two bolts (arrowed) at the front

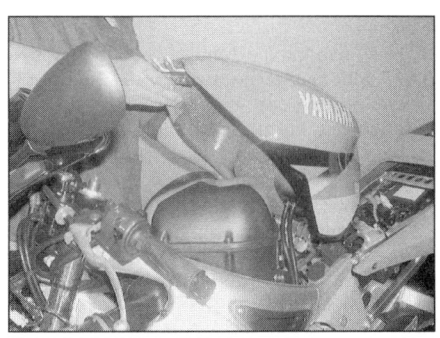

2.3 Raise the front of the tank . . .

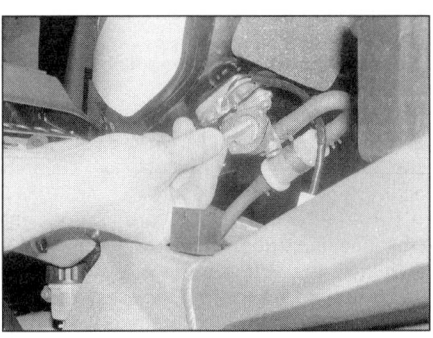

2.4a . . . and turn OFF the fuel tap . . .

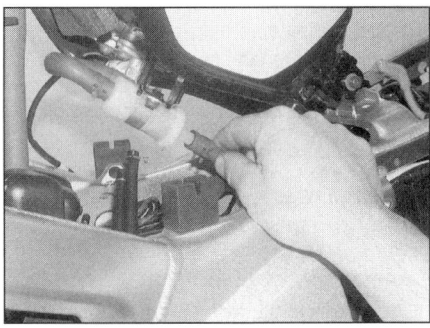

2.4b . . . then disconnect the fuel hose . . .

2.5 . . . and the breather and overflow hoses

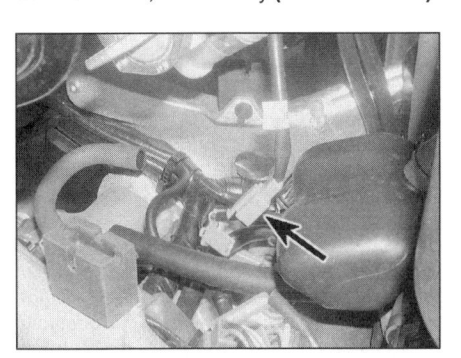

2.6 Disconnect the fuel level sender wiring connector . . .

2.7 . . . then remove the rear bolt and lift off the tank

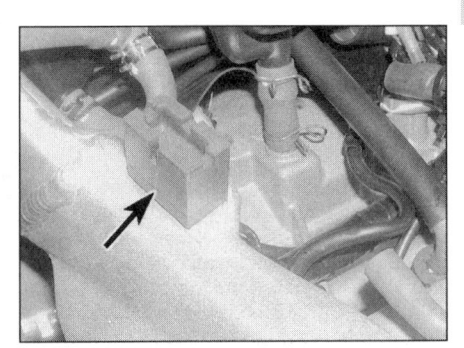

2.8 Check the condition of the tank mounting rubbers (arrowed)

4•4 Fuel and exhaust systems

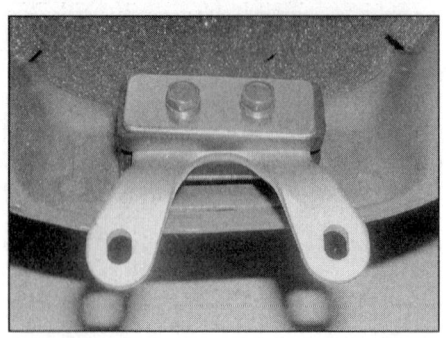

2.9a Ensure the front mounting bracket is secure

2.9b Don't forget to turn the fuel tap ON

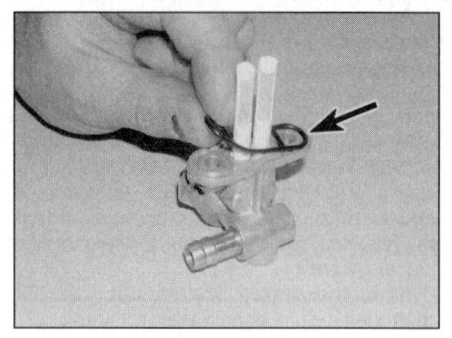

2.10 Fuel tap joint is sealed by an O-ring (arrowed)

Installation

9 Installation is the reverse of removal, noting the following:
- Ensure that the front mounting bracket is secure **(see illustration)**.
- Make sure the hoses are properly attached and secured by their clips. Make sure the level sender wiring connector is securely connected.
- Turn the fuel tap ON before lowering the tank **(see illustration)**.
- Ensure that the overflow hose and the breather hose are not trapped or kinked.
- Tighten the mounting bolts to the torque settings specified at the beginning of this Chapter.
- Start the engine and check that there is no sign of fuel leakage, then shut if off.

Fuel tap

10 The tap should not be removed unnecessarily from the tank, otherwise there is a possibility of damaging the O-ring or strainer. If the fuel tap to tank joint is leaking, ensure that the retaining screws are tightened to the specified torque setting. If leakage persists, remove the tap (see Steps 13 to 15) and renew the O-ring **(see illustration)**.
11 If the tap body is leaking, first ensure that the body screws are tight. If leakage persists, remove the screws, front plate, lever and O-ring. Clean any sediment out of the tap body, then fit a new O-ring and reassemble the lever, front plate and screws. Tighten the screws securely.

12 If fuel starvation is evident remove the fuel tap as described below and clean the fuel strainers.
13 Remove the fuel tank as described above.
14 Connect a drain hose to the fuel outlet union on the tap and insert its end in a container suitable and large enough for storing the fuel in the tank. Turn the fuel tap ON and allow the tank to drain. When the tank has drained, turn the tap OFF.
15 Remove the screws securing the tap to the tank and withdraw the tap assembly **(see illustration)**. Discard the O-ring, as a new one must be used.
16 Use a new O-ring when refitting the tap **(see illustration 2.10)**. Tighten the screws to the torque setting specified at the beginning of this Chapter.
17 Install the fuel tank (see above).

Fuel filter

18 The in-line fuel filter is mounted on the underside of the tank next to the fuel tap. The filter should be renewed at the specified service interval or sooner if it becomes dirty or clogged (see Chapter 1).

3 Fuel tank – cleaning and repair

1 All repairs to the fuel tank should be carried out by a professional who has experience in this critical and potentially dangerous work.

Even after cleaning and flushing of the fuel system, explosive fumes can remain and ignite during repair of the tank.
2 If the fuel tank is removed from the bike, it should not be placed in an area where sparks or open flames could ignite the fumes coming out of the tank. Be especially careful inside garages where a natural gas-type appliance is located, because the pilot light could cause an explosion.

4 Air filter housing – removal and installation

Removal

1 Remove the fuel tank (see Section 2).
2 Release the clips securing the air filter housing breather hose and the crankcase breather hose and detach them from the filter housing, noting which fits where **(see illustration)**.
3 Where fitted, release the clip securing the AIS hose and detach it.
4 Unscrew the bolt securing the front of the housing to the frame, noting the collar and grommet **(see illustration)**. Loosen the clamp screws securing the housing to the carburettor intakes **(see illustration)**.
5 Release the clips securing the left and right-hand air intake ducts to the front of the filter housing and detach the ducts **(see illustration)**.
6 Unscrew the screw securing the filter housing catch tank to the filter housing **(see illustration)**.

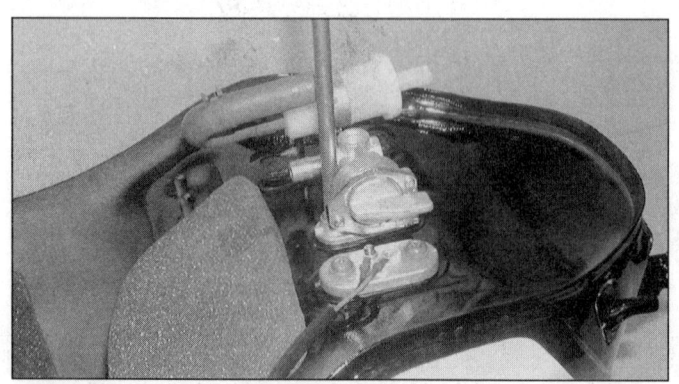

2.15 Fuel tap is secured to the tank by two screws with sealing washers

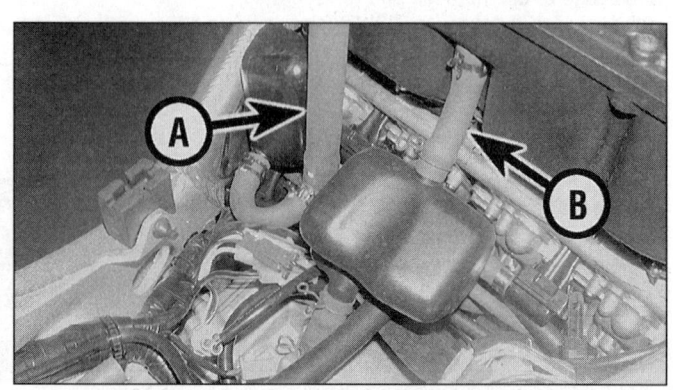

4.2 Detach the air filter housing (A) and crankcase (B) breather hoses

Fuel and exhaust systems 4•5

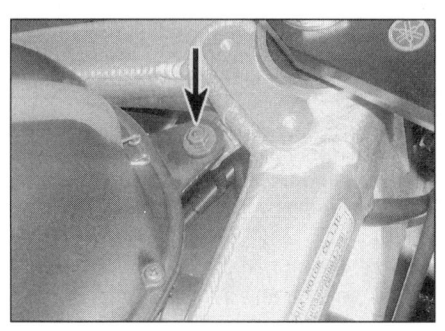

4.4a Unscrew the front mounting bolt . . .

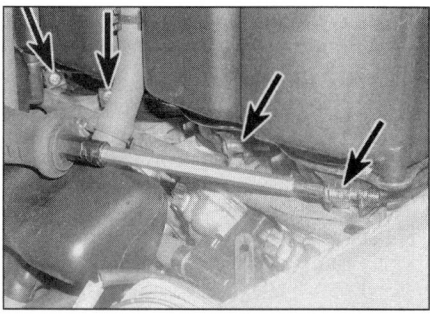

4.4b . . . and loosen the carburettor intake clamps (arrowed)

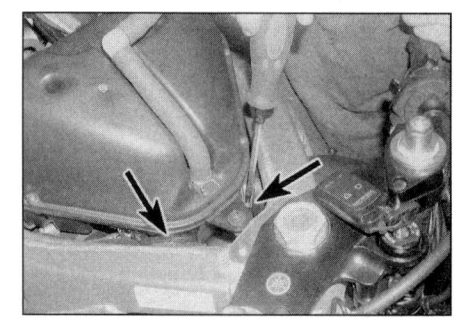

4.5 Detach the air intake ducts (arrowed) . . .

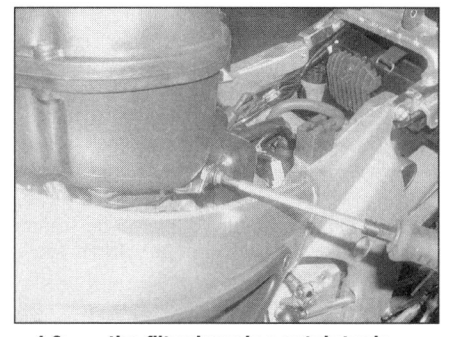

4.6 . . . the filter housing catch tank . . .

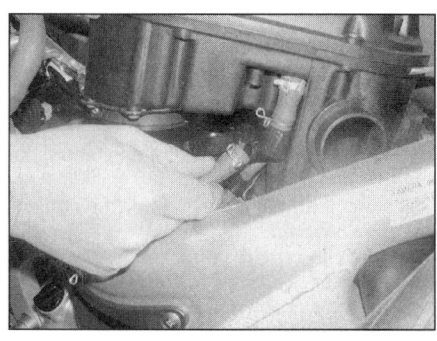

4.7a . . . and the carburettor balance hoses . . .

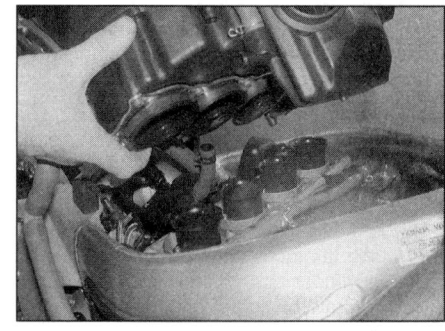

4.7b . . . then lift the housing off the carburettors

7 Release the clips securing the left and right-hand carburettor balance hoses and detach the hoses, then lift the housing up carefully and, ensuring that all the hoses are completely detached, lift the housing off the motorcycle (see illustrations).

Installation

8 Installation is the reverse of removal. Check the condition of the various hoses and their clamps and replace them with new ones, if necessary. Check the layout of the hoses before installing the filter housing and check that all the carburettor intake clamps are in place and the screws are correctly aligned (see illustrations).

5 Air/fuel mixture adjustment – general information

UK market models

1 If the engine runs extremely roughly at idle or continually stalls, and if cleaning the air filter, adjusting the throttle cables and adjusting the carburettor synchronisation (see Chapter 1) and a carburettor overhaul (see Section 6) does not cure the problem, the pilot screws may require adjustment. It is worth noting at this point that unless you have the experience to carry this out on a multi-cylinder machine it is best to entrust the task to a motorcycle dealer, tuner or fuel systems specialist. Note that you will need a long thin flexible drive screwdriver with an angled end to access the pilot screws (see

4.8a Before installation, check the layout of the hoses . . .

4.8b . . . and the position of the clamps and screws

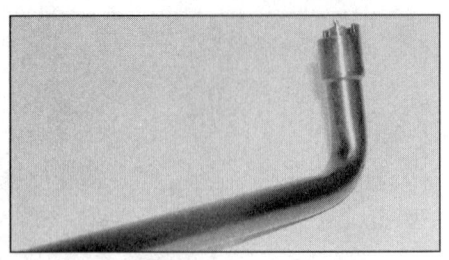

4•6 Fuel and exhaust systems

5.1 Pilot screw adjusting tool

illustration), an auxiliary fuel supply to run the engine with the fuel tank removed and ideally a tachometer that can be attached independently to the terminals of each ignition coil in turn.

2 Warm the engine up to normal working temperature, then stop the engine and remove the fuel tank (see Section 2) and the fairing side panels (see Chapter 8).

3 Screw in all four pilot screws **(see illustration 8.14)** until they seat lightly, then back them out to the number of turns specified at the beginning of this Chapter. This is the base position for adjustment.

4 Attach the tachometer to the ignition coil of No. 1 cylinder and connect the auxiliary fuel supply. Start the engine and set the idle speed by the motorcycle's tachometer as close to the correct level as possible (see Chapter 1).

5 Working on the carburettor of No. 1 cylinder, observe the tachometer reading for this cylinder and, if necessary, turn the pilot screw by a small amount either side of the base position until the tachometer reading matches the correct idle speed.

6 Stop the engine and attach the tachometer to the ignition coil of No. 2 cylinder and repeat the procedure.

⚠️ **Warning: Always stop the engine before disconnecting the tachometer from the ignition coil.**

Repeat the procedure on the other two carburettors in turn, then reset the idle speed to the specified level. **Note:** *As each carburettor is tuned in turn the engine should run noticeably smoother and the idle speed will rise.*

7 Attach the tachometer to the ignition coil of No. 1 cylinder and ensure that the tachometer reading still matches the correct idle speed. Adjust the pilot screw if necessary, then repeat the procedure on the other three carburettors.

8 Adjust the idle speed and check the adjustment on the throttle cables (see Chapter 1).

Other markets

9 Due to the increased emphasis on controlling exhaust emissions in certain world markets, regulations have been formulated which prevent adjustment of the air/fuel mixture. On such models the pilot screw positions are pre-set at the factory and in some cases have a limiter cap fitted to prevent tampering. Where adjustment is possible, it should only be made in conjunction with an exhaust gas analyser to ensure that the machine does not exceed the emissions regulations.

6 Carburettor overhaul – general information

1 Poor engine performance, hesitation, hard starting, stalling, flooding and backfiring are all signs that major carburettor maintenance may be required.

2 Keep in mind that many so-called carburettor problems are really not carburettor problems at all, but mechanical problems within the engine or ignition system malfunctions. Try to establish for certain that the carburettors are in need of maintenance before beginning a major overhaul.

3 Check the fuel tap and filter, the fuel hoses, the fuel pump, the intake manifold joint clamps, the air filter, the ignition system, the spark plugs and carburettor synchronisation before assuming that a carburettor overhaul is required.

4 Most carburettor problems are caused by dirt particles, varnish and other deposits which build up in and block the fuel and air passages. Also, in time, gaskets and O-rings shrink or deteriorate and cause fuel and air leaks which lead to poor performance.

5 When overhauling the carburettors, disassemble them completely and clean the parts thoroughly with a carburettor cleaning solvent and dry them with filtered, unlubricated compressed air. Blow through the fuel and air passages with compressed air to force out any dirt that may have been loosened but not removed by the solvent. Once the cleaning process is complete, reassemble the carburettor using new gaskets and O-rings.

6 Before disassembling the carburettors, make sure you have all the necessary O-rings and other parts, some carburettor cleaner, a supply of clean rags, some means of blowing out the carburettor passages and a clean place to work. It is recommended that only one carburettor be overhauled at a time to avoid mixing up parts.

7 Carburettors – removal and installation

⚠️ **Warning: Refer to the precautions given in Section 1 before starting work.**

Removal

1 Remove the fairing side panels and frame side panels from each side of the motorcycle (see Chapter 8). Remove the fuel tank (see Section 2) and the air filter housing (see Section 4).

2 Drain the cooling system on models equipped with a carburettor warmer system (see Chapter 1).

3 Detach the throttle cables from the carburettors (see Section 11).

4 Detach the choke cable from the carburettors (see Section 12).

5 Place a rag beneath the fuel supply union to the carburettors, then release the clip securing the fuel supply hose to the union and detach the hose **(see illustration)**. Be prepared to catch any residual fuel.

6 Release the tie securing the hoses at the back of the cylinder block **(see illustration)**. Where fitted, release the clips securing the carburettor heater hoses to the back of the cylinder head and the radiator neck, then detach the hoses **(see illustrations)**; be prepared to catch any residual coolant.

7 Release the idle speed adjuster from its bracket on the top of the clutch cover **(see illustration)**.

8 Disconnect the throttle position sensor wiring connector **(see illustration)**.

9 Using a long reach Allen key, fully loosen the clamps on the cylinder head intake stubs. Note that the clamp screws for Nos. 1, 2 and 3 cylinders are accessible from the front; the clamp screw for No. 4 cylinder is accessible

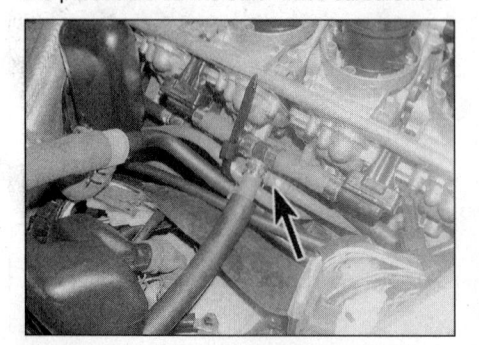

7.5 Detach the fuel supply hose to the carburettors at the union (arrowed)

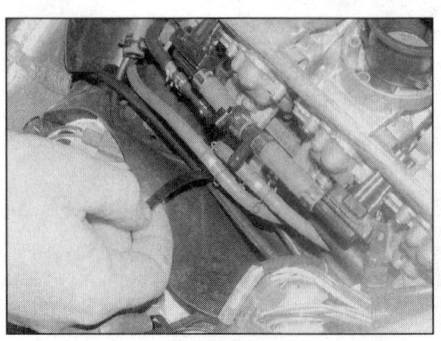

7.6a Release the tie securing the hoses . . .

7.6b . . . and detach the carburettor heater hose

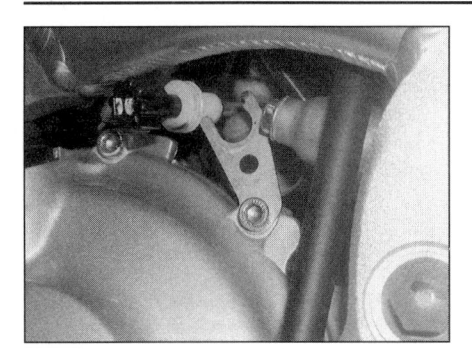

Fuel and exhaust systems 4•7

7.7 Detach the idle speed adjuster from its bracket ...

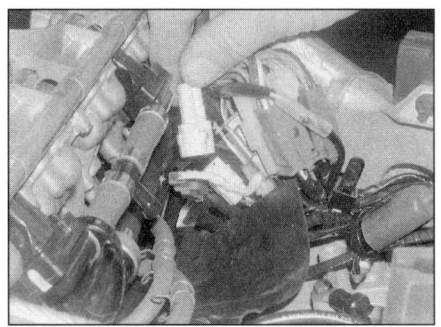

7.8 ... and disconnect the throttle position sensor wiring

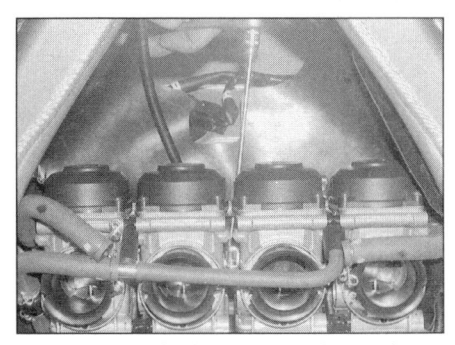

7.9a Access the intake stub clamps from the front ...

7.9b ... and the right-hand side with a long reach Allen key

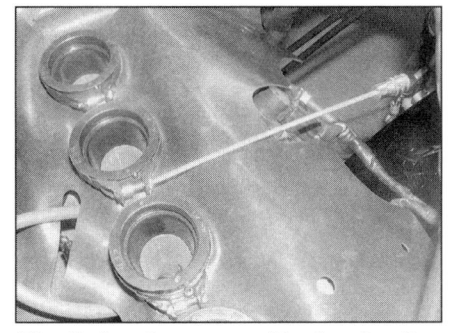

7.9c Carburettors removed to show location of stub clamps above the heat shield

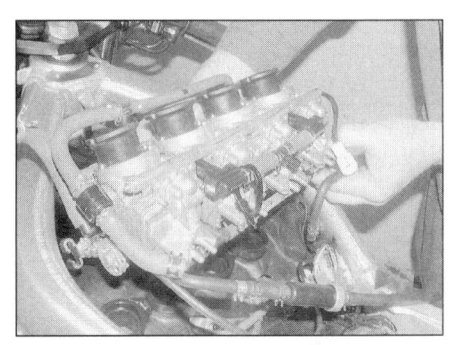

7.10 All four carburettors come off the stubs together

through the right-hand side of the frame **(see illustrations)**.

10 Ease the carburettors off the intake stubs and remove them **(see illustration)**. **Note:** *Keep the carburettors level to prevent fuel spillage from the float chambers and the possibility of the piston diaphragms being damaged.*

Caution: Stuff clean rag into each cylinder head intake after removing the carburettor to prevent anything from falling in.

11 Place a suitable container below the float chambers, then slacken the drain bolt on each chamber in turn and drain all the fuel from the carburettors. Tighten the drain screws securely once all the fuel has been drained.

Installation

12 Installation is the reverse of removal, noting the following.
● Check for cracks or splits in the cylinder

head intake stubs and replace them with new ones, if necessary.
● Make sure the carburettors are fully engaged with the cylinder head intake stubs – they can be difficult to engage, so a squirt of WD-40 or a smear of grease inside the stubs

will ease fitting. Make sure the clamps are positioned so their indents locate over the ridges on the stubs **(see illustration)**. Tighten the clamp screws securely.
● Make sure all hoses are correctly routed and secured and not trapped or kinked.

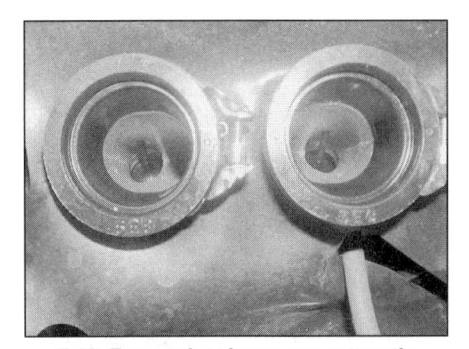

7.12 Ensure the clamps are correctly positioned before installing the carburettors

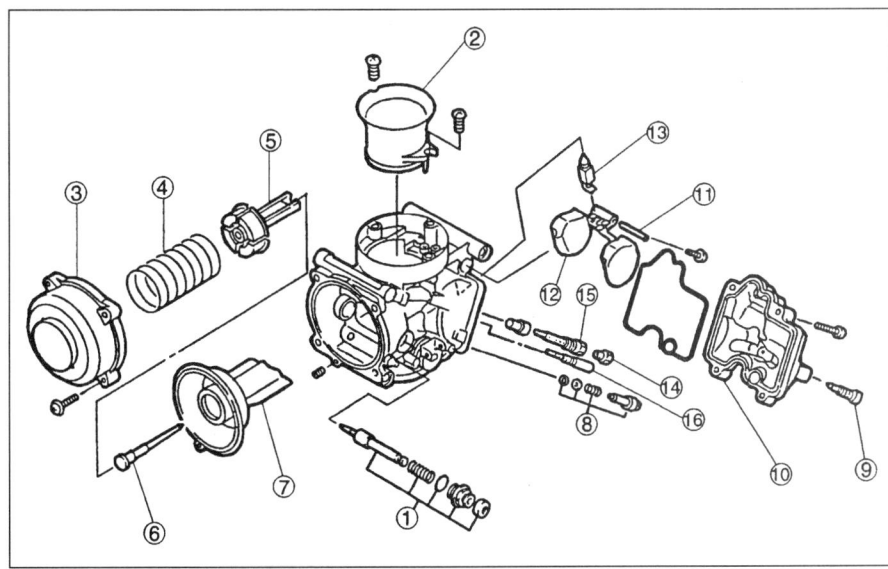

8.1 Carburettor components

1 Choke plunger assembly
2 Intake venturi
3 Top cover
4 Spring
5 Jet needle holder
6 Needle
7 Piston/slide
8 Pilot screw assembly
9 Drain bolt
10 Float chamber
11 Float pivot pin
12 Float
13 Needle valve
14 Main jet
15 Emulsion tube
16 Pilot jet

4•8 Fuel and exhaust systems

8.2a Unhook the choke linkage return spring . . .

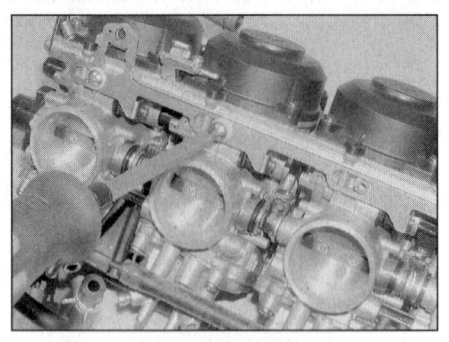

8.2b . . . then remove the screws . . .

8.2c . . . and the plastic washers

● Do not forget to connect the throttle position sensor wiring connector.
● Refer to Section 11 for installation of the throttle cables, and Section 12 for the choke cable. Check the operation of the cables and adjust them as necessary (see Chapter 1).
● Check idle speed and carburettor synchronisation and adjust as necessary (see Chapter 1).
● Refill the cooling system (see Chapter 1).

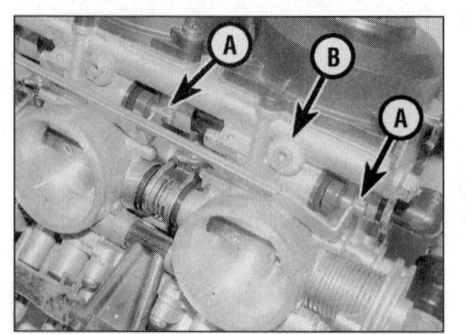

8.3 Remove the bar, noting how it fits on the choke plungers (A), and the washers (B)

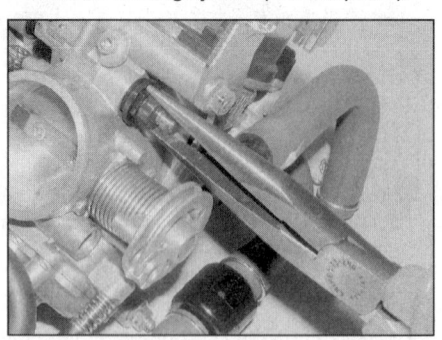

8.4a Unscrew the choke plunger nut . . .

8.4b . . . and withdraw the choke plunger assembly

8.5a Remove the carburettor top cover . . .

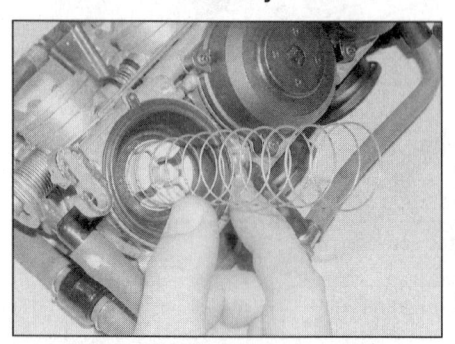

8.5b . . . then withdraw the spring

8.6a Note how the piston diaphragm locates around the air passage (arrowed) . . .

8.6b . . . and how the piston and slide locate in the carburettor body

8 Carburettors – disassembly, cleaning and inspection

> **Warning:** Refer to the precautions given in Section 1 before starting work.

Disassembly

1 Remove the carburettors from the machine as described in Section 7. **Note:** *Do not separate the carburettors unless absolutely necessary; each carburettor can be dismantled sufficiently for all normal cleaning and adjustments while in place on the mounting brackets. Dismantle the carburettors separately to avoid interchanging parts* **(see illustration on page 4•7).**

2 Unhook the choke linkage bar return spring, noting how it fits, then unscrew and remove the screws securing the linkage bar to the carburettors and remove the plastic washers **(see illustrations)**. **Note:** *On the machine photographed, only three of the carburettors were fitted with screws and washers.*

3 Remove the bar, noting how the forked tabs locate on the choke plungers, and remove the second set of plastic washers **(see illustration)**.

4 Unscrew the choke plunger nut, using a pair of thin-nosed pliers if access is too restricted for a spanner, and withdraw the plunger assembly from the carburettor body **(see illustrations)**. If any of the choke plungers are difficult to withdraw due to

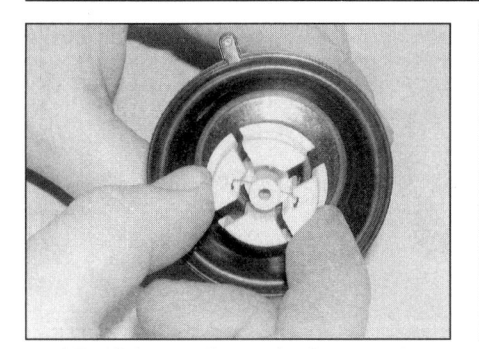

Fuel and exhaust systems 4•9

8.7a Squeeze the marked segments together to release the needle holder

8.7b Withdraw the jet needle from the top of the piston

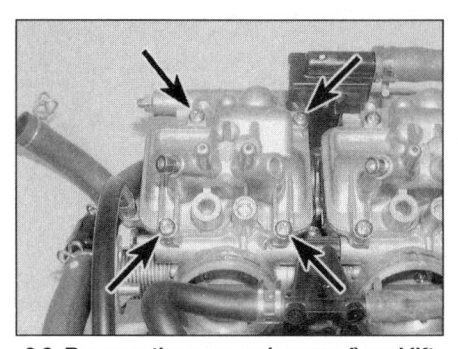

8.8 Remove the screws (arrowed) and lift off the float chamber

limited clearance, separate the carburettors as described in Section 10.

5 Unscrew and remove the top cover retaining screws and remove the cover, then remove the spring from inside the piston **(see illustrations)**.

6 Note how the tab on the piston diaphragm locates around the air passage in the carburettor body **(see illustration)**. Carefully peel the rim of the diaphragm out of its sealing groove and withdraw the piston assembly, noting how the piston and slide locate in the carburettor body **(see illustration)**.

Caution: Do not use a sharp instrument to displace the diaphragm from its groove, as it is easily damaged.

7 Squeeze the marked segments of the jet needle holder (marked with arrows) together and withdraw the needle holder from the piston, then push the jet needle up from the bottom of the piston and withdraw it from the top **(see illustrations)**.

8 Remove the screws securing the float chamber to the carburettor body and remove the float chamber, noting how it fits **(see illustration)**. Discard the gasket as a new one must be fitted on reassembly.

9 Unscrew and remove the screw retaining the float pivot pin and lift the float assembly out of the carburettor **(see illustrations)**. Remove the pivot pin if it is loose. Unhook the needle valve from the tab on the float, noting how it fits.

10 Unscrew and remove the pilot jet **(see illustration)**.

11 Unscrew and remove the main jet **(see illustration)**.

12 Unscrew and remove the emulsion tube **(see illustration)**.

13 Unscrew and remove the emulsion tube holder **(see illustration)**.

14 The pilot screw assembly can be removed from the carburettor if necessary, but note that its setting will be disturbed **(see Haynes Hint overleaf)**. Unscrew and remove the pilot screw along with its spring, washer and O-ring **(see illustration)**. Individual components are not available separately and the pilot screw assembly has to be renewed as a set.

8.9a Remove the retaining screw (arrowed) . . .

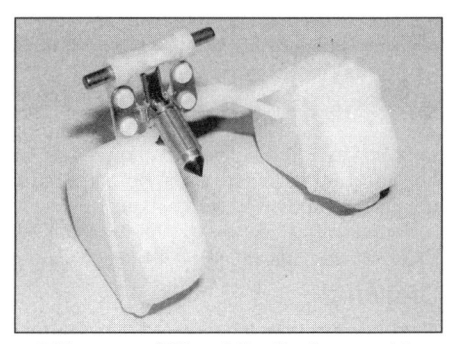

8.9b . . . and lift out the float assembly

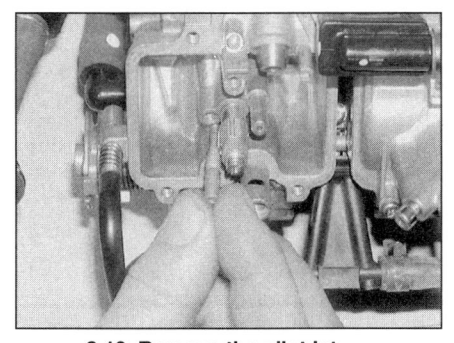

8.10 Remove the pilot jet . . .

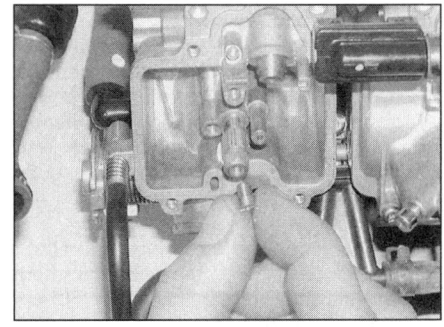

8.11 . . . the main jet . . .

8.12 . . . the emulsion tube . . .

8.13 . . . and the emulsion tube holder

8.14 Remove the pilot screw assembly (arrowed) only if necessary

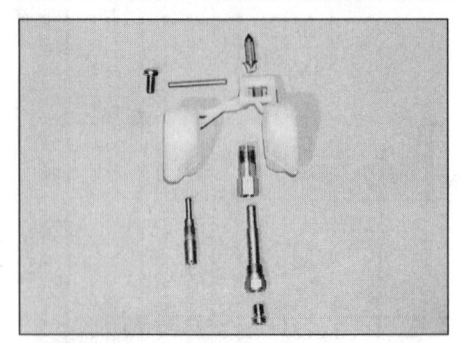

4•10 Fuel and exhaust systems

8.16 Clean the carburettor components carefully to remove varnish – never clean the jets with wire

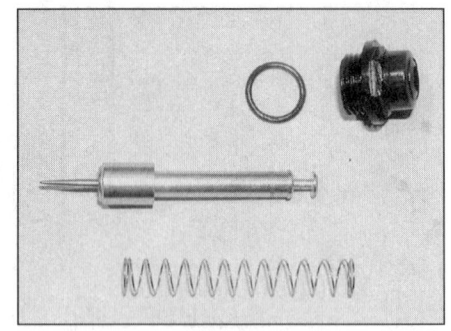

8.18 Components of the choke plunger assembly

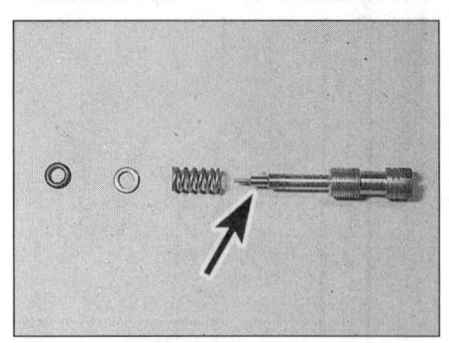

8.19 Check the tapered portion (arrowed) of the pilot screw for wear

> **HAYNES HINT**
> To record the pilot screw's current setting, turn the screw in until it seats lightly, counting the number of turns necessary to achieve this, then fully unscrew it. On installation, the screw is simply backed out the number of turns you've recorded.

15 A throttle position sensor is mounted on the outside of the right-hand carburettor. Do not remove the sensor from the carburettor unless it is known to be faulty and is being replaced with a new one. Refer to Chapter 5 for check and adjustment of the sensor.

Cleaning

Caution: Use only a dedicated carburettor cleaner or petroleum-based solvent for carburettor cleaning. Do not use caustic cleaners.

16 Soak the carburettor body and individual components in the cleaner to loosen and dissolve the varnish and other deposits (always check the directions for use of solvent products, especially when applying them to non-metallic items) **(see illustration)**. Then use a nylon-bristle brush to remove the stubborn deposits, rinse, and dry the components with compressed air.

17 Use compressed air to blow out all the fuel and air passages in the carburettor body and the jets and emulsion tube.

Caution: Never clean the jets or passages with a piece of wire or a drill bit, as they will be enlarged, causing the fuel and air metering rates to be upset.

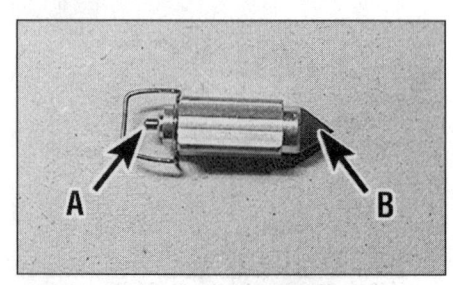

Inspection

18 Check the operation of the choke plunger assembly. If it doesn't move smoothly, inspect the needle on the end of the plunger, the spring and the plunger linkage bar **(see illustration)**. Replace the plunger assembly with a new one if any component is worn, damaged or bent – individual parts are not available.

19 If removed, check the tapered portion of the pilot screw and the spring and O-ring for wear or damage **(see illustration)**. Replace the pilot screw assembly with a new one if necessary – individual parts are not available.

20 Check the carburettor body, float chamber and top cover for cracks, distorted sealing surfaces and other damage. If any defects are found, replace the faulty component with a new one, although replacement of the entire carburettor may be necessary (check with a Yamaha dealer on the availability of separate components).

21 Check the piston diaphragm for splits, holes, creases and general deterioration. Holding it up to a light will help to reveal defects of this nature. Replace it with a new one if necessary.

22 Insert the piston into the carburettor body and check that it moves up and down smoothly. Check the surface of the piston and slide for wear. If it is worn excessively or doesn't move smoothly in the body, replace it with a new one.

23 Check the jet needle for straightness by rolling it on a flat surface such as a piece of glass. Replace it with a new one if it is bent, or if the tip is worn.

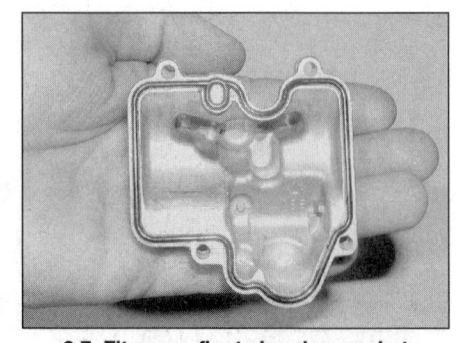

8.24 Check the valve's spring loaded plunger (A) and tip (B)

9.7 Fit a new float chamber gasket

24 Check the tip of the float needle valve for grooves or scratches or other signs of wear. Gently push down on the plunger on the top of the valve then release it – it should spring back immediately. If any defects are found, replace the needle valve with a new one **(see illustration)**

25 Check the float for damage. This will usually be apparent by the presence of fuel inside the float. If the float is damaged, replace it with a new one.

26 Operate the throttle shaft to make sure the throttle butterfly valve opens and closes smoothly. If it doesn't, cleaning the throttle linkage may help. Otherwise, renew the carburettor.

9 Carburettors – reassembly and fuel level check

⚠️ **Warning: Refer to the precautions given in Section 1 before proceeding.**

Note: *When reassembling the carburettors renew all O-rings and seals. Do not overtighten the carburettor jets and screws, as they are easily damaged.*

Reassembly

1 If removed, install the pilot screw along with its spring, washer and O-ring, turning it in until it seats lightly. Now, turn the screw out the number of turns previously recorded, or as specified at the beginning of this Chapter if a new screw is being fitted.

2 Install the tube holder **(see illustration 8.13)**.

3 Install the emulsion tube **(see illustration 8.12)**.

4 Install the main jet **(see illustration 8.11)**.

5 Install the pilot jet **(see illustration 8.10)**.

6 If removed, install the float pivot pin. Hook the float needle valve onto the tab on the float assembly, then position the float assembly in the carburettor, making sure the needle valve locates in its seat. Install the retaining screw and tighten it securely **(see illustration 8.9b and a)**.

7 Fit a new gasket onto the float chamber, making sure it is seated properly in its groove, then install the chamber on the carburettor and tighten its screws securely **(see illustration)**.

Fuel and exhaust systems 4•11

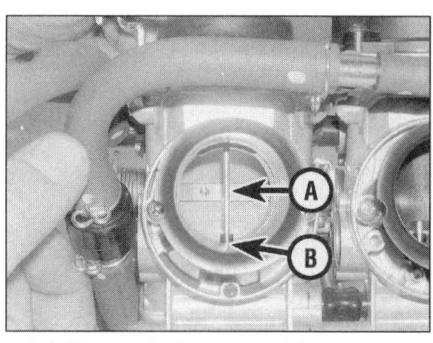

9.8 Ensure the jet needle (A) is aligned with the needle jet (B)

8 Fit the jet needle into the piston, then install the needle holder, pressing the holder down until it clicks into place in the piston. Slide the piston assembly into the carburettor, making sure the needle is correctly aligned with the needle jet **(see illustration)**.

9 Align the tab on the piston diaphragm with the air passage in the carburettor body and press the rim of the diaphragm into its groove, making sure it is correctly seated **(see illustration 8.6a)**.

10 Fit the spring into the piston and into the recess in the top cover, then fit the cover onto the carburettor and tighten the screws securely **(see illustrations 8.5b and a)**. Check that the piston moves smoothly in the carburettor body by pushing it up with your finger; note that the piston should descend slowly and smoothly as the diaphragm draws air into the chamber – it should not drop sharply under spring pressure.

11 Fit the choke plunger assembly into the carburettor body and tighten it securely **(see illustration 8.4b and a)**. Install the plastic washers for the choke linkage bar, then fit the bar, making sure the tabs locate correctly on each choke plunger. Fit the second set of washers and install the screws, tightening them securely. Fit the linkage bar return spring and check the operation of the mechanism **(see illustrations 8.3 and 8.2a, b and c)**.

12 Install the carburettors. If new float assembly components have been fitted check the fuel level (see below).

Fuel level check

13 To check the fuel level, position the motorcycle on level ground and support it using an auxiliary stand so that it is vertical. If not already done, remove the fuel tank (see Section 2) and the air filter housing (see Section 4), then arrange a temporary fuel supply to the carburettors.

14 Yamaha produce a fuel level gauge (Part No. 90890-01312 for Europe, or YM-01312-A for USA), or alternatively a suitable length of clear plastic tubing can be used. Attach the gauge or tubing to the drain hose union on the bottom of the float chamber of No. 1 carburettor and secure the calibrated section vertically alongside the carburettors **(see illustration)**.

15 Turn the fuel supply ON and slacken the

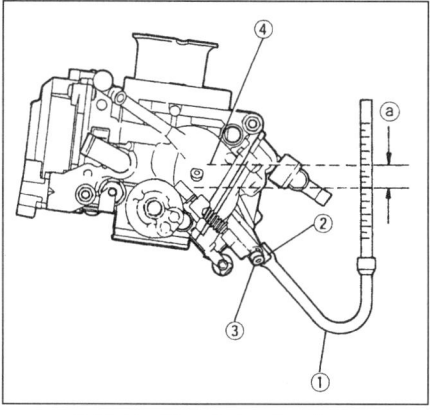

9.14 Fuel level check set-up

1 Gauge assembly
2 Union
3 Drain screw
4 Level line on casting
a) Fuel level measurement

drain screw to allow the fuel to flow into the tube. The level at which the fuel stabilises in the tubing indicates the level of the fuel in the float chamber of No. 1 carburettor. Refer to the Specifications at the beginning of this Chapter and measure the level relative to the fuel level line on the casting.

16 If the level is incorrect, detach the fuel supply and drain the carburettors, then remove the float from the chamber (see Section 8), and adjust the float height by carefully bending the float tab **(see illustration)** a little at a time until the correct height is obtained. Repeat the

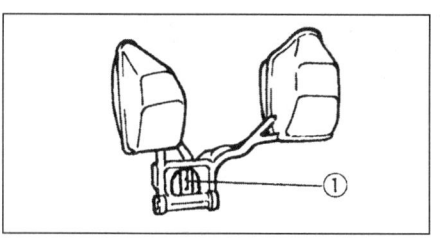

9.16 Adjust fuel level by bending the float tab (1)

procedure for the other carburettors. **Note:** *Bending the tab up lowers the fuel level – bending it down raises the fuel level.*

10 Carburettors – separation and joining

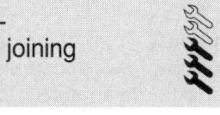

⚠ **Warning: Refer to the precautions given in Section 1 before proceeding.**

Separation

1 The carburettors do not need to be separated for normal overhaul. If you need to separate them (to replace a carburettor body with a new one, for example), refer to the following procedure.

2 Remove the carburettors from the machine (see Section 7). Mark the body of each carburettor with its cylinder location to ensure that it is positioned correctly on reassembly **(see illustration)**.

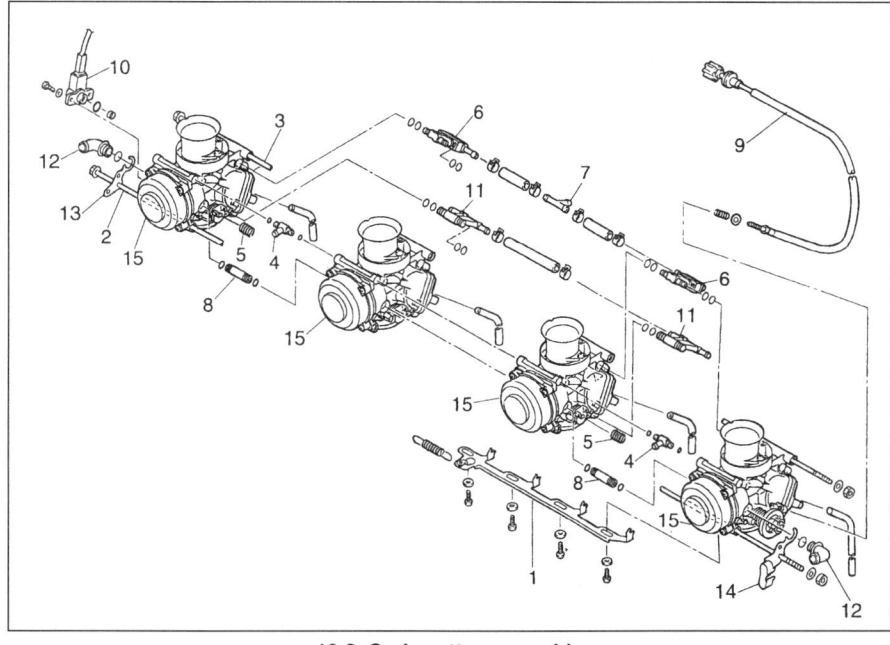

10.2 Carburettor assembly

1 Choke linkage bar
2 Connecting bolt
3 Connecting bolt
4 Hose joint
5 Spring
6 Fuel pipe joint
7 Fuel pipe union
8 Joint pipe
9 Idle adjuster
10 Throttle position sensor
11 Heater pipe joint
12 Balance pipe
13 Balance pipe bracket
14 Throttle cable bracket
15 Carburettor body

4•12 Fuel and exhaust systems

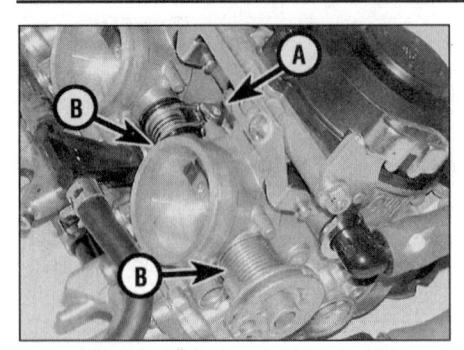

10.3a Note the arrangement of the synchronisation (A) and linkage springs (B) . . .

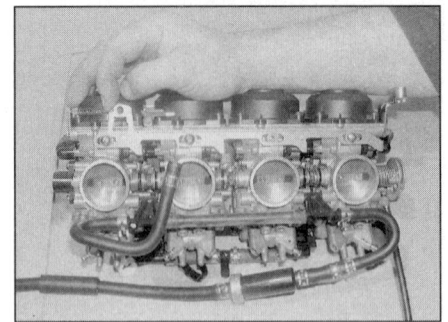

10.3b . . . and the fuel, heater and vent hose unions

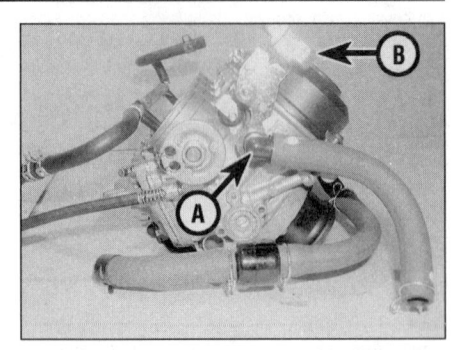

10.11 Ensure the balance pipe (A) and throttle cable (B) brackets are in place before tightening the through-bolt nuts

3 Make a note of how the throttle linkage springs and synchronisation springs and screws are arranged, to ensure that they are fitted correctly on reassembly (see illustration). Also note the arrangement of the fuel supply and heater unions, and the vacuum chamber and float chamber vent unions (see illustration).

4 Remove the choke linkage bar (see Section 8). Grip the clips on the fuel and heater hoses and slide them off the union/hose joints to a mid-way point between adjacent carburettors.

5 The carburettors are held together by two long bolts which pass through them from the right-hand side (see illustration 10.2). Unscrew and remove the nuts and the throttle cable bracket, then withdraw the bolts carefully; remove any spacers from between the carburettors, noting which fits where. Slide the spacers back onto the bolts in the order of assembly and remove the balance pipe bracket from the No. 4 carburettor.

6 Gently separate No. 1 and No. 2 carburettors, noting how the throttle linkage is connected and how the throttle lever engages on the synchronising screw. Ease the hoses off the fuel and heater unions, then pull the fuel, heater and vent unions out of the carburettor body(s). Note that the fuel and heater unions have two O-rings on each branch to the carburettor(s) and the vent unions have one O-ring on each branch. The O-rings should be renewed on reassembly.

7 If required, unscrew the idle speed adjuster and remove it from the No. 1 carburettor. Note the spring and washer on the end of the cable.

8 Repeat the procedure in Step 6, separating Nos. 2 and 3 carburettors, and Nos. 3 and 4 carburettors in turn as required.

Joining

9 Fit new O-rings onto the fuel, heater and vent unions. Lubricate the O-rings with a light film of oil and install the unions in their respective locations, making sure they seat completely. Also fit the hose joints.

10 Position the coil springs between the carburettors, gently push the carburettors together, then make sure the throttle linkages are correctly engaged. Check the fuel, heater and vent unions to make sure they have engaged properly.

11 Install the balance pipe bracket on No. 4 carburettor and install the two through-bolts with their spacers (where fitted). Install the throttle cable bracket and the through-bolt nuts, and tighten the nuts finger-tight (see illustration).

12 Engage the throttle levers with the synchronising screws, then operate the throttle cable pulley by hand to check that all the linkages are correctly engaged (see illustration).

13 Install the choke linkage bar (see Section 9). Install the fuel and heater hoses and secure them with their clips.

14 Set the carburettor assembly on a surface plate or sheet of glass, intake manifold side down, to check alignment; loosen the through-bolt nuts if necessary to adjust the alignment. Press down evenly on the assembly and tighten the through-bolt nuts to the torque setting specified at the beginning of this Chapter.

15 If removed, install the idle speed adjuster. Check the operation of the throttle and choke mechanisms and make sure they both operate smoothly, and return quickly under spring pressure. Visually check the synchronisation of the throttle butterfly valves (see illustration). If necessary, adjust the synchronising screws to equalise the clearance between the butterfly valves and the throttle bores of each carburettor.

16 Install the carburettors (see Section 7) and check carburettor synchronisation and idle speed (see Chapter 1).

10.12 Operate the throttle pulley to ensure all the linkages are engaged

10.15 Check the synchronisation of the throttle butterfly valves

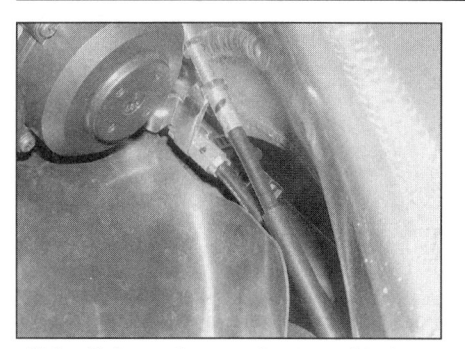

Fuel and exhaust systems 4•13

11.3a Release the accelerator cable from the bracket . . .

11.3b . . . and detach the cable nipple (arrowed) from the pulley

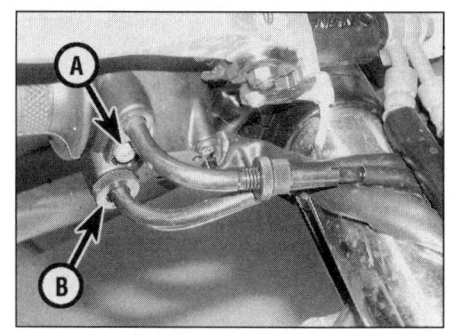

11.5a Unscrew the accelerator cable elbow retaining screw (A) and decelerator cable lockring (B)

11 Throttle cables – removal and installation

Warning: Refer to the precautions given in Section 1 before proceeding.

Removal

1 Remove the fuel tank (see Section 2), the air filter housing (see Section 4), the left-hand fairing side panel and the left-hand frame side panel (see Chapter 8).
2 Label each cable according to its location at both ends. If new cables are being fitted, match them to the old cables to ensure they are correctly installed.
3 Slacken the nuts on the accelerator (opening) cable adjuster either side of the cable bracket on the left-hand side of the carburettors and release the cable from the bracket. Detach the cable nipple from the throttle pulley **(see illustrations)**.
4 Slacken the locknut on the end of the decelerator (closing) cable and release the cable from the bracket, then detach the cable nipple from the throttle pulley. Withdraw both cables from the machine, noting the correct routing of each cable.
5 Remove the screw retaining the accelerator cable elbow to the twistgrip and unscrew the decelerator cable lockring. Remove the twistgrip/switch unit screws and separate the halves of the unit **(see illustrations)**. Detach both cable nipples from the throttle pulley and withdraw the cables from the unit **(see illustration)**.

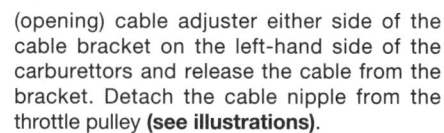

Installation

6 Lubricate the cable nipples with multi-purpose grease and install the ends of the cables through the lower half of the twistgrip into the throttle pulley. Fit the cable elbows into the unit, making sure they locate correctly, tighten the decelerator cable lockring finger-tight and install the accelerator cable elbow retaining screw. Join the unit halves, making sure the pin in the upper half locates in the hole in the handlebar, and tighten the screws **(see illustration)**.
7 Feed the cables through to the carburettors, making sure they are correctly routed. The cables must not interfere with any other component and should not be kinked or bent sharply.
8 Lubricate the accelerator cable nipple with multi-purpose grease and fit it into the upper socket on the carburettor throttle pulley, then fit the accelerator cable adjuster into the upper bracket **(see illustrations 11.3b and a)**. Lubricate the decelerator cable nipple with multi-purpose grease and fit it into the lower socket on the pulley, then fit the decelerator cable into the bracket and tighten the locknut **(see illustration)**. Adjust the throttle cables as described in Chapter 1 to obtain the correct amount of twistgrip freeplay.
9 Operate the throttle to check that it opens and closes freely. Turn the handlebars back and forth to make sure the cables don't cause the steering to bind.
10 Tighten the decelerator cable lock ring and the accelerator cable elbow screw, then install the remaining components in the reverse order of removal.
11 Start the engine and check that the idle speed does not rise as the handlebars are turned. If it does, the throttle cables are routed incorrectly. Correct the problem before riding the motorcycle.

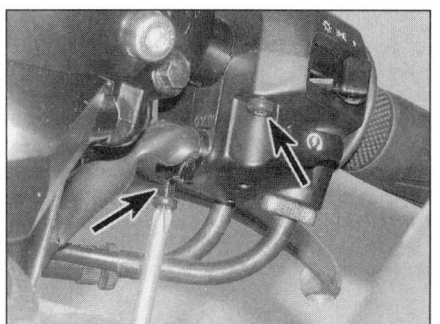

11.5b Remove the screws (arrowed) and split the twistgrip/switch unit . . .

11.5c . . . then detach the cable nipples

11.6 Pin (arrowed) locates in handlebar

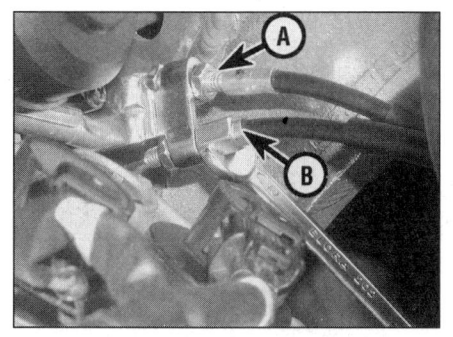

11.8 Install the accelerator (A) and decelerator (B) cables in the bracket

12 Choke cable – removal and installation

Removal

1 Remove the fuel tank (see Section 2) and the air filter housing (see Section 4).

4•14 Fuel and exhaust systems

12.2a Free the choke cable from its bracket (arrowed) . . .

12.2b . . . then detach the cable nipple . . .

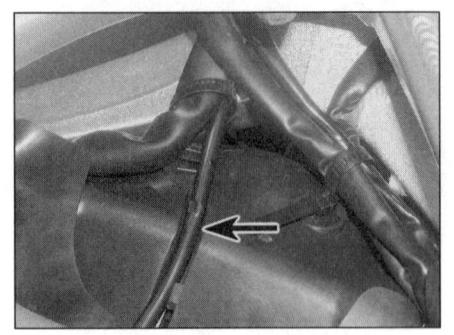

12.2c . . . and unclip the cable (arrowed) from the radiator cover

12.3a Remove the screws (arrowed) . . .

12.3b . . . and split the switch/choke lever unit

2 Slacken the choke outer cable bracket screw and free the cable from the bracket on the front of the carburettors, then detach the inner cable nipple from the choke linkage bar **(see illustrations)**. Unclip the cable from the channel in the radiator cover and withdraw the cable from the machine, noting the correct routing **(see illustration)**.
3 Unscrew the two handlebar switch/choke lever unit screws and separate the two halves of the unit **(see illustrations)**.
4 Separate the cable elbow and choke lever from the unit, noting how they fit, and detach the cable nipple from the lever **(see illustration)**.

Installation

5 Lubricate the cable nipple with multi-purpose grease and attach it to the choke lever **(see illustrations 12.4)**. Fit the lever and cable elbow into the unit, then fit the two halves of the unit onto the handlebar, making sure the lever fits correctly, and the pin in the front half of the unit locates in the hole in the front of the handlebar **(see illustration)**. Install the screws and tighten them securely **(see illustration 12.3a)**.

6 Install the cable, making sure it is correctly routed. The cable must not interfere with any other component and should not be kinked or bent sharply.
7 Lubricate the cable nipple with multi-purpose grease and attach it to the choke linkage bar on the carburettors **(see illustration 12.2b)**. Fit the outer cable into its bracket, making sure there is a small amount of freeplay in the inner cable, and tighten the screw.
8 Check the operation of the choke cable (see Chapter 1), then clip the cable into the channel in the radiator cover.
9 Install the remaining components in the reverse order of removal.

13 Exhaust system – removal and installation

⚠️ *Warning: If the engine has been running the exhaust system will be very hot. Allow the system to cool before carrying out any work.*

Silencer

1 Remove the lower fairing (see Chapter 8).

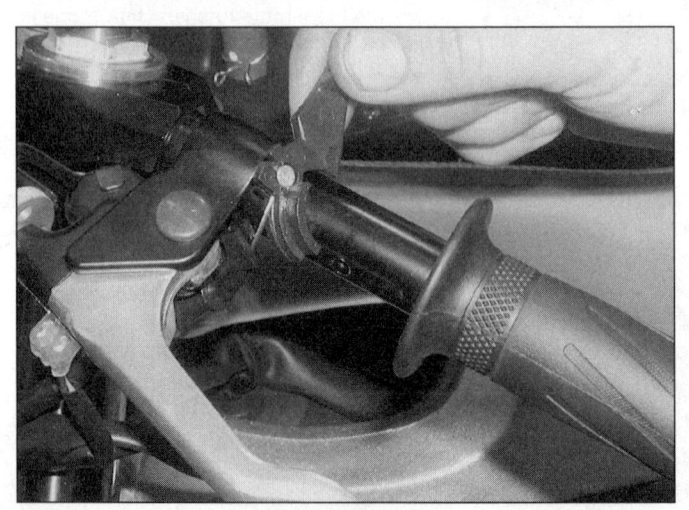

12.4 Separate the choke lever from the unit and detach the cable nipple

12.5 Pin (arrowed) locates in handlebar

Fuel and exhaust systems 4•15

13.1 Loosen the silencer clamp bolt

13.2a Undo the silencer mounting bolt . . .

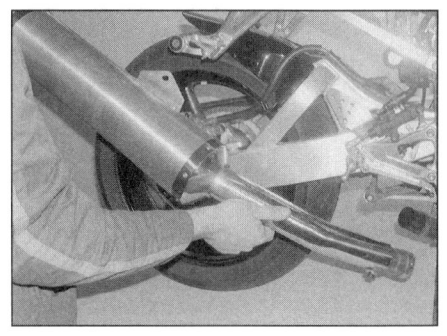

13.2b . . . and pull the silencer off the pipe

Loosen the clamp bolt securing the silencer to the exhaust system **(see illustration)**.

2 Unscrew and remove the silencer mounting nut and bolt, then pull the silencer off the exhaust pipe **(see illustrations)**. Remove the sealing ring from inside the end of the silencer and discard it, as a new one should be fitted on reassembly **(see illustration)**.

3 Check the condition of the silencer mounting rubber bush in the footrest bracket and replace it with a new one if it is damaged, deformed or deteriorated **(see illustration)**. Check that the spacer is fitted inside the bush.

4 Fit the new sealing ring into the end of the silencer and press it up against the internal ridge **(see illustration)**. Fit the silencer onto the exhaust pipe, making sure it is pushed fully home. Align the silencer bracket with the mounting bracket and install the bolt; tighten the nut finger-tight **(see illustration)**.

5 Tighten the clamp bolt first, then the silencer mounting nut and bolt, to the torque settings specified at the beginning of this Chapter **(see illustration)**.

6 Run the engine and check the system for leaks; remedy any defects before installing the lower fairing (see Chapter 8).

Complete system

Removal

7 Remove the lower fairing and the fairing side panels (see Chapter 8), and the radiator (see Chapter 3). Slacken the silencer mounting nut and bolt but do not remove

them yet. Unscrew the bolt securing the rear of the exhaust system to the hanging bracket behind the engine unit **(see illustration)**.

8 Unscrew the eight downpipe flange nuts

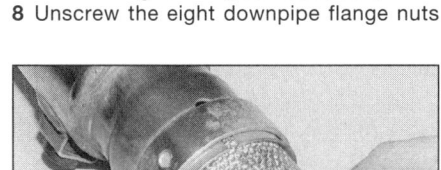

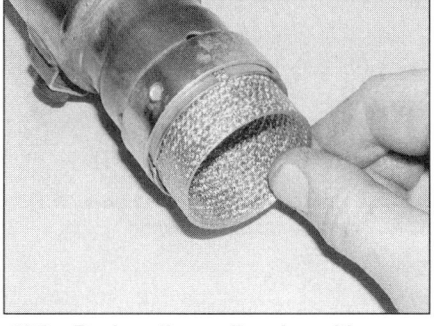

13.2c Replace the sealing ring with a new one

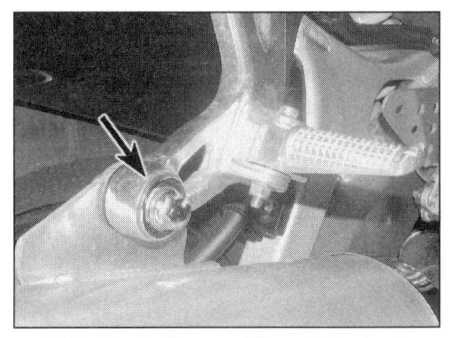

13.4a Press the new seal in against the internal ridge

13.5 Counter-hold the nut (arrowed) while tightening the bolt

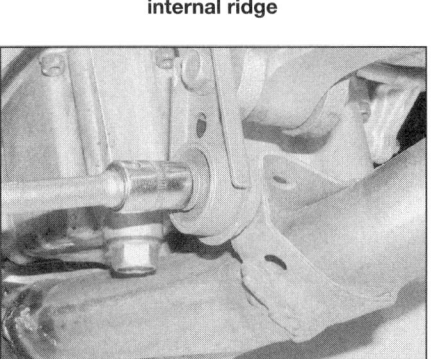

13.7 Detach the rear of the exhaust system from the hanging bracket

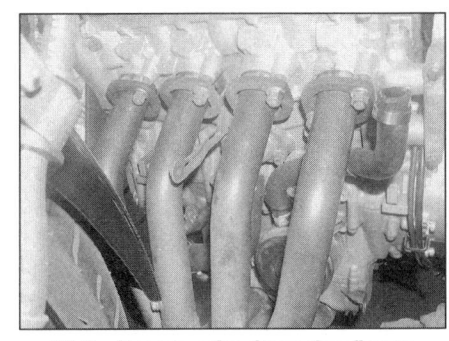

and draw the flanges off the studs **(see illustrations)**.

9 Supporting the system, remove the silencer mounting nut and bolt, then pull the

13.3 Check the condition of the bush (arrowed) inside the silencer bracket

13.4b Push the silencer fully home on the pipe

13.8a Unscrew the downpipe flange nuts . . .

4•16 Fuel and exhaust systems

13.8b ... and pull the flanges off the studs

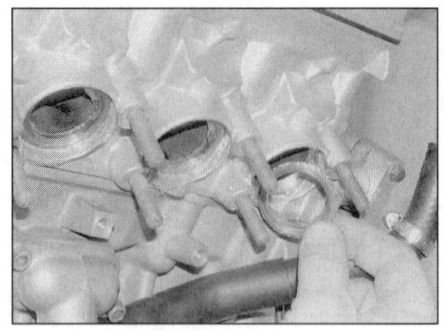

13.13 Install new gaskets in the exhaust ports

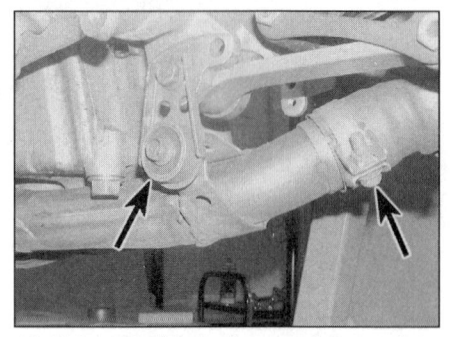

13.14 Install all bolts (arrowed) finger-tight to start with

downpipes away from the cylinder head and remove the complete system.

10 Remove the gasket from each port in the cylinder head and discard it, as a new one must be fitted.

Installation

11 Check the condition of the silencer mounting rubber bush in the footrest bracket and replace it with a new one if it is damaged, deformed or deteriorated **(see illustration 13.3)**. Check that the spacer is fitted inside the bush. Check the condition of the rubber bushing in the hanging bracket and fit a new bracket if the bushing is deformed or deteriorated.

12 Scrape any excess carbon out of the downpipe recesses in the cylinder head and clean any corrosion off the flange studs. Lubricate the flange studs with copper based grease.

13 Fit a new gasket into each of the cylinder head ports **(see illustration)**. If necessary, apply a smear of grease to the gaskets to keep them in place whilst fitting the downpipes.

14 Manoeuvre the exhaust system into position so that the head of each downpipe is located in its recess in the cylinder head. Install the silencer mounting nut and bolt and the rear exhaust system bolt, but do not tighten them yet **(see illustration)**.

15 Locate the downpipe flanges onto the studs, then fit the nuts and tighten them to the torque setting specified at the beginning of this Chapter **(see illustration)**. Now tighten the other bolts to the specified torques.

16 Install the radiator (see Chapter 3), then run the engine and check that there are no exhaust gas leaks. Remedy any defects before installing the fairing panels (see Chapter 8).

14 Fuel pump and relay – check, removal and installation

⚠️ **Warning: Refer to the precautions given in Section 1 before starting work.**

Check

1 The fuel pump is powered by the ignition control unit via the fuel pump relay. It will run whenever the ignition is switched ON and the ignition is operative (i.e. only when the engine is turning over). As soon as the ignition is killed, power to its relay is cut off so that there is no risk of fuel being sprayed out under pressure in the event of an accident.

2 The fuel pump is mounted inside the right-hand side of the frame alongside the rear shock absorber **(see illustration)**. If fuel is not being delivered to the carburettors, first check that fuel is flowing from the tank to the pump. Raise the front of the fuel tank (see Section 2) and turn the tap OFF, then release the clip securing the fuel supply hose to the pump and disconnect the hose at the pump. Place the end of the hose in a container suitable for holding petrol (gasoline), turn the fuel tap ON and lower the tank back into place. Fuel should flow into the container; if it does not, check the tank breather hose and fuel system for blockages (see Section 2). Turn the fuel tap OFF, then reconnect the hose to the pump and secure it with the clip.

3 If fuel is reaching the pump, check the components of the fuel pump system in the following order. Remove the fuel tank (see Section 2) and check the main and ignition fuses, the pump wiring (see Chapter 9) and the battery condition (see Chapter 9). If they are all good, identify the relay assembly unit which is mounted near the battery under the rider's seat, disconnect its multi-pin connector and check for loose or corroded connections or physical damage **(see illustration)**.

4 The relay assembly is a sealed unit – it houses the fuel pump relay, starter interlock relay and diodes. To check the operation of the relay, disconnect its wire connector and remove the relay from the motorcycle **(see illustration 14.3)**. First connect a multimeter set to the ohms x 100 range, or a continuity tester, between the blue/black and red/black wire terminals of the relay. There should be no continuity.

5 Leave the multimeter or continuity tester connected to the relay. Now, using a fully charged 12V battery and two suitable jumper wires, connect the battery positive (+ve) terminal to the relay's red/black wire terminal and the battery negative (–ve) terminal to the relay's blue/red wire terminal. With voltage applied, the test equipment should show

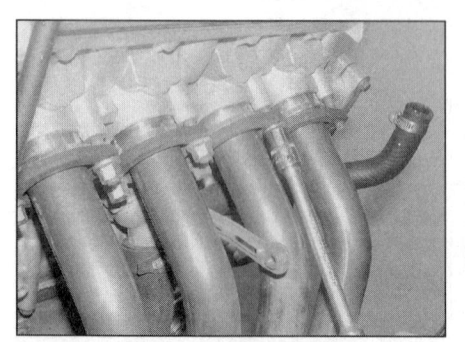

13.15 Tighten the flange nuts to the specified torque

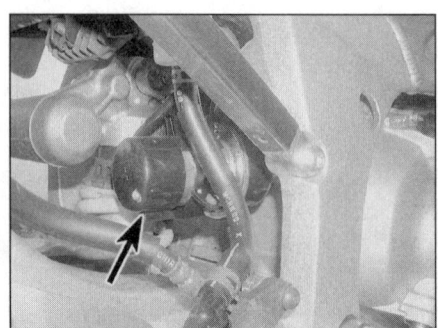

14.2 The fuel pump (arrowed) is located on the right-hand side of the rear shock

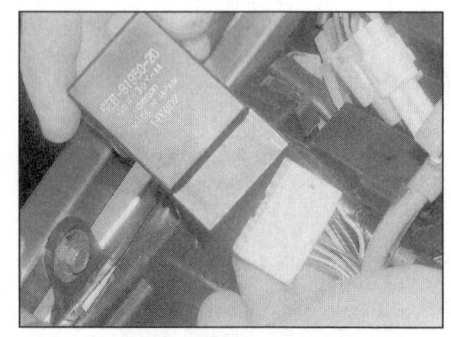

14.3 Check the relay assembly for loose connections

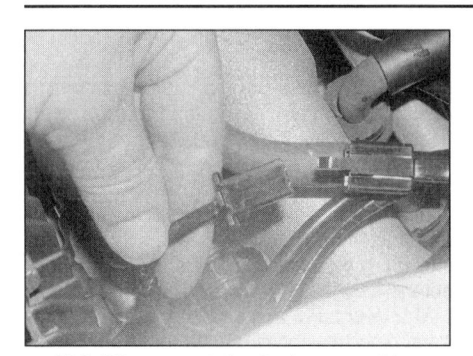

Fuel and exhaust systems 4•17

14.6 Disconnect the fuel pump wiring connector

14.7a Disconnect the fuel hose to the carburettors (arrowed)

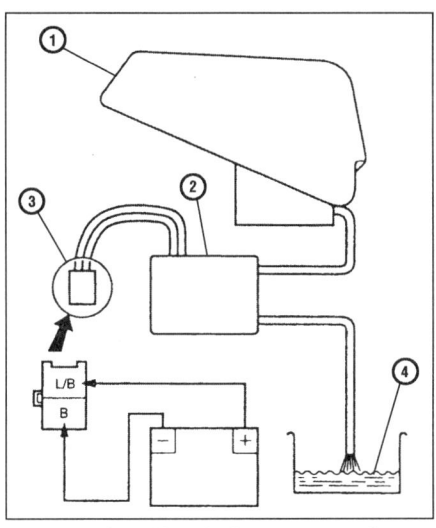

14.7b Checking fuel pump operation

1 Fuel tank
2 Fuel pump
3 Wiring connector
4 Suitable container

continuity. If it doesn't, replace the relay assembly with a new one.

6 To check the fuel pump, first test the fuel pump's resistance with the multimeter set to ohms. Trace the wiring from the pump and disconnect it at the connector **(see illustration)**. Connect the multimeter positive (+ve) probe to the pump's blue/black terminal, and the negative (–ve) probe to the pump's black terminal. If the reading is not as specified at the beginning of this Chapter, replace the pump with a new one.

7 To check the pump's operation, release the clip securing the fuel delivery hose (pump to carburettors) to the pump and disconnect the hose at the pump **(see illustration)**. Connect a length of fuel hose to the pump and secure it with a clip; place the end of the hose in a container suitable for storing petrol (gasoline) **(see illustration)**.

8 Use jumper wires to connect the battery positive (+ve) terminal to the pump's blue/black terminal and the battery negative (–ve) terminal to the pump's black terminal. Fuel should flow into the container; if it doesn't, replace the pump with a new one.

Removal

9 Make sure the ignition is switched OFF. Remove the fuel tank (see Section 2), then trace the wiring from the fuel pump and disconnect it at the connector **(see illustration 14.6)**. Disconnect the cable tie securing the pump wiring to the wiring loom.

10 Make a note of which fuel hose fits where (supply from the tank and delivery to the carburettors) as an aid to installation. Using a rag to mop up any spilled fuel, release the clips securing the hoses to the pump and disconnect the hoses. Unscrew the bolts securing the pump to the frame and remove the pump and its mounting sleeve **(see illustration 14.7a)**. Separate the pump from the sleeve.

11 To remove the relay assembly, disconnect the battery negative (–ve) lead, then displace the relay from its mounting and disconnect the wiring connector **(see illustration 14.3)**.

Installation

12 Installation is a reverse of the removal procedure. Make sure the fuel hoses are fitted correctly and secured to the pump with the clips. Secure the relay assembly with its clip and secure the pump wiring with its clip. Start the engine and check carefully that there are no leaks at the hose connections.

15 Fuel warning light and sender – check and renewal

Check

1 When the ignition is first switched ON, or while the engine is running, the ignition control unit performs its own self-diagnosis of the fuel level warning circuit. If a fault occurs, the tachometer will display zero rpm for 3 seconds, then the condition code '8000 rpm' for 2.5 seconds, then the actual engine speed for 3 seconds, whereupon it will repeat the cycle until the engine is switched OFF. If the engine is not running, the engine speed is displayed as zero rpm.

2 The circuit consists of the sender mounted in the fuel tank and the warning light LED mounted in the instrument panel. If the system malfunctions, check first that the battery is fully charged and that the fuses are good.

3 To check the fuel sender, remove the fuel tank (see Section 2). Using a multimeter, check for continuity between the green and black terminals on the sender side of the wiring connector coming from the fuel tank **(see illustration 2.6)**. There should be continuity. If not, replace the sender with a new one (see below).

4 Check all the relevant wiring and wiring connectors (see Chapter 9), referring to the Wiring Diagrams at the end of Chapter 9.

5 Check the warning light LED (see Chapter 9). If the LED has failed, take the instrument cluster to a Yamaha dealer for further assessment. The instrument cluster is a sealed unit and in the event of a component failure a new cluster may have to be fitted.

Renewal

6 Refer to Chapter 9 for removal of the instrument cluster.

7 To renew the sender, remove the fuel tank (see Section 2) and drain it. Remove the screws securing the sender and draw it out of the tank **(see illustration)**. Fit a new O-ring onto the new sender and install it in the tank, then tighten the screws to the torque setting specified at the beginning of this Chapter **(see illustration)**.

8 Install the tank (see Section 2), and check carefully that there are no fuel leaks. Rectify any leaks immediately.

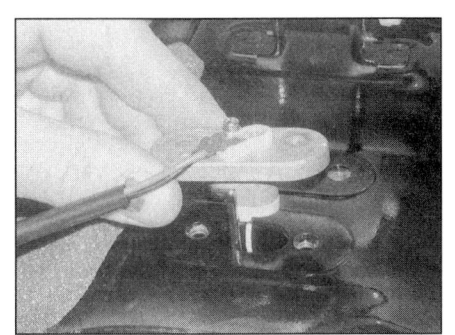

15.7a Undo the fixing screws and pull the sender out of the fuel tank

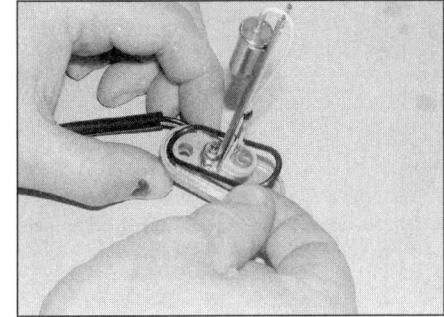

15.7b Fit a new O-ring before installing the sender

4•18 Fuel and exhaust systems

16 Air induction system (AIS) – function, disassembly and reassembly

Function

1 The air induction system (AIS) is fitted to California models **(see illustration 16.1)**. The system sucks fresh air into the exhaust ports where it burns unburnt gases, thereby reducing the emission of hydrocarbons into the atmosphere. Reed valves control the flow of air into the ports, opening when there is negative pressure, and preventing exhaust gases flowing back into the AIS. An air cut-off valve is operated by intake manifold pressure and shuts off the flow of air during deceleration, preventing backfiring.

Disassembly

2 Remove the fairing side panels (see Chapter 8) and the exhaust system (see Section 13).

3 To remove the air cut-off valve, disconnect the large-bore hose which goes to the air filter housing, the small-bore vacuum hose which goes to No. 3 carburettor, then the two short hoses which link the cut-off valve to the reed valves. Release the air cut-off valve from its retaining clip and rubber damper.

4 Inspect the air cut-off valve for signs of damage; inspect the hoses and clips and renew any parts that are damaged, cracked or deteriorated.

5 The reed valve units can be removed after detaching the hoses which link them to the cut-off valve and the individual short hoses which link the reed valves to the metal pipes. The reed valve units are retained to the crankcase by three bolts. The metal pipes can be detached from the front of the cylinders by removing their retaining bolts and gaskets. Make a sketch of the pipe routing prior to removal to aid reassembly.

6 To inspect the reed valves, unscrew the reed valve cover bolts, then unscrew the bolts securing the reed itself and remove the reed, noting how it fits. Check the reeds for cracks, warpage and any other damage or deterioration. Also check the contact areas between the reeds and the reed holders, and the holders themselves, for any signs of damage or deterioration. Any carbon deposits or other foreign particles can be cleaned off using a high flash-point solvent. Note that individual parts are not available for the reed valve units.

Reassembly

7 Reassemble the system components, making sure all the components are correctly positioned and the hoses are secured at each end by their clips. If removed, clean the threads of the air cut-off valve mounting bracket bolt and the metal pipe manifold bolts and lubricate them with copper-based grease. Use new gaskets at the joints between the metal pipe manifolds and cylinder.

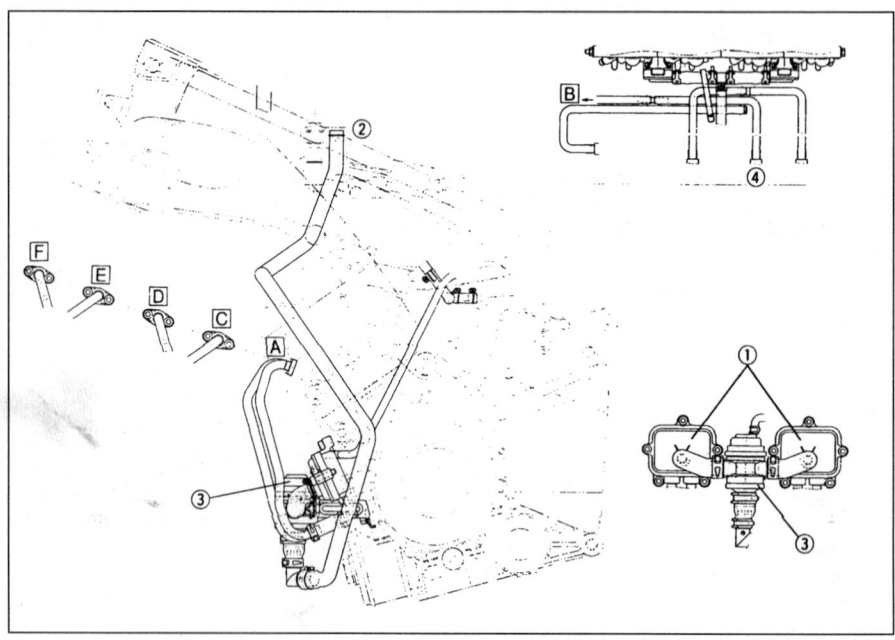

16.1 Air induction system (AIS)

1 Reed valves
2 Hose connection to the air filter
3 Air cut-off valve
4 Hose connection to No. 3 carburettor
A Metal pipes to the cylinders
B Vacuum hose from the carburettors
C No. 1 cylinder connection
D No. 2 cylinder connection
E No. 3 cylinder connection
F No. 4 cylinder connection

Chapter 5
Ignition system

Contents

General information	1	Neutral switch – check and renewal	see Chapter 9
Ignition (main) switch – check, removal and installation	see Chapter 9	Pick-up coil – check and renewal	4
		Relay assembly – check and renewal	see Chapter 9
Ignition control unit – check, removal and installation	6	Sidestand switch – check and renewal	see Chapter 9
Ignition HT coils – check, removal and installation	3	Spark plugs – gap check/adjustment, and renewal	see Chapter 1
Ignition system – check	2	Throttle position sensor – check, adjustment and renewal	5
Ignition timing – general information and check	7		

Degrees of difficulty

Easy, suitable for novice with little experience	Fairly easy, suitable for beginner with some experience	Fairly difficult, suitable for competent DIY mechanic	Difficult, suitable for experienced DIY mechanic	Very difficult, suitable for expert DIY or professional

Specifications

General information
Cylinder numbering .... 1 to 4 from left to right
Spark plugs .... see Chapter 1

Ignition timing
At idle
  1999 models .... 10° BTDC @ 1100 rpm
  2000-on models .... 10° BTDC @ 1300 rpm
Full advance .... 55° BTDC @ 5250 rpm

Pick-up coil
Resistance .... 248 to 372 ohms

Ignition HT coils
1999 models
  Primary resistance .... 0.238 to 0.322 ohms @ 20°C
  Secondary resistance .... 8.16 to 11.04 K-ohms @ 20°C
2000-on models
  Primary resistance .... 0.204 to 0.276 ohms @ 20°C
  Secondary resistance .... 8.5 to 11.5 K-ohms @ 20°C
Minimum spark gap (see Section 2) .... 6 mm

Throttle position sensor
Maximum resistance .... 4.0 to 6.0 K-ohms
Resistance range .... Zero to 5.0 ± 1.0 K-ohms @ 20°C

Torque wrench settings
Pick-up coil bolts .... 10 Nm
Ignition rotor cover bolts .... 12 Nm

5•2 Ignition system

1 General information

All models are fitted with a fully electronic dc CDI ignition system which, due to its lack of mechanical parts, is totally maintenance-free. The system comprises a trigger, pick-up coil, ignition control unit and ignition HT coils (refer to *Wiring Diagrams* at the end of Chapter 9 for details). All models are fitted with four 'stick' style HT coils which are integral with the spark plug caps. A throttle position sensor provides information on throttle opening to the ignition control unit.

The ignition trigger, which is on the rotor on the right-hand end of the crankshaft, magnetically operates the pick-up coil as the crankshaft rotates. The pick-up coil sends a signal to the ignition control unit, which then supplies the ignition HT coils with the power necessary to produce a spark at the plugs.

The ignition control unit incorporates an electronic advance system controlled by signals from the ignition trigger and pick-up coil and from the throttle position sensor.

The system also incorporates a safety interlock circuit which will cut the ignition if the sidestand is extended whilst the engine is running and in gear, or if a gear is selected whilst the engine is running and the sidestand is extended. It also prevents the engine from being started if the engine is in gear unless the clutch lever is pulled in (see Chapter 9).

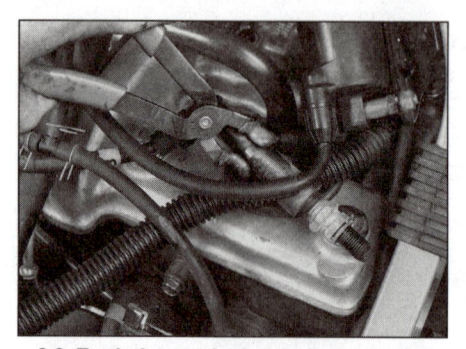

Because of their nature, the individual ignition system components can be checked but not repaired. If ignition system troubles occur, and the faulty component can be isolated, the only cure for the problem is to replace the part with a new one. Keep in mind that most electrical parts, once purchased, cannot be returned. To avoid unnecessary expense, make very sure the faulty component has been positively identified before buying a replacement part.

Note that there is no provision for adjusting the ignition timing on these models.

2 Ignition system – check

⚠️ **Warning:** *The energy levels in electronic systems can be very high. On no account should the ignition be switched on whilst the plugs or plug caps are being held. Shocks from the HT circuit can be most unpleasant. Secondly, it is vital that the engine is not turned over or run with any of the plug caps removed, and that the plugs are soundly earthed (grounded) when the system is checked for sparking. The ignition system components can be seriously damaged if the HT circuit becomes isolated.*

1 As no means of adjustment is available, any failure of the system can be traced to failure of a system component or a simple wiring fault. Of the two possibilities, the latter is by far the most likely. In the event of failure, check the system in a logical fashion, as described below.

2 Disconnect the wiring connector on the coil for No. 1 cylinder and pull the coil off the spark plug (see Section 3). Reconnect the wiring connector and connect the coil to a spare spark plug (preferably use a new plug, properly gapped – see Chapter 1). Lay the plug on the engine with the threads contacting the engine **(see illustration)**. If necessary, hold the spark plug with an insulated tool.

⚠️ **Warning:** *Do not remove any of the spark plugs from the engine to perform this check – atomised fuel being pumped out of the open spark plug hole could ignite, causing severe injury!*

3 Check that the kill switch is in the RUN position and the transmission is in neutral, then turn the ignition switch ON and turn the engine over on the starter motor. If the system is in good condition a regular, fat blue spark should be evident at the plug electrodes. If the spark appears thin or yellowish, or is non-existent, further investigation will be necessary. Turn the ignition off and repeat the test for each coil in turn.

4 The ignition system must be able to produce a spark which is capable of jumping a particular size gap. Yamaha specify that a healthy system should produce a spark capable of jumping at least 6 mm. A simple testing tool can be made to test the minimum gap across which the spark will jump **(see Tool Tip)** or, alternatively, it is possible to buy an ignition spark gap tester tool, some of which are adjustable to alter the spark gap **(see illustration)**.

5 Connect the coil of No. 1 cylinder to the protruding contact on the test tool, and clip the tool to a good earth (ground) on the engine or frame **(see illustration)**. Check that the kill switch is in the RUN position, turn the ignition switch ON and turn the engine over on the starter motor. If the system is in good condition a regular, fat blue spark will be seen to jump the gap between the electrodes. Repeat the test for the other coils. If the test results are good the entire ignition system can be considered good. If the spark appears thin or yellowish, or is non-existent, further investigation will be necessary.

6 Ignition faults can be divided into two categories, namely those where the ignition system has failed completely, and those which are due to a partial failure. The likely faults are listed below, starting with the most probable source of failure. Work through the list systematically, referring to the appropriate

2.2 Earth the spark plug and operate the starter – bright blue sparks should be visible

TOOL TIP

A simple spark gap testing tool can be made from a block of wood, a large alligator clip and two nails, one of which is fashioned so that a spark plug cap or bare HT lead end can be connected to its end. Make sure the gap between the two nail ends is the same as specified.

2.4 An adjustable spark gap tester

2.5 Connect the tester as shown – when the engine is cranked sparks should jump the gap between the nails

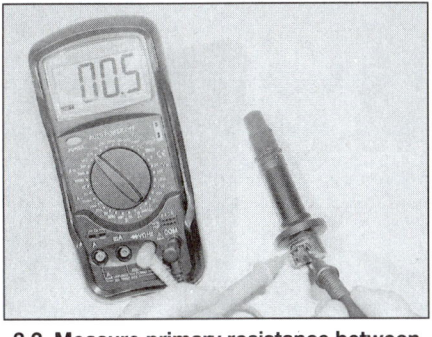

Ignition system 5•3

3.2 Measure primary resistance between the terminals on the coil

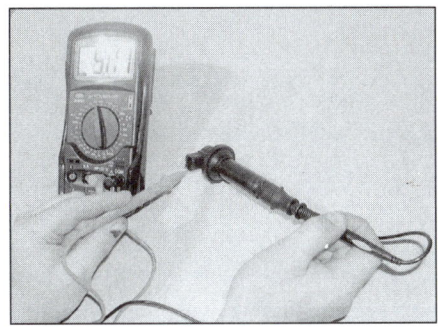

3.3 Measure secondary resistance between the spark plug terminal and one of the primary terminals

Sections of this Chapter (or other Chapters, as indicated) for full details of the necessary checks and tests. **Note:** *Before checking the following items ensure that the battery is fully charged and that all fuses are in good condition.*

  Loose, corroded or damaged wiring connections; broken or shorted wiring between any of the component parts of the ignition system (see Chapter 9).
  Faulty spark plug, dirty, worn or corroded plug electrodes, or incorrect gap between electrodes.
  Faulty ignition (main) switch or engine kill switch (see Chapter 9).
  Faulty neutral, clutch or sidestand switch, or starter cut-off relay (see Chapter 9).
  Faulty pick-up coil or damaged trigger.
  Faulty ignition HT coil(s).
  Faulty ignition control unit.

7 If the above checks don't reveal the cause of the problem, have the ignition system tested by a Yamaha dealer.

3 Ignition HT coils – check, removal and installation

Check

1 Check each coil visually for cracks and other damage. Inspect the wiring terminals and the spark plug terminal.

2 Measure the primary circuit resistance with a multimeter as follows. Set the meter to the ohms x 1 scale and measure the resistance between the terminals on the coil **(see illustration)**. If the reading obtained is not within the range shown in the Specifications, it is likely that the coil is defective.

3 Measure the secondary circuit resistance with a multimeter as follows. Set the meter to the K-ohm scale. Connect one meter probe to one primary circuit terminal and the other probe to the spark plug terminal **(see illustration)**. If the reading obtained is not within the range shown in the Specifications, it is likely that the coil is defective.

4 If a coil is confirmed to be faulty, it must be replaced with a new one: the coils are sealed units and cannot therefore be repaired.

Removal and installation

5 Remove the fairing side panels (see Chapter 8), the air filter housing (see Chapter 4) and the radiator cover (see Chapter 3, Section 7). Disconnect the battery negative (–ve) lead (see Chapter 9).

6 Disconnect the primary circuit wiring connectors on the coils and pull the coils off the spark plugs **(see illustrations)**.

7 Installation is the reverse of removal. Make sure the coils are pushed down firmly onto the spark plugs and that the wiring connectors are securely connected.

4 Pick-up coil – check and renewal

Check

1 Disconnect the battery negative (–ve) lead (see Chapter 9).

2 Trace the wiring from the pick-up coil on the right-hand side of the engine and disconnect it at the white 2-pin connector **(see illustration)**. Using a multimeter set to the ohms x 100 scale, measure the resistance between the terminals on the pick-up coil side of the connector.

3 Compare the reading obtained with that given in the Specifications at the beginning of this Chapter. The pick-up coil must be replaced with a new one if the reading obtained differs greatly from that given, particularly if the meter indicates a short circuit (no measurable resistance) or an open circuit (infinite, or very high resistance).

4 If the pick-up coil is thought to be faulty, first remove the lower fairing and the right-hand fairing side panel (see Chapter 8), and check that the wiring from the coil to the connector is not damaged. Pinched or broken wires can usually be repaired. If the wiring is good, replace the pick-up coil with a new one.

Renewal

5 Remove the lower fairing and the right-hand fairing side panel (see Chapter 8), and disconnect the battery negative (–ve) lead (Chapter 9).

6 Trace the wiring from the pick-up coil on the right-hand side of the engine and disconnect it at the 2-pin connector **(see illustration 4.2)**. Feed the wiring back to the coil, noting its routing and releasing it from any clips.

7 Unscrew the bolts securing the ignition rotor cover on the right-hand side of the engine and remove the cover, noting the guide for the coolant hose and the clutch cable bracket. Discard the gasket, as a new one must be used. Remove the dowels from either the crankcase or the cover if they are loose.

3.6a Disconnect the wiring connector (arrowed) . . .

3.6b . . . and pull the coil off the spark plug

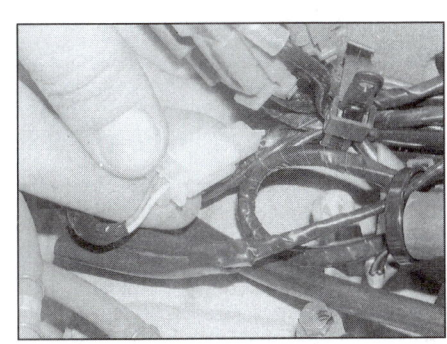

4.2 Pick-up coil wiring connector

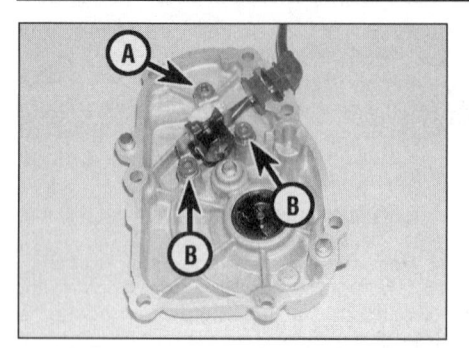

5•4 Ignition system

4.8 Release the wiring clamp (A) and remove the bolts (B)

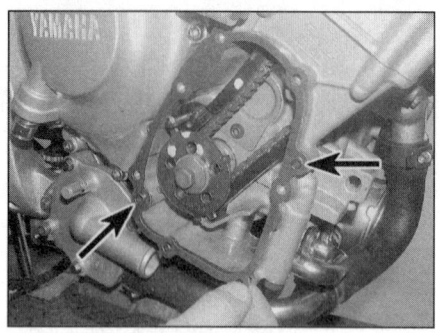

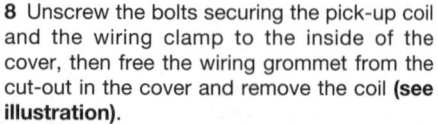

4.10a Install the new gasket on the dowels (arrowed)

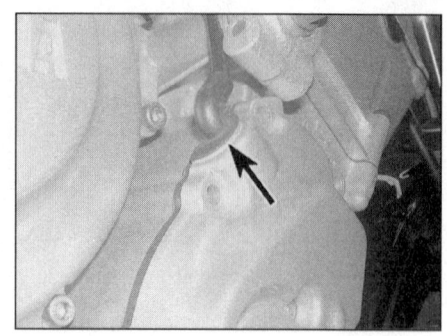

4.10b Ensure the grommet (arrowed) seats properly when the cover is fitted

8 Unscrew the bolts securing the pick-up coil and the wiring clamp to the inside of the cover, then free the wiring grommet from the cut-out in the cover and remove the coil (see illustration).
9 Fit the coil and the wiring grommet into their locations in the cover. Apply a suitable non-permanent thread locking compound to the coil bolts and tighten them to the torque setting specified at the beginning of this Chapter. Install the wiring clamp and tighten the clamp bolt securely.
10 If removed, install the cover dowels into the crankcase and fit a new gasket (see illustration). Fit the cover, ensuring that the cam chain tensioner blade pivot pin locates in the hole in the cover and that the wiring grommet is properly seated (see illustration). Install the coolant hose guide and the clutch cable bracket and tighten the cover bolts to the torque setting specified at the beginning of this Chapter.
11 Feed the pick-up coil wiring up to the connector, securing it with any clips, and reconnect it (see illustration 4.2).
12 Reconnect the battery negative (–ve) terminal and install the remaining components in the reverse order of removal.

5 Throttle position sensor – check, adjustment and renewal

1 The throttle position sensor is mounted on the outside of the right-hand (No. 4) carburettor and is keyed to the throttle shaft. The sensor provides the ignition control unit with information on throttle position and rate of opening or closing.
2 When the ignition is first switched ON, or while the engine is running, the ignition control unit performs its own self-diagnosis of the throttle position sensor. If a fault occurs, the tachometer will be seen to display zero rpm for 3 seconds, then 3000 rpm for 2.5 seconds, then the actual engine speed for 3 seconds, whereupon it will repeat the cycle until the engine is switched off. Note that the motorcycle can be ridden even though a fault has been diagnosed, though a difference in performance will be noticed.

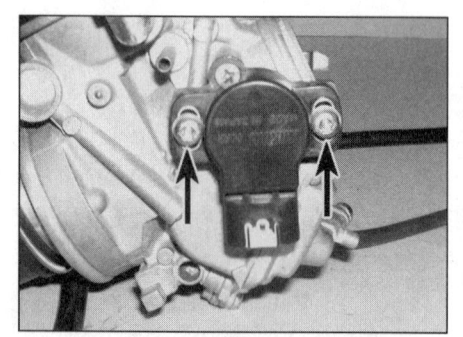

Check

Note: *Check that engine idle speed before carrying out this procedure (see Chapter 1).*
3 Remove the fuel tank (see Chapter 4), the right-hand fairing side panel and the right-hand frame side panel (see Chapter 8). The throttle sensor is mounted on the outside of the right-hand (No. 4) carburettor (see illustration).
4 Make sure the ignition is switched OFF, then trace the wiring from the sensor and disconnect it at the connector (see illustration).
5 Using a multimeter set to the K-ohms range, measure the sensor's maximum resistance by connecting the meter positive probe to the blue wire terminal and its negative probe to the black/blue wire terminal on the sensor side of the connector. Compare the reading obtained with that given in the Specifications at the beginning of this Chapter; if it differs greatly, replace the sensor with a new one.
6 Now measure the sensor's resistance range by connecting the positive meter probe to the yellow wire terminal and the negative probe to the black/blue wire terminal, and slowly open the throttle from fully closed to fully open. If the readings obtained differ greatly from those specified at the beginning of this Chapter, replace the sensor with a new one. **Note:** *When checking the resistance range, it is more important that there is a smooth and constant change in the resistance as the throttle is opened, than that the figures themselves are exactly as specified.*
7 If the checks made in Steps 5 and 6 produce different readings from those specified, remove the sensor from the carburettor as described below. Inspect the sensor for signs of damage and wear, especially the slot where the throttle shaft connects. Repeat the checks described in Steps 5 and 6 with the sensor moved to the bench; turn the sensor drive by hand in Step 6. If the test results are still outside of those specified, the sensor should be renewed.
8 If the sensor test results are within specification, yet a fault is still indicated, check the wiring between the sensor connector and the ignition control unit. Use a multimeter to check for continuity, referring to *Wiring Diagrams* at the end of Chapter 9. If continuity does not exist, this is probably due to a damaged or broken wire between the connectors: pinched or broken wires can usually be repaired. Also check the connectors for loose or corroded terminals. If the wiring and connectors are good, check the adjustment of the sensor as described below.

Adjustment

9 Before adjusting the sensor, check the idle speed and carburettor synchronisation (see Chapter 1).
10 Locate the sensor wiring connector (see Step 4). Turn the ignition ON, then disconnect and then reconnect the sensor wiring connector. The tachometer is now in throttle position sensor adjustment mode. If the

5.3 The throttle position sensor is mounted on No. 4 carburettor

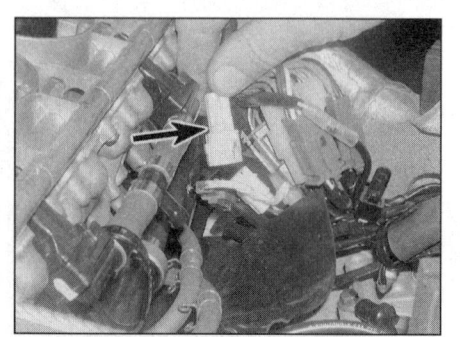

5.4 Disconnect the sensor wiring connector (arrowed)

Ignition system 5•5

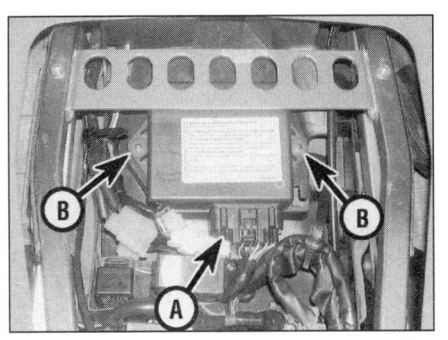

6.3 Disconnect the wiring connectors (A) and undo the fixing screws (B)

sensor angle is correct, the tachometer will read 5000 rpm.

11 If the tachometer reads 0 rpm, loosen the sensor mounting screws **(see illustration 5.3)** and rotate the sensor clockwise until it reads 5000 rpm. If the tachometer reads 10,000 rpm, loosen the screws and rotate the sensor anticlockwise until it reads 5000 rpm. If the sensor cannot be adjusted to obtain the correct reading, replace it with a new one.

12 Tighten the sensor mounting screws securely and turn the ignition OFF. The tachometer will exit the sensor adjustment mode when the ignition is turned off.

Renewal

13 Remove the fuel tank (see Chapter 4), the right-hand fairing side panel and the right-hand frame side panel (see Chapter 8). The throttle sensor is mounted on the outside of the right-hand (No. 4) carburettor.

14 Make sure the ignition is switched OFF, then trace the wiring from the sensor and disconnect it at the connector **(see illustration 5.4)**. Unscrew the sensor mounting screws and remove the sensor, noting how it fits **(see illustration 5.3)**.

15 Install the sensor, ensuring it is keyed correctly onto the throttle shaft, and tighten the screws lightly. Connect the wiring connector and adjust the sensor as described in Steps 9 to 12.

16 Install the remaining components in the reverse order of removal.

6 Ignition control unit – check, removal and installation

Check

1 If the tests shown in the preceding Sections have failed to isolate the cause of an ignition fault, it is possible that the ignition control unit itself is faulty. No details are available with which the unit can be tested. The best way to determine whether it is faulty or not is to substitute it with a known good one, having first checked all other components in the ignition system. Otherwise, take the unit to a Yamaha dealer for assessment.

Removal

2 Remove the rider's seat (see Chapter 8). Disconnect the battery negative (–ve) lead.

3 Disconnect the wiring connectors from the ignition control unit, then remove its fixing screws **(see illustration)**.

Installation

4 Installation is the reverse of removal. Make sure the wiring connectors are correctly and securely connected.

7 Ignition timing – general information and check

General information

1 Since no provision exists for adjusting the ignition timing, and since no ignition component is subject to mechanical wear, there is no need for regular checks. However, the ignition timing be checked if investigating a fault such as a loss of power or a misfire, but only after a thorough examination of all the other ignition system components and wiring.

2 The ignition timing is checked dynamically (engine running) using a stroboscopic lamp. The inexpensive neon lamps should be adequate in theory, but in practice may produce a pulse of such low intensity that the timing mark remains indistinct. If possible, one of the more precise xenon tube lamps should be used, powered by an external source of the appropriate voltage. **Note:** *Do not use the machine's own battery, as an incorrect reading may result from stray impulses within the machine's electrical system.*

Check

3 Remove the lower fairing and the fairing right-hand side panel (see Chapter 8). Warm the engine up to normal operating temperature, then stop it.

4 Unscrew the timing inspection bolt (the small bolt, not the large slotted plug) from the centre of the ignition rotor cover on the right-hand side of the engine **(see illustration)**.

5 The mark on the ignition rotor which indicates the firing point at idle speed for the No. 1 cylinder is an 'H' mark on its side **(see illustration)**. The static timing marks with which this should align are the cut-outs in the inspection hole.

6 Connect the timing light to the No. 1 cylinder ignition coil as described in the manufacturer's instructions.

> **HAYNES HiNT** *The timing marks can be highlighted with white paint to make them more visible under the stroboscope light.*

7 Start the engine and aim the light at the inspection hole.

8 With the machine idling at the specified speed, the 'H' timing mark should appear precisely in the middle of the two static timing marks **(see illustration)**. **Note:** *It is essential that the reading is taken at the specified idling speed.*

9 If the ignition timing is incorrect, or suspected of being incorrect, one of the ignition system components is at fault, and the system must be tested as described in the preceding Sections of this Chapter.

10 When the check is complete, install the timing inspection bolt, using a new sealing washer if the old one is damaged or deformed, and tighten it securely. Install the remaining components in the reverse order of removal.

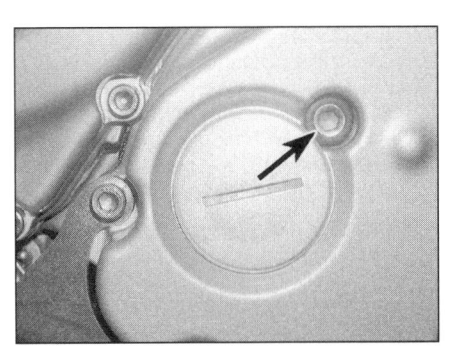

7.4 Timing inspection bolt (arrowed) in rotor cover

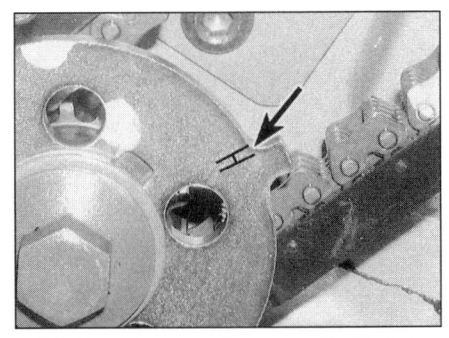

7.5 Cover removed to show the timing mark (arrowed) on the rotor

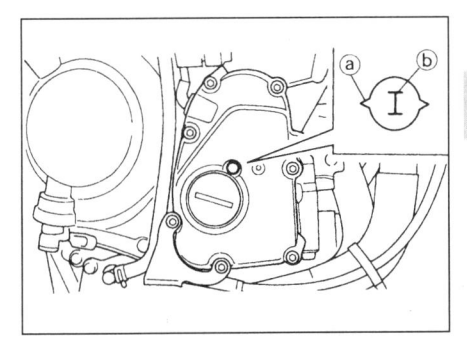

7.8 Timing mark alignment
a Static timing marks   b H mark

Notes

Chapter 6
Frame, suspension and final drive

Contents

Drive chain – removal and installation	15	Sidestand – check and pivot lubrication	see Chapter 1
Drive chain and sprockets – check, adjustment and lubrication	see Chapter 1	Sidestand – removal and installation	4
		Sidestand switch – check and renewal	see Chapter 9
Footrests, brake pedal and gearchange lever – removal and installation	3	Sprockets – check and renewal	16
Forks – disassembly, inspection and reassembly	7	Steering head bearings – freeplay check and adjustment	see Chapter 1
Forks – oil change	see Chapter 1	Steering head bearings – inspection and renewal	9
Forks – removal and installation	6	Steering head bearings – re-greasing	see Chapter 1
Frame – inspection and repair	2	Steering stem – removal and installation	8
General information	1	Suspension – adjustments	12
Handlebar switches – check, removal and installation	see Chapter 9	Suspension – check	see Chapter 1
Handlebars and levers – removal and installation	5	Swingarm – inspection and bearing renewal	14
Rear shock absorber – removal, inspection and installation	10	Swingarm – removal and installation	13
Rear sprocket coupling/rubber dampers – check and renewal	17	Swingarm and suspension linkage bearings – re-greasing	see Chapter 1
Rear suspension linkage – removal, inspection and installation	11		

Degrees of difficulty

Easy, suitable for novice with little experience	Fairly easy, suitable for beginner with some experience	Fairly difficult, suitable for competent DIY mechanic	Difficult, suitable for experienced DIY mechanic	Very difficult, suitable for expert DIY or professional

Specifications

Front forks
Fork oil type .... Yamaha suspension oil '01' or equivalent
Fork oil capacity (per leg) .... 476 cc
Fork oil level* .... 107 mm
Fork springs
   Free length .... 251.8 mm
   Service limit .... 246 mm
*Oil level is measured from the top of the tube with the fork spring removed and the leg fully compressed.

Rear suspension
Shock absorber spring installed length .... 169.5 mm

Final drive
Chain type .... DID 532ZLV (116 links)
Chain freeplay and stretch limit .... see Chapter 1
Sprocket sizes .... Front 16T, Rear 48T (46T on later California models)

6•2 Frame, suspension and final drive

Torque wrench settings

Footrest bracket bolts	28 Nm
Fork clamp bolts	
Bottom yoke	23 Nm
Top yoke	25 Nm
Fork damper cartridge bolt	40 Nm
Fork damper cartridge rod-to-top bolt locknut	15 Nm
Fork top bolt	23 Nm
Front axle pinch bolt	23 Nm
Front master cylinder clamp bolts	13 Nm
Front sprocket cover bolts	10 Nm
Front sprocket nut	70 Nm
Handlebar clamp bolts	33 Nm
Handlebar positioning bolts	13 Nm
Rear master cylinder mounting bolts	23 Nm
Rear shock absorber nuts	40 Nm
Rear sprocket nuts	69 Nm
Rear sub-frame mounting bolts	41 Nm
Rear suspension linkage plate and linkage arm nuts	40 Nm
Sidestand bolt	60 Nm
Steering head bearing adjuster nut	
Initial setting	17 Nm
Final setting	9 Nm
Steering stem nut	115 Nm
Swingarm pivot bolt nut	95 Nm

1 General information

All models use a twin spar box-section Deltabox II style aluminium frame, incorporating the engine as a stressed member.

Front suspension is by a pair of oil-damped, telescopic forks with internal coil springs. The forks are adjustable for spring pre-load and both rebound and compression damping.

At the rear, an aluminium alloy swingarm acts on a single shock absorber via a three-way linkage. The Bilstein shock absorber is adjustable for spring pre-load and for both rebound and compression damping.

The drive to the rear wheel is by chain and sprockets.

2 Frame – inspection and repair

1 The frame should not require attention unless accident damage has occurred. In most cases, frame renewal is the only satisfactory remedy for such damage. A few frame specialists have the jigs and other equipment necessary for straightening the frame to the required standard of accuracy, but even then there is no simple way of assessing to what extent the frame may have been over-stressed.

2 After the machine has covered a high mileage, the frame should be examined closely for signs of cracking or splitting at the welded joints. Loose engine mount bolts can cause ovaling or fracturing of the mounts themselves. Minor damage can often be repaired by welding, depending on the extent and nature of the damage, but this is a task for an expert.

3 Remember that a frame which is out of alignment will cause handling problems. If misalignment is suspected as the result of an accident, first check the wheel alignment (see Chapter 7). To have the frame checked thoroughly it will be necessary to strip the machine completely.

4 If the rear sub-frame is ever removed, note that the four aluminium bolts which retain it to the main frame must be renewed – they are not re-usable. When installing the new bolts note that the underside of each bolt head must be lubricated with a smear of engine oil or grease before tightening them to the specified torque setting.

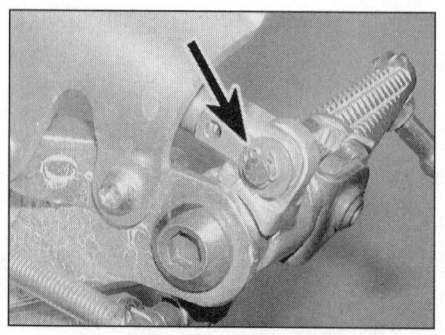

3.1 Remove the split pin and washer (arrowed) to withdraw clevis pin

3 Footrests, brake pedal and gearchange lever – removal and installation

Brake pedal and rider's right-hand footrest

Removal

1 Remove the split pin and washer from the clevis pin connecting the brake pedal to the master cylinder pushrod (see illustration). Remove the clevis pin and separate the pushrod from the pedal. Discard the split pin, as a new one must be used on reassembly.

2 Unhook the pedal return spring and brake light switch spring from the lug on the back of the pedal, then unscrew the bolt securing the brake light switch to the footrest bracket and remove the bolt and washer (see illustration).

3 Unscrew the bolts securing the rear brake master cylinder to the footrest bracket and

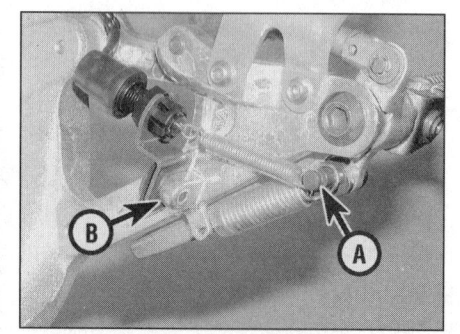

3.2 Unhook the springs from the lug (A) and undo the brake light switch bolt (B)

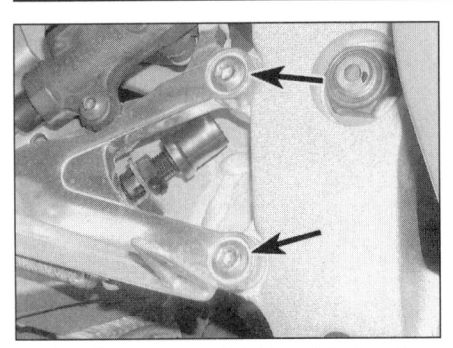

Frame, suspension and final drive 6•3

3.4 Remove the right-hand footrest bracket bolts (arrowed)

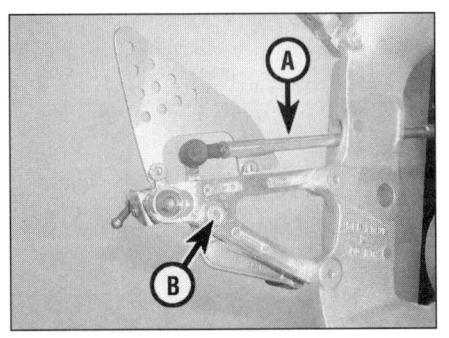

3.7 Remove the gearchange rod (A), then unscrew the lever pivot bolt (B)

3.8 Remove the left-hand footrest bracket bolts (arrowed)

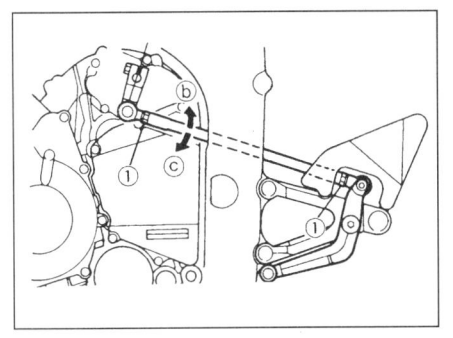

3.9 Gearchange lever height adjustment

1 Locknuts
b turn this way to increase rod length
c turn this way to reduce rod length

remove the bolts. To prevent straining the hydraulic hose, use a cable tie to secure the master cylinder to the frame clear of the bracket.
4 Unscrew the bolts securing the footrest bracket to the frame and remove the bracket (see illustration). Unscrew the footrest bolt, then remove the footrest from the bracket and remove the pedal. Note the washer fitted between the pedal and the footrest bracket. The heel plate is secured to the footrest bracket by two bolts.

Installation

5 Installation is the reverse of removal. Apply grease to the brake pedal pivot. Use a new split pin on the clevis pin securing the brake pedal to the master cylinder pushrod.

Note: *See Chapter 7 for details of adjusting the lever height.* Tighten the footrest bracket bolts and the master cylinder bolts to the torque setting specified at the beginning of this Chapter. Check the operation of the rear brake light switch (see Chapter 1, Section 13).

Gearchange lever and rider's left-hand footrest

Removal

6 Loosen the gearchange linkage rod locknuts, then unscrew the rod and separate it from the lever and the arm (the rod is reverse-threaded on the lever end, so will unscrew from both lever and arm simultaneously when turned in the one direction – see Chapter 2). Withdraw the rod from the frame.
7 Unscrew the gearchange lever pivot bolt and remove the bolt, washer and lever (see illustration).
8 Unscrew the bolts securing the footrest bracket to the frame and remove the bracket (see illustration). Unscrew the footrest bolt, then remove the footrest from the bracket. The heel plate is secured to the footrest bracket by two bolts.

Installation

9 Installation is the reverse of removal. Apply grease to the gearchange lever pivot. Tighten the footrest bracket bolts to the torque setting specified at the beginning of this Chapter. To adjust the gearchange lever position, first loosen both locknuts on the linkage rod. Rotate the rod in one direction or the other to either raise or lower the lever height (see illustration). Make sure the linkage rod length is within the 242 mm specification advised by Yamaha, then tighten both locknuts securely.

Passenger footrests

10 Unscrew the footrest pivot bolt and nut, then withdraw the bolt and remove the footrest (see illustration). Note the fitting of the detent plates, ball, spring and bolt spacer – take care that they do not fall out when removing the footrest.
11 If required, remove the seat cowling (see Chapter 8), then unscrew the bolts securing the footrest bracket to the frame and remove the bracket. Note: *The right-hand bracket supports the exhaust silencer – see Chapter 4 to remove the silencer.*
12 Installation is the reverse of removal.

4 Sidestand – removal and installation

1 Support the motorcycle securely in an upright position using an auxiliary stand.
2 Release the breather hoses from the guide on the stand spring bracket, then unhook the stand spring, noting how it fits (see illustration).
3 Unscrew the stand centre bolt and remove the bolt, washer, spring bracket, stand and washer (see illustration). Note how the

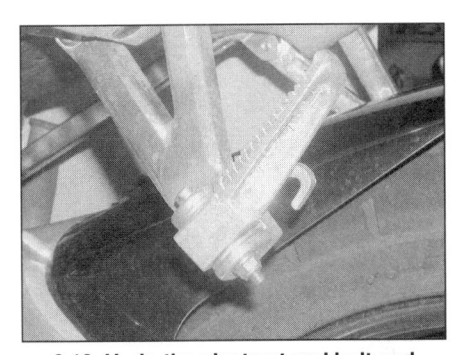

3.10 Undo the pivot nut and bolt and remove the passenger footrest

4.2 Unhook the sidestand spring at the top and bottom lugs (arrowed)

4.3a Unscrew the centre bolt (arrowed) to remove the stand

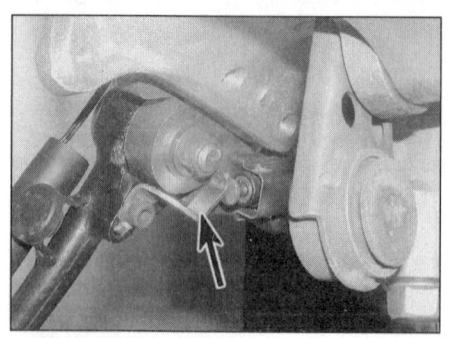

6•4 Frame, suspension and final drive

4.3b Plate (arrowed) actuates sidestand switch

5.1a Fluid reservoir mounting bolt (arrowed)

5.1b Remove the two bolts (arrowed) to free the master cylinder clamp

contact plate on the stand locates against the switch plunger when the stand is lowered **(see illustration)**.

4 If required, counter-hold the stand pivot stub and unscrew the nut on the back of the stand bracket; remove the nut and washer and withdraw the pivot stub from the bracket. Unscrew the bracket bolts and remove the bracket from the frame.

5 Installation is the reverse of removal, noting the following points:

- Apply a suitable thread locking compound to the bracket bolts before installation and tighten the bolts securely.
- Tighten the stand centre bolt to the specified torque setting.
- Ensure the stand contact plate actuates the switch when the stand is lowered.
- Check the spring tension – it must hold the stand up when it is not in use. If the spring has sagged, renew it.

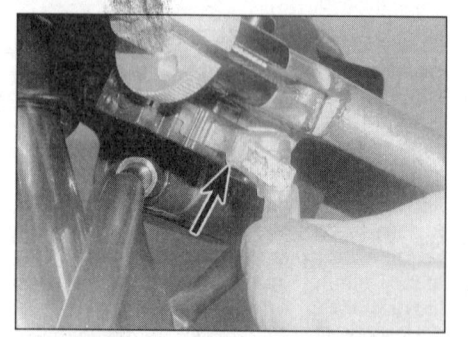

● Check the operation of the sidestand switch (see Chapter 1).

5 Handlebars and levers – removal and installation

Handlebars

Removal

Note: *The left-hand handlebar can be displaced from the forks without having to remove the clutch lever or switch assembly. The front brake assembly must be removed from the right-hand handlebar before displacing the handlebar.*

1 To remove the right handlebar, first remove the bolt securing the reservoir to its bracket on the top yoke **(see illustration)**. Unscrew the master cylinder clamp bolts and remove

the clamp, noting how it fits, then lift the master cylinder away from the handlebar **(see illustration)**. There is no need to disconnect the hydraulic hose between the reservoir and the master cylinder. Keep the reservoir upright to prevent fluid spillage and make sure no strain is placed on the hose.

2 Displace the throttle twistgrip housing from the handlebar and detach both cable nipples from the throttle pulley (see Chapter 4, Section 11, Step 5).

3 Unscrew the handlebar end weight and remove the weight, then slide the twistgrip off the handlebar.

4 To remove the left handlebar, displace the handlebar switch housing and the choke lever (see Chapter 4, Section 12, Steps 3 and 4).

5 If required, unscrew the handlebar end weight and pull the grip off the bar. Push a screwdriver between the grip and the bar and blow compressed air or spray lubricant inside the grip to loosen it. If the grip has been bonded in place you may need to cut it free.

6 Disconnect the clutch switch wiring connector **(see illustration)**. Detach the clutch cable from the lever (see Chapter 2, Section 14, Step 4), then slacken the lever bracket pinch bolt and slide the lever off the bar end.

7 Remove the blanking caps from the heads of the handlebar positioning bolts using a small flat-bladed screwdriver, then unscrew the bolts **(see illustrations)**.

8 Slacken the handlebar clamp bolts and ease the handlebars up and off the fork legs **(see illustrations)**.

5.6 Disconnect the clutch switch wiring connectors (arrowed)

5.7a Remove the blanking cap (arrowed) . . .

5.7b . . . then unscrew the handlebar positioning bolts . . .

5.8a . . . slacken the clamp bolts . . .

5.8b . . . and ease the handlebar off the fork leg

Frame, suspension and final drive 6•5

5.10a Thread the adjuster fully in . . .

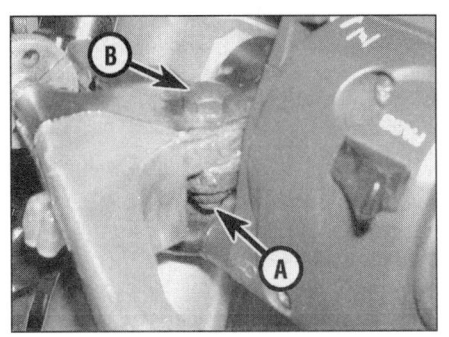

5.10b . . . then unscrew nut (A), remove bolt (B) and slide the lever out of the bracket

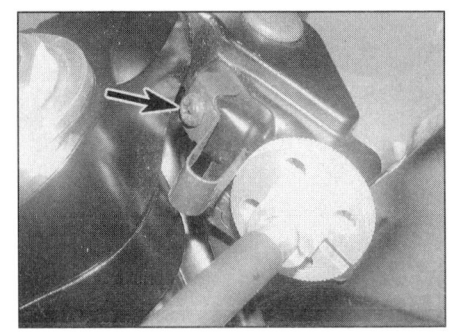

5.11 Cable adjuster spring is retained by the screw (arrowed)

Installation

9 Installation is the reverse of removal, noting the following.
- Tighten the handlebar positioning bolts, handlebar clamp bolts, and brake master cylinder clamp bolts to the torque settings specified at the beginning of this Chapter, in that order.
- Lubricate the right-hand bar before sliding on the throttle twistgrip. Apply grease to the clutch, throttle and choke cable ends.
- Refer to the relevant Chapters (as directed) for the installation of the handlebar mounted assemblies. Align the slit in the clutch lever bracket with the punch mark on the underside of the handlebar.
- Do not forget to reconnect the front brake light switch and clutch switch wiring connectors.
- Adjust throttle and clutch cable freeplay (see Chapter 1).
- Check the operation of all switches and the front brake and clutch before taking the machine on the road.

Clutch lever

10 Thread the clutch cable adjuster fully into the bracket to provide maximum freeplay in the cable **(see illustration)**. Unscrew the lever pivot bolt locknut, then push the pivot bolt out of the bracket and remove the lever, detaching the cable nipple as you do so **(see illustration)**. Note the bush inside the lever and remove it if it is loose.

11 If required, remove the screw retaining the cable adjuster spring plate and remove the spring **(see illustration)**.

12 Installation is the reverse of removal. Apply grease to the pivot bolt shaft, the bush and the contact areas between the lever and its bracket, and to the clutch cable nipple. Adjust the clutch cable freeplay (see Chapter 1).

Front brake lever

13 Unscrew the lever pivot bolt locknut, then push the pivot bolt out of the bracket and remove the lever **(see illustration)**.

14 Installation is the reverse of removal. Apply grease to the pivot bolt shaft and the contact areas between the lever and its bracket.

6 Forks – removal and installation

Removal

Note: *Although not strictly necessary, before removing the forks it is recommended that all the fairing panels and air intake ducting are removed (see Chapter 8). This will improve access and prevent accidental damage to the paintwork should a tool slip.*

1 Support the motorcycle with an auxiliary stand so that the front wheel is off the ground. Remove the fairing and the fairing side panels (see Chapter 8).

2 Displace the front brake calipers (see Chapter 7). There is no need to disconnect the hydraulic hoses but support the calipers with cable ties to prevent straining the hoses.

3 Remove the front wheel (see Chapter 7).

4 Remove the front mudguard (see Chapter 8).

5 Remove the handlebars – the clutch lever and switch assemblies can remain in place (see Section 5).

6 Work on each fork leg individually. Note the routing of the various cables and hoses around the forks.

7 Note how much above the top yoke the fork tube protrudes, then loosen the fork clamp bolt in the top yoke **(see illustrations)**. If the fork legs are to be disassembled, or if the fork oil is being changed, loosen the fork top bolt at this stage, but don't remove it.

8 Support the fork leg, then loosen but do not remove the fork clamp bolts in the bottom yoke **(see illustration)**. Remove the fork leg

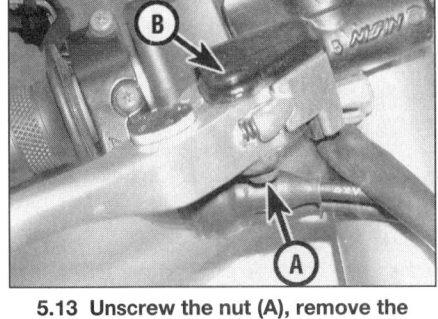

5.13 Unscrew the nut (A), remove screw (B) and slide the lever out of the bracket

6.7a Note how far the leg protrudes above the top yoke . . .

6.7b . . . then loosen the fork clamp bolt

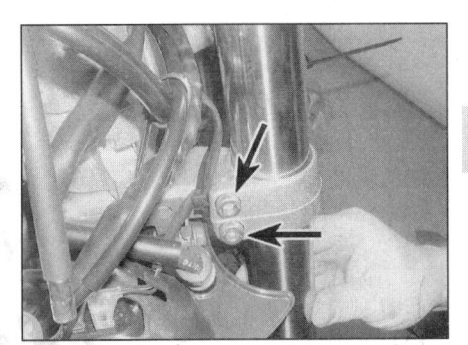

6.8 Loosen the clamp bolts (arrowed) and remove the leg

6•6 Frame, suspension and final drive

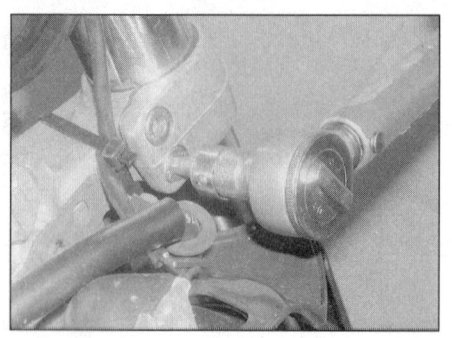

6.10 Tighten the bolts to the specified torque

by twisting it and pulling it downwards. Note which fork leg fits on which side.

> **HAYNES HINT**
> If the fork legs are seized in the yokes, spray the area with penetrating oil and allow time for it to soak in before trying again.

Installation

9 Remove all traces of corrosion from the fork tubes and the yokes. Slide the fork leg up through the bottom yoke and into the top yoke, making sure the wiring, cables and hoses are the correct side of the leg as noted on removal. Make sure that the leg with the threaded section for the axle is on the left, and the leg with the axle pinch bolt is on the right. Check that the amount of protrusion of the fork tube above the top yoke is as noted on removal and equal on both sides – the tops of the tubes should be flush with the tops of the handlebar clamps when they are fitted **(see illustration 6.7a)**.

10 Tighten the fork clamp bolts in the bottom yoke to the torque setting specified at the beginning of this Chapter **(see illustration)**. If the fork leg has been dismantled or if the oil has been changed, tighten the top bolt to the specified torque setting. Now tighten the clamp bolt in the top yoke to the specified torque setting **(see illustration 6.7b)**.

11 Install the remaining components in the reverse order of removal.

12 Check the operation of the front forks and brakes before taking the machine out on the road.

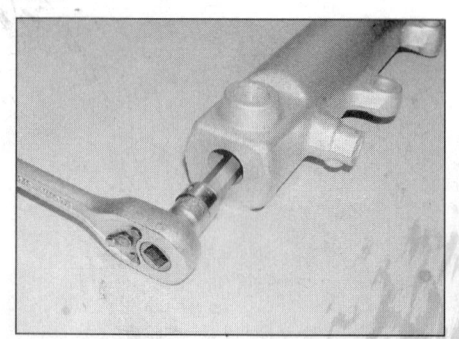

7.2 Loosen the damper cartridge bolt

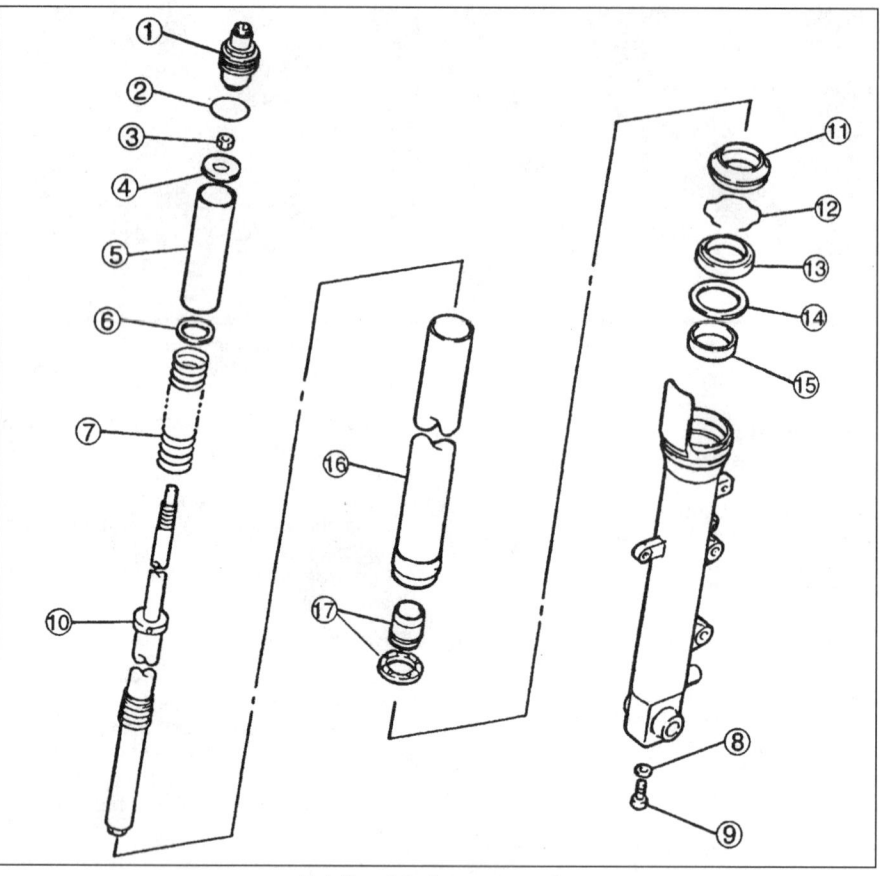

7.1 Front fork components

1 Top bolt
2 O-ring
3 Lock nut
4 Washer
5 Spacer
6 Spring seat
7 Spring
8 Sealing washer
9 Damper cartridge bolt
10 Damper cartridge assembly
11 Dust seal
12 Retaining clip
13 Oil seal
14 Washer
15 Top bush
16 Fork tube
17 Damper cartridge seat

7 Forks – disassembly, inspection and reassembly

Disassembly

1 Always dismantle the fork legs separately to avoid interchanging any parts and thus causing an accelerated rate of wear. Store all components in separate, clearly marked containers **(see illustration)**.

2 Before dismantling the fork leg, it is advised that the damper cartridge bolt be loosened at this stage. Invert the leg and compress the fork tube in the slider so that the spring exerts the maximum pressure on the damper cartridge head, then slacken the damper cartridge bolt in the base of the fork slider **(see illustration)**.

3 If the fork top bolt was not loosened with the fork on the motorcycle, carefully clamp the fork tube in a vice equipped with soft jaws, taking care not to overtighten or score the tube's surface, and loosen the top bolt.

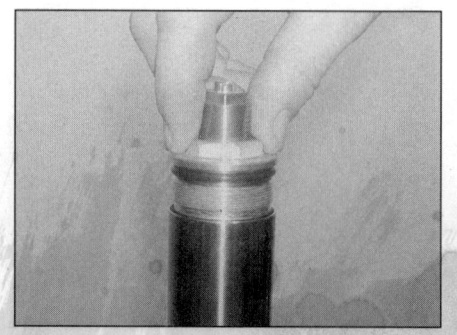

4 Unscrew the top bolt from the fork leg **(see illustration)**. The damper cartridge rod will remain threaded to the top bolt.

> ⚠ **Warning:** The fork spring is pressing on the fork top bolt with considerable pressure. Unscrew the bolt very carefully, keeping a downward pressure on it and release it slowly as it is likely to spring clear. It is advisable to wear some form of eye and face protection when carrying out this operation.

7.4 Unscrew the top bolt . . .

Frame, suspension and final drive 6•7

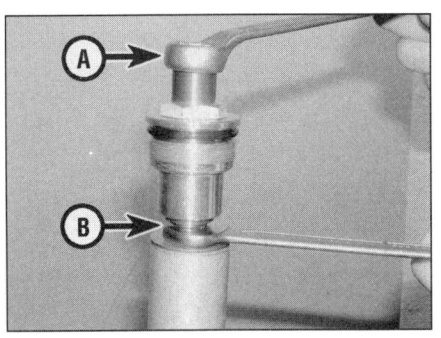

7.5a ... then counter-hold the spring pre-load bolt (A) and loosen the locknut (B) ...

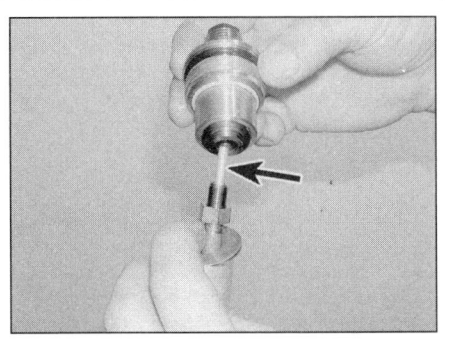

7.5b ... and unscrew the top bolt. Note the rebound damping adjuster (arrowed)

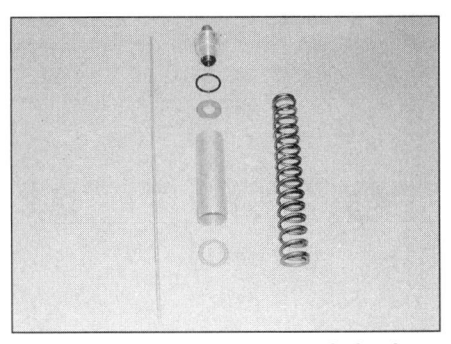

7.6 Components of the inner fork tube assembly

5 Counter-hold the spring pre-load bolt and loosen the damper cartridge rod locknut, then unscrew the top bolt from the rod **(see illustrations)**. Note the rebound damping adjuster inside the damper cartridge rod. Discard the O-ring as a new one must be fitted on reassembly.

6 Withdraw the washer, spacer, spring seat, spring and damping adjuster in that order from the fork leg **(see illustration)**.

7 Invert the fork leg over a suitable container and pump the fork vigorously to expel as much fork oil as possible.

8 Remove the previously slackened damper cartridge bolt and its copper sealing washer from the bottom of the slider **(see illustration 7.2)**. Discard the sealing washer as a new one must be used on reassembly. If the damper cartridge bolt was not slackened before dismantling the fork, it may be necessary to re-install the spring assembly (see Step 6) and top bolt to prevent the damper cartridge from turning. Yamaha produce a service tool (Part No. 90890-01425 or YM-01425) which passes down over the damper cartridge rod and engages the head of the cartridge body to hold it in place.

9 Withdraw the damper cartridge from inside the fork tube **(see illustration)**.

10 Prise the stoneguard off the top of the fork slider, then prise out the dust seal from the top of the slider to gain access to the oil seal retaining clip and remove the clip **(see illustrations)**. Take care not to scratch the fork leg. Discard the dust seal as a new one must be used.

11 To separate the tube from the slider it is necessary to displace the oil seal and top bush in the slider. The bottom bush will not pass through the top bush, and this can be used to good effect. Push the tube gently inwards until it stops against the damper cartridge seat. Take care not to do this forcibly or the seat may be damaged. Then pull the tube sharply outwards until the bottom bush strikes the top bush. Repeat this operation until the seal, seal washer and top bush are tapped out of the slider and the tube can be fully withdrawn from the slider **(see illustration)**.

12 Slide the oil seal, its washer and the top bush off the fork tube, noting which way up they fit **(see illustration)**. Discard the oil seal as a new one must be fitted on reassembly.

Note: *Yamaha recommend that both the top and bottom bushes should be renewed when the forks are disassembled.*

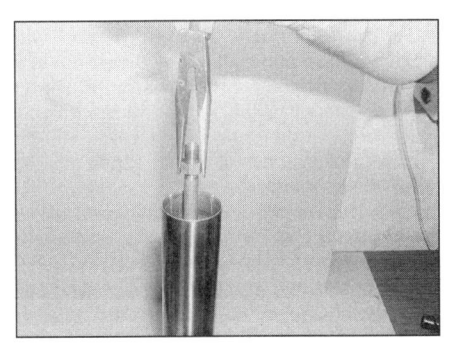

7.9 Withdraw the damper cartridge

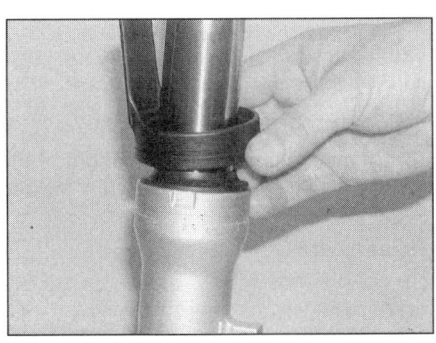

7.10a Prise off the stoneguard ...

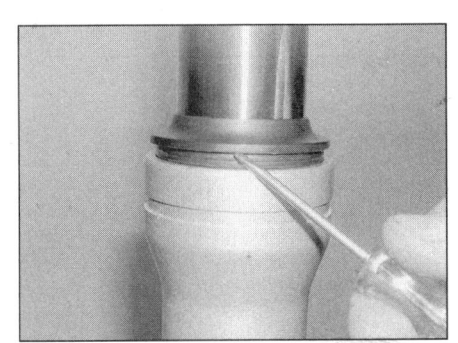

7.10b ... then the dust deal ...

7.10c ... and the oil seal retaining clip

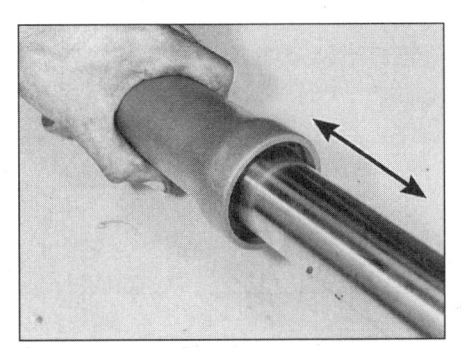

7.11 Separate the tube from the slider by pulling them apart firmly several times

7.12 The oil seal (1), washer (2), top bush (3) and bottom bush (4) will come out with the fork tube

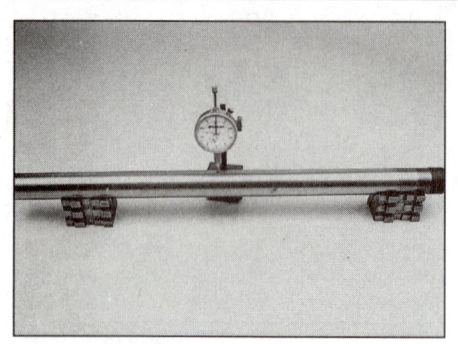

6•8 Frame, suspension and final drive

7.15 Check the fork tube runout using V-blocks and a dial gauge

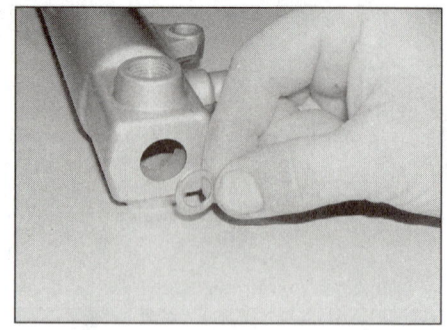

7.21 Fit a new sealing washer to the damper cartridge bolt

7.22 Install the top bush . . .

13 Tip the damper cartridge seat out of the slider, noting which way up it fits.

Inspection

14 Clean all parts in solvent and blow them dry with compressed air, if available. Check the fork tube for score marks; scratches, flaking or pitted chrome finish and excessive or abnormal wear. Renew the tube in both forks if any dents are found. Check the fork seal seat for nicks, gouges and scratches. If damage is evident, leaks will occur. Also check the oil seal washer for damage or distortion; renew damaged or worn parts as necessary.

15 Check the fork tube for runout (bending) using V-blocks and a dial gauge, or have it done by a Yamaha dealer or suspension specialist **(see illustration)**. Yamaha do not specify a runout limit, but if the tube is bent beyond the generally accepted limit of 0.2 mm, seek the advice of a suspension specialist.

⚠️ **Warning: If the tube is bent, it should not be straightened – replace it with a new one.**

16 Check the spring for cracks and other damage. Measure the spring free length and compare the measurement to the specifications at the beginning of this Chapter. If a spring is defective or has sagged below the service limit, replace the springs in both fork legs with new ones. Never renew only one spring.

17 Examine the working surfaces of the two bushes; if worn or scuffed they must be renewed (see Step 12). Note that separation of the fork may damage the bushes and it is advisable to renew them as a matter of course. The bottom bush (on the fork tube) can be removed by gently opening out its slit with a large flat-bladed screwdriver so that it can be slid off the end of the fork tube; use the same method to install the new bush.

18 Check the damper cartridge for damage and wear, and renew it if necessary. If available, blow compressed air through the oil passages.

19 Examine the seat on the bottom of the damper cartridge and renew it if it is worn or distorted.

Reassembly

20 Insert the damper cartridge into the fork tube and slide it into place so that it projects fully from the bottom of the tube, then install the seat on the bottom of the damper cartridge.

21 Oil the fork tube and bottom bush with the specified fork oil and insert the assembly into the slider. Fit a new copper sealing washer to the damper cartridge bolt and apply a few drops of a suitable non-permanent thread-locking compound, then install the bolt into the bottom of the slider **(see illustration)**. Tighten the bolt to the specified torque setting. If the damper cartridge rotates inside the tube, hold the rod with spring pressure or the service tool as on disassembly (see Step 8).

22 Push the fork tube fully into the slider, then oil the top bush and slide it down over the tube **(see illustration)**. Press the bush squarely into its recess in the slider. Use a hammer and a suitable piece of tubing to tap the bush lightly into place; note that excessive force should be unnecessary and will damage the bush.

23 Install the oil seal washer on top of the bush, then lubricate the **new** oil seal with lithium grease and slide it down over the tube with its markings facing upwards. Press the seal squarely into the slider and tap it lightly into place as described in Step 22 until the retaining clip groove is visible above the seal **(see illustrations)**.

24 Fit the retaining clip, making sure it is correctly located in its groove **(see illustration)**.

25 Lubricate the inside of the new dust seal then slide it down the fork tube and press it into position **(see illustration)**.

Note: *Take care not to scratch the fork tube during reassembly; if the fork tube is pushed*

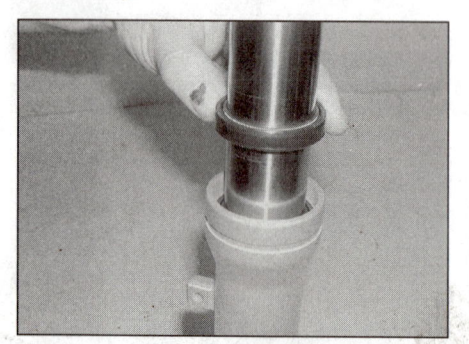

7.23a . . . followed by the washer . . .

7.23b . . . then install the new oil seal . . .

7.24 . . . and ensure that its retaining clip is correctly seated

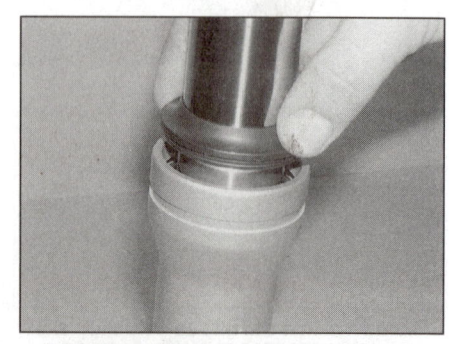

7.25 Press the dust seal into place . . .

Frame, suspension and final drive 6•9

7.26 ... and then the stoneguard, noting the location recess (arrowed)

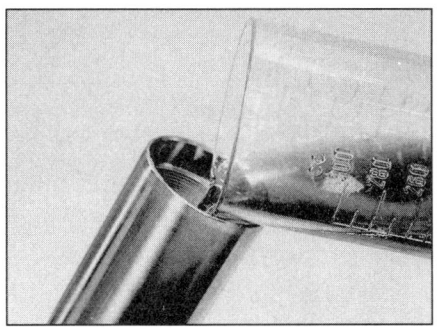

7.27 Pour the fork oil into the top of the tube

7.28 Measure the oil level with the fork held upright and fully compressed

fully into the slider any accidental scratching is confined to the area above the oil seal.

26 Fit the stoneguard **(see illustration)**.
27 Fully compress the fork tube in the slider, then slowly pour in the correct quantity of the specified grade of fork oil and carefully pump the damper cartridge rod at least ten times to distribute the oil **(see illustration)**. Now pump the fork tube in the slider using short strokes no longer than 100 mm, and leave the leg upright for ten minutes to allow any air bubbles to disperse.
28 Ensure the fork tube is still fully compressed into the slider; measure the fork oil level from the top of the tube **(see illustration)**. Add or subtract fork oil until it is at the level specified at the beginning of this Chapter.
29 Pull the fork tube out of the slider to its full extension and install the spring, followed by the spring seat, spacer, washer and damping adjuster in that order **(see illustrations)**.
30 Position the damper cartridge rod locknut so that the distance between the top of the nut and the top of the rod is 11 mm **(see illustration)**.
31 Lubricate a new O-ring with fork oil and fit it onto the top bolt, then thread the top bolt onto the damper cartridge rod until it seats against the locknut **(see illustration)**. Counter-hold the spring pre-load bolt and tighten the locknut securely against it, to the

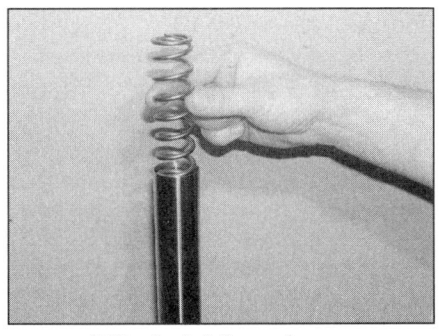

7.29a Install the spring ...

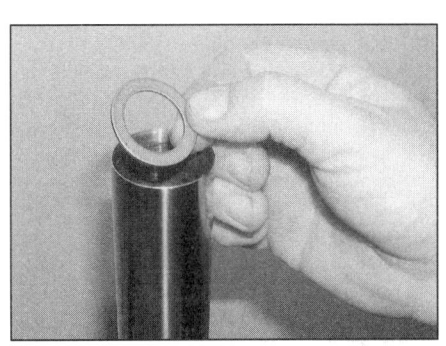

7.29b ... the spring seat ...

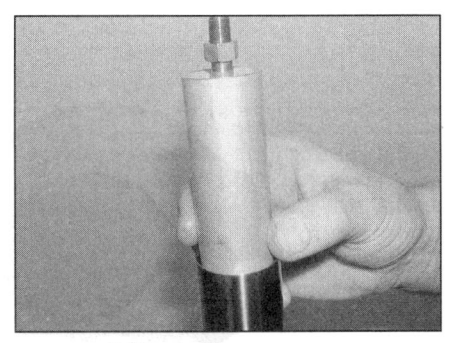

7.29c ... the spacer ...

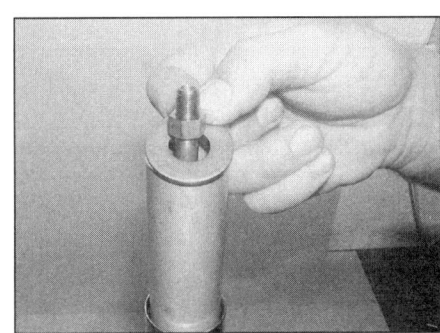

7.29d ... the washer ...

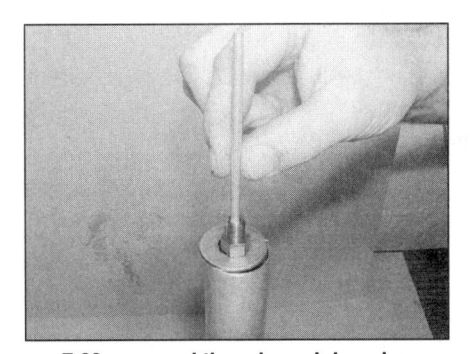

7.29e ... and the rebound damping adjuster

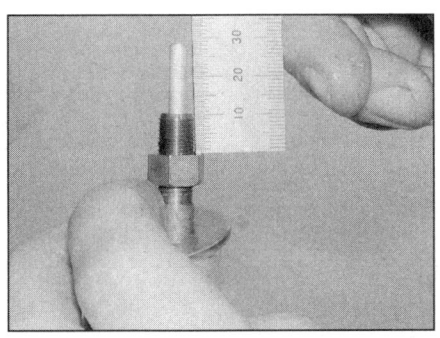

7.30 Measure the position of the damper rod locknut

7.31 Install a new O-ring on the top bolt

6•10 Frame, suspension and final drive

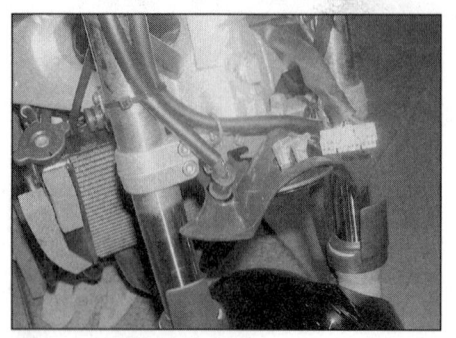

8.4 Displace the horn bracket

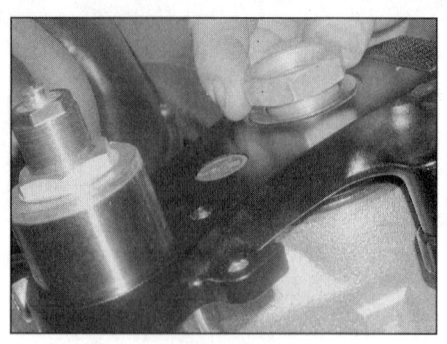

8.5a Remove the steering stem nut...

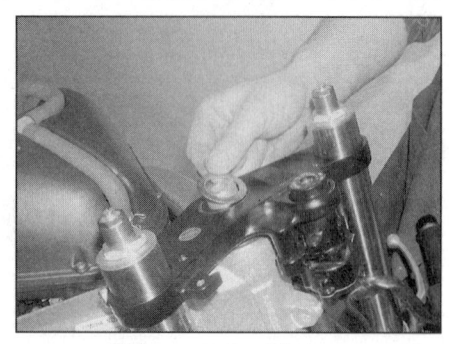

8.5b ...and washer...

specified torque if the correct tools are available **(see illustration 7.5a)**.

32 Fully extend the outer tube and carefully screw the top bolt into the tube, making sure it is not cross-threaded. **Note:** *The top bolt can be tightened to the specified torque setting at this stage if the tube is held between the padded jaws of a vice, but do not risk distorting the tube by doing so. A better method is to tighten the top bolt when the fork leg has been installed and is securely held in the yokes.*

TOOL TIP *Use a ratchet-type tool when installing the fork top bolt. This makes it unnecessary to remove the tool from the bolt whilst threading it in.*

33 Install the forks as described in Section 6. Set the spring pre-load and rebound damping as required (see Section 12).

8 Steering stem – removal and installation

Removal

1 Remove the fairing panels and air intake ducting (see Chapter 8). It is also advisable to remove the fuel tank to avoid the possibility of scratching it (see Chapter 4).
2 Remove the front forks (see Section 6).
3 Trace the wiring from the ignition switch and disconnect it at the connector. Disconnect the horn wiring connectors.
4 Unscrew the bolts securing the bracket for the horn and brake hose guides to the bottom yoke and displace the bracket **(see illustration)**.
5 Unscrew the steering stem nut and remove it and its washer, then lift the top yoke up off the steering stem **(see illustrations)**.
6 Remove the tabbed lockwasher, noting how it fits, then unscrew and remove the locknut using, if necessary, either a C-spanner, a peg spanner or a drift located in one of the notches (though it shouldn't be tight and can probably be undone with your fingers) **(see illustrations)**. Remove the rubber washer **(see illustration)**.
7 Supporting the bottom yoke, unscrew the adjuster nut using either a C-spanner, a peg-spanner or a drift located in one of the notches, then remove the adjuster nut and the bearing cover from the steering stem **(see illustrations)**.

8.5c ...then lift off the top yoke

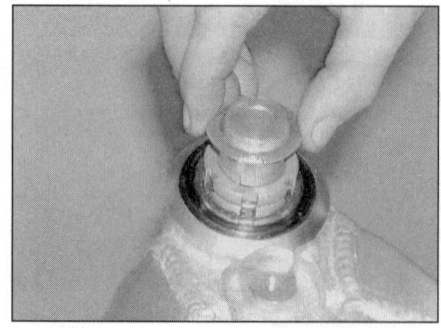

8.6a Remove the tabbed washer...

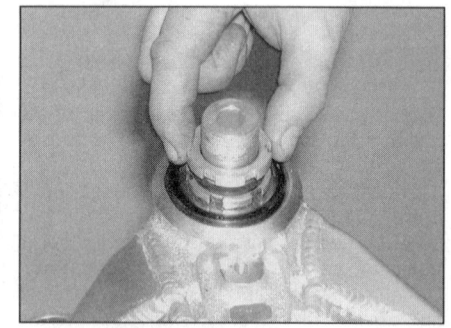

8.6b ...the locknut...

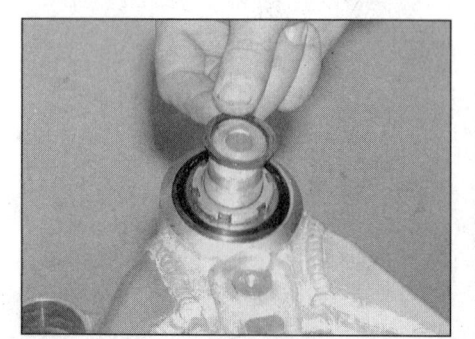

8.6c ...and the rubber washer

8.7a Unscrew the adjuster nut...

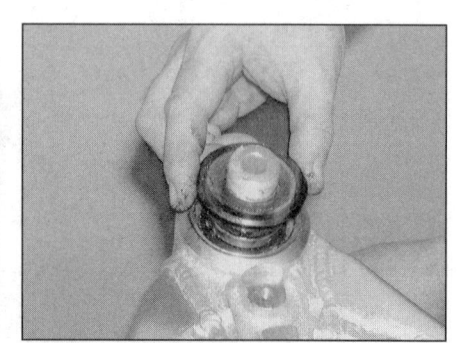

8.7b ...and remove the bearing cover

Frame, suspension and final drive 6•11

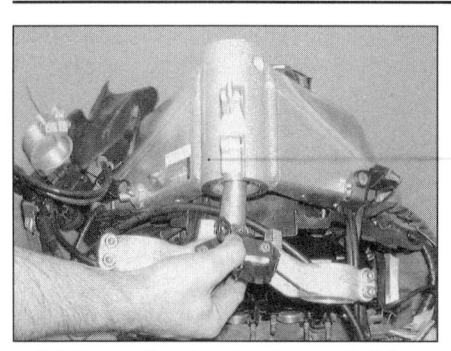

8.8 Lower the steering stem out of the frame

8.9a Remove the inner race ...

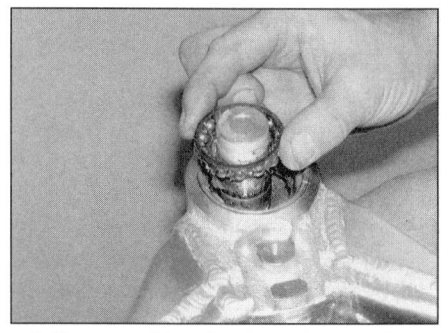

8.9b ... and bearing from the steering head

8 Gently lower the bottom yoke and steering stem out of the frame **(see illustration)**.

9 Remove the inner race and bearing from the top of the steering head **(see illustrations)**.

10 Remove the bearing and dust seal from the base of the steering stem **(see illustrations)**. Discard the dust seal as a new one must be fitted on reassembly. Use a suitable solvent to remove all traces of old grease from the bearings and races and check them for wear or damage as described in Section 9. **Note:** *Do not remove the races from the steering head or the steering stem unless they are to be replaced with new ones – do not re-use the races if they have been removed.*

Installation

11 Smear a liberal quantity of lithium-based grease onto the bearing races and work some grease well into both the upper and lower bearings. Fit the new dust seal over the lower bearing inner race on the steering stem, then fit the bearing **(see illustration 8.10b and a)**.

12 Carefully lift the bottom yoke and steering stem up through the steering head, and install the upper bearing and the inner race into the top of the steering head **(see illustrations 8.9b and a)**. Fit the bearing cover, then thread the adjuster nut onto the steering stem and adjust the bearings as described in Chapter 1, Section 17, noting that you may need to carry out the procedure several times if new bearings have been fitted to allow them to settle.

13 Install the rubber washer and the locknut **(see illustrations 8.6c and b)**. Tighten the locknut finger-tight, then tighten it further until its notches align with those in the adjuster nut. If necessary, counter-hold the adjuster nut to prevent it turning. Install the tabbed lockwasher so that the tabs fit into the notches in both the locknut and adjuster nut **(see illustration)**.

14 Fit the top yoke onto the steering stem, then install the washer and steering stem nut and tighten it finger-tight.

15 Install the fork legs to align the top and bottom yokes, and temporarily tighten the bottom yoke pinch bolts. Now tighten the steering stem nut to the torque setting specified at the beginning of this Chapter **(see illustration)**.

16 Ensure that the fork legs are correctly positioned in the yokes, then tighten the bottom yoke pinch bolts and then the top yoke pinch bolts to the recommended torque settings.

17 Install the remaining components in the reverse order of removal. Carry out a check of the steering head bearing freeplay as described in Chapter 1, and if necessary re-adjust.

9 Steering head bearings – inspection and renewal

Inspection

1 Remove the steering stem (see Section 8) and use a suitable solvent to remove all traces of old grease from the bearings and races.

3 Check for wear or damage; the races should be polished and free from indentations. Inspect the bearing balls for signs of wear, damage or discoloration, and examine the retainer cages for cracks or splits. Spin the bearing balls by hand. They should spin freely and smoothly. If there are signs of wear on any of the above components, both upper and lower bearing assemblies must be renewed as a set. **Note:** *Do not remove the races from the steering head or the steering stem unless they are to be replaced with new ones – do not re-use the races if they have been removed.*

Renewal

4 The outer races are an interference fit in the

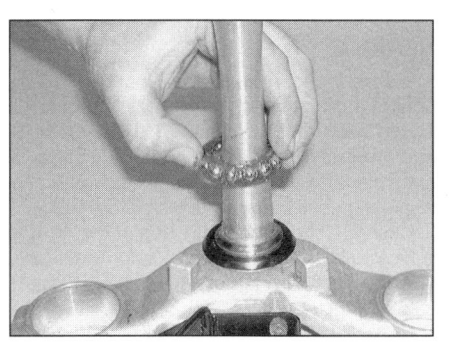

8.10a Remove the bearing ...

8.10b ... and dust seal

8.13 Align the notches and fit the tabbed washer

8.15 Tighten the steering stem nut to the specified torque

6•12 Frame, suspension and final drive

9.4a Locate the end of the drift in the cutout (arrowed) . . .

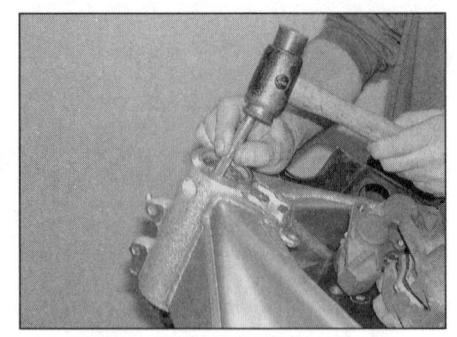

9.4b . . . and drive the race out

steering head and can be tapped out with a suitable drift located in the cutouts in the head **(see illustrations)**. Alternate between the left and right-hand cutouts so that the race is driven out squarely. It may prove advantageous to curve the end of the drift slightly to improve access.

5 Alternatively, the races can be removed using a slide-hammer type bearing extractor – these can often be hired from tool shops.

6 The new outer races can be installed in the head using a drawbolt arrangement **(see illustration)**, or by using a large diameter tubular drift. Ensure that the drawbolt washer or drift (as applicable) bears only on the outer edge of the race and does not contact the bearing surface.

HAYNES HINT *Installation of new bearing outer races is made much easier if the races are left overnight in the freezer. This causes them to contract slightly making them a looser fit. Alternatively, use a freeze spray.*

7 To remove the lower bearing race from the steering stem, first drive a chisel between the base of the race and the bottom yoke. Work the chisel around the race to ensure it lifts squarely. Once there is clearance beneath the race, use two levers placed on opposite sides of the race to work it free, using blocks of wood to improve leverage and protect the yoke **(see illustration)**. If the race is firmly in place it will be necessary to use a bearing puller **(see illustration)**. Alternatively, take the steering stem to a Yamaha dealer.

8 Fit the new lower race onto the steering stem. A length of tubing with an internal diameter slightly larger than the steering stem will be needed to tap the new race into position **(see illustration)**.

9 Install the steering stem (see Section 8).

10 Rear shock absorber – removal, inspection and installation

⚠ *Warning: Do not attempt to disassemble this shock absorber. It is nitrogen-charged*

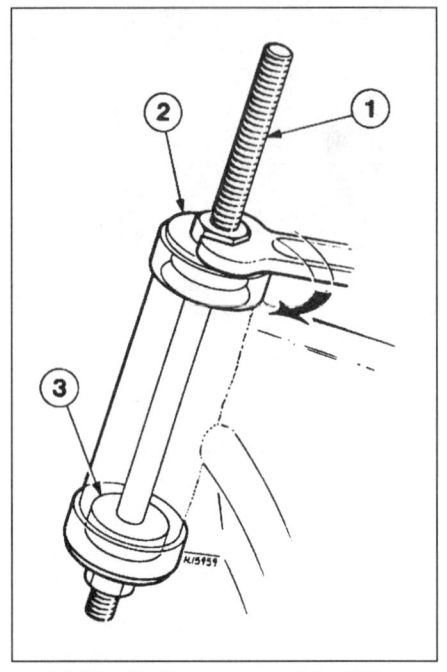

9.6 Drawbolt arrangement for fitting steering stem races

1 Long bolt or threaded bar
2 Thick washer
3 Guide for lower race

under high pressure. Improper disassembly could result in serious injury. Take the shock to a Yamaha dealer or suspension specialist for servicing and disposal.

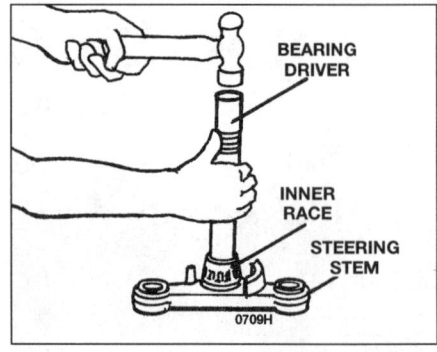

Removal

1 Support the motorcycle securely in an upright position using an auxiliary stand.

2 Remove the lower fairing (see Chapter 8) and the rear wheel (see Chapter 7). Support the swingarm so that it does not drop when the linkage bolts are removed.

3 Unscrew the nut on the bolt securing the linkage plates to the lower end of the shock **(see illustration)**. Remove the nut and washer and withdraw the bolt.

4 Unscrew the nut on the bolt securing the linkage plates to the link arm, then remove the nut and washer and withdraw the bolt **(see**

9.7a Lever the lower race off the steering stem . . .

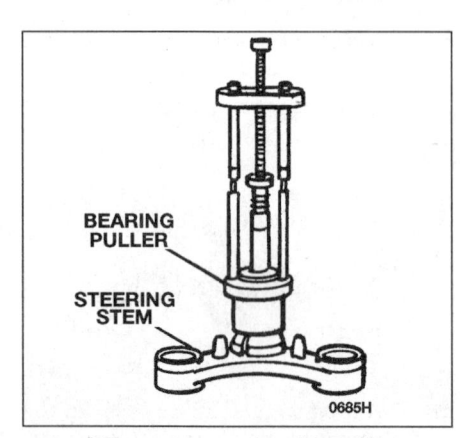

9.7b . . . or use a bearing puller

9.8 Install the lower race using a suitable driver of length of tubing

10.3 Unscrew the nut and withdraw the shock lower mounting bolt

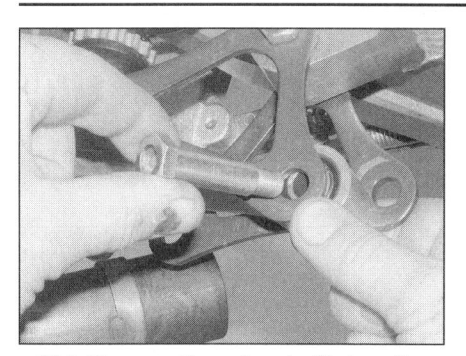

Frame, suspension and final drive 6•13

10.4 Unscrew the nut and withdraw the linkage arm bolt

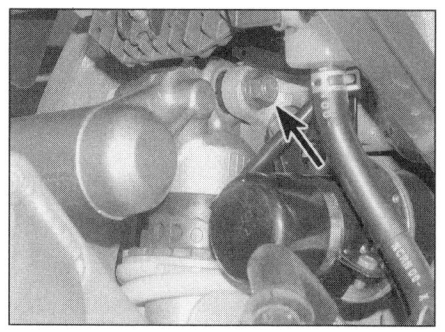

10.5 Loosen the shock upper mounting fixing (arrowed)

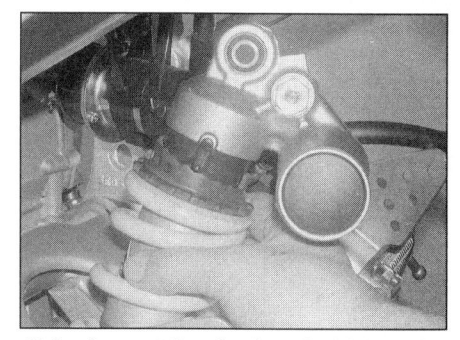

10.6a Support the shock and withdraw the upper bolt

illustration). Lower the plates and the link arm to provide clearance for the shock.

5 On 1999 models, remove the R-clip on the shock upper mounting pin and remove the washer. On 2000-on models, unscrew the nut on the shock absorber upper mounting bolt.

6 Support the shock absorber and withdraw the upper mounting pin or bolt **(see illustration)**. Raise the swingarm and lower the shock out of the frame. Remove the collar from inside the shock upper mounting for safekeeping **(see illustration)**.

Inspection

7 Inspect the body of the shock absorber for obvious physical damage and the coil spring for looseness, cracks or signs of fatigue.
8 Inspect the shock damper rod for signs of bending, pitting and oil leakage.
9 Inspect the gas cylinder for damage.
10 Inspect the pivot collar in the upper mounting for wear and renew it if necessary.
11 Inspect the bearing seals and needle bearing and collar in the lower mounting. If necessary, prise out the seals and remove the collar. The bearing can be pressed out with a suitably sized socket if a new one has to be fitted (see *Tools and Workshop Tips* in the *Reference* section). Discard the seals as new ones must be fitted on reassembly.
12 On 1999 models, inspect the upper mounting pin R-clip and replace it with a new one if it is damaged or corroded.
13 Ensure that the spring pre-load adjusting ring is clean and free to rotate; inspect the indents on the ring for wear.
14 Ensure that the rebound damping and compression damping adjusters are clean and free to rotate.
15 The shock cannot be dismantled for the replacement of individual components. If it is worn or damaged, it must be replaced with a new one.

Installation

16 Installation is the reverse of removal. Clean and grease the needle bearing in the lower mounting and install new bearing seals. Apply lithium-based grease to the shock absorber and link arm pivot points. Install the bolts and nuts finger-tight only until all components are in position, then tighten the nuts to the torque settings specified at the beginning of this Chapter.

11 Rear suspension linkage – removal, inspection and installation

Removal

1 Support the motorcycle securely in an upright position using an auxiliary stand.
2 Remove the lower fairing (see Chapter 8) and the rear wheel (see Chapter 7). Support the swingarm so that it does not drop when the linkage bolts are removed.
3 Unscrew the nuts on the bolts securing the

10.6b Note the collar inside the upper mounting

linkage plates to the lower end of the shock and the link arm **(see illustration)**. Remove the nuts and washers and withdraw the bolts.
4 Note the position of the FWD markings on the lower edge of the linkage plates **(see illustration)**. Unscrew the nut on the bolt securing the plates to the swingarm. Remove the nut and washer, then support the plates and withdraw the bolt.
5 Unscrew the nut and withdraw the bolt securing the link arm to the frame and remove the arm; note which way round the arm fits **(see illustration)**. Remove the spacer from the link arm. Note that the exhaust system bracket can remain in place.

Inspection

6 Remove the collars from the bearings in each end of the link arm and also from the

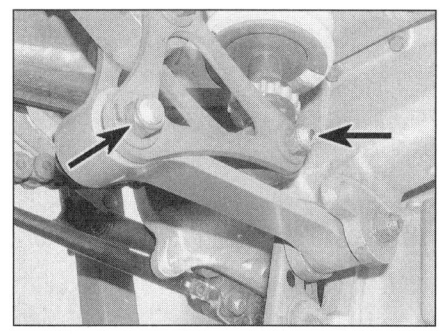

11.3 Undo the bolts (arrowed) connecting the plates to the shock and the linkage arm

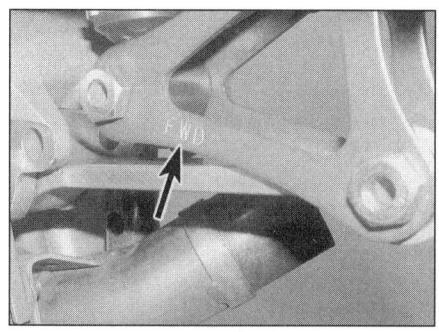

11.4 The linkage plates are marked FWD (arrowed) to aid reassembly

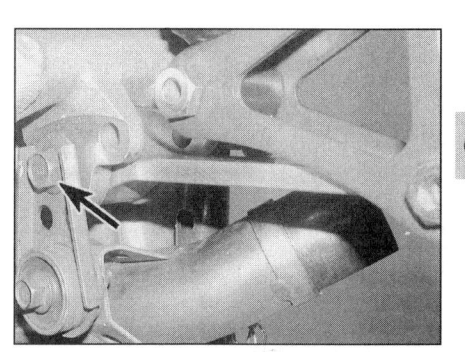

11.5 Remove the bolt (arrowed) to release the link arm

6

6•14 Frame, suspension and final drive

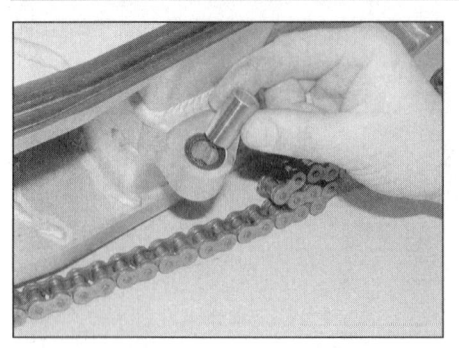

11.6a Press the collars out of the swingarm . . .

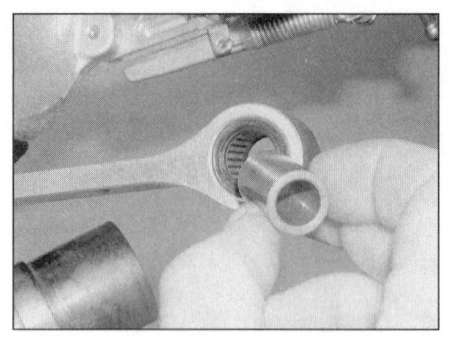

11.6b . . . and the link arm . . .

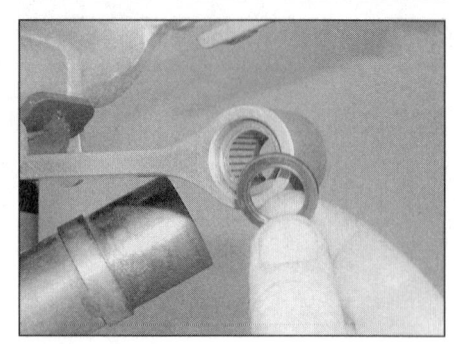

11.6c . . . and prise out the bearing seals

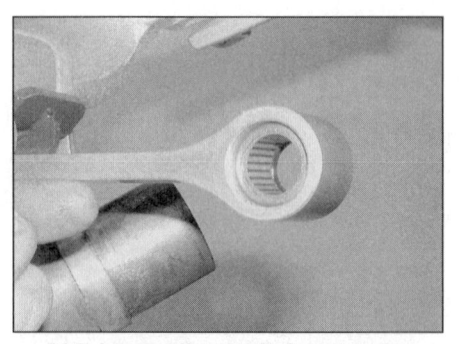

11.7 Inspect the needle bearings for freeplay

linkage plate mounting point in the swingarm. Prise out the bearing seals **(see illustrations)**. Thoroughly clean all components with a suitable solvent, removing all traces of dirt, corrosion and grease.

7 Inspect all components closely, looking for obvious signs of wear such as heavy scoring, or for damage such as cracks or distortion **(see illustration)**. Inspect the bolt holes in the linkage plates for elongation. Slip each collar back into its bearing and check that there is not an excessive amount of freeplay between the two components (see *Tools and Workshop Tips* in the *Reference* section).

8 The bearings can be drifted out of their bores, but only remove them if new bearings are to be fitted. Take care when fitting new bearings; do not drift the bearings into place – a suitable drawbolt tool can be made up as described in *Tools and*

Workshop Tips (Section 5) in the *Reference* section.

Installation

9 Installation is the reverse of removal, noting the following:
● Lubricate the needle roller bearings and the collars with lithium-based grease.
● Lubricate the new bearing seals with grease and press the seals squarely into place so that their marked side faces outwards.
● Don't forget to install the exhaust bracket when bolting the link arm to the frame.
● Assemble the linkage plates with the FWD markings on the lower edge **(see illustration 11.4)**.
● Install the nuts, bolts and washers finger-tight only until all components are in position, then tighten the nuts to the torque settings specified at the beginning of the Chapter.

12 Suspension – adjustments

Note: *Refer to the Owner's Manual supplied with the machine for recommended front and rear suspension settings to suit loading.*
Caution: *Never attempt to turn an adjuster beyond the minimum or maximum setting.*

Front forks

1 The front forks are adjustable for spring pre-load, rebound damping, and compression damping.

2 Spring pre-load is adjusted using a suitable spanner on the adjuster flats on the top of the forks; the amount of pre-load is indicated by lines on the adjuster **(see illustration)**. There are eight lines. The standard position is with the 5th line (1999 models) or 7th line (2000-on models) just visible above the fork top bolt hex. Turn the adjuster clockwise to increase pre-load, and anti-clockwise to decrease it. Always make sure both adjusters are set equally.

3 Rebound damping is adjusted using a screwdriver in the slot in the adjuster protruding from the spring pre-load adjuster **(see illustration)**. Turn the adjuster clockwise to increase damping and anti-clockwise to decrease it. There are twelve positions. To establish the current setting, turn the adjuster in (clockwise) until it stops, counting the number of clicks, then reset it as required by turning it out (anti-clockwise). The standard position is six clicks out. The maximum position is one click out. The minimum setting is 11 clicks (1999 models) or 9 clicks (2000-on models) out. Always make sure both adjusters are set equally.

4 Compression damping is adjusted using a screwdriver in the slot in the adjuster on the base of each fork slider **(see illustration)**. Turn the adjuster clockwise to increase damping and anti-clockwise to decrease it. There are eleven positions. To establish the current setting, turn the adjuster in (clockwise) until it

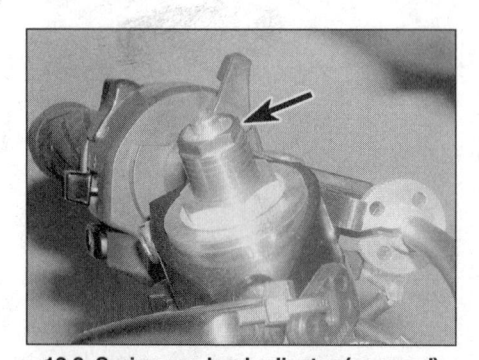

12.2 Spring pre-load adjuster (arrowed)

12.3 Adjusting the rebound damping

12.4 Adjusting the compression damping

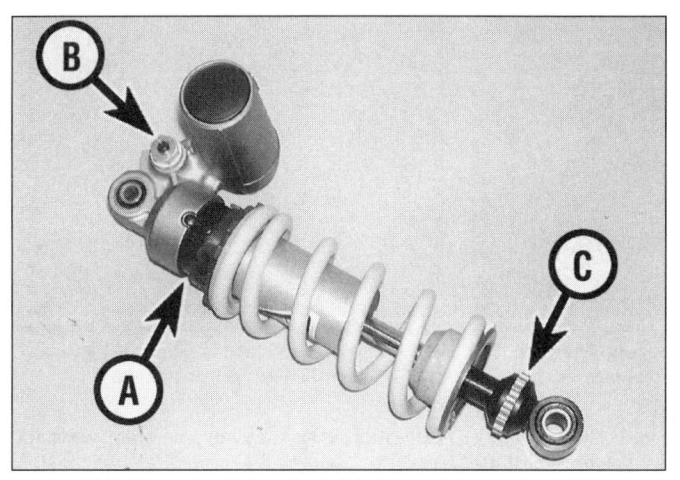

Frame, suspension and final drive 6•15

12.5 Rear shock is adjustable for spring pre-load (A), compression damping (B) and rebound damping (C)

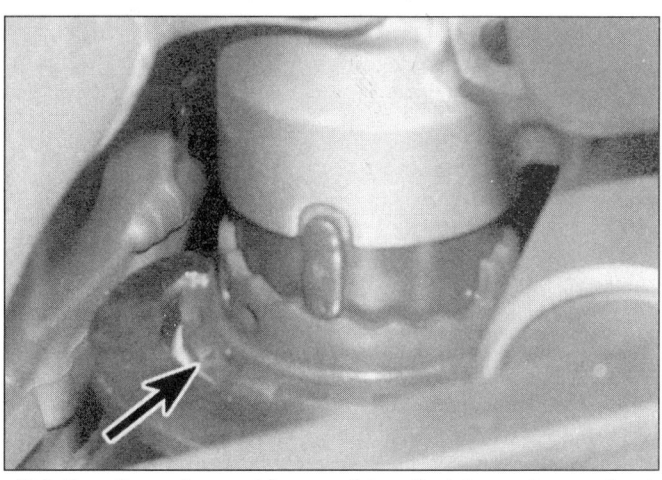

12.6 Turn the spring seat (arrowed) to adjust the spring pre-load

12.7 Turn the adjuster (arrowed) to set the rebound damping

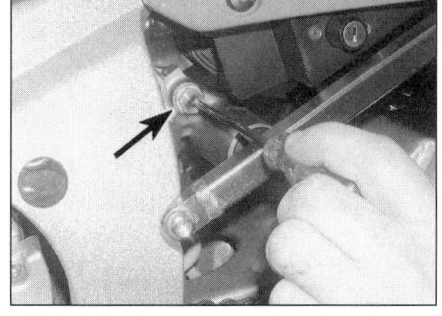

12.8 Adjusting compression damping at the top of the shock

stops, counting the number of clicks, then reset it as required by turning it out (anti-clockwise). The standard position is six clicks out. The maximum position is one click out. The minimum setting is 12 clicks (1999 models) or 10 clicks (2000-on models) out. Always make sure both adjusters are set equally.

Rear shock absorber

5 The rear shock absorber is adjustable for spring pre-load, rebound damping, and compression damping **(see illustration)**.
6 Spring pre-load is adjusted using a suitable C-spanner (one is provided in the bike's toolkit) to turn the spring seat on the top of the shock absorber **(see illustration)**. There are nine positions. Position 1 is the softest setting, position 4 is the standard, position 9 is the hardest. Align the setting required with the adjustment stopper. Turn the spring seat anti-clockwise to increase pre-load and clockwise to decrease it.
7 Rebound damping is adjusted by turning the adjuster on the base of the shock absorber **(see illustration)**. Turn the adjuster clockwise to increase damping and anti-clockwise to decrease it. There are twenty-five positions. To establish the current setting, turn the adjuster clockwise until it stops, counting the number of clicks, then reset it as required by turning it anti-clockwise. The standard position is nine clicks anti-clockwise, the maximum position is one click anti-clockwise and the minimum is 25 clicks anti-clockwise.

8 Compression damping is adjusted using a screwdriver in the slot in the adjuster on the top of the shock absorber **(see illustration)**. Turn the adjuster clockwise to increase damping and anti-clockwise to decrease it. There are thirteen positions. To establish the current setting, turn the adjuster in (clockwise) until it stops, counting the number of clicks, then reset it as required by turning it out (anti-clockwise). The standard position is seven clicks out, the maximum position is one click out and the minimum is 13 clicks out.

13 Swingarm – removal and installation

Removal

Note: *This motorcycle has a drive chain with a staked-type master link (see Section 15). Only break the chain to remove it from the swingarm if the chain or the swingarm are going to be renewed.*

1 Support the motorcycle securely in an upright position using an auxiliary stand.
2 Remove the exhaust silencer (see Chapter 4), shock absorber (see Section 10) and the front sprocket (see Section 16).
3 Unscrew the bolts securing the chainguard to the swingarm and remove it, noting how it fits **(see illustrations)**.

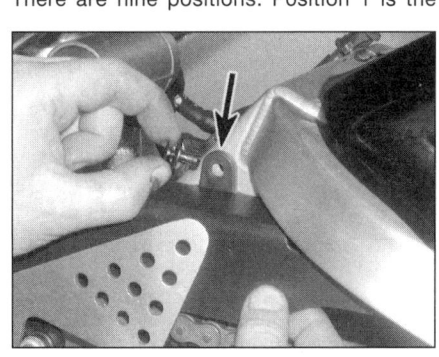

13.3a Undo the bolts at the front . . .

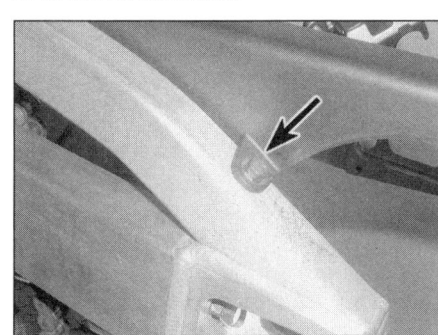

13.3b . . . rear and . . .

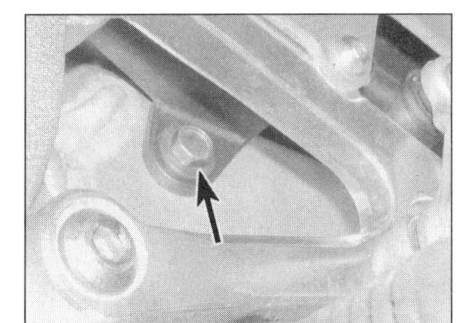

13.3c . . . lower edge of the chainguard

6•16 Frame, suspension and final drive

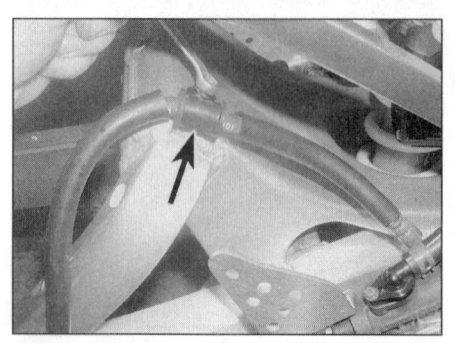

13.4a Undo the bolts securing the brake hose guide (arrowed) . . .

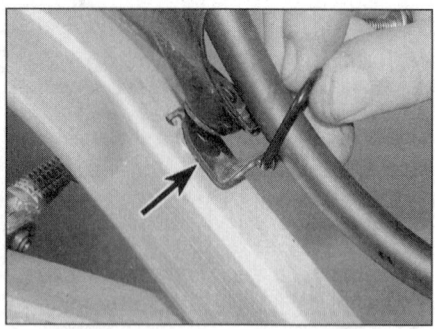

13.4b . . . and the hose guide and mudguard (arrowed)

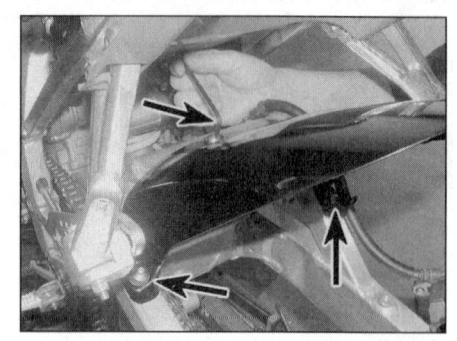

13.4c The mudguard is secured by three button-head bolts (arrowed)

4 Unscrew the bolts securing the brake hose guides to the swingarm, then unscrew the bolts securing the mudguard (hugger) to the swingarm and remove it (see illustrations).
5 Before removing the swingarm it is advisable to check for play in the bearings (see Chapter 1). Any problems which were not evident with the other suspension components attached may now show up.
6 Unscrew the nut on the end of the swingarm pivot bolt and remove the washer (see illustrations).
7 Loosen the swingarm pivot adjuster (see illustration). Yamaha provide a shaft wrench for this purpose (Part No. 90890 – 01471) but a suitable tool can easily be made as illustrated. Support the swingarm, then withdraw the pivot bolt and remove the swingarm, along with the drive chain (see illustration). Knock the pivot bolt through using a large drift if required, but be careful not to damage the threaded end; note how the flat sides on the bolt head locate in the recess in the frame (see illustration).
8 If necessary, unscrew the bolt securing the chain slider to the swingarm and remove the slider, noting how it fits (see illustration). If the slider is badly worn or damaged, it should be replaced with a new one.
9 Inspect all components for wear and damage as described in Section 14.

Installation

10 Remove the bearing cover from the left-hand side of the swingarm and check the condition of the seal inside the cover (see illustration). If the seal is in good condition, the cover can be reused, otherwise discard it and fit a new one on reassembly.
11 Remove the collar from inside the seal on the right-hand side of the swingarm, then

13.6a Unscrew the nut (arrowed) . . .

13.6b . . . and remove the washer . . .

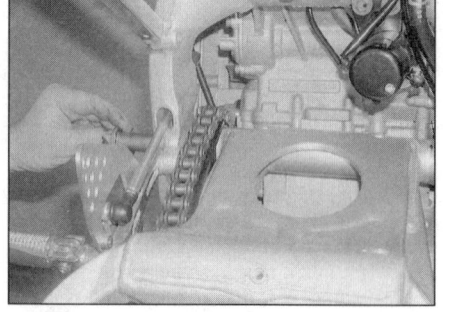

13.7a . . . then loosen the pivot adjuster . . .

13.7b . . . and withdraw the pivot bolt . . .

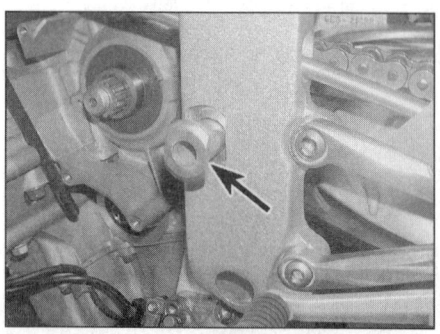

13.7c . . . noting how its head (arrowed) locates in the frame recess

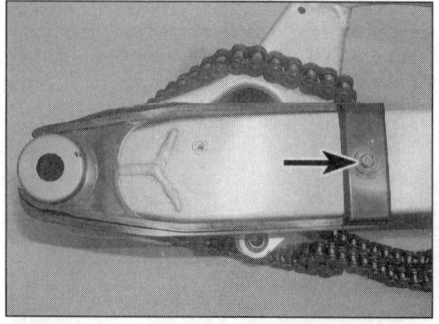

13.8 Undo bolt (arrowed) to remove the chain slider

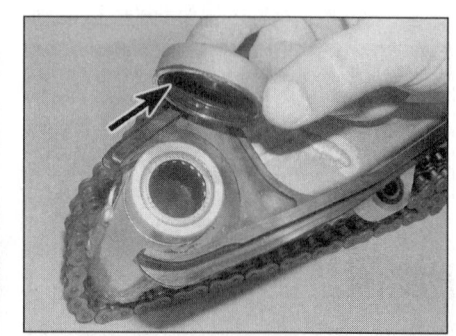

13.10 Check the condition of the seal (arrowed)

Frame, suspension and final drive 6•17

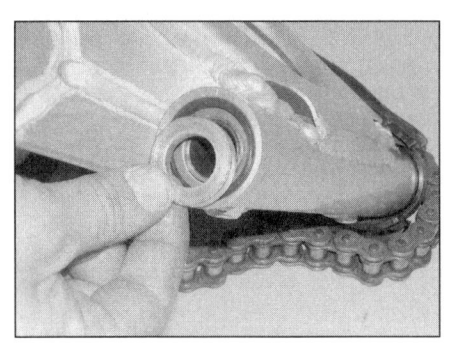

13.11a Remove the collar . . .

13.11b . . . the seal . . .

13.11c . . . and the shim . . .

carefully remove the seal and the shim **(see illustrations)**. If the seal is in good condition, it can be reused; otherwise discard the seal and fit a new one on reassembly.

12 Withdraw the swingarm long inner sleeve **(see illustration)**. Wipe the old grease from the inner sleeve and bearings, then apply fresh lithium-based grease to their surfaces.

13 Install the long inner sleeve through the bearings. Install the shim in the right-hand side of the swingarm; lubricate the seal with grease and install the seal, then install the collar. Grease the inside of the left-hand bearing cover and install the cover. Lubricate the suspension linkage bearing on the underside of the swingarm (see Section 11) and grease the swingarm pivot bolt.

14 If removed, install the chain slider and tighten the bolt securely **(see illustration 13.8)**. Ensure the pivot adjuster is backed-off sufficiently to allow easy installation of the swingarm **(see illustration)**. Loop the drive chain over the slider and the swingarm pivot, then install the swingarm and slide the pivot bolt through from the left-hand side. Locating the head of the bolt correctly in the frame **(see illustration 13.7c)**.

15 Tighten the swingarm pivot adjuster finger-tight, then install the washer and nut on the pivot bolt and tighten the nut to the torque setting specified at the beginning of this Chapter.

16 Install the remaining components in the reverse order of removal. Check and adjust the drive chain slack (see Chapter 1), and check the operation of the rear suspension before taking the machine on the road.

14 Swingarm – inspection and bearing renewal

Inspection

1 Thoroughly clean the swingarm, removing all traces of dirt, corrosion and grease. Pay particular attention to the area covered by the chain slider and the slots for the rear axle and the chain adjuster plates. Unscrew the chain adjusters and check the condition of the threads in the swingarm; if they are damaged consult a specialist engineer or a Yamaha dealer to have them repaired.

2 If not already done, remove the bearing cover from the left-hand side of the swingarm and check the condition of the internal seal (see Section 13).

3 Remove the collar from inside the seal on the right-hand side of the swingarm, then carefully remove the seal and the shim (see Section 13). Withdraw the long inner sleeve and clean any old grease off the bearings.

4 Clean all components thoroughly and then inspect them for signs of wear such as heavy scoring, and cracks or distortion due to accident damage. Check the bearings for roughness, looseness and any other damage, referring to *Tools and Workshop Tips* (Section 5) in the *Reference* section **(see illustration)**. Any damaged or worn component must be renewed.

5 Remove any corrosion from the swingarm pivot bolt and the inner sleeve with steel wool. Check them for straightness by rolling them on a flat surface such as a piece of plate glass. If available, measure the runout with V-blocks and replace either component with a new one if it is bent.

Bearing renewal

6 The two needle bearings can be drawn or drifted out of their bores, but note that removal will make them unusable; new bearings should be obtained before work commences. Pass a long drift with a hooked end through one side of the swingarm and locate it on the inside edge of the bearing on the opposite side. Tap the drift around the bearing's inside edge to ensure that it is driven out of its bore squarely. Use the same method to extract both bearings. A preferable alternative, if available, is a slide-hammer with knife-edged bearing puller.

7 Inspect the bearing seats and remove any scoring or corrosion carefully with steel wool or a suitable scraper.

8 The new bearings should be pressed or drawn into their bores, rather than driven into position. In the absence of a press, a suitable drawbolt arrangement can be made up as described in *Tools and Workshop Tips* (Section 5) in the *Reference* section. Lubricate the bearings with lithium-based grease.

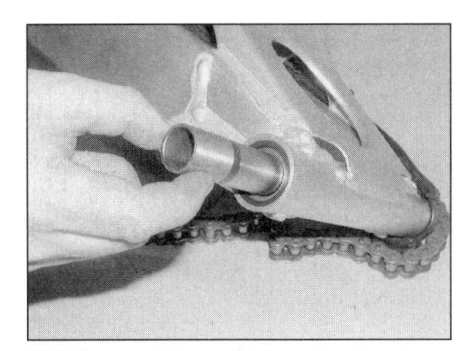

13.12 . . . and then withdraw the long inner sleeve

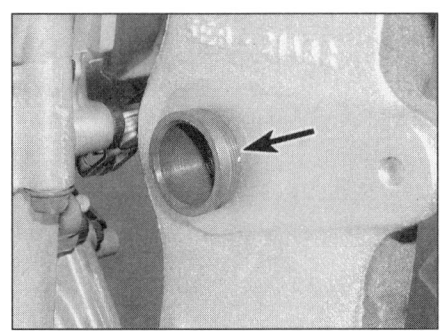

13.14 Back-off the adjuster (arrowed) to allow easy installation of the swingarm

14.4 Clean and examine both swingarm bearings

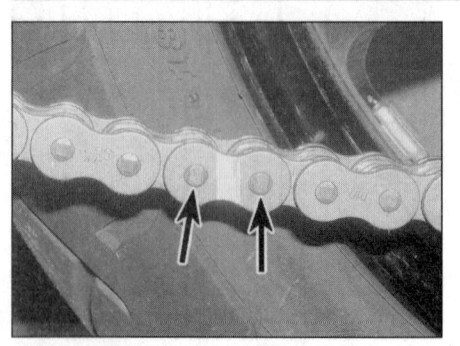

6•18 Frame, suspension and final drive

15.2 Joining link is identified by paint and centre-punched pins (arrowed)

16.2 Ensure the lockwasher (arrowed) is correctly bent over the sprocket nut

16.7 Bend back the lockwasher tabs with a small chisel

15 Drive chain – removal and installation

Removal

Note: *All models are fitted with a staked-type master (joining) link which can be disassembled using one of several commercially-available drive chain cutting/staking tools. Such chains can be recognised by the master link side plate's identification marks (and usually its different colour), as well as by the staked ends of the link's two pins which look as if they have been deeply centre-punched, instead of peened over as with all the other pins.*

⚠️ **Warning:** *Use ONLY the correct service tools to disassemble and assemble the staked-type of master link – if you do not have access to such tools or do not have the skill to operate them correctly, have the old chain removed and a new one fitted by a dealer service department or bike repair shop.*

1 Remove the front sprocket cover (see Chapter 2, Section 17, Steps 1 to 4).
2 Place the joining link in a suitable position for working on, by rotating the back wheel **(see illustration)**.
3 Slacken the drive chain as described in Chapter 1.
4 Split the chain at the joining link using the chain cutter, following the manufacturer's operating instructions carefully (see also Section 8 in *Tools and Workshop Tips* in the *Reference* Section). Remove the chain from the bike, noting its routing through the swingarm.

Installation

⚠️ **Warning:** *NEVER install a drive chain which uses a clip-type master (split) link. Use ONLY the correct service tools to secure the staked-type of master link – if you do not have access to such tools or do not have the skill to operate them correctly, have the chain installed by a dealer service department or bike repair shop to be sure of having it securely installed.*

5 Route the drive chain through the swingarm sections and around the front and rear sprockets, leaving the two ends in a convenient position to work on.
6 Refer to Section 8 in *Tools and Workshop Tips* in the *Reference* Section. Fit an O-ring onto each pin on the **new** joining link, then slide the link through from the inside and fit the other two O-rings. Install the new side plate with its identification marks facing out. Stake the new link using the drive chain cutting/staking tool, following the instructions of both the chain manufacturer and the tool manufacturer carefully. DO NOT re-use old joining link components.
7 After staking, check the joining link and staking for any signs of cracking. If there is any evidence of cracking, the joining link, O-rings and side plate must be renewed.
8 Install the sprocket cover (see Section 16).
9 On completion, adjust and lubricate the chain following the procedures described in Chapter 1.

16 Sprockets – check and renewal

Check

1 Remove the front sprocket cover (see Chapter 2, Section 17, Steps 1 to 4).
2 Check that the lockwasher is correctly installed on the front sprocket nut and that the nut is tight **(see illustration)**.

3 Check that the rear wheel sprocket nuts are tightened to the torque setting specified at the beginning of this Chapter.
4 Check the wear pattern on the front and rear wheel sprockets **(see illustration 1.7 in Chapter 1)**. Whenever the sprockets are inspected, the drive chain should also be inspected. If the sprocket teeth are worn excessively, or you are fitting a new chain, renew the chain and sprockets as a set.
5 Adjust and lubricate the chain following the procedures described in Chapter 1.

Renewal

Front sprocket

6 Remove the front sprocket cover (see Chapter 2, Section 17, Steps 1 to 4).
7 Bend back the tabs on the sprocket nut lockwasher **(see illustration)**. Have an assistant apply the rear brake hard, then unscrew the nut and remove the washer. Discard the washer, as a new one must be used on reassembly. Adjust the chain so that it is fully slack (see Chapter 1, Section 1).
8 Slide the sprocket and chain off the shaft and slip the sprocket out of the chain **(see illustration)**. If there is not enough slack in the chain to disengage the sprocket, slip the chain off the rear wheel sprocket **(see illustration)**. **Note:** *If the sprocket is not being replaced with a new one, mark its outside face with a scratch, or dab of paint, so that it can be installed the same way round.*
9 Engage the new sprocket with the chain and slide it on the shaft. If removed, install the

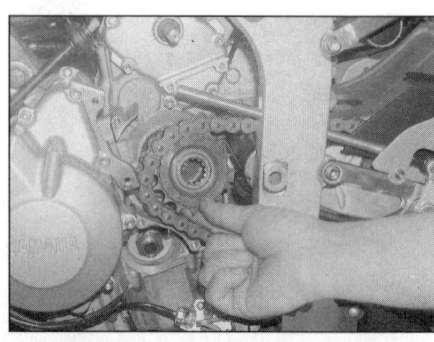

16.8a Slide the sprocket off the shaft

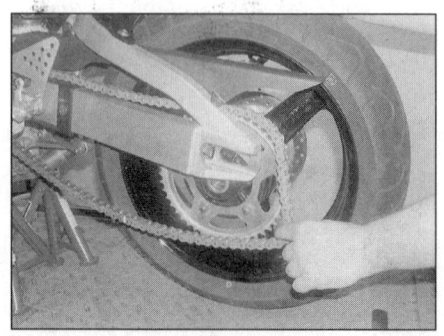

16.8b Slip the chain off the rear sprocket to gain more slack

Frame, suspension and final drive 6•19

16.10a Fit the new lockwasher...

16.10b ...and tighten the nut to the specified torque...

16.10c ...then bend the washer tabs against the nut

chain on the rear sprocket and take up the slack in the chain (see Chapter 1).
10 Install the **new** lockwasher, then fit the nut with the shouldered side facing in and tighten it to the torque setting specified at the beginning of this Chapter, applying the rear brake to prevent the sprocket from turning **(see illustrations)**. Bend the tabs of the lockwasher up against the nut flats **(see illustration)**.
11 Install the front sprocket cover.
12 Install the remaining components in the reverse order of removal.

Rear sprocket

13 Remove the rear wheel (see Chapter 7). *Caution: Don't lay the wheel down and allow it to rest on the disc or the sprocket – they could become warped. Set the wheel on wood blocks so the wheel rim supports the weight of the wheel. Don't operate the brake pedal with the wheel removed.*
14 Unscrew the nuts securing the sprocket to the hub assembly **(see illustration)**. Remove the sprocket, noting which way round it fits. *Note: The size of the sprocket (i.e. its number of teeth) is stamped on the outside face of the sprocket* **(see illustration)**.
15 Install the sprocket onto the hub with the stamped mark facing out. Tighten the nuts evenly and in a criss-cross sequence to the

16.14a Unscrew the nuts (arrowed)

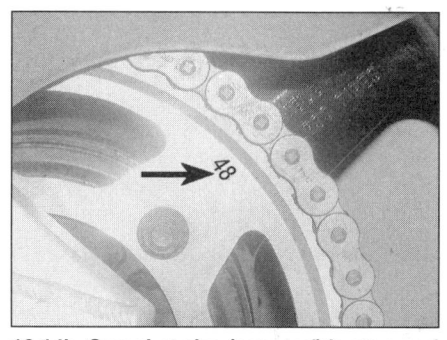

16.14b Sprocket size (arrowed) is stamped on the outside face

torque setting specified at the beginning of this Chapter.
16 Install the rear wheel (see Chapter 7).

17 Rear sprocket coupling/rubber dampers – check and renewal

1 Remove the rear wheel (see Chapter 7). *Caution: Don't lay the wheel down and allow it to rest on the disc or the sprocket – they could become warped. Set the wheel on wood blocks so the wheel rim supports the weight of the wheel. Don't operate the brake pedal with the wheel removed.*

2 Lift the sprocket coupling out of the hub, leaving the rubber dampers in position in the hub, and check the coupling for cracks or any obvious signs of damage **(see illustrations)**. Also check the sprocket studs for looseness, wear or damage.
3 Lift the rubber damper segments from the hub and check them for cracks, hardening, wear and general deterioration **(see illustration)**. Renew the rubber dampers as a set, if necessary.
4 Checking and renewal procedures for the sprocket coupling bearing are described in Chapter 7.
5 Installation is the reverse of removal.
6 Install the rear wheel (see Chapter 7).

17.2a Lift the sprocket coupling out of the hub...

17.2b ...and check the coupling for damage...

17.3 ...then lift the damper segments out of the hub

Notes

Chapter 7
Brakes, wheels and tyres

Contents

Brake fluid level check . . . . .see *Daily (pre-ride) checks*	
Brake hoses and unions – inspection and renewal 10	
Brake light switches – check and renew . . . . .see Chapter 9	
Brake pad wear check . . . . .see Chapter 1	
Brake system – bleeding and fluid change 11	
Brake system check . . . . .see Chapter 1	
Front brake calipers – removal, overhaul and installation 3	
Front brake discs – inspection, removal and installation 4	
Front brake master cylinder – removal, overhaul and installation . . . 5	
Front brake pads – renewal 2	
Front wheel – removal and installation 14	
General information 1	
Rear brake caliper – removal, overhaul and installation 7	
Rear brake disc – inspection, removal and installation 8	
Rear brake master cylinder – removal, overhaul and installation . . . 9	
Rear brake pads – renewal 6	
Rear wheel – removal and installation 15	
Tyres – general information and fitting 17	
Tyres – pressure, tread depth and condition . . . . .see *Daily (pre-ride) checks*	
Wheel bearings – check . . . . .see Chapter 1	
Wheel bearings – removal, inspection and installation 16	
Wheels – alignment check 13	
Wheels – general check . . . . .see Chapter 1	
Wheels – inspection and repair 12	

Degrees of difficulty

Easy, suitable for novice with little experience	**Fairly easy,** suitable for beginner with some experience	**Fairly difficult,** suitable for competent DIY mechanic	**Difficult,** suitable for experienced DIY mechanic	**Very difficult,** suitable for expert DIY or professional

Specifications

Brakes

Brake fluid type	DOT 4
Brake pad friction material wear limit	see Chapter 1
Front caliper bore ID	
Upper bore	30.2 mm
Lower bore	27.0 mm
Front disc thickness	
Standard	5.0 mm
Service limit	4.5 mm
Front disc maximum runout	0.1 mm
Front master cylinder bore ID	14.0 mm
Rear caliper bore ID	
Upper bore	27.0 mm
Lower bore	22.2 mm
Rear disc thickness	
Standard	5.0 mm
Service limit	4.5 mm
Rear disc maximum runout	0.1 mm
Rear master cylinder bore ID	12.7 mm

Wheels

Rim size	
Front	17 x MT3.50
Rear	17 x MT5.50
Wheel runout (max)	
Axial (side-to-side)	0.5 mm
Radial (out-of-round)	1.0 mm

7•2 Brakes, wheels and tyres

Tyres

Tyre pressures	see *Daily (pre-ride) checks*
Tyre sizes*	
Front	120/60-ZR17 (55W)
Rear	180/55-ZR17 (73W)

Refer to the owners manual or your Yamaha dealer for approved tyre brands.

Torque wrench settings

Brake caliper bleed valves	6 Nm
Brake hose banjo bolts	30 Nm
Brake hose-to-front mudguard clamp bolt	6 Nm
Front axle	72 Nm
Front axle pinch bolt	23 Nm
Front brake caliper mounting bolts	40 Nm
Front brake disc bolts	18 Nm
Front brake master cylinder clamp bolts	13 Nm
Rear axle nut	150 Nm
Rear brake caliper bracket-to-swingarm anchor bolt	40 Nm
Rear brake caliper mounting bolts	27 Nm
Rear brake disc bolts	18 Nm
Rear brake master cylinder mounting bolts	23 Nm

1 General information

All models are fitted with cast alloy wheels designed for tubeless tyres only.

Both front and rear brakes are hydraulically-operated disc brakes.

The front brakes are twin floating discs with twin, opposed-piston calipers. The rear brake is a single disc with a two-piston sliding caliper.

Caution: Disc brake components rarely require disassembly. Do not disassemble components unless absolutely necessary. If a hydraulic brake line is loosened, the entire system must be disassembled, drained, cleaned and then properly filled and bled upon reassembly. Do not use solvents on internal brake components. Solvents will cause the seals to swell and distort. Use only clean brake fluid or denatured alcohol for cleaning. Use care when working with brake fluid as it can injure your eyes and it will damage painted surfaces and plastic parts.

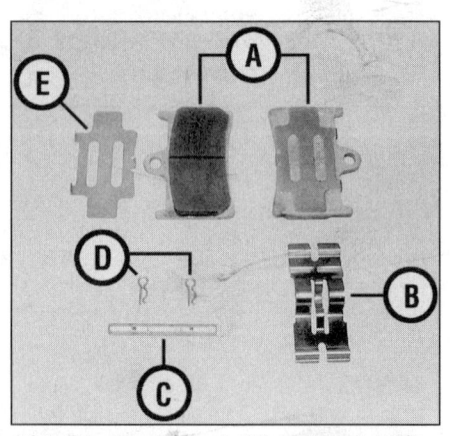

2.1 Front brake pads (A), pad spring (B), retaining pin (C), R-clips (D) and anti-chatter shim (E)

2.2 Remove the R-clips . . .

2 Front brake pads – renewal

Warning: The dust created by the brake system may contain asbestos, which is harmful to your health. Never blow it out with compressed air and don't inhale any of it. An approved filtering mask should be worn when working on the brakes.

1 If new pads are being installed, displace the calipers from the discs (see Section 3) – this makes it easier to push the pistons back into the caliper to allow for the extra thickness of new pads. Otherwise, the pads can be removed with the caliper in place **(see illustration)**.

2 Remove the R-clip from each end of the pad retaining pin **(see illustration)**. If the clips are distorted or corroded, discard them and fit new ones on reassembly.

3 Withdraw the pin, noting how it fits through the pad spring and remove the pad spring, noting which way round it fits **(see illustrations)**. Withdraw the pads from the top of the caliper, noting how they fit **(see illustration)**. If required, remove the anti-chatter shim from the back of each pad,

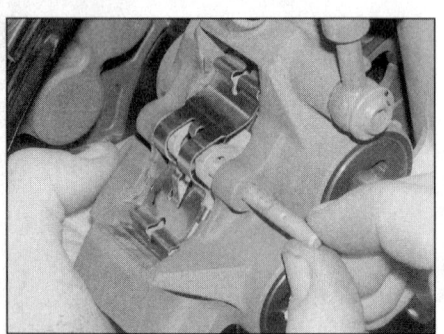

2.3a . . . then pull out the pin . . .

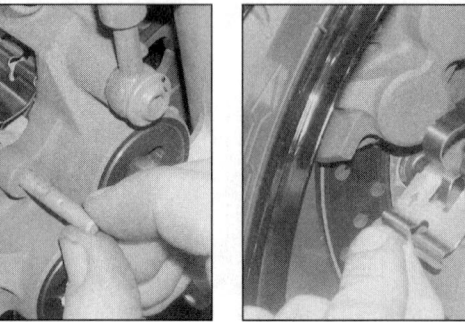

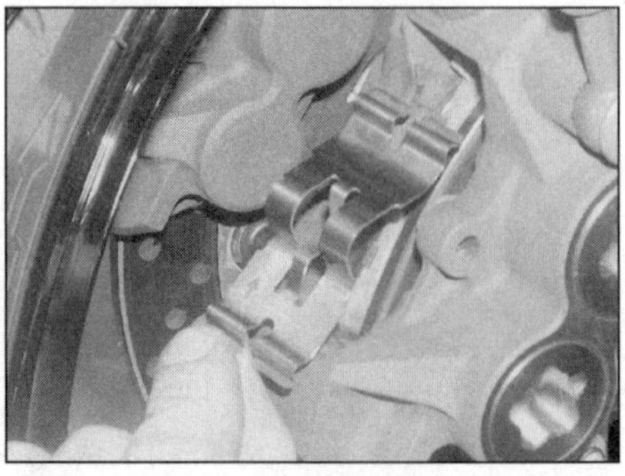

2.3b . . . the pad spring . . .

2.3c . . . and the pads

Brakes, wheels and tyres 7•3

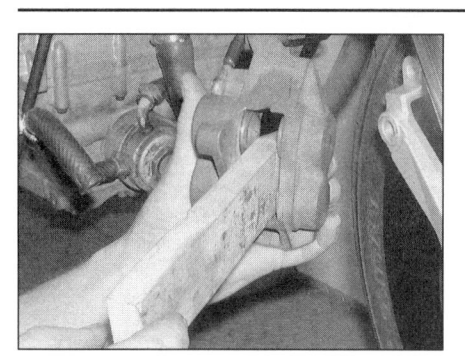

2.9a Pushing the pistons back into the caliper using a piece of wood

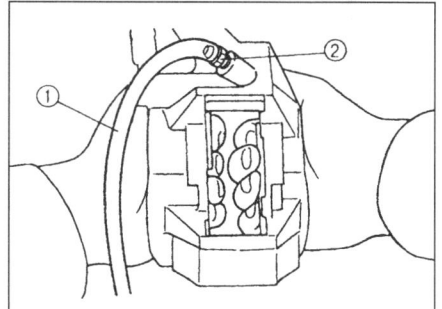

2.9b Using finger pressure to push all four pistons evenly back into the caliper

Note the tube (1) fitted to the bleed valve (2) – open the bleed valve slightly to allow displaced fluid to escape, then tighten the valve

noting how it fits. **Note:** *Do not operate the brake lever while the pads are out of the caliper.*

4 Inspect the surface of each pad for contamination and check that the friction material has not worn to or beyond its wear limit (see Chapter 1, Section 12). If either pad is worn down to or beyond the limit, is fouled with oil or grease, or is heavily scored or damaged by dirt and debris, both pads in each caliper must be renewed. Note that it is not possible to degrease the friction material; if the pads are contaminated in any way, new ones must be fitted.

5 Check that each pad has worn evenly at each end, and that each has the same amount of wear as the other. If uneven wear is noticed, one of the pistons is probably sticking in the caliper, in which case the caliper must be overhauled (see Section 3).

6 If the pads are in good condition clean them carefully, using a fine wire brush which is completely free of oil and grease, to remove all traces of road dirt and corrosion. Using a pointed instrument, clean out the groove in the friction material and dig out any embedded particles of foreign matter. Remove any areas of glazing using emery cloth. Spray the caliper with a dedicated brake cleaner to remove any dust and remove any traces of corrosion which might cause sticking of the caliper/pad operation.

7 Check the condition of the brake disc (see Section 4).

8 Remove all traces of corrosion from the pad retaining pin. Check it for signs of wear and renew it if necessary.

9 If new pads are being installed, push the pistons as far back into the caliper as possible, using hand pressure or a piece of wood as leverage **(see illustration)**. **Note:** *If the caliper is still in place, under no circumstances must you lever against the brake disc to push the pistons back into the caliper as damage to the disc will result.* This will displace brake fluid back into the hydraulic reservoir, so it may be necessary to remove the reservoir cap, plate and diaphragm and siphon out some fluid (depending on how much fluid was in there in the first place and how far the pistons have to be pushed in). If the pistons are difficult to push back, attach a length of clear hose to the bleed valve and place the open end in a suitable container, then open the valve and try again **(see illustration)**. Take great care not to draw any air into the system. If in doubt, bleed the brakes afterwards (see Section 11). **Note:** *Yamaha recommend that new pad shims and pad springs should be fitted whenever the pads are renewed.*

10 Smear the backs of the pads and the pad pins lightly with copper-based grease, making sure that none gets on the front or sides of the pads.

11 If removed, fit the shim onto the back of each pad **(see illustration)**. Insert the pads into the caliper so that the friction material faces the disc. Fit the pad spring onto the pads, making sure the arrow points in the direction of normal disc rotation **(see illustration 2.3b)**. Insert the pad retaining pin through the hole in the outer pad, then press down on the pad spring and push the pin through the spring and the hole in the inner pad. Install the R-clips, using new ones if necessary **(see illustration)**.

12 If displaced, install the calipers (see Section 3). Top-up fluid reservoir if necessary (see *Daily (pre-ride) checks*).

13 Operate the brake lever several times to bring the pads into contact with the discs. Check the operation of the brake before riding the motorcycle.

3 Front brake calipers – removal, overhaul and installation

⚠ **Warning:** *If a caliper indicates the need for an overhaul (usually due to leaking fluid or sticky operation), all old brake fluid should be flushed from the system. Also, the dust created by the brake system may contain asbestos, which is harmful to your health. Never blow it out with compressed air and do not inhale any of it. An approved filtering mask should be worn when working on the brakes. Do not, under any circumstances, use petroleum-based solvents to clean brake parts. Use clean brake fluid of the type specified, dedicated brake cleaner or denatured alcohol only, as described.*

Removal

1 If the caliper is just being displaced or removed, the pads can be left in place. If the caliper is being overhauled, remove the brake pads (see Section 2).

2 Unscrew and remove the bolt securing the brake hose guide to the mudguard **(see illustration)**.

3 If the caliper is just being displaced, do not disconnect the brake hose. If the caliper is being completely removed or overhauled, unscrew the brake hose banjo bolt and detach the banjo fitting, noting its alignment with the

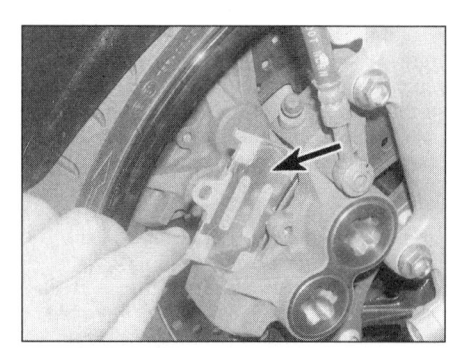

2.11a Install the pad with the shim (arrowed) in place

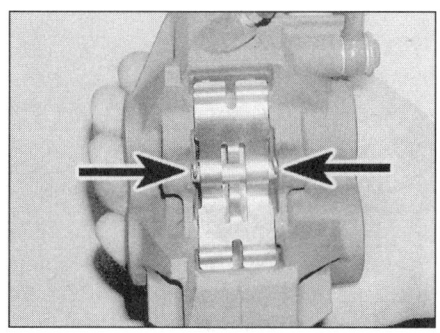

2.11b Fit the R-clips (arrowed) in the pad retaining pin

3.2 Unscrew the bolt securing the brake hose guide (arrowed) to the mudguard

7•4 Brakes, wheels and tyres

3.3 Detach the banjo union, noting its alignment (arrowed) with the caliper

3.4 Unscrew the caliper mounting bolts (arrowed)

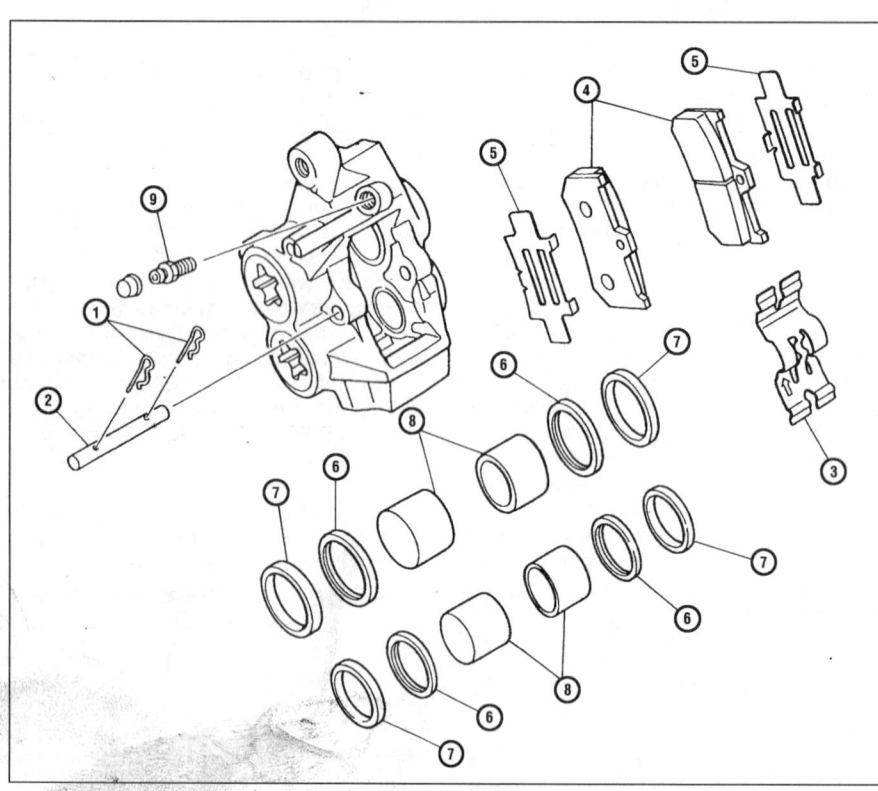

3.5 Front brake caliper components

1 R-clip
2 Pad retaining pin
3 Pad spring
4 Pad
5 Anti-chatter shim
6 Dust seal
7 Piston seal
8 Piston
9 Bleed valve

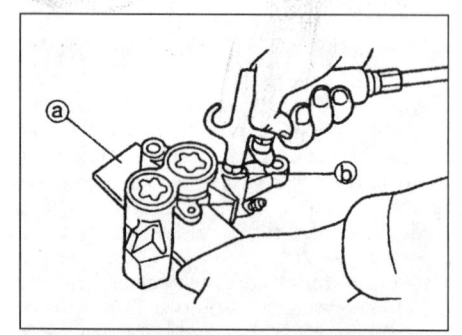

3.6 Using a block of wood (a) and compressed air through the fluid inlet (b) to expel the pistons on one side at a time

3.8 Use a plastic or wooden tool to remove the seals

caliper **(see illustration)**. Discard the sealing washers, as new ones must be used on reassembly. Wrap a clean plastic bag tightly around the end of the hose to prevent dirt entering the system, and secure it in an upright position to minimise fluid loss. **Note:** *If you are planning to overhaul the caliper and do not have a source of compressed air to blow out the pistons, just loosen the banjo bolt at this stage and retighten it lightly. The hydraulic system can then be used to force the pistons out of the caliper once the pads have been removed. Disconnect the hose once the pistons have been sufficiently displaced.*

4 Unscrew the caliper mounting bolts and slide the caliper off the disc **(see illustration)**. If the caliper is just being displaced, secure it to the motorcycle with a cable tie to avoid straining the hydraulic hose. **Note:** *Do not operate the brake lever while the caliper is off the disc.*

Overhaul

5 Clean the exterior of the caliper with denatured alcohol or brake system cleaner **(see illustration)**. **Note:** *The pistons are of two different sizes (see Specifications at the beginning of this Chapter). Mark each piston head and the caliper body with a suitable marker to ensure that the pistons can be matched to their original bores on reassembly.*

6 Displace the pistons from their bores using either compressed air **(see illustration)** or by carefully operating the front brake lever to pump them out. Ensure that all the pistons are moving freely and evenly. If the pistons are being displaced hydraulically, it may be necessary to top-up the hydraulic reservoir during the procedure. Also, have some clean rag ready to catch any spilled hydraulic fluid when the pistons reach the end of their bores. **Note:** *If the compressed air method is used, direct the air into the fluid inlet on the caliper. Use only low pressure to ease the pistons out – if the air pressure is too high and the pistons are forced out, the caliper and/or pistons may be damaged.*

⚠ **Warning:** *Never place your fingers in front of the pistons in an attempt to catch or protect them when applying compressed air, as serious injury could result.*

7 If a piston sticks in its bore, first remove the other pistons and pack their bores with clean rag. If not already done, disconnect the brake hose (see Step 3) then try and displace the stuck piston with compressed air (see Step 6). If the piston cannot be displaced, the caliper will have to be replaced with a new one.

Caution: *Do not try to remove the pistons by levering them out, or by using pliers or any other grips. Do not attempt to remove the coloured caliper bore plugs on the outside of the caliper.*

8 Remove the dust seals and the piston seals from the piston bores using a soft wooden or plastic tool to avoid scratching the bores **(see illustration)**. Discard the seals as new ones must be fitted on reassembly.

Brakes, wheels and tyres 7•5

4.2 Measuring the disc thickness with a micrometer

4.3 Set-up for checking brake disc runout

4.5 Undo the bolts (arrowed) and remove the disc

9 Clean the pistons and bores with clean brake fluid of the specified type. If compressed air is available, blow it through the fluid galleries in the caliper to ensure they are clear and use it to dry the parts thoroughly (make sure it is filtered and unlubricated).
Caution: Do not, under any circumstances, use a petroleum-based solvent to clean brake parts.
10 Inspect the caliper bores and pistons for signs of corrosion, nicks and burrs and loss of plating. If surface defects are present, the caliper assembly must be renewed. If the caliper is in bad shape the master cylinder should also be checked.
11 Lubricate the new piston seals with clean brake fluid and install them in their grooves in the caliper bores. Compare the seals and measure them if necessary to ensure that the correct seals are fitted in the correct bores (see Specifications). The same applies when fitting the new dust seals and pistons.
12 Lubricate the new dust seals with clean brake fluid and install them in their grooves in the caliper bores.
13 Lubricate the pistons with clean brake fluid and install them, closed-end first, into the caliper bores. Using your thumbs, push the pistons all the way in, making sure they enter the bores squarely.

Installation

14 Slide the caliper onto the brake disc. If they weren't removed, make sure the pads sit squarely each side of the disc.
15 Install the caliper mounting bolts and tighten them to the torque setting specified at the beginning of this Chapter.
16 If removed, connect the brake hose to the caliper, using **new** sealing washers on each side of the banjo fitting. Align the fitting as noted on removal. Tighten the banjo bolt to the torque setting specified at the beginning of this Chapter.
17 Install the bolt in the brake hose guide and attach the guide to the mudguard. Tighten the bolt to the specified torque setting.
18 If removed, install the brake pads (see Section 2).
19 Top-up the hydraulic reservoir with new DOT 4 brake fluid (see *Daily (pre-ride) checks*) and bleed the system as described in Section 11. Check that there are no fluid leaks and thoroughly test the operation of the brake before riding the motorcycle.

4 Front brake discs – inspection, removal and installation

Inspection

1 Visually inspect the surface of the disc for score marks and other damage. Light scratches are normal after use and will not affect brake operation, but deep grooves and heavy score marks will reduce braking efficiency and accelerate pad wear. If a disc is badly grooved it must be machined, or a new one fitted.
2 The disc must not be machined or allowed to wear down to a thickness less than the service limit as listed in this Chapter's Specifications. The thickness of the disc can be checked with a micrometer or vernier caliper **(see illustration)**. If the thickness of the disc is less than the service limit, a new one must be fitted.
3 To check disc runout, position the bike on an auxiliary stand and support it so that the front wheel is raised off the ground. Mount a dial gauge to a fork leg, with the plunger of the gauge touching the surface of the disc about 10 mm (1/2 in) from the outer edge **(see illustration)**. Rotate the wheel and watch the gauge needle, comparing the reading with the limit listed in the Specifications at the beginning of this Chapter. If the runout is greater than the service limit, check the wheel bearings for play (see Chapter 1). If the bearings are worn, install new ones (see Section 16) and repeat this check. If the disc runout is still excessive, a new disc will have to be fitted.

Removal

4 Remove the wheel (see Section 14).
Caution: Don't lay the wheel down and allow it to rest on the disc – the disc could become warped. Set the wheel on wood blocks so the wheel rim supports the weight of the wheel.
5 If you are not replacing the disc with a new one, mark the relationship of the disc to the wheel so that it can be installed in the same position. Unscrew the disc retaining bolts, loosening them evenly and a little at a time in a criss-cross pattern to avoid distorting the disc, then remove the disc from the wheel **(see illustration)**.

Installation

6 Before installing the disc, make sure there is no dirt or corrosion where the disc seats on the hub, particularly right in the angle of the seat. If the disc does not sit flat when it is bolted down, it will appear to be warped when checked or when the front brake is used.
7 Install the disc on the wheel; align the previously applied register marks if you are reinstalling the original disc.
8 Clean the threads of the disc mounting bolts, then apply a suitable non-permanent thread locking compound. Install the bolts and tighten them evenly and a little at a time in a criss-cross pattern to the torque setting specified at the beginning of this Chapter. Clean the brake disc using acetone or brake system cleaner. If a new brake disc has been installed, remove any protective coating from its working surfaces.
9 Install the front wheel (see Section 14).
10 Operate the brake lever several times to bring the pads into contact with the disc. Check the operation of the brakes carefully before riding the motorcycle.

5 Front brake master cylinder – removal, overhaul and installation

1 If the brake lever does not feel firm when the brake is applied, and the hydraulic hose and brake caliper are in good condition and bleeding the brake does not help (see Section 11), or if the master cylinder is leaking fluid, then master cylinder overhaul is recommended.
2 Before disassembling the master cylinder, read through the entire procedure and make sure that you have obtained all the new parts required including some new DOT 4 brake fluid, some clean rags and internal circlip pliers.

7•6 Brakes, wheels and tyres

5.4 Undo the clamp (A) and loosen the cap, then unscrew the mounting bolt (B)

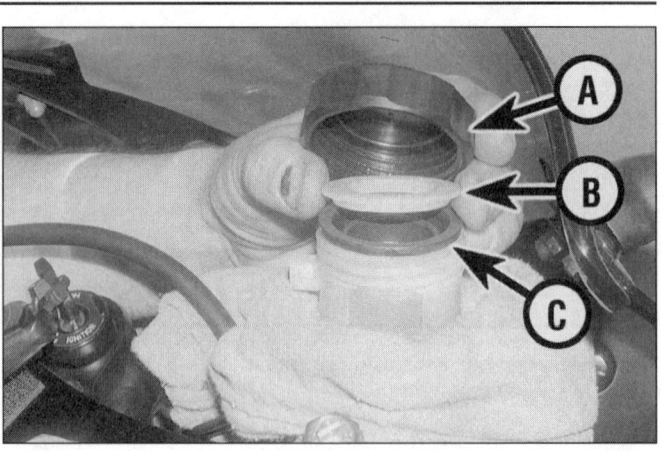

5.5a Remove the cap (A), diaphragm plate (B) and diaphragm (C)

Caution: Disassembly, overhaul and reassembly of the brake master cylinder must be done in a spotlessly clean work area to avoid contamination and possible failure of the brake hydraulic system components. To prevent damage to the paint from spilled brake fluid, always cover the fuel tank and fairing when working on the master cylinder.

Removal

Note: *If the master cylinder is just being displaced and not completely removed from the motorcycle, unscrew the bolt securing the hydraulic reservoir to its bracket on the top yoke and follow Step 7. Secure the master cylinder to the motorcycle with a cable tie to avoid straining the hydraulic hose. Keep the reservoir upright to prevent air entering the system.*

3 Disconnect the brake light switch wiring connectors and remove the front brake lever (see Chapter 6).
4 Remove the fluid reservoir cap clamp and loosen the cap, then unscrew the bolt securing the reservoir to its bracket on the top yoke **(see illustration)**.
5 Remove the reservoir cap and lift off the diaphragm plate and the diaphragm **(see illustration)**. Drain the brake fluid into a suitable container. Release the clip securing the reservoir hose to the union on the master cylinder and detach the hose **(see illustration)**. Wipe any remaining fluid out of the reservoir with a clean rag and replace the diaphragm, diaphragm plate and cap temporarily.
6 Unscrew the brake hose banjo bolt and separate the hose banjo fittings from the master cylinder, noting their alignment **(see illustration)**. Discard the sealing washers from each side of, and between, the banjo fittings as new ones must be used on reassembly. Wrap a clean plastic bag tightly around the ends of the hoses to prevent dirt entering the system and secure them in an upright position. Alternatively, bend the hoses down carefully and place the open ends in a clean container. The objective is to prevent excessive loss of brake fluid, fluid spills and system contamination.
7 Unscrew the master cylinder clamp bolts and remove the clamp, noting how it fits, then lift the master cylinder away from the handlebar **(see illustration)**.
8 If required, remove the screw securing the brake light switch and remove the switch **(see illustration)**.

Overhaul

9 Remove the reservoir hose union dust cover, then remove the circlip and detach the union from the master cylinder. Discard the O-ring as a new one must be used on reassembly. Inspect the reservoir hose for cracks or splits and renew it if necessary. Check the hose clips; renew them if they are distorted or corroded.
10 Carefully remove the dust boot from the master cylinder to reveal the pushrod retaining circlip **(see illustration)**.

5.5b Detach the reservoir hose (arrowed)

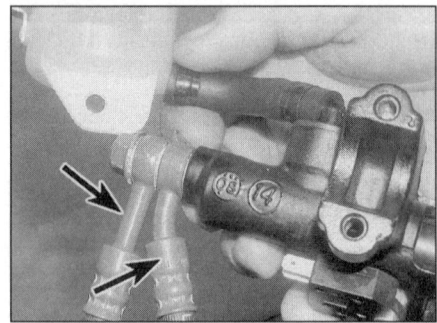

5.6 Note the alignment of the banjo fittings (arrowed)

5.7 Unscrew the master cylinder clamp bolts (arrowed)

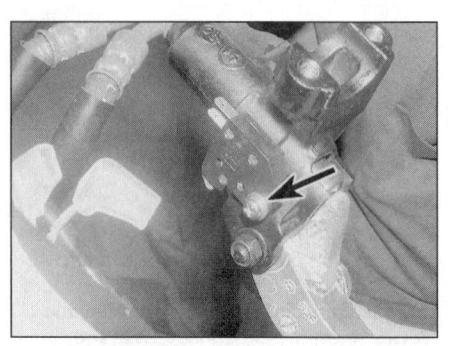

5.8 Undo the screw (arrowed) to remove the front brake light switch

5.10 Remove the dust boot from the end of the master cylinder

Brakes, wheels and tyres 7•7

1 Dust boot
2 Circlip
3 Piston assembly and spring
4 Master cylinder

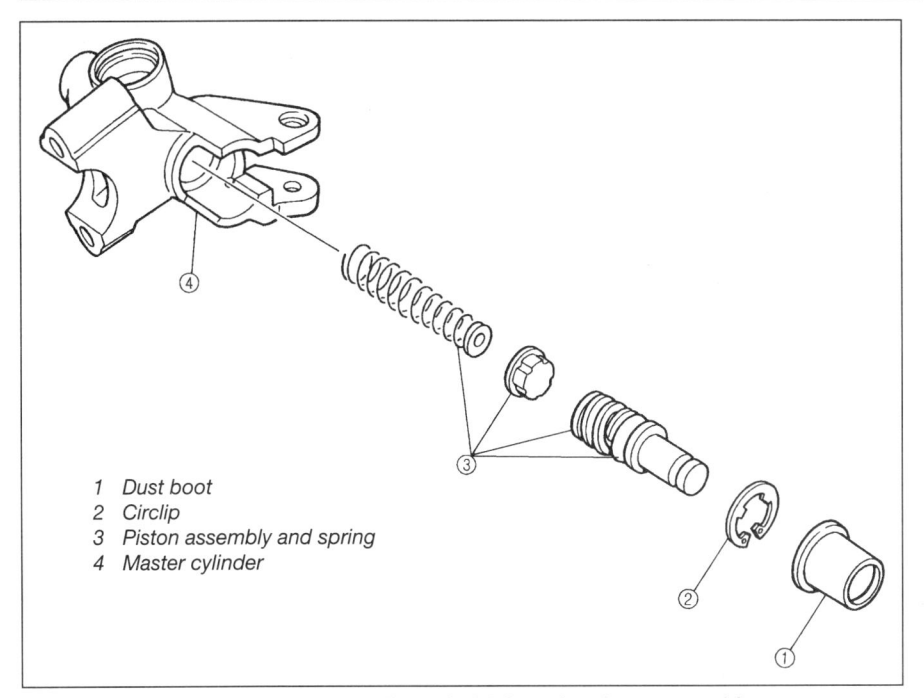

5.11 Remove the circlip and withdraw the piston assembly

11 Depress the pushrod and use circlip pliers to remove the circlip, then slide out the piston assembly and the spring, noting how they fit **(see illustration)**. If they are difficult to remove, apply low pressure compressed air to the fluid outlet. Lay the parts out in the proper order to prevent confusion during reassembly.

12 Clean all parts with clean brake fluid. If compressed air is available, blow it through the fluid galleries to ensure they are clear and use it to dry the parts thoroughly (make sure the air is filtered and unlubricated).

Caution: Do not, under any circumstances, use a petroleum-based solvent to clean brake parts.

13 Check the master cylinder bore for corrosion, scratches, nicks and score marks. If damage or wear is evident, the master cylinder must be replaced with a new one. If the master cylinder is in poor condition, then the calipers should be checked as well.

14 The dust boot, circlip, piston assembly and spring are included in the master cylinder rebuild kit. Use all of the new parts, regardless of the apparent condition of the old ones. Fit them according to the layout of the old piston assembly **(see illustration 5.11)**.

15 Fit the spring into the master cylinder with its narrow end facing out. Lubricate the piston assembly with clean brake fluid and fit the assembly into the master cylinder, making sure it is the correct way round. Make sure the lips on the cup do not turn inside out when they are slipped into the bore. Depress the piston and install the new circlip, making sure it is properly located in the groove.

16 Install the dust boot, making sure the lip is seated properly in the groove **(see illustration 5.10)**.

17 Fit a new O-ring onto the reservoir hose union, then press the union into the master cylinder and secure it with the circlip. Fit the dust cover over the union.

18 Inspect the fluid reservoir cap, diaphragm plate and diaphragm and renew any parts if they are damaged or deteriorated.

Installation

19 Installation is the reverse of removal, noting the following points:

● Attach the fluid reservoir to the top yoke, then attach the master cylinder to the handlebar and fit the clamp with its UP mark facing up **(see illustration)**, aligning the top mating surfaces of the clamp with the punch mark on the handlebar **(see illustration)**. Tighten the upper bolt first, then the lower bolt to the torque setting specified at the beginning of this Chapter.

● Connect the brake hose banjo fittings to the master cylinder, using new sealing washers on each side of, and between, the fittings, and aligning the fittings as noted on removal. Tighten the banjo bolt to the torque setting specified at the beginning of this Chapter **(see illustration 5.6)**.

● Fill the fluid reservoir with new DOT 4 brake fluid as described in *Daily (pre-ride) checks*. Refer to Section 11 of this Chapter and bleed the air from the system.

● Ensure the reservoir diaphragm is correctly seated, and that the cap and cap clamp are tightened securely.

● Check the operation of the front brake before riding the motorcycle.

6 Rear brake pads – renewal

Warning: The dust created by the brake system may contain asbestos, which is harmful to your health. Never blow it out with compressed air and do not inhale any of it. An approved filtering mask should be worn when working on the brakes.

1 Remove the exhaust silencer (see Chapter 4), then displace the rear brake caliper (see Section 7) – there is no need to disconnect the hose. The brake pads, shims and pad springs will remain inside the caliper bracket **(see illustration)**

2 Remove the brake pads from the caliper

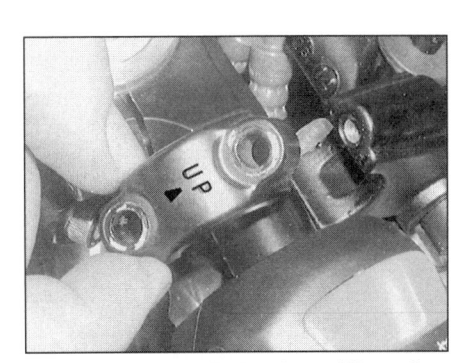

5.19a Master cylinder clamp UP mark must face upwards

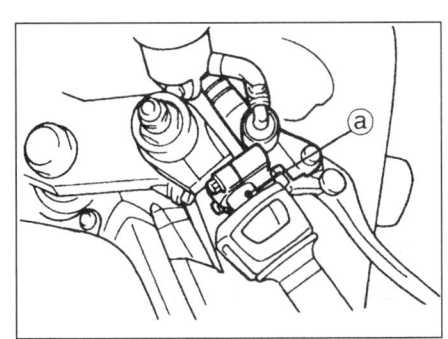

5.19b Align the clamp joint at the top with the punch mark (a) on the handlebar

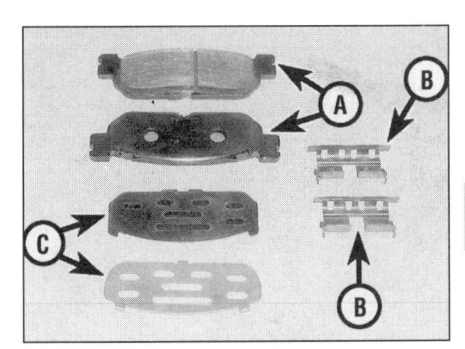

6.1 Rear brake pads (A), springs (B) and anti-chatter shims (C)

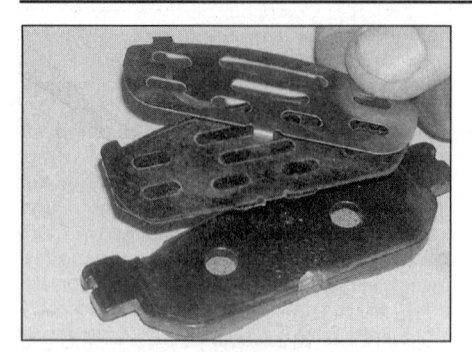

7•8 Brakes, wheels and tyres

6.2 Each pad is fitted with a two-piece anti-chatter shim

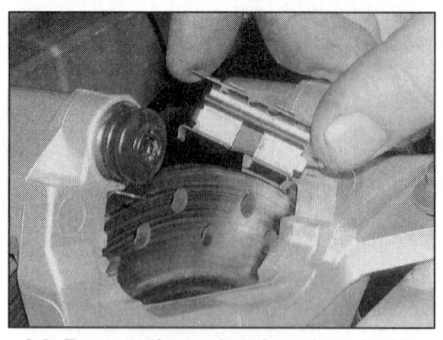

6.3 Remove the pad springs from inside the caliper bracket

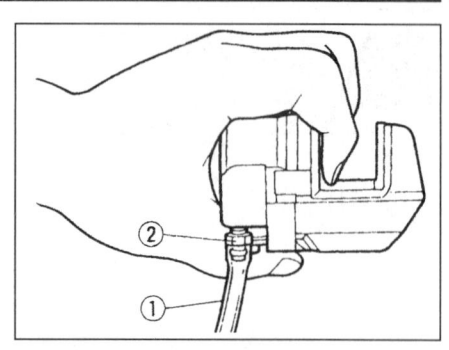

6.8 Push the pistons back into the caliper using finger pressure

Note the tube (1) fitted to the bleed valve (2) – open the bleed valve slightly to allow displaced fluid to escape, then tighten the valve

bracket. If required, remove the two anti-chatter shims from the back of each pad, noting how they fit **(see illustration)**.

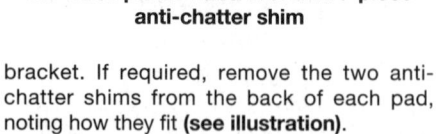

3 Remove the pad springs from inside the caliper bracket, noting how they fit **(see illustration)**.

4 Inspect the surface of each pad for contamination and check that the friction material has not worn beyond its wear limit (see Chapter 1, Section 12). If either pad is worn down to or beyond the limit, is fouled with oil or grease, or is heavily scored or damaged by dirt and debris, both pads must be renewed as a set. Note that it is not possible to degrease the friction material; if the pads are contaminated in any way, new ones must be fitted.

5 Check that each pad has worn evenly at each end, and that each has the same amount of wear as the other. If uneven wear is noticed, one of the pistons is probably sticking in the caliper, in which case the caliper must be overhauled (see Section 7).

6 If the pads are in good condition, clean them carefully using a fine wire brush which is completely free of oil and grease, to remove all traces of road dirt and corrosion. Using a pointed instrument, dig out any embedded particles of foreign matter. Any areas of glazing may be removed using emery cloth. Spray the caliper with a dedicated brake cleaner to remove any dust and remove any traces of corrosion which might cause sticking of the caliper/pad operation.

7 Check the condition of the brake disc (see Section 8).

8 If new pads are being installed, push the pistons as far back into the caliper as possible using hand pressure or a piece of wood as leverage. This will displace brake fluid back into the fluid reservoir, so it may be necessary to remove the reservoir cap, plate and diaphragm, and siphon out some fluid (depending on how much fluid was in there in the first place and how far the pistons have to be pushed in). If the pistons are difficult to push back, attach a length of clear tubing to the bleed valve and place the open end in a suitable container, then open the valve and try again **(see illustration)**. Take great care not to draw any air into the system. If in doubt, bleed the brakes afterwards (see Section 11). **Note:** *Yamaha recommend that new pad shims and pad springs should be fitted whenever the pads are renewed.*

9 Smear the backs of the pads with copper-based grease, making sure that none gets on the front or sides of the pads. Fit the anti-chatter shims (one plain, one slotted) onto the back of each pad **(see illustration 6.2)**.

10 Install the pad springs into the caliper bracket, then insert the pads into the bracket so that the friction material of each pad is facing the disc **(see illustrations)**.

11 Install the caliper (see Section 7). Top-up the hydraulic reservoir if necessary (see *Daily (pre-ride) checks*).

12 Operate the brake pedal several times to bring the pads into contact with the disc. Check the operation of the brake before riding the motorcycle.

7 Rear brake caliper – removal, overhaul and installation

⚠ **Warning:** *If a caliper indicates the need for an overhaul (usually due to leaking fluid or sticky operation), all old brake fluid should be flushed from the system. Also, the dust created by the brake system may contain asbestos, which is harmful to your health. Never blow it out with compressed air and do not inhale any of it. An approved filtering mask should be worn when working on the brakes. Do not, under any circumstances, use petroleum-based solvents to clean brake parts. Use the specified clean brake fluid, dedicated brake cleaner or denatured alcohol only, as described.*

Removal

1 Remove the exhaust silencer (see Chapter 4), then unscrew and remove the bolts securing the brake hose guides to the swingarm **(see illustration)**.

2 If the caliper is just being displaced, do not disconnect the brake hose. If the caliper is being completely removed or overhauled, unscrew the brake hose banjo bolt and detach the banjo fitting, noting its alignment with the

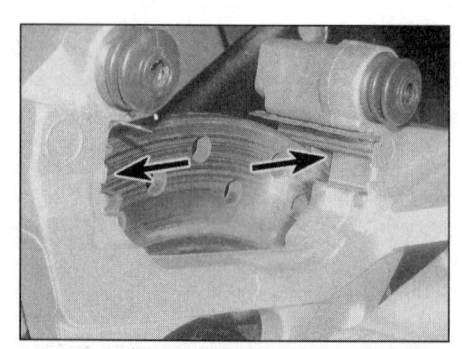

6.10a Fit the pad springs (arrowed) into the caliper bracket . . .

6.10b . . . then fit the pads

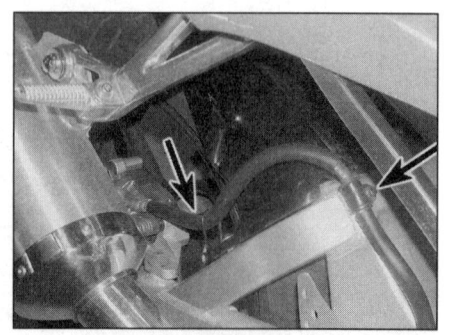

7.1 Detach the rear brake hose guides from the swingarm

Brakes, wheels and tyres 7•9

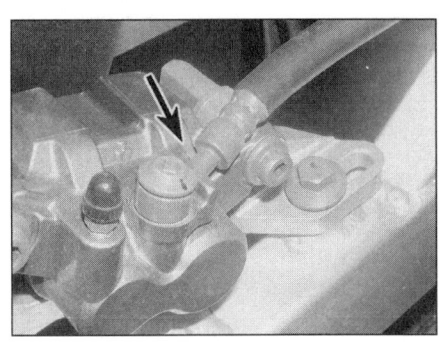

7.2 Detach the banjo union, noting its alignment (arrowed) with the caliper

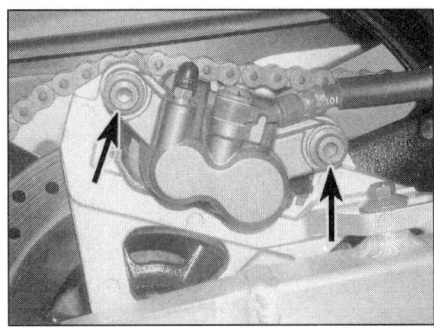

7.3a Unscrew the caliper mounting bolts (arrowed)

7.3b ... and slide the caliper off the disc

caliper **(see illustration)**. Discard the sealing washers, as new ones must be used on reassembly. Wrap a clean plastic bag tightly around the end of the hose to prevent dirt entering the system, and secure it in an upright position to minimise fluid loss. **Note:** *If you are planning to overhaul the caliper and do not have a source of compressed air to blow out the pistons, just loosen the banjo bolt at this stage and retighten it lightly. The hydraulic system can then be used to force the pistons out of the caliper once the pads have been removed. Disconnect the hose once the pistons have been sufficiently displaced.*

3 Unscrew the caliper mounting bolts, and slide the caliper off the disc **(see illustrations)**. The brake pads will be retained in the caliper bracket. If the caliper is just being displaced, secure it to the motorcycle with a cable tie to avoid straining the hydraulic hose. **Note:** *Do not operate the brake pedal while the caliper is off the disc.*

Overhaul

4 Clean the exterior of the caliper with denatured alcohol or brake system cleaner **(see illustration)**. **Note:** *The pistons are of two different sizes (see Specifications at the beginning of this Chapter).*

5 Displace the pistons from their bores using either compressed air or by carefully operating the rear brake pedal to pump them out **(see illustration)**. Ensure that both the pistons are moving freely and evenly. If the pistons are being displaced hydraulically, it may be necessary to top-up the hydraulic reservoir during the procedure. Also, have some clean rag ready to catch any spilled hydraulic fluid when the pistons reach the end of their bores. **Note:** *If the compressed air method is used, direct the air into the fluid inlet on the caliper. Use only low pressure to ease the pistons out – if the air pressure is too high and the pistons are forced out, the caliper and/or pistons may be damaged.*

⚠️ **Warning:** *Never place your fingers in front of the pistons in an attempt to catch or protect them when applying compressed air, as serious injury could result.*

6 If a piston sticks in its bore, first remove the other piston and pack its bore with clean rag. If not already done, disconnect the brake hose (see Step 2) then try and displace the stuck piston with compressed air (see Step 5). ***Caution: Do not try to remove the pistons by levering them out, or by using pliers or any other grips. Do not attempt to remove the coloured caliper bore plugs on the outside of the caliper.***

7 Remove the dust seals and the piston seals from the piston bores using a wooden or plastic tool to avoid scratching the bores **(see illustration 3.8)**. Discard the seals as new ones must be fitted on reassembly.

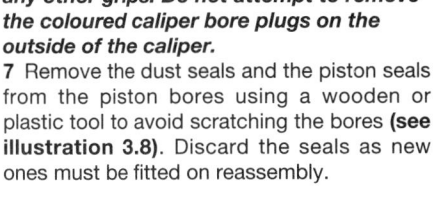

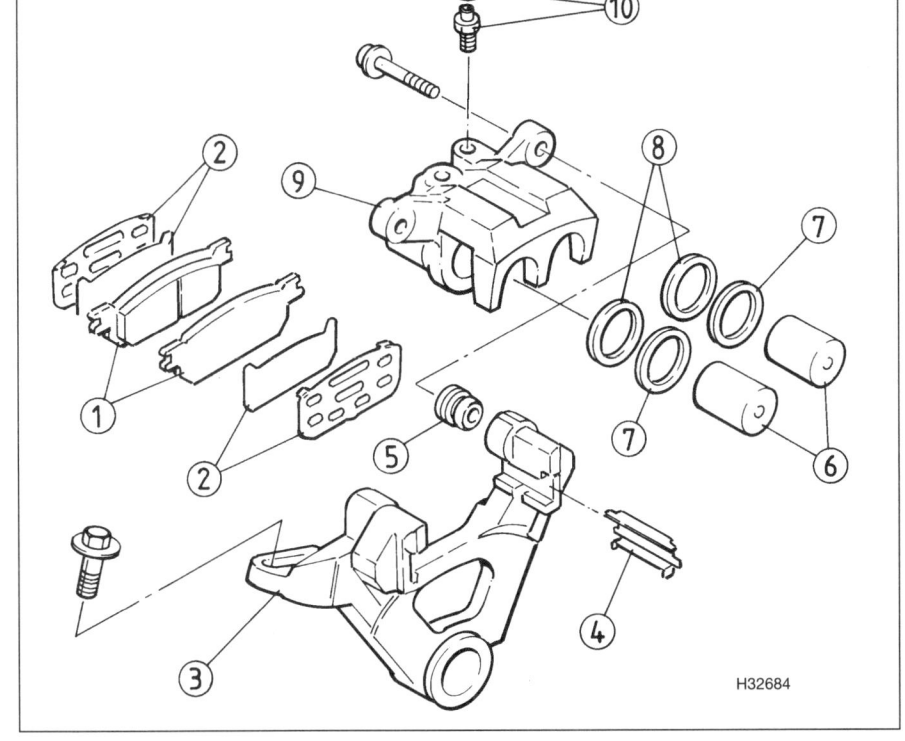

7.4 Rear brake caliper components

1 Pads
2 Anti-chatter shim sets
3 Caliper bracket
4 Pad spring - 2 off
5 Dust boot - 2 off
6 Pistons
7 Piston dust seals
8 Piston fluid seals
9 Caliper body
10 Bleed valve

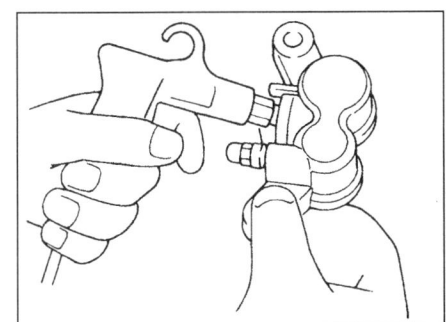

7.5 Using compressed air via the fluid inlet to expel the pistons

7

7•10 Brakes, wheels and tyres

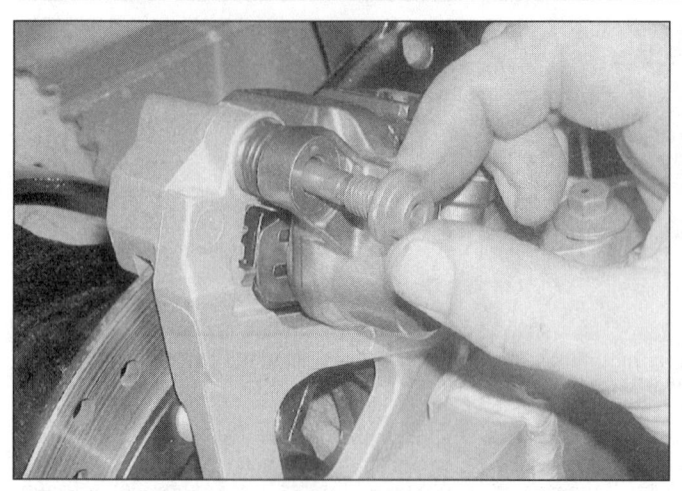

7.16 Install the bolts and tighten them to the specified torque

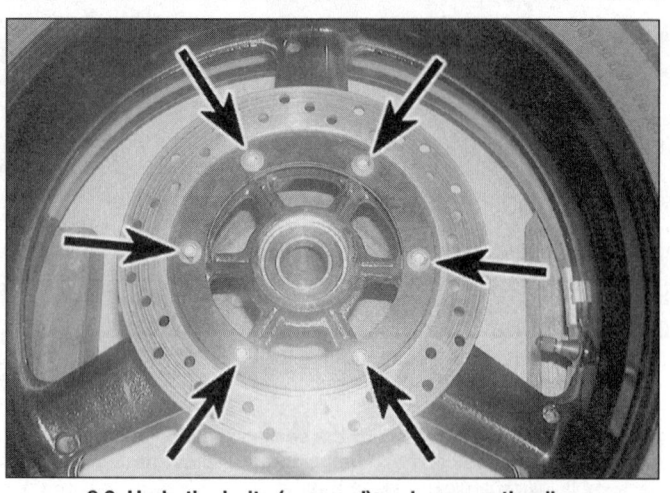

8.3 Undo the bolts (arrowed) and remove the disc

8 Clean the pistons and bores with clean brake fluid of the specified type. If compressed air is available, blow it through the fluid galleries in the caliper to ensure they are clear and use it to dry the parts thoroughly (make sure it is filtered and unlubricated).
Caution: Do not, under any circumstances, use a petroleum-based solvent to clean brake parts.
9 Inspect the caliper bores and pistons for signs of corrosion, nicks and burrs and loss of plating. If surface defects are present, the caliper assembly must be renewed. If the caliper is in bad shape the master cylinder should also be checked.
10 Lubricate the new piston seals with clean brake fluid and install them in their grooves in the caliper bores. Compare the seals and measure them if necessary to ensure that the correct seals are fitted in the correct bores (see Specifications). The same applies when fitting the new dust seals and pistons.
11 Lubricate the new dust seals with clean brake fluid and install them in their grooves in the caliper bores.
12 Lubricate the pistons with clean brake fluid and install them, closed-end first, into the caliper bores. Using your thumbs, push the pistons all the way in, making sure they enter their bores squarely.
13 Ensure that the caliper mounting bolts are clean and free from corrosion, especially on their plain pins which locate in the caliper bracket bores. If the bolts show signs of wear, renew them. Similarly inspect the corresponding bores in the caliper bracket. Clean off all old grease and apply a smear of copper-based grease to the bores and mounting bolt pins. Check the condition of the two dust boots on the bracket and renew them if cracked or perished.

Installation

14 If necessary, push the pistons a little way back into the caliper as described in Section 6, Step 8.

15 Ensure that the brake pads are installed squarely each side of the disc, then slide the caliper onto the brake disc.
16 Lightly smear the caliper mounting bolt pins with copper-based grease, then install the bolts and tighten them to the torque setting specified at the beginning of this Chapter **(see illustration)**.
17 If detached, connect the brake hose to the caliper, using new sealing washers on each side of the banjo union and tighten the banjo bolt to the torque setting specified at the beginning of this Chapter **(see illustration 7.2)**. Install the brake hose guides.
18 Top-up the hydraulic reservoir with DOT 4 brake fluid (see Daily (pre-ride) checks) and bleed the system as described in Section 11.
19 Check that there are no fluid leaks and thoroughly test the operation of the brake before riding the motorcycle.

8 Rear brake disc – inspection, removal and installation

Inspection

1 Refer to Section 4 of this Chapter, noting that the dial gauge should be attached to the swingarm.

Removal

2 Remove the rear wheel (see Section 15).
Caution: Don't lay the wheel down and allow it to rest on the disc or the sprocket – they could become warped. Set the wheel on wood blocks so the wheel rim supports the weight of the wheel.
3 If you are not replacing the disc with a new one, mark the relationship of the disc to the wheel so that it can be installed in the same position. Unscrew the disc retaining bolts, loosening them evenly and a little at a time in a criss-cross pattern to avoid distorting the disc, then remove the disc from the wheel **(see illustration)**.

Installation

4 Before installing the disc, make sure there is no dirt or corrosion where the disc seats on the hub, particularly right in the angle of the seat. If the disc does not sit flat when it is bolted down, it will appear to be warped when checked or when the rear brake is used.
5 Install the disc on the wheel; align the previously applied register marks if you are reinstalling the original disc.
6 Clean the threads of the disc mounting bolts, then apply a suitable non-permanent thread locking compound. Install the bolts and tighten them evenly and a little at a time in a criss-cross pattern to the torque setting specified at the beginning of this Chapter **(see illustration 8.3)**. Clean the brake disc using acetone or brake system cleaner. If a new brake disc has been installed, remove any protective coating from its working surfaces.
7 Install the rear wheel (see Section 15).
8 Operate the brake pedal several times to bring the pads into contact with the disc. Check the operation of the brake carefully before riding the motorcycle.

9 Rear brake master cylinder – removal, overhaul and installation

1 If the brake pedal does not firm feel when the brake is applied, and the hydraulic hose and brake caliper are in good condition and bleeding the brakes does not help (see Section 11), or if the master cylinder is leaking fluid, then master cylinder overhaul is recommended.
2 Before disassembling the master cylinder, read through the entire procedure and make sure that you have obtained all the new parts required including some new DOT 4 brake fluid, some clean rags and internal circlip pliers.
Caution: Disassembly, overhaul and reassembly of the brake master cylinder

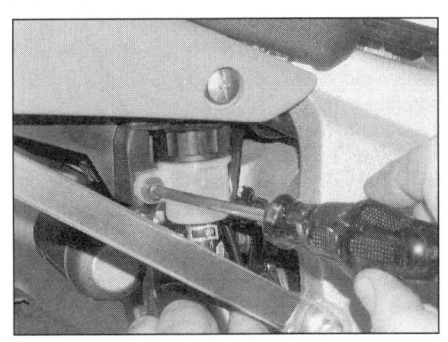

Brakes, wheels and tyres 7•11

9.3a Detach the fluid reservoir from the frame ...

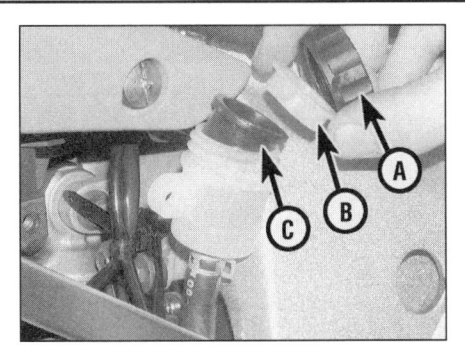

9.3b ... and remove the cap (A), diaphragm plate (B) and diaphragm (C)

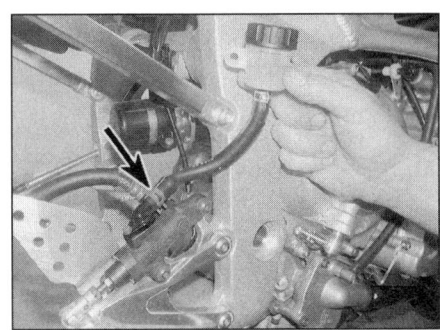

9.3c Release the clip (arrowed) and detach the hose

must be done in a spotlessly clean work area to avoid contamination and possible failure of the brake hydraulic system components. To prevent damage to the paint from spilled brake fluid, always cover or remove the lower fairing when working on the master cylinder.

Removal

Note: *If the master cylinder is just being displaced and not completely removed from the motorcycle, remove the screw securing the fluid reservoir to the frame and follow Steps 5 and 6. Secure the master cylinder to the motorcycle with a cable tie to avoid straining the hydraulic hose and keep the reservoir upright to prevent air entering the system.*

3 Remove the screw securing the fluid reservoir to the frame, then remove the reservoir cap, diaphragm plate and diaphragm (see illustrations). Drain the brake fluid into a suitable container. Release the clip securing the reservoir hose to the union on the master cylinder and detach the hose (see illustration). Wipe any remaining fluid out of the reservoir with a clean rag and refit the diaphragm, diaphragm plate and cap temporarily.
4 Unscrew the brake hose banjo bolt and separate the hose banjo fitting from the master cylinder, noting its alignment (see illustration). Discard the sealing washers, as new ones must be used on reassembly. Wrap a clean plastic bag tightly around the end of

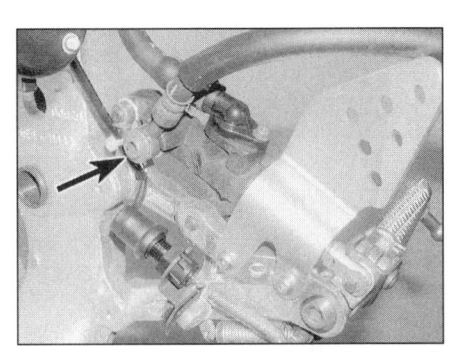

9.4 Disconnect the banjo fitting (arrowed) from the master cylinder

the hose to prevent dirt entering the system and secure it in an upright position. Alternatively, bend the hose down carefully and place the open end in a clean container. The objective is to prevent excessive loss of brake fluid, fluid spills and system contamination.
5 Remove the split pin and washer from the clevis pin connecting the brake pedal to the master cylinder pushrod (see illustration). Remove the clevis pin and separate the pushrod from the pedal. Discard the split pin, as a new one must be used on reassembly.
6 Unscrew the two bolts securing the master cylinder to the footrest bracket and remove the master cylinder (see illustration).

Overhaul

7 Remove the reservoir hose union retaining screw and washer, then remove the union

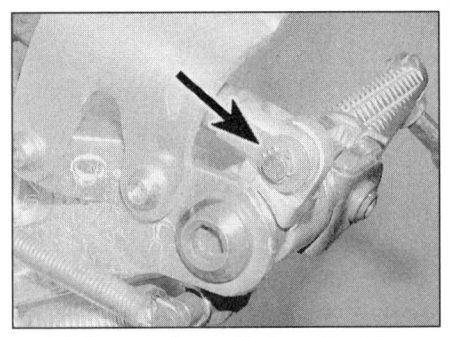

9.5 Remove the split pin and washer (arrowed) to disconnect the brake pedal

from the master cylinder. Discard the O-ring as a new one must be used on reassembly. Inspect the reservoir hose for cracks or splits and renew it if necessary. Check the hose clips; renew them if they are sprained or corroded.
8 If required, measure the position of the clevis on the pushrod, then slacken the locknut and thread the clevis and nut off the pushrod. Carefully remove the dust boot from the end of the master cylinder to reveal the pushrod retaining circlip (see illustration).
9 Depress the pushrod and use circlip pliers to remove the circlip, then slide out the pushrod, piston assembly and spring, noting how they fit (see illustration). If they are difficult to remove, apply low pressure compressed air to the fluid outlet. Lay the parts out in the proper order to prevent

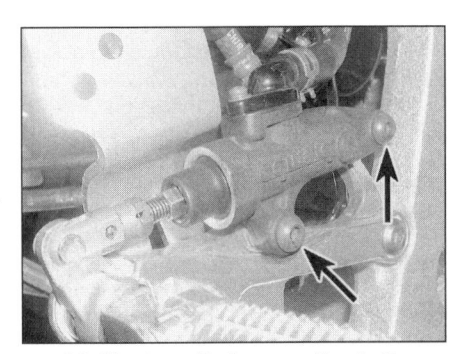

9.6 Master cylinder mounting bolts (arrowed)

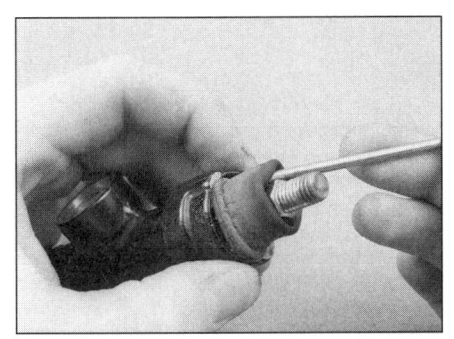

9.8 Remove the dust boot from the end of the master cylinder ...

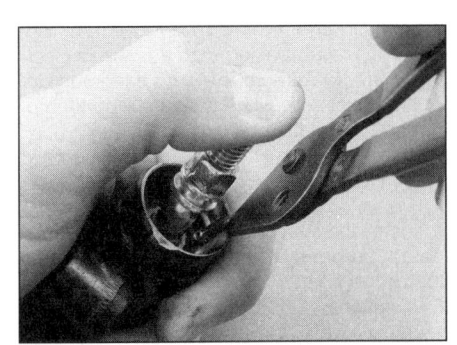

9.9a ... then remove the circlip and withdraw the piston assembly

7•12 Brakes, wheels and tyres

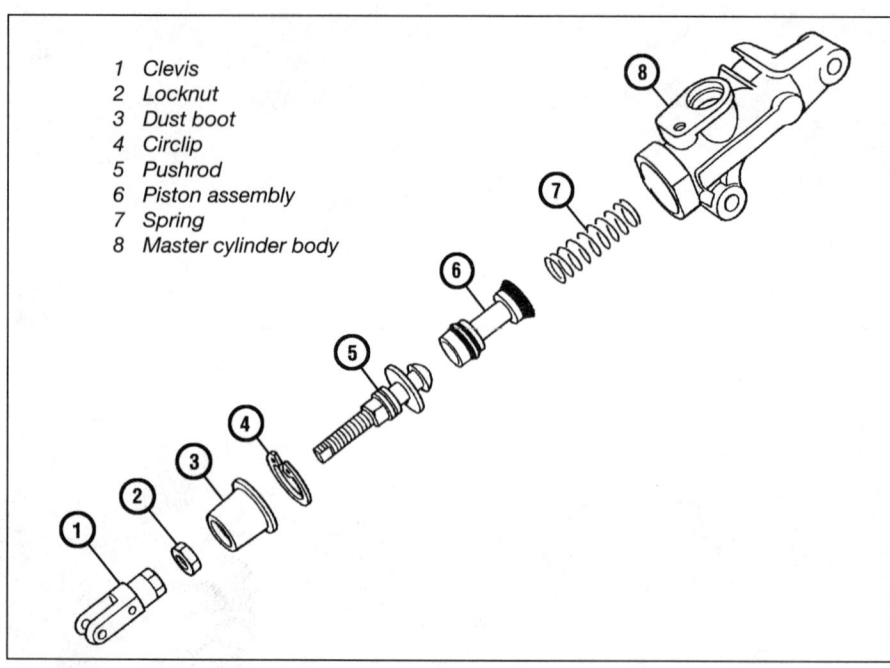

1 Clevis
2 Locknut
3 Dust boot
4 Circlip
5 Pushrod
6 Piston assembly
7 Spring
8 Master cylinder body

9.9b Master cylinder components

confusion during reassembly **(see illustration)**.

10 Clean all of the parts with clean brake fluid. If compressed air is available, blow it through the fluid galleries to ensure they are clear and use it to dry the parts thoroughly (make sure the air is filtered and unlubricated). *Caution: Do not, under any circumstances, use a petroleum-based solvent to clean brake parts.*

11 Check the master cylinder bore for corrosion, scratches, nicks and score marks. If damage or wear is evident, the master cylinder must be replaced with a new one. If the master cylinder is in poor condition, then the caliper should be checked as well.

12 The dust boot, circlip, pushrod, piston assembly and spring are included in the master cylinder rebuild kit. Use all of the new parts, regardless of the apparent condition of the old ones. Fit them according to the layout of the old piston assembly **(see illustration 9.9b)**.

13 Fit the spring into the master cylinder. Lubricate the piston assembly with clean brake fluid and fit the assembly into the master cylinder, making sure it is the correct way round. Make sure the lips on the cup do not turn inside out when they are slipped into the bore. Install the pushrod.

14 Depress the pushrod and install the new circlip, making sure it is properly located in its groove.

15 Install the dust boot, making sure the lip is seated properly in the groove **(see illustration 9.8)**.

16 If removed, thread the clevis locknut and the clevis onto the pushrod. Position the clevis as noted on removal (see Step 8), then tighten the locknut securely.

17 Fit a new O-ring onto the reservoir hose union, then press the union into the master cylinder and secure it with the washer and screw.

18 Inspect the fluid reservoir cap, diaphragm plate and diaphragm and renew any parts if they are damaged or deteriorated.

Installation

19 Installation is the reverse of removal, noting the following points:
● Fit the master cylinder onto the footrest bracket and tighten its mounting bolts to the torque setting specified at the beginning of this Chapter.
● Secure the master cylinder pushrod clevis pin with a new split pin **(see illustration 9.5)**.
● Connect the brake hose banjo fitting to the master cylinder, using new sealing washers on each side of the banjo fitting, and aligning the fitting as noted on removal **(see illustration 9.4)**. Tighten the banjo bolt to the specified torque setting.
● Attach the fluid reservoir in position temporarily; ensure that the hose is correctly routed, then connect it to the union on the master cylinder and secure it with the clip **(see illustration 9.3c)**.
● Fill the fluid reservoir with new DOT 4 brake fluid (see *Daily (pre-ride) checks*). Refer to Section 11 of this Chapter and bleed the air from the system.
● Ensure the reservoir diaphragm is correctly seated, and that the cap is tightened securely.
● Check the operation of the rear brake before riding the motorcycle.

10 Brake hoses and unions – inspection and renewal

Inspection

1 Brake hose condition should be checked regularly and the hoses renewed at the specified interval (see Chapter 1).

2 Twist and flex the hoses while looking for cracks, bulges and seeping hydraulic fluid **(see illustration)**. Check extra carefully around the areas where the hoses connect with the banjo fittings, as these are common areas for hose failure.

3 Check the banjo fittings connected to the brake hoses. If the fittings are rusted, scratched or cracked, fit new hoses.

Renewal

4 The brake hoses have banjo fittings on each end. Cover the surrounding area with plenty of rags and unscrew the banjo bolt at each end of the hose, noting the alignment of the fitting with the master cylinder or brake caliper **(see illustrations 3.3, 5.6, 7.2 and 9.4)**. Free the hose from any clips or guides and remove it, noting its routing. Discard the sealing washers.

5 Position the new hose, making sure it is not twisted or otherwise strained, and ensure that it is correctly routed through any clips or guides and is clear of all moving components.

6 Check that the fittings align correctly, then install the banjo bolts, using new sealing washers on both sides of the fittings. Tighten the banjo bolts to the torque setting specified at the beginning of this Chapter.

7 Flush the old brake fluid from the system, refill with new DOT 4 brake fluid (see *Daily (pre-ride) checks*) and bleed the air from the system (see Section 11).

8 Check the operation of the brakes before riding the motorcycle.

11 Brake system – bleeding and fluid change

Bleeding air from the system

1 Bleeding the brakes is simply the process of removing air from the brake fluid reservoir, the hose and the brake caliper. Bleeding is

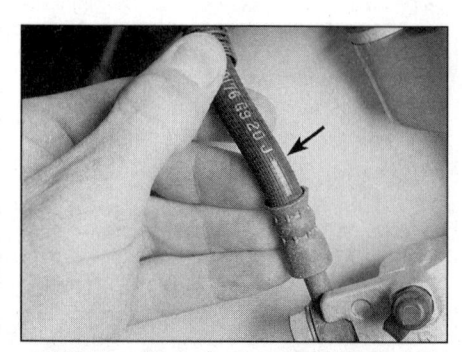

10.2 Flex the brake hose and check for cracks, bulges and seeping fluid

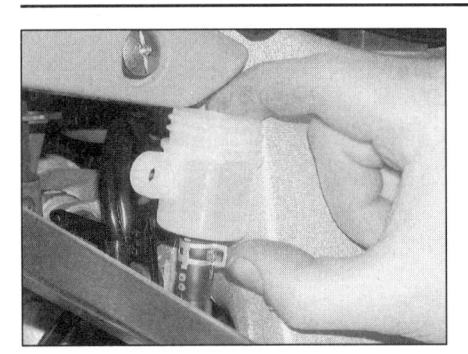

Brakes, wheels and tyres 7•13

11.4 Have an assistant hold the rear fluid reservoir upright while bleeding the brake

11.6a Bleed valve (arrowed) for the front left-hand caliper

11.6b Bleed valve (arrowed) for the rear caliper

11.6c Attach one end of the hose to the bleed valve and submerge the other end in the brake fluid

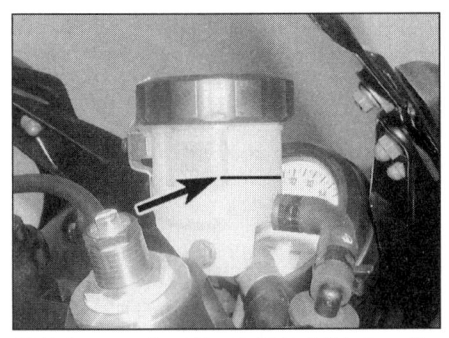

11.7 Do not allow the fluid to fall below the lower level mark (arrowed)

necessary whenever a brake system hydraulic connection is loosened, after a component or hose is renewed, or when the master cylinder or caliper is overhauled. Leaks in the system may also allow air to enter, but leaking brake fluid will reveal their presence and warn you of the need for repair.

2 To bleed the brakes, you will need some new DOT 4 brake fluid, a length of clear vinyl or plastic hose, a small container partially filled with clean brake fluid, some rags and a spanner to fit the brake caliper bleed valve.

3 Cover the fuel tank and other painted components to prevent damage in the event that brake fluid is spilled.

4 When bleeding the rear brake, remove the screw securing the fluid reservoir to the frame and have an assistant hold the reservoir upright to prevent air entering the system (see illustration).

5 Remove the reservoir cap, diaphragm plate and diaphragm and slowly pump the brake lever (front brake) or pedal (rear brake) a few times, until no air bubbles can be seen floating up from the holes in the bottom of the reservoir. This bleeds the air from the master cylinder end of the line. Temporarily refit the reservoir cap.

6 Pull the dust cap off the bleed valve (see illustrations). Attach one end of the clear vinyl or plastic hose to the bleed valve and submerge the other end in the clean brake fluid in the container (see illustration). **Note:** *To avoid damaging the bleed valve during the procedure, loosen it and then tighten it temporarily with a ring spanner before attaching the hose. With the hose attached, the valve can then be opened and closed with an open-ended spanner.*

7 Remove the reservoir cap and check the fluid level. Do not allow the fluid level to drop below the lower mark during the procedure (see illustration).

8 Carefully pump the brake lever or pedal three or four times and hold it in (front) or down (rear) while opening the caliper bleed valve. When the valve is opened, brake fluid will flow out of the caliper into the clear tubing, and the lever will move toward the handlebar, or the pedal will move down. If there is air in the system you will see air bubbles in the brake fluid coming out of the caliper.

9 Retighten the bleed valve, then release the brake lever or pedal gradually. Top-up the reservoir and repeat the process until no air bubbles are visible in the brake fluid leaving the caliper, and the lever or pedal is firm when applied. On completion, disconnect the hose, then tighten the bleed valve to the torque setting specified at the beginning of this Chapter and install the dust cap. If bleeding the front brake, go on to bleed air from the other caliper.

> **HAYNES HINT:** *If it is not possible to produce a firm feel to the lever or pedal, the fluid may be aerated. Let the brake fluid in the system stabilise for a few hours and then repeat the procedure when the tiny bubbles in the system have settled out.*

10 Top-up the reservoir, install the diaphragm, diaphragm plate and cap, and wipe up any spilled brake fluid. Attach the rear brake hydraulic reservoir to the frame and tighten the retaining screw securely. Check the entire system for fluid leaks.

11 Check the operation of the brakes before riding the motorcycle.

Changing the fluid

12 Changing the brake fluid is a similar process to bleeding the brakes and requires the same materials plus a suitable tool for siphoning the fluid out of the hydraulic reservoir. Also ensure that the container is large enough to take all the old fluid when it is flushed out of the system.

13 Follow Steps 3, 4 and 6, then remove the reservoir cap, diaphragm plate and diaphragm and siphon the old fluid out of the reservoir. Fill the reservoir with new brake fluid, then follow Step 8.

14 Retighten the bleed valve, then release the brake lever or pedal gradually. Keep the reservoir topped-up with new fluid to above the LOWER level at all times or air may enter the system and greatly increase the length of the task. Repeat the process until new fluid can be seen emerging from the bleed valve.

> **HAYNES HINT:** *Old brake fluid is invariably much darker in colour than new fluid, making it easy to see when all old fluid has been expelled from the system.*

15 Disconnect the hose, then tighten the bleed valve to the specified torque setting and install the dust cap.

16 Top-up the reservoir, install the diaphragm, diaphragm plate and cap, and wipe up any spilled brake fluid. Attach the rear brake hydraulic reservoir to the frame and tighten the retaining screw securely. Check the entire system for fluid leaks.

17 Check the operation of the brakes before riding the motorcycle.

12 Wheels – inspection and repair

1 In order to carry out a proper inspection of the wheels, it is necessary to support the bike

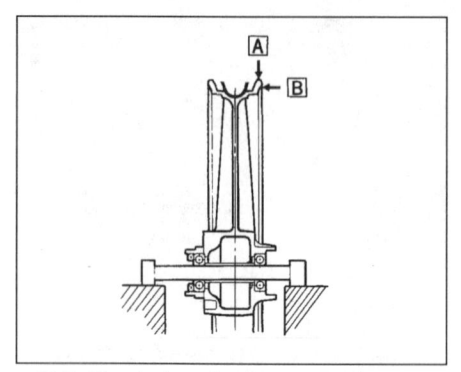

7•14 Brakes, wheels and tyres

12.2 Check the wheel for radial (out-of-round) runout (A) and axial (side-to-side) runout (B)

upright so that the wheel being inspected is raised off the ground. Position the motorcycle on an auxiliary stand. Clean the wheels thoroughly to remove mud and dirt that may interfere with the inspection procedure or mask defects. Make a general check of the wheels (see Chapter 1) and tyres (see *Daily (pre-ride) checks*).

2 Attach a dial gauge to the fork or the swingarm and position its tip against the side of the wheel rim **(see illustration)**. Spin the wheel slowly and check the axial (side-to-side) runout at the rim.

3 In order to accurately check radial (out of round) runout with the dial gauge, remove the wheel from the machine, and the tyre from the wheel. With the axle clamped in a vice and the dial gauge positioned on the top of the rim, the wheel can be rotated to check the runout.

4 An easier, though slightly less accurate, method is to attach a stiff wire pointer to the fork or the swingarm and position the end a fraction of an inch from the edge of the wheel rim where the wheel and tyre join. If the wheel is true, the distance from the pointer to the rim will be constant as the wheel is rotated. **Note:** *If wheel runout is excessive, check the wheel bearings very carefully before renewing the wheel.*

5 The wheels should also be inspected for cracks, flat spots on the rim and other damage. Look very closely for dents in the area where the tyre bead contacts the rim. Dents in this area may prevent complete sealing of the tyre against the rim, which leads to deflation of the tyre over a period of time. If damage is evident, or if runout in either direction is excessive, the wheel will have to be replaced with a new one. Never attempt to repair a damaged cast alloy wheel.

13 Wheels – alignment check

1 Misalignment of the wheels due to a bent frame or forks can cause strange and possibly serious handling problems. If the frame or forks are at fault, repair by a frame specialist or replacement with new parts are the only options.

2 To check wheel alignment you will need an assistant, a length of string or a perfectly straight piece of wood and a ruler. A plumb bob or spirit level for checking that the wheels are vertical will also be required.

3 In order to make a proper check of the wheels it is necessary to support the bike in an upright position, using an auxiliary stand. First ensure that the chain adjuster markings coincide on each side of the swingarm (see Chapter 1, Section 1). Next, measure the width of both tyres at their widest points. Subtract the smaller measurement from the larger measurement, then divide the difference by two. The result is the amount of offset that should exist between the front and rear tyres on both sides of the machine.

4 If a string is used, have your assistant hold one end of it about halfway between the floor and the rear axle, with the string touching the back edge of the rear tyre sidewall.

5 Run the other end of the string forward and pull it tight so that it is roughly parallel to the floor **(see illustration)**. Slowly bring the string into contact with the front edge of the rear tyre sidewall, then turn the front wheel until it is parallel with the string. Measure the distance from the front tyre sidewall to the string.

6 Repeat the procedure on the other side of the motorcycle. The distance from the front tyre sidewall to the string should be equal on both sides.

7 As previously mentioned, a perfectly straight length of wood or metal bar may be substituted for the string **(see illustration)**.

8 If the distance between the string and tyre is greater on one side, or if the rear wheel appears to be out of alignment, have your machine checked by a Yamaha dealer.

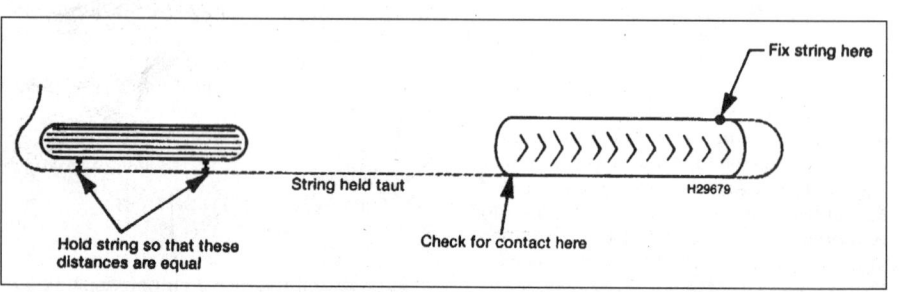

9 If the front-to-back alignment is correct, the wheels still may be out of alignment vertically.

10 Using a plumb bob or spirit level, check the rear wheel to make sure it is vertical. To do this, hold the string of the plumb bob against the tyre upper sidewall and allow the weight to settle just off the floor. If the string touches both the upper and lower tyre sidewalls and is perfectly straight, the wheel is vertical. If it is not, adjust the stand until it is.

11 Once the rear wheel is vertical, check the front wheel in the same manner. If both wheels are not perfectly vertical, the frame and/or major suspension components are bent.

14 Front wheel – removal and installation

Removal

1 Remove the lower fairing (see Chapter 8). Using an auxiliary stand, support the

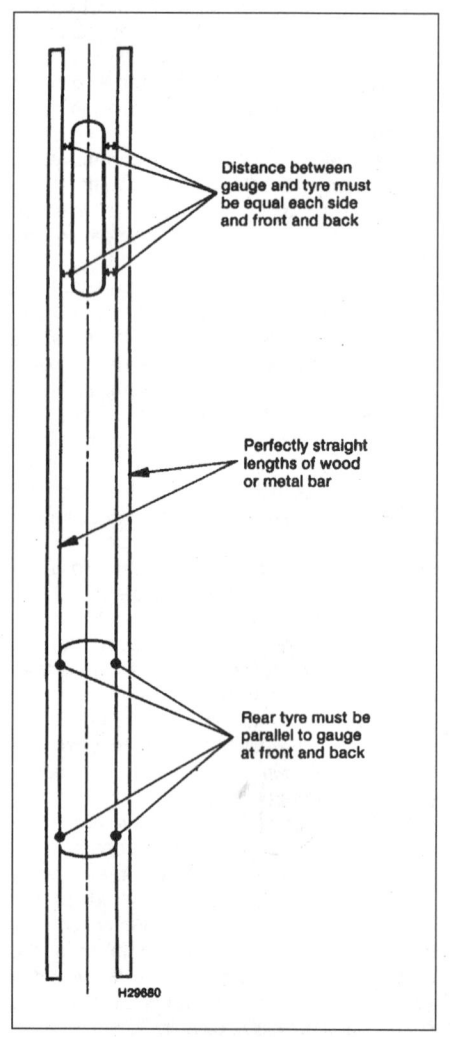

13.5 Wheel alignment check using string

13.7 Wheel alignment check using a straight-edge

Brakes, wheels and tyres 7•15

14.3a Slacken the pinch bolt (arrowed) . . .

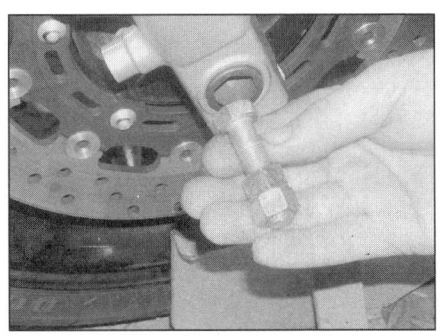

14.3b . . . and unscrew the axle using a bolt and two locknuts

14.5 Remove the axle spacers from inside the seals

14.10 Install the axle from the right-hand side . . .

14.11 . . . and ensure it aligns with the threaded hole (arrowed) in the left-hand fork . . .

14.12 . . . then tighten it to the specified torque

motorcycle securely in an upright position with the front wheel off the ground.
2 Displace the front brake calipers (see Section 3).
3 Slacken the axle pinch bolt on the bottom of the right-hand fork slider, then unscrew the axle, using an automotive 18 mm sump plug tool or an 18 mm bolt with two locknuts, as shown **(see illustrations)**.
4 Support the wheel, then withdraw the axle from the right-hand side and remove the wheel from between the forks.
5 Remove the axle spacers from both sides of the wheel, noting how they fit inside the bearing seals **(see illustration)**.
Caution: Don't lay the wheel down and allow it to rest on the brake disc – the disc could become warped. Set the wheel on wood blocks so the wheel rim supports the weight of the wheel, or keep the wheel upright. Don't operate the brake lever with the wheel removed.
6 Clean the axle and remove any corrosion using steel wool. Check the axle for straightness by rolling it on a flat surface such as a piece of plate glass. If available, place the axle in V-blocks and check for runout using a dial gauge. If the axle is bent, replace it with a new one.
7 Wipe any old grease off the bearing seals and check the condition of the seals and the wheel bearings (see Section 16).

8 Clean the axle spacers and remove any corrosion with steel wool. The spacers should be perfectly smooth where they locate in the seals.

Installation

9 Apply lithium-based grease to the insides of the bearing seals, then fit the spacers into the seals with the shouldered end of the spacers facing out.
10 Apply a thin coat of lithium-based grease to the axle, then lift the wheel into position between the forks, making sure the spacers remain in place, and slide the axle in from the right-hand side **(see illustration)**.
11 Ensure that the axle aligns correctly with the threaded hole in the left-hand fork **(see illustration)** and tighten the axle to half the torque setting specified at the beginning of this Chapter, then take the bike off its auxiliary stand and compress the forks by pressing down on the handlebars to align the wheel and the suspension.
12 Tighten the axle to the full specified torque setting, then tighten the pinch bolt on the bottom of the right-hand fork slider to the specified torque setting **(see illustration)**.
13 Install the brake calipers, making sure the pads sit squarely on each side of the discs (see Section 3), and install the lower fairing (see Chapter 8).
14 Apply the front brake to bring the pads back into contact with the discs.

15 Check the operation of the front brake before riding the motorcycle.

15 Rear wheel – removal and installation

Removal

1 Using and auxiliary stand, support the motorcycle securely in an upright position with the rear wheel off the ground.
2 Displace the rear brake caliper (see Section 7) and loosen the brake caliper bracket anchor bolt **(see illustration)**.
3 Loosen the chain adjuster locknuts and turn

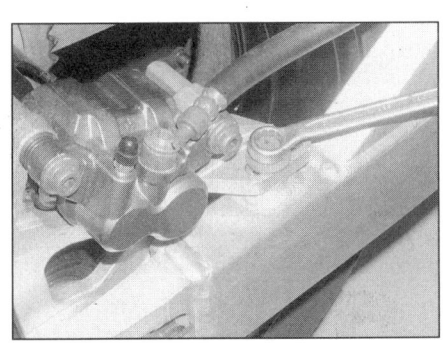

15.2 Loosen the brake caliper anchor bolt

7•16 Brakes, wheels and tyres

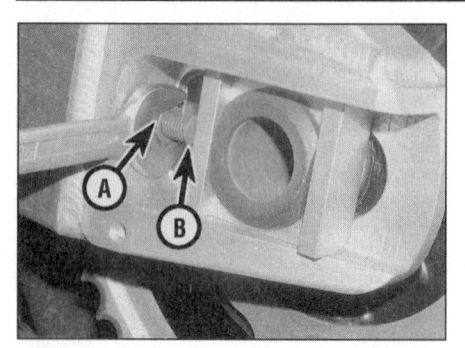

15.3 Loosen the locknuts (A) and turn the adjusters (B) in

15.4a Unscrew the axle nut . . .

15.4b . . . and remove the washer . . .

the adjusters in to provide some slack in the chain **(see illustration)**.

4 Unscrew the axle nut and remove the nut, washer and right-hand chain adjuster plate **(see illustrations)**.

5 Support the wheel, then withdraw the axle along with the left-hand chain adjuster plate and lower the wheel to the ground **(see illustration)**. Note how the caliper bracket locates between the wheel and the swingarm, then unscrew the anchor bolt and remove the bracket **(see illustration)**.

6 Slide the adjuster plate off the axle, noting how it fits. **Note:** *The left and right-hand adjuster plates are different and must not be swapped around on reassembly.*

7 Disengage the chain from the rear wheel sprocket and remove the wheel from the swingarm **(see illustration)**.

8 Remove the axle spacers from each side of the wheel, noting how they fit inside the bearing seals **(see illustration)**.

Caution: Don't lay the wheel down and allow it to rest on the disc or the sprocket – they could become warped. Set the wheel on wood blocks so the wheel rim supports the weight of the wheel, or keep the wheel upright. Don't operate the brake pedal with the wheel removed.

9 Clean the axle and remove any corrosion using steel wool. Check the axle for straightness by rolling it on a flat surface such as a piece of plate glass. If available, place the axle in V-blocks and check for runout using a dial gauge. If the axle is bent, replace it with a new one.

10 Wipe any old grease off the bearing seals and check the condition of the seals and the wheel bearings (see Section 16). Lift the sprocket coupling out of the hub to check the left-hand side wheel bearing.

11 Clean the axle spacers and remove any corrosion with steel wool. The spacers should be perfectly smooth where they locate in the seals.

Installation

12 Install the sprocket coupling. Apply lithium-based grease to the insides of the bearing seals, then fit the axle spacers into the seals.

13 Manoeuvre the wheel into place in the swingarm and engage the drive chain on the sprocket.

14 Locate the brake caliper bracket on the swingarm and tighten the anchor bolt finger-tight.

15 Slide the left-hand chain adjuster plate onto the axle and align the flats on the axle head with the plate. Apply a thin coat of lithium-based grease to the axle.

16 Lift the wheel into position, making sure the spacers remain in place, and slide the axle through from the left-hand side **(see illustration 15.5a)**. Ensure the axle passes through the caliper bracket.

17 Locate the left-hand chain adjuster plate

15.4c . . . and the right-hand chain adjuster plate

15.5a Withdraw the axle and lower the wheel . . .

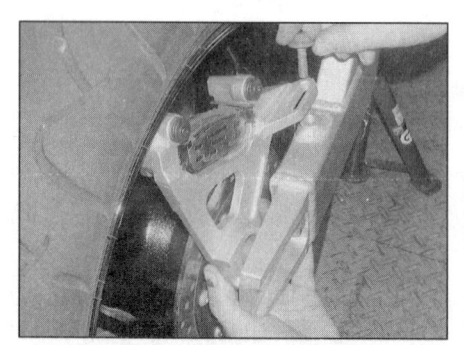

15.5b . . . then undo the anchor bolt and remove the caliper bracket

15.7 Disengage the chain and remove the wheel

15.8 Remove the axle spacers, noting how they fit

Brakes, wheels and tyres 7•17

15.17 Raised sides (arrowed) of the plate must be vertical

16.2 Lever out the seals . . .

16.3a . . . then drive out the bearings with a drift . . .

in the slot in the swingarm with the raised sections on the plate vertical **(see illustration)**.
18 Fit the right-hand chain adjuster plate with its tapered side facing the swingarm, then fit the washer and the axle nut.
19 Adjust the chain tension as described in Chapter 1, then tighten the axle nut and the caliper anchor bolt to the torque settings specified at the beginning of this Chapter.
20 Install the brake caliper (see Section 7).
21 Apply the rear brake to bring the pads into contact with the disc. Check the operation of the rear brake before riding the motorcycle.

16 Wheel bearings – removal, inspection and installation

Front wheel bearings

Note: *Always renew the wheel bearings in sets, never individually. Avoid using a high pressure cleaner on the wheel bearing area.*
1 Remove the wheel (see Section 14).
2 Lever out the bearing seals from both sides of the hub using a large, flat-bladed screwdriver and a piece of wood, taking care not to damage the hub **(see illustration)**. Discard the seals as new ones must be fitted on reassembly.
3 Using a metal rod (preferably a brass punch) inserted through the centre of the bearing on one side of the hub, tap evenly around the outer race of the bearing on the other side to drive it from the hub **(see illustrations)**.
4 The bearing spacer will drop out of position once the first bearing has been removed.
5 Turn the wheel over and drive out the remaining bearing using the same procedure.
6 Check the condition of the bearings – see *Tools and Workshop Tips (Section 5)* in the *Reference* section.
7 Thoroughly clean the hub area of the wheel with a suitable solvent and inspect the bearing seats for scoring and wear. If the seats are damaged, consult a Yamaha dealer before reassembling the wheel.
8 Install a bearing into its seat in one side of the hub, with the marked or sealed side facing outwards. Using an old bearing (if new ones are being fitted), a bearing driver or a socket large enough to contact the outer race of the bearing, drive it in until it's completely seated **(see illustrations)**.
9 Turn the wheel over, install the bearing spacer and drive the other bearing into place.
10 Lubricate the bearing seals with lithium-based grease and press them into the hub, using a bearing driver or a suitable socket **(see illustration)**. Level the seals with the inner rim of the hub with a small block of wood **(see illustration)**.
11 Clean the brake discs using acetone or brake system cleaner, then install the wheel (see Section 14).

Rear wheel bearings

12 Remove the rear wheel (see Section 15) and lift the sprocket coupling out of the hub.

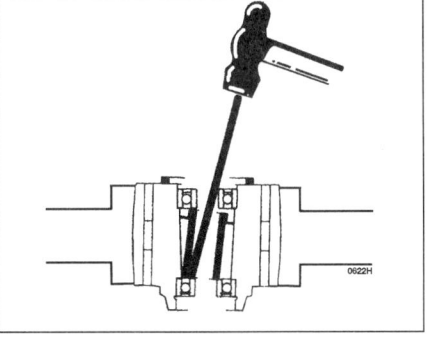

16.3b . . . locating it as shown

16.8a Position the bearing with its sealed side facing outwards . . .

16.8b . . . and drive it in with a suitable driver

16.10a Lubricate the seal and press it into place . . .

16.10b . . . then level it with a block of wood

7

7•18 Brakes, wheels and tyres

16.14 Remove the circlip

16.15a Remove the needle bearing collar...

16.15b ...then drive out the caged ball bearing

13 A caged ball bearing is fitted in the right-hand side of the hub and a needle roller bearing is fitted in the left-hand side.
14 Set the wheel on wooden blocks with the disc (right-hand side) facing up, then lever out the bearing seal using a large flat-bladed screwdriver and a piece of wood, taking care not to damage the hub **(see illustration 16.2)**. Discard the seal as a new one must be fitted on reassembly. Remove the circlip securing the bearing **(see illustration)**.
15 Turn the wheel over and rest it on the wooden blocks. Remove the collar from inside the needle bearing **(see illustration)**. Using a metal rod (preferably a brass punch) inserted through the centre of the needle bearing, tap evenly around the outer race of the caged ball bearing to drive it from the hub **(see illustration)**. The bearing spacer will also come out.
16 Turn the wheel over and drive the needle bearing out of the hub using the same procedure. **Note:** *Removing a needle roller bearing makes it unfit for further use – a new bearing must be installed, whatever the condition of the old one.*
17 Check the condition of the ball bearing – see *Tools and Workshop Tips (Section 5)* in the *Reference* section.
18 Thoroughly clean the hub area of the wheel with a suitable solvent and inspect the bearing seats for scoring and wear. If the seats are damaged, consult a Yamaha dealer before reassembling the wheel.
19 First install the caged ball bearing into its recess in the right-hand side of the hub, with the marked or sealed side facing outwards. Using an old bearing (if new ones are being fitted), a bearing driver or a socket large enough to contact the outer race of the bearing, drive it in squarely until it is completely seated **(see illustrations 16.8a and b)**. Fit the circlip, making sure it locates correctly in its groove.
20 Lubricate the right-hand bearing seal with lithium-based grease and press it into the hub, using a bearing driver or a suitable socket. Level the seal with the inner rim of the hub with a small block of wood **(see illustration 16.10b)**.
21 Turn the wheel over and install the bearing spacer **(see illustration)**. Fit the new needle bearing; needle bearings should be pressed or drawn, rather than driven, into position. In the absence of a press, a suitable drawbolt arrangement can be made up as described in *Tools and Workshop Tips (Section 5)* in the *Reference* section. Fit the collar into the needle bearing **(see illustration 16.15a)**.
22 Clean the brake disc using acetone or brake system cleaner.
23 Install the sprocket coupling assembly and install the wheel (see Section 15).

Sprocket coupling bearing

24 Remove the rear wheel (see Section 15) and lift the sprocket coupling out of the hub.
25 Lever out the bearing seal using a large flat-bladed screwdriver and a piece of wood, taking care not to damage the rim of the coupling **(see illustration)**. Discard the seal as a new one must be fitted on reassembly.
26 Support the coupling on blocks of wood and drive the bearing out from the inside using a bearing driver or socket **(see illustration)**.
27 Check the condition of the bearing – see *Tools and Workshop Tips (Section 5)* in the *Reference* section.
28 Thoroughly clean the bearing seat with a suitable solvent and inspect the seat for scoring and wear. If the seat is damaged, consult a Yamaha dealer before reassembling the wheel.
29 Install the bearing into the coupling, with the marked or sealed side facing out. Using the old bearing (if a new one is being fitted), a bearing driver or a socket large enough to contact the outer race of the bearing, drive it in until it is completely seated **(see illustration)**.
30 Lubricate the new seal with lithium-base grease and press it into the coupling, using a

16.21 Install the bearing spacer

16.25 Lever the seal out of the coupling

16.26 Drive the bearing out from the inside

16.29 A socket can be used to drive in the bearing

Brakes, wheels and tyres 7•19

16.30 Lubricate the new seal and press it into the coupling

bearing driver or a suitable socket **(see illustration)**.
31 Inspect the sprocket coupling rubber dampers (see Chapter 6, Section 17).
32 Clean the brake disc using acetone or brake system cleaner, then install the sprocket coupling assembly and install the wheel (see Section 15).

17 Tyres – general information and fitting

General information

1 The wheels fitted on all models are designed to take tubeless tyres only. Tyre sizes are given in the Specifications at the beginning of this chapter.
2 Refer to *Daily (pre-ride) checks* at the beginning of this manual for tyre maintenance and pressures.

Fitting new tyres

3 When selecting new tyres, refer to the tyre information in the Owner's Manual. Ensure that front and rear tyre types are compatible, and of the correct size and speed rating; if necessary, seek advice from a Yamaha dealer or motorcycle tyre specialist **(see illustration)**.
4 It is recommended that tyres are fitted by a motorcycle tyre specialist and that this is not attempted in the home workshop. This is particularly relevant in the case of tubeless tyres because the force required to break the seal between the wheel rim and tyre bead is substantial, and is usually beyond the capabilities of an individual working with normal tyre levers. Additionally, the specialist will be able to balance the wheels after tyre fitting.
5 Note that punctured tubeless tyres can in some cases be repaired. Seek the advice of a Yamaha dealer or a motorcycle tyre specialist concerning tyre repairs.

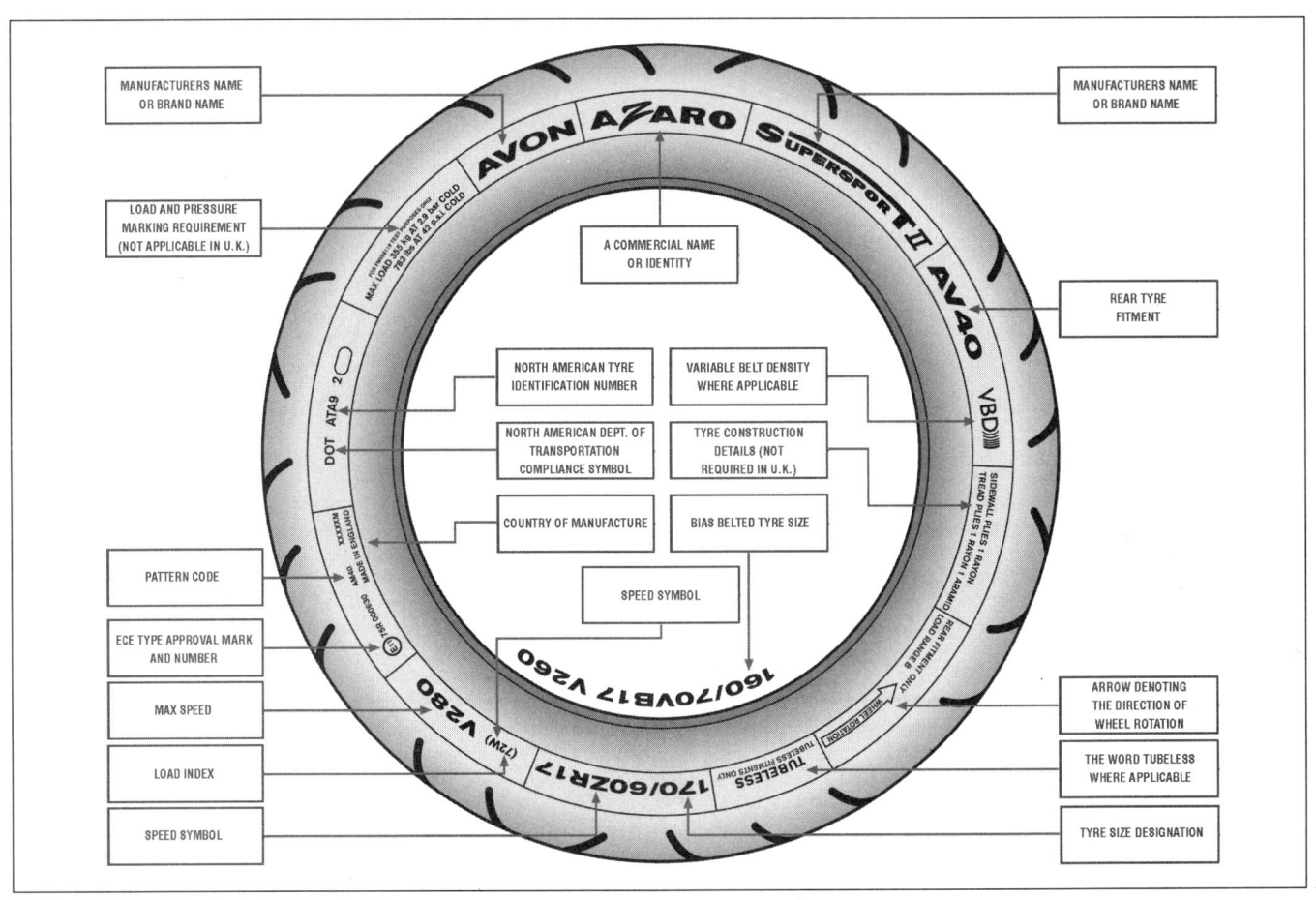

17.3 Common tyre sidewall markings

Notes

Chapter 8
Bodywork

Contents

Fairing and body panels – removal and installation 3
Front mudguard – removal and installation 6
General information 1
Rear view mirrors – removal and installation 4
Seats – removal and installation 2
Windshield – removal and installation 5

Degrees of difficulty

| **Easy,** suitable for novice with little experience | **Fairly easy,** suitable for beginner with some experience | **Fairly difficult,** suitable for competent DIY mechanic | **Difficult,** suitable for experienced DIY mechanic | **Very difficult,** suitable for expert DIY or professional |

1 General information

1 This Chapter covers the procedures necessary to remove and install the body parts. Since many service and repair operations on these motorcycles require the removal of the body parts, the procedures are grouped here and referred to from other Chapters.
2 In the case of damage to the body parts, it is usually necessary to remove the broken component and replace it with a new (or used) one. The material from which the body panels are made does not lend itself to conventional repair techniques. There are, however, some shops that specialise in 'plastic welding', so it may be worthwhile seeking the advice of one of these specialists before consigning an expensive component to the bin. There are also fairing repair kits available for DIY use.
3 When attempting to remove any body panel, first study it closely, noting any fasteners and associated fittings, to be sure of returning everything to its correct place on installation. In some cases the aid of an assistant will be required when removing panels, to help avoid the risk of damage to paintwork. Once the evident fasteners have been removed, try to withdraw the panel as described but DO NOT FORCE IT – if it will not release, check that all fasteners have been removed and try again. Where a panel engages another by means of tabs, be careful not to break the tab or its mating slot or to damage the paintwork. Remember that a few moments of patience at this stage will save you a lot of money in replacing broken fairing panels! To remove trim clips, push the centre into the body, then draw the clip out of the panel **(see illustration)**. To undo quick-release screws, turn them 90° anti-clockwise.
4 When installing a body panel, first study it closely, noting any fasteners and associated fittings removed with it, to be sure of returning everything to its correct place. Check that all fasteners are in good condition, including all trim clips and rubber mounts; any of these

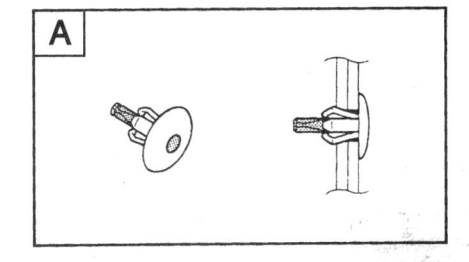

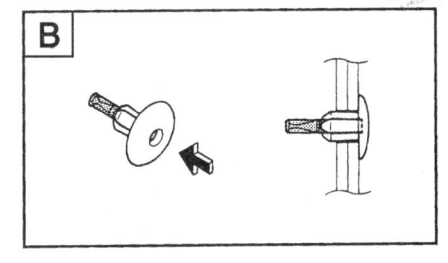

1.3 Trim clip removal
A Clip installed
B Clip with centre pin pushed in and ready for removal from panel

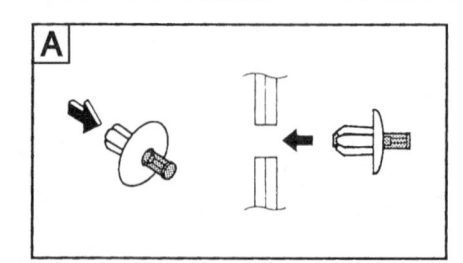

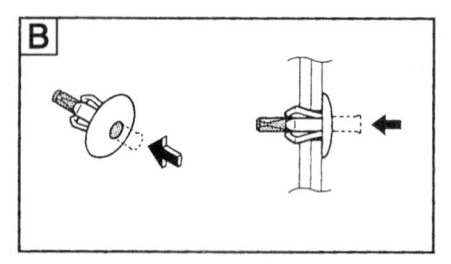

8•2 Bodywork

1.4 Trim clip installation
A Clip ready for installation
B Clip being secured in panel

that are faulty must be replaced with new ones before the panel is reassembled. Check also that all mounting brackets are straight, and repair or renew them if necessary before attempting to install the panel. Where assistance was required to remove a panel, make sure your assistant is on hand to install it. To install trim clips, first push the centre back out so that it protrudes from the top of the clip **(see illustration)**. Fit the clip into its hole, then push the centre in so that it is flush with the top of the clip. To install quick-release screws, turn them 90° clockwise.

5 Tighten the fasteners securely, but be careful not to overtighten any of them or the panel may break (not always immediately) due to the uneven stress.

2 Seats – removal and installation

1 To remove the passenger seat, insert the ignition key into the seat lock located on the left-hand side of the bike, and turn it anti-clockwise to unlock the seat **(see illustration)**. Lift up the front of the seat and draw it forwards, noting how the tab at the back locates **(see illustration)**.

2 To remove the rider's seat, pull up each rear corner of the seat to access the bolts that retain it, then unscrew the bolts and remove the seat, noting how the tab at the front locates under the tank bracket **(see illustrations)**.

3 Installation is the reverse of removal. Push down on the front of the passenger seat to engage the latch.

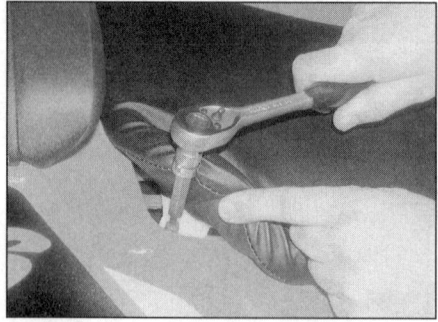

3 Fairing and body panels – removal and installation

Seat cowling

1 Remove the seats (see Section 2).
2 Release and remove the six trim clips on the underside of the seat cowling (three on each side) **(see illustration)**.
3 Remove the screw on each side at the front of the cowling; note the bush in the cowling panel. Remove the screws on the top of the cowling at the back, then carefully draw the cowling back and off the bike **(see illustrations)**.
4 Installation is the reverse of removal.

Under seat panel (2001-on models)

5 Later models are fitted with a separate panel on the underside of the tail assembly. The under seat panel houses the LED tail light unit.
6 Remove the seat cowling (see above).
7 Unscrew the bolts securing the passenger

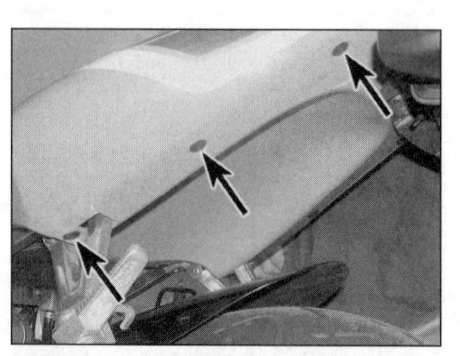

2.1a Turn key anti-clockwise to release seat catch

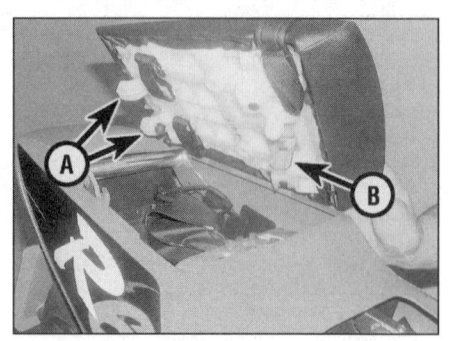

2.1b Note locating tabs (A) and seat lock latch (B)

2.2a Unscrew the bolt from each rear corner . . .

2.2b . . . then lift the rear of the seat and pull it back

3.2 Release the trim clips, three on each side . . .

3.3a . . . then remove the screws at the front, one each side . . .

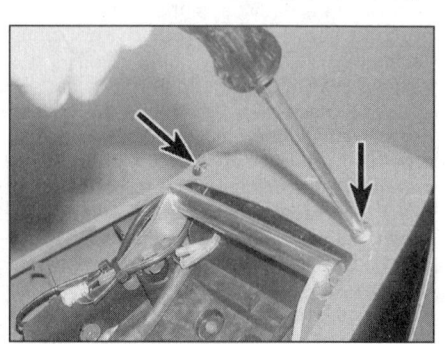

3.3b . . . the two at the rear . . .

Bodywork 8•3

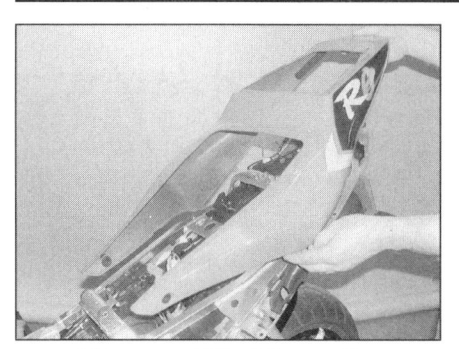

3.3c . . . and lift off the cowling

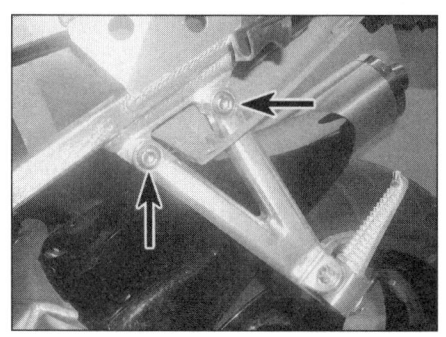

3.7a Unscrew the passenger footrest bracket bolts . . .

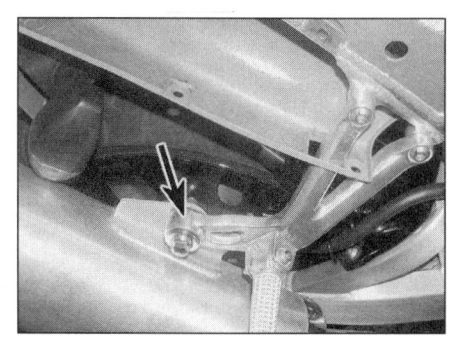

3.7b . . . and the silencer bolt

footrest brackets to the frame and the nut and bolt securing the exhaust silencer to the right-hand footrest bracket, and remove the brackets **(see illustrations)**.

8 Remove the two trim clips on the front corners of the panel **(see illustration)**.

9 Trace the wiring from the rear turn signals and the rear light unit and disconnect it at the connectors. Release the wiring from the wiring clips on the panel **(see illustration)**.

10 Unscrew the bolts securing the number plate/turn signal bracket to the frame and remove the bolts, then lower the under seat panel and number plate/ turn signal bracket away from the motorcycle **(see illustrations)**. Thread the turn signal wiring through the grommet in the under seat panel to separate the components. **Note:** *The bolts screw into a threaded plate inside the number plate/turn signal bracket – note how the plate fits to aid reassembly.*

11 Installation is the reverse of removal.

Lower fairing

12 Release the three quick-release screws securing each side of the lower fairing to each side panel, and undo the two screws securing each side of the lower fairing to the frame **(see illustrations)**.

13 Carefully lower the fairing and remove it, noting how it engages with the side panels along its top edge. **Note:** *The lower fairing is a three-piece assembly. If required, the left and right-*

3.8 Remove the trim clips, one each side . . .

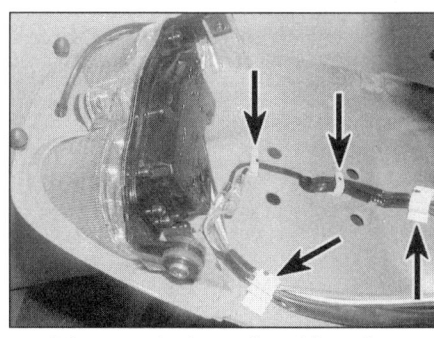

3.9 . . . and release the wiring clips

3.10a Unscrew the bracket bolts . . .

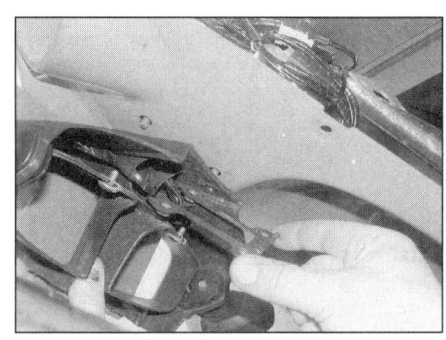

3.10b . . . then remove the bracket and the seat panel

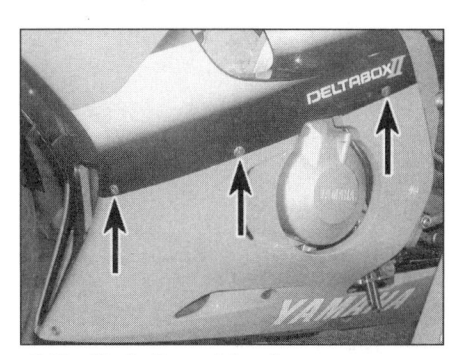

3.12a Undo the quick-release screws . . .

3.12b . . . and the front . . .

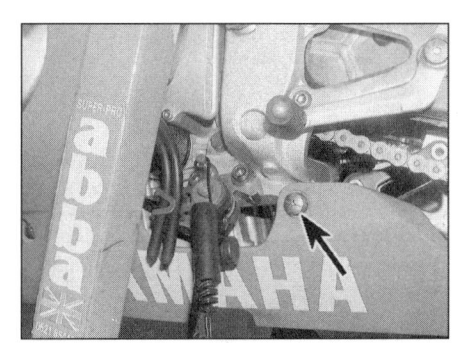

3.12c . . . and rear fairing-to-frame screws

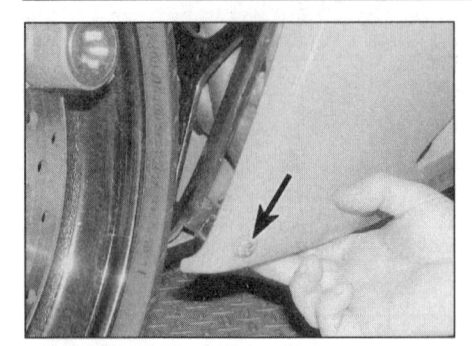

8•4 Bodywork

3.13a Undo the quick-release screw . . .

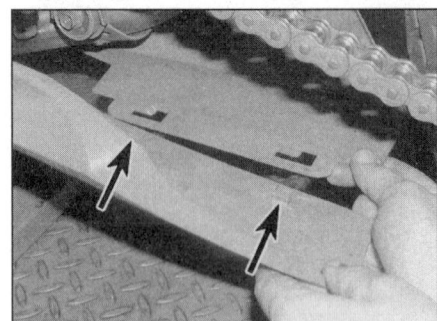

3.13b . . . and unclip the tabs

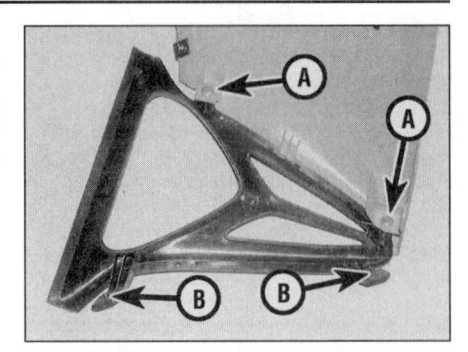

3.13c The front section is retained by screws (A) and clips (B)

hand sections can be separated while the fairing is still on the machine by releasing the quick-release screw on the lower front edge of the left-hand section, then unclipping the tabs on the adjoining middle edges **(see illustrations)**. The front section is clipped to the left-hand side and fixed to the right-hand section by two self-tapping screws **(see illustration)**.

14 Installation is the reverse of removal.

Inner trim panels

15 Release the two quick-release screws, then ease the panel back to release the tab on the side panel. Lift the lower edge of the trim panel from underneath the edge of the fairing side panel and lift the trim panel out. Be careful not to break the tab on the inner edge of the side panel **(see illustrations)**.

16 Installation is the reverse of removal. Make sure the panel locates correctly with the fairing and fairing side panel.

Fairing side panels

17 Remove the lower fairing and the inner trim panel (see above).

18 Disconnect the turn signal wiring connectors **(see illustration)**.

19 Remove the trim clip situated underneath the front of the fairing that secures the panel to the fairing, and the trim clip on the inside of the side panel forward of the radiator that secures the panel to the lower edge of the air intake duct **(see illustrations)**.

20 Release the three quick-release screws securing the side panel to the fairing, and undo the screw securing the side panel to the frame **(see illustrations)**.

21 Carefully draw the panel away, noting how it engages with the fairing along its top edge **(see illustration)**. Note the foam cushion for the panel down the side of the radiator.

22 Installation is the reverse of removal.

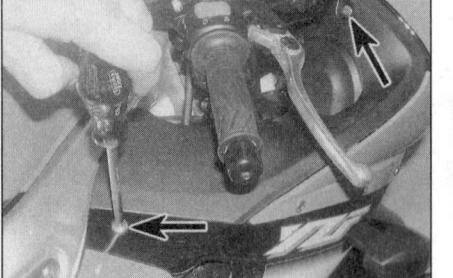

3.15a Release the screws (arrowed) . . .

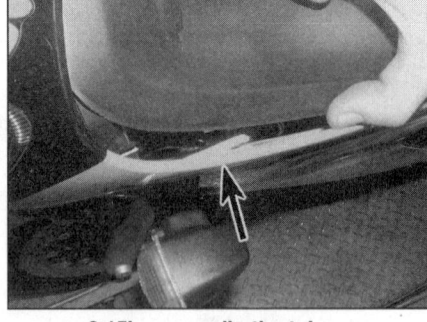

3.15b . . . unclip the tab . . .

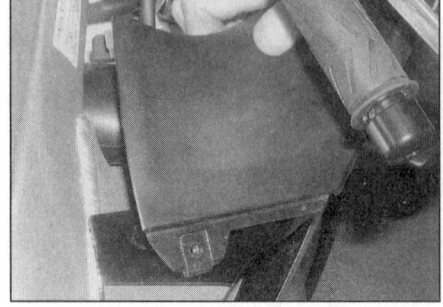

3.15c . . . and lift out the panel

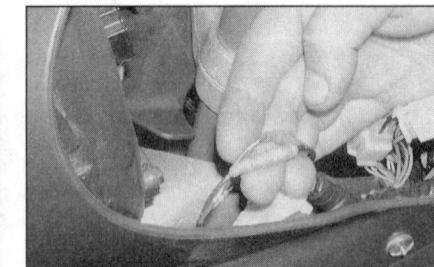

3.18 Disconnect the turn signal wiring connectors

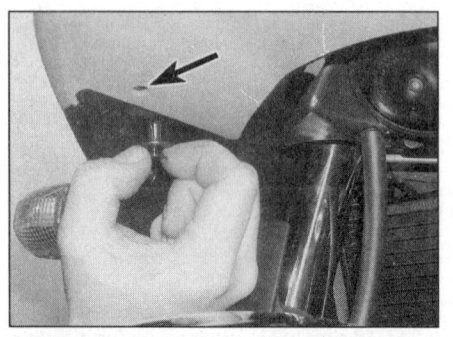

3.19a Remove the trim clip under the front of the fairing . . .

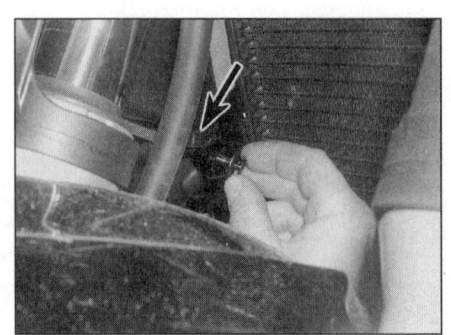

3.19b . . . and inside the fairing . . .

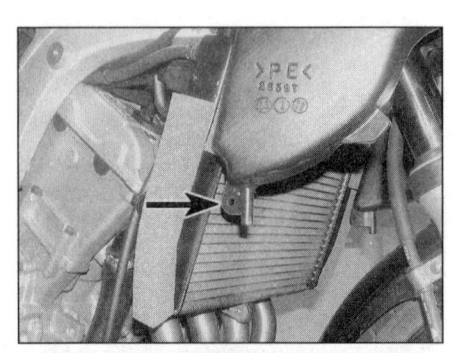

3.19c . . . securing the side panel to the air intake duct – panel removed for clarity

Bodywork 8•5

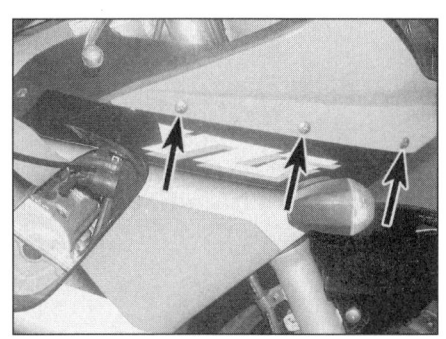

3.20a Undo the quick-release screws...

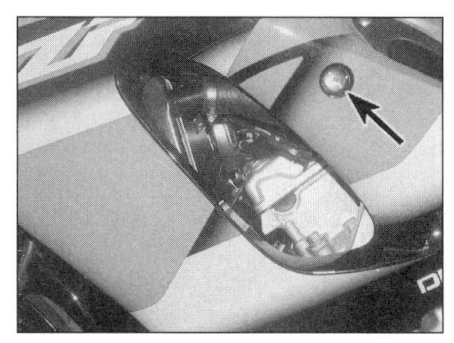

3.20b ...and the fairing-to-frame screw...

3.21 ...then lift the panel off

Fairing

Note: *Although not essential, it is easier to remove the fairing having first removed the lower fairing and side panels.*

23 Remove both inner trim panels (see above).
24 Disconnect the white instrument cluster wiring connector, lighting wiring connectors and turn signal connectors **(see illustration)**.
25 Loosen the clips securing the air intake tubes to the ducts inside the fairing **(see illustration)**.
26 If not already done, release the quick-release screws securing the side panels to the fairing (see Step 20), and remove the trim clips securing the side panels to the fairing (see Step 19).
27 Support the fairing and remove the two bolts securing the fairing stay to the steering head **(see illustration)**. Carefully lift the fairing assembly up and draw it forwards, disconnect the air intake tubes from the ducts and remove the fairing – the headlights, instrument cluster and intake ducts come away with the fairing **(see illustration)**.
28 To remove the fairing stay, first remove the rear view mirrors (see Section 4).
29 Unscrew the four bolts securing the fairing stay to the fairing and remove the bolts and the stay **(see illustration)**. Remove the pads with collars for the rear view mirror bolts from inside the fairing **(see illustration)**. **Note:** *The instrument cluster is mounted on the fairing stay – disconnect the multi-pin wiring connector at the back of the cluster to separate the fairing stay completely. The air intake ducts are also mounted on the fairing stay – note the position of the intake grill in the front of the fairing when the stay assembly is removed.*
30 If required, remove the screws securing

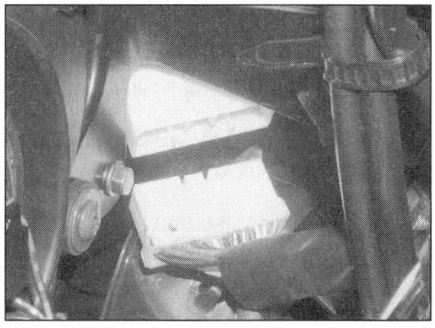

3.24 The instrument cluster connector is attached to the fairing bracket

3.25 Loosen the screws on the air intake tubing

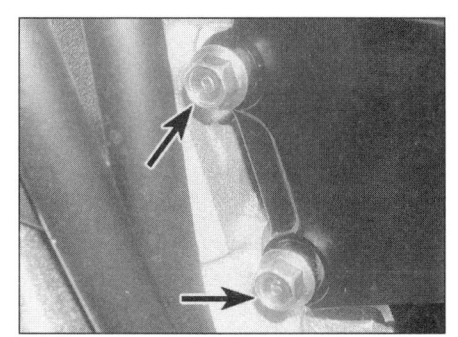

3.27a Remove the fairing stay bolts (arrowed)...

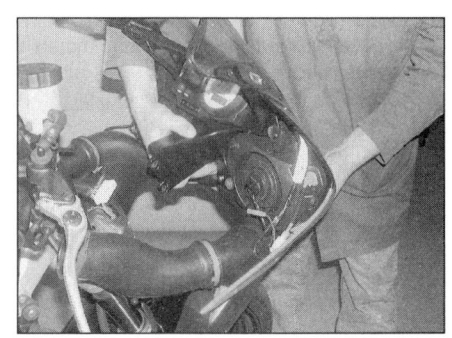

3.27b ...and lift the fairing off

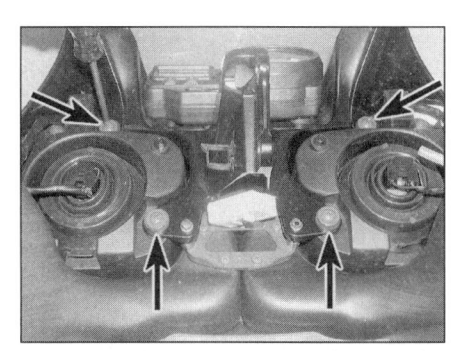

3.29a Fairing mounting bolts (arrowed)

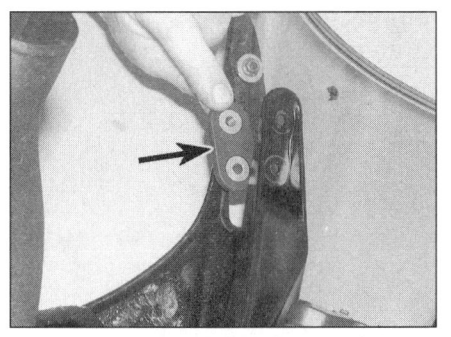

3.29b Pad with collars (arrowed) fits between the fairing and the stay

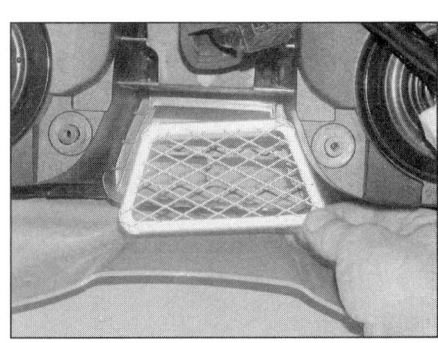

3.29c intake grill is retained by fairing stay

8

8•6 Bodywork

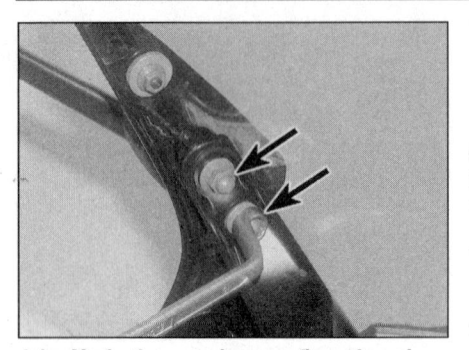

4.1a Undo the nuts (arrowed) on the mirror stay...

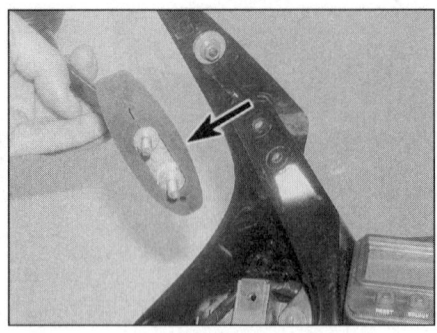

4.1b ...and remove the mirror, noting the pad (arrowed)

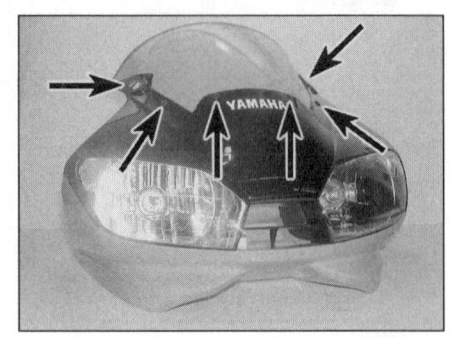

5.1 Windshield is secured by six screws

the instrument cluster and intake ducts to the fairing stay and separate the components. Remove the screws securing the headlight unit in the fairing and remove the unit.

31 Installation is the reverse of removal. Make sure the instrument cluster wiring connector is connected and the air intake grill is in position before installing the fairing bracket.

4 Rear view mirrors – removal and installation

1 Unscrew the two nuts securing each mirror and remove the mirror along with its rubber insulator pad **(see illustration)**. Note the rubber pad with collars for the mirror bolts fixed between the fairing and fairing mounting stay **(illustration 3.29b)**.
2 Installation is the reverse of removal.

5 Windshield – removal and installation

1 Remove the rear view mirrors (see Section 4). Remove the six screws securing the windshield to the fairing and remove the windshield, noting how it fits **(see illustration)**. Note that the two rear screws are retained by a plain washer and nut on the inside edge of the fairing; the four front screws thread into wellnuts set in the screen.
2 Installation is the reverse of removal. Do not overtighten the screws.

6 Front mudguard – removal and installation

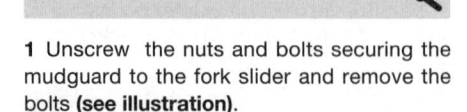

1 Unscrew the nuts and bolts securing the mudguard to the fork slider and remove the bolts **(see illustration)**.
2 Draw the mudguard forward from between the forks and remove it from the motorcycle **(see illustration)**.
3 Note the collars and bushes in the mudguard mounting holes and remove them if they are loose. The bushes should be a tight fit in the mudguard; replace them if they are worn or perished.
4 Installation is the reverse of removal.

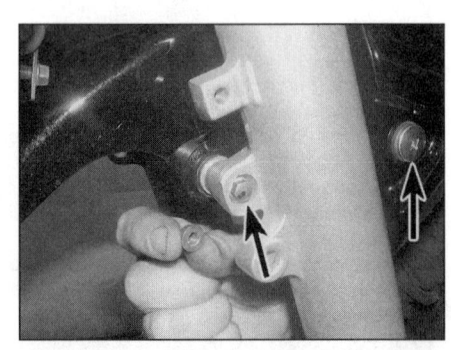

6.1 Unscrew the bolts (arrowed) on both sides...

6.2 ...and draw the mudguard forward

Chapter 9
Electrical system

Contents

Alternator rotor and stator – check, removal and installation	32
Battery – charging	4
Battery – removal, installation, inspection and maintenance	3
Brake light switches – check and renewal	14
Brake/tail light bulbs – renewal	9
Charging system – leakage and output test	31
Charging system testing – general information and precautions	30
Clutch switch – check and renewal	23
Coolant temperature display, warning light and sender	see Chapter 3
Cooling fan switch – check and renewal	see Chapter 3
Electrical system – fault finding	2
Fuel pump and relay	see Chapter 4
Fuses – check and renewal	5
General information	1
Handlebar switches – check	19
Handlebar switches – removal and installation	20
Headlight aim – check and adjustment	see Chapter 1
Headlight bulbs and sidelight bulbs – renewal	7
Headlight unit – removal and installation	8
Horn – check and renewal	25
Ignition (main) switch – check, removal and installation	18
Ignition system components	see Chapter 5
Instrument cluster – removal and installation	15
Instruments – check and renewal	16
Lighting system – check	6
Neutral switch – check, removal and installation	21
Oil level sensor and relay – check, removal and installation	26
Regulator/rectifier – check and renewal	33
Relay assembly – check and renewal	24
Sidestand switch – check and renewal	22
Starter motor – disassembly, inspection and reassembly	29
Starter motor – removal and installation	28
Starter relay – check and renewal	27
Tail light unit – removal and installation	10
Turn signal assemblies – removal and installation	13
Turn signal bulbs – renewal	12
Turn signal circuit – check	11
Warning lights – renewal	17

Degrees of difficulty

Easy, suitable for novice with little experience	Fairly easy, suitable for beginner with some experience	Fairly difficult, suitable for competent DIY mechanic	Difficult, suitable for experienced DIY mechanic	Very difficult, suitable for expert DIY or professional

Specifications

Battery
Capacity
- 1999 and 2000 models 12V, 10Ah
- 2001-on models 12V, 8Ah

Type
- 1999 and 2000 models GT12B-4
- 2001-on models GT9B-4

Charge condition
- Fully charged 12.8V
- Half-charged 12.4V
- Discharged .... 12V or less

Charging time .... Until fully charged (12.8V) (see Section 4)
Current leakage .... 1mA (max)

Alternator
Nominal output .... 14V, 320W @ 5000 rpm
Stator coil resistance .... 0.27 to 0.33 ohms @ 20°C

Regulator/rectifier
Regulated voltage output (no load) .... 14.1 to 14.9V @ 5000 rpm

Starter relay
Resistance .... 4.18 to 4.62 ohms @ 20°C

Starter motor
Brush length
- Standard .... 10 mm
- Service limit (min) .... 3.5 mm

Commutator diameter
- Standard .... 28 mm
- Service limit (min) .... 27 mm

Mica undercut .... 0.7 mm
Commutator resistance .... 0.012 to 0.022 ohms

Fuses
Main 30A
Headlight 20A
Signal 20A
Ignition 15A
Cooling fan 7.5A
Backup fuse (odometer) 7.5A

Bulbs
Headlight .... 60/55W halogen x 2
Sidelight .... 5W x 2
Brake/tail light
- 1999 and 2000 models .... 21/5W x 2
- 2001-on models .... LED

Turn signal lights
- UK models .... 21W x 4
- US models .... 27/8W x 2 (front with running light), 27W x 2 (rear)

Instrument cluster illumination lights .... 1.4W x 2
Instrument warning lights .... LED

Torque wrench settings
Alternator cover bolts .... 12 Nm
Alternator rotor bolt .... 65 Nm
Alternator stator bolts .... 10 Nm
Neutral switch .... 20 Nm
Oil level sensor bolts .... 10 Nm
Starter motor long bolts .... 5 Nm
Starter motor mounting bolts .... 7 Nm

1 General information

All models have a 12 volt electrical system charged by a three-phase alternator with a separate regulator/rectifier.

The regulator maintains the charging system output within the specified range to prevent overcharging, and the rectifier converts the ac (alternating current) output of the alternator to dc (direct current) to power the lights and other components and to charge the battery. The alternator rotor is mounted on the left-hand end of the crankshaft.

The starting system includes the starter motor, the battery, the relay and the various wires and switches. If the engine kill switch is in the RUN position and the ignition (main) switch is ON, the starter relay allows the starter motor to operate only if the transmission is in neutral (neutral switch on) or, if the transmission is in gear, if the clutch lever is pulled into the handlebar and the sidestand is up. The starter motor is mounted on the top of the crankcase.

Note: *Keep in mind that electrical parts, once purchased, cannot be returned. To avoid unnecessary expense, make very sure the faulty component has been positively identified before buying a replacement part.*

2 Electrical system – fault finding

Warning: *To prevent the risk of short circuits, the ignition (main) switch must always be OFF and the battery negative (–ve) terminal should be disconnected before any of the bike's other electrical components are disturbed. Don't forget to reconnect the terminal securely once work is finished or if battery power is needed for circuit testing.*

1 A typical electrical circuit consists of an electrical component, the switches, relays, etc. related to that component and the wiring and connectors that link the component to both the battery and the frame. To aid in locating a problem in any electrical circuit, refer to *Wiring Diagrams* at the end of this Chapter.

2 Before tackling any troublesome electrical circuit, first study the wiring diagram (see end of Chapter) thoroughly to get a complete picture of what makes up that individual circuit. Faults can often be tracked down by noting if other components related to that circuit are operating properly or not. If several components or circuits fail at one time, it may be that the fault lies in the fuse or earth (ground) connection, as several circuits are often routed through the same fuse and earth (ground) connections.

3 Electrical problems often stem from simple causes, such as loose or corroded connections or a blown fuse. Prior to any electrical fault finding, always check the condition of the fuse, wires and connections in the problem circuit visually. Intermittent failures can be especially frustrating, since you cannot always duplicate the failure when it is convenient to do a test. In such situations, it is good practice to clean all connections and terminals in the affected circuit, whether or not they appear to be good, and ensure that the connectors fit together tightly.

4 If testing instruments are going to be used,

Electrical system 9•3

study the wiring diagram to plan where you will make the necessary connections in order to pinpoint the trouble spot accurately.

5 The basic tools needed for electrical fault finding include a battery and bulb test circuit, a continuity tester, a test light, and jumper wires. A multimeter capable of reading volts, ohms and amps is also very useful as an alternative to the above, and is necessary for performing more extensive tests and checks.

> **HAYNES HiNT**: Refer to Fault Finding Equipment in the Reference section for details of how to use electrical test equipment.

3 Battery – removal, installation, inspection and maintenance

Caution: Be extremely careful when handling or working around the battery. The electrolyte gel is very caustic and an explosive gas (hydrogen) is given off when the battery is charging.

Removal and installation

1 Remove the rider's seat (see Chapter 8).
2 Unscrew the negative (–ve) terminal bolt first and disconnect the lead from the battery **(see illustration)**. Lift up the insulating cover to access the positive (+ve) terminal, then unscrew the bolt and disconnect the lead. Release the battery strap and remove the battery from the bike **(see illustration)**.
3 On installation, ensure the battery terminals and lead ends are clean, then reconnect the leads, connecting the positive (+ve) terminal first.
4 Install the seat (see Chapter 8).

> **HAYNES HiNT**: Battery corrosion can be kept to a minimum by applying a layer of petroleum jelly to the terminals after the cables have been connected.

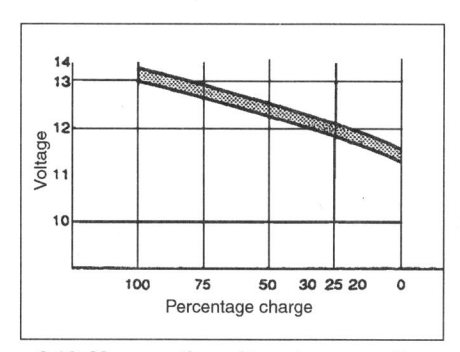

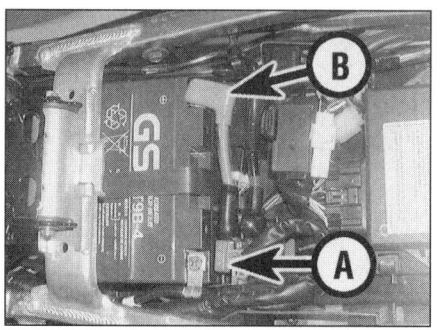

3.2a First disconnect negative (–ve) (A) then positive (+ve) (B) terminals ...

Inspection and maintenance

5 The battery is of the maintenance-free (sealed) gel type, therefore requiring no specific maintenance. Do not attempt to open the battery as resulting damage will mean it will be unfit for further use. However, the following checks should still be regularly performed.
6 Check the battery terminals and leads for tightness and corrosion. If corrosion is evident, unscrew the terminal bolts and disconnect the leads from the battery, disconnecting the negative (–ve) terminal first. Clean the terminals and lead ends with a wire brush or penknife and steel wool. Reconnect the leads, connecting the negative (–ve) terminal last, and apply a thin coat of petroleum jelly to the connections to slow further corrosion.
7 The battery case should be kept clean to prevent current leakage, which can discharge the battery over a period of time (especially when it sits unused). Remove the battery from the motorcycle and wash the outside of the case with a solution of baking soda and water. Rinse the battery thoroughly, then dry it.
8 Look for cracks in the case and renew the battery if any are found.
9 If the motorcycle sits unused for long periods of time, disconnect the leads from the battery terminals, negative (–ve) terminal first. Refer to Section 4 and charge the battery once every month to six weeks.
10 The condition of the battery can be

3.2b ... then release the strap (arrowed) and lift out the battery

assessed by measuring the voltage present at the battery terminals, and comparing the figure against the chart **(see illustration)**. Connect the voltmeter positive (+ve) probe to the battery positive (+ve) terminal, and the negative (–ve) probe to the battery negative (–ve) terminal. When fully charged, there should be 12.8 volts (or more) present. If the voltage falls below 12.0 volts the battery must be removed, disconnecting the negative (–ve) terminal first, and recharged as described in Section 4.

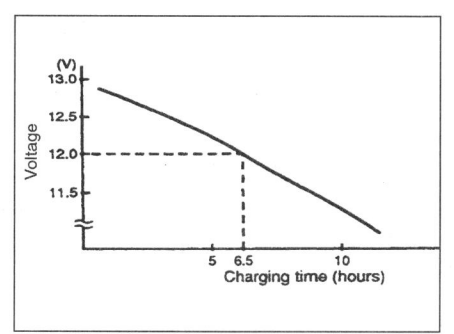

4 Battery – charging

Caution: Be extremely careful when handling or working around the battery. The electrolyte gel is very caustic and an explosive gas (hydrogen) is given off when the battery is charging.

1 Ensure the charger is suitable for charging a 12V battery.
2 Remove the battery from the motorcycle (see Section 3). If not already done, refer to Section 3, Step 10, and check the open circuit voltage of the battery. Refer to the chart **(see illustration)** and read off the charging time required according to the voltage reading taken.
3 Connect the charger to the battery BEFORE switching the charger ON. Make sure that the positive (+ve) lead on the charger is connected to the positive (+ve) terminal on the battery, and the negative (–ve) lead is connected to the negative (–ve) terminal. The battery should be charged for the specified time, or until the voltage across the terminals reaches 12.8V (allow the battery to stabilise for 30 minutes after charging, before taking a voltage reading). Note that exceeding this charging time can cause the battery to overheat, buckling the plates and rendering it useless.
4 Few owners will have access to an expensive current controlled charger, so if a normal domestic charger is used check that after a possible initial peak, the charge rate

3.10 Measure the voltage to assess the condition of the battery from the chart

4.2 Measure the voltage to determine the charging time required

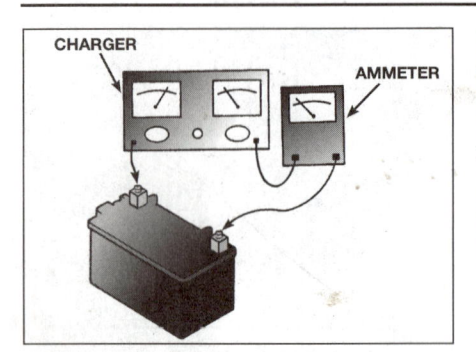

9•4 Electrical system

4.4 If the charger has no built-in ammeter, connect one in series as shown. DO NOT connect the ammeter between the battery terminals or it will be ruined

falls to a safe level **(see illustration)**. If the battery becomes hot during charging **STOP**. Further charging will cause damage. **Note:** *In emergencies the battery can be charged at a higher rate of around 3.0 amps for a period of 1 hour. However, this is not recommended and the low amp charge is by far the safer method of charging the battery.*

5 If the recharged battery discharges rapidly when left disconnected it is likely that an internal short caused by physical damage or sulphation has occurred. A new battery will be required. A sound battery will tend to lose its charge at about 1% per day.
6 Install the battery (see Section 3).
7 If the motorcycle sits unused for long periods of time, charge the battery once every month to six weeks and leave it disconnected. Alternatively, remove the battery and store it in as cool, dry place.

5 Fuses – check and renewal

1 The electrical system is protected by fuses of different ratings. All except the main fuse are housed in the fusebox, which is located under the rider's seat to the rear of the battery **(see illustration)**. The main fuse is integral with the starter relay, which is located under the rider's seat on the left-hand side.

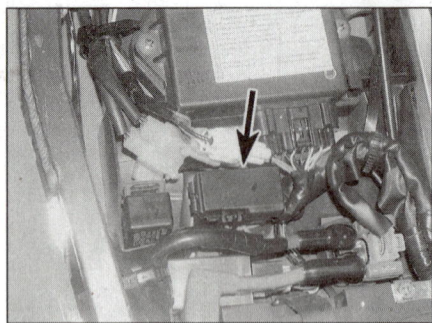

5.1 Fusebox location (arrowed)

2 To access the fusebox fuses, remove the rider's seat (see Chapter 8) and unclip the fusebox lid **(see illustration)**. To access the main fuse, remove the rider's seat and disconnect the starter relay wiring connector **(see illustration)**.
3 The fuses can be removed and checked visually. If you can't pull the fuse out with your fingertips, use a suitable pair of pliers. A blown fuse is easily identified by a break in the element **(see illustration)**, or the fuse can be tested for continuity using an ohmmeter or continuity tester – if there is no continuity, it has blown. Each fuse is clearly marked with its rating and must only be replaced by a fuse of the same rating. Spare fuses are housed in the fusebox, and a spare main fuse is housed in the starter relay. If a spare fuse is used, always replace it with a new one so that a spare of each rating is carried on the bike at all times.

⚠ **Warning: Never put in a fuse of a higher rating or bridge the terminals with any other substitute, however temporary it may be. Serious damage may be done to the circuit, or a fire may start.**

4 If a fuse blows, be sure to check the wiring circuit very carefully for evidence of a short-circuit. Look for bare wires and chafed, melted or burned insulation. If the fuse is renewed before the cause is located, the new fuse will blow immediately.
5 Occasionally a fuse will blow or cause an open-circuit for no obvious reason. Corrosion of the fuse ends and fusebox terminals may occur and cause poor fuse contact. If this happens, remove the corrosion with a penknife or steel wool, then spray the fuse end and terminals with electrical contact cleaner.

6 Lighting system – check

Note: *If the ignition is switched ON for any checks, remember to switch it OFF again before proceeding further or removing any electrical component from the system.*

1 The battery provides power for operation of the headlight, tail light, brake light, turn signals and instrument cluster lights. If none of the lights operate, always check battery condition before proceeding. Low battery voltage indicates either a faulty battery or a defective charging system. Refer to Section 3 for battery checks and Sections 30 and 31 for charging system tests. Also, check the condition of the fuses (see Section 5). When checking for a blown filament in a bulb, it is advisable to back up a visual check with a continuity test of the filament as it is not always apparent that a bulb has blown. When testing for continuity, remember that on tail light and turn signal bulbs it is often the metal body of the bulb that is the ground or earth.

Headlight and relays

2 If the headlight fails to work, check the bulb first (see Section 7), and then the main fuse, signal fuse and headlight fuse. Next disconnect the headlight wiring connector and check for battery voltage on the supply side of the wiring connector with a test light or multimeter. Refer to *Wiring Diagrams* at the end of this Chapter, then connect the negative probe of the multimeter to earth (black wire) and the positive probe to first the high beam terminal (yellow wire on 1999/2000 models, black/yellow wire on 2001-on models) and then the low beam terminal (green wire on 1999/2000 models, black/green on 2001-on models) with the ignition switch and light switch (where fitted) ON. Don't forget to select either high or low beam at the handlebar switch while conducting this test.

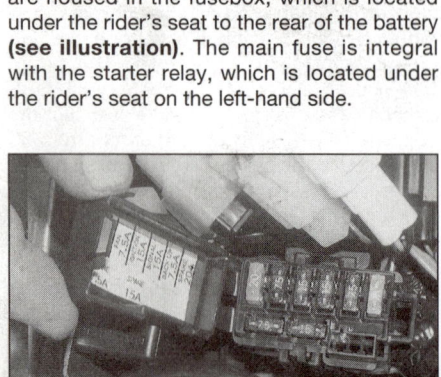

5.2a Unclip fusebox lid to access fuses

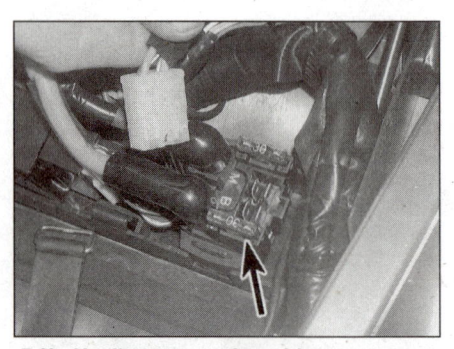

5.2b Unclip starter relay wiring connector to access main fuse (arrowed)

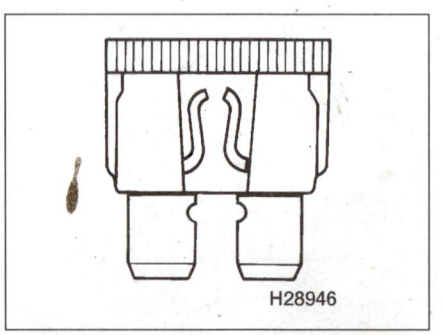

5.3 A blown fuse can be identified by a break in its element

Electrical system 9•5

6.5 Headlight relays (arrowed)

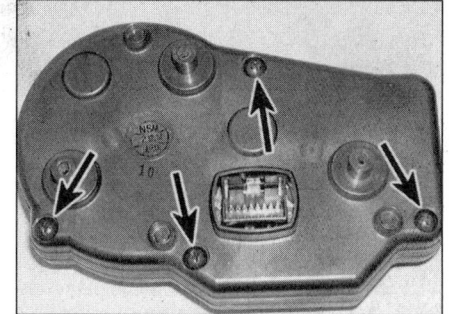

6.25a Undo the screws...

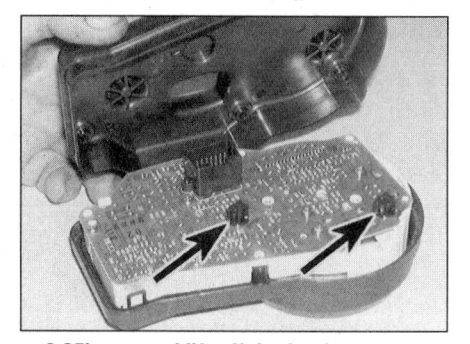

6.25b ...and lift off the back cover to access the bulbholders

3 If no voltage is indicated at either terminal, check the wiring between the headlight connector, relays, light switches and the ignition switch, then check the switches themselves.

4 If voltage is indicated, check for continuity between the black wire connector terminal and earth (ground). If there is no continuity, check the earth (ground) circuit for an open or poor connection.

5 To check the headlight relays, first remove the fairing (see Chapter 8); the relays are mounted between the headlights **(see illustration)**. Disconnect the relevant relay wiring connector and make the checks on the relay side of the connector. Use a continuity tester (or a multimeter set to the resistance range) and a 12V battery with insulated jumper wires according to the relevant procedure below.

6 On 1999 and 2000 models, two relays are fitted, one for the low beam circuit and another for the high beam circuit. To test, connect the meter between the relay red/yellow wire terminal and either the yellow wire terminal (high beam relay) or green wire terminal (low beam relay); there should be no continuity.

7 Leaving the meter in place, use the jumper wires to connect the battery negative (–ve) terminal to the relay black wire terminal and the battery positive (+ve) terminal to either the white/yellow wire terminal (high beam relay) or the white/green wire terminal (low beam relay). The relay should now close and continuity (0 ohms) should be shown on the meter.

8 On 2001-on models onwards, the primary relay (4 wires) works in conjunction with the lighting switch and the secondary relay (5 wires) and switches the current between the high beam and low beam circuits. Test the primary relay by connecting the multimeter probes between the relay red/yellow and black/blue wire terminals; there should be no continuity.

9 Leaving the meter in place, use the jumper wires to connect the battery positive (+ve) terminal to the relay blue/black wire terminal and the battery negative (–ve) terminal to the relay black wire terminal. The relay should now close and continuity (0 ohms) should be shown on the meter.

10 Test the secondary relay low beam circuit by connecting the meter probes between the relay black/blue and black/green wire terminals; there should be no continuity.

Leaving the meter in place, use the jumper wires to connect the battery positive (+ve) terminal to the relay yellow wire terminal and the battery negative (-ve) terminal to the relay black wire terminal; continuity (0 ohms) should be shown on the meter.

11 Test the secondary relay high beam circuit by connecting the meter probes between the relay black/blue and black/yellow wire terminals; there should be no continuity. Leaving the meter in place, use the jumper wires to connect the battery positive (+ve) terminal to the relay yellow wire terminal and the battery negative (–ve) terminal to the relay black wire terminal; continuity (0 ohms) should be shown on the meter.

Tail light

12 On 1999 and 2000 models, if the tail light fails to work and the battery, main fuse and signal fuse are good, check the bulb and the bulb terminals and the wiring connector (see Section 9). Next check for battery voltage at the blue/red wire terminal on the supply side of the tail light wiring connector, with the ignition switch and light switch (where fitted) ON.

13 If no voltage is indicated, check the wiring between the tail light, the light switch and the ignition switch, then check the switches themselves.

14 If voltage is indicated, check for continuity between the wiring connector terminals on the tail light side of the wiring connector and the corresponding terminals in the bulbholder; no continuity indicates a break in the circuit. If continuity is present, check for continuity between the black wire terminal and earth (ground). If there is no continuity, check the earth (ground) circuit for a broken or poor connection.

15 On 2001-on models, the tail light consists of a number of LEDs in a sealed unit. When a single LED fails it cannot be renewed, however the failure of one LED will not affect the function of the others. If the tail light fails to work completely, follow Steps 12 to 14. When sufficient LEDs have failed so as to impair the safe operation of the motorcycle, renew the tail light unit.

Sidelight (European models)

16 If the sidelight fails to work and the battery, main fuse and signal fuse are good, check the bulb and the bulb terminals and wiring connector (see Section 7). Next check for battery voltage at the blue/red wire terminal on the supply side of the sidelight wiring connector, with the ignition switch and light switch ON.

17 If no voltage is indicated, check the wiring between the sidelight, the light switch and the ignition switch, then check the switches themselves.

18 If voltage is indicated, check for continuity between the wiring connector terminals on the sidelight side of the wiring connector and the corresponding terminals in the bulbholder; no continuity indicates a break in the circuit. If continuity is present, check for continuity between the black wire terminal and earth (ground). If there is no continuity, check the earth (ground) circuit for a broken or poor connection.

Brake light

19 If the brake light fails to work and the battery, main fuse and signal fuse are good, check the bulb and the bulb terminals and wiring connector (see Section 9). Next check for battery voltage at the yellow wire terminal on the supply side of the tail light wiring connector, with the ignition switch ON and the brake lever or pedal applied.

20 If no voltage is indicated, check the brake light switches (see Section 14), then the wiring between the tail light and the switches.

21 If voltage is indicated, check for continuity between the black wire terminal and earth (ground). If there is no continuity, check the earth (ground) circuit for a broken or poor connection.

Turn signal lights

22 If one light fails to work, check the bulb and the bulb terminals (see Section 12), then the wiring connectors. If none of the turn signals work, first check the battery, main fuse and signal fuse.

23 If the fuse is good, check the turn signal circuit (see Section 11).

Instrument cluster lights

24 Remove the instrument cluster (see Section 15).

25 Unscrew the four screws that retain the back of the instrument cluster case and lift the back off **(see illustrations)**. Take care not to

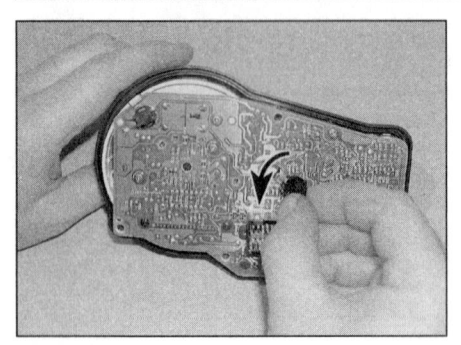

9•6 Electrical system

6.26a Turn the bulbholder to release it ...

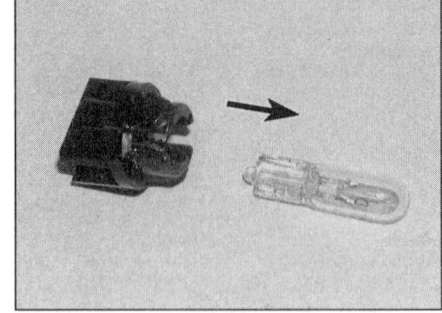

6.26b ... then pull out the bulb

7.2 Pull off the headlight bulb connector (A) and remove the dust cover (B)

damage the instrument cluster circuit board or the tachometer needle while the case is open.

26 Release the bulb holder by twisting it and pulling it out of the circuit board **(see illustration)**. Pull the bulb out of the holder and install the new one **(see illustration)**.

7 Headlight bulbs and sidelight bulbs – renewal

Note: *The headlight bulb is of the quartz-halogen type. Do not touch the bulb glass as skin acids will shorten the bulb's service life. If the bulb is accidentally touched, it should be wiped carefully when cold with a rag soaked in methylated spirit and dried before fitting.*

Warning: *Allow the bulb time to cool before removing it if the headlight has been on.*

Headlight

1 Remove the inner trim panel (see Chapter 8).
2 Disconnect the wiring connector from the back of the headlight bulb and remove the rubber dust cover, noting how it fits **(see illustration)**.
3 Release the bulb retaining clip, noting how it fits, then remove the bulb from the back of the reflector **(see illustrations)**.
4 Fit the new bulb, bearing in mind the information in the **Note** above. Make sure the tabs on the bulb flange are aligned with the slots in the back of the reflector, and secure the bulb in position with the retaining clip.
5 Install the dust cover, making sure it is correctly seated with the TOP mark at the top, then connect the wiring connector **(see illustration)**.
6 Check the operation of the headlight, then install the inner trim panel.

Sidelight (European models)

7 Remove the inner trim panel (see Chapter 8).
8 Turn the bulbholder anti-clockwise and pull it out of the back of the headlight unit, then carefully pull the bulb out of the holder **(see illustrations)**.
9 Fit the new bulb and check the operation of the sidelight, then install the bulbholder in the back of the headlight unit and turn it clockwise to lock it in place.
10 Install the inner trim panel.

HAYNES HiNT *Always use a paper towel or dry cloth when handling new bulbs to prevent injury if the bulb should break, and to increase bulb life.*

8 Headlight unit – removal and installation

Removal

1 Remove the fairing then remove the fairing stay (see Chapter 8).
2 Remove the four screws securing the

7.3a Release the retaining clip (arrowed) ...

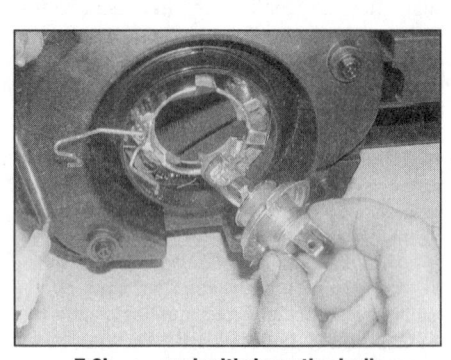

7.3b ... and withdraw the bulb

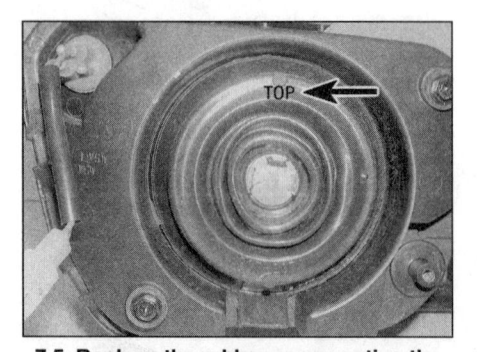

7.5 Replace the rubber cover, noting the TOP mark (arrowed)

7.8a Turn the bulbholder ...

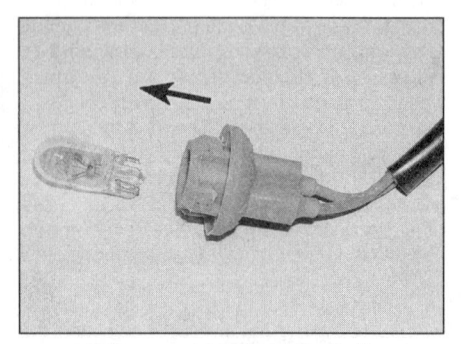

7.8b ... and pull out the bulb

Electrical system 9•7

headlight unit and lift it out of the fairing **(see illustrations)**.
3 Disconnect the headlight wiring connector, remove the sidelight bulbs and unclip the relays from the front of the headlight unit, then remove the wiring sub-loom, noting how it fits. Remove the headlight bulbs.

Installation

4 Installation is the reverse of removal. Make sure all the wiring is correctly connected and secured. Check the operation of the headlight and sidelight. Check the headlight aim (see Chapter 1).

9 Brake/tail light bulbs – renewal

Note: *1999 and 2000 models use conventional bulbs, 2001-on models use LEDs in a sealed light unit. The LEDs cannot be renewed individually (see Section 6, Step 15).*
1 Remove the passenger seat (see Chapter 8).
2 Turn the bulbholder anti-clockwise and withdraw it from the light unit **(see illustration)**. Push the bulb into the holder and twist it anti-clockwise to remove it **(see illustration)**.
3 Check the socket terminals for corrosion and clean them if necessary. Line up the pins of the new bulb with the slots in the socket, then push the bulb in and turn it clockwise until it locks into place. **Note:** *The pins on the bulb are offset so it can only be installed one*

8.2a Undo the screws (arrowed) . . .

way. *It is a good idea to use a paper towel or dry cloth when handling the new bulb to prevent injury if the bulb should break, and to increase bulb life.*
4 Check the operation of the brake/tail light, then install the bulbholder in the light unit and turn it clockwise to secure it.
5 Install the seat (see Chapter 8).

10 Tail light unit – removal and installation

Removal

1 Remove the seat cowling (see Chapter 8).
2 On 1999 and 2000 models, release the turn signal wiring from the clip on each side of the tail light bracket, then disconnect the tail light wiring connector **(see illustration)**.

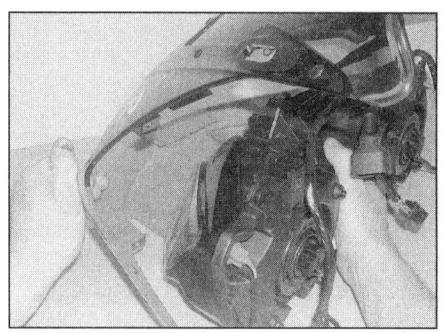

8.2b . . . and remove the headlight unit

3 Unscrew the two screws and release the trim clips securing the light unit to the main under seat moulding and remove it. Refer to Chapter 8, Section 1 for details on how to release the trim clips, if required.
4 If required, unscrew the three screws and separate the lens from the tail light unit **(see illustration)**.
5 On 2001-on models, remove the under seat panel (see Chapter 8).
6 Unscrew the two screws securing the light unit to the under seat panel and pull the unit off the panel, noting how the peg on the light unit locates in the bush on the panel **(see illustrations)**.

Installation

7 Installation is the reverse of removal. Check the operation of the tail light and the brake light, then replace the seat cowling.

9.2a Release the bulbholder from the light unit . . .

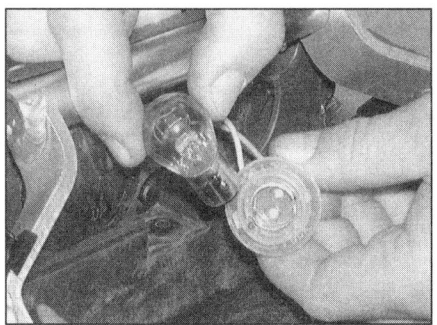

9.2b . . . then release the bulb from the holder

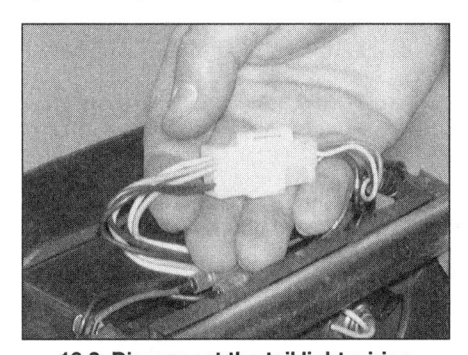

10.2 Disconnect the tail light wiring connector

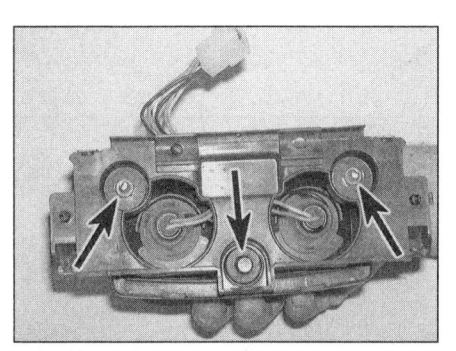

10.4 Undo the screws (arrowed) and separate the lens from the light unit

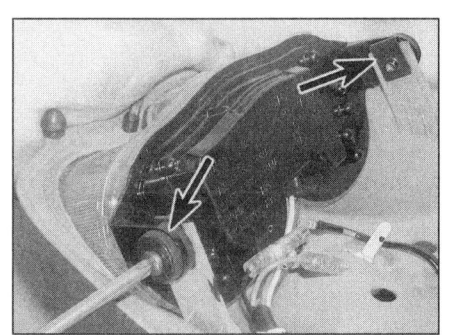

10.6a Light unit is secure by two screws (arrowed)

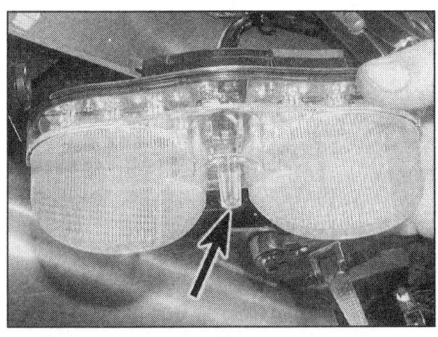

10.6b Peg (arrowed) locates in bush on seat panel

9•8 Electrical system

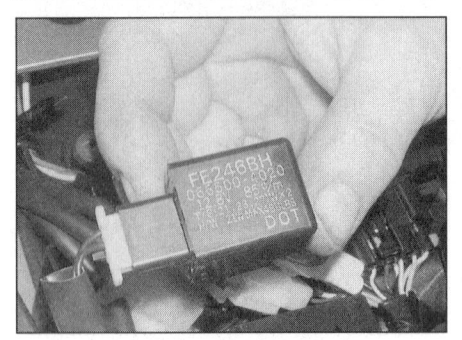

11.3 Turn signal relay

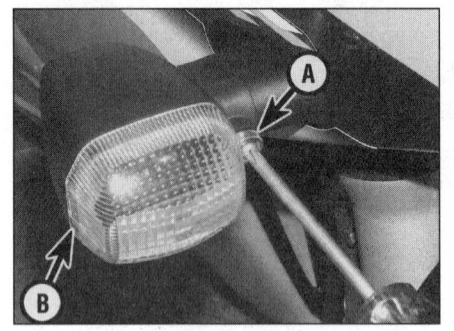

12.1 Turn signal lens is retained by screw (A) and tab (B)

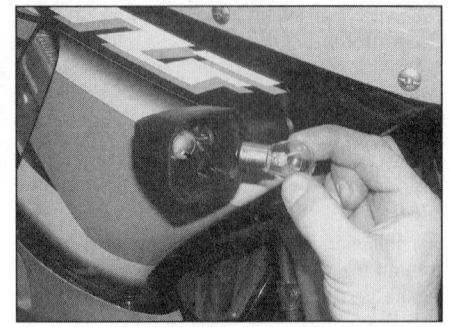

12.2 Push the bulb in and twist anti-clockwise to remove it

11 Turn signal circuit – check

Note: *If the ignition is switched ON for any checks, remember to switch it OFF again before proceeding further or removing any electrical component from the system.*

1 Most turn signal problems are the result of a burned-out bulb or corroded socket. This is especially true when the turn signals function properly in one direction, but fail to flash in the other direction. Check the bulbs and the sockets (see Section 12) and the wiring connectors. Also, check the main fuse and signal fuse (see Section 5) and the switch (see Section 19).

2 The battery provides power for operation of the turn signals, so if they do not operate, check the battery voltage. Low battery voltage indicates either a faulty battery or a defective charging system. Refer to Section 3 for battery checks and Sections 30 and 31 for charging system tests.

3 If the bulbs, sockets, connectors, fuses, switch and battery are good, check the turn signal relay, which is mounted under the rider's seat **(see illustration)**. Remove the rider's seat (see Chapter 8) and locate the relay.

4 Disconnect the relay connector and check for voltage at the brown wire terminal in the connector with the ignition ON. If no voltage is indicated, refer to the appropriate wiring diagram at the end of this Chapter and check the wiring between the relay and the ignition (main) switch for continuity.

5 If voltage is indicated, check for voltage at the brown/white wire terminal in the connector with the ignition ON, and with the signal switch turned to either LEFT or RIGHT. **Note:** *The relay must be connected to the wiring connector for this check.*

6 If no voltage is indicated, replace the relay with a new one.

7 If voltage is indicated, check the wiring between the relay, turn signal switch and turn signal lights for continuity.

12 Turn signal bulbs – renewal

1 Remove the screw securing the turn signal lens and remove the lens, noting how it fits **(see illustration)**.

2 Push the bulb into the holder and twist it anti-clockwise to remove it **(see illustration)**. Check the socket terminals for corrosion and clean them, if necessary. Line up the pins of the new bulb with the slots in the socket, then push the bulb in and turn it clockwise until it locks into place. **Note:** *US models fitted with front running lights, use dual filament bulbs which have offset pins and can only be fitted one way in their holders.*

3 Fit the lens onto the holder, making sure the tab locates correctly. Do not overtighten the screw as the lens or threads could be damaged.

13 Turn signal assemblies – removal and installation

Front

1 Remove the fairing side panel from the side concerned (see Chapter 8)

2 Unscrew the screw securing the turn signal on the inside of the fairing, and remove the screw, washer and backing plate **(see illustration)**. Remove the turn signal from the panel, noting how it fits. Take care not to snag the wiring as you pull it through the panel.

3 Installation is the reverse of removal. Make sure the wiring is correctly routed and securely connected. Check the operation of the turn signals.

Rear

4 Remove the seat cowling (see Chapter 8)

5 Trace the wiring back from the turn signal and disconnect it at the connectors **(see illustration)**. Release the wiring from its clip and feed it through to the turn signal.

13.2 Front turn signal is retained by a single screw (arrowed)

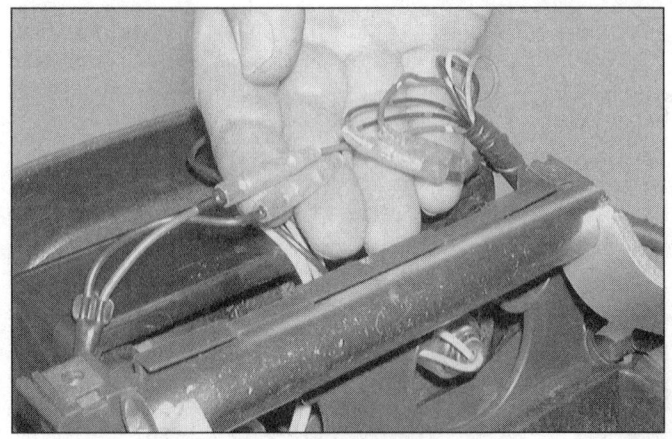

13.5 Rear turn signal wiring connectors

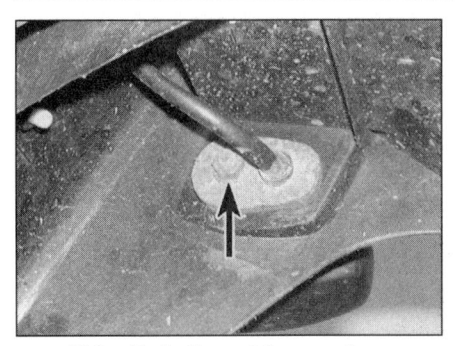

Electrical system 9•9

13.6a Undo the nut (arrowed) . . .

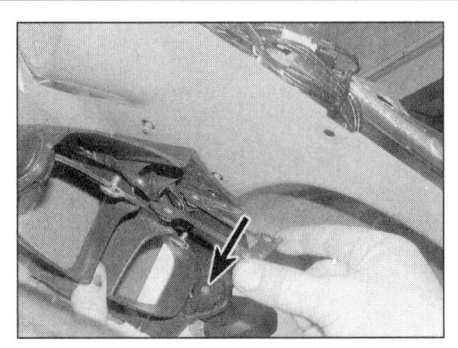

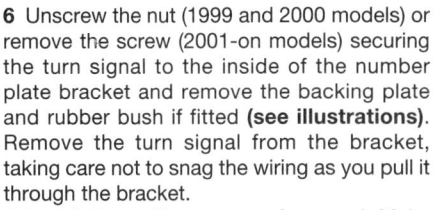

13.6b . . . or the screw (arrowed) to remove the turn signal

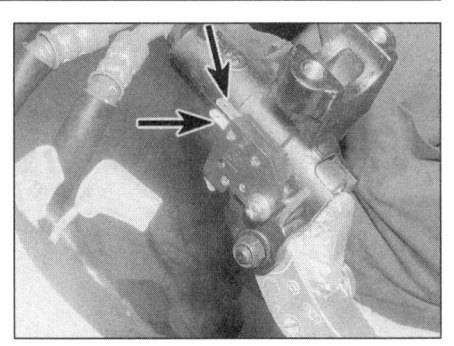

14.2 Test the front brake switch at the terminals (arrowed)

6 Unscrew the nut (1999 and 2000 models) or remove the screw (2001-on models) securing the turn signal to the inside of the number plate bracket and remove the backing plate and rubber bush if fitted **(see illustrations)**. Remove the turn signal from the bracket, taking care not to snag the wiring as you pull it through the bracket.

7 Installation is the reverse of removal. Make sure the wiring is correctly routed and securely connected. Check the operation of the turn signals.

14 Brake light switches – check and renewal

Circuit check

Note: *If the ignition is switched ON for any checks, remember to switch it OFF again before proceeding further or removing any electrical component from the system.*

1 Before checking the switches, check the brake light circuit (see Section 6).
2 The front brake light switch is mounted on the underside of the brake master cylinder. Disconnect the wiring connectors from the switch. Using a continuity tester, connect its probes to the terminals of the switch **(see illustration)**. With the brake lever at rest, there should be no continuity. With the brake lever applied, there should be continuity. If the switch does not behave as described, replace it with a new one.

3 The rear brake light switch is mounted on the right-hand side, above the brake pedal **(see illustration)**. Remove the fuel tank (see Chapter 4) to access the wiring connector. Trace the wiring from the switch and disconnect it at the connector. Using a continuity tester, connect the probes to the two terminals on the switch side of the wiring connector. With the brake pedal at rest, there should be no continuity. With the brake pedal applied, there should be continuity. If the switch does not behave as described, replace it with a new one.

4 If the switches are good, connect the wiring and check for voltage at the brown wire terminal on the supply side of the connector with the ignition switch ON. If no voltage is indicated, check the wiring between the switch and the ignition switch (see *Wiring Diagrams* at the end of this Chapter).

Switch renewal

Front brake light switch

5 The switch is mounted on the underside of the brake master cylinder. Disconnect the wiring connectors from the switch **(see illustration 14.2)**.

6 Remove the single screw and washers securing the switch to the bottom of the master cylinder and remove the switch.
7 Installation is the reverse of removal. The switch is not adjustable.

Rear brake light switch

8 The switch is mounted on the back of the right-hand footrest bracket. Remove the fuel tank (see Chapter 4) to access the wiring connector, then trace the wiring from the switch and disconnect it at the connector. Free the wiring from any ties and feed it through to the switch.
9 Detach the lower end of the switch spring from the pin on the back of the brake pedal **(see illustration)**. Unscrew the bolt securing the switch bracket to the footrest bracket and remove the bolt and switch; note the bush and spacer in the switch bracket and remove them if they are loose.
10 Installation is the reverse of removal, noting the following:
• Renew the switch bracket bush if it is worn or perished.
• Ensure the end of the switch spring is correctly located in the groove on the brake pedal pin.
• Secure the wiring with new cable ties.
• Adjust the switch as necessary (see Chapter 1, Section 13).

14.3 Rear brake switch location

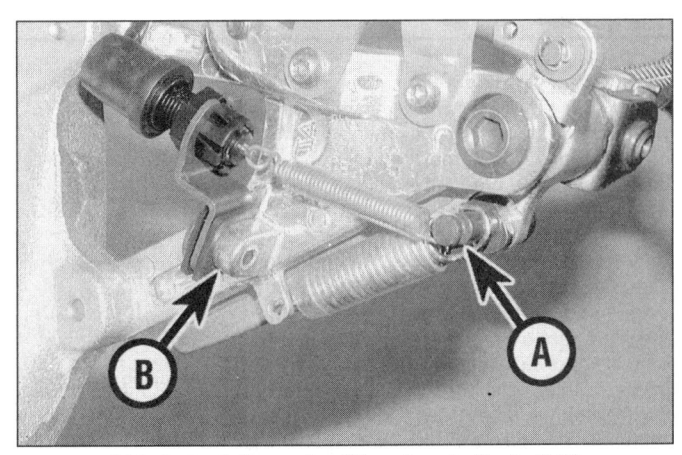

14.9 Detach the spring (A) and undo the bolt (B)

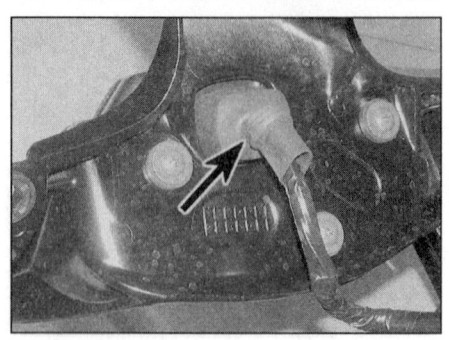

9•10 Electrical system

15.2a Pull back the cover (arrowed) . . .

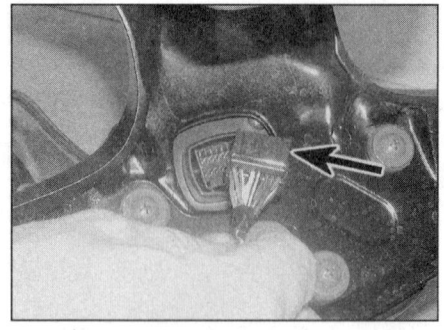

15.2b . . . and disconnect the multi-pin connector

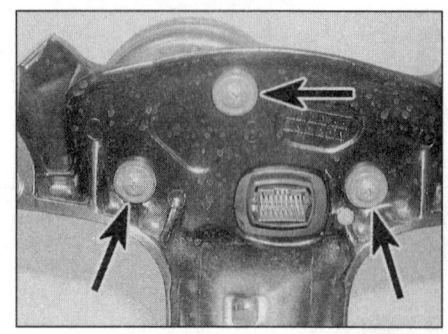

15.3a Undo the screws (arrowed)

15 Instrument cluster – removal and installation

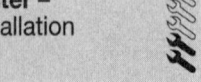

Removal

1 Remove the fairing, then remove the fairing stay (see Chapter 8).
2 Pull back the rubber cover and disconnect the multi-pin wiring connector at the back of the instrument cluster **(see illustrations)**.
3 Unscrew the screws securing the instrument cluster to the fairing stay and remove the screws and washers. Pull the cluster off the fairing stay and note the three pins on the back of the cluster that locate in three bushes on the stay **(see illustrations)**.

Installation

4 Installation is the reverse of removal. If the bushes in the stay are worn or perished replace them with new ones, and ensure the rubber cover is securely located over the wiring connector.

16 Instruments – check and renewal

Check

Tachometer

1 If the tachometer fails to display engine rpm when the engine is running, first check the signal fuse, then check for voltage at the brown wire terminal of the white instrument cluster connector inside the fairing and the cluster multi-pin connector with the ignition switched ON.
2 If the fuse is good and voltage is indicated, refer to the wiring diagram at the end of this Chapter and check for continuity between each end of the yellow/black wire which runs from the tachometer to the ignition control unit. If there is continuity, yet the fault still exists, either the tachometer or ignition control unit is faulty; seek the advice of a Yamaha dealer for checking of these components.

3 The tachometer performs a dual function as part of the ignition control unit's self-diagnosing system for the throttle position sensor and the fuel level warning circuit. If there is a fault with the throttle position sensor (see Chapter 5, Section 5) and/or the fuel level warning circuit (see Chapter 4, Section 15), the tachometer will display the respective condition code in rpm when the ignition is switched ON, whether the engine is running or not.

Oil level display

4 The oil level display is controlled by the oil level sensor – refer to Section 26 for test details.

Coolant temperature display

5 The coolant temperature display is controlled by the temperature sender (see Chapter 3, Section 5).

Speedometer

6 The speedometer is controlled by the speed sensor, which is mounted in the top of the crankcase underneath the starter motor. To test the output from the sensor, place the motorcycle on an auxiliary stand so the rear wheel is off the ground. Make sure the transmission is in neutral.
7 Connect the positive (+ve) probe of a multimeter set to the DC20V scale to the blue/yellow wire terminal on the sensor side of the instrument cluster connector, and connect the negative (–ve) probe to the black/blue wire terminal. Turn the ignition ON. Turn the rear wheel in its normal direction of rotation and check the reading on the multimeter – it

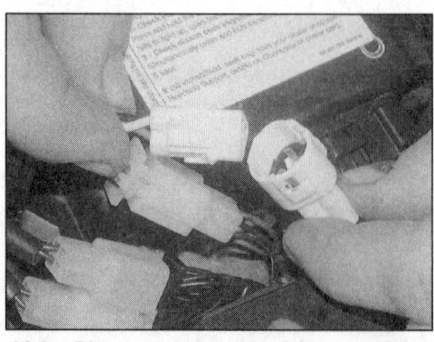

15.3b Check the condition of the mounting bushes before installing the instrument cluster

should be seen to fluctuate between zero and 5 volts as the wheel is turned. If not, and if the wiring between the speed sensor and the connector is good, replace the speed sensor with a new one.
8 If the multimeter reading is correct, refer to *Wiring Diagrams* at the end of this Chapter and check that the wiring and connectors between the sensor and related electrical components is good. If no fault can be found, the speedometer may be faulty; take the instruments to a Yamaha dealer for further assessment.
9 To fit a new sensor, first remove the starter motor (see Section 28). Trace the wiring from the sensor and disconnect it at the wiring connector **(see illustration)**. Remove the screw and withdraw the sensor from the crankcase **(see illustration)**. Discard the O-ring.

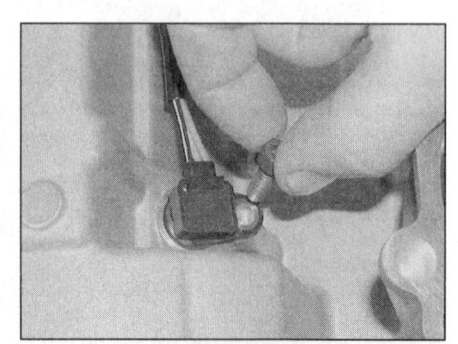

16.9a Disconnect the speed sensor wiring connector

16.9b Speed sensor

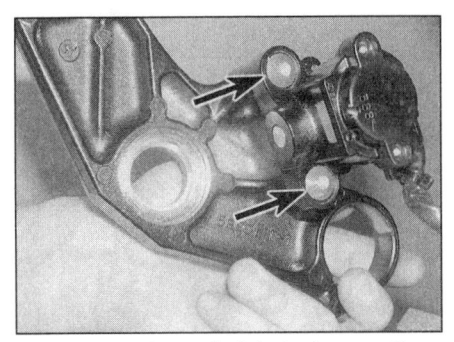

Electrical system 9•11

18.6 Ignition switch bolts (arrowed)

19.3 The handlebar switch wiring connectors are secured to the right-hand side of the frame

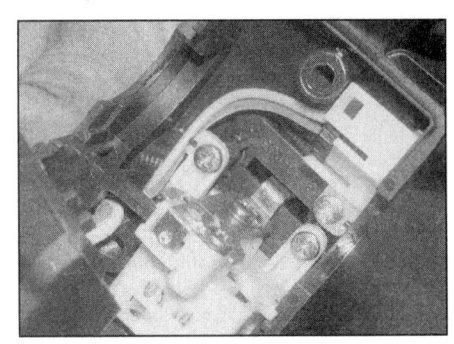

19.5 Keep switch internals clean and corrosion free

10 Install the sensor using a new O-ring, and tighten the fixing screw securely. Connect the sensor wiring connector, then install the starter motor.

Renewal

11 The instruments are mounted on a circuit board inside the cluster housing. Yamaha do not list any of the instruments as separate components, so in the event of an instrument failure the instrument circuit board will have to be removed and replaced with a new one (see Section 15).

17 Warning lights – check and renewal

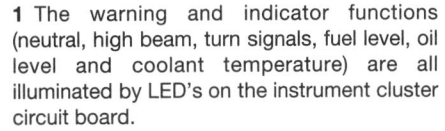

1 The warning and indicator functions (neutral, high beam, turn signals, fuel level, oil level and coolant temperature) are all illuminated by LED's on the instrument cluster circuit board.

2 The fuel level indicator light should come on for a few seconds when the ignition is switched ON as a check of the LED, and then go off. If the light does not go off, first check the fuel level, and if the level is good check the LED circuit (see Step 4). If the light does not come on, test the LED as described below.

3 The combined warning LED for the engine oil level and coolant temperature should also come on as a check of the LED, and then go off. Refer to Chapter 26 of this Chapter and Section 5 of Chapter 3 for checking of the circuits.

4 To test whether an LED has failed, remove the instrument cluster (see Section 15). Using a fully charged 12V battery and two suitable jumper wires, refer to *Wiring Diagrams* at the end of this Chapter and connect the positive (+ve) and negative (-ve) battery terminals to the relevant terminals on the instrument cluster for the LED being tested.

5 If the LED comes on, the fault lies elsewhere in the electrical circuit for the LED in question. Check the signal fuse and wiring, and the operation of the component linked to the LED.

6 If the LED has failed a new instrument circuit board must be installed.

18 Ignition (main) switch – check, removal and installation

Warning: To prevent the risk of short circuits, disconnect the battery negative (–ve) lead before making any ignition (main) switch checks.

Check

1 Remove the fuel tank (see Chapter 4). Trace the ignition (main) switch wiring back from the switch and disconnect it at the connector on the right-hand side of the frame. Make the checks on the switch side of the connector.

2 Using a multimeter or a continuity tester, check the continuity of the connector terminal pairs (see *Wiring Diagrams* at the end of this Chapter). Continuity should exist between the terminals connected by a solid line on the diagram when the switch key is turned to the indicated position.

3 If the switch fails any of the tests, replace it with a new one.

Removal

4 Disconnect the battery negative (–ve) lead. Remove the fuel tank (see Chapter 4), trace the ignition (main) switch wiring back from the switch and disconnect it at the connector on the right-hand side of the frame. Release the wiring from any cable ties and feed it back to the switch noting the correct routing.

5 Remove the fairing (see Chapter 8), the handlebars and the top yoke (see Chapter 6, Section 8).

6 Two shear-head bolts mount the switch to the underside of the top yoke **(see illustration)**. The heads of the bolts must be tapped around using a suitable punch or drift, or drilled off, before the switch can be removed. To do this, mount the yoke in a vice equipped with soft jaws to avoid damaging the yoke.

7 Remove the bolts and discard them as new ones must be used on reassembly, then withdraw the switch from the top yoke.

Installation

8 Installation is the reverse of removal, noting the following:
● Ensure the switch is installed in the yoke the correct way round before tightening the shear-head bolts.
● Obtain the correct type shear-head bolts from a Yamaha dealer – do not use another type of bolt. Tighten the bolts until their heads shear off.
● Ensure the wiring is securely connected and correctly routed and tied to the frame.
● Ensure all nuts and bolts are tightened to the torque settings specified in the relevant Chapters.

19 Handlebar switches – check

1 Generally speaking, the handlebar switch units are reliable and trouble-free. Most problems, when they do occur, are caused by dirty or corroded contacts, but wear and breakage of internal parts is a possibility that should not be overlooked. If breakage does occur, the entire switch unit and related wiring harness will have to be replaced with a new one, as individual parts are not available.

2 The switches can be checked for continuity using an multimeter or a continuity tester.

3 Remove the fuel tank to access the switch wiring connectors (see Chapter 4). Trace the wiring harness of the switch in question back to its connectors and disconnect it **(see illustration)**.

4 Check for continuity between the terminals of the switch harness with the switch in the various positions (i.e. switch OFF – no continuity, switch ON – continuity) – see *Wiring Diagrams* at the end of this Chapter.

5 If the continuity check indicates a problem exists, refer to Section 20, remove the switch and spray the switch contacts with electrical contact cleaner. If they are accessible, the contacts can be scraped clean with a penknife or polished with steel wool **(see illustration)**. If switch components are damaged or broken, it should be obvious when the switch is disassembled.

9•12 Electrical system

20 Handlebar switches – removal and installation

Removal

1 If the switch unit is to be removed from the motorcycle, rather than just displaced from the handlebar, remove the fuel tank (see Chapter 4) and trace the wiring harness of the switch in question back to its connector and disconnect it **(see illustration 19.3)**. Feed the wiring back to the switch, freeing it from any clips and ties and noting its correct routing.

2 Disconnect the wiring connectors from the brake light switch (if removing the right-hand switch unit) or the clutch switch (if removing the left-hand switch unit) **(see illustration 14.2 or 23.2)**.

3 Unscrew the switch unit screws and free the unit from the handlebar by separating the halves **(see illustrations)**. When removing the left-hand switch, remove the choke cable lever from the unit, noting how it fits.

Installation

4 Installation is the reverse of removal. Refer to Chapter 4 for installation of the choke cable, if required. Make sure the locating pin in the switch unit locates in the hole in the handlebar. Make sure the wiring is securely connected and correctly routed and tied to the frame.

21 Neutral switch – check, removal and installation

Check

1 Before checking the electrical circuit, check the signal fuse (see Section 5).

2 The switch is located on the back of the engine **(see illustration)**. Make sure the transmission is in neutral. To access the neutral switch wiring connector, remove the fuel tank (see Chapter 4). Trace the wiring from the switch and disconnect it at the connector **(see illustration)**.

20.3a Left-hand switch unit splits vertically . . .

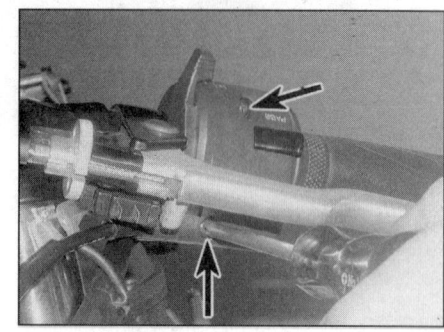

20.3c Right-hand switch unit splits horizontally . . .

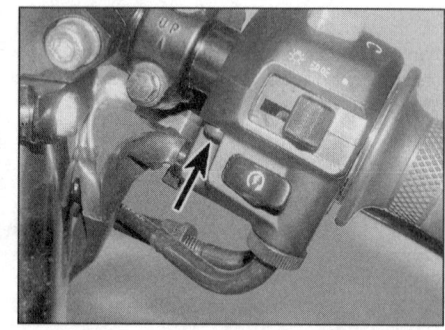

3 With the connector disconnected and the ignition switched ON, the neutral light should be out. If not, the wire between the connector and instrument cluster must be earthed (grounded) at some point.

4 Check for continuity between the light blue wire terminal on the switch side of the wiring connector, and the crankcase. With the transmission in neutral, there should be continuity. With the transmission in gear, there should be no continuity. If there is continuity when in gear, check that the wire is not earthed (grounded). If there is no continuity when in neutral, check for a break in the wire, then remove the switch (see below), and check that the contact plunger is not damaged or seized in the switch body **(see illustration)**.

5 If the switch and wiring are good, check for battery voltage at the brown wire terminal on

20.3b . . . with the screws fitted from the front

20.3d . . . with the screws fitted from underneath

the wiring loom side of the instrument cluster connector with the ignition ON.

6 If no voltage is indicated, refer to the wiring diagram at the end of this Chapter and check for continuity between the connector and the signal fuse.

7 If voltage is indicated, check the LED in the instrument cluster (see Section 17), then check the starter circuit cut-off relay (Section 24) and other components in the starter circuit as described in the relevant Sections of this Chapter. If all components are good, check the wiring between the various components (see *Wiring Diagrams* at the end of this Chapter).

Removal and installation

8 The switch is located on the back of the engine. Pull the wire connector off the switch terminal, then unscrew the switch and

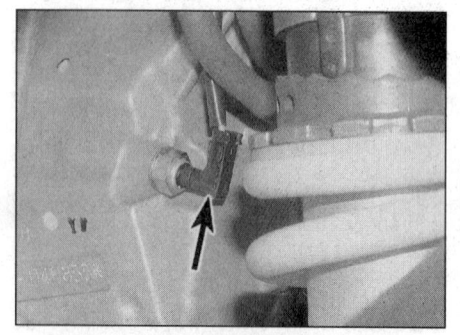

21.2a The neutral switch (arrowed) is located on the back of the engine

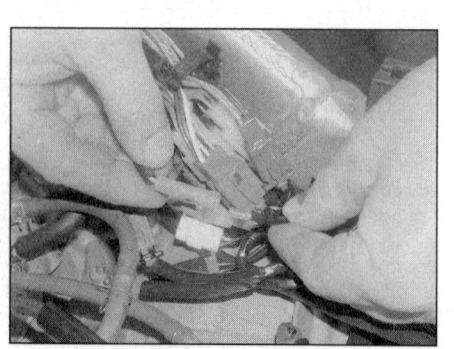

21.2b Disconnect the neutral switch wiring connector

21.4 Check the plunger in the end of the switch

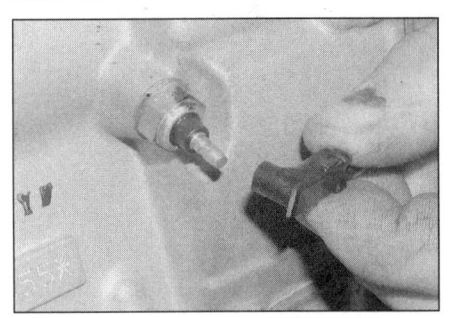

Electrical system 9•13

21.9 Install the switch with a new sealing washer and ensure the wiring connector is tight

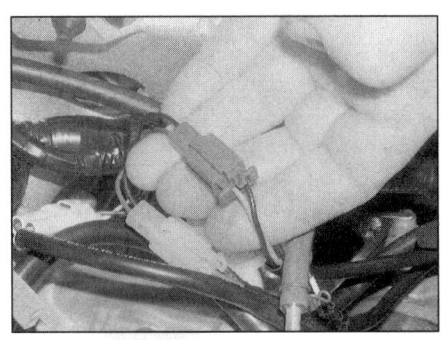

22.2 Sidestand switch wiring connector

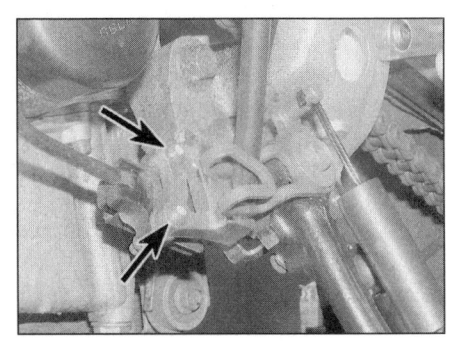

22.7 Sidestand switch mounting bolts

withdraw it from the casing. Discard the sealing washer as a new one must be used on reassembly.

9 Install the switch using a new sealing washer and tighten it to the torque setting specified at the beginning of this Chapter.

10 Connect the wire to the switch terminal and check the operation of the neutral light, then install the fuel tank.

22 Sidestand switch – check and renewal

Check

1 The sidestand switch is mounted on the back of the sidestand bracket. The switch is part of the safety circuit which prevents or stops the engine running if the transmission is in gear whilst the sidestand is down, and prevents the engine from starting if the transmission is in gear unless the sidestand is up and the clutch lever is pulled in. Before checking the electrical circuit, check the main and ignition fuses (see Section 5).

2 To access the wiring connector, remove the fuel tank (see Chapter 4). Trace the wiring from the switch and disconnect it at the connector **(see illustration)**.

3 Check the operation of the switch using a multimeter or continuity tester. Connect the meter probes to the terminals on the switch side of the connector. With the sidestand up there should be continuity (zero resistance) between the terminals, and with the stand down there should be no continuity (infinite resistance).

4 If the switch does not perform as expected, it is defective and must be renewed.

5 If the switch is good, check the starter circuit cut-off relay (Section 24) and other components in the starter circuit as described in the relevant Sections of this Chapter. If all components are good, check the wiring between the various components (see Wiring Diagrams at the end of this Chapter).

Renewal

6 The sidestand switch is mounted on the back of the sidestand bracket. Remove the fuel tank (see Chapter 4), then trace the wiring

from the switch and disconnect it at the connector **(see illustration 22.2)**. Release the wiring from any cable ties and feed it back to the switch noting the correct routing.

7 Remove the lower fairing (see Chapter 8), then unscrew the bolts securing the switch to the bracket and remove the switch **(see illustration)**.

8 Install the new switch and tighten the bolts securely. Ensure the tab on the sidestand engages the switch plunger correctly.

9 Make sure the wiring is correctly routed up to the connector and retained by all the necessary clips and ties. Reconnect the wiring connector and check the operation of the switch, then install the fuel tank and lower fairing.

23 Clutch switch – check and renewal

Check

1 The clutch switch is mounted on the underside of the clutch lever bracket. The switch is part of the safety circuit which prevents or stops the engine running if the transmission is in gear whilst the sidestand is down, and prevents the engine from starting if the transmission is in gear unless the sidestand is up and the clutch lever is pulled in. The switch is not adjustable.

2 To check the switch, disconnect the wiring connectors **(see illustration)**. Connect the probes of a multimeter or a continuity tester to the two switch terminals. There should be continuity (zero resistance) with the clutch

lever pulled in, and no continuity (infinite resistance) with the clutch lever out.

3 If the switch is good, check the starter circuit cut-off relay (Section 24) and other components in the starter circuit as described in the relevant Sections of this Chapter. If all components are good, check the wiring between the various components (see Wiring Diagrams at the end of this Chapter).

Renewal

4 The clutch switch is mounted on the underside of the clutch lever bracket.

5 Disconnect the wiring connectors **(see illustration 23.2)**, then remove the screw and detach the switch.

6 Installation is the reverse of removal.

24 Relay assembly – check and renewal

Starter circuit cut-out relay

Check

1 The starter circuit cut-out relay is part of the safety circuit which prevents or stops the engine running if the transmission is in gear whilst the sidestand is down, and prevents the engine from starting if the transmission is in gear unless the sidestand is up and the clutch lever is pulled in.

2 The starter circuit cut-out relay and its diodes are contained within the relay assembly, which is mounted below the rider's seat **(see illustration)**. Remove the rider's seat for access (see Chapter 8).

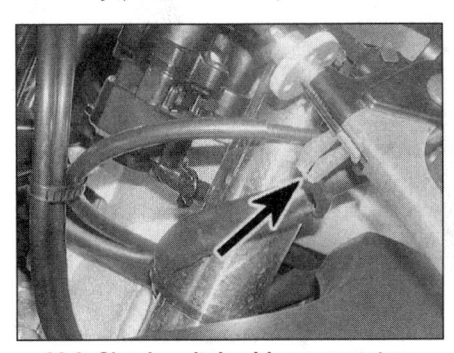

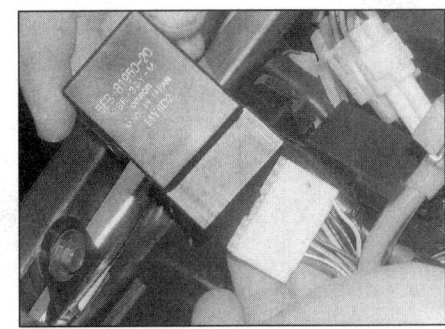

23.2 Clutch switch wiring connectors (arrowed)

24.2 Relay assembly location

9•14 Electrical system

25.2 The horn is mounted on the bottom yoke

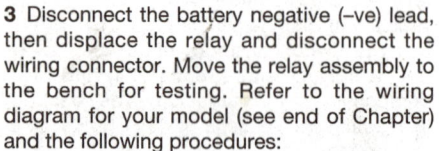

25.3 The wiring terminals (arrowed) are on the back of the horn

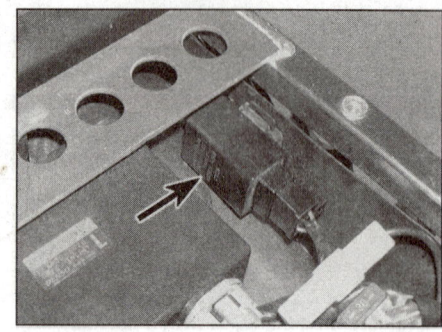

26.4 Oil level sensor relay (arrowed)

3 Disconnect the battery negative (–ve) lead, then displace the relay and disconnect the wiring connector. Move the relay assembly to the bench for testing. Refer to the wiring diagram for your model (see end of Chapter) and the following procedures:

4 To check the operation of the relay, first connect a multimeter set to the ohms x 1 scale, or a continuity tester, between the blue/white and blue (1999 and 2000 models) or blue/white and black (2001-on models) wire terminals of the relay. There should be no continuity.

5 Leave the multimeter or continuity tester connected to the relay. Now, using a fully charged 12V battery and two suitable jumper wires, connect the battery positive (+ve) terminal to the relay's red/black wire terminal and the battery negative (–ve) terminal to the relay's black/yellow wire terminal. With voltage applied, the test equipment should show continuity. If it doesn't, replace the relay assembly with a new one.

6 The diodes contained within the relay assembly can be checked by performing a continuity test. Refer to the appropriate wiring diagram at the end of this Chapter and connect the multimeter (set to ohms) or continuity tester across the wire terminals for the diode being tested. The diodes should show continuity in one direction and no continuity when the meter or tester probes are reversed. If any diode shows the same condition in both directions it should be considered faulty, and the relay assembly must be replaced with a new one.

7 If the cut-out relay and diodes are good, but the starting system fault still exists, check all other components in the starting circuit (i.e. the neutral switch, side stand switch, clutch switch, starter switch and starter relay) as described in the relevant Sections of this Chapter. If all components are good, check the wiring between the various components (see *Wiring Diagrams* at the end of this Chapter).

8 Installation is the reverse of removal.

Fuel pump relay

9 The fuel pump relay is housed within the relay assembly. Refer to Chapter 4, Section 14 for test details.

25 Horn – check and renewal

Check

1 If the horn doesn't work, first check the signal fuse (see Section 5) and the battery (see Section 3).

2 The horn is mounted on the bottom yoke **(see illustration)**. Remove either the left or right-hand fairing side panel for best access to it (see Chapter 8).

3 Pull the wiring connectors off the horn terminals **(see illustration)**. Using two jumper wires, apply battery voltage directly to the terminals on the horn. If the horn sounds, check the switch (see Section 19) and the wiring between the switch and the horn (see *Wiring Diagrams* at the end of this Chapter).

4 If the horn doesn't sound, replace it with a new one.

Renewal

5 Remove either the left or right-hand fairing side panel (see Chapter 8) for best access to the horn and pull the wiring connectors off the horn terminals.

6 Unscrew the bolt securing the horn to the bottom fork yoke and remove it from the bike.

7 Install the horn and tighten the bolt securely. Connect the wiring connectors and check the operation of the horn, then install the fairing panel.

26 Oil level sensor and relay – check, removal and installation

Check

1 The combined oil level/coolant temperature warning light will come on for a few seconds when the ignition is switched ON as a check of the warning light LED. It should then go out and the motorcycle can be started. If the warning light remains on and/or the oil level symbol in the digital display remains illuminated, check the oil level as described in *Daily (pre-ride) checks*. If the oil level is correct, check the sensor and relay (1999 and 2000 models only) as described below. Equally if the warning light comes on (and/or flashes) and the oil level symbol flashes whilst the motorcycle is being ridden, stop the engine and check the oil level immediately.

2 If the warning light does not come on during the self-checking procedure described above, check the LED as described in Section 17).

3 To check the sensor, remove it from the sump (see Steps 9 to 11). Connect one probe of a multimeter or continuity tester to the sensor wire and the other probe to the base of the sensor. With the sensor in its normal installed position (wiring at the bottom), there should be continuity. Turn the sensor upside down. There should be no continuity. If either condition does not occur, replace the sensor with a new one.

4 To check the relay (1999 and 2000 models only), remove the rider's seat (see Chapter 8). Trace the wire from the sensor to the relay, then disconnect the relay wiring connector and release the relay from its holder **(see illustration)**.

5 Connect a multimeter set to the ohms x 1 scale, or a continuity tester, between the red/blue and black wire terminals of the relay. There should be no continuity.

6 Leave the multimeter or continuity tester connected to the relay. Now, using a fully-charged 12V battery and two suitable jumper wires, connect the battery positive (+ve) lead to the relay's brown wire terminal and the negative (–ve) lead to the relay's white wire terminal. With voltage applied, the test equipment should show continuity. If it doesn't, replace the relay with a new one.

> **HAYNES HiNT**: On all models the warning light may flicker during sudden acceleration or deceleration or when riding up or down hill. Note that this is a characteristic of the system and provided the oil level is correct, does not indicate a fault.

Removal

7 To remove the oil level sensor, first drain the engine oil (see Chapter 1).

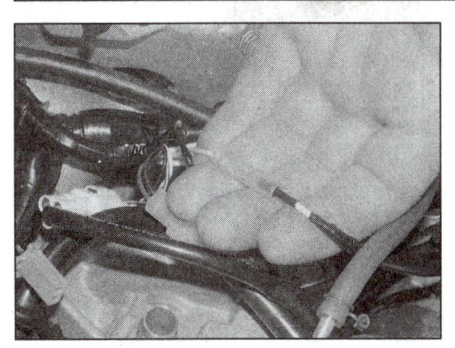

Electrical system 9•15

26.8 Oil level sensor wiring connector

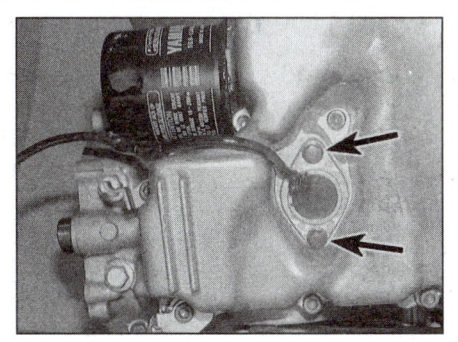

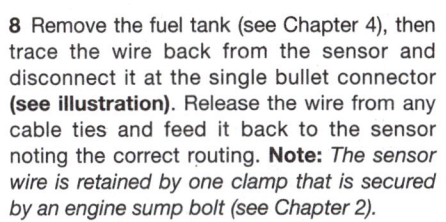

26.9 Unscrew the bolts (arrowed) to remove the sensor

27.2 Starter relay (arrowed)

8 Remove the fuel tank (see Chapter 4), then trace the wire back from the sensor and disconnect it at the single bullet connector **(see illustration)**. Release the wire from any cable ties and feed it back to the sensor noting the correct routing. **Note:** *The sensor wire is retained by one clamp that is secured by an engine sump bolt (see Chapter 2).*

9 Unscrew the two bolts securing the sensor to the bottom of the sump and withdraw it from the sump, being prepared to catch any residual oil **(see illustration)**. Check the condition of the O-ring and replace it with a new one if it is damaged, deformed or deteriorated.

10 To remove the relay (1999 and 2000 models), remove the rider's seat (see Chapter 8), then disconnect the relay wiring connector and release the relay from its holder **(see illustration 26.4)**.

Installation

11 Fit a new O-ring onto the oil level sensor. Smear the O-ring with lithium grease, then fit the sensor into the sump. Tighten its bolts to the torque setting specified at the beginning of this Chapter.

12 Feed the wiring to the connector **(see illustration 26.8)** and secure it with the cable ties. Don't forget to install the clamp and sump bolt.

13 Fill the engine with oil (see Chapter 1) and check the operation of the sensor. Install the fuel tank.

14 Fit the relay into its holder and connect the wiring connector **(see illustration 26.4)**, then install the rider's seat.

27 Starter relay – check and renewal

Check

1 If the starter circuit is faulty, first check the main fuse and ignition fuse (see Section 5).

2 Remove the rider's seat (see Chapter 8). The starter relay is located behind the battery **(see illustration)**. Lift the terminal cover and unscrew the bolt securing the thick starter motor lead to the terminal marked M; position the lead away from the relay terminal. With the ignition switch ON, the engine kill switch in the RUN position, and the transmission in neutral, press the starter switch. The relay should be heard to click.

3 If the relay doesn't click, switch the ignition OFF, remove the relay (see Steps 8 and 9) and test it as follows.

4 Connect a multimeter set to the ohms x 1 scale, or a continuity tester, between the relay's starter motor (M) and battery (B) lead terminals **(see illustration)**. There should be no continuity.

5 Leave the multimeter or continuity tester connected to the relay. Now, using a fully-charged 12V battery and two suitable jumper wires, connect the battery positive (+ve) terminal to the relay's red/white wire terminal, and the battery negative (–ve) terminal to the relay's blue/white wire terminal. With voltage applied, the relay should be heard to click and the test equipment should show continuity. Disconnect the battery and test meter.

6 If the relay does not click when battery voltage is applied and indicates no continuity (infinite resistance) across its terminals, it is faulty and must be replaced with a new one. The relay coil resistance can be checked by connecting a multimeter set to the ohms x 1 range across the red-white and blue-white terminals of the relay wire connector; the value should be as specified at the beginning of this Chapter.

7 If the relay is good, check for battery voltage at the red/white wire terminal on the loom side of the relay wiring connector when the starter button is pressed with the ignition switched ON. If voltage is present, check the other components in the starter circuit as described in the relevant Sections of this Chapter. If no voltage is present, check the wiring between the various components (see *Wiring Diagrams* at the end of this Chapter).

Renewal

8 Remove the rider's seat (see Chapter 8). The starter relay is located behind the battery. Disconnect the battery negative (–ve) lead before removing the relay.

9 Disconnect the relay wiring connector **(see illustration)**. Unscrew the two bolts securing the starter motor and battery leads to the

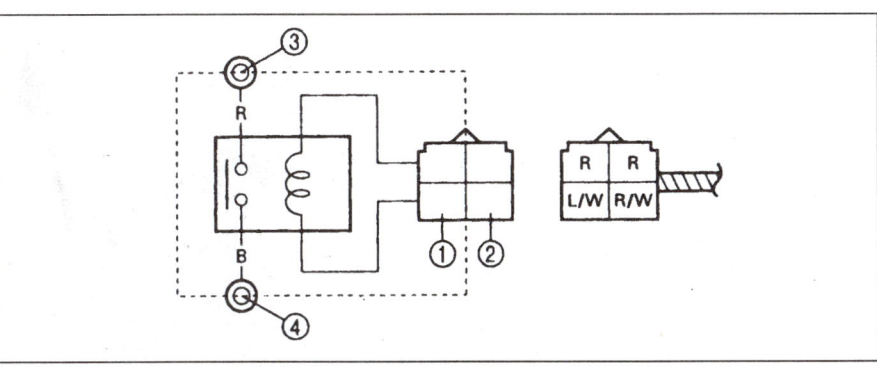

27.4 Relay test set-up

1 Red/white wire terminal
2 Blue/white wire terminal
3 Battery lead terminal (B)
4 Starter motor lead terminal (M)

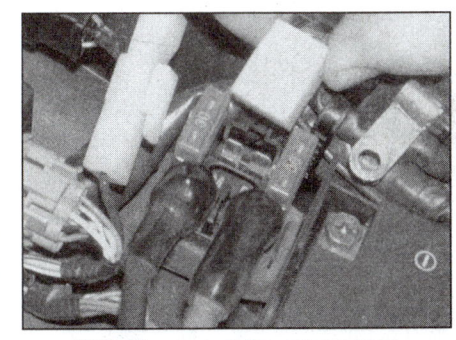

27.9 Disconnect the relay wiring connector

9•16 Electrical system

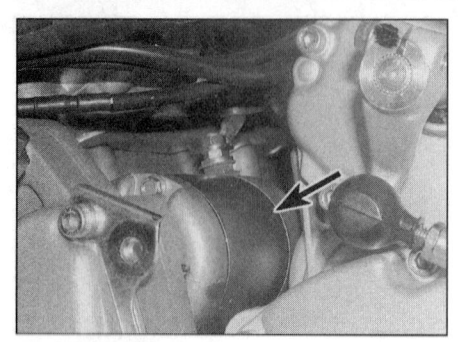

28.1 The starter motor (arrowed) is located behind the cylinder block

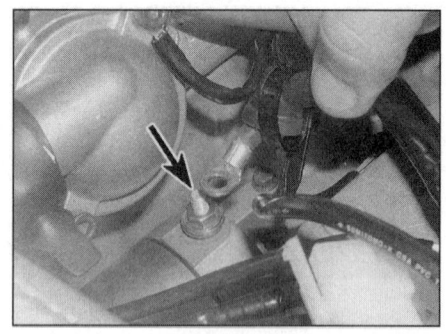

28.2 Disconnect the starter motor terminal (arrowed)

28.3a Unscrew the fixing bolts . . .

relay and detach the leads. Remove the relay with its rubber sleeve from its mounting lug on the frame.

10 Installation is the reverse of removal. The starter motor lead connects to the terminal marked M, and the battery lead to the terminal marked B **(see illustration 27.4)**. Make sure the terminal bolts are tightened securely. Connect the negative (–ve) lead last when reconnecting the battery.

28 Starter motor – removal and installation

28.3b . . . and remove the starter motor

28.5 Fit a new O-ring and smear it with grease

Removal

1 Remove the carburettors (see Chapter 4) and disconnect the battery negative (–ve) lead. The starter motor is mounted on the crankcase, behind the cylinder block **(see illustration)**.
2 Peel back the terminal boot and unscrew the nut securing the lead to the starter motor terminal and detach the lead **(see illustration)**.
3 Unscrew the two bolts securing the starter motor and draw the starter motor out of the crankcase and remove it from the machine **(see illustrations)**.
4 Remove the O-ring on the end of the starter motor and discard it, as a new one must be used.

Installation

5 Fit a new O-ring onto the end of the starter motor, making sure it is seated in its groove, and smear it with grease **(see illustration)**.
6 Manoeuvre the motor into position and slide it into the crankcase **(see illustration)**. Ensure that the starter motor teeth mesh correctly with those of the starter idler gear. Install the mounting bolts and tighten them to the torque setting specified at the beginning of this Chapter.
7 Connect the lead to the starter motor terminal and secure it with the nut. Make sure the boot is correctly seated over the terminal.
8 Connect the battery negative (–ve) lead and install the carburettors (see Chapter 4).

29 Starter motor – disassembly, inspection and reassembly

Disassembly

1 Remove the starter motor (see Section 28).
2 Note the alignment marks between the main housing and the front and rear covers, or make your own if they are unclear, then unscrew the two long bolts and remove the bolts and O-rings (if fitted) **(see illustration)**.
3 Remove the front cover from the motor **(see illustration)**.
4 Remove the tabbed washer from inside

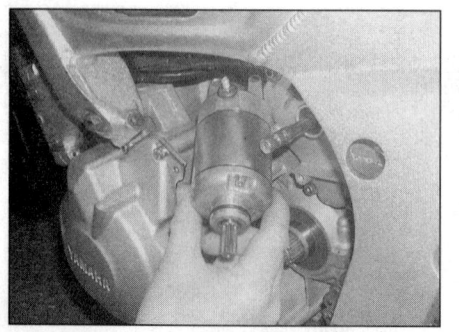

28.6 Manoeuvre the starter motor back into place

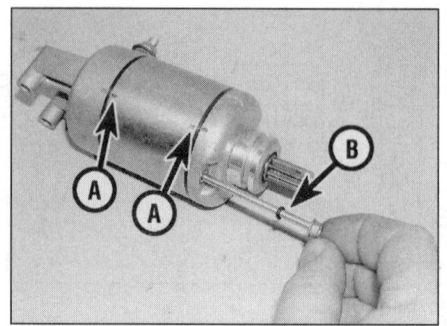

29.2 Note the alignment marks (A) and the O-ring (B)

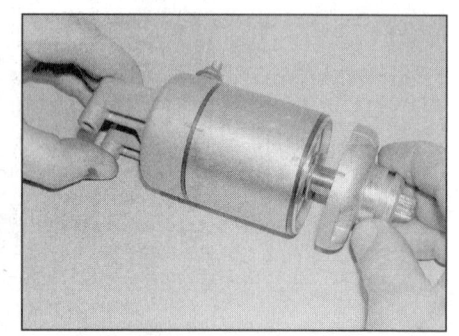

29.3 Remove the front cover . . .

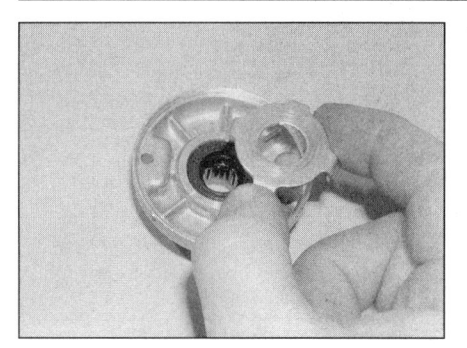

Electrical system 9•17

29.4a ... the tabbed washer from inside the cover ...

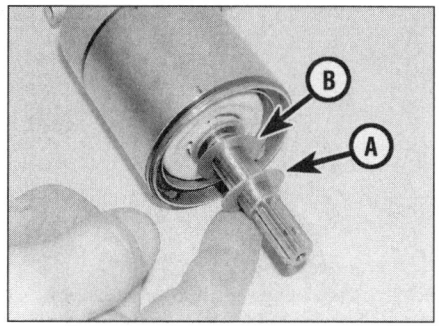

29.4b ... and the insulating washer (A) and shims (B) from the armature

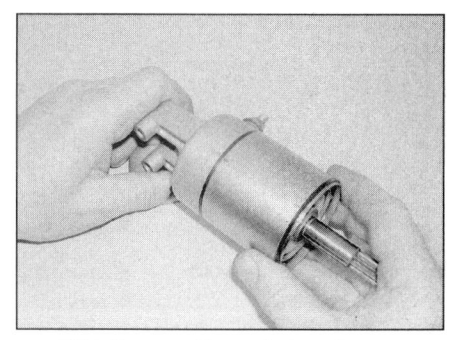

29.5 Remove the main housing ...

the cover and slide the insulating washer and shim(s) from the front end of the armature, noting the order in which they are fitted **(see illustrations)**.

5 Remove the main housing and remove the cover O-rings from the housing and discard them as new ones must be fitted on reassembly **(see illustration)**.

6 Remove the rear cover and brushplate assembly from the armature commutator **(see illustration)**. Remove the shim(s) from the rear end of the armature shaft **(see illustration)**.

7 Noting the order in which they are fitted, unscrew the terminal nut and remove it along with its washer and insulating washers **(see illustrations)**.

8 Withdraw the terminal and brushplate assembly from the rear cover and remove the O-ring and square insulating washer from the terminal **(see illustrations)**.

9 Lift the brush springs and slide the brushes out from their holders, noting that one brush is attached to the terminal and the other is attached to the brushplate **(see illustration)**.

Inspection

10 Check the general condition of all the starter motor components **(see**

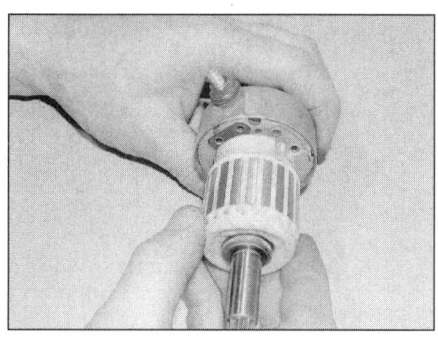

29.6a ... the rear cover and brushplate ...

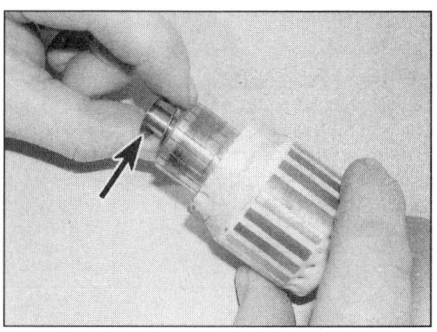

29.6b ... and the shims (arrowed) from the end of the armature

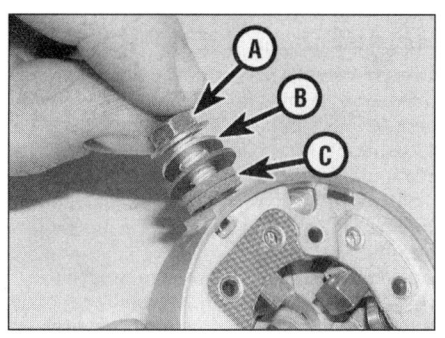

29.7 Unscrew the terminal nut (A) and remove the washer (B) and insulating washers (C)

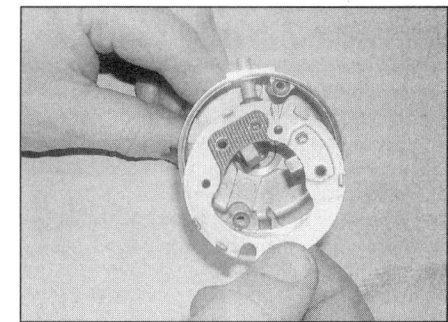

29.8a Remove the terminal and brushplate ...

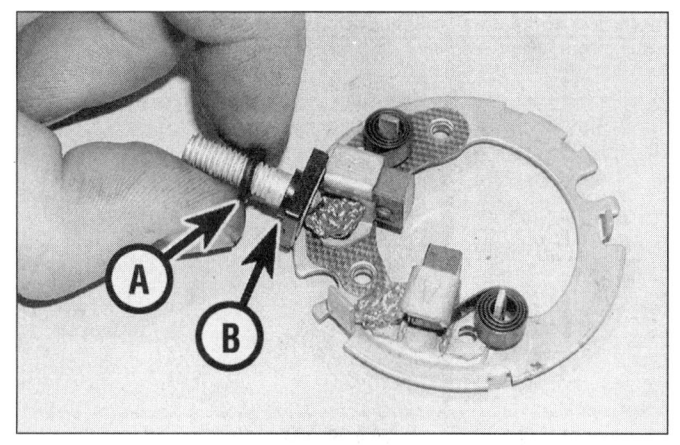

29.8b ... and remove the O-ring (A) and insulating washer (B) from the terminal

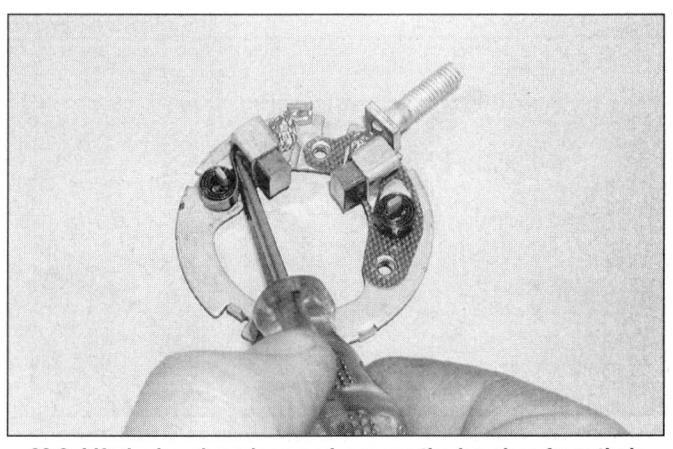

29.9 Lift the brush springs and remove the brushes from their holders

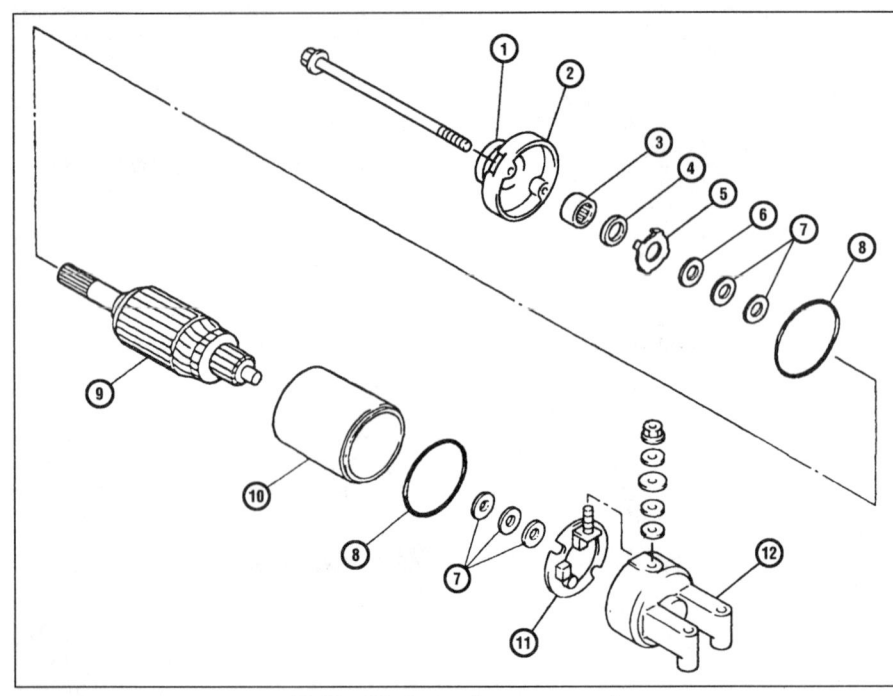

9•18 Electrical system

29.10a Starter motor components

1 O-ring
2 Front cover
3 Bearing
4 Oil seal
5 Tabbed washer
6 Insulating washer
7 Shims
8 O-rings
9 Armature
10 Housing
11 Brushplate and terminal
12 Rear cover

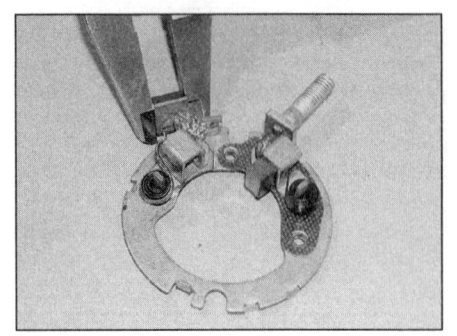

29.10b Measuring the starter motor brushes with a vernier caliper

illustration). The parts that are most likely to require attention are the brushes. Measure the length of the brushes and compare the results to the brush length listed in this Chapter's Specifications **(see illustration)**. If either of the brushes are worn beyond the service limit, renew the brushplate assembly. If the brushes are not worn excessively, cracked, chipped, or otherwise damaged, they may be re-used.

11 Inspect the commutator bars on the armature for scoring, scratches and discoloration. The commutator can be cleaned and polished with steel wool, but do not use sandpaper or emery paper. After cleaning, wipe away any residue with a cloth soaked in electrical system cleaner or denatured alcohol.

12 Using a multimeter or a continuity tester, check for continuity between the commutator bars **(see illustration)**. Continuity should exist (Yamaha specify 0.012 to 0.022 ohms) between each bar and all of the others.

13 Check for continuity between the commutator bars and the armature shaft **(see illustration)**. There should be no continuity (infinite resistance – Yamaha specify a resistance of over 1 M-ohm); if the checks indicate otherwise, the armature is defective.

14 Check the depth of the insulating mica undercut between the commutator bars **(see illustration)** – if it is less than the amount specified at the beginning of this Chapter, scrape the mica away using a suitably shaped hacksaw blade until it is correct.

15 Measure the diameter of the commutator and replace the starter motor with a new one if it has worn below the minimum diameter specified.

16 Check the starter pinion gear for worn, cracked, chipped and broken teeth. If the gear is damaged or worn, replace the starter motor with a new one.

17 Inspect the end covers for signs of cracks or wear. Check the oil seal and needle bearing in the front cover and the bush in the rear cover for wear and damage. Inspect the magnets in the main housing and the housing itself for cracks.

18 Inspect the terminal insulating washers, the O-ring and square insulating washer for signs of damage, and renew them if necessary.

Reassembly

19 Slide the brushes back into their holders and place the brush spring ends onto the brushes.

20 Fit the square insulating washer and O-ring onto the terminal and install the terminal and brushplate assembly into the rear cover **(see illustration 29.8b)**.

21 Fit the insulating washers onto the terminal, followed by the plain washer and nut, and tighten the nut securely.

22 Slide the shims onto the rear end of the armature shaft **(see illustration 29.6b)**. Lubricate the shaft with a smear of grease, then insert the shaft into the rear cover, locating the brushes on the commutator as you do, taking care not to damage the

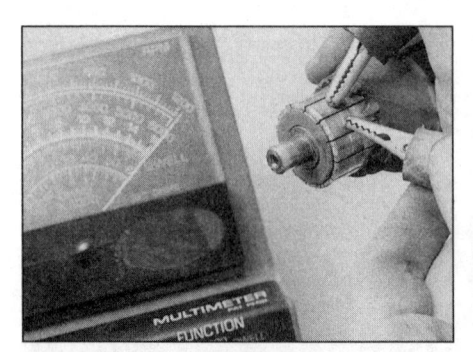

29.12 Continuity should exist between the commutator bars

29.13 There should be no continuity between the commutator bars and the armature shaft

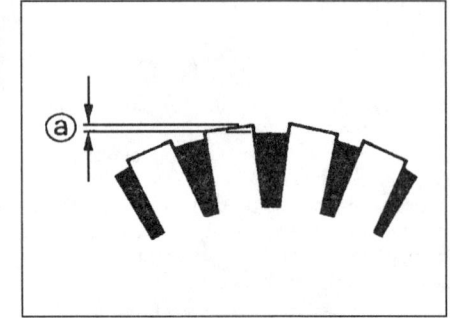

29.14 Mica undercut depth (a)

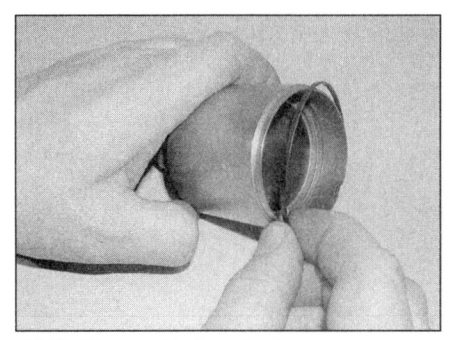

Electrical system 9•19

29.23 Fit new O-rings to the starter motor housing

29.25 Ensure the cover marks are aligned and tighten the long bolts

brushes **(see illustration 29.6a)**. Check that each brush is securely pressed against the commutator by its spring and is free to move easily in its holder.
23 Fit new O-rings onto the main housing, then fit the housing over the armature and onto the rear cover, aligning the marks made on removal **(see illustration)**.
24 Slide the shims and then the insulating washer onto the front end of the armature shaft and lubricate the shaft with a smear of grease. Apply a smear of grease to the inside of the front cover oil seal and fit the tabbed washer into the cover, making sure the tabs locate correctly **(see illustrations 29.4b and a)**. Install the cover onto the main housing, aligning the marks made on removal (see Step 2).
25 If fitted, slide a new O-ring onto each of the long bolts. Check that the marks on the rear cover, main housing and front cover are correctly aligned, then install the bolts and tighten them to the specified torque setting **(see illustration)**.
26 Install the starter motor (see Section 28).

30 Charging system testing – general information and precautions

1 If the performance of the charging system is suspect, the system as a whole should be checked first, followed by testing of the individual components. **Note:** *Before beginning the checks, make sure the battery is fully charged and that all system connections are clean and tight.*
2 Checking the output of the charging system and the performance of the various components within the charging system requires the use of a multimeter (with voltage, current and resistance checking facilities).
3 When making the checks, follow the procedures carefully to prevent incorrect connections or short circuits, as irreparable damage to electrical system components may result if short circuits occur.
4 If a multimeter is not available, the job of checking the charging system should be left to a Yamaha dealer or automotive electrician.

31 Charging system – leakage and output test

1 If the charging system of the machine is thought to be faulty, remove the rider's seat (see Chapter 8) and perform the following checks.

Leakage test

Caution: Always connect an ammeter in series, never in parallel with the battery, otherwise it will be damaged. Do not turn the ignition ON or operate the starter motor when the ammeter is connected – a sudden surge in current will blow the meter's fuse.
2 Turn the ignition switch OFF and disconnect the lead from the battery negative (–ve) terminal.
3 Set the multimeter to the Amps function and connect its negative (–ve) probe to the battery negative (–ve) terminal, and positive (+ve) probe to the disconnected negative (–ve) lead **(see illustration)**. Always set the meter to a high amps range initially and then bring it down to the mA (milli Amps) range; if there is a high current flow in the circuit it may blow the meter's fuse.
4 No current flow should be indicated. If

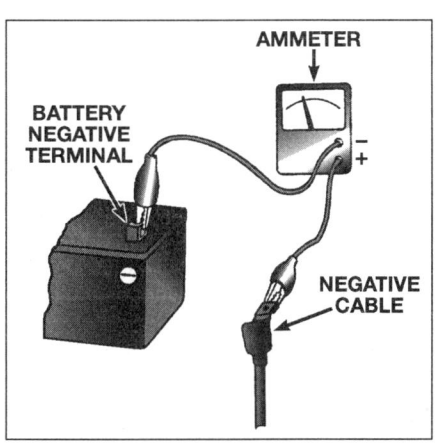

31.3 Checking the charging system leakage rate

current leakage is indicated (generally greater than 1mA, but may be more if an alarm is fitted), there is a short circuit in the wiring. Using the wiring diagrams at the end of this Chapter, systematically disconnect individual electrical components, checking the meter each time until the source is identified.
5 If no leakage is indicated, disconnect the meter and connect the negative (–ve) lead to the battery, tightening it securely.

Output test

6 Start the engine and warm it up to normal operating temperature.
7 To check the regulated voltage output, allow the engine to idle and connect a multimeter set to the 0 to 20 volts DC scale (voltmeter) across the terminals of the battery, positive (+ve) lead to battery positive (+ve) terminal, negative (–ve) lead to battery negative (–ve) terminal. Slowly increase the engine speed to 5000 rpm and note the reading obtained.
8 The regulated voltage should be 14V. If the voltage is outside these limits, check the alternator, then the regulator/rectifier (see Sections 32 and 33).
9 Stop the engine and disconnect the test meter.

32 Alternator rotor and stator – check, removal and installation

Check

1 Remove the fuel tank (see Chapter 4).
2 Trace the wiring back from the alternator cover on the left-hand side of the engine and disconnect it at the white connector containing the three white wires **(see illustration)**.
3 Using a multimeter set to the ohms x 1 (ohmmeter) scale, measure the resistance between the centre wire and each of the other two on the alternator side of the connector, taking a total of two readings, then check for continuity between each terminal and ground

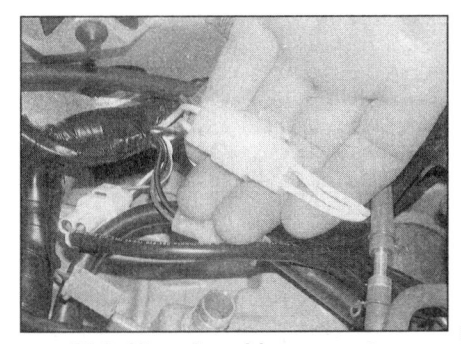

32.2 Alternator wiring connector

9•20 Electrical system

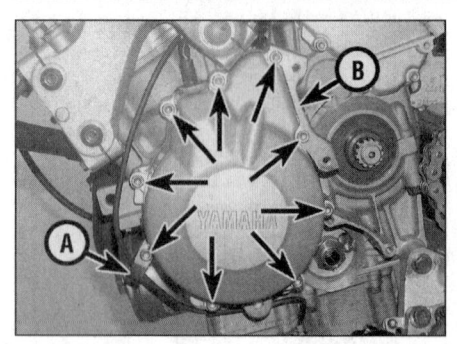

32.6 Unscrew the cover bolts (arrowed) and remove the wiring guide (A) and coolant reservoir bracket (B)

32.7 Avoid contacting the raised sections (arrowed) on the rotor

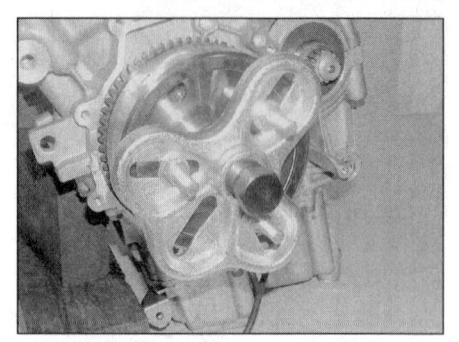

32.8 Removing the rotor using a commercially available puller

(earth). If the stator coil windings are in good condition the resistance readings should be within the range shown in the Specifications at the beginning of this Chapter and there should be no continuity (infinite resistance) between the terminals and ground (earth). If not, check the fault is not due to damaged wiring between the connector and coils. If the wiring is good, the alternator stator coil assembly is at fault and should be replaced with a new one.

Removal

4 Drain the engine oil (see Chapter 1) and remove the fuel tank (see Chapter 4) and the fairing left-hand side panel (see Chapter 8).
5 Trace the wiring back from the alternator cover on the left-hand side of the engine and

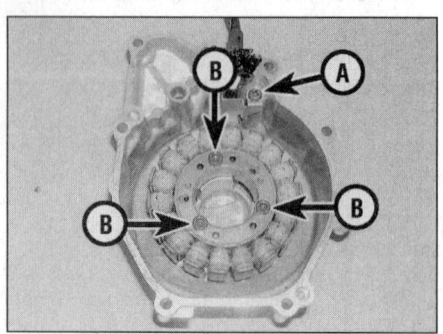

32.9 Remove the wiring clamp (A) and the stator bolts (B)

disconnect it at the white connector containing the three white wires **(see illustration 32.2)**. Free the wiring from any clips or guides and feed it through to the alternator cover.
6 Working in a criss-cross pattern, unscrew the bolts securing the alternator cover and remove the cover, the wiring guide and the coolant reservoir bracket **(see illustration)**. Note the dowels in the cover or the crankcase, and remove them if they are loose. Discard the gasket, as a new one must be used on reassembly.
7 To remove the rotor bolt it is necessary to stop the rotor from turning. If a rotor holding strap or tool is not available, and if the engine is still in the frame, place the transmission in gear and have an assistant apply the rear brake, then unscrew the bolt **(see illustration 32.13b)**. **Note:** *If a rotor holding strap is used, make sure it does not contact the raised sections on the outside of the rotor* **(see illustration)**.
8 To remove the rotor from the shaft it is necessary to use a rotor puller. Yamaha provide a special tool (Part Nos. 90890-01362 and 90890-04089 or YU-33270 and YM-33282), or alternatively a similar tool can be obtained commercially **(see illustration)**. **Note:** *The rotor has three threaded holes designed to accept the bolts of the puller.*
9 To remove the stator, remove the bolt securing the wiring clamp and the three bolts

securing the stator to the inside of the cover, then remove the assembly, noting how the wiring grommet locates in the edge of the cover **(see illustration)**.

Installation

10 Install the stator, aligning the wiring grommet with the recess in the cover. Apply a suitable non-permanent thread locking compound to the stator bolt threads, then install the bolts and tighten them to the torque setting specified at the beginning of this Chapter.
11 Apply a suitable sealant to the wiring grommet, then press it into the recess in the cover and secure the wiring with the clamp.
12 Clean the tapered end of the crankshaft and the corresponding mating surface on the inside of the rotor with a suitable solvent. Make sure that no metal objects have attached themselves to the magnet on the inside of the rotor, then slide the rotor onto the shaft **(see illustration)**.
13 Apply some clean engine oil to the rotor bolt threads, fit the washer onto the bolt and tighten the bolt to the torque setting specified at the beginning of this Chapter **(see illustration)**. Use the method employed on removal to prevent the rotor from turning **(see illustration)**.
14 If removed, install the dowels in the crankcase and fit the new gasket, making sure it locates onto the dowels **(see**

32.12 Slide the rotor onto the shaft

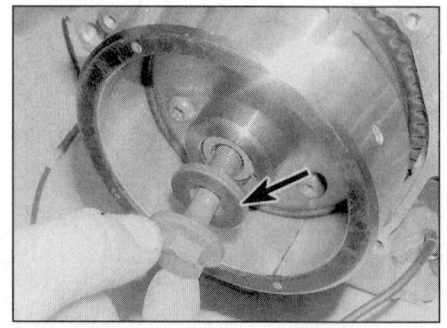

32.13a Install the rotor bolt washer . . .

32.13b . . . then tighten the bolt to the specified torque

illustration). Install the cover and the coolant reservoir bracket, and tighten the bolts evenly in a criss-cross pattern to the specified torque setting **(see illustration 32.6)**.
15 Feed the wiring to the connector, making sure it is correctly routed and secured by the cable ties **(see illustration 32.2)**.
16 Fill the engine up the specified level with oil (see Chapter 1 and *Daily (pre-ride) checks*). Install the fairing left-hand side panel (see Chapter 8), and the fuel tank (see Chapter 4).

33 Regulator/rectifier – check and renewal

Check

1 Yamaha provide no test specifications for the regulator/rectifier other than the charging system output test (see Section 31). If the regulator/rectifier is suspected of being faulty, first check all other components and the wiring and connectors in the charging circuit, referring to the relevant Sections in this Chapter and to the wiring diagrams at the end.

32.14 Fit a new gasket over the crankcase dowels

2 If all other components and the wiring are good, remove the unit (see below) and take it to a Yamaha dealer for testing. Alternatively, substitute the suspect unit with a known good one and see if the fault is cured.

HAYNES HiNT *Clues to a faulty regulator are constantly blowing bulbs, with brightness varying considerably with engine speed, and battery overheating.*

33.3 The regulator/rectifier wiring connector (arrowed)

Renewal

3 The regulator/rectifier is mounted to the frame underneath the rear mounting for the fuel tank – remove the tank for access (see Chapter 4). Disconnect the wiring connector **(see illustration)**.
4 Unscrew the two bolts securing the regulator/rectifier and remove it.
5 Install the new unit and tighten its bolts securely. Connect the wiring connector. Install the fuel tank (see Chapter 4).

9•22 Wiring diagrams

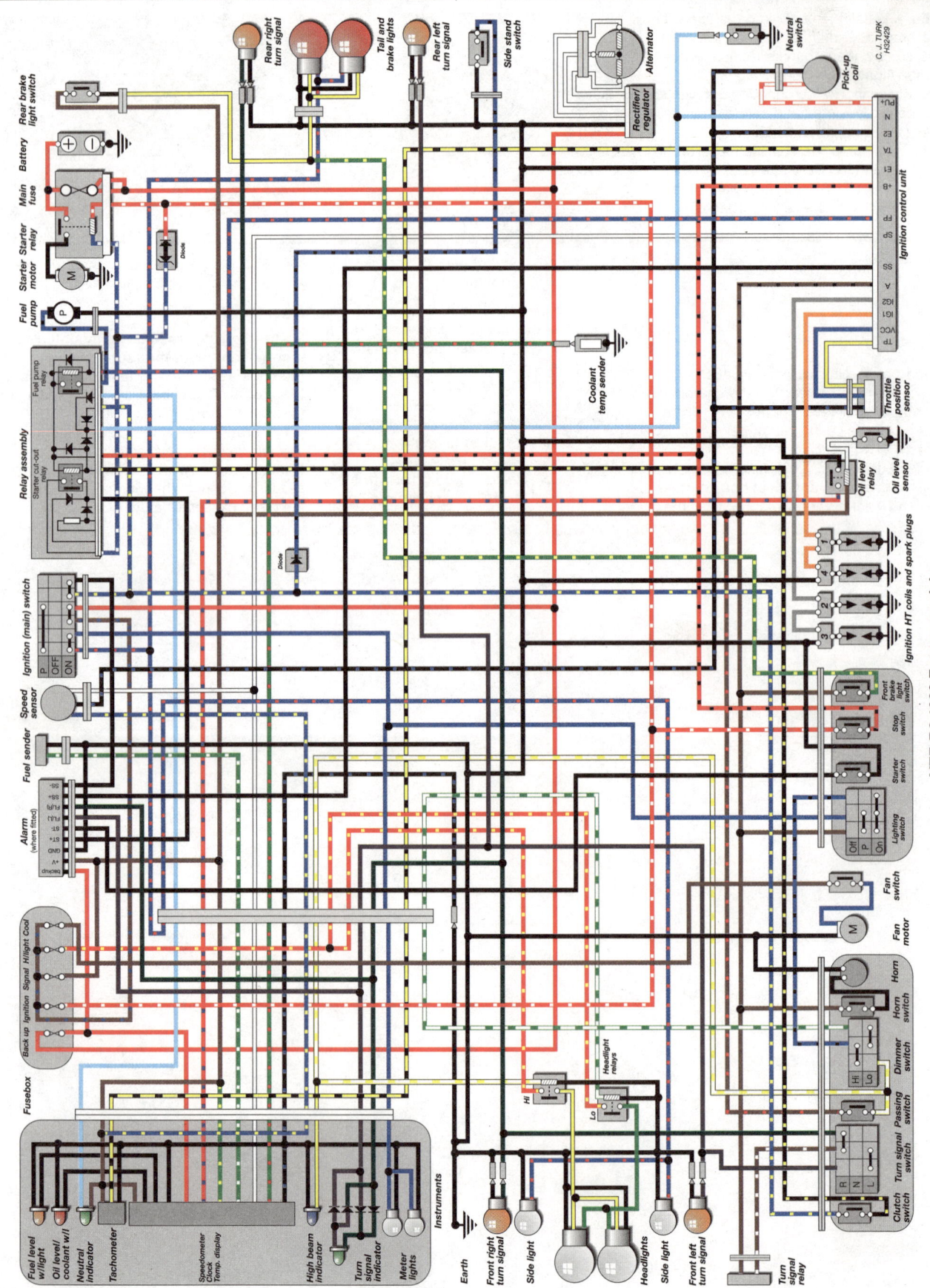

YZF-R6 1999 Europe models

Wiring diagrams 9•23

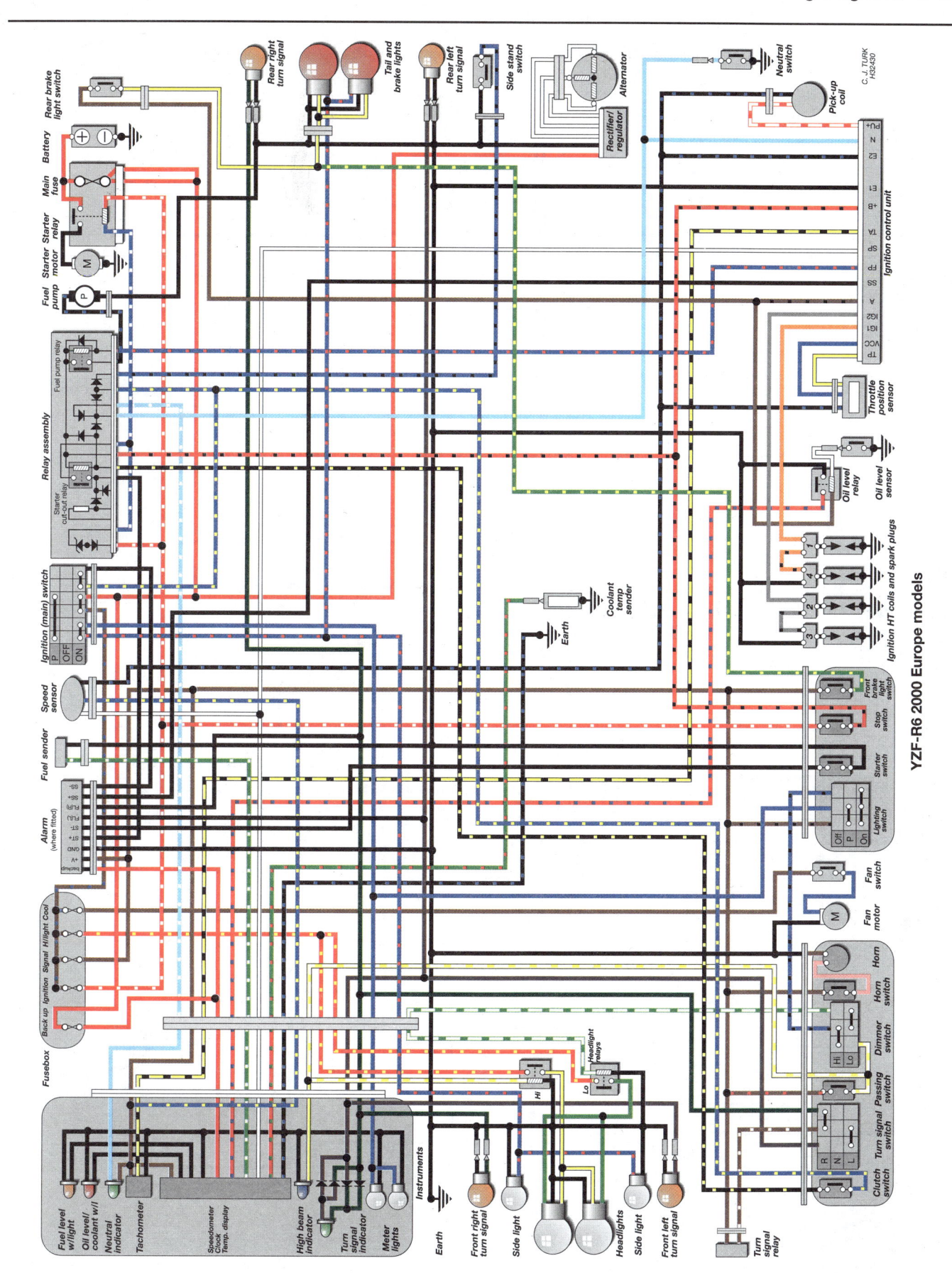

9•24 Wiring diagrams

YZF-R6 2001 and 2002 Europe models

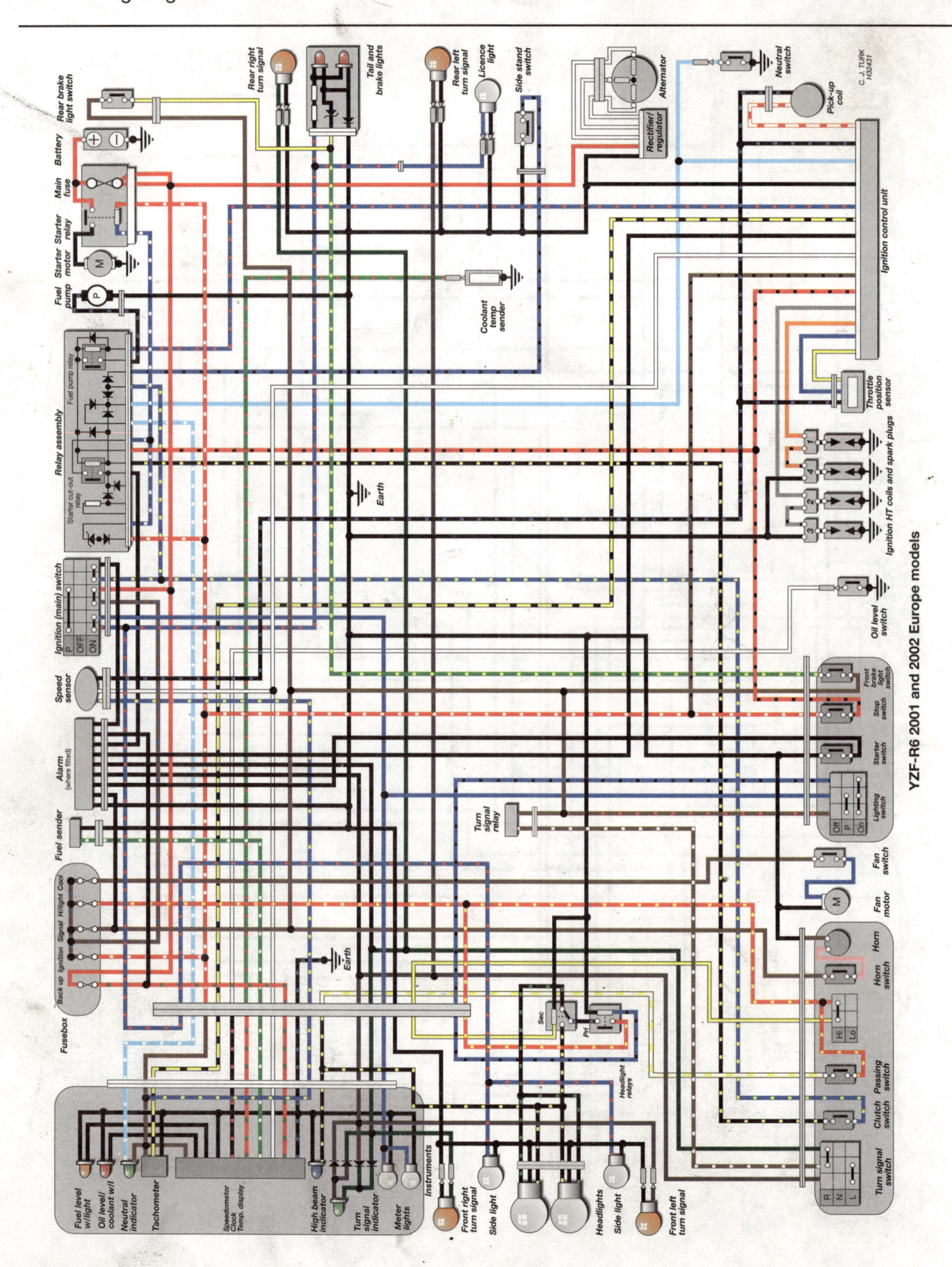

Wiring diagrams 9•25

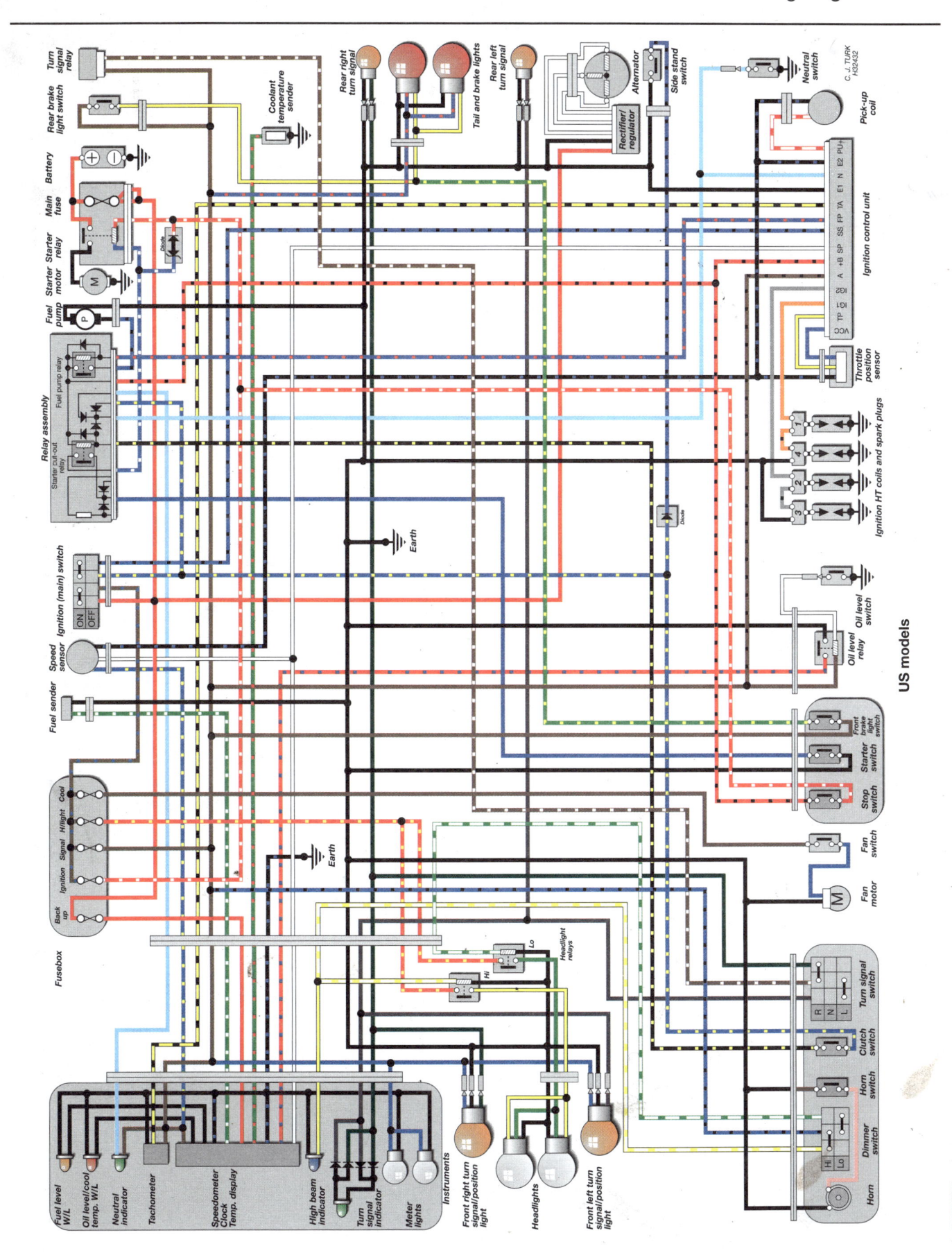

US models

REF•1

Reference

Tools and Workshop Tips — REF•2
- Building up a tool kit and equipping your workshop ● Using tools ● Understanding bearing, seal, fastener and chain sizes and markings ● Repair techniques

Security — REF•20
- Locks and chains ● U-locks ● Disc locks ● Alarms and immobilisers ● Security marking systems ● Tips on how to prevent bike theft

Lubricants and fluids — REF•23
- Engine oils ● Transmission (gear) oils ● Coolant/anti-freeze ● Fork oils and suspension fluids ● Brake/clutch fluids ● Spray lubes, degreasers and solvents

Conversion Factors — REF•26

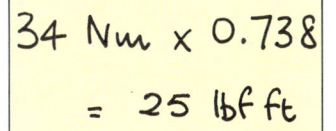

34 Nm × 0.738 = 25 lbf ft

- Formulae for conversion of the metric (SI) units used throughout the manual into Imperial measures

MOT Test Checks — REF•27
- A guide to the UK MOT test ● Which items are tested ● How to prepare your motorcycle for the test and perform a pre-test check

Storage — REF•32
- How to prepare your motorcycle for going into storage and protect essential systems ● How to get the motorcycle back on the road

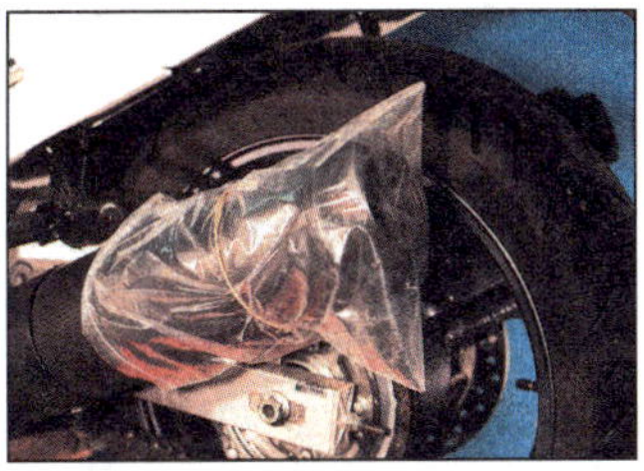

Fault Finding — REF•35
- Common faults and their likely causes ● How to check engine cylinder compression ● How to make electrical tests and use test meters

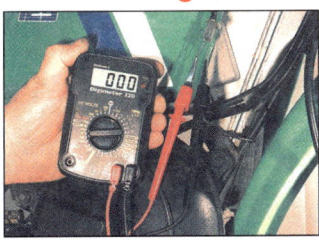

Technical Terms Explained — REF•49
- Component names, technical terms and common abbreviations explained

Index — REF•53

REF•2 Tools and Workshop Tips

Buying tools

A toolkit is a fundamental requirement for servicing and repairing a motorcycle. Although there will be an initial expense in building up enough tools for servicing, this will soon be offset by the savings made by doing the job yourself. As experience and confidence grow, additional tools can be added to enable the repair and overhaul of the motorcycle. Many of the specialist tools are expensive and not often used so it may be preferable to hire them, or for a group of friends or motorcycle club to join in the purchase.

As a rule, it is better to buy more expensive, good quality tools. Cheaper tools are likely to wear out faster and need to be renewed more often, nullifying the original saving.

Warning: To avoid the risk of a poor quality tool breaking in use, causing injury or damage to the component being worked on, always aim to purchase tools which meet the relevant national safety standards.

The following lists of tools do not represent the manufacturer's service tools, but serve as a guide to help the owner decide which tools are needed for this level of work. In addition, items such as an electric drill, hacksaw, files, soldering iron and a workbench equipped with a vice, may be needed. Although not classed as tools, a selection of bolts, screws, nuts, washers and pieces of tubing always come in useful.

For more information about tools, refer to the Haynes *Motorcycle Workshop Practice TechBook* (Bk. No. 3470).

Manufacturer's service tools

Inevitably certain tasks require the use of a service tool. Where possible an alternative tool or method of approach is recommended, but sometimes there is no option if personal injury or damage to the component is to be avoided. Where required, service tools are referred to in the relevant procedure.

Service tools can usually only be purchased from a motorcycle dealer and are identified by a part number. Some of the commonly-used tools, such as rotor pullers, are available in aftermarket form from mail-order motorcycle tool and accessory suppliers.

Maintenance and minor repair tools

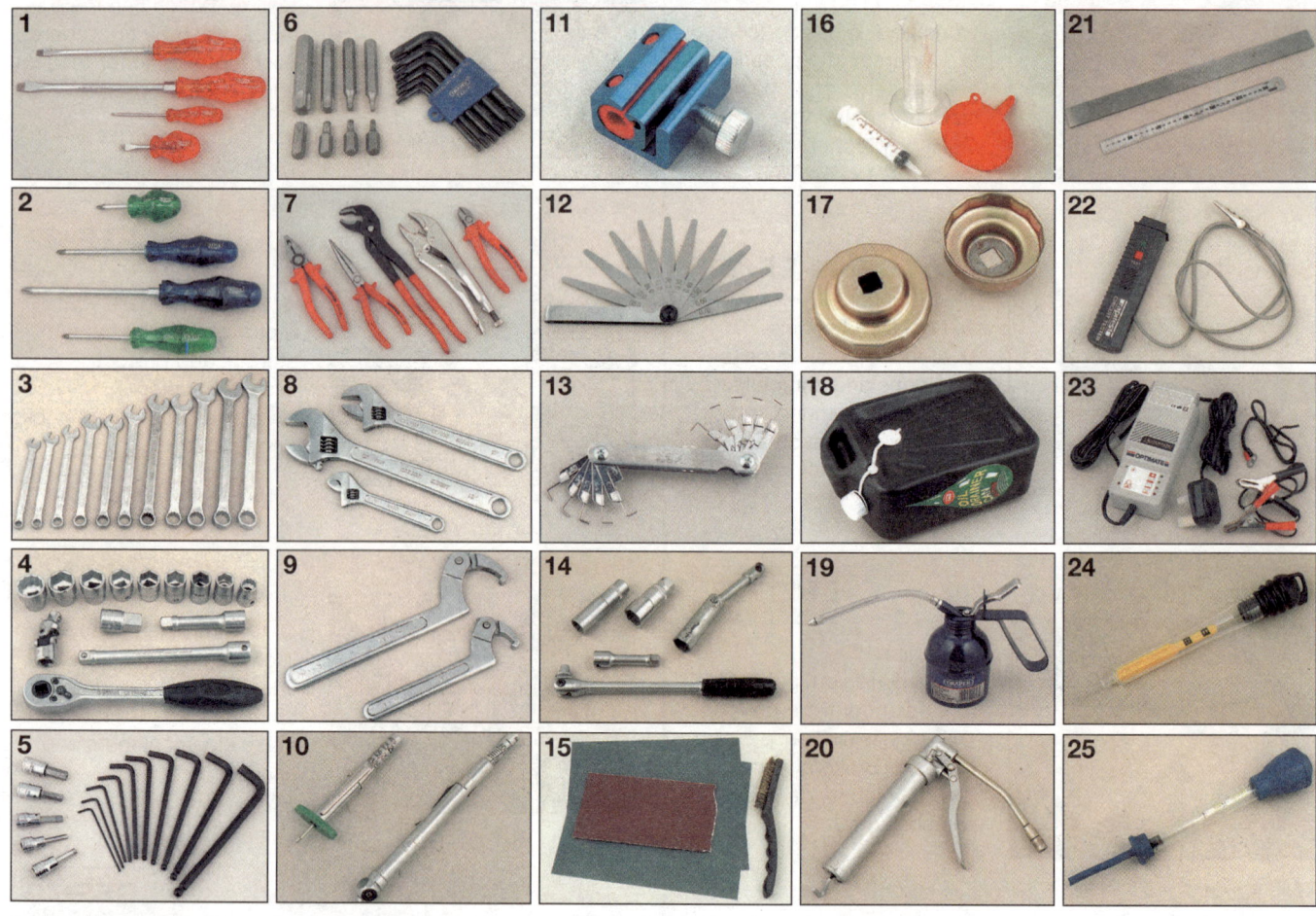

1. Set of flat-bladed screwdrivers
2. Set of Phillips head screwdrivers
3. Combination open-end and ring spanners
4. Socket set (3/8 inch or 1/2 inch drive)
5. Set of Allen keys or bits
6. Set of Torx keys or bits
7. Pliers, cutters and self-locking grips (Mole grips)
8. Adjustable spanners
9. C-spanners
10. Tread depth gauge and tyre pressure gauge
11. Cable oiler clamp
12. Feeler gauges
13. Spark plug gap measuring tool
14. Spark plug spanner or deep plug sockets
15. Wire brush and emery paper
16. Calibrated syringe, measuring vessel and funnel
17. Oil filter adapters
18. Oil drainer can or tray
19. Pump type oil can
20. Grease gun
21. Straight-edge and steel rule
22. Continuity tester
23. Battery charger
24. Hydrometer (for battery specific gravity check)
25. Anti-freeze tester (for liquid-cooled engines)

Tools and Workshop Tips REF•3

Repair and overhaul tools

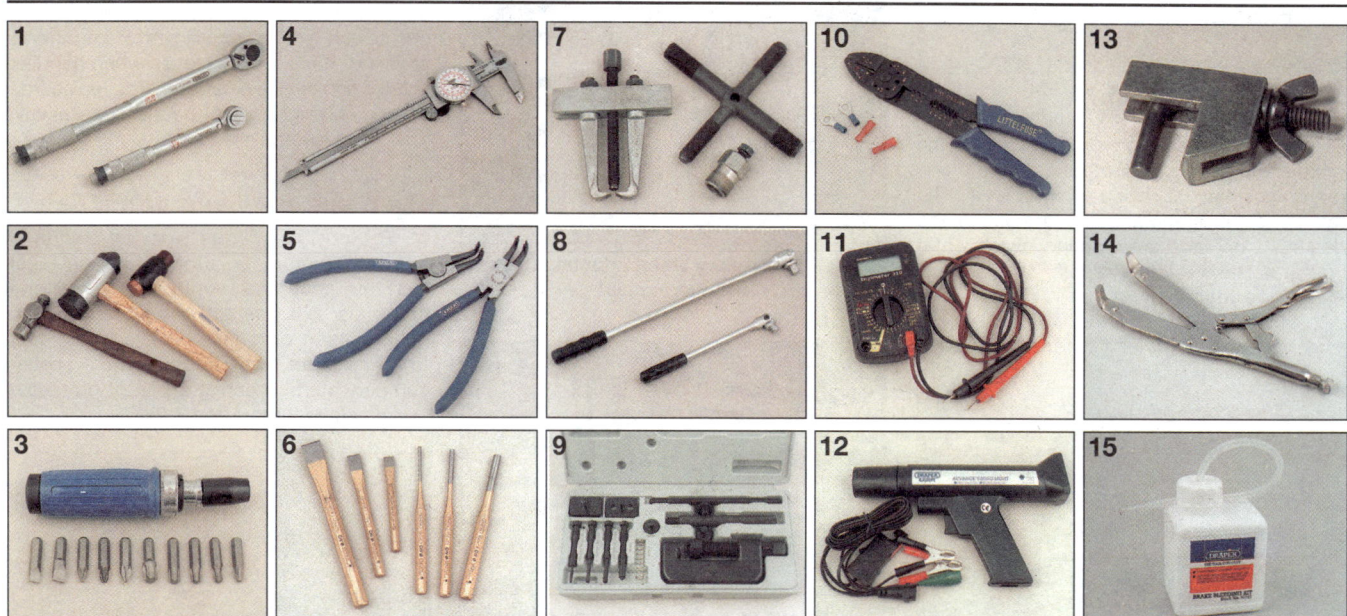

1 Torque wrench (small and mid-ranges)
2 Conventional, plastic or soft-faced hammers
3 Impact driver set
4 Vernier gauge
5 Circlip pliers (internal and external, or combination)
6 Set of cold chisels and punches
7 Selection of pullers
8 Breaker bars
9 Chain breaking/riveting tool set
10 Wire stripper and crimper tool
11 Multimeter (measures amps, volts and ohms)
12 Stroboscope (for dynamic timing checks)
13 Hose clamp (wingnut type shown)
14 Clutch holding tool
15 One-man brake/clutch bleeder kit

Specialist tools

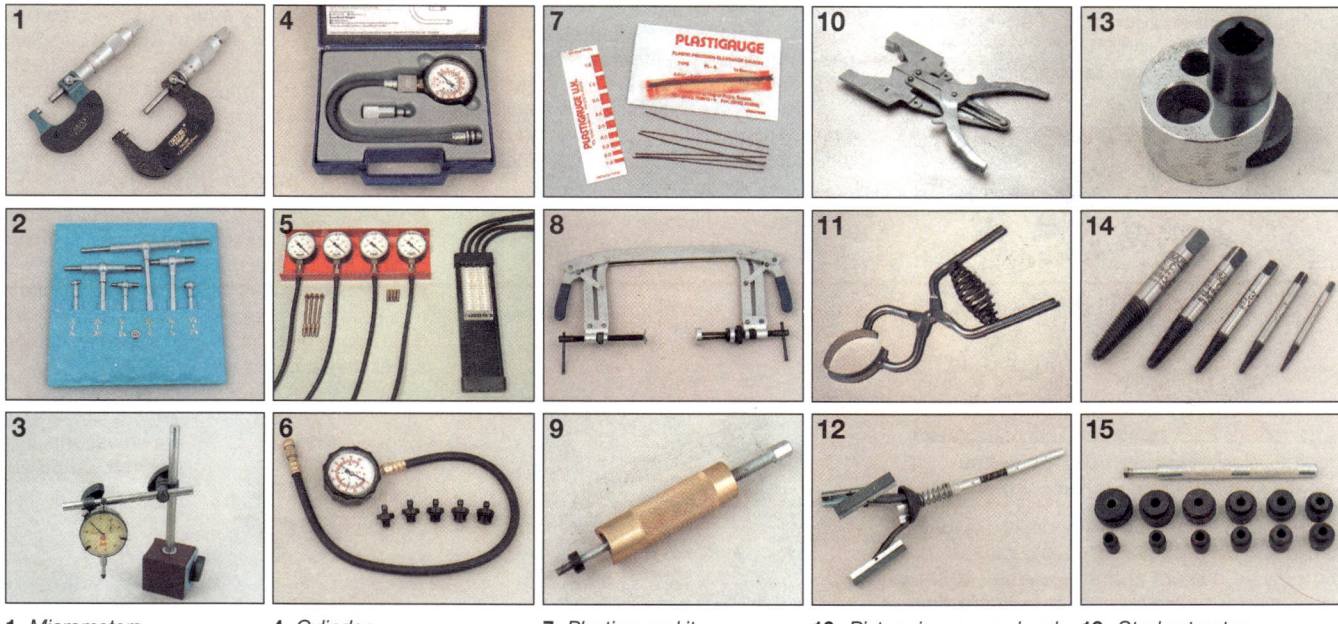

1 Micrometers (external type)
2 Telescoping gauges
3 Dial gauge
4 Cylinder compression gauge
5 Vacuum gauges (left) or manometer (right)
6 Oil pressure gauge
7 Plastigauge kit
8 Valve spring compressor (4-stroke engines)
9 Piston pin drawbolt tool
10 Piston ring removal and installation tool
11 Piston ring clamp
12 Cylinder bore hone (stone type shown)
13 Stud extractor
14 Screw extractor set
15 Bearing driver set

REF•4 Tools and Workshop Tips

1 Workshop equipment and facilities

The workbench

● Work is made much easier by raising the bike up on a ramp - components are much more accessible if raised to waist level. The hydraulic or pneumatic types seen in the dealer's workshop are a sound investment if you undertake a lot of repairs or overhauls **(see illustration 1.1)**.

1.3 This auxiliary stand attaches to the swingarm pivot

1.1 Hydraulic motorcycle ramp

● If raised off ground level, the bike must be supported on the ramp to avoid it falling. Most ramps incorporate a front wheel locating clamp which can be adjusted to suit different diameter wheels. When tightening the clamp, take care not to mark the wheel rim or damage the tyre - use wood blocks on each side to prevent this.
● Secure the bike to the ramp using tie-downs **(see illustration 1.2)**. If the bike has only a sidestand, and hence leans at a dangerous angle when raised, support the bike on an auxiliary stand.

1.2 Tie-downs are used around the passenger footrests to secure the bike

● Auxiliary (paddock) stands are widely available from mail order companies or motorcycle dealers and attach either to the wheel axle or swingarm pivot **(see illustration 1.3)**. If the motorcycle has a centrestand, you can support it under the crankcase to prevent it toppling whilst either wheel is removed **(see illustration 1.4)**.

1.4 Always use a block of wood between the engine and jack head when supporting the engine in this way

Fumes and fire

● Refer to the Safety first! page at the beginning of the manual for full details. Make sure your workshop is equipped with a fire extinguisher suitable for fuel-related fires (Class B fire - flammable liquids) - it is not sufficient to have a water-filled extinguisher.
● Always ensure adequate ventilation is available. Unless an exhaust gas extraction system is available for use, ensure that the engine is run outside of the workshop.
● If working on the fuel system, make sure the workshop is ventilated to avoid a build-up of fumes. This applies equally to fume build-up when charging a battery. Do not smoke or allow anyone else to smoke in the workshop.

Fluids

● If you need to drain fuel from the tank, store it in an approved container marked as suitable for the storage of petrol (gasoline) **(see illustration 1.5)**. Do not store fuel in glass jars or bottles.

1.5 Use an approved can only for storing petrol (gasoline)

● Use proprietary engine degreasers or solvents which have a high flash-point, such as paraffin (kerosene), for cleaning off oil, grease and dirt - never use petrol (gasoline) for cleaning. Wear rubber gloves when handling solvent and engine degreaser. The fumes from certain solvents can be dangerous - always work in a well-ventilated area.

Dust, eye and hand protection

● Protect your lungs from inhalation of dust particles by wearing a filtering mask over the nose and mouth. Many frictional materials still contain asbestos which is dangerous to your health. Protect your eyes from spouts of liquid and sprung components by wearing a pair of protective goggles **(see illustration 1.6)**.

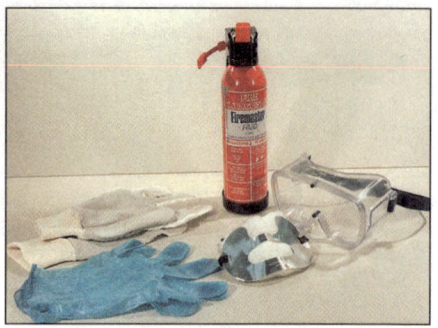

1.6 A fire extinguisher, goggles, mask and protective gloves should be at hand in the workshop

● Protect your hands from contact with solvents, fuel and oils by wearing rubber gloves. Alternatively apply a barrier cream to your hands before starting work. If handling hot components or fluids, wear suitable gloves to protect your hands from scalding and burns.

What to do with old fluids

● Old cleaning solvent, fuel, coolant and oils should not be poured down domestic drains or onto the ground. Package the fluid up in old oil containers, label it accordingly, and take it to a garage or disposal facility. Contact your local authority for location of such sites or ring the oil care hotline.

OIL CARE — FOLLOW THE CODE — OIL BANK LINE **0800 66 33 66** www.oilbankline.org.uk

Note: It is antisocial and illegal to dump oil down the drain. To find the location of your local oil recycling bank, call this number free.

In the USA, note that any oil supplier must accept used oil for recycling.

Tools and Workshop Tips

2 Fasteners - screws, bolts and nuts

Fastener types and applications

Bolts and screws

● Fastener head types are either of hexagonal, Torx or splined design, with internal and external versions of each type (see illustrations 2.1 and 2.2); splined head fasteners are not in common use on motorcycles. The conventional slotted or Phillips head design is used for certain screws. Bolt or screw length is always measured from the underside of the head to the end of the item (see illustration 2.11).

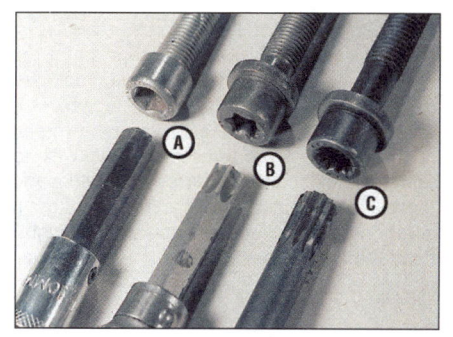

2.1 Internal hexagon/Allen (A), Torx (B) and splined (C) fasteners, with corresponding bits

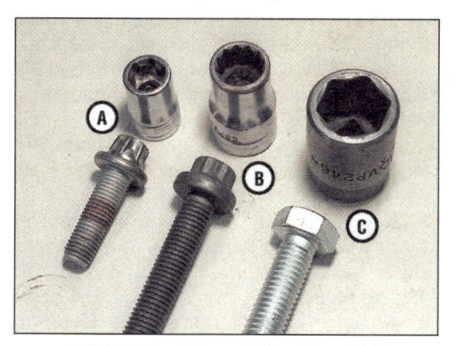

2.2 External Torx (A), splined (B) and hexagon (C) fasteners, with corresponding sockets

● Certain fasteners on the motorcycle have a tensile marking on their heads, the higher the marking the stronger the fastener. High tensile fasteners generally carry a 10 or higher marking. Never replace a high tensile fastener with one of a lower tensile strength.

Washers (see illustration 2.3)

● Plain washers are used between a fastener head and a component to prevent damage to the component or to spread the load when torque is applied. Plain washers can also be used as spacers or shims in certain assemblies. Copper or aluminium plain washers are often used as sealing washers on drain plugs.

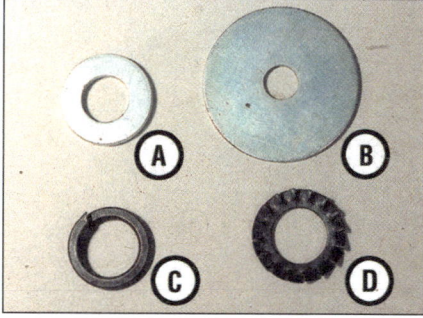

2.3 Plain washer (A), penny washer (B), spring washer (C) and serrated washer (D)

● The split-ring spring washer works by applying axial tension between the fastener head and component. If flattened, it is fatigued and must be renewed. If a plain (flat) washer is used on the fastener, position the spring washer between the fastener and the plain washer.

● Serrated star type washers dig into the fastener and component faces, preventing loosening. They are often used on electrical earth (ground) connections to the frame.

● Cone type washers (sometimes called Belleville) are conical and when tightened apply axial tension between the fastener head and component. They must be installed with the dished side against the component and often carry an OUTSIDE marking on their outer face. If flattened, they are fatigued and must be renewed.

● Tab washers are used to lock plain nuts or bolts on a shaft. A portion of the tab washer is bent up hard against one flat of the nut or bolt to prevent it loosening. Due to the tab washer being deformed in use, a new tab washer should be used every time it is disturbed.

● Wave washers are used to take up endfloat on a shaft. They provide light springing and prevent excessive side-to-side play of a component. Can be found on rocker arm shafts.

Nuts and split pins

● Conventional plain nuts are usually six-sided (see illustration 2.4). They are sized by thread diameter and pitch. High tensile nuts carry a number on one end to denote their tensile strength.

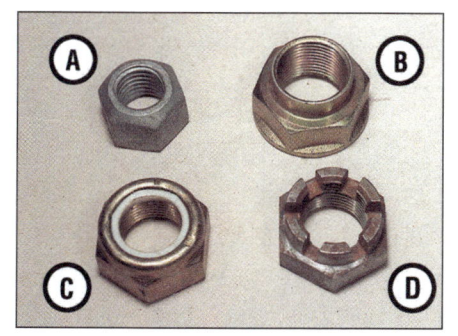

2.4 Plain nut (A), shouldered locknut (B), nylon insert nut (C) and castellated nut (D)

● Self-locking nuts either have a nylon insert, or two spring metal tabs, or a shoulder which is staked into a groove in the shaft - their advantage over conventional plain nuts is a resistance to loosening due to vibration. The nylon insert type can be used a number of times, but must be renewed when the friction of the nylon insert is reduced, ie when the nut spins freely on the shaft. The spring tab type can be reused unless the tabs are damaged. The shouldered type must be renewed every time it is disturbed.

● Split pins (cotter pins) are used to lock a castellated nut to a shaft or to prevent slackening of a plain nut. Common applications are wheel axles and brake torque arms. Because the split pin arms are deformed to lock around the nut a new split pin must always be used on installation - always fit the correct size split pin which will fit snugly in the shaft hole. Make sure the split pin arms are correctly located around the nut (see illustrations 2.5 and 2.6).

2.5 Bend split pin (cotter pin) arms as shown (arrows) to secure a castellated nut

2.6 Bend split pin (cotter pin) arms as shown to secure a plain nut

Caution: If the castellated nut slots do not align with the shaft hole after tightening to the torque setting, tighten the nut until the next slot aligns with the hole - never slacken the nut to align its slot.

● R-pins (shaped like the letter R), or slip pins as they are sometimes called, are sprung and can be reused if they are otherwise in good condition. Always install R-pins with their closed end facing forwards (see illustration 2.7).

Tools and Workshop Tips

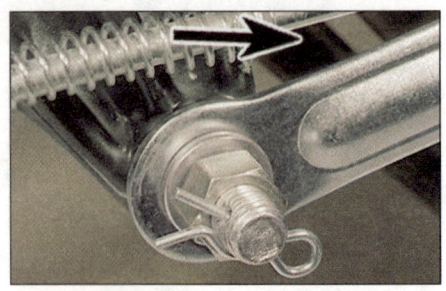

2.7 Correct fitting of R-pin. Arrow indicates forward direction

Circlips (see illustration 2.8)

● Circlips (sometimes called snap-rings) are used to retain components on a shaft or in a housing and have corresponding external or internal ears to permit removal. Parallel-sided (machined) circlips can be installed either way round in their groove, whereas stamped circlips (which have a chamfered edge on one face) must be installed with the chamfer facing away from the direction of thrust load **(see illustration 2.9)**.

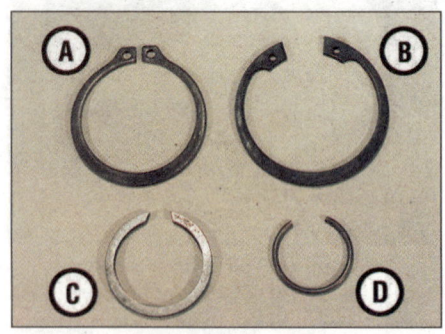

2.8 External stamped circlip (A), internal stamped circlip (B), machined circlip (C) and wire circlip (D)

● Always use circlip pliers to remove and install circlips; expand or compress them just enough to remove them. After installation, rotate the circlip in its groove to ensure it is securely seated. If installing a circlip on a splined shaft, always align its opening with a shaft channel to ensure the circlip ends are well supported and unlikely to catch **(see illustration 2.10)**.

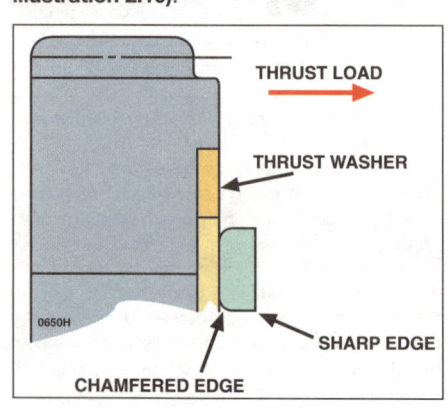

2.9 Correct fitting of a stamped circlip

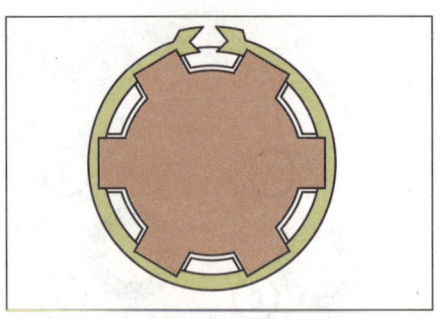

2.10 Align circlip opening with shaft channel

● Circlips can wear due to the thrust of components and become loose in their grooves, with the subsequent danger of becoming dislodged in operation. For this reason, renewal is advised every time a circlip is disturbed.

● Wire circlips are commonly used as piston pin retaining clips. If a removal tang is provided, long-nosed pliers can be used to dislodge them, otherwise careful use of a small flat-bladed screwdriver is necessary. Wire circlips should be renewed every time they are disturbed.

Thread diameter and pitch

● Diameter of a male thread (screw, bolt or stud) is the outside diameter of the threaded portion **(see illustration 2.11)**. Most motorcycle manufacturers use the ISO (International Standards Organisation) metric system expressed in millimetres, eg M6 refers to a 6 mm diameter thread. Sizing is the same for nuts, except that the thread diameter is measured across the valleys of the nut.

● Pitch is the distance between the peaks of the thread **(see illustration 2.11)**. It is expressed in millimetres, thus a common bolt size may be expressed as 6.0 x 1.0 mm (6 mm thread diameter and 1 mm pitch). Generally pitch increases in proportion to thread diameter, although there are always exceptions.

● Thread diameter and pitch are related for conventional fastener applications and the accompanying table can be used as a guide. Additionally, the AF (Across Flats), spanner or socket size dimension of the bolt or nut **(see illustration 2.11)** is linked to thread and pitch specification. Thread pitch can be measured with a thread gauge **(see illustration 2.12)**.

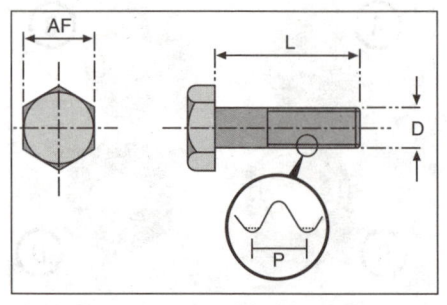

2.11 Fastener length (L), thread diameter (D), thread pitch (P) and head size (AF)

2.12 Using a thread gauge to measure pitch

AF size	Thread diameter x pitch (mm)
8 mm	M5 x 0.8
8 mm	M6 x 1.0
10 mm	M6 x 1.0
12 mm	M8 x 1.25
14 mm	M10 x 1.25
17 mm	M12 x 1.25

● The threads of most fasteners are of the right-hand type, ie they are turned clockwise to tighten and anti-clockwise to loosen. The reverse situation applies to left-hand thread fasteners, which are turned anti-clockwise to tighten and clockwise to loosen. Left-hand threads are used where rotation of a component might loosen a conventional right-hand thread fastener.

Seized fasteners

● Corrosion of external fasteners due to water or reaction between two dissimilar metals can occur over a period of time. It will build up sooner in wet conditions or in countries where salt is used on the roads during the winter. If a fastener is severely corroded it is likely that normal methods of removal will fail and result in its head being ruined. When you attempt removal, the fastener thread should be heard to crack free and unscrew easily - if it doesn't, stop there before damaging something.

● A smart tap on the head of the fastener will often succeed in breaking free corrosion which has occurred in the threads **(see illustration 2.13)**.

● An aerosol penetrating fluid (such as WD-40) applied the night beforehand may work its way down into the thread and ease removal. Depending on the location, you may be able to make up a Plasticine well around the fastener head and fill it with penetrating fluid.

2.13 A sharp tap on the head of a fastener will often break free a corroded thread

Tools and Workshop Tips REF•7

• If you are working on an engine internal component, corrosion will most likely not be a problem due to the well lubricated environment. However, components can be very tight and an impact driver is a useful tool in freeing them **(see illustration 2.14)**.

2.14 Using an impact driver to free a fastener

• Where corrosion has occurred between dissimilar metals (eg steel and aluminium alloy), the application of heat to the fastener head will create a disproportionate expansion rate between the two metals and break the seizure caused by the corrosion. Whether heat can be applied depends on the location of the fastener - any surrounding components likely to be damaged must first be removed **(see illustration 2.15)**. Heat can be applied using a paint stripper heat gun or clothes iron, or by immersing the component in boiling water - wear protective gloves to prevent scalding or burns to the hands.

2.15 Using heat to free a seized fastener

• As a last resort, it is possible to use a hammer and cold chisel to work the fastener head unscrewed **(see illustration 2.16)**. This will damage the fastener, but more importantly extreme care must be taken not to damage the surrounding component.

Caution: Remember that the component being secured is generally of more value than the bolt, nut or screw - when the fastener is freed, do not unscrew it with force, instead work the fastener back and forth when resistance is felt to prevent thread damage.

2.16 Using a hammer and chisel to free a seized fastener

Broken fasteners and damaged heads

• If the shank of a broken bolt or screw is accessible you can grip it with self-locking grips. The knurled wheel type stud extractor tool or self-gripping stud puller tool is particularly useful for removing the long studs which screw into the cylinder mouth surface of the crankcase or bolts and screws from which the head has broken off **(see illustration 2.17)**. Studs can also be removed by locking two nuts together on the threaded end of the stud and using a spanner on the lower nut **(see illustration 2.18)**.

2.17 Using a stud extractor tool to remove a broken crankcase stud

2.18 Two nuts can be locked together to unscrew a stud from a component

• A bolt or screw which has broken off below or level with the casing must be extracted using a screw extractor set. Centre punch the fastener to centralise the drill bit, then drill a hole in the fastener **(see illustration 2.19)**. Select a drill bit which is approximately half to three-quarters the

2.19 When using a screw extractor, first drill a hole in the fastener ...

diameter of the fastener and drill to a depth which will accommodate the extractor. Use the largest size extractor possible, but avoid leaving too small a wall thickness otherwise the extractor will merely force the fastener walls outwards wedging it in the casing thread.

• If a spiral type extractor is used, thread it anti-clockwise into the fastener. As it is screwed in, it will grip the fastener and unscrew it from the casing **(see illustration 2.20)**.

2.20 ... then thread the extractor anti-clockwise into the fastener

• If a taper type extractor is used, tap it into the fastener so that it is firmly wedged in place. Unscrew the extractor (anti-clockwise) to draw the fastener out.

> **Warning: Stud extractors are very hard and may break off in the fastener if care is not taken - ask an engineer about spark erosion if this happens.**

• Alternatively, the broken bolt/screw can be drilled out and the hole retapped for an oversize bolt/screw or a diamond-section thread insert. It is essential that the drilling is carried out squarely and to the correct depth, otherwise the casing may be ruined - if in doubt, entrust the work to an engineer.

• Bolts and nuts with rounded corners cause the correct size spanner or socket to slip when force is applied. Of the types of spanner/socket available always use a six-point type rather than an eight or twelve-point type - better grip

REF•8 Tools and Workshop Tips

2.21 Comparison of surface drive ring spanner (left) with 12-point type (right)

is obtained. Surface drive spanners grip the middle of the hex flats, rather than the corners, and are thus good in cases of damaged heads **(see illustration 2.21)**.

● Slotted-head or Phillips-head screws are often damaged by the use of the wrong size screwdriver. Allen-head and Torx-head screws are much less likely to sustain damage. If enough of the screw head is exposed you can use a hacksaw to cut a slot in its head and then use a conventional flat-bladed screwdriver to remove it. Alternatively use a hammer and cold chisel to tap the head of the fastener around to slacken it. Always replace damaged fasteners with new ones, preferably Torx or Allen-head type.

HAYNES HiNT

A dab of valve grinding compound between the screw head and screwdriver tip will often give a good grip.

Thread repair

● Threads (particularly those in aluminium alloy components) can be damaged by overtightening, being assembled with dirt in the threads, or from a component working loose and vibrating. Eventually the thread will fail completely, and it will be impossible to tighten the fastener.

● If a thread is damaged or clogged with old locking compound it can be renovated with a thread repair tool (thread chaser) **(see illustrations 2.22 and 2.23)**; special thread

2.22 A thread repair tool being used to correct an internal thread

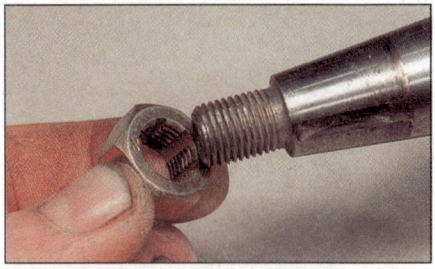

2.23 A thread repair tool being used to correct an external thread

chasers are available for spark plug hole threads. The tool will not cut a new thread, but clean and true the original thread. Make sure that you use the correct diameter and pitch tool. Similarly, external threads can be cleaned up with a die or a thread restorer file **(see illustration 2.24)**.

2.24 Using a thread restorer file

● It is possible to drill out the old thread and retap the component to the next thread size. This will work where there is enough surrounding material and a new bolt or screw can be obtained. Sometimes, however, this is not possible - such as where the bolt/screw passes through another component which must also be suitably modified, also in cases where a spark plug or oil drain plug cannot be obtained in a larger diameter thread size.

● The diamond-section thread insert (often known by its popular trade name of Heli-Coil) is a simple and effective method of renewing the thread and retaining the original size. A kit can be purchased which contains the tap, insert and installing tool **(see illustration 2.25)**. Drill out the damaged thread with the size drill specified **(see illustration 2.26)**. Carefully retap the thread **(see illustration 2.27)**. Install the

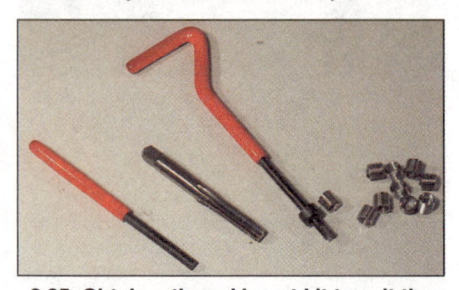

2.25 Obtain a thread insert kit to suit the thread diameter and pitch required

2.26 To install a thread insert, first drill out the original thread . . .

2.27 . . . tap a new thread . . .

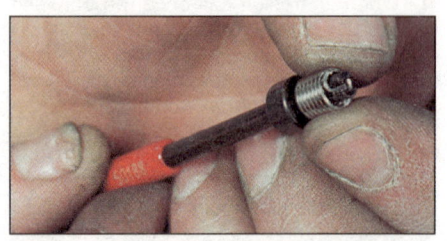

2.28 . . . fit insert on the installing tool . . .

2.29 . . . and thread into the component . . .

2.30 . . . break off the tang when complete

insert on the installing tool and thread it slowly into place using a light downward pressure **(see illustrations 2.28 and 2.29)**. When positioned between a 1/4 and 1/2 turn below the surface withdraw the installing tool and use the break-off tool to press down on the tang, breaking it off **(see illustration 2.30)**.

● There are epoxy thread repair kits on the market which can rebuild stripped internal threads, although this repair should not be used on high load-bearing components.

Tools and Workshop Tips REF•9

Thread locking and sealing compounds

● Locking compounds are used in locations where the fastener is prone to loosening due to vibration or on important safety-related items which might cause loss of control of the motorcycle if they fail. It is also used where important fasteners cannot be secured by other means such as lockwashers or split pins.

● Before applying locking compound, make sure that the threads (internal and external) are clean and dry with all old compound removed. Select a compound to suit the component being secured - a non-permanent general locking and sealing type is suitable for most applications, but a high strength type is needed for permanent fixing of studs in castings. Apply a drop or two of the compound to the first few threads of the fastener, then thread it into place and tighten to the specified torque. Do not apply excessive thread locking compound otherwise the thread may be damaged on subsequent removal.

● Certain fasteners are impregnated with a dry film type coating of locking compound on their threads. Always renew this type of fastener if disturbed.

● Anti-seize compounds, such as copper-based greases, can be applied to protect threads from seizure due to extreme heat and corrosion. A common instance is spark plug threads and exhaust system fasteners.

3 Measuring tools and gauges

Feeler gauges

● Feeler gauges (or blades) are used for measuring small gaps and clearances **(see illustration 3.1)**. They can also be used to measure endfloat (sideplay) of a component on a shaft where access is not possible with a dial gauge.

● Feeler gauge sets should be treated with care and not bent or damaged. They are etched with their size on one face. Keep them clean and very lightly oiled to prevent corrosion build-up.

3.1 Feeler gauges are used for measuring small gaps and clearances - thickness is marked on one face of gauge

● When measuring a clearance, select a gauge which is a light sliding fit between the two components. You may need to use two gauges together to measure the clearance accurately.

Micrometers

● A micrometer is a precision tool capable of measuring to 0.01 or 0.001 of a millimetre. It should always be stored in its case and not in the general toolbox. It must be kept clean and never dropped, otherwise its frame or measuring anvils could be distorted resulting in inaccurate readings.

● External micrometers are used for measuring outside diameters of components and have many more applications than internal micrometers. Micrometers are available in different size ranges, eg 0 to 25 mm, 25 to 50 mm, and upwards in 25 mm steps; some large micrometers have interchangeable anvils to allow a range of measurements to be taken. Generally the largest precision measurement you are likely to take on a motorcycle is the piston diameter.

● Internal micrometers (or bore micrometers) are used for measuring inside diameters, such as valve guides and cylinder bores. Telescoping gauges and small hole gauges are used in conjunction with an external micrometer, whereas the more expensive internal micrometers have their own measuring device.

External micrometer

Note: *The conventional analogue type instrument is described. Although much easier to read, digital micrometers are considerably more expensive.*

● Always check the calibration of the micrometer before use. With the anvils closed (0 to 25 mm type) or set over a test gauge (for the larger types) the scale should read zero **(see illustration 3.2)**; make sure that the anvils (and test piece) are clean first. Any discrepancy can be adjusted by referring to the instructions supplied with the tool. Remember that the micrometer is a precision measuring tool - don't force the anvils closed, use the ratchet (4) on the end of the micrometer to close it. In this way, a measured force is always applied.

● To use, first make sure that the item being measured is clean. Place the anvil of the micrometer (1) against the item and use the thimble (2) to bring the spindle (3) lightly into contact with the other side of the item **(see illustration 3.3)**. Don't tighten the thimble down because this will damage the micrometer - instead use the ratchet (4) on the end of the micrometer. The ratchet mechanism applies a measured force preventing damage to the instrument.

● The micrometer is read by referring to the linear scale on the sleeve and the annular scale on the thimble. Read off the sleeve first to obtain the base measurement, then add the fine measurement from the thimble to obtain the overall reading. The linear scale on the sleeve represents the measuring range of the micrometer (eg 0 to 25 mm). The annular scale

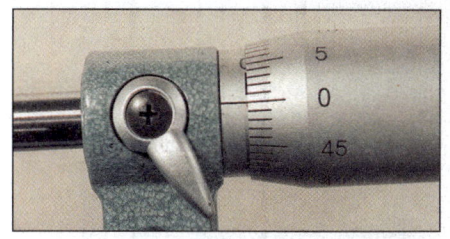

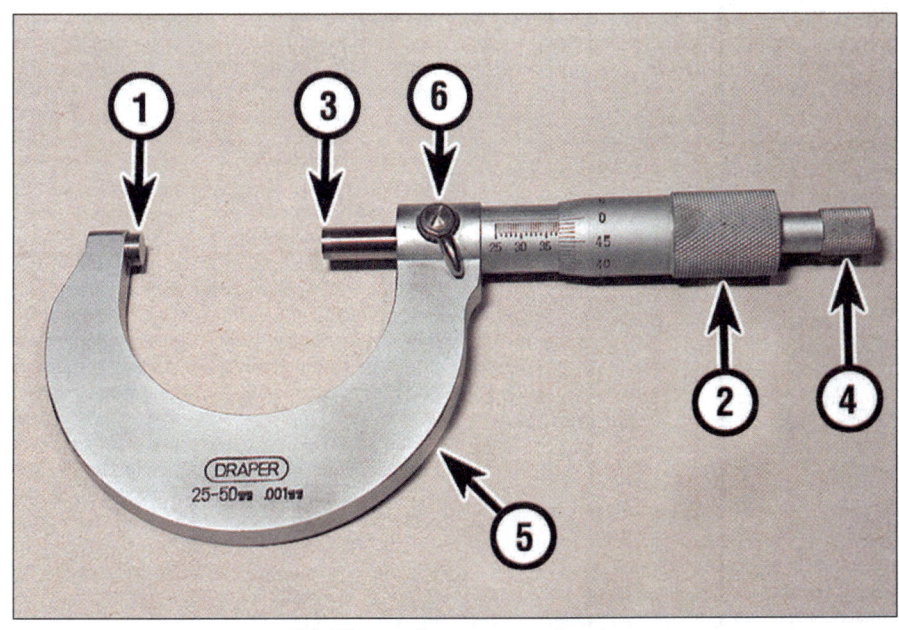

3.2 Check micrometer calibration before use

3.3 Micrometer component parts

1 Anvil
2 Thimble
3 Spindle
4 Ratchet
5 Frame
6 Locking lever

REF•10 Tools and Workshop Tips

on the thimble will be in graduations of 0.01 mm (or as marked on the frame) - one full revolution of the thimble will move 0.5 mm on the linear scale. Take the reading where the datum line on the sleeve intersects the thimble's scale. Always position the eye directly above the scale otherwise an inaccurate reading will result.

In the example shown the item measures 2.95 mm **(see illustration 3.4)**:

Linear scale	2.00 mm
Linear scale	0.50 mm
Annular scale	0.45 mm
Total figure	**2.95 mm**

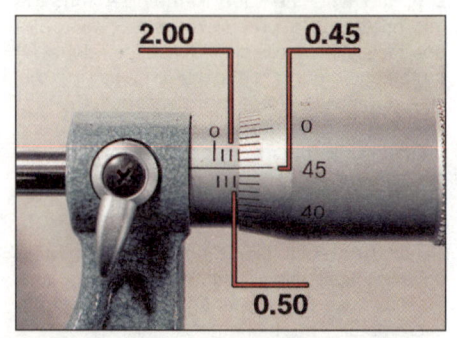

3.4 Micrometer reading of 2.95 mm

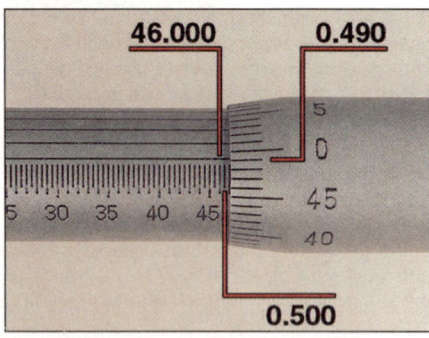

3.5 Micrometer reading of 46.99 mm on linear and annular scales . . .

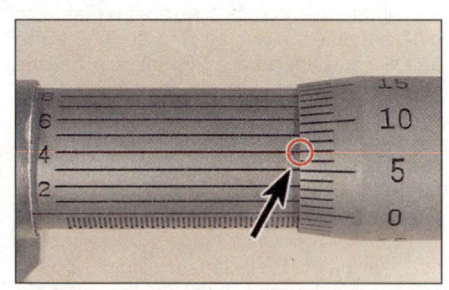

3.6 . . . and 0.004 mm on vernier scale

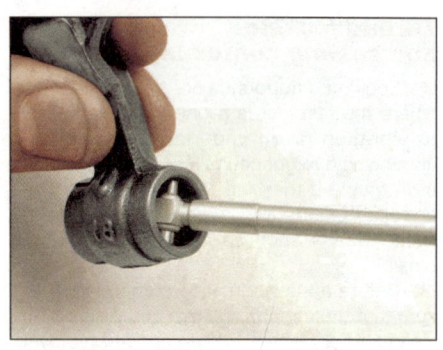

3.7 Expand the telescoping gauge in the bore, lock its position . . .

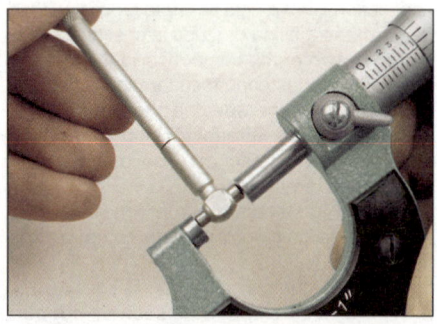

3.8 . . . then measure the gauge with a micrometer

3.9 Expand the small hole gauge in the bore, lock its position . . .

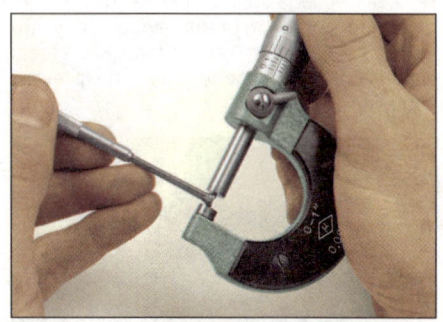

3.10 . . . then measure the gauge with a micrometer

Most micrometers have a locking lever (6) on the frame to hold the setting in place, allowing the item to be removed from the micrometer.

● Some micrometers have a vernier scale on their sleeve, providing an even finer measurement to be taken, in 0.001 increments of a millimetre. Take the sleeve and thimble measurement as described above, then check which graduation on the vernier scale aligns with that of the annular scale on the thimble **Note:** *The eye must be perpendicular to the scale when taking the vernier reading - if necessary rotate the body of the micrometer to ensure this.* Multiply the vernier scale figure by 0.001 and add it to the base and fine measurement figures.

In the example shown the item measures 46.994 mm **(see illustrations 3.5 and 3.6)**:

Linear scale (base)	46.000 mm
Linear scale (base)	00.500 mm
Annular scale (fine)	00.490 mm
Vernier scale	00.004 mm
Total figure	**46.994 mm**

Internal micrometer

● Internal micrometers are available for measuring bore diameters, but are expensive and unlikely to be available for home use. It is suggested that a set of telescoping gauges and small hole gauges, both of which must be used with an external micrometer, will suffice for taking internal measurements on a motorcycle.

● Telescoping gauges can be used to measure internal diameters of components. Select a gauge with the correct size range, make sure its ends are clean and insert it into the bore. Expand the gauge, then lock its position and withdraw it from the bore **(see illustration 3.7)**. Measure across the gauge ends with a micrometer **(see illustration 3.8)**.

● Very small diameter bores (such as valve guides) are measured with a small hole gauge. Once adjusted to a slip-fit inside the component, its position is locked and the gauge withdrawn for measurement with a micrometer **(see illustrations 3.9 and 3.10)**.

Vernier caliper

Note: *The conventional linear and dial gauge type instruments are described. Digital types are easier to read, but are far more expensive.*

● The vernier caliper does not provide the precision of a micrometer, but is versatile in being able to measure internal and external diameters. Some types also incorporate a depth gauge. It is ideal for measuring clutch plate friction material and spring free lengths.

● To use the conventional linear scale vernier, slacken off the vernier clamp screws (1) and set its jaws over (2), or inside (3), the item to be measured **(see illustration 3.11)**. Slide the jaw into contact, using the thumb-wheel (4) for fine movement of the sliding scale (5) then tighten the clamp screws (1). Read off the main scale (6) where the zero on the sliding scale (5) intersects it, taking the whole number to the left of the zero; this provides the base measurement. View along the sliding scale and select the division which lines up exactly with any of the divisions on the main scale, noting that the divisions usually represents 0.02 of a millimetre. Add this fine measurement to the base measurement to obtain the total reading.

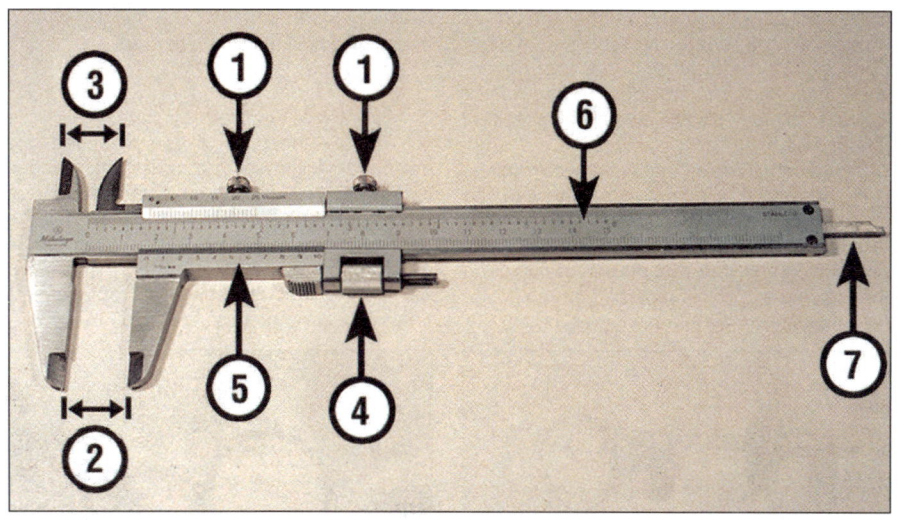

Tools and Workshop Tips REF•11

3.11 Vernier component parts (linear gauge)

1 Clamp screws
2 External jaws
3 Internal jaws
4 Thumbwheel
5 Sliding scale
6 Main scale
7 Depth gauge

In the example shown the item measures 55.92 mm **(see illustration 3.12)**:

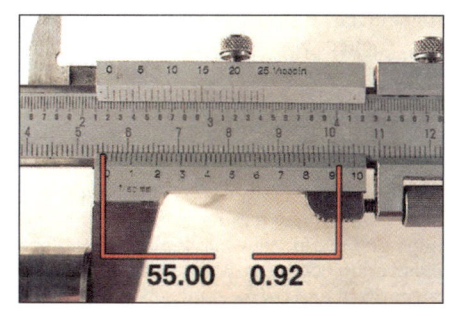

Base measurement	55.00 mm
Fine measurement	00.92 mm
Total figure	**55.92 mm**

3.12 Vernier gauge reading of 55.92 mm

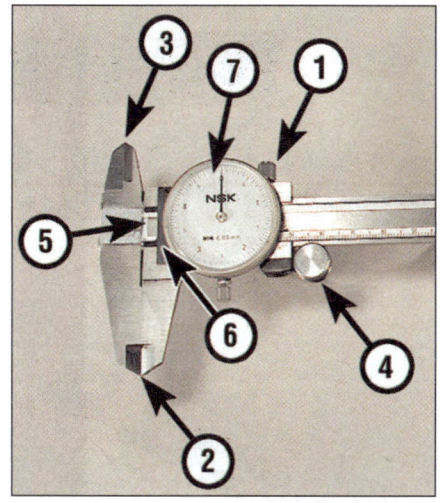

- Some vernier calipers are equipped with a dial gauge for fine measurement. Before use, check that the jaws are clean, then close them fully and check that the dial gauge reads zero. If necessary adjust the gauge ring accordingly. Slacken the vernier clamp screw (1) and set its jaws over (2), or inside (3), the item to be measured **(see illustration 3.13)**. Slide the jaws into contact, using the thumbwheel (4) for fine movement. Read off the main scale (5) where the edge of the sliding scale (6) intersects it, taking the whole number to the left of the zero; this provides the base measurement. Read off the needle position on the dial gauge (7) scale to provide the fine measurement; each division represents 0.05 of a millimetre. Add this fine measurement to the base measurement to obtain the total reading.

In the example shown the item measures 55.95 mm **(see illustration 3.14)**:

Base measurement	55.00 mm
Fine measurement	00.95 mm
Total figure	**55.95 mm**

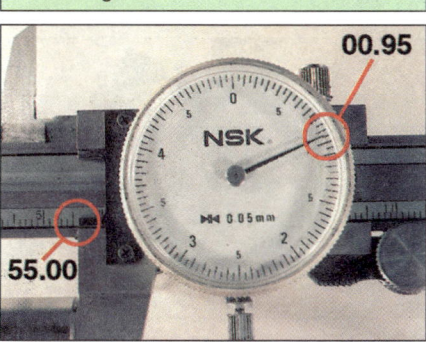

3.13 Vernier component parts (dial gauge)

1 Clamp screw
2 External jaws
3 Internal jaws
4 Thumbwheel
5 Main scale
6 Sliding scale
7 Dial gauge

3.14 Vernier gauge reading of 55.95 mm

Plastigauge

- Plastigauge is a plastic material which can be compressed between two surfaces to measure the oil clearance between them. The width of the compressed Plastigauge is measured against a calibrated scale to determine the clearance.

- Common uses of Plastigauge are for measuring the clearance between crankshaft journal and main bearing inserts, between crankshaft journal and big-end bearing inserts, and between camshaft and bearing surfaces. The following example describes big-end oil clearance measurement.

- Handle the Plastigauge material carefully to prevent distortion. Using a sharp knife, cut a length which corresponds with the width of the bearing being measured and place it carefully across the journal so that it is parallel with the shaft **(see illustration 3.15)**. Carefully install both bearing shells and the connecting rod. Without rotating the rod on the journal tighten its bolts or nuts (as applicable) to the specified torque. The connecting rod and bearings are then disassembled and the crushed Plastigauge examined.

3.15 Plastigauge placed across shaft journal

- Using the scale provided in the Plastigauge kit, measure the width of the material to determine the oil clearance **(see illustration 3.16)**. Always remove all traces of Plastigauge after use using your fingernails.

Caution: Arriving at the correct clearance demands that the assembly is torqued correctly, according to the settings and sequence (where applicable) provided by the motorcycle manufacturer.

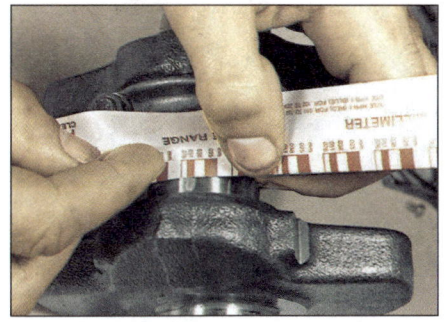

3.16 Measuring the width of the crushed Plastigauge

Tools and Workshop Tips

Dial gauge or DTI (Dial Test Indicator)

● A dial gauge can be used to accurately measure small amounts of movement. Typical uses are measuring shaft runout or shaft endfloat (sideplay) and setting piston position for ignition timing on two-strokes. A dial gauge set usually comes with a range of different probes and adapters and mounting equipment.

● The gauge needle must point to zero when at rest. Rotate the ring around its periphery to zero the gauge.

● Check that the gauge is capable of reading the extent of movement in the work. Most gauges have a small dial set in the face which records whole millimetres of movement as well as the fine scale around the face periphery which is calibrated in 0.01 mm divisions. Read off the small dial first to obtain the base measurement, then add the measurement from the fine scale to obtain the total reading.

In the example shown the gauge reads 1.48 mm (see illustration 3.17):

Base measurement	1.00 mm
Fine measurement	0.48 mm
Total figure	**1.48 mm**

3.17 Dial gauge reading of 1.48 mm

● If measuring shaft runout, the shaft must be supported in vee-blocks and the gauge mounted on a stand perpendicular to the shaft. Rest the tip of the gauge against the centre of the shaft and rotate the shaft slowly whilst watching the gauge reading **(see illustration 3.18)**. Take several measurements along the length of the shaft and record the maximum gauge reading as the amount of runout in the shaft. **Note:** *The reading obtained will be total runout at that point - some manufacturers specify that the runout figure is halved to compare with their specified runout limit.*

● Endfloat (sideplay) measurement requires that the gauge is mounted securely to the surrounding component with its probe touching the end of the shaft. Using hand pressure, push and pull on the shaft noting the maximum endfloat recorded on the gauge **(see illustration 3.19)**.

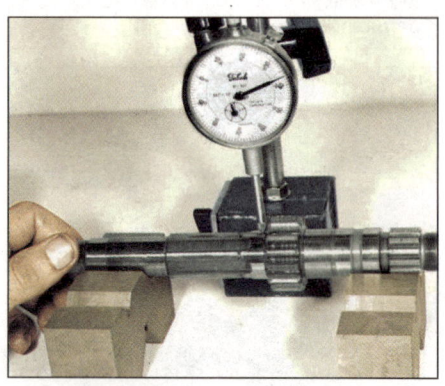

3.18 Using a dial gauge to measure shaft runout

3.19 Using a dial gauge to measure shaft endfloat

● A dial gauge with suitable adapters can be used to determine piston position BTDC on two-stroke engines for the purposes of ignition timing. The gauge, adapter and suitable length probe are installed in the place of the spark plug and the gauge zeroed at TDC. If the piston position is specified as 1.14 mm BTDC, rotate the engine back to 2.00 mm BTDC, then slowly forwards to 1.14 mm BTDC.

Cylinder compression gauges

● A compression gauge is used for measuring cylinder compression. Either the rubber-cone type or the threaded adapter type can be used. The latter is preferred to ensure a perfect seal against the cylinder head. A 0 to 300 psi (0 to 20 Bar) type gauge (for petrol/gasoline engines) will be suitable for motorcycles.

● The spark plug is removed and the gauge either held hard against the cylinder head (cone type) or the gauge adapter screwed into the cylinder head (threaded type) **(see illustration 3.20)**. Cylinder compression is measured with the engine turning over, but not running - carry out the compression test as described in *Fault Finding Equipment*. The gauge will hold the reading until manually released.

3.20 Using a rubber-cone type cylinder compression gauge

Oil pressure gauge

● An oil pressure gauge is used for measuring engine oil pressure. Most gauges come with a set of adapters to fit the thread of the take-off point **(see illustration 3.21)**. If the take-off point specified by the motorcycle manufacturer is an external oil pipe union, make sure that the specified replacement union is used to prevent oil starvation.

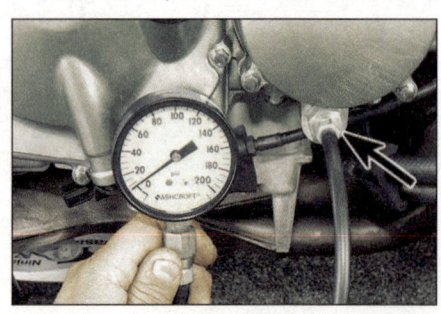

3.21 Oil pressure gauge and take-off point adapter (arrow)

● Oil pressure is measured with the engine running (at a specific rpm) and often the manufacturer will specify pressure limits for a cold and hot engine.

Straight-edge and surface plate

● If checking the gasket face of a component for warpage, place a steel rule or precision straight-edge across the gasket face and measure any gap between the straight-edge and component with feeler gauges **(see illustration 3.22)**. Check diagonally across the component and between mounting holes **(see illustration 3.23)**.

3.22 Use a straight-edge and feeler gauges to check for warpage

3.23 Check for warpage in these directions

Tools and Workshop Tips

- Checking individual components for warpage, such as clutch plain (metal) plates, requires a perfectly flat plate or piece or plate glass and feeler gauges.

4 Torque and leverage

What is torque?

- Torque describes the twisting force about a shaft. The amount of torque applied is determined by the distance from the centre of the shaft to the end of the lever and the amount of force being applied to the end of the lever; distance multiplied by force equals torque.
- The manufacturer applies a measured torque to a bolt or nut to ensure that it will not slacken in use and to hold two components securely together without movement in the joint. The actual torque setting depends on the thread size, bolt or nut material and the composition of the components being held.
- Too little torque may cause the fastener to loosen due to vibration, whereas too much torque will distort the joint faces of the component or cause the fastener to shear off. Always stick to the specified torque setting.

Using a torque wrench

- Check the calibration of the torque wrench and make sure it has a suitable range for the job. Torque wrenches are available in Nm (Newton-metres), kgf m (kilograms-force metre), lbf ft (pounds-feet), lbf in (inch-pounds). Do not confuse lbf ft with lbf in.
- Adjust the tool to the desired torque on the scale (see illustration 4.1). If your torque wrench is not calibrated in the units specified, carefully convert the figure (see Conversion Factors). A manufacturer sometimes gives a torque setting as a range (8 to 10 Nm) rather than a single figure - in this case set the tool midway between the two settings. The same torque may be expressed as 9 Nm ± 1 Nm. Some torque wrenches have a method of locking the setting so that it isn't inadvertently altered during use.

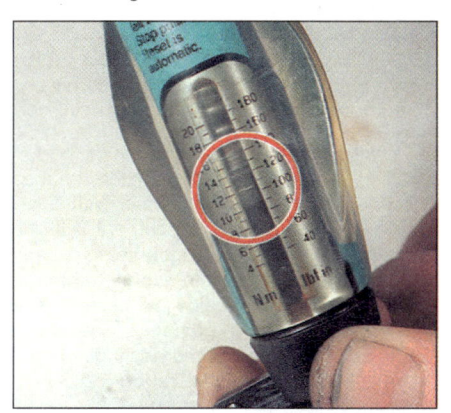

- Install the bolts/nuts in their correct location and secure them lightly. Their threads must be clean and free of any old locking compound. Unless specified the threads and flange should be dry - oiled threads are necessary in certain circumstances and the manufacturer will take this into account in the specified torque figure. Similarly, the manufacturer may also specify the application of thread-locking compound.
- Tighten the fasteners in the specified sequence until the torque wrench clicks, indicating that the torque setting has been reached. Apply the torque again to double-check the setting. Where different thread diameter fasteners secure the component, as a rule tighten the larger diameter ones first.
- When the torque wrench has been finished with, release the lock (where applicable) and fully back off its setting to zero - do not leave the torque wrench tensioned. Also, do not use a torque wrench for slackening a fastener.

Angle-tightening

- Manufacturers often specify a figure in degrees for final tightening of a fastener. This usually follows tightening to a specific torque setting.
- A degree disc can be set and attached to the socket (see illustration 4.2) or a protractor can be used to mark the angle of movement on the bolt/nut head and the surrounding casting (see illustration 4.3).

4.2 Angle tightening can be accomplished with a torque-angle gauge . . .

4.1 Set the torque wrench index mark to the setting required, in this case 12 Nm

4.3 . . . or by marking the angle on the surrounding component

Loosening sequences

- Where more than one bolt/nut secures a component, loosen each fastener evenly a little at a time. In this way, not all the stress of the joint is held by one fastener and the components are not likely to distort.
- If a tightening sequence is provided, work in the REVERSE of this, but if not, work from the outside in, in a criss-cross sequence (see illustration 4.4).

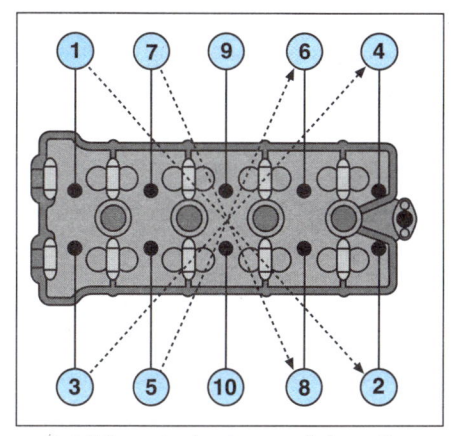

4.4 When slackening, work from the outside inwards

Tightening sequences

- If a component is held by more than one fastener it is important that the retaining bolts/nuts are tightened evenly to prevent uneven stress build-up and distortion of sealing faces. This is especially important on high-compression joints such as the cylinder head.
- A sequence is usually provided by the manufacturer, either in a diagram or actually marked in the casting. If not, always start in the centre and work outwards in a criss-cross pattern (see illustration 4.5). Start off by securing all bolts/nuts finger-tight, then set the torque wrench and tighten each fastener by a small amount in sequence until the final torque is reached. By following this practice,

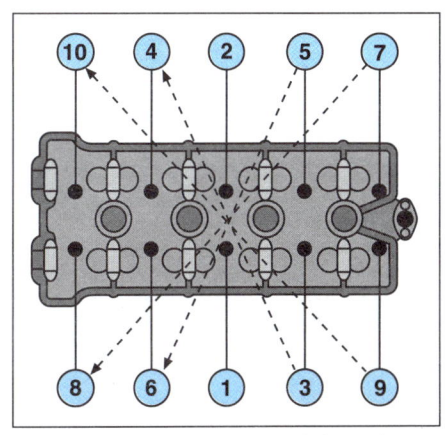

4.5 When tightening, work from the inside outwards

Tools and Workshop Tips

the joint will be held evenly and will not be distorted. Important joints, such as the cylinder head and big-end fasteners often have two- or three-stage torque settings.

Applying leverage

● Use tools at the correct angle. Position a socket wrench or spanner on the bolt/nut so that you pull it towards you when loosening. If this can't be done, push the spanner without curling your fingers around it (see illustration 4.6) - the spanner may slip or the fastener loosen suddenly, resulting in your fingers being crushed against a component.

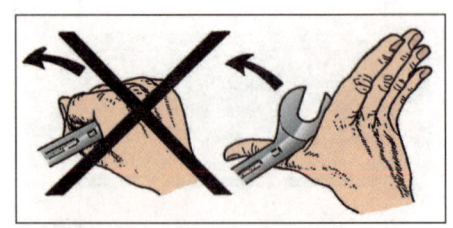

4.6 If you can't pull on the spanner to loosen a fastener, push with your hand open

● Additional leverage is gained by extending the length of the lever. The best way to do this is to use a breaker bar instead of the regular length tool, or to slip a length of tubing over the end of the spanner or socket wrench.
● If additional leverage will not work, the fastener head is either damaged or firmly corroded in place (see Fasteners).

5 Bearings

Bearing removal and installation

Drivers and sockets

● Before removing a bearing, always inspect the casing to see which way it must be driven out - some casings will have retaining plates or a cast step. Also check for any identifying markings on the bearing and if installed to a certain depth, measure this at this stage. Some roller bearings are sealed on one side - take note of the original fitted position.
● Bearings can be driven out of a casing using a bearing driver tool (with the correct size head) or a socket of the correct diameter. Select the driver head or socket so that it contacts the outer race of the bearing, not the balls/rollers or inner race. Always support the casing around the bearing housing with wood blocks, otherwise there is a risk of fracture. The bearing is driven out with a few blows on the driver or socket from a heavy mallet. Unless access is severely restricted (as with wheel bearings), a pin-punch is not recommended unless it is moved around the bearing to keep it square in its housing.

● The same equipment can be used to install bearings. Make sure the bearing housing is supported on wood blocks and line up the bearing in its housing. Fit the bearing as noted on removal - generally they are installed with their marked side facing outwards. Tap the bearing squarely into its housing using a driver or socket which bears only on the bearing's outer race - contact with the bearing balls/rollers or inner race will destroy it (see illustrations 5.1 and 5.2).
● Check that the bearing inner race and balls/rollers rotate freely.

5.1 Using a bearing driver against the bearing's outer race

5.2 Using a large socket against the bearing's outer race

Pullers and slide-hammers

● Where a bearing is pressed on a shaft a puller will be required to extract it (see illustration 5.3). Make sure that the puller clamp or legs fit securely behind the bearing and are unlikely to slip out. If pulling a bearing

5.3 This bearing puller clamps behind the bearing and pressure is applied to the shaft end to draw the bearing off

off a gear shaft for example, you may have to locate the puller behind a gear pinion if there is no access to the race and draw the gear pinion off the shaft as well (see illustration 5.4).

Caution: Ensure that the puller's centre bolt locates securely against the end of the shaft and will not slip when pressure is applied. Also ensure that puller does not damage the shaft end.

5.4 Where no access is available to the rear of the bearing, it is sometimes possible to draw off the adjacent component

● Operate the puller so that its centre bolt exerts pressure on the shaft end and draws the bearing off the shaft.
● When installing the bearing on the shaft, tap only on the bearing's inner race - contact with the balls/rollers or outer race with destroy the bearing. Use a socket or length of tubing as a drift which fits over the shaft end (see illustration 5.5).

5.5 When installing a bearing on a shaft use a piece of tubing which bears only on the bearing's inner race

● Where a bearing locates in a blind hole in a casing, it cannot be driven or pulled out as described above. A slide-hammer with knife-edged bearing puller attachment will be required. The puller attachment passes through the bearing and when tightened expands to fit firmly behind the bearing (see illustration 5.6). By operating the slide-hammer part of the tool the bearing is jarred out of its housing (see illustration 5.7).
● It is possible, if the bearing is of reasonable weight, for it to drop out of its housing if the casing is heated as described opposite. If this

Tools and Workshop Tips REF•15

5.6 Expand the bearing puller so that it locks behind the bearing . . .

5.7 . . . attach the slide hammer to the bearing puller

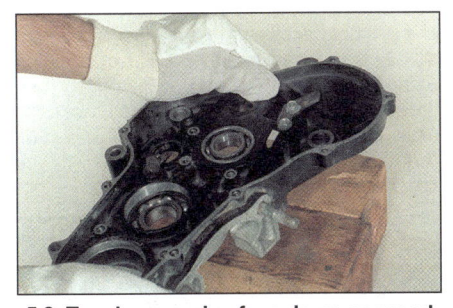

5.8 Tapping a casing face down on wood blocks can often dislodge a bearing

● Bearings can be installed in blind holes using the driver or socket method described above.

Drawbolts

● Where a bearing or bush is set in the eye of a component, such as a suspension linkage arm or connecting rod small-end, removal by drift may damage the component. Furthermore, a rubber bushing in a shock absorber eye cannot successfully be driven out of position. If access is available to a engineering press, the task is straightforward. If not, a drawbolt can be fabricated to extract the bearing or bush.

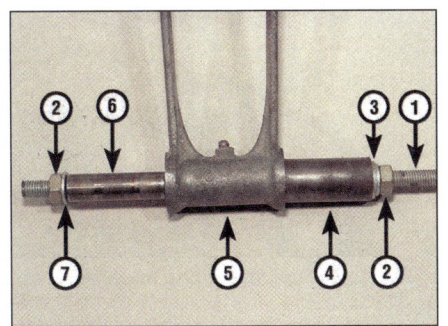

5.9 Drawbolt component parts assembled on a suspension arm

1. Bolt or length of threaded bar
2. Nuts
3. Washer (external diameter greater than tubing internal diameter)
4. Tubing (internal diameter sufficient to accommodate bearing)
5. Suspension arm with bearing
6. Tubing (external diameter slightly smaller than bearing)
7. Washer (external diameter slightly smaller than bearing)

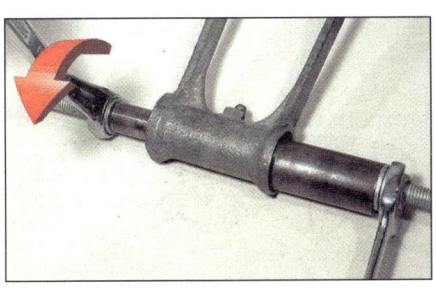

5.10 Drawing the bearing out of the suspension arm

● To extract the bearing/bush you will need a long bolt with nut (or piece of threaded bar with two nuts), a piece of tubing which has an internal diameter larger than the bearing/bush, another piece of tubing which has an external diameter slightly smaller than the bearing/bush, and a selection of washers **(see illustrations 5.9 and 5.10)**. Note that the pieces of tubing must be of the same length, or longer, than the bearing/bush.

● The same kit (without the pieces of tubing) can be used to draw the new bearing/bush back into place **(see illustration 5.11)**.

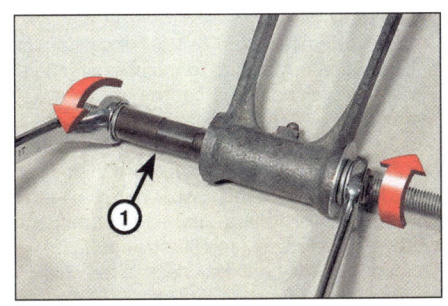

5.11 Installing a new bearing (1) in the suspension arm

Temperature change

● If the bearing's outer race is a tight fit in the casing, the aluminium casing can be heated to release its grip on the bearing. Aluminium will expand at a greater rate than the steel bearing outer race. There are several ways to do this, but avoid any localised extreme heat (such as a blow torch) - aluminium alloy has a low melting point.

● Approved methods of heating a casing are using a domestic oven (heated to 100°C) or immersing the casing in boiling water **(see illustration 5.12)**. Low temperature range localised heat sources such as a paint stripper heat gun or clothes iron can also be used **(see illustration 5.13)**. Alternatively, soak a rag in boiling water, wring it out and wrap it around the bearing housing.

> ⚠ **Warning: All of these methods require care in use to prevent scalding and burns to the hands. Wear protective gloves when handling hot components.**

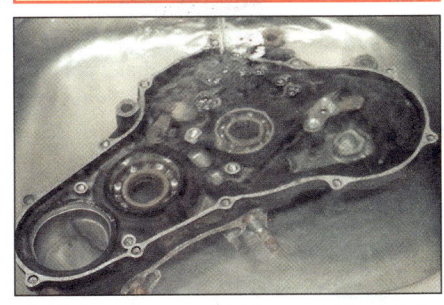

5.12 A casing can be immersed in a sink of boiling water to aid bearing removal

5.13 Using a localised heat source to aid bearing removal

● If heating the whole casing note that plastic components, such as the neutral switch, may suffer - remove them beforehand.

● After heating, remove the bearing as described above. You may find that the expansion is sufficient for the bearing to fall out of the casing under its own weight or with a light tap on the driver or socket.

● If necessary, the casing can be heated to aid bearing installation, and this is sometimes the recommended procedure if the motorcycle manufacturer has designed the housing and bearing fit with this intention.

method is attempted, first prepare a work surface which will enable the casing to be tapped face down to help dislodge the bearing - a wood surface is ideal since it will not damage the casing's gasket surface. Wearing protective gloves, tap the heated casing several times against the work surface to dislodge the bearing under its own weight **(see illustration 5.8)**.

REF•16 Tools and Workshop Tips

- Installation of bearings can be eased by placing them in a freezer the night before installation. The steel bearing will contract slightly, allowing easy insertion in its housing. This is often useful when installing steering head outer races in the frame.

Bearing types and markings

- Plain shell bearings, ball bearings, needle roller bearings and tapered roller bearings will all be found on motorcycles (see illustrations 5.14 and 5.15). The ball and roller types are usually caged between an inner and outer race, but uncaged variations may be found.

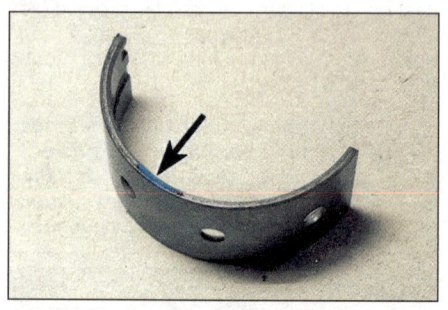

5.14 Shell bearings are either plain or grooved. They are usually identified by colour code (arrow)

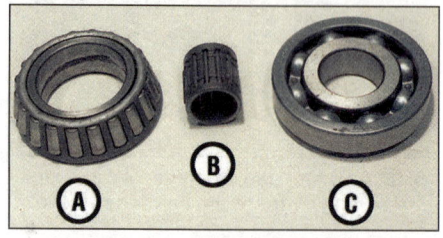

5.15 Tapered roller bearing (A), needle roller bearing (B) and ball journal bearing (C)

- Shell bearings (often called inserts) are usually found at the crankshaft main and connecting rod big-end where they are good at coping with high loads. They are made of a phosphor-bronze material and are impregnated with self-lubricating properties.
- Ball bearings and needle roller bearings consist of a steel inner and outer race with the balls or rollers between the races. They require constant lubrication by oil or grease and are good at coping with axial loads. Taper roller bearings consist of rollers set in a tapered cage set on the inner race; the outer race is separate. They are good at coping with axial loads and prevent movement along the shaft - a typical application is in the steering head.
- Bearing manufacturers produce bearings to ISO size standards and stamp one face of the bearing to indicate its internal and external diameter, load capacity and type (see illustration 5.16).
- Metal bushes are usually of phosphor-bronze material. Rubber bushes are used in suspension mounting eyes. Fibre bushes have also been used in suspension pivots.

5.16 Typical bearing marking

Bearing fault finding

- If a bearing outer race has spun in its housing, the housing material will be damaged. You can use a bearing locking compound to bond the outer race in place if damage is not too severe.
- Shell bearings will fail due to damage of their working surface, as a result of lack of lubrication, corrosion or abrasive particles in the oil (see illustration 5.17). Small particles of dirt in the oil may embed in the bearing material whereas larger particles will score the bearing and shaft journal. If a number of short journeys are made, insufficient heat will be generated to drive off condensation which has built up on the bearings.

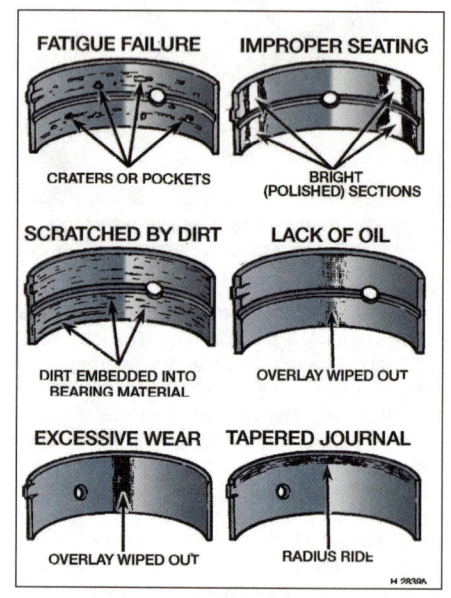

5.17 Typical bearing failures

- Ball and roller bearings will fail due to lack of lubrication or damage to the balls or rollers. Tapered-roller bearings can be damaged by overloading them. Unless the bearing is sealed on both sides, wash it in paraffin (kerosene) to remove all old grease then allow it to dry. Make a visual inspection looking to dented balls or rollers, damaged cages and worn or pitted races (see illustration 5.18).
- A ball bearing can be checked for wear by listening to it when spun. Apply a film of light oil to the bearing and hold it close to the ear - hold the outer race with one hand and spin the inner race with the other hand (see illustration 5.19). The bearing should be almost silent when spun; if it grates or rattles it is worn.

5.18 Example of ball journal bearing with damaged balls and cages

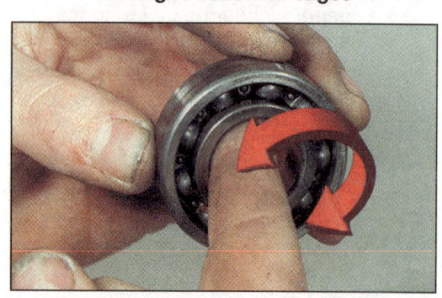

5.19 Hold outer race and listen to inner race when spun

6 Oil seals

Oil seal removal and installation

- Oil seals should be renewed every time a component is dismantled. This is because the seal lips will become set to the sealing surface and will not necessarily reseal.
- Oil seals can be prised out of position using a large flat-bladed screwdriver (see illustration 6.1). In the case of crankcase seals, check first that the seal is not lipped on the inside, preventing its removal with the crankcases joined.

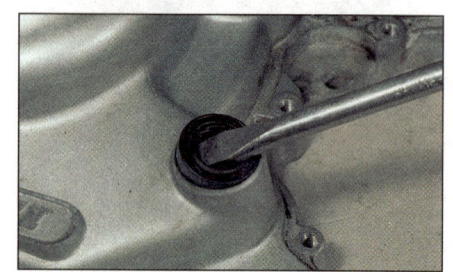

6.1 Prise out oil seals with a large flat-bladed screwdriver

- New seals are usually installed with their marked face (containing the seal reference code) outwards and the spring side towards the fluid being retained. In certain cases, such as a two-stroke engine crankshaft seal, a double lipped seal may be used due to there being fluid or gas on each side of the joint.

Tools and Workshop Tips　REF•17

- Use a bearing driver or socket which bears only on the outer hard edge of the seal to install it in the casing - tapping on the inner edge will damage the sealing lip.

Oil seal types and markings

- Oil seals are usually of the single-lipped type. Double-lipped seals are found where a liquid or gas is on both sides of the joint.
- Oil seals can harden and lose their sealing ability if the motorcycle has been in storage for a long period - renewal is the only solution.
- Oil seal manufacturers also conform to the ISO markings for seal size - these are moulded into the outer face of the seal **(see illustration 6.2)**.

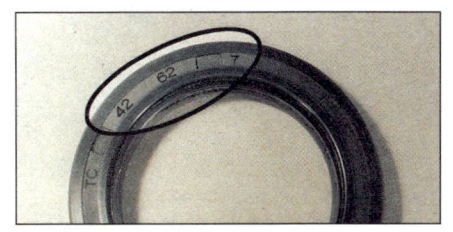

6.2 These oil seal markings indicate inside diameter, outside diameter and seal thickness

7　Gaskets and sealants

Types of gasket and sealant

- Gaskets are used to seal the mating surfaces between components and keep lubricants, fluids, vacuum or pressure contained within the assembly. Aluminium gaskets are sometimes found at the cylinder joints, but most gaskets are paper-based. If the mating surfaces of the components being joined are undamaged the gasket can be installed dry, although a dab of sealant or grease will be useful to hold it in place during assembly.
- RTV (Room Temperature Vulcanising) silicone rubber sealants cure when exposed to moisture in the atmosphere. These sealants are good at filling pits or irregular gasket faces, but will tend to be forced out of the joint under very high torque. They can be used to replace a paper gasket, but first make sure that the width of the paper gasket is not essential to the shimming of internal components. RTV sealants should not be used on components containing petrol (gasoline).
- Non-hardening, semi-hardening and hard setting liquid gasket compounds can be used with a gasket or between a metal-to-metal joint. Select the sealant to suit the application: universal non-hardening sealant can be used on virtually all joints; semi-hardening on joint faces which are rough or damaged; hard setting sealant on joints which require a permanent bond and are subjected to high temperature and pressure. **Note:** *Check first if the paper gasket has a bead of sealant impregnated in its surface before applying additional sealant.*
- When choosing a sealant, make sure it is suitable for the application, particularly if being applied in a high-temperature area or in the vicinity of fuel. Certain manufacturers produce sealants in either clear, silver or black colours to match the finish of the engine. This has a particular application on motorcycles where much of the engine is exposed.
- Do not over-apply sealant. That which is squeezed out on the outside of the joint can be wiped off, whereas an excess of sealant on the inside can break off and clog oilways.

Breaking a sealed joint

- Age, heat, pressure and the use of hard setting sealant can cause two components to stick together so tightly that they are difficult to separate using finger pressure alone. Do not resort to using levers unless there is a pry point provided for this purpose **(see illustration 7.1)** or else the gasket surfaces will be damaged.
- Use a soft-faced hammer **(see illustration 7.2)** or a wood block and conventional hammer to strike the component near the mating surface. Avoid hammering against cast extremities since they may break off. If this method fails, try using a wood wedge between the two components.

Caution: If the joint will not separate, double-check that you have removed all the fasteners.

7.1 If a pry point is provided, apply gently pressure with a flat-bladed screwdriver

7.2 Tap around the joint with a soft-faced mallet if necessary - don't strike cooling fins

Removal of old gasket and sealant

- Paper gaskets will most likely come away complete, leaving only a few traces stuck on

HAYNES HiNT

Most components have one or two hollow locating dowels between the two gasket faces. If a dowel cannot be removed, do not resort to gripping it with pliers - it will almost certainly be distorted. Install a close-fitting socket or Phillips screwdriver into the dowel and then grip the outer edge of the dowel to free it.

the sealing faces of the components. It is imperative that all traces are removed to ensure correct sealing of the new gasket.

- Very carefully scrape all traces of gasket away making sure that the sealing surfaces are not gouged or scored by the scraper **(see illustrations 7.3, 7.4 and 7.5)**. Stubborn deposits can be removed by spraying with an aerosol gasket remover. Final preparation of

7.3 Paper gaskets can be scraped off with a gasket scraper tool . . .

7.4 . . . a knife blade . . .

7.5 . . . or a household scraper

REF•18 Tools and Workshop Tips

7.6 Fine abrasive paper is wrapped around a flat file to clean up the gasket face

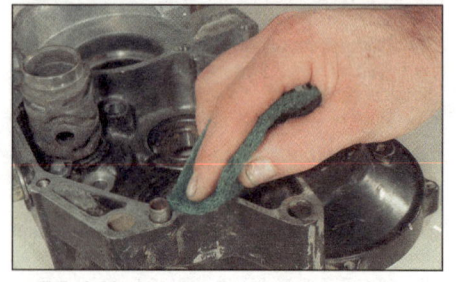

7.7 A kitchen scourer can be used on stubborn deposits

8.1 Tighten the chain breaker to push the pin out of the link . . .

8.2 . . . withdraw the pin, remove the tool . . .

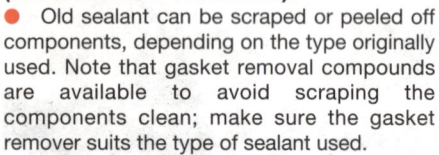

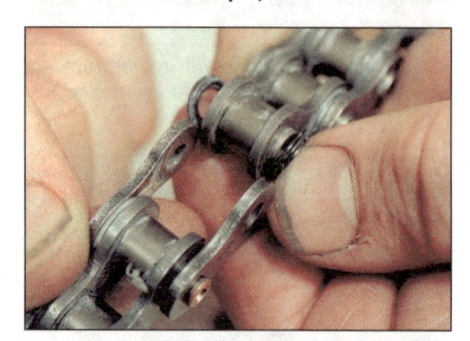

8.3 . . . and separate the chain link

8.4 Insert the new soft link, with O-rings, through the chain ends . . .

8.5 . . . install the O-rings over the pin ends . . .

8.6 . . . followed by the sideplate

8.7 Push the sideplate into position using a clamp

the gasket surface can be made with very fine abrasive paper or a plastic kitchen scourer **(see illustrations 7.6 and 7.7)**.

● Old sealant can be scraped or peeled off components, depending on the type originally used. Note that gasket removal compounds are available to avoid scraping the components clean; make sure the gasket remover suits the type of sealant used.

8 Chains

Breaking and joining final drive chains

● Drive chains for all but small bikes are continuous and do not have a clip-type connecting link. The chain must be broken using a chain breaker tool and the new chain securely riveted together using a new soft rivet-type link. Never use a clip-type connecting link instead of a rivet-type link, except in an emergency. Various chain breaking and riveting tools are available, either as separate tools or combined as illustrated in the accompanying photographs - read the instructions supplied with the tool carefully.

> ⚠ **Warning: The need to rivet the new link pins correctly cannot be overstressed - loss of control of the motorcycle is very likely to result if the chain breaks in use.**

● Rotate the chain and look for the soft link. The soft link pins look like they have been deeply centre-punched instead of peened over like all the other pins **(see illustration 8.9)** and its sideplate may be a different colour. Position the soft link midway between the sprockets and assemble the chain breaker tool over one of the soft link pins **(see illustration 8.1)**. Operate the tool to push the pin out through the chain **(see illustration 8.2)**. On an O-ring chain, remove the O-rings **(see illustration 8.3)**. Carry out the same procedure on the other soft link pin.

> *Caution: Certain soft link pins (particularly on the larger chains) may require their ends to be filed or ground off before they can be pressed out using the tool.*

● Check that you have the correct size and strength (standard or heavy duty) new soft link - do not reuse the old link. Look for the size marking on the chain sideplates **(see illustration 8.10)**.

● Position the chain ends so that they are engaged over the rear sprocket. On an O-ring chain, install a new O-ring over each pin of the link and insert the link through the two chain ends **(see illustration 8.4)**. Install a new O-ring over the end of each pin, followed by the sideplate (with the chain manufacturer's marking facing outwards) **(see illustrations 8.5 and 8.6)**. On an unsealed chain, insert the link through the two chain ends, then install the sideplate with the chain manufacturer's marking facing outwards.

● Note that it may not be possible to install the sideplate using finger pressure alone. If using a joining tool, assemble it so that the plates of the tool clamp the link and press the sideplate over the pins **(see illustration 8.7)**. Otherwise, use two small sockets placed over

Tools and Workshop Tips   REF•19

8.8 Assemble the chain riveting tool over one pin at a time and tighten it fully

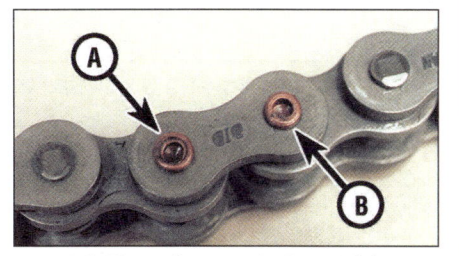

8.9 Pin end correctly riveted (A), pin end unriveted (B)

the rivet ends and two pieces of the wood between a G-clamp. Operate the clamp to press the sideplate over the pins.
● Assemble the joining tool over one pin (following the maker's instructions) and tighten the tool down to spread the pin end securely **(see illustrations 8.8 and 8.9)**. Do the same on the other pin.

> **Warning: Check that the pin ends are secure and that there is no danger of the sideplate coming loose. If the pin ends are cracked the soft link must be renewed.**

Final drive chain sizing

● Chains are sized using a three digit number, followed by a suffix to denote the chain type **(see illustration 8.10)**. Chain type is either standard or heavy duty (thicker sideplates), and also unsealed or O-ring/X-ring type.
● The first digit of the number relates to the pitch of the chain, ie the distance from the centre of one pin to the centre of the next pin **(see illustration 8.11)**. Pitch is expressed in eighths of an inch, as follows:

8.10 Typical chain size and type marking

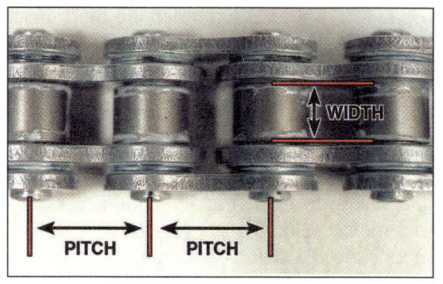

8.11 Chain dimensions

Sizes commencing with a 4 (eg 428) have a pitch of 1/2 inch (12.7 mm)

Sizes commencing with a 5 (eg 520) have a pitch of 5/8 inch (15.9 mm)

Sizes commencing with a 6 (eg 630) have a pitch of 3/4 inch (19.1 mm)

● The second and third digits of the chain size relate to the width of the rollers, again in imperial units, eg the 525 shown has 5/16 inch (7.94 mm) rollers **(see illustration 8.11)**.

9 Hoses

Clamping to prevent flow

● Small-bore flexible hoses can be clamped to prevent fluid flow whilst a component is worked on. Whichever method is used, ensure that the hose material is not permanently distorted or damaged by the clamp.
  a) A brake hose clamp available from auto accessory shops **(see illustration 9.1)**.
  b) A wingnut type hose clamp **(see illustration 9.2)**.
  c) Two sockets placed each side of the hose and held with straight-jawed self-locking grips **(see illustration 9.3)**.
  d) Thick card each side of the hose held between straight-jawed self-locking grips **(see illustration 9.4)**.

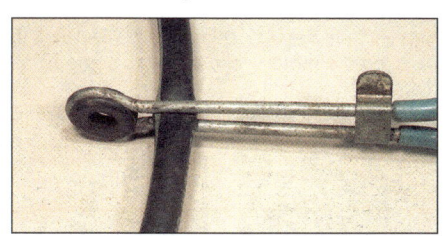

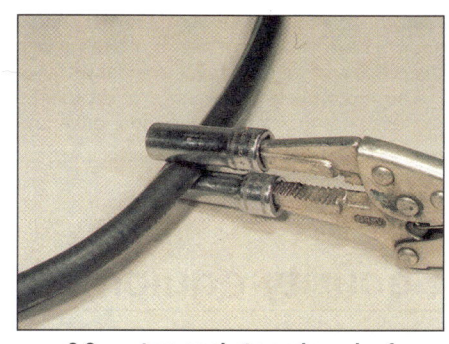

9.1 Hoses can be clamped with an automotive brake hose clamp . . .

9.2 . . . a wingnut type hose clamp . . .

9.3 . . . two sockets and a pair of self-locking grips . . .

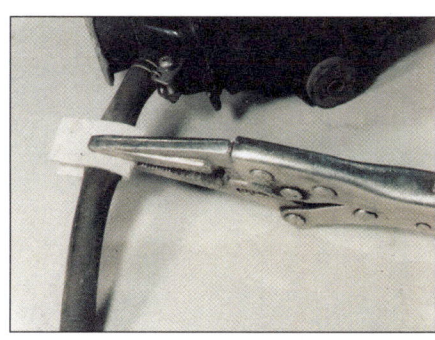

9.4 . . . or thick card and self-locking grips

Freeing and fitting hoses

● Always make sure the hose clamp is moved well clear of the hose end. Grip the hose with your hand and rotate it whilst pulling it off the union. If the hose has hardened due to age and will not move, slit it with a sharp knife and peel its ends off the union **(see illustration 9.5)**.
● Resist the temptation to use grease or soap on the unions to aid installation; although it helps the hose slip over the union it will equally aid the escape of fluid from the joint. It is preferable to soften the hose ends in hot water and wet the inside surface of the hose with water or a fluid which will evaporate.

9.5 Cutting a coolant hose free with a sharp knife

REF•20 Security

Introduction

In less time than it takes to read this introduction, a thief could steal your motorcycle. Returning only to find your bike has gone is one of the worst feelings in the world. Even if the motorcycle is insured against theft, once you've got over the initial shock, you will have the inconvenience of dealing with the police and your insurance company.

The motorcycle is an easy target for the professional thief and the joyrider alike and the official figures on motorcycle theft make for depressing reading; on average a motorcycle is stolen every 16 minutes in the UK!

Motorcycle thefts fall into two categories, those stolen 'to order' and those taken by opportunists. The thief stealing to order will be on the look out for a specific make and model and will go to extraordinary lengths to obtain that motorcycle. The opportunist thief on the other hand will look for easy targets which can be stolen with the minimum of effort and risk.

Whilst it is never going to be possible to make your machine 100% secure, it is estimated that around half of all stolen motorcycles are taken by opportunist thieves. Remember that the opportunist thief is always on the look out for the easy option: if there are two similar motorcycles parked side-by-side, they will target the one with the lowest level of security. By taking a few precautions, you can reduce the chances of your motorcycle being stolen.

Security equipment

There are many specialised motorcycle security devices available and the following text summarises their applications and their good and bad points.

Once you have decided on the type of security equipment which best suits your needs, we recommended that you read one of the many equipment tests regularly carried out by the motorcycle press. These tests compare the products from all the major manufacturers and give impartial ratings on their effectiveness, value-for-money and ease of use.

No one item of security equipment can provide complete protection. It is highly recommended that two or more of the items described below are combined to increase the security of your motorcycle (a lock and chain plus an alarm system is just about ideal). The more security measures fitted to the bike, the less likely it is to be stolen.

Lock and chain

Pros: *Very flexible to use; can be used to secure the motorcycle to almost any immovable object. On some locks and chains, the lock can be used on its own as a disc lock (see below).*

Cons: *Can be very heavy and awkward to carry on the motorcycle, although some types will be supplied with a carry bag which can be strapped to the pillion seat.*

● Heavy-duty chains and locks are an excellent security measure **(see illustration 1)**. Whenever the motorcycle is parked, use the lock and chain to secure the machine to a solid, immovable object such as a post or railings. This will prevent the machine from being ridden away or being lifted into the back of a van.

● When fitting the chain, always ensure the chain is routed around the motorcycle frame or swingarm **(see illustrations 2 and 3)**. Never merely pass the chain around one of the wheel rims; a thief may unbolt the wheel and lift the rest of the machine into a van, leaving you with just the wheel! Try to avoid having excess chain free, thus making it difficult to use cutting tools, and keep the chain and lock off the ground to prevent thieves attacking it with a cold chisel. Position the lock so that its lock barrel is facing downwards; this will make it harder for the thief to attack the lock mechanism.

1 Ensure the lock and chain you buy is of good quality and long enough to shackle your bike to a solid object

2 Pass the chain through the bike's frame, rather than just through a wheel . . .

3 . . . and loop it around a solid object

Security REF•21

U-locks

Pros: *Highly effective deterrent which can be used to secure the bike to a post or railings. Most U-locks come with a carrier which allows the lock to be easily carried on the bike.*

Cons: *Not as flexible to use as a lock and chain.*

● These are solid locks which are similar in use to a lock and chain. U-locks are lighter than a lock and chain but not so flexible to use. The length and shape of the lock shackle limit the objects to which the bike can be secured **(see illustration 4)**.

U-locks can be used to secure the bike to a solid object – ensure you purchase one which is long enough

Disc locks

Pros: *Small, light and very easy to carry; most can be stored underneath the seat.*

Cons: *Does not prevent the motorcycle being lifted into a van. Can be very embarrassing if you forget to remove the lock before attempting to ride off!*

● Disc locks are designed to be attached to the front brake disc. The lock passes through one of the holes in the disc and prevents the wheel rotating by jamming against the fork/brake caliper **(see illustration 5)**. Some are equipped with an alarm siren which sounds if the disc lock is moved; this not only acts as a theft deterrent but also as a handy reminder if you try to move the bike with the lock still fitted.

● Combining the disc lock with a length of cable which can be looped around a post or railings provides an additional measure of security **(see illustration 6)**.

A typical disc lock attached through one of the holes in the disc

Alarms and immobilisers

Pros: *Once installed it is completely hassle-free to use. If the system is 'Thatcham' or 'Sold Secure-approved', insurance companies may give you a discount.*

Cons: *Can be expensive to buy and complex to install. No system will prevent the motorcycle from being lifted into a van and taken away.*

● Electronic alarms and immobilisers are available to suit a variety of budgets. There are three different types of system available: pure alarms, pure immobilisers, and the more expensive systems which are combined alarm/immobilisers **(see illustration 7)**.

● An alarm system is designed to emit an audible warning if the motorcycle is being tampered with.

● An immobiliser prevents the motorcycle being started and ridden away by disabling its electrical systems.

● When purchasing an alarm/immobiliser system, check the cost of installing the system unless you are able to do it yourself. If the motorcycle is not used regularly, another consideration is the current drain of the system. All alarm/immobiliser systems are powered by the motorcycle's battery; purchasing a system with a very low current drain could prevent the battery losing its charge whilst the motorcycle is not being used.

A disc lock combined with a security cable provides additional protection

A typical alarm/immobiliser system

REF•22 Security

Indelible markings can be applied to most areas of the bike – always apply the manufacturer's sticker to warn off thieves

Chemically-etched code numbers can be applied to main body panels . . .

. . . again, always ensure that the kit manufacturer's sticker is applied in a prominent position

Security marking kits

Pros: *Very cheap and effective deterrent. Many insurance companies will give you a discount on your insurance premium if a recognised security marking kit is used on your motorcycle.*

Cons: *Does not prevent the motorcycle being stolen by joyriders.*

● There are many different types of security marking kits available. The idea is to mark as many parts of the motorcycle as possible with a unique security number (see illustrations 8, 9 and 10). A form will be included with the kit to register your personal details and those of the motorcycle with the kit manufacturer. This register is made available to the police to help them trace the rightful owner of any motorcycle or components which they recover should all other forms of identification have been removed. Always apply the warning stickers provided with the kit to deter thieves.

Ground anchors, wheel clamps and security posts

Pros: *An excellent form of security which will deter all but the most determined of thieves.*

Cons: *Awkward to install and can be expensive.*

● Whilst the motorcycle is at home, it is a good idea to attach it securely to the floor or a solid wall, even if it is kept in a securely locked garage. Various types of ground anchors, security posts and wheel clamps are available for this purpose (see illustration 11). These security devices are either bolted to a solid concrete or brick structure or can be cemented into the ground.

Permanent ground anchors provide an excellent level of security when the bike is at home

Security at home

A high percentage of motorcycle thefts are from the owner's home. Here are some things to consider whenever your motorcycle is at home:

✔ Where possible, always keep the motorcycle in a securely locked garage. Never rely solely on the standard lock on the garage door, these are usual hopelessly inadequate. Fit an additional locking mechanism to the door and consider having the garage alarmed. A security light, activated by a movement sensor, is also a good investment.

✔ Always secure the motorcycle to the ground or a wall, even if it is inside a securely locked garage.

✔ Do not regularly leave the motorcycle outside your home, try to keep it out of sight wherever possible. If a garage is not available, fit a motorcycle cover over the bike to disguise its true identity.

✔ It is not uncommon for thieves to follow a motorcyclist home to find out where the bike is kept. They will then return at a later date. Be aware of this whenever you are returning home on your motorcycle. If you suspect you are being followed, do not return home, instead ride to a garage or shop and stop as a precaution.

✔ When selling a motorcycle, do not provide your home address or the location where the bike is normally kept. Arrange to meet the buyer at a location away from your home. Thieves have been known to pose as potential buyers to find out where motorcycles are kept and then return later to steal them.

Security away from the home

As well as fitting security equipment to your motorcycle here are a few general rules to follow whenever you park your motorcycle.

✔ Park in a busy, public place.
✔ Use car parks which incorporate security features, such as CCTV.
✔ At night, park in a well-lit area, preferably directly underneath a street light.
✔ Engage the steering lock.
✔ Secure the motorcycle to a solid, immovable object such as a post or railings with an additional lock. If this is not possible, secure the bike to a friend's motorcycle. Some public parking places provide security loops for motorcycles.
✔ Never leave your helmet or luggage attached to the motorcycle. Take them with you at all times.

Lubricants and fluids

A wide range of lubricants, fluids and cleaning agents is available for motor-cycles. This is a guide as to what is available, its applications and properties.

Four-stroke engine oil

● Engine oil is without doubt the most important component of any four-stroke engine. Modern motorcycle engines place a lot of demands on their oil and choosing the right type is essential. Using an unsuitable oil will lead to an increased rate of engine wear and could result in serious engine damage. Before purchasing oil, always check the recommended oil specification given by the manufacturer. The manufacturer will state a recommended 'type or classification' and also a specific 'viscosity' range for engine oil.

● The oil 'type or classification' is identified by its API (American Petroleum Institute) rating. The API rating will be in the form of two letters, e.g. SG. The S identifies the oil as being suitable for use in a petrol (gasoline) engine (S stands for spark ignition) and the second letter, ranging from A to J, identifies the oil's performance rating. The later this letter, the higher the specification of the oil; for example API SG oil exceeds the requirements of API SF oil. **Note:** *On some oils there may also be a second rating consisting of another two letters, the first letter being C, e.g. API SF/CD. This rating indicates the oil is also suitable for use in a diesel engines (the C stands for compression ignition) and is thus of no relevance for motorcycle use.*

● The 'viscosity' of the oil is identified by its SAE (Society of Automotive Engineers) rating. All modern engines require multigrade oils and the SAE rating will consist of two numbers, the first followed by a W, e.g. 10W/40. The first number indicates the viscosity rating of the oil at low temperatures (W stands for winter – tested at –20°C) and the second number represents the viscosity of the oil at high temperatures (tested at 100°C). The lower the number, the thinner the oil. For example an oil with an SAE 10W/40 rating will give better cold starting and running than an SAE 15W/40 oil.

● As well as ensuring the 'type' and 'viscosity' of the oil match the recommendations, another consideration to make when buying engine oil is whether to purchase a standard mineral-based oil, a semi-synthetic oil (also known as a synthetic blend or synthetic-based oil) or a fully-synthetic oil. Although all oils will have a similar rating and viscosity, their cost will vary considerably; mineral-based oils are the cheapest, the fully-synthetic oils the most expensive with the semi-synthetic oils falling somewhere in-between. This decision is very much up to the owner, but it should be noted that modern synthetic oils have far better lubricating and cleaning qualities than traditional mineral-based oils and tend to retain these properties for far longer. Bearing in mind the operating conditions inside a modern, high-revving motorcycle engine it is highly recommended that a fully synthetic oil is used. The extra expense at each service could save you money in the long term by preventing premature engine wear.

● As a final note always ensure that the oil is specifically designed for use in motorcycle engines. Engine oils designed primarily for use in car engines sometimes contain additives or friction modifiers which could cause clutch slip on a motorcycle fitted with a wet-clutch.

Two-stroke engine oil

● Modern two-stroke engines, with their high power outputs, place high demands on their oil. If engine seizure is to be avoided it is essential that a high-quality oil is used. Two-stroke oils differ hugely from four-stroke oils. The oil lubricates only the crankshaft and piston(s) (the transmission has its own lubricating oil) and is used on a total-loss basis where it is burnt completely during the combustion process.

● The Japanese have recently introduced a classification system for two-stroke oils, the JASO rating. This rating is in the form of two letters, either FA, FB or FC – FA is the lowest classification and FC the highest. Ensure the oil being used meets or exceeds the recommended rating specified by the manufacturer.

● As well as ensuring the oil rating matches the recommendation, another consideration to make when buying engine oil is whether to purchase a standard mineral-based oil, a semi-synthetic oil (also known as a synthetic blend or synthetic-based oil) or a fully-synthetic oil. The cost of each type of oil varies considerably; mineral-based oils are the cheapest, the fully-synthetic oils the most expensive with the semi-synthetic oils falling somewhere in-between. This decision is very much up to the owner, but it should be noted that modern synthetic oils have far better lubricating properties and burn cleaner than traditional mineral-based oils. It is therefore recommended that a fully synthetic oil is used. The extra expense could save you money in the long term by preventing premature engine wear, engine performance will be improved, carbon deposits and exhaust smoke will be reduced.

Lubricants and fluids

- Always ensure that the oil is specifically designed for use in an injector system. Many high quality two-stroke oils are designed for competition use and need to be pre-mixed with fuel. These oils are of a much higher viscosity and are not designed to flow through the injector pumps used on road-going two-stroke motorcycles.

Transmission (gear) oil

- On a two-stroke engine, the transmission and clutch are lubricated by their own separate oil bath which must be changed in accordance with the Maintenance Schedule.
- Although the engine and transmission units of most four-strokes use a common lubrication supply, there are some exceptions where the engine and gearbox have separate oil reservoirs and a dry clutch is used.
- Motorcycle manufacturers will either recommend a monograde transmission oil or a four-stroke multigrade engine oil to lubricate the transmission.
- Transmission oils, or gear oils as they are often called, are designed specifically for use in transmission systems. The viscosity of these oils is represented by an SAE number, but the scale of measurement applied is different to that used to grade engine oils. As a rough guide a SAE90 gear oil will be of the same viscosity as an SAE50 engine oil.

Shaft drive oil

- On models equipped with shaft final drive, the shaft drive gears are will have their own oil supply. The manufacturer will state a recommended 'type or classification' and also a specific 'viscosity' range in the same manner as for four-stroke engine oil.
- Gear oil classification is given by the number which follows the API GL (GL standing for gear lubricant) rating, the higher the number, the higher the specification of the oil, e.g. API GL5 oil is a higher specification than API GL4 oil. Ensure the oil meets or exceeds the classification specified and is of the correct viscosity. The viscosity of gear oils is also represented by an SAE number but the scale of measurement used is different to that used to grade engine oils. As a rough guide an SAE90 gear oil will be of the same viscosity as an SAE50 engine oil.
- If the use of an EP (Extreme Pressure) gear oil is specified, ensure the oil purchased is suitable.

Fork oil and suspension fluid

- Conventional telescopic front forks are hydraulic and require fork oil to work. To ensure the forks function correctly, the fork oil must be changed in accordance with the Maintenance Schedule.
- Fork oil is available in a variety of viscosities, identified by their SAE rating; fork oil ratings vary from light (SAE 5) to heavy (SAE 30). When purchasing fork oil, ensure the viscosity rating matches that specified by the manufacturer.
- Some lubricant manufacturers also produce a range of high-quality suspension fluids which are very similar to fork oil but are designed mainly for competition use. These fluids may have a different viscosity rating system which is not to be confused with the SAE rating of normal fork oil. Refer to the manufacturer's instructions if in any doubt.

Brake and clutch fluid

- All disc brake systems and some clutch systems are hydraulically operated. To ensure correct operation, the hydraulic fluid must be changed in accordance with the Maintenance Schedule.
- Brake and clutch fluid is classified by its DOT rating with most motorcycle manufacturers specifying DOT 3 or 4 fluid. Both fluid types are glycol-based and can be mixed together without adverse effect; DOT 4 fluid exceeds the requirements of DOT 3 fluid. Although it is safe to use DOT 4 fluid in a system designed for use with DOT 3 fluid, never use DOT 3 fluid in a system which specifies the use of DOT 4 as this will adversely affect the system's performance. The type required for the system will be marked on the fluid reservoir cap.
- Some manufacturers also produce a DOT 5 hydraulic fluid. DOT 5 hydraulic fluid is silicone-based and is not compatible with the glycol-based DOT 3 and 4 fluids. Never mix DOT 5 fluid with DOT 3 or 4 fluid as this will seriously affect the performance of the hydraulic system.

Coolant/antifreeze

- When purchasing coolant/antifreeze, always ensure it is suitable for use in an aluminium engine and contains corrosion inhibitors to prevent possible blockages of the internal coolant passages of the system. As a general rule, most coolants are designed to be used neat and should not be diluted whereas antifreeze can be mixed with distilled water to provide a coolant solution of the required strength. Refer to the manufacturer's instructions on the bottle.
- Ensure the coolant is changed in accordance with the Maintenance Schedule.

Chain lube

- Chain lube is an aerosol-type spray lubricant specifically designed for use on motorcycle final drive chains. Chain lube has two functions, to minimise friction between the final drive chain and sprockets and to prevent corrosion of the chain. Regular use of a good-quality chain lube will extend the life of the drive chain and sprockets and thus maximise the power being transmitted from the transmission to the rear wheel.
- When using chain lube, always allow some time for the solvents in the lube to evaporate before riding the motorcycle. This will minimise the amount of lube which will

Lubricants and fluids REF•25

'fling' off from the chain when the motorcycle is used. If the motorcycle is equipped with an 'O-ring' chain, ensure the chain lube is labelled as being suitable for use on 'O-ring' chains.

Degreasers and solvents

● There are many different types of solvents and degreasers available to remove the grime and grease which accumulate around the motorcycle during normal use. Degreasers and solvents are usually available as an aerosol-type spray or as a liquid which you apply with a brush. Always closely follow the manufacturer's instructions and wear eye protection during use. Be aware that many solvents are flammable and may give off noxious fumes; take adequate precautions when using them (see Safety First!).

● For general cleaning, use one of the many solvents or degreasers available from most motorcycle accessory shops. These solvents are usually applied then left for a certain time before being washed off with water.

Brake cleaner is a solvent specifically designed to remove all traces of oil, grease and dust from braking system components. Brake cleaner is designed to evaporate quickly and leaves behind no residue.

Carburettor cleaner is an aerosol-type solvent specifically designed to clear carburettor blockages and break down the hard deposits and gum often found inside carburettors during overhaul.

Contact cleaner is an aerosol-type solvent designed for cleaning electrical components. The cleaner will remove all traces of oil and dirt from components such as switch contacts or fouled spark plugs and then dry, leaving behind no residue.

Gasket remover is an aerosol-type solvent designed for removing stubborn gaskets from engine components during overhaul. Gasket remover will minimise the amount of scraping required to remove the gasket and therefore reduce the risk of damage to the mating surface.

Spray lubricants

● Aerosol-based spray lubricants are widely available and are excellent for lubricating lever pivots and exposed cables and switches. Try to use a lubricant which is of the dry-film type as the fluid evaporates, leaving behind a dry-film of lubricant. Lubricants which leave behind an oily residue will attract dust and dirt which will increase the rate of wear of the cable/lever.

● Most lubricants also act as a moisture dispersant and a penetrating fluid. This means they can also be used to 'dry out' electrical components such as wiring connectors or switches as well as helping to free seized fasteners.

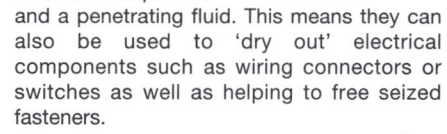

Greases

● Grease is used to lubricate many of the pivot-points. A good-quality multi-purpose grease is suitable for most applications but some manufacturers will specify the use of specialist greases for use on components such as swingarm and suspension linkage bushes. These specialist greases can be purchased from most motorcycle (or car) accessory shops; commonly specified types include molybdenum disulphide grease, lithium-based grease, graphite-based grease, silicone-based grease and high-temperature copper-based grease.

Gasket sealing compounds

● Gasket sealing compounds can be used in conjunction with gaskets, to improve their sealing capabilities, or on their own to seal metal-to-metal joints. Depending on their type, sealing compounds either set hard or stay relatively soft and pliable.

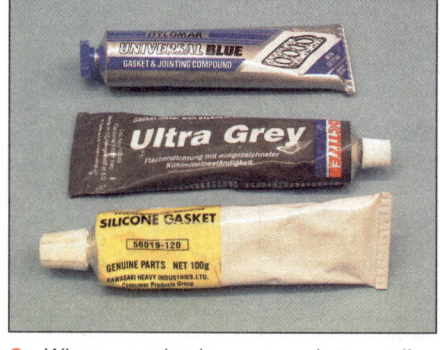

● When purchasing a gasket sealing compound, ensure that it is designed specifically for use on an internal combustion engine. General multi-purpose sealants available from DIY stores may appear visibly similar but they are not designed to withstand the extreme heat or contact with fuel and oil encountered when used on an engine (see 'Tools and Workshop Tips' for further information).

Thread locking compound

● Thread locking compounds are used to secure certain threaded fasteners in position to prevent them from loosening due to vibration. Thread locking compounds can be purchased from most motorcycle (and car) accessory shops. Ensure the threads of the both components are completely clean and dry before sparingly applying the locking compound (see 'Tools and Workshop Tips' for further information).

Fuel additives

● Fuel additives which protect and clean the fuel system components are widely available. These additives are designed to remove all traces of deposits that build up on the carburettors/injectors and prevent wear, helping the fuel system to operate more efficiently. If a fuel additive is being used, check that it is suitable for use with your motorcycle, especially if your motorcycle is equipped with a catalytic converter.

● Octane boosters are also available. These additives are designed to improve the performance of highly-tuned engines being run on normal pump-fuel and are of no real use on standard motorcycles.

Conversion Factors

Length (distance)
Inches (in)	x 25.4	= Millimetres (mm)	x 0.0394	= Inches (in)
Feet (ft)	x 0.305	= Metres (m)	x 3.281	= Feet (ft)
Miles	x 1.609	= Kilometres (km)	x 0.621	= Miles

Volume (capacity)
Cubic inches (cu in; in^3)	x 16.387	= Cubic centimetres (cc; cm^3)	x 0.061	= Cubic inches (cu in; in^3)
Imperial pints (Imp pt)	x 0.568	= Litres (l)	x 1.76	= Imperial pints (Imp pt)
Imperial quarts (Imp qt)	x 1.137	= Litres (l)	x 0.88	= Imperial quarts (Imp qt)
Imperial quarts (Imp qt)	x 1.201	= US quarts (US qt)	x 0.833	= Imperial quarts (Imp qt)
US quarts (US qt)	x 0.946	= Litres (l)	x 1.057	= US quarts (US qt)
Imperial gallons (Imp gal)	x 4.546	= Litres (l)	x 0.22	= Imperial gallons (Imp gal)
Imperial gallons (Imp gal)	x 1.201	= US gallons (US gal)	x 0.833	= Imperial gallons (Imp gal)
US gallons (US gal)	x 3.785	= Litres (l)	x 0.264	= US gallons (US gal)

Mass (weight)
Ounces (oz)	x 28.35	= Grams (g)	x 0.035	= Ounces (oz)
Pounds (lb)	x 0.454	= Kilograms (kg)	x 2.205	= Pounds (lb)

Force
Ounces-force (ozf; oz)	x 0.278	= Newtons (N)	x 3.6	= Ounces-force (ozf; oz)
Pounds-force (lbf; lb)	x 4.448	= Newtons (N)	x 0.225	= Pounds-force (lbf; lb)
Newtons (N)	x 0.1	= Kilograms-force (kgf; kg)	x 9.81	= Newtons (N)

Pressure
Pounds-force per square inch (psi; lbf/in^2; lb/in^2)	x 0.070	= Kilograms-force per square centimetre (kgf/cm^2; kg/cm^2)	x 14.223	= Pounds-force per square inch (psi; lbf/in^2; lb/in^2)
Pounds-force per square inch (psi; lbf/in^2; lb/in^2)	x 0.068	= Atmospheres (atm)	x 14.696	= Pounds-force per square inch (psi; lbf/in^2; lb/in^2)
Pounds-force per square inch (psi; lbf/in^2; lb/in^2)	x 0.069	= Bars	x 14.5	= Pounds-force per square inch (psi; lbf/in^2; lb/in^2)
Pounds-force per square inch (psi; lbf/in^2; lb/in^2)	x 6.895	= Kilopascals (kPa)	x 0.145	= Pounds-force per square inch (psi; lbf/in^2; lb/in^2)
Kilopascals (kPa)	x 0.01	= Kilograms-force per square centimetre (kgf/cm^2; kg/cm^2)	x 98.1	= Kilopascals (kPa)
Millibar (mbar)	x 100	= Pascals (Pa)	x 0.01	= Millibar (mbar)
Millibar (mbar)	x 0.0145	= Pounds-force per square inch (psi; lbf/in^2; lb/in^2)	x 68.947	= Millibar (mbar)
Millibar (mbar)	x 0.75	= Millimetres of mercury (mmHg)	x 1.333	= Millibar (mbar)
Millibar (mbar)	x 0.401	= Inches of water (inH$_2$O)	x 2.491	= Millibar (mbar)
Millimetres of mercury (mmHg)	x 0.535	= Inches of water (inH$_2$O)	x 1.868	= Millimetres of mercury (mmHg)
Inches of water (inH$_2$O)	x 0.036	= Pounds-force per square inch (psi; lbf/in^2; lb/in^2)	x 27.68	= Inches of water (inH$_2$O)

Torque (moment of force)
Pounds-force inches (lbf in; lb in)	x 1.152	= Kilograms-force centimetre (kgf cm; kg cm)	x 0.868	= Pounds-force inches (lbf in; lb in)
Pounds-force inches (lbf in; lb in)	x 0.113	= Newton metres (Nm)	x 8.85	= Pounds-force inches (lbf in; lb in)
Pounds-force inches (lbf in; lb in)	x 0.083	= Pounds-force feet (lbf ft; lb ft)	x 12	= Pounds-force inches (lbf in; lb in)
Pounds-force feet (lbf ft; lb ft)	x 0.138	= Kilograms-force metres (kgf m; kg m)	x 7.233	= Pounds-force feet (lbf ft; lb ft)
Pounds-force feet (lbf ft; lb ft)	x 1.356	= Newton metres (Nm)	x 0.738	= Pounds-force feet (lbf ft; lb ft)
Newton metres (Nm)	x 0.102	= Kilograms-force metres (kgf m; kg m)	x 9.804	= Newton metres (Nm)

Power
Horsepower (hp)	x 745.7	= Watts (W)	x 0.0013	= Horsepower (hp)

Velocity (speed)
Miles per hour (miles/hr; mph)	x 1.609	= Kilometres per hour (km/hr; kph)	x 0.621	= Miles per hour (miles/hr; mph)

Fuel consumption*
Miles per gallon (mpg)	x 0.354	= Kilometres per litre (km/l)	x 2.825	= Miles per gallon (mpg)

Temperature

Degrees Fahrenheit = (°C x 1.8) + 32   Degrees Celsius (Degrees Centigrade; °C) = (°F - 32) x 0.56

*It is common practice to convert from miles per gallon (mpg) to litres/100 kilometres (l/100km), where mpg x l/100 km = 282

MOT Test Checks REF•27

About the MOT Test

In the UK, all vehicles more than three years old are subject to an annual test to ensure that they meet minimum safety requirements. A current test certificate must be issued before a machine can be used on public roads, and is required before a road fund licence can be issued. Riding without a current test certificate will also invalidate your insurance.

For most owners, the MOT test is an annual cause for anxiety, and this is largely due to owners not being sure what needs to be checked prior to submitting the motorcycle for testing. The simple answer is that a fully roadworthy motorcycle will have no difficulty in passing the test.

This is a guide to getting your motorcycle through the MOT test. Obviously it will not be possible to examine the motorcycle to the same standard as the professional MOT tester, particularly in view of the equipment required for some of the checks. However, working through the following procedures will enable you to identify any problem areas before submitting the motorcycle for the test.

It has only been possible to summarise the test requirements here, based on the regulations in force at the time of printing. Test standards are becoming increasingly stringent, although there are some exemptions for older vehicles. More information about the MOT test can be obtained from the TSO publications, *How Safe is your Motorcycle* and *The MOT Inspection Manual for Motorcycle Testing*.

Many of the checks require that one of the wheels is raised off the ground. If the motorcycle doesn't have a centre stand, note that an auxiliary stand will be required. Additionally, the help of an assistant may prove useful.

Certain exceptions apply to machines under 50 cc, machines without a lighting system, and Classic bikes - if in doubt about any of the requirements listed below seek confirmation from an MOT tester prior to submitting the motorcycle for the test.

Check that the frame number is clearly visible.

> **HAYNES HiNT** *If a component is in borderline condition, the tester has discretion in deciding whether to pass or fail it. If the motorcycle presented is clean and evidently well cared for, the tester may be more inclined to pass a borderline component than if the motorcycle is scruffy and apparently neglected.*

Electrical System

Lights, turn signals, horn and reflector

✔ With the ignition on, check the operation of the following electrical components. **Note:** *The electrical components on certain small-capacity machines are powered by the generator, requiring that the engine is run for this check.*

a) *Headlight and tail light. Check that both illuminate in the low and high beam switch positions.*
b) *Position lights. Check that the front position (or sidelight) and tail light illuminate in this switch position.*
c) *Turn signals. Check that all flash at the correct rate, and that the warning light(s) function correctly. Check that the turn signal switch works correctly.*
d) *Hazard warning system (where fitted). Check that all four turn signals flash in this switch position.*
e) *Brake stop light. Check that the light comes on when the front and rear brakes are independently applied. Models first used on or after 1st April 1986 must have a brake light switch on each brake.*
f) *Horn. Check that the sound is continuous and of reasonable volume.*

✔ Check that there is a red reflector on the rear of the machine, either mounted separately or as part of the tail light lens.
✔ Check the condition of the headlight, tail light and turn signal lenses.

Headlight beam height

✔ The MOT tester will perform a headlight beam height check using specialised beam setting equipment **(see illustration 1)**. This equipment will not be available to the home mechanic, but if you suspect that the headlight is incorrectly set or may have been maladjusted in the past, you can perform a rough test as follows.
✔ Position the bike in a straight line facing a brick wall. The bike must be off its stand, upright and with a rider seated. Measure the height from the ground to the centre of the headlight and mark a horizontal line on the wall at this height. Position the motorcycle 3.8 metres from the wall and draw a vertical line up the wall central to the centreline of the motorcycle. Switch to dipped beam and check that the beam pattern falls slightly lower than the horizontal line and to the left of the vertical line **(see illustration 2)**.

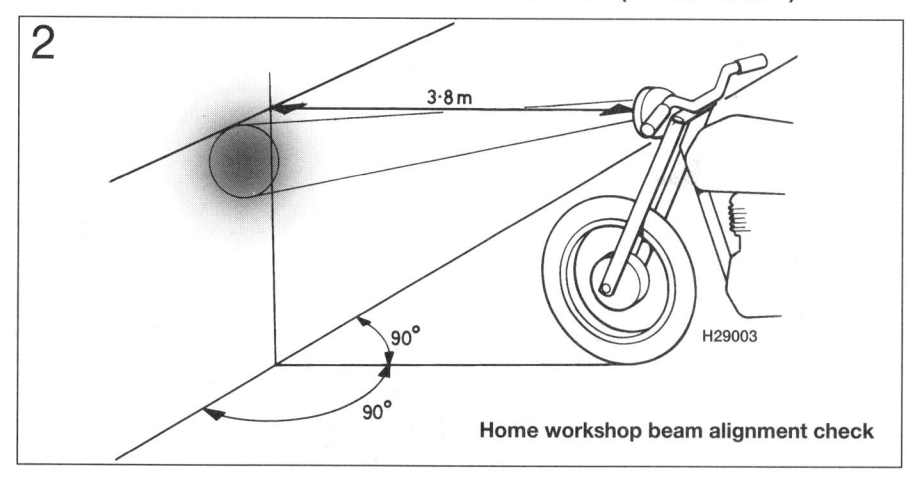

1

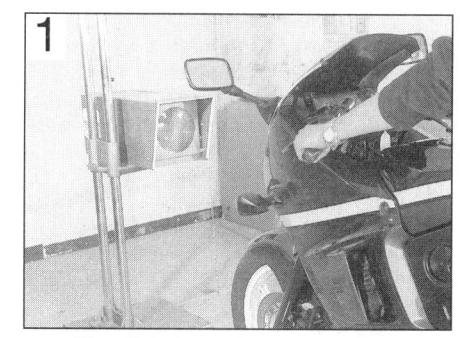

Headlight beam height checking equipment

2

Home workshop beam alignment check

REF•28 MOT Test Checks

Exhaust System and Final Drive

Exhaust

✔ Check that the exhaust mountings are secure and that the system does not foul any of the rear suspension components.
✔ Start the motorcycle. When the revs are increased, check that the exhaust is neither holed nor leaking from any of its joints. On a linked system, check that the collector box is not leaking due to corrosion.
✔ Note that the exhaust decibel level ("loudness" of the exhaust) is assessed at the discretion of the tester. If the motorcycle was first used on or after 1st January 1985 the silencer must carry the BSAU 193 stamp, or a marking relating to its make and model, or be of OE (original equipment) manufacture. If the silencer is marked NOT FOR ROAD USE, RACING USE ONLY or similar, it will fail the MOT.

Final drive

✔ On chain or belt drive machines, check that the chain/belt is in good condition and does not have excessive slack. Also check that the sprocket is securely mounted on the rear wheel hub. Check that the chain/belt guard is in place.
✔ On shaft drive bikes, check for oil leaking from the drive unit and fouling the rear tyre.

Steering and Suspension

Steering

✔ With the front wheel raised off the ground, rotate the steering from lock to lock. The handlebar or switches must not contact the fuel tank or be close enough to trap the rider's hand. Problems can be caused by damaged lock stops on the lower yoke and frame, or by the fitting of non-standard handlebars.
✔ When performing the lock to lock check, also ensure that the steering moves freely without drag or notchiness. Steering movement can be impaired by poorly routed cables, or by overtight head bearings or worn bearings. The tester will perform a check of the steering head bearing lower race by mounting the front wheel on a surface plate, then performing a lock to lock check with the weight of the machine on the lower bearing (see illustration 3).
✔ Grasp the fork sliders (lower legs) and attempt to push and pull on the forks (see illustration 4). Any play in the steering head bearings will be felt. Note that in extreme cases, wear of the front fork bushes can be misinterpreted for head bearing play.
✔ Check that the handlebars are securely mounted.
✔ Check that the handlebar grip rubbers are secure. They should by bonded to the bar left end and to the throttle cable pulley on the right end.

Front wheel mounted on a surface plate for steering head bearing lower race check

Front suspension

✔ With the motorcycle off the stand, hold the front brake on and pump the front forks up and down (see illustration 5). Check that they are adequately damped.

Checking the steering head bearings for freeplay

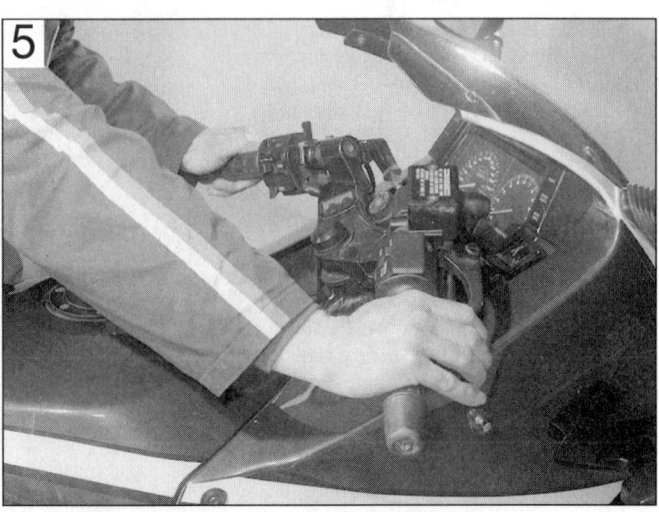

Hold the front brake on and pump the front forks up and down to check operation

MOT Test Checks REF•29

Inspect the area around the fork dust seal for oil leakage (arrow)

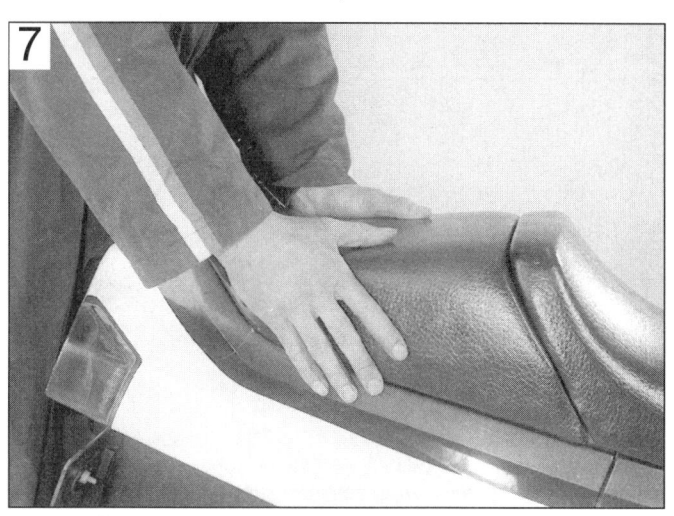

Bounce the rear of the motorcycle to check rear suspension operation

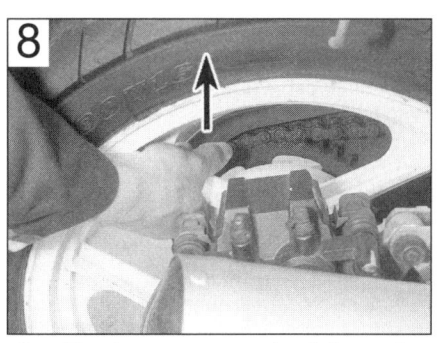

Checking for rear suspension linkage play

✔ Inspect the area above and around the front fork oil seals **(see illustration 6)**. There should be no sign of oil on the fork tube (stanchion) nor leaking down the slider (lower leg). On models so equipped, check that there is no oil leaking from the anti-dive units.

✔ On models with swingarm front suspension, check that there is no freeplay in the linkage when moved from side to side.

Rear suspension

✔ With the motorcycle off the stand and an assistant supporting the motorcycle by its handlebars, bounce the rear suspension **(see illustration 7)**. Check that the suspension components do not foul on any of the cycle parts and check that the shock absorber(s) provide adequate damping.

✔ Visually inspect the shock absorber(s) and check that there is no sign of oil leakage from its damper. This is somewhat restricted on certain single shock models due to the location of the shock absorber.

✔ With the rear wheel raised off the ground, grasp the wheel at the highest point and attempt to pull it up **(see illustration 8)**. Any play in the swingarm pivot or suspension linkage bearings will be felt as movement. **Note:** *Do not confuse play with actual suspension movement.* Failure to lubricate suspension linkage bearings can lead to bearing failure **(see illustration 9)**.

✔ With the rear wheel raised off the ground, grasp the swingarm ends and attempt to move the swingarm from side to side and forwards and backwards - any play indicates wear of the swingarm pivot bearings **(see illustration 10)**.

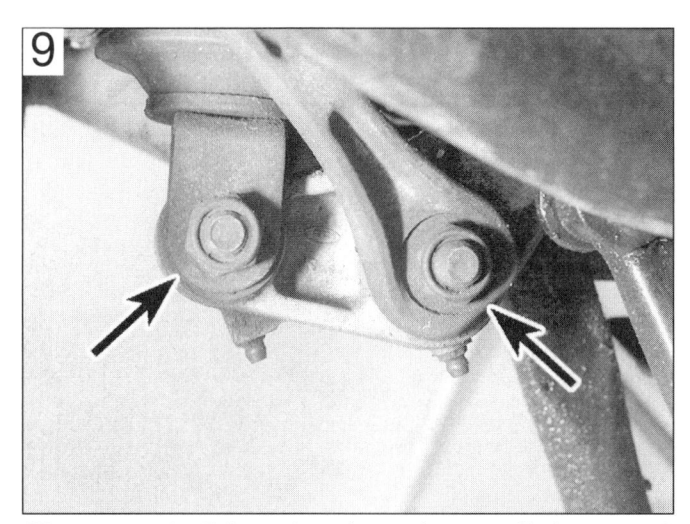

Worn suspension linkage pivots (arrows) are usually the cause of play in the rear suspension

Grasp the swingarm at the ends to check for play in its pivot bearings

REF•30 MOT Test Checks

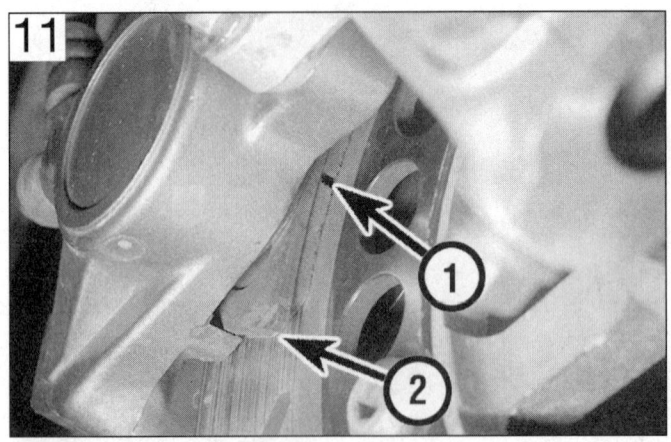

Brake pad wear can usually be viewed without removing the caliper. Most pads have wear indicator grooves (1) and some also have indicator tangs (2)

On drum brakes, check the angle of the operating lever with the brake fully applied. Most drum brakes have a wear indicator pointer and scale.

Brakes, Wheels and Tyres

Brakes

✔ With the wheel raised off the ground, apply the brake then free it off, and check that the wheel is about to revolve freely without brake drag.
✔ On disc brakes, examine the disc itself. Check that it is securely mounted and not cracked.
✔ On disc brakes, view the pad material through the caliper mouth and check that the pads are not worn down beyond the limit **(see illustration 11)**.
✔ On drum brakes, check that when the brake is applied the angle between the operating lever and cable or rod is not too great **(see illustration 12)**. Check also that the operating lever doesn't foul any other components.
✔ On disc brakes, examine the flexible hoses from top to bottom. Have an assistant hold the brake on so that the fluid in the hose is under pressure, and check that there is no sign of fluid leakage, bulges or cracking. If there are any metal brake pipes or unions, check that these are free from corrosion and damage. Where a brake-linked anti-dive system is fitted, check the hoses to the anti-dive in a similar manner.
✔ Check that the rear brake torque arm is secure and that its fasteners are secured by self-locking nuts or castellated nuts with split-pins or R-pins **(see illustration 13)**.
✔ On models with ABS, check that the self-check warning light in the instrument panel works.
✔ The MOT tester will perform a test of the motorcycle's braking efficiency based on a calculation of rider and motorcycle weight. Although this cannot be carried out at home, you can at least ensure that the braking systems are properly maintained. For hydraulic disc brakes, check the fluid level, lever/pedal feel (bleed of air if its spongy) and pad material. For drum brakes, check adjustment, cable or rod operation and shoe lining thickness.

Wheels and tyres

✔ Check the wheel condition. Cast wheels should be free from cracks and if of the built-up design, all fasteners should be secure. Spoked wheels should be checked for broken, corroded, loose or bent spokes.
✔ With the wheel raised off the ground, spin the wheel and visually check that the tyre and wheel run true. Check that the tyre does not foul the suspension or mudguards.
✔ With the wheel raised off the ground, grasp the wheel and attempt to move it about the axle (spindle) **(see illustration 14)**. Any play felt here indicates wheel bearing failure.

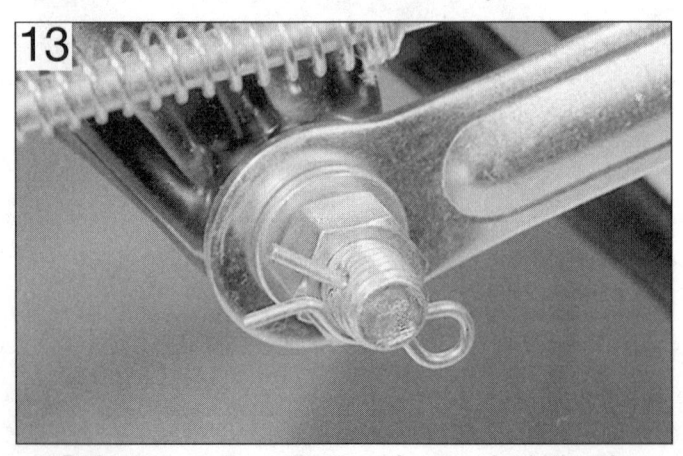

Brake torque arm must be properly secured at both ends

Check for wheel bearing play by trying to move the wheel about the axle (spindle)

MOT Test Checks REF•31

Checking the tyre tread depth

Tyre direction of rotation arrow can be found on tyre sidewall

Castellated type wheel axle (spindle) nut must be secured by a split pin or R-pin

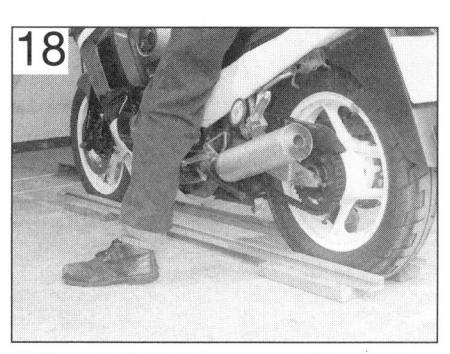

Two straightedges are used to check wheel alignment

✔ Check the tyre tread depth, tread condition and sidewall condition **(see illustration 15)**.
✔ Check the tyre type. Front and rear tyre types must be compatible and be suitable for road use. Tyres marked NOT FOR ROAD USE, COMPETITION USE ONLY or similar, will fail the MOT.

✔ If the tyre sidewall carries a direction of rotation arrow, this must be pointing in the direction of normal wheel rotation **(see illustration 16)**.
✔ Check that the wheel axle (spindle) nuts (where applicable) are properly secured. A self-locking nut or castellated nut with a split-pin or R-pin can be used **(see illustration 17)**.
✔ Wheel alignment is checked with the motorcycle off the stand and a rider seated. With the front wheel pointing straight ahead, two perfectly straight lengths of metal or wood and placed against the sidewalls of both tyres **(see illustration 18)**. The gap each side of the front tyre must be equidistant on both sides. Incorrect wheel alignment may be due to a cocked rear wheel (often as the result of poor chain adjustment) or in extreme cases, a bent frame.

General checks and condition

✔ Check the security of all major fasteners, bodypanels, seat, fairings (where fitted) and mudguards.

✔ Check that the rider and pillion footrests, handlebar levers and brake pedal are securely mounted.

✔ Check for corrosion on the frame or any load-bearing components. If severe, this may affect the structure, particularly under stress.

Sidecars

A motorcycle fitted with a sidecar requires additional checks relating to the stability of the machine and security of attachment and swivel joints, plus specific wheel alignment (toe-in) requirements. Additionally, tyre and lighting requirements differ from conventional motorcycle use. Owners are advised to check MOT test requirements with an official test centre.

REF•32 Storage

Preparing for storage

Before you start

If repairs or an overhaul is needed, see that this is carried out now rather than left until you want to ride the bike again.

Give the bike a good wash and scrub all dirt from its underside. Make sure the bike dries completely before preparing for storage.

Engine

● Remove the spark plug(s) and lubricate the cylinder bores with approximately a teaspoon of motor oil using a spout-type oil can **(see illustration 1)**. Reinstall the spark plug(s). Crank the engine over a couple of times to coat the piston rings and bores with oil. If the bike has a kickstart, use this to turn the engine over. If not, flick the kill switch to the OFF position and crank the engine over on the starter **(see illustration 2)**. If the nature on the ignition system prevents the starter operating with the kill switch in the OFF position, remove the spark plugs and fit them back in their caps; ensure that the plugs are earthed (grounded) against the cylinder head when the starter is operated **(see illustration 3)**.

Warning: It is important that the plugs are earthed (grounded) away from the spark plug holes otherwise there is a risk of atomised fuel from the cylinders igniting.

HAYNES HINT *On a single cylinder four-stroke engine, you can seal the combustion chamber completely by positioning the piston at TDC on the compression stroke.*

● Drain the carburettor(s) otherwise there is a risk of jets becoming blocked by gum deposits from the fuel **(see illustration 4)**.

● If the bike is going into long-term storage, consider adding a fuel stabiliser to the fuel in the tank. If the tank is drained completely, corrosion of its internal surfaces may occur if left unprotected for a long period. The tank can be treated with a rust preventative especially for this purpose. Alternatively, remove the tank and pour half a litre of motor oil into it, install the filler cap and shake the tank to coat its internals with oil before draining off the excess. The same effect can also be achieved by spraying WD40 or a similar water-dispersant around the inside of the tank via its flexible nozzle.

● Make sure the cooling system contains the correct mix of antifreeze. Antifreeze also contains important corrosion inhibitors.

● The air intakes and exhaust can be sealed off by covering or plugging the openings. Ensure that you do not seal in any condensation; run the engine until it is hot,

Squirt a drop of motor oil into each cylinder

Flick the kill switch to OFF . . .

. . . and ensure that the metal bodies of the plugs (arrows) are earthed against the cylinder head

Connect a hose to the carburettor float chamber drain stub (arrow) and unscrew the drain screw

Storage REF•33

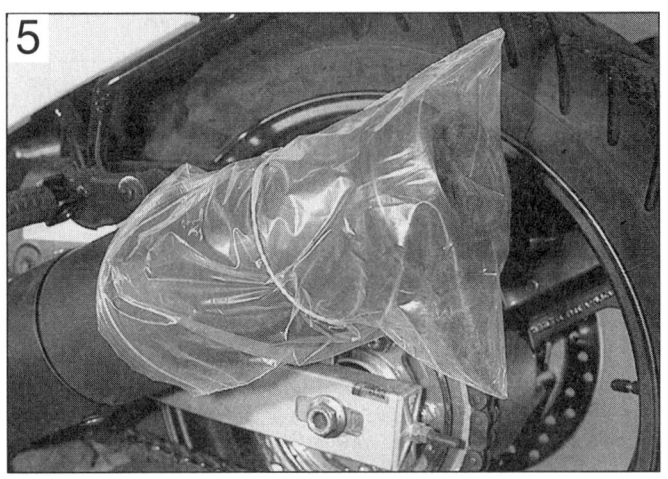

Exhausts can be sealed off with a plastic bag

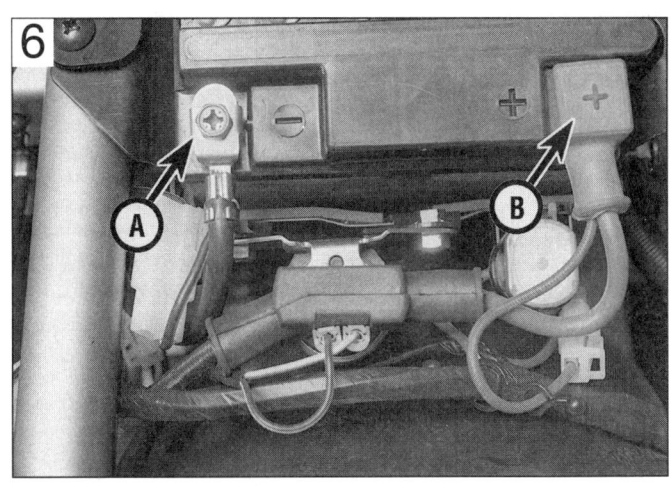

Disconnect the negative lead (A) first, followed by the positive lead (B)

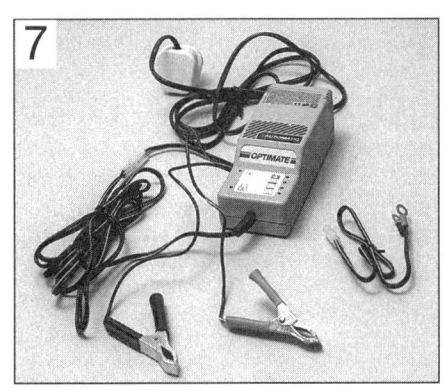

Use a suitable battery charger - this kit also assess battery condition

then switch off and allow to cool. Tape a piece of thick plastic over the silencer end(s) **(see illustration 5)**. Note that some advocate pouring a tablespoon of motor oil into the silencer(s) before sealing them off.

Battery

● Remove it from the bike - in extreme cases of cold the battery may freeze and crack its case **(see illustration 6)**.

● Check the electrolyte level and top up if necessary (conventional refillable batteries). Clean the terminals.
● Store the battery off the motorcycle and away from any sources of fire. Position a wooden block under the battery if it is to sit on the ground.
● Give the battery a trickle charge for a few hours every month **(see illustration 7)**.

Tyres

● Place the bike on its centrestand or an auxiliary stand which will support the motorcycle in an upright position. Position wood blocks under the tyres to keep them off the ground and to provide insulation from damp. If the bike is being put into long-term storage, ideally both tyres should be off the ground; not only will this protect the tyres, but will also ensure that no load is placed on the steering head or wheel bearings.
● Deflate each tyre by 5 to 10 psi, no more or the beads may unseat from the rim, making subsequent inflation difficult on tubeless tyres.

Pivots and controls

● Lubricate all lever, pedal, stand and footrest pivot points. If grease nipples are fitted to the rear suspension components, apply lubricant to the pivots.
● Lubricate all control cables.

Cycle components

● Apply a wax protectant to all painted and plastic components. Wipe off any excess, but don't polish to a shine. Where fitted, clean the screen with soap and water.
● Coat metal parts with Vaseline (petroleum jelly). When applying this to the fork tubes, do not compress the forks otherwise the seals will rot from contact with the Vaseline.
● Apply a vinyl cleaner to the seat.

Storage conditions

● Aim to store the bike in a shed or garage which does not leak and is free from damp.
● Drape an old blanket or bedspread over the bike to protect it from dust and direct contact with sunlight (which will fade paint). This also hides the bike from prying eyes. Beware of tight-fitting plastic covers which may allow condensation to form and settle on the bike.

Getting back on the road

Engine and transmission

● Change the oil and replace the oil filter. If this was done prior to storage, check that the oil hasn't emulsified - a thick whitish substance which occurs through condensation.
● Remove the spark plugs. Using a spout-type oil can, squirt a few drops of oil into the cylinder(s). This will provide initial lubrication as the piston rings and bores comes back into contact. Service the spark plugs, or fit new ones, and install them in the engine.

● Check that the clutch isn't stuck on. The plates can stick together if left standing for some time, preventing clutch operation. Engage a gear and try rocking the bike back and forth with the clutch lever held against the handlebar. If this doesn't work on cable-operated clutches, hold the clutch lever back against the handlebar with a strong elastic band or cable tie for a couple of hours **(see illustration 8)**.
● If the air intakes or silencer end(s) were blocked off, remove the bung or cover used.
● If the fuel tank was coated with a rust

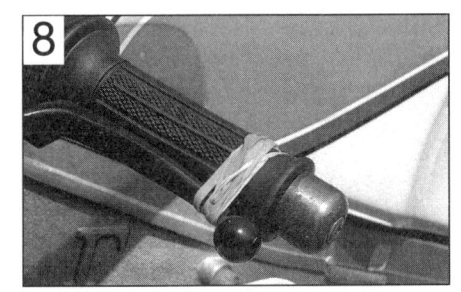

Hold clutch lever back against the handlebar with elastic bands or a cable tie

Storage

preventative, oil or a stabiliser added to the fuel, drain and flush the tank and dispose of the fuel sensibly. If no action was taken with the fuel tank prior to storage, it is advised that the old fuel is disposed of since it will go off over a period of time. Refill the fuel tank with fresh fuel.

Frame and running gear

- Oil all pivot points and cables.
- Check the tyre pressures. They will definitely need inflating if pressures were reduced for storage.
- Lubricate the final drive chain (where applicable).
- Remove any protective coating applied to the fork tubes (stanchions) since this may well destroy the fork seals. If the fork tubes weren't protected and have picked up rust spots, remove them with very fine abrasive paper and refinish with metal polish.
- Check that both brakes operate correctly. Apply each brake hard and check that it's not possible to move the motorcycle forwards, then check that the brake frees off again once released. Brake caliper pistons can stick due to corrosion around the piston head, or on the sliding caliper types, due to corrosion of the slider pins. If the brake doesn't free after repeated operation, take the caliper off for examination. Similarly drum brakes can stick due to a seized operating cam, cable or rod linkage.
- If the motorcycle has been in long-term storage, renew the brake fluid and clutch fluid (where applicable).
- Depending on where the bike has been stored, the wiring, cables and hoses may have been nibbled by rodents. Make a visual check and investigate disturbed wiring loom tape.

Battery

- If the battery has been previously removal and given top up charges it can simply be reconnected. Remember to connect the positive cable first and the negative cable last.
- On conventional refillable batteries, if the battery has not received any attention, remove it from the motorcycle and check its electrolyte level. Top up if necessary then charge the battery. If the battery fails to hold a charge and a visual checks show heavy white sulphation of the plates, the battery is probably defective and must be renewed. This is particularly likely if the battery is old. Confirm battery condition with a specific gravity check.
- On sealed (MF) batteries, if the battery has not received any attention, remove it from the motorcycle and charge it according to the information on the battery case - if the battery fails to hold a charge it must be renewed.

Starting procedure

- If a kickstart is fitted, turn the engine over a couple of times with the ignition OFF to distribute oil around the engine. If no kickstart is fitted, flick the engine kill switch OFF and the ignition ON and crank the engine over a couple of times to work oil around the upper cylinder components. If the nature of the ignition system is such that the starter won't work with the kill switch OFF, remove the spark plugs, fit them back into their caps and earth (ground) their bodies on the cylinder head. Reinstall the spark plugs afterwards.
- Switch the kill switch to RUN, operate the choke and start the engine. If the engine won't start don't continue cranking the engine - not only will this flatten the battery, but the starter motor will overheat. Switch the ignition off and try again later. If the engine refuses to start, go through the fault finding procedures in this manual. **Note:** *If the bike has been in storage for a long time, old fuel or a carburettor blockage may be the problem. Gum deposits in carburettors can block jets - if a carburettor cleaner doesn't prove successful the carburettors must be dismantled for cleaning.*
- Once the engine has started, check that the lights, turn signals and horn work properly.
- Treat the bike gently for the first ride and check all fluid levels on completion. Settle the bike back into the maintenance schedule.

Fault Finding REF•35

This Section provides an easy reference-guide to the more common faults that are likely to afflict your machine. Obviously, the opportunities are almost limitless for faults to occur as a result of obscure failures, and to try and cover all eventualities would require a book. Indeed, a number have been written on the subject.

Successful troubleshooting is not a mysterious 'black art' but the application of a bit of knowledge combined with a systematic and logical approach to the problem. Approach any troubleshooting by first accurately identifying the symptom and then checking through the list of possible causes, starting with the simplest or most obvious and progressing in stages to the most complex.

Take nothing for granted, but above all apply liberal quantities of common sense.

The main symptom of a fault is given in the text as a major heading below which are listed the various systems or areas which may contain the fault. Details of each possible cause for a fault and the remedial action to be taken are given, in brief, in the paragraphs below each heading. Further information should be sought in the relevant Chapter.

1 Engine doesn't start or is difficult to start
- [ ] Starter motor doesn't rotate
- [ ] Starter motor rotates but engine does not turn over
- [ ] Starter works but engine won't turn over (seized)
- [ ] No fuel flow
- [ ] Engine flooded
- [ ] No spark or weak spark
- [ ] Compression low
- [ ] Stalls after starting
- [ ] Rough idle

2 Poor running at low speed
- [ ] Spark weak
- [ ] Fuel/air mixture incorrect
- [ ] Compression low
- [ ] Poor acceleration

3 Poor running or no power at high speed
- [ ] Firing incorrect
- [ ] Fuel/air mixture incorrect
- [ ] Compression low
- [ ] Knocking or pinging
- [ ] Miscellaneous causes

4 Overheating
- [ ] Engine overheats
- [ ] Firing incorrect
- [ ] Fuel/air mixture incorrect
- [ ] Compression too high
- [ ] Engine load excessive
- [ ] Lubrication inadequate
- [ ] Miscellaneous causes

5 Clutch problems
- [ ] Clutch slipping
- [ ] Clutch not disengaging completely

6 Gearchanging problems
- [ ] Doesn't go into gear, or lever doesn't return
- [ ] Jumps out of gear
- [ ] Overshifts

7 Abnormal engine noise
- [ ] Knocking or pinking
- [ ] Piston slap or rattling
- [ ] Valve noise
- [ ] Other noise

8 Abnormal driveline noise
- [ ] Clutch noise
- [ ] Transmission noise
- [ ] Final drive noise

9 Abnormal frame and suspension noise
- [ ] Front end noise
- [ ] Shock absorber noise
- [ ] Brake noise

10 Excessive exhaust smoke
- [ ] White smoke
- [ ] Black smoke
- [ ] Brown smoke

11 Poor handling or stability
- [ ] Handlebar hard to turn
- [ ] Handlebar shakes or vibrates excessively
- [ ] Handlebar pulls to one side
- [ ] Poor shock absorbing qualities

12 Braking problems
- [ ] Brakes are spongy, don't hold
- [ ] Brake lever or pedal pulsates
- [ ] Brakes drag

13 Electrical problems
- [ ] Battery dead or weak
- [ ] Battery overcharged

REF•36 Fault Finding

1 Engine doesn't start or is difficult to start

Starter motor doesn't rotate

- [ ] Engine kill switch OFF.
- [ ] Fuse blown. Check main fuse and ignition circuit fuse (Chapter 9).
- [ ] Battery voltage low. Check and recharge battery (Chapter 9).
- [ ] Starter motor defective. Make sure the wiring to the starter is secure. Make sure the starter relay clicks when the start button is pushed. If the relay clicks, then the fault is in the wiring or motor.
- [ ] Starter relay faulty. Check it according to the procedure in Chapter 9.
- [ ] Starter switch not contacting. The contacts could be wet, corroded or dirty. Disassemble and clean the switch (Chapter 9).
- [ ] Wiring open or shorted. Check all wiring connections and harnesses to make sure that they are dry, tight and not corroded. Also check for broken or frayed wires that can cause a short to ground (earth) (see wiring diagram, Chapter 9).
- [ ] Ignition (main) switch defective. Check the switch according to the procedure in Chapter 9. Replace the switch with a new one if it is defective.
- [ ] Engine kill switch defective. Check for wet, dirty or corroded contacts. Clean or replace the switch as necessary (Chapter 9).
- [ ] Faulty neutral, side stand or clutch switch. Check the wiring to each switch and the switch itself according to the procedures in Chapter 9.

Starter motor rotates but engine does not turn over

- [ ] Starter motor clutch defective. Inspect and repair or replace (Chapter 2).
- [ ] Damaged idler or starter gears. Inspect and replace the damaged parts (Chapter 2).

Starter works but engine won't turn over (seized)

- [ ] Seized engine caused by one or more internally damaged components. Failure due to wear, abuse or lack of lubrication. Damage can include seized valves, followers, camshafts, pistons, crankshaft, connecting rod bearings, or transmission gears or bearings. Refer to Chapter 2 for engine disassembly.

No fuel flow

- [ ] No fuel in tank.
- [ ] Fuel tank breather hose obstructed.
- [ ] Fuel tap strainer or in-line filter clogged. Remove the tap and clean it and check the filter (Chapters 1 and 4).
- [ ] Fuel line clogged. Pull the fuel line loose and carefully blow through it.
- [ ] Float needle valve clogged. For all of the valves to be clogged, either a very bad batch of fuel with an unusual additive has been used, or some other foreign material has entered the tank. Many times after a machine has been stored for many months without running, the fuel turns to a varnish-like liquid and forms deposits on the inlet needle valves and jets. The carburettors should be removed and overhauled if draining the float chambers doesn't solve the problem.
- [ ] Fuel pump faulty. Check the fuel pump flow and renew the pump if necessary (Chapter 4).

Engine flooded

- [ ] Fuel level (float height) too high. Check as described in Chapter 4.
- [ ] Float needle valve worn or stuck open. A piece of dirt, rust or other debris can cause the valve to seat improperly, causing excess fuel to be admitted to the float chamber. In this case, the float chamber should be cleaned and the needle valve and seat inspected. If the needle and seat are worn, then the leaking will persist and the parts should be replaced with new ones (Chapter 4).
- [ ] Starting technique incorrect. Under normal circumstances (i.e., if all the carburettor functions are sound) the machine should start with little or no throttle. When the engine is cold, the choke should be operated and the engine started without opening the throttle. When the engine is at operating temperature, only a very slight amount of throttle should be necessary. If the engine is flooded, turn the fuel tap OFF and hold the throttle open while cranking the engine. This will allow additional air to reach the cylinders. Remember to turn the fuel tap back ON afterwards.

No spark or weak spark

- [ ] Ignition switch OFF.
- [ ] Engine kill switch turned to the OFF position.
- [ ] Battery voltage low. Check and recharge the battery as necessary (Chapter 9).
- [ ] Spark plugs dirty, defective or worn out. Locate reason for fouled plugs using spark plug condition chart and follow the plug maintenance procedures (Chapter 1).
- [ ] Spark plug caps or secondary (HT) wiring faulty. Check condition. Renew either or both components if cracks or deterioration are evident (Chapter 5).
- [ ] Spark plug caps not making good contact. Make sure that the plug caps fit snugly over the plug ends.
- [ ] Ignition control unit defective. Check the unit (Chapter 5).
- [ ] Pick-up coil defective. Check the unit (Chapter 5).
- [ ] Ignition HT coils/plug caps defective. Check the coils (Chapter 5).
- [ ] Ignition or kill switch shorted. This is usually caused by water, corrosion, damage or excessive wear. The switches can be disassembled and cleaned with electrical contact cleaner. If cleaning does not help, renew the switches (Chapter 9).
- [ ] Wiring shorted or broken between:
    - a) Ignition (main) switch and engine kill switch (or blown fuse)
    - b) Ignition control unit and engine kill switch
    - c) Ignition control unit and ignition HT coils/plug caps
    - d) Ignition control unit and pick-up coil
- [ ] Make sure that all wiring connections are clean, dry and tight. Look for chafed and broken wires (Chapters 5 and 9).

Compression low

- [ ] Spark plugs loose. Remove the plugs and inspect their threads. Reinstall and tighten to the specified torque (Chapter 1).
- [ ] Cylinder head not sufficiently tightened down. If the cylinder head is suspected of being loose, then there's a chance that the gasket or head is damaged if the problem has persisted for any length of time. The head bolts should be tightened to the proper torque in the correct sequence (Chapter 2).
- [ ] Improper valve clearance. This means that the valve is not closing completely and compression pressure is leaking past the valve. Check and adjust the valve clearances (Chapter 1).
- [ ] Cylinder and/or piston worn. Excessive wear will cause compression pressure to leak past the rings. This is usually accompanied by worn rings as well. A top-end overhaul is necessary (Chapter 2).
- [ ] Piston rings worn, weak, broken, or sticking. Broken or sticking piston rings usually indicate a lubrication or carburation problem that causes excess carbon deposits or seizures to form on the pistons and rings. Top-end overhaul is necessary (Chapter 2).
- [ ] Piston ring-to-groove clearance excessive. This is caused by excessive wear of the piston ring lands. Piston renewal is necessary (Chapter 2).
- [ ] Cylinder head gasket damaged. If the head is allowed to become loose, or if excessive carbon build-up on the piston crown and combustion chamber causes extremely high compression, the head gasket may leak. Retorquing the head is not always sufficient to restore the seal, so gasket renewal is necessary (Chapter 2).
- [ ] Cylinder head warped. This is caused by overheating or improperly tightened head bolts. Machine shop resurfacing or head renewal is necessary (Chapter 2).

Fault Finding

1 Engine doesn't start or is difficult to start (continued)

- ☐ Valve spring broken or weak. Caused by component failure or wear; the springs must be renewed (Chapter 2).
- ☐ Valve not seating properly. This is caused by a bent valve (from over-revving or improper valve adjustment), burned valve or seat (improper carburation) or an accumulation of carbon deposits on the seat (from carburation or lubrication problems). The valves must be cleaned and/or replaced and the seats serviced if possible (Chapter 2).

Stalls after starting

- ☐ Improper choke action. Make sure the choke linkage shaft is getting a full stroke and staying in the out position (Chapter 4).
- ☐ Ignition malfunction (Chapter 5).
- ☐ Carburettor malfunction (Chapter 4).
- ☐ Fuel contaminated. The fuel can be contaminated with either dirt or water, or can change chemically if the machine is allowed to sit for several months or more. Drain the tank and float chambers (Chapter 4).
- ☐ Intake air leak. Check for loose carburettor-to-intake manifold connections, loose or missing vacuum gauge adapter hose plugs, or loose carburettor tops (Chapter 4).
- ☐ Engine idle speed incorrect. Turn idle adjusting screw until the engine idles at the specified rpm (Chapter 1).

Rough idle

- ☐ Ignition malfunction (Chapter 5).
- ☐ Idle speed incorrect (Chapter 1).
- ☐ Carburettors not synchronised. Adjust carburettors with vacuum gauge or manometer set as described in Chapter 1.
- ☐ Carburettor malfunction (Chapter 4).
- ☐ Fuel contaminated. The fuel can be contaminated with either dirt or water, or can change chemically if the machine is allowed to sit for several months or more. Drain the tank and float chambers (Chapter 4).
- ☐ Intake air leak. Check for loose carburettor-to-intake manifold connections, loose or missing vacuum gauge adapter hose plugs or hoses, or loose carburettor tops (Chapter 4).
- ☐ Air filter clogged. Renew the air filter element (Chapter 1).

2 Poor running at low speeds

Spark weak

- ☐ Battery voltage low. Check and recharge battery (Chapter 9).
- ☐ Spark plugs fouled, defective or worn out. Refer to Chapter 1 for spark plug maintenance.
- ☐ HT coil/plug cap or wiring defective. Refer to Chapters 1 and 5 for details on the ignition system.
- ☐ Spark plug caps not making contact. Make sure they are securely pushed on to the plugs.
- ☐ Incorrect spark plugs. Wrong type, heat range or cap configuration. Check and install correct plugs listed in Chapter 1.
- ☐ Ignition control unit defective (Chapter 5).
- ☐ Pick-up coil defective (Chapter 5).

Fuel/air mixture incorrect

- ☐ Pilot screws out of adjustment (Chapter 4).
- ☐ Pilot jet or air passage clogged. Remove and overhaul the carburettors (Chapter 4).
- ☐ Air bleed holes clogged. Remove carburettor and blow out all passages (Chapter 4).
- ☐ Air filter clogged, poorly sealed or missing (Chapter 1).
- ☐ Air filter housing poorly sealed. Look for cracks, holes or loose clamps and renew or repair defective parts.
- ☐ Fuel level too high or too low. Check the level (Chapter 4).
- ☐ Fuel tank breather hose obstructed.
- ☐ Carburettor intake manifolds loose. Check for cracks, breaks, tears or loose clamps. Renew the rubber intake manifold joints if split or perished.

Compression low

- ☐ Spark plugs loose. Remove the plugs and inspect their threads. Reinstall and tighten to the specified torque (Chapter 1).
- ☐ Cylinder head not sufficiently tightened down. If the cylinder head is suspected of being loose, then there's a chance that the gasket and head are damaged if the problem has persisted for any length of time. The head bolts should be tightened to the proper torque in the correct sequence (Chapter 2).
- ☐ Improper valve clearance. This means that the valve is not closing completely and compression pressure is leaking past the valve. Check and adjust the valve clearances (Chapter 1).
- ☐ Cylinder and/or piston worn. Excessive wear will cause compression pressure to leak past the rings. This is usually accompanied by worn rings as well. A top-end overhaul is necessary (Chapter 2).
- ☐ Piston rings worn, weak, broken, or sticking. Broken or sticking piston rings usually indicate a lubrication or carburation problem that causes excess carbon deposits or seizures to form on the pistons and rings. Top-end overhaul is necessary (Chapter 2).
- ☐ Piston ring-to-groove clearance excessive. This is caused by excessive wear of the piston ring lands. Piston renewal is necessary (Chapter 2).
- ☐ Cylinder head gasket damaged. If the head is allowed to become loose, or if excessive carbon build-up on the piston crown and combustion chamber causes extremely high compression, the head gasket may leak. Retorquing the head is not always sufficient to restore the seal, so gasket renewal is necessary (Chapter 2).
- ☐ Cylinder head warped. This is caused by overheating or improperly tightened head bolts. Machine shop resurfacing or head renewal is necessary (Chapter 2).
- ☐ Valve spring broken or weak. Caused by component failure or wear; the springs must be renewed (Chapter 2).
- ☐ Valve not seating properly. This is caused by a bent valve (from over-revving or improper valve adjustment), burned valve or seat (improper carburation) or an accumulation of carbon deposits on the seat (from carburation, lubrication problems). The valves must be cleaned and/or replaced and the seats serviced if possible (Chapter 2).

Poor acceleration

- ☐ Carburettors leaking or dirty. Overhaul the carburettors (Chapter 4).
- ☐ Timing not advancing. The pick-up coil or the ignition control unit may be defective. If so, they must be renewed, as they can't be repaired.
- ☐ Carburettors not synchronised. Adjust them with a vacuum gauge set or manometer (Chapter 1).
- ☐ Engine oil viscosity too high. Using a heavier oil than that recommended in Chapter 1 can damage the oil pump or lubrication system and cause drag on the engine.
- ☐ Brakes dragging. Usually caused by debris which has entered the brake piston seals, or from a warped disc or bent axle. Repair as necessary (Chapter 7).
- ☐ Fuel pump flow rate insufficient. Check the pump (Chapter 4).

REF•38 Fault Finding

3 Poor running or no power at high speed

Firing incorrect
- [ ] Air filter restricted. Clean or renew filter (Chapter 1).
- [ ] Spark plugs fouled, defective or worn out. See Chapter 1 for spark plug maintenance.
- [ ] HT coil/plug cap or wiring defective. See Chapters 1 and 5 for details of the ignition system.
- [ ] Spark plug caps not in good contact (Chapter 5).
- [ ] Incorrect spark plugs. Wrong type, heat range or cap configuration. Check and install correct plugs listed in Chapter 1.
- [ ] Ignition control unit defective (Chapter 5).

Fuel/air mixture incorrect
- [ ] Main jet clogged. Dirt, water or other contaminants can clog the main jets. Clean the fuel tap strainer, the float chamber area, and the jets and carburettor orifices (Chapter 4). Renew the in-line fuel filter (Chapter 1).
- [ ] Main jet wrong size. The standard jetting is for sea level atmospheric pressure and oxygen content.
- [ ] Throttle shaft-to-carburettor body clearance excessive. Refer to Chapter 4 for inspection and part renewal procedures.
- [ ] Air bleed holes clogged. Remove and overhaul carburettors (Chapter 4).
- [ ] Air filter clogged, poorly sealed, or missing (Chapter 1).
- [ ] Air filter housing poorly sealed. Look for cracks, holes or loose clamps, and renew or repair defective parts.
- [ ] Fuel level too high or too low. Check the level (Chapter 4).
- [ ] Fuel tank breather hose obstructed.
- [ ] Carburettor intake manifolds loose. Check for cracks, breaks, tears or loose clamps. Renew the rubber intake manifolds if they are split or perished (Chapter 4).

Compression low
- [ ] Spark plugs loose. Remove the plugs and inspect their threads. Reinstall and tighten to the specified torque (Chapter 1).
- [ ] Cylinder head not sufficiently tightened down. If the cylinder head is suspected of being loose, then there's a chance that the gasket and head are damaged if the problem has persisted for any length of time. The head bolts should be tightened to the proper torque in the correct sequence (Chapter 2).
- [ ] Improper valve clearance. This means that the valve is not closing completely and compression pressure is leaking past the valve. Check and adjust the valve clearances (Chapter 1).
- [ ] Cylinder and/or piston worn. Excessive wear will cause compression pressure to leak past the rings. This is usually accompanied by worn rings as well. A top-end overhaul is necessary (Chapter 2).
- [ ] Piston rings worn, weak, broken, or sticking. Broken or sticking piston rings usually indicate a lubrication or carburation problem that causes excess carbon deposits or seizures to form on the pistons and rings. Top-end overhaul is necessary (Chapter 2).
- [ ] Piston ring-to-groove clearance excessive. This is caused by excessive wear of the piston ring lands. Piston renewal is necessary (Chapter 2).
- [ ] Cylinder head gasket damaged. If the head is allowed to become loose, or if excessive carbon build-up on the piston crown and combustion chamber causes extremely high compression, the head gasket may leak. Retorquing the head is not always sufficient to restore the seal, so gasket renewal is necessary (Chapter 2).
- [ ] Cylinder head warped. This is caused by overheating or improperly tightened head bolts. Machine shop resurfacing or head renewal is necessary (Chapter 2).
- [ ] Valve spring broken or weak. Caused by component failure or wear; the springs must be renewed (Chapter 2).
- [ ] Valve not seating properly. This is caused by a bent valve (from over-revving or improper valve adjustment), burned valve or seat (improper carburation) or an accumulation of carbon deposits on the seat (from carburation or lubrication problems). The valves must be cleaned and/or renewed and the seats serviced if possible (Chapter 2).

Knocking or pinking
- [ ] Carbon build-up in combustion chamber. Use of a fuel additive that will dissolve the adhesive bonding the carbon particles to the crown and chamber is the easiest way to remove the build-up. Otherwise, the cylinder head will have to be removed and decarbonised (Chapter 2).
- [ ] Incorrect or poor quality fuel. Old or improper grades of fuel can cause detonation. This causes the piston to rattle, thus the knocking or pinking sound. Drain old fuel and always use the recommended fuel grade.
- [ ] Spark plug heat range incorrect. Uncontrolled detonation indicates the plug heat range is too hot. The plug in effect becomes a glow plug, raising cylinder temperatures. Install the proper heat range plug (Chapter 1).
- [ ] Improper air/fuel mixture. This will cause the cylinders to run hot, which leads to detonation. Clogged jets or an air leak can cause this imbalance. See Chapter 4.

Miscellaneous causes
- [ ] Throttle valve doesn't open fully. Adjust the throttle grip freeplay (Chapter 1).
- [ ] Clutch slipping. May be caused by loose or worn clutch components. Refer to Chapter 2 for clutch overhaul procedures.
- [ ] Engine oil viscosity too high. Using a heavier oil than the one recommended in Chapter 1 can damage the oil pump or lubrication system and cause drag on the engine.
- [ ] Brakes dragging. Usually caused by debris which has entered the brake piston seals, or from a warped disc or bent axle. Repair as necessary.
- [ ] Fuel pump flow rate insufficient. Check the pump (Chapter 4).

Fault Finding REF•39

4 Overheating

Engine overheats
- ☐ Coolant level low. Check and add coolant (Chapter 1).
- ☐ Leak in cooling system. Check cooling system hoses and radiator for leaks and other damage. Repair or renew parts as necessary (Chapter 3).
- ☐ Thermostat sticking open or closed. Check and renew as described in Chapter 3.
- ☐ Faulty radiator cap. Remove the cap and have it pressure tested.
- ☐ Coolant passages clogged. Have the entire system drained and flushed, then refill with fresh coolant.
- ☐ Water pump defective. Remove the pump and check the components (Chapter 3).
- ☐ Clogged radiator fins. Clean them by blowing compressed air through the fins from the backside.
- ☐ Cooling fan or fan switch fault (Chapter 3).

Firing incorrect
- ☐ Spark plugs fouled, defective or worn out. See Chapter 1 for spark plug maintenance.
- ☐ Incorrect spark plugs.
- ☐ Ignition control unit defective (Chapter 5).
- ☐ Faulty ignition HT coils/plug caps (Chapter 5).

Fuel/air mixture incorrect
- ☐ Main jet clogged. Dirt, water and other contaminants can clog the main jets. Clean the fuel tap strainer, the float chamber area and the jets and carburettor orifices (Chapter 4). Renew the in-line fuel filter (Chapter 1).
- ☐ Main jet wrong size. The standard jetting is for sea level atmospheric pressure and oxygen content.
- ☐ Air filter clogged, poorly sealed or missing (Chapter 1).
- ☐ Air filter housing poorly sealed. Look for cracks, holes or loose clamps and renew or repair.
- ☐ Fuel level too low. Check the level (Chapter 4).
- ☐ Fuel tank breather hose obstructed.
- ☐ Carburettor intake manifolds loose. Check for cracks, breaks, tears or loose clamps. Renew the rubber intake manifold joints if split or perished.

Compression too high
- ☐ Carbon build-up in combustion chamber. Use of a fuel additive that will dissolve the adhesive bonding the carbon particles to the piston crown and chamber is the easiest way to remove the build-up. Otherwise, the cylinder head will have to be removed and decarbonised (Chapter 2).
- ☐ Improperly machined head surface or installation of incorrect gasket during engine assembly.

Engine load excessive
- ☐ Clutch slipping. Can be caused by damaged, loose or worn clutch components. Refer to Chapter 2 for overhaul procedures.
- ☐ Engine oil level too high. The addition of too much oil will cause pressurisation of the crankcase and inefficient engine operation. Check Specifications and drain to proper level (Chapter 1).
- ☐ Engine oil viscosity too high. Using a heavier oil than the one recommended in Chapter 1 can damage the oil pump or lubrication system as well as cause drag on the engine.
- ☐ Brakes dragging. Usually caused by debris which has entered the brake piston seals, or from a warped disc or bent axle. Repair as necessary.

Lubrication inadequate
- ☐ Engine oil level too low. Friction caused by intermittent lack of lubrication or from oil that is overworked can cause overheating. The oil provides a definite cooling function in the engine. Check the oil level (Chapter 1).
- ☐ Poor quality engine oil or incorrect viscosity or type. Oil is rated not only according to viscosity but also according to type. Some oils are not rated high enough for use in this engine. Check the Specifications section and change to the correct oil (Chapter 1).

Miscellaneous causes
- ☐ Modification to exhaust system. Most aftermarket exhaust systems cause the engine to run leaner, which make them run hotter. When installing an accessory exhaust system, always rejet the carburettors.

5 Clutch problems

Clutch slipping
- ☐ Incorrectly adjusted cable (see Chapter 1).
- ☐ Friction plates worn or warped. Overhaul the clutch assembly (Chapter 2).
- ☐ Plain plates warped (Chapter 2).
- ☐ Clutch release mechanism defective. Renew any defective parts (Chapter 2).
- ☐ Clutch centre or housing unevenly worn. This causes improper engagement of the plates. Renew the damaged or worn parts (Chapter 2).

Clutch not disengaging completely
- ☐ Incorrectly adjusted cable (see Chapter 1).
- ☐ Clutch plates warped or damaged. This will cause clutch drag, which in turn will cause the machine to creep. Overhaul the clutch assembly (Chapter 2).
- ☐ Clutch springs broken or weak (Chapter 2).
- ☐ Engine oil deteriorated. Old, thin, worn out oil will not provide proper lubrication for the plates, causing the clutch to drag. Change the oil and filter (Chapter 1).
- ☐ Engine oil viscosity too high. Using a heavier oil than recommended in Chapter 1 can cause the plates to stick together, putting a drag on the engine. Change to the correct weight oil (Chapter 1).
- ☐ Clutch needle bearing seized on input shaft. Lack of lubrication, severe wear or damage can cause the bearing centre to seize on the shaft. Overhaul of the clutch, and perhaps transmission, may be necessary to repair the damage (Chapter 2).
- ☐ Clutch release mechanism defective. Overhaul it (Chapter 2).
- ☐ Loose clutch centre nut. Causes housing and centre misalignment putting a drag on the engine. Engagement adjustment continually varies. Overhaul the clutch assembly (Chapter 2).

REF•40 Fault Finding

6 Gearchanging problems

Doesn't go into gear or lever doesn't return
- [ ] Clutch not disengaging. See above.
- [ ] Selector fork(s) bent or seized. Often caused by dropping the machine or from lack of lubrication. Overhaul the transmission (Chapter 2).
- [ ] Gear(s) stuck on shaft. Most often caused by a lack of lubrication or excessive wear in transmission gears and bushes. Overhaul the transmission (Chapter 2).
- [ ] Selector drum binding. Caused by lubrication failure or excessive wear. Renew the drum and bearing (Chapter 2).
- [ ] Gearchange shaft centralising spring weak or broken (Chapter 2).
- [ ] Gearchange lever broken. Splines stripped out of lever or shaft, caused by allowing the lever to get loose or from dropping the machine. Renew necessary parts (Chapter 2).
- [ ] Gearchange mechanism stopper arm broken or worn. Full engagement and rotary movement of selector drum results. Renew the arm (Chapter 2).
- [ ] Stopper arm spring broken. Allows arm to float, causing sporadic gearchange operation. Renew spring (Chapter 2).

Jumps out of gear
- [ ] Selector fork(s) worn. Overhaul the transmission (Chapter 2).
- [ ] Gear groove(s) worn. Overhaul the transmission (Chapter 2).
- [ ] Gear dogs or dog slots worn or damaged. The gears should be inspected and renewed. No attempt should be made to service the worn parts.

Overselects
- [ ] Stopper arm spring weak or broken (Chapter 2).
- [ ] Gearchange shaft centralising spring locating pin broken or distorted (Chapter 2).

7 Abnormal engine noise

Knocking or pinking
- [ ] Carbon build-up in combustion chamber. Use of a fuel additive that will dissolve the adhesive bonding the carbon particles to the piston crown and chamber is the easiest way to remove the build-up. Otherwise, the cylinder head will have to be removed and decarbonised (Chapter 2).
- [ ] Incorrect or poor quality fuel. Old or improper fuel can cause detonation. This causes the pistons to rattle, thus the knocking or pinking sound. Drain the old fuel and always use the recommended grade fuel (Chapter 4).
- [ ] Spark plug heat range incorrect. Uncontrolled detonation indicates that the plug heat range is too hot. The plug in effect becomes a glow plug, raising cylinder temperatures. Install the proper heat range plug (Chapter 1).
- [ ] Improper air/fuel mixture. This will cause the cylinders to run hot and lead to detonation. Clogged jets or an air leak can cause this imbalance. See Chapter 4.

Piston slap or rattling
- [ ] Cylinder-to-piston clearance excessive. Caused by improper assembly. Inspect and overhaul top-end parts (Chapter 2).
- [ ] Connecting rod bent. Caused by over-revving, trying to start a badly flooded engine or from ingesting a foreign object into the combustion chamber. Renew the damaged parts (Chapter 2).
- [ ] Piston pin or piston pin bore worn or seized from wear or lack of lubrication. Renew damaged parts (Chapter 2).
- [ ] Piston ring(s) worn, broken or sticking. Overhaul the top-end (Chapter 2).
- [ ] Piston seizure damage. Usually from lack of lubrication or overheating. Renew the pistons and crankcases, as necessary (Chapter 2).
- [ ] Connecting rod upper or lower end clearance excessive. Caused by excessive wear or lack of lubrication. Renew worn parts.

Valve noise
- [ ] Incorrect valve clearances. Adjust the clearances by referring to Chapter 1.
- [ ] Valve spring broken or weak. Check and renew weak valve springs (Chapter 2).
- [ ] Camshaft or cylinder head worn or damaged. Lack of lubrication at high rpm is usually the cause of damage. Insufficient oil or failure to change the oil at the recommended intervals are the chief causes. Since there are no replaceable bearings in the head, the head itself will have to be renewed if there is excessive wear or damage (Chapter 2).

Other noise
- [ ] Cylinder head gasket leaking.
- [ ] Exhaust pipe leaking at cylinder head connection. Caused by improper fit of pipe(s) or loose exhaust flange. All exhaust fasteners should be tightened evenly and carefully. Failure to do this will lead to a leak.
- [ ] Crankshaft runout excessive. Caused by a bent crankshaft (from over-revving) or damage from an upper cylinder component failure. Can also be attributed to dropping the machine on either of the crankshaft ends.
- [ ] Engine mounting bolts loose. Tighten all engine mount bolts (Chapter 2).
- [ ] Crankshaft bearings worn (Chapter 2).
- [ ] Cam chain worn, tensioner faulty or chain guides worn (Chapter 2)..

Fault Finding REF•41

8 Abnormal driveline noise

Clutch noise
- [ ] Clutch housing/friction plate clearance excessive (Chapter 2).
- [ ] Loose or damaged clutch pressure plate and/or bolts (Chapter 2).

Transmission noise
- [ ] Bearings/bushes worn. Also includes the possibility that the shafts are worn. Overhaul the transmission (Chapter 2).
- [ ] Gears worn or chipped (Chapter 2).
- [ ] Metal chips jammed in gear teeth. Probably pieces from a broken clutch, gear or selector mechanism that were picked up by the gears. This will cause early bearing failure (Chapter 2).
- [ ] Engine oil level too low. Causes a howl from transmission. Also affects engine power and clutch operation (Chapter 1).

Final drive noise
- [ ] Chain not adjusted properly (Chapter 1).
- [ ] Front or rear sprocket loose. Tighten fasteners (Chapter 6).
- [ ] Sprockets worn. Renew sprockets (Chapter 6).
- [ ] Rear sprocket warped. Renew sprockets (Chapter 6).
- [ ] Loose or worn rear wheel or sprocket coupling bearings. Check and renew as needed (Chapter 7).

9 Abnormal frame and suspension noise

Front end noise
- [ ] Low fluid level or improper viscosity oil in forks. This can sound like spurting and is usually accompanied by irregular fork action (Chapter 6).
- [ ] Spring weak or broken. Makes a clicking or scraping sound. Fork oil, when drained, will have a lot of metal particles in it (Chapter 6).
- [ ] Steering head bearings loose or damaged. Clicks when braking. Check and adjust or renew as necessary (Chapters 1 and 6).
- [ ] Fork yokes loose. Make sure all clamp pinch bolts are tightened to the specified torque (Chapter 6).
- [ ] Fork tube bent. Good possibility if machine has been dropped. Replace tube with a new one (Chapter 6).
- [ ] Front axle bolt or axle clamp bolt loose. Tighten them to the specified torque (Chapter 7).
- [ ] Loose or worn wheel bearings. Check and renew as needed (Chapter 7).

Shock absorber noise
- [ ] Fluid level incorrect. Indicates a leak caused by defective seal. Shock will be covered with oil. Renew shock or seek advice on repair from a Yamaha dealer (Chapter 6).
- [ ] Defective shock absorber with internal damage. This is in the body of the shock and can't be remedied. The shock must be replaced with a new one (Chapter 6).
- [ ] Bent or damaged shock body. Replace the shock with a new one (Chapter 6).
- [ ] Loose or worn suspension linkage components. Check and renew as necessary (Chapter 6).

Brake noise
- [ ] Squeal caused by pad shim not installed or positioned correctly (Chapter 7).
- [ ] Squeal caused by dust on brake pads. Usually found in combination with glazed pads. Clean using brake cleaning solvent (Chapter 7).
- [ ] Contamination of brake pads. Oil, brake fluid or dirt causing brake to chatter or squeal. Clean or renew pads (Chapter 7).
- [ ] Pads glazed. Caused by excessive heat from prolonged use or from contamination. Do not use sandpaper, emery cloth, carborundum cloth or any other abrasive to roughen the pad surfaces as abrasives will stay in the pad material and damage the disc. A very fine flat file can be used, but pad renewal is suggested as a cure (Chapter 7).
- [ ] Disc warped. Can cause a chattering, clicking or intermittent squeal. Usually accompanied by a pulsating lever and uneven braking. Renew the disc (Chapter 7).
- [ ] Loose or worn wheel bearings. Check and renew as needed (Chapter 7).

REF•42 Fault Finding

10 Excessive exhaust smoke

White smoke

- ☐ Piston oil ring worn. The ring may be broken or damaged, causing oil from the crankcase to be pulled past the piston into the combustion chamber. Replace the rings with new ones (Chapter 2).
- ☐ Cylinders worn, cracked, or scored. Caused by overheating or oil starvation. Check the cylinder bores, lubrication system and cooling system (see Chapters 2 and 3).
- ☐ Valve oil seal damaged or worn. Replace oil seals with new ones (Chapter 2).
- ☐ Valve guide worn. Perform a complete valve job (Chapter 2).
- ☐ Engine oil level too high, which causes the oil to be forced past the rings. Drain oil to the proper level (Chapter 1).
- ☐ Head gasket broken between oil return and cylinder. Causes oil to be pulled into the combustion chamber. Replace the head gasket and check the head for warpage (Chapter 2).
- ☐ Abnormal crankcase pressurisation, which forces oil past the rings. Clogged breather is usually the cause.

Black smoke

- ☐ Air filter clogged. Clean or replace the element (Chapter 1).
- ☐ Main jet too large or loose. Compare the jet size to the Specifications (Chapter 4).
- ☐ Choke cable or linkage shaft stuck, causing fuel to be pulled through choke circuit (Chapter 4).
- ☐ Fuel level too high. Check and adjust the float height(s) as necessary (Chapter 4).
- ☐ Float needle valve held off needle seat. Clean the float chambers and fuel line and replace the needles and seats if necessary (Chapter 4).

Brown smoke

- ☐ Main jet too small or clogged. Lean condition caused by wrong size main jet or by a restricted orifice. Clean float chambers and jets and compare jet size to Specifications (Chapter 4).
- ☐ Fuel flow insufficient - float needle valve stuck closed due to chemical reaction with old fuel; fuel level incorrect; restricted fuel line; faulty fuel pump (Chapter 4).
- ☐ Carburettor intake manifold clamps loose (Chapter 4).
- ☐ Air filter poorly sealed or not installed (Chapter 1).

11 Poor handling or stability

Handlebar hard to turn

- ☐ Steering head bearing adjuster nut too tight. Check adjustment as described in Chapter 1.
- ☐ Bearings damaged. Roughness can be felt as the bars are turned from side-to-side. Renew bearings and races (Chapter 6).
- ☐ Races dented or worn. Denting results from wear in only one position (e.g., straight ahead), from a collision or hitting a pothole or from dropping the machine. Renew races and bearings (Chapter 6
- ☐ Steering stem lubrication inadequate. Causes are grease getting hard from age or being washed out by high pressure car washes. Disassemble steering head and repack bearings (Chapter 6).
- ☐ Steering stem bent. Caused by a collision, hitting a pothole or by dropping the machine. Renew damaged part. Don't try to straighten the steering stem (Chapter 6).
- ☐ Front tyre air pressure too low (Chapter 1).

Handlebar shakes or vibrates excessively

- ☐ Tyres worn or out of balance (Chapter 7).
- ☐ Swingarm bearings worn. Renew worn bearings (Chapter 6).
- ☐ Wheel rim(s) warped or damaged. Inspect wheels for runout (Chapter 7).
- ☐ Wheel bearings worn. Worn front or rear wheel bearings can cause poor tracking. Worn front bearings will cause wobble (Chapter 7).
- ☐ Handlebar clamp bolts loose (Chapter 6).
- ☐ Fork yoke bolts loose. Tighten them to the specified torque (Chapter 6).
- ☐ Engine mounting bolts loose. Will cause excessive vibration with increased engine rpm (Chapter 2).

Handlebar pulls to one side

- ☐ Frame bent. Definitely suspect this if the machine has been dropped. May or may not be accompanied by cracking near the bend. Renew the frame (Chapter 6).
- ☐ Wheels out of alignment. Caused by improper location of axle spacers or from bent steering stem or frame (Chapter 6).
- ☐ Swingarm bent or twisted. Caused by age (metal fatigue) or impact damage. Renew the arm (Chapter 6).
- ☐ Steering stem bent. Caused by impact damage or by dropping the motorcycle. Renew the steering stem (Chapter 6).
- ☐ Fork tube bent. Disassemble the forks and renew the damaged parts (Chapter 6).
- ☐ Fork oil level uneven. Check and add or drain as necessary (Chapter 6).

Poor shock absorbing qualities

- ☐ Too hard:
  - a) Fork oil level excessive (Chapter 6).
  - b) Fork oil viscosity too high. Use a lighter oil (see the Specifications in Chapter 6).
  - c) Fork tube bent. Causes a harsh, sticking feeling (Chapter 6).
  - d) Fork internal damage (Chapter 6).
  - e) Shock shaft or body bent or damaged (Chapter 6).
  - f) Shock internal damage.
  - g) Tyre pressure too high (Chapter 1).
- ☐ Too soft:
  - a) Fork or shock oil insufficient and/or leaking (Chapter 6).
  - b) Fork oil level too low (Chapter 6).
  - c) Fork oil viscosity too light (Chapter 6).
  - d) Fork springs weak or broken (Chapter 6).
  - e) Shock internal damage or leakage (Chapter 6).

Fault Finding REF•43

12 Braking problems

Brakes are spongy, don't hold
- ☐ Air in brake line. Caused by inattention to master cylinder fluid level or by leakage. Locate problem and bleed brakes (Chapter 7).
- ☐ Pad or disc worn (Chapters 1 and 7).
- ☐ Brake fluid leak. See paragraph 1.
- ☐ Contaminated pads. Caused by contamination with oil, grease, brake fluid, etc. Clean or renew pads. Clean disc thoroughly with brake cleaner (Chapter 7).
- ☐ Brake fluid deteriorated. Fluid is old or contaminated. Drain system, replenish with new fluid and bleed the system (Chapter 7).
- ☐ Master cylinder internal parts worn or damaged causing fluid to bypass (Chapter 7).
- ☐ Master cylinder bore scratched by foreign material or broken spring. Repair or renew master cylinder (Chapter 7).
- ☐ Disc warped. Renew disc (Chapter 7).

Brake lever or pedal pulsates
- ☐ Disc warped. Renew disc (Chapter 7).
- ☐ Axle bent. Renew axle (Chapter 7).
- ☐ Brake caliper bolts loose (Chapter 7).
- ☐ Wheel warped or otherwise damaged (Chapter 7).
- ☐ Wheel bearings damaged or worn (Chapter 7).

Brakes drag
- ☐ Master cylinder piston seized. Caused by wear or damage to piston or cylinder bore (Chapter 7).
- ☐ Lever balky or stuck. Check pivot and lubricate (Chapter 7).
- ☐ Brake caliper piston seized in bore. Caused by wear or ingestion of dirt past deteriorated seal (Chapter 7).
- ☐ Brake caliper sticking due to lack of lubrication on mounting bolt pins (rear caliper only) (Chapter 7).
- ☐ Brake pad damaged. Pad material separated from backing plate. Usually caused by faulty manufacturing process or from contact with chemicals. Renew pads (Chapter 7).
- ☐ Pads improperly installed (Chapter 7).

13 Electrical problems

Battery dead or weak
- ☐ Battery faulty. Caused by sulphated plates which are shorted through sedimentation. Also, broken battery terminal making only occasional contact (Chapter 9).
- ☐ Battery cables making poor contact (Chapter 9).
- ☐ Load excessive. Caused by addition of high wattage lights or other electrical accessories.
- ☐ Ignition (main) switch defective. Switch either grounds (earths) internally or fails to shut off system. Renew the switch (Chapter 9).
- ☐ Regulator/rectifier defective (Chapter 9).
- ☐ Alternator stator coil open or shorted (Chapter 9).
- ☐ Wiring faulty. Wiring grounded (earthed) or connections loose in ignition, charging or lighting circuits (Chapter 9).

Battery overcharged
- ☐ Regulator/rectifier defective. Overcharging is noticed when battery gets excessively warm (Chapter 9).
- ☐ Battery defective. Renew battery (Chapter 9).
- ☐ Battery amperage too low, wrong type or size. Install manufacturer's specified amp-hour battery to handle charging load (Chapter 9).

REF•44 Fault Finding Notes

Fault Finding Equipment REF•45

Checking engine compression

● Low compression will result in exhaust smoke, heavy oil consumption, poor starting and poor performance. A compression test will provide useful information about an engine's condition and if performed regularly, can give warning of trouble before any other symptoms become apparent.
● A compression gauge will be required, along with an adapter to suit the spark plug hole thread size. Note that the screw-in type gauge/adapter set up is preferable to the rubber cone type.
● Before carrying out the test, first check the valve clearances as described in Chapter 1.

1 Run the engine until it reaches normal operating temperature, then stop it and remove the spark plug(s), taking care not to scald your hands on the hot components.
2 Install the gauge adapter and compression gauge in No. 1 cylinder spark plug hole **(see illustration 1)**.

Screw the compression gauge adapter into the spark plug hole, then screw the gauge into the adapter

3 On kickstart-equipped motorcycles, make sure the ignition switch is OFF, then open the throttle fully and kick the engine over a couple of times until the gauge reading stabilises.
4 On motorcycles with electric start only, the procedure will differ depending on the nature of the ignition system. Flick the engine kill switch (engine stop switch) to OFF and turn the ignition switch ON; open the throttle fully and crank the engine over on the starter motor for a couple of revolutions until the gauge reading stabilises. If the starter will not operate with the kill switch OFF, turn the ignition switch OFF and refer to the next paragraph.
5 Install the spark plugs back into their suppressor caps and arrange the plug electrodes so that their metal bodies are earthed (grounded) against the cylinder head; this is essential to prevent damage to the ignition system as the engine is spun over **(see illustration 2)**. Position the plugs well

All spark plugs must be earthed (grounded) against the cylinder head

away from the plug holes otherwise there is a risk of atomised fuel escaping from the combustion chambers and igniting. As a safety precaution, cover the top of the valve cover with rag. Now turn the ignition switch ON and kill switch ON, open the throttle fully and crank the engine over on the starter motor for a couple of revolutions until the gauge reading stabilises.
6 After one or two revolutions the pressure should build up to a maximum figure and then stabilise. Take a note of this reading and on multi-cylinder engines repeat the test on the remaining cylinders.
7 The correct pressures are given in Chapter 2 Specifications. If the results fall within the specified range and on multi-cylinder engines all are relatively equal, the engine is in good condition. If there is a marked difference between the readings, or if the readings are lower than specified, inspection of the top-end components will be required.
8 Low compression pressure may be due to worn cylinder bores, pistons or rings, failure of the cylinder head gasket, worn valve seals, or poor valve seating.
9 To distinguish between cylinder/piston wear and valve leakage, pour a small quantity of oil into the bore to temporarily seal the piston rings, then repeat the compression tests **(see illustration 3)**. If the readings show

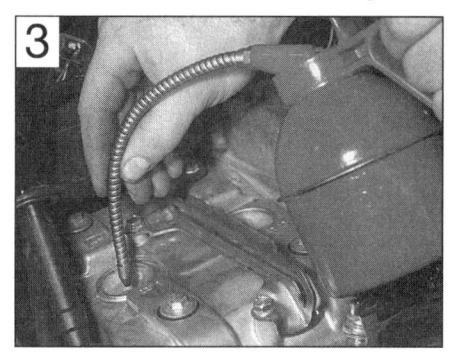

Bores can be temporarily sealed with a squirt of motor oil

a noticeable increase in pressure this confirms that the cylinder bore, piston, or rings are worn. If, however, no change is indicated, the cylinder head gasket or valves should be examined.
10 High compression pressure indicates excessive carbon build-up in the combustion chamber and on the piston crown. If this is the case the cylinder head should be removed and the deposits removed. Note that excessive carbon build-up is less likely with the used on modern fuels.

Checking battery open-circuit voltage

⚠ *Warning: The gases produced by the battery are explosive - never smoke or create any sparks in the vicinity of the battery. Never allow the electrolyte to contact your skin or clothing - if it does, wash it off and seek immediate medical attention.*

REF•46 Fault Finding Equipment

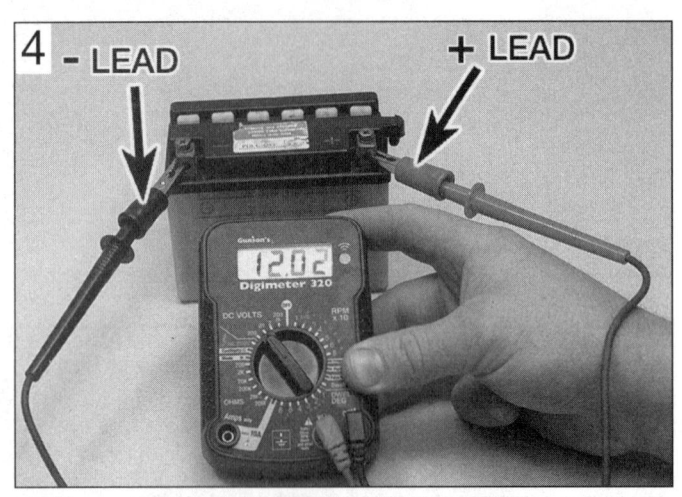

Measuring open-circuit battery voltage

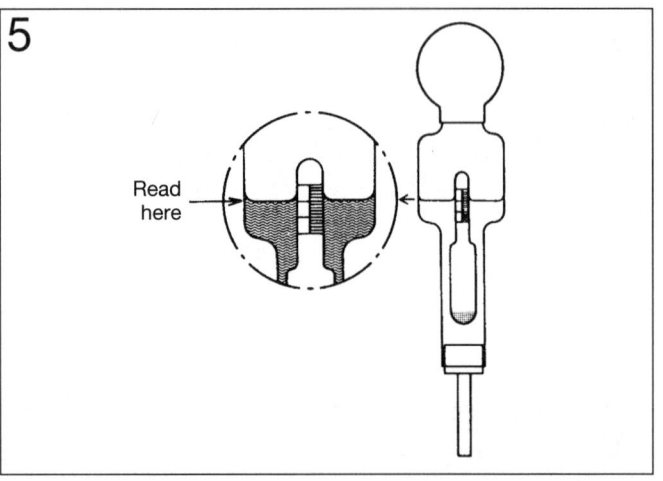

Float-type hydrometer for measuring battery specific gravity

- Before any electrical fault is investigated the battery should be checked.
- You'll need a dc voltmeter or multimeter to check battery voltage. Check that the leads are inserted in the correct terminals on the meter, red lead to positive (+ve), black lead to negative (-ve). Incorrect connections can damage the meter.
- A sound fully-charged 12 volt battery should produce between 12.3 and 12.6 volts across its terminals (12.8 volts for a maintenance-free battery). On machines with a 6 volt battery, voltage should be between 6.1 and 6.3 volts.

1 Set a multimeter to the 0 to 20 volts dc range and connect its probes across the battery terminals. Connect the meter's positive (+ve) probe, usually red, to the battery positive (+ve) terminal, followed by the meter's negative (-ve) probe, usually black, to the battery negative terminal (-ve) **(see illustration 4)**.

2 If battery voltage is low (below 10 volts on a 12 volt battery or below 4 volts on a six volt battery), charge the battery and test the voltage again. If the battery repeatedly goes flat, investigate the motorcycle's charging system.

Checking battery specific gravity (SG)

Warning: The gases produced by the battery are explosive - never smoke or create any sparks in the vicinity of the battery. Never allow the electrolyte to contact your skin or clothing - if it does, wash it off and seek immediate medical attention.

- The specific gravity check gives an indication of a battery's state of charge.
- A hydrometer is used for measuring specific gravity. Make sure you purchase one which has a small enough hose to insert in the aperture of a motorcycle battery.
- Specific gravity is simply a measure of the electrolyte's density compared with that of water. Water has an SG of 1.000 and fully-charged battery electrolyte is about 26% heavier, at 1.260.
- Specific gravity checks are not possible on maintenance-free batteries. Testing the open-circuit voltage is the only means of determining their state of charge.

1 To measure SG, remove the battery from the motorcycle and remove the first cell cap. Draw

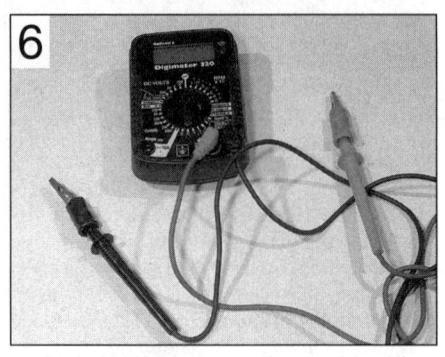

Digital multimeter can be used for all electrical tests

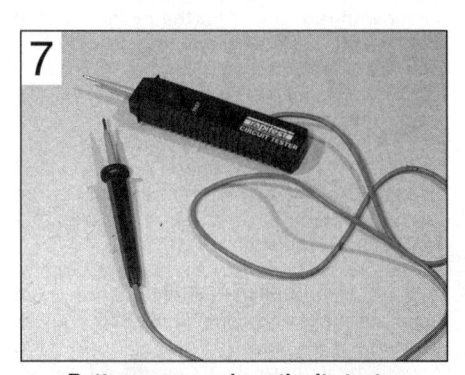

Battery-powered continuity tester

some electrolyte into the hydrometer and note the reading **(see illustration 5)**. Return the electrolyte to the cell and install the cap.

2 The reading should be in the region of 1.260 to 1.280. If SG is below 1.200 the battery needs charging. Note that SG will vary with temperature; it should be measured at 20°C (68°F). Add 0.007 to the reading for every 10°C above 20°C, and subtract 0.007 from the reading for every 10°C below 20°C. Add 0.004 to the reading for every 10°F above 68°F, and subtract 0.004 from the reading for every 10°F below 68°F.

3 When the check is complete, rinse the hydrometer thoroughly with clean water.

Checking for continuity

- The term continuity describes the uninterrupted flow of electricity through an electrical circuit. A continuity check will determine whether an **open-circuit** situation exists.
- Continuity can be checked with an ohmmeter, multimeter, continuity tester or battery and bulb test circuit **(see illustrations 6, 7 and 8)**.

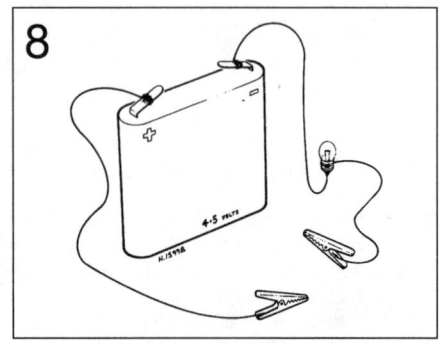

Battery and bulb test circuit

Fault Finding Equipment REF•47

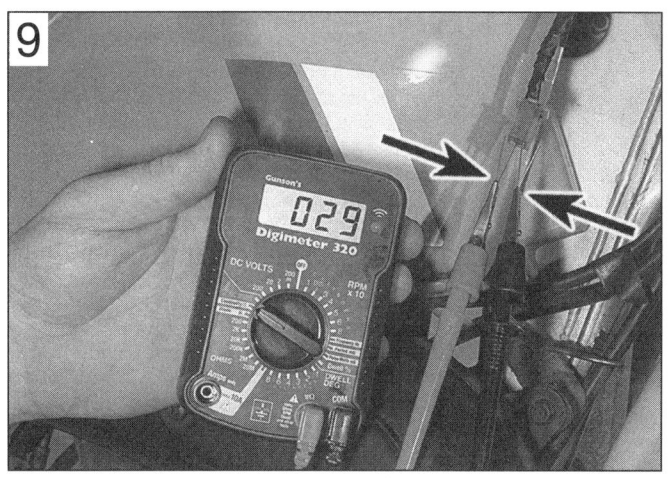

Continuity check of front brake light switch using a meter - note split pins used to access connector terminals

Continuity check of rear brake light switch using a continuity tester

- All of these instruments are self-powered by a battery, therefore the checks are made with the ignition OFF.
- As a safety precaution, always disconnect the battery negative (-ve) lead before making checks, particularly if ignition switch checks are being made.
- If using a meter, select the appropriate ohms scale and check that the meter reads infinity (∞). Touch the meter probes together and check that meter reads zero; where necessary adjust the meter so that it reads zero.
- After using a meter, always switch it OFF to conserve its battery.

Switch checks

1 If a switch is at fault, trace its wiring up to the wiring connectors. Separate the wire connectors and inspect them for security and condition. A build-up of dirt or corrosion here will most likely be the cause of the problem - clean up and apply a water dispersant such as WD40.

2 If using a test meter, set the meter to the ohms x 10 scale and connect its probes across the wires from the switch **(see illustration 9)**. Simple ON/OFF type switches, such as brake light switches, only have two wires whereas combination switches, like the ignition switch, have many internal links. Study the wiring diagram to ensure that you are connecting across the correct pair of wires. Continuity (low or no measurable resistance - 0 ohms) should be indicated with the switch ON and no continuity (high resistance) with it OFF.

3 Note that the polarity of the test probes doesn't matter for continuity checks, although care should be taken to follow specific test procedures if a diode or solid-state component is being checked.

4 A continuity tester or battery and bulb circuit can be used in the same way. Connect its probes as described above **(see illustration 10)**. The light should come on to indicate continuity in the ON switch position, but should extinguish in the OFF position.

Wiring checks

- Many electrical faults are caused by damaged wiring, often due to incorrect routing or chaffing on frame components.
- Loose, wet or corroded wire connectors can also be the cause of electrical problems, especially in exposed locations.

1 A continuity check can be made on a single length of wire by disconnecting it at each end and connecting a meter or continuity tester across both ends of the wire **(see illustration 11)**.

2 Continuity (low or no resistance - 0 ohms) should be indicated if the wire is good. If no continuity (high resistance) is shown, suspect a broken wire.

Checking for voltage

- A voltage check can determine whether current is reaching a component.
- Voltage can be checked with a dc voltmeter, multimeter set on the dc volts scale, test light or buzzer **(see illustrations 12 and 13)**. A meter has the advantage of being able to measure actual voltage.
- When using a meter, check that its leads are inserted in the correct terminals on the meter, red to positive (+ve), black to negative (-ve). Incorrect connections can damage the meter.
- A voltmeter (or multimeter set to the dc volts scale) should always be connected in parallel (across the load). Connecting it in series will destroy the meter.
- Voltage checks are made with the ignition ON.

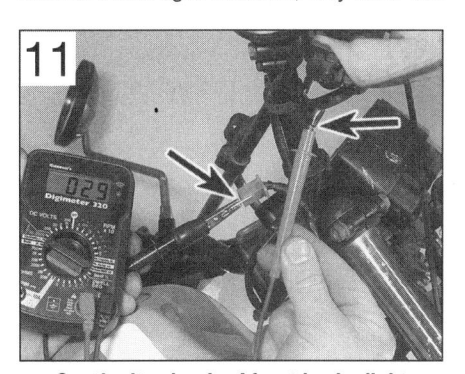

Continuity check of front brake light switch sub-harness

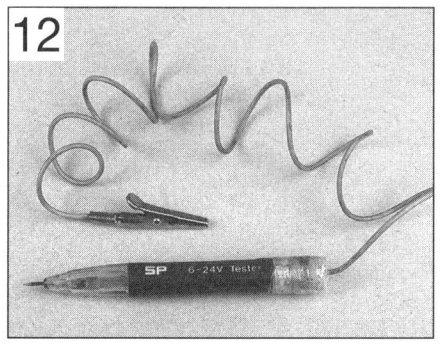

A simple test light can be used for voltage checks

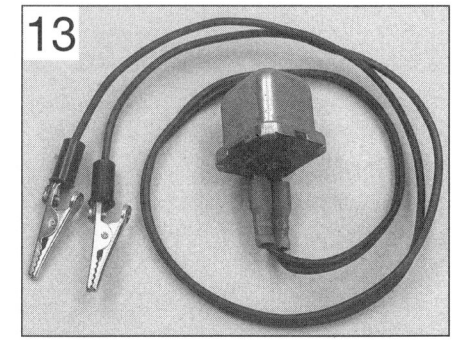

A buzzer is useful for voltage checks

REF•48 Fault Finding Equipment

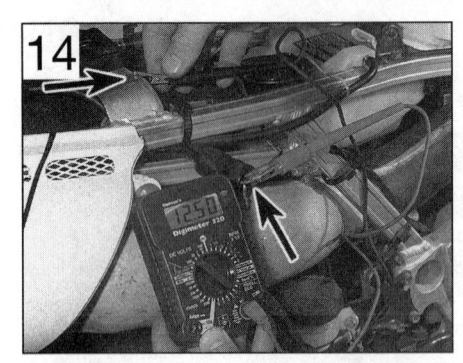

Checking for voltage at the rear brake light power supply wire using a meter . . .

1 First identify the relevant wiring circuit by referring to the wiring diagram at the end of this manual. If other electrical components share the same power supply (ie are fed from the same fuse), take note whether they are working correctly - this is useful information in deciding where to start checking the circuit.
2 If using a meter, check first that the meter leads are plugged into the correct terminals on the meter (see above). Set the meter to the dc volts function, at a range suitable for the battery voltage. Connect the meter red probe (+ve) to the power supply wire and the black probe to a good metal earth (ground) on the motorcycle's frame or directly to the battery negative (-ve) terminal **(see illustration 14)**. Battery voltage should be shown on the meter

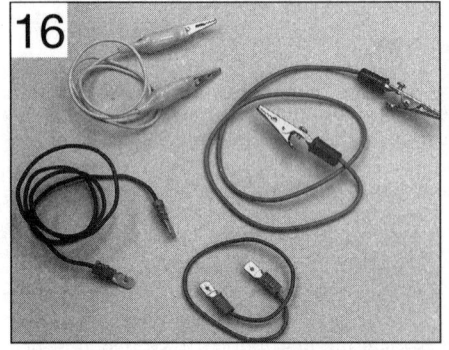

A selection of jumper wires for making earth (ground) checks

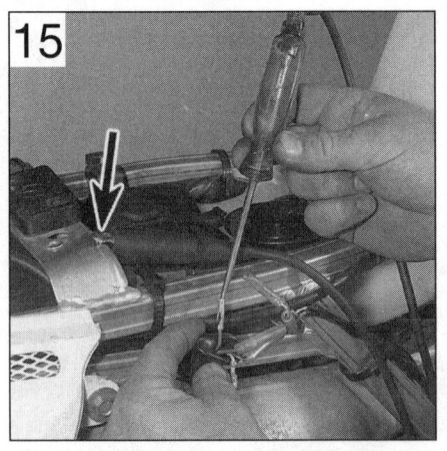

. . . or a test light - note the earth connection to the frame (arrow)

with the ignition switched ON.
3 If using a test light or buzzer, connect its positive (+ve) probe to the power supply terminal and its negative (-ve) probe to a good earth (ground) on the motorcycle's frame or directly to the battery negative (-ve) terminal **(see illustration 15)**. With the ignition ON, the test light should illuminate or the buzzer sound.
4 If no voltage is indicated, work back towards the fuse continuing to check for voltage. When you reach a point where there is voltage, you know the problem lies between that point and your last check point.

Checking the earth (ground)

● Earth connections are made either directly to the engine or frame (such as sensors, neutral switch etc. which only have a positive feed) or by a separate wire into the earth circuit of the wiring harness. Alternatively a short earth wire is sometimes run directly from the component to the motorcycle's frame.
● Corrosion is often the cause of a poor earth connection.
● If total failure is experienced, check the security of the main earth lead from the negative (-ve) terminal of the battery and also the main earth (ground) point on the wiring harness. If corroded, dismantle the connection and clean all surfaces back to bare metal.
1 To check the earth on a component, use an insulated jumper wire to temporarily bypass its earth connection **(see illustration 16)**. Connect one end of the jumper wire between the earth terminal or metal body of the component and the other end to the motorcycle's frame.
2 If the circuit works with the jumper wire installed, the original earth circuit is faulty. Check the wiring for open-circuits or poor connections. Clean up direct earth connections, removing all traces of corrosion and remake the joint. Apply petroleum jelly to the joint to prevent future corrosion.

Tracing a short-circuit

● A short-circuit occurs where current shorts to earth (ground) bypassing the circuit components. This usually results in a blown fuse.

● A short-circuit is most likely to occur where the insulation has worn through due to wiring chafing on a component, allowing a direct path to earth (ground) on the frame.

1 Remove any bodypanels necessary to access the circuit wiring.
2 Check that all electrical switches in the circuit are OFF, then remove the circuit fuse and connect a test light, buzzer or voltmeter (set to the dc scale) across the fuse terminals. No voltage should be shown.
3 Move the wiring from side to side whilst observing the test light or meter. When the test light comes on, buzzer sounds or meter shows voltage, you have found the cause of the short. It will usually shown up as damaged or burned insulation.
4 Note that the same test can be performed on each component in the circuit, even the switch.

Technical Terms Explained REF•49

A

ABS (Anti-lock braking system) A system, usually electronically controlled, that senses incipient wheel lockup during braking and relieves hydraulic pressure at wheel which is about to skid.
Aftermarket Components suitable for the motorcycle, but not produced by the motorcycle manufacturer.
Allen key A hexagonal wrench which fits into a recessed hexagonal hole.
Alternating current (ac) Current produced by an alternator. Requires converting to direct current by a rectifier for charging purposes.
Alternator Converts mechanical energy from the engine into electrical energy to charge the battery and power the electrical system.
Ampere (amp) A unit of measurement for the flow of electrical current. Current = Volts ÷ Ohms.
Ampere-hour (Ah) Measure of battery capacity.
Angle-tightening A torque expressed in degrees. Often follows a conventional tightening torque for cylinder head or main bearing fasteners **(see illustration)**.

Angle-tightening cylinder head bolts

Antifreeze A substance (usually ethylene glycol) mixed with water, and added to the cooling system, to prevent freezing of the coolant in winter. Antifreeze also contains chemicals to inhibit corrosion and the formation of rust and other deposits that would tend to clog the radiator and coolant passages and reduce cooling efficiency.
Anti-dive System attached to the fork lower leg (slider) to prevent fork dive when braking hard.
Anti-seize compound A coating that reduces the risk of seizing on fasteners that are subjected to high temperatures, such as exhaust clamp bolts and nuts.
API American Petroleum Institute. A quality standard for 4-stroke motor oils.
Asbestos A natural fibrous mineral with great heat resistance, commonly used in the composition of brake friction materials. Asbestos is a health hazard and the dust created by brake systems should never be inhaled or ingested.
ATF Automatic Transmission Fluid. Often used in front forks.
ATU Automatic Timing Unit. Mechanical device for advancing the ignition timing on early engines.
ATV All Terrain Vehicle. Often called a Quad.
Axial play Side-to-side movement.
Axle A shaft on which a wheel revolves. Also known as a spindle.

B

Backlash The amount of movement between meshed components when one component is held still. Usually applies to gear teeth.
Ball bearing A bearing consisting of a hardened inner and outer race with hardened steel balls between the two races.
Bearings Used between two working surfaces to prevent wear of the components and a build-up of heat. Four types of bearing are commonly used on motorcycles: plain shell bearings, ball bearings, tapered roller bearings and needle roller bearings.
Bevel gears Used to turn the drive through 90°. Typical applications are shaft final drive and camshaft drive **(see illustration)**.

Bevel gears are used to turn the drive through 90°

BHP Brake Horsepower. The British measurement for engine power output. Power output is now usually expressed in kilowatts (kW).
Bias-belted tyre Similar construction to radial tyre, but with outer belt running at an angle to the wheel rim.
Big-end bearing The bearing in the end of the connecting rod that's attached to the crankshaft.
Bleeding The process of removing air from an hydraulic system via a bleed nipple or bleed screw.
Bottom-end A description of an engine's crankcase components and all components contained there-in.
BTDC Before Top Dead Centre in terms of piston position. Ignition timing is often expressed in terms of degrees or millimetres BTDC.
Bush A cylindrical metal or rubber component used between two moving parts.
Burr Rough edge left on a component after machining or as a result of excessive wear.

C

Cam chain The chain which takes drive from the crankshaft to the camshaft(s).
Canister The main component in an evaporative emission control system (California market only); contains activated charcoal granules to trap vapours from the fuel system rather than allowing them to vent to the atmosphere.
Castellated Resembling the parapets along the top of a castle wall. For example, a castellated wheel axle or spindle nut.
Catalytic converter A device in the exhaust system of some machines which converts certain pollutants in the exhaust gases into less harmful substances.
Charging system Description of the components which charge the battery, ie the alternator, rectifer and regulator.
Circlip A ring-shaped clip used to prevent endwise movement of cylindrical parts and shafts. An internal circlip is installed in a groove in a housing; an external circlip fits into a groove on the outside of a cylindrical piece such as a shaft. Also known as a snap-ring.
Clearance The amount of space between two parts. For example, between a piston and a cylinder, between a bearing and a journal, etc.
Coil spring A spiral of elastic steel found in various sizes throughout a vehicle, for example as a springing medium in the suspension and in the valve train.
Compression Reduction in volume, and increase in pressure and temperature, of a gas, caused by squeezing it into a smaller space.
Compression damping Controls the speed the suspension compresses when hitting a bump.
Compression ratio The relationship between cylinder volume when the piston is at top dead centre and cylinder volume when the piston is at bottom dead centre.
Continuity The uninterrupted path in the flow of electricity. Little or no measurable resistance.
Continuity tester Self-powered bleeper or test light which indicates continuity.
Cp Candlepower. Bulb rating commonly found on US motorcycles.
Crossply tyre Tyre plies arranged in a criss-cross pattern. Usually four or six plies used, hence 4PR or 6PR in tyre size codes.
Cush drive Rubber damper segments fitted between the rear wheel and final drive sprocket to absorb transmission shocks **(see illustration)**.

Cush drive rubbers dampen out transmission shocks

D

Degree disc Calibrated disc for measuring piston position. Expressed in degrees.
Dial gauge Clock-type gauge with adapters for measuring runout and piston position. Expressed in mm or inches.
Diaphragm The rubber membrane in a master cylinder or carburettor which seals the upper chamber.
Diaphragm spring A single sprung plate often used in clutches.
Direct current (dc) Current produced by a dc generator.

Technical Terms Explained

Decarbonisation The process of removing carbon deposits - typically from the combustion chamber, valves and exhaust port/system.
Detonation Destructive and damaging explosion of fuel/air mixture in combustion chamber instead of controlled burning.
Diode An electrical valve which only allows current to flow in one direction. Commonly used in rectifiers and starter interlock systems.
Disc valve (or rotary valve) A induction system used on some two-stroke engines.
Double-overhead camshaft (DOHC) An engine that uses two overhead camshafts, one for the intake valves and one for the exhaust valves.
Drivebelt A toothed belt used to transmit drive to the rear wheel on some motorcycles. A drivebelt has also been used to drive the camshafts. Drivebelts are usually made of Kevlar.
Driveshaft Any shaft used to transmit motion. Commonly used when referring to the final driveshaft on shaft drive motorcycles.

E

Earth return The return path of an electrical circuit, utilising the motorcycle's frame.
ECU (Electronic Control Unit) A computer which controls (for instance) an ignition system, or an anti-lock braking system.
EGO Exhaust Gas Oxygen sensor. Sometimes called a Lambda sensor.
Electrolyte The fluid in a lead-acid battery.
EMS (Engine Management System) A computer controlled system which manages the fuel injection and the ignition systems in an integrated fashion.
Endfloat The amount of lengthways movement between two parts. As applied to a crankshaft, the distance that the crankshaft can move side-to-side in the crankcase.
Endless chain A chain having no joining link. Common use for cam chains and final drive chains.
EP (Extreme Pressure) Oil type used in locations where high loads are applied, such as between gear teeth.
Evaporative emission control system Describes a charcoal filled canister which stores fuel vapours from the tank rather than allowing them to vent to the atmosphere. Usually only fitted to California models and referred to as an EVAP system.
Expansion chamber Section of two-stroke engine exhaust system so designed to improve engine efficiency and boost power.

F

Feeler blade or gauge A thin strip or blade of hardened steel, ground to an exact thickness, used to check or measure clearances between parts.
Final drive Description of the drive from the transmission to the rear wheel. Usually by chain or shaft, but sometimes by belt.
Firing order The order in which the engine cylinders fire, or deliver their power strokes, beginning with the number one cylinder.
Flooding Term used to describe a high fuel level in the carburettor float chambers, leading to fuel overflow. Also refers to excess fuel in the combustion chamber due to incorrect starting technique.

Free length The no-load state of a component when measured. Clutch, valve and fork spring lengths are measured at rest, without any preload.
Freeplay The amount of travel before any action takes place. The looseness in a linkage, or an assembly of parts, between the initial application of force and actual movement. For example, the distance the rear brake pedal moves before the rear brake is actuated.
Fuel injection The fuel/air mixture is metered electronically and directed into the engine intake ports (indirect injection) or into the cylinders (direct injection). Sensors supply information on engine speed and conditions.
Fuel/air mixture The charge of fuel and air going into the engine. See **Stoichiometric ratio**.
Fuse An electrical device which protects a circuit against accidental overload. The typical fuse contains a soft piece of metal which is calibrated to melt at a predetermined current flow (expressed as amps) and break the circuit.

G

Gap The distance the spark must travel in jumping from the centre electrode to the side electrode in a spark plug. Also refers to the distance between the ignition rotor and the pickup coil in an electronic ignition system.
Gasket Any thin, soft material - usually cork, cardboard, asbestos or soft metal - installed between two metal surfaces to ensure a good seal. For instance, the cylinder head gasket seals the joint between the block and the cylinder head.
Gauge An instrument panel display used to monitor engine conditions. A gauge with a movable pointer on a dial or a fixed scale is an analogue gauge. A gauge with a numerical readout is called a digital gauge.
Gear ratios The drive ratio of a pair of gears in a gearbox, calculated on their number of teeth.
Glaze-busting see **Honing**
Grinding Process for renovating the valve face and valve seat contact area in the cylinder head.
Gudgeon pin The shaft which connects the connecting rod small-end with the piston. Often called a piston pin or wrist pin.

H

Helical gears Gear teeth are slightly curved and produce less gear noise that straight-cut gears. Often used for primary drives.

Installing a Helicoil thread insert in a cylinder head

Helicoil A thread insert repair system. Commonly used as a repair for stripped spark plug threads **(see illustration)**.
Honing A process used to break down the glaze on a cylinder bore (also called glaze-busting). Can also be carried out to roughen a rebored cylinder to aid ring bedding-in.
HT (High Tension) Description of the electrical circuit from the secondary winding of the ignition coil to the spark plug.
Hydraulic A liquid filled system used to transmit pressure from one component to another. Common uses on motorcycles are brakes and clutches.
Hydrometer An instrument for measuring the specific gravity of a lead-acid battery.
Hygroscopic Water absorbing. In motorcycle applications, braking efficiency will be reduced if DOT 3 or 4 hydraulic fluid absorbs water from the air - care must be taken to keep new brake fluid in tightly sealed containers.

I

lbf ft Pounds-force feet. An imperial unit of torque. Sometimes written as ft-lbs.
lbf in Pound-force inch. An imperial unit of torque, applied to components where a very low torque is required. Sometimes written as in-lbs.
IC Abbreviation for Integrated Circuit.
Ignition advance Means of increasing the timing of the spark at higher engine speeds. Done by mechanical means (ATU) on early engines or electronically by the ignition control unit on later engines.
Ignition timing The moment at which the spark plug fires, expressed in the number of crankshaft degrees before the piston reaches the top of its stroke, or in the number of millimetres before the piston reaches the top of its stroke.
Infinity (∞) Description of an open-circuit electrical state, where no continuity exists.
Inverted forks (upside down forks) The sliders or lower legs are held in the yokes and the fork tubes or stanchions are connected to the wheel axle (spindle). Less unsprung weight and stiffer construction than conventional forks.

J

JASO Quality standard for 2-stroke oils.
Joule The unit of electrical energy.
Journal The bearing surface of a shaft.

K

Kickstart Mechanical means of turning the engine over for starting purposes. Only usually fitted to mopeds, small capacity motorcycles and off-road motorcycles.
Kill switch Handebar-mounted switch for emergency ignition cut-out. Cuts the ignition circuit on all models, and additionally prevent starter motor operation on others.
km Symbol for kilometre.
kmh Abbreviation for kilometres per hour.

L

Lambda (λ) sensor A sensor fitted in the exhaust system to measure the exhaust gas oxygen content (excess air factor).

Technical Terms Explained REF•51

Lapping see **Grinding**.
LCD Abbreviation for Liquid Crystal Display.
LED Abbreviation for Light Emitting Diode.
Liner A steel cylinder liner inserted in a aluminium alloy cylinder block.
Locknut A nut used to lock an adjustment nut, or other threaded component, in place.
Lockstops The lugs on the lower triple clamp (yoke) which abut those on the frame, preventing handlebar-to-fuel tank contact.
Lockwasher A form of washer designed to prevent an attaching nut from working loose.
LT Low Tension Description of the electrical circuit from the power supply to the primary winding of the ignition coil.

M

Main bearings The bearings between the crankshaft and crankcase.
Maintenance-free (MF) battery A sealed battery which cannot be topped up.
Manometer Mercury-filled calibrated tubes used to measure intake tract vacuum. Used to synchronise carburettors on multi-cylinder engines.
Micrometer A precision measuring instrument that measures component outside diameters **(see illustration)**.

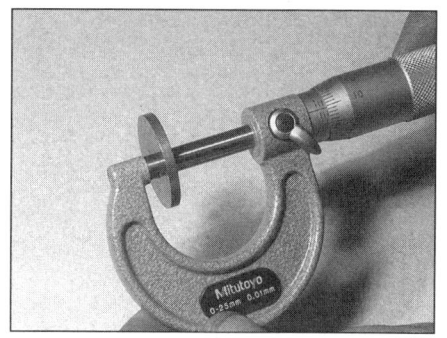

Tappet shims are measured with a micrometer

MON (Motor Octane Number) A measure of a fuel's resistance to knock.
Monograde oil An oil with a single viscosity, eg SAE80W.
Monoshock A single suspension unit linking the swingarm or suspension linkage to the frame.
mph Abbreviation for miles per hour.
Multigrade oil Having a wide viscosity range (eg 10W40). The W stands for Winter, thus the viscosity ranges from SAE10 when cold to SAE40 when hot.
Multimeter An electrical test instrument with the capability to measure voltage, current and resistance. Some meters also incorporate a continuity tester and buzzer.

N

Needle roller bearing Inner race of caged needle rollers and hardened outer race. Examples of uncaged needle rollers can be found on some engines. Commonly used in rear suspension applications and in two-stroke engines.
Nm Newton metres.
NOx Oxides of Nitrogen. A common toxic pollutant emitted by petrol engines at higher temperatures.

O

Octane The measure of a fuel's resistance to knock.
OE (Original Equipment) Relates to components fitted to a motorcycle as standard or replacement parts supplied by the motorcycle manufacturer.
Ohm The unit of electrical resistance. Ohms = Volts ÷ Current.
Ohmmeter An instrument for measuring electrical resistance.
Oil cooler System for diverting engine oil outside of the engine to a radiator for cooling purposes.
Oil injection A system of two-stroke engine lubrication where oil is pump-fed to the engine in accordance with throttle position.
Open-circuit An electrical condition where there is a break in the flow of electricity - no continuity (high resistance).
O-ring A type of sealing ring made of a special rubber-like material; in use, the O-ring is compressed into a groove to provide the sealing action.
Oversize (OS) Term used for piston and ring size options fitted to a rebored cylinder.
Overhead cam (sohc) engine An engine with single camshaft located on top of the cylinder head.
Overhead valve (ohv) engine An engine with the valves located in the cylinder head, but with the camshaft located in the engine block or crankcase.
Oxygen sensor A device installed in the exhaust system which senses the oxygen content in the exhaust and converts this information into an electric current. Also called a Lambda sensor.

P

Plastigauge A thin strip of plastic thread, available in different sizes, used for measuring clearances. For example, a strip of Plastigauge is laid across a bearing journal. The parts are assembled and dismantled; the width of the crushed strip indicates the clearance between journal and bearing.
Polarity Either negative or positive earth (ground), determined by which battery lead is connected to the frame (earth return). Modern motorcycles are usually negative earth.
Pre-ignition A situation where the fuel/air mixture ignites before the spark plug fires. Often due to a hot spot in the combustion chamber caused by carbon build-up. Engine has a tendency to 'run-on'.
Pre-load (suspension) The amount a spring is compressed when in the unloaded state. Preload can be applied by gas, spacer or mechanical adjuster.
Premix The method of engine lubrication on older two-stroke engines. Engine oil is mixed with the petrol in the fuel tank in a specific ratio. The fuel/oil mix is sometimes referred to as "petroil".
Primary drive Description of the drive from the crankshaft to the clutch. Usually by gear or chain.
PS Pfedestärke - a German interpretation of BHP.
PSI Pounds-force per square inch. Imperial measurement of tyre pressure and cylinder pressure measurement.
PTFE Polytetrafluroethylene. A low friction substance.
Pulse secondary air injection system A process of promoting the burning of excess fuel present in the exhaust gases by routing fresh air into the exhaust ports.

Q

Quartz halogen bulb Tungsten filament surrounded by a halogen gas. Typically used for the headlight **(see illustration)**.

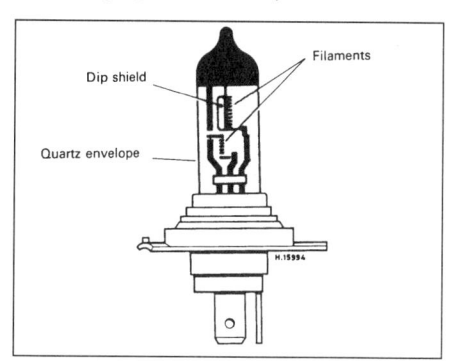

Quartz halogen headlight bulb construction

R

Rack-and-pinion A pinion gear on the end of a shaft that mates with a rack (think of a geared wheel opened up and laid flat). Sometimes used in clutch operating systems.
Radial play Up and down movement about a shaft.
Radial ply tyres Tyre plies run across the tyre (from bead to bead) and around the circumference of the tyre. Less resistant to tread distortion than other tyre types.
Radiator A liquid-to-air heat transfer device designed to reduce the temperature of the coolant in a liquid cooled engine.
Rake A feature of steering geometry - the angle of the steering head in relation to the vertical **(see illustration)**.

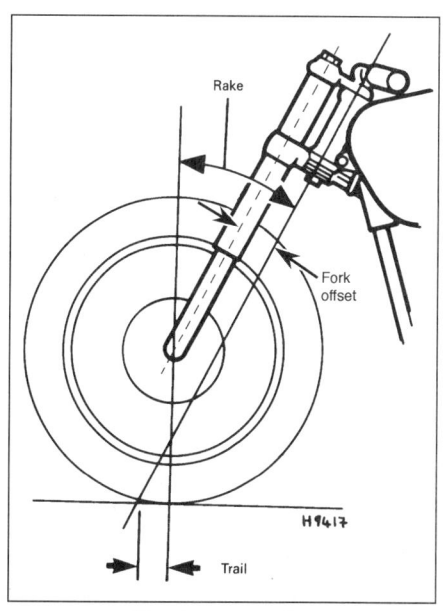

Steering geometry

Technical Terms Explained

Rebore Providing a new working surface to the cylinder bore by boring out the old surface. Necessitates the use of oversize piston and rings.

Rebound damping A means of controlling the oscillation of a suspension unit spring after it has been compressed. Resists the spring's natural tendency to bounce back after being compressed.

Rectifier Device for converting the ac output of an alternator into dc for battery charging.

Reed valve An induction system commonly used on two-stroke engines.

Regulator Device for maintaining the charging voltage from the generator or alternator within a specified range.

Relay A electrical device used to switch heavy current on and off by using a low current auxiliary circuit.

Resistance Measured in ohms. An electrical component's ability to pass electrical current.

RON (Research Octane Number) A measure of a fuel's resistance to knock.

rpm revolutions per minute.

Runout The amount of wobble (in-and-out movement) of a wheel or shaft as it's rotated. The amount a shaft rotates 'out-of-true'. The out-of-round condition of a rotating part.

S

SAE (Society of Automotive Engineers) A standard for the viscosity of a fluid.

Sealant A liquid or paste used to prevent leakage at a joint. Sometimes used in conjunction with a gasket.

Service limit Term for the point where a component is no longer useable and must be renewed.

Shaft drive A method of transmitting drive from the transmission to the rear wheel.

Shell bearings Plain bearings consisting of two shell halves. Most often used as big-end and main bearings in a four-stroke engine. Often called bearing inserts.

Shim Thin spacer, commonly used to adjust the clearance or relative positions between two parts. For example, shims inserted into or under tappets or followers to control valve clearances. Clearance is adjusted by changing the thickness of the shim.

Short-circuit An electrical condition where current shorts to earth (ground) bypassing the circuit components.

Skimming Process to correct warpage or repair a damaged surface, eg on brake discs or drums.

Slide-hammer A special puller that screws into or hooks onto a component such as a shaft or bearing; a heavy sliding handle on the shaft bottoms against the end of the shaft to knock the component free.

Small-end bearing The bearing in the upper end of the connecting rod at its joint with the gudgeon pin.

Spalling Damage to camshaft lobes or bearing journals shown as pitting of the working surface.

Specific gravity (SG) The state of charge of the electrolyte in a lead-acid battery. A measure of the electrolyte's density compared with water.

Straight-cut gears Common type gear used on gearbox shafts and for oil pump and water pump drives.

Stanchion The inner sliding part of the front forks, held by the yokes. Often called a fork tube.

Stoichiometric ratio The optimum chemical air/fuel ratio for a petrol engine, said to be 14.7 parts of air to 1 part of fuel.

Sulphuric acid The liquid (electrolyte) used in a lead-acid battery. Poisonous and extremely corrosive.

Surface grinding (lapping) Process to correct a warped gasket face, commonly used on cylinder heads.

T

Tapered-roller bearing Tapered inner race of caged needle rollers and separate tapered outer race. Examples of taper roller bearings can be found on steering heads.

Tappet A cylindrical component which transmits motion from the cam to the valve stem, either directly or via a pushrod and rocker arm. Also called a cam follower.

TCS Traction Control System. An electronically-controlled system which senses wheel spin and reduces engine speed accordingly.

TDC Top Dead Centre denotes that the piston is at its highest point in the cylinder.

Thread-locking compound Solution applied to fastener threads to prevent slackening. Select type to suit application.

Thrust washer A washer positioned between two moving components on a shaft. For example, between gear pinions on gearshaft.

Timing chain See **Cam Chain**.

Timing light Stroboscopic lamp for carrying out ignition timing checks with the engine running.

Top-end A description of an engine's cylinder block, head and valve gear components.

Torque Turning or twisting force about a shaft.

Torque setting A prescribed tightness specified by the motorcycle manufacturer to ensure that the bolt or nut is secured correctly. Undertightening can result in the bolt or nut coming loose or a surface not being sealed. Overtightening can result in stripped threads, distortion or damage to the component being retained.

Torx key A six-point wrench.

Tracer A stripe of a second colour applied to a wire insulator to distinguish that wire from another one with the same colour insulator. For example, Br/W is often used to denote a brown insulator with a white tracer.

Trail A feature of steering geometry. Distance from the steering head axis to the tyre's central contact point.

Triple clamps The cast components which extend from the steering head and support the fork stanchions or tubes. Often called fork yokes.

Turbocharger A centrifugal device, driven by exhaust gases, that pressurises the intake air. Normally used to increase the power output from a given engine displacement.

TWI Abbreviation for Tyre Wear Indicator. Indicates the location of the tread depth indicator bars on tyres.

U

Universal joint or U-joint (UJ) A double-pivoted connection for transmitting power from a driving to a driven shaft through an angle. Typically found in shaft drive assemblies.

Unsprung weight Anything not supported by the bike's suspension (ie the wheel, tyres, brakes, final drive and bottom (moving) part of the suspension).

V

Vacuum gauges Clock-type gauges for measuring intake tract vacuum. Used for carburettor synchronisation on multi-cylinder engines.

Valve A device through which the flow of liquid, gas or vacuum may be stopped, started or regulated by a moveable part that opens, shuts or partially obstructs one or more ports or passageways. The intake and exhaust valves in the cylinder head are of the poppet type.

Valve clearance The clearance between the valve tip (the end of the valve stem) and the rocker arm or tappet/follower. The valve clearance is measured when the valve is closed. The correct clearance is important - if too small the valve won't close fully and will burn out, whereas if too large noisy operation will result.

Valve lift The amount a valve is lifted off its seat by the camshaft lobe.

Valve timing The exact setting for the opening and closing of the valves in relation to piston position.

Vernier caliper A precision measuring instrument that measures inside and outside dimensions. Not quite as accurate as a micrometer, but more convenient.

VIN Vehicle Identification Number. Term for the bike's engine and frame numbers.

Viscosity The thickness of a liquid or its resistance to flow.

Volt A unit for expressing electrical "pressure" in a circuit. Volts = current x ohms.

W

Water pump A mechanically-driven device for moving coolant around the engine.

Watt A unit for expressing electrical power. Watts = volts x current.

Wear limit see **Service limit**

Wet liner A liquid-cooled engine design where the pistons run in liners which are directly surrounded by coolant **(see illustration)**.

Wet liner arrangement

Wheelbase Distance from the centre of the front wheel to the centre of the rear wheel.

Wiring harness or loom Describes the electrical wires running the length of the motorcycle and enclosed in tape or plastic sheathing. Wiring coming off the main harness is usually referred to as a sub harness.

Woodruff key A key of semi-circular or square section used to locate a gear to a shaft. Often used to locate the alternator rotor on the crankshaft.

Wrist pin Another name for gudgeon or piston pin.

Index REF•53

Note: *References throughout this index are in the form - "Chapter number" • "Page number"*

A

Air filter – 1•8
Air filter housing – 4•4
Air induction system – 1•10, 4•18
Air/fuel mixture adjustment – 4•5
Alternator – 9•19

B

Battery
  checking and charging – 1•18, 9•3
  specifications – 9•1
Body panels – 8•1 *et seq*
Brake
  bleeding and fluid change – 7•12
  calipers – 7•3
  discs – 7•5
  fluid change – 1•22
  fluid level check – 0•14
  master cylinders – 7•5
  hoses and unions – 1•23, 7•12
  pads – 1•14, 7•2
  pedal – 6•2
  seal renewal – 1•22
  specifications – 7•1
  system check – 1•14
Brake light
  bulb renewal – 9•7
  check – 9•5, 9•9
  switches – 9•9

Bulbs
  brake/tail lights – 9•7
  headlights – 9•6
  instrument cluster lights – 9•5
  sidelights – 9•6
  turn signals – 9•8
  wattages – 9•2

C

Cables
  choke – 1•11, 4•13
  clutch – 1•11, 2•20
  lubrication – 1•12
  throttle – 1•10, 4•13
Calipers (brake) – 7•3, 7•8
Cam chain tensioner – 2•10
Cam chain, tensioner blade and guides – 2•14
Camshafts – 2•10
Carburettors
  fuel level check – 4•11
  overhaul – 4•6, 4•8, 4•10
  removal and installation – 4•6
  separation and joining – 4•11
  synchronisation – 1•9
Chain (cam) – 2•14
Chain (final drive)
  check, adjustment and lubrication – 1•6
  pre-ride check – 0•15
  removal and installation – 6•18
  specifications – 6•1

Charging system – 9•19
Choke cable – 1•10, 4•13
Clutch – 2•21
Clutch cable – 1•11, 2•20
Clutch switch – 9•13
Coil (pick-up) – 5•3
Coils (HT) – 5•3
Connecting rods – 2•36
Coolant level check – 0•15
Coolant reservoir – 3•2
Cooling system
  check – 1•12
  draining, flushing and refilling – 1•22
  fan and fan switch – 3•2
  hoses, pipes and unions – 3•8
  temperature display/light and sender – 3•3, 9•10
  thermostat – 3•4
Control unit (ignition) – 5•5
Conversion factors – REF•26
Crankcase halves and cylinder bores – 2•33, 2•51
Crankshaft and main bearings – 2•41
Cush drive – 6•19
Cylinder compression check – 1•23, REF•45
Cylinder head – 2•15, 2•16

D

Dimensions – 0•10
Discs (brake) – 7•5, 7•10

Index

Drive chain
 check, adjustment and lubrication – 1•6
 pre-ride check – 0•15
 removal and installation – 6•18
 sprockets – 6•18

E

Electrical system
 fault finding – 9•2, REF•43
 specifications – 9•1
Engine number – 0•9
Engine/transmission
 cam chain tensioner – 2•10
 cam chain, tensioner blade and guides – 2•14
 camshafts – 2•10
 connecting rods – 2•36
 crankcase halves and cylinder bores – 2•33, 2•51
 crankshaft and main bearings – 2•41
 cylinder compression check – 1•23
 cylinder head – 2•15, 2•16
 followers – 2•10
 idle speed – 1•9
 main and connecting rod bearings – 2•35
 oil change – 1•13
 oil cooler – 2•29
 oil filter change – 1•19
 oil level check – 0•13
 oil pressure check – 1•24
 oil pressure relief valve – 2•30
 oil pump – 2•31
 oil sump – 2•30
 oil strainer – 2•30
 pistons and rings – 2•39, 2•40
 removal and refitting – 2•5
 running-in procedure – 2•53
 specifications – 2•1
 valve clearance check – 1•20
 valve cover – 2•9
 valves/valve seats/valve guides – 2•15, 2•16
Exhaust system – 4•14

F

Fairing – 8•2, 8•5
Fan and fan switch – 3•2
Fault finding – REF•35 et seq
Filter
 air – 1•8
 oil – 1•19
 fuel – 1•19
Final drive
 check, adjustment and lubrication – 1•6
 pre-ride check – 0•15
 removal and installation – 6•18
 specifications – 6•1
 sprockets – 6•18
Followers (cam) – 2•10
Footrests – 6•2
Frame – 6•2
Frame number – 0•9

Front brake
 calipers – 7•3
 discs – 7•5
 master cylinder – 7•5
 pads – 1•14, 7•2
Front mudguard – 8•6
Front suspension (forks)
 adjustment – 6•14
 check – 1•15
 oil change – 1•24
 overhaul – 6•6
 removal and installation – 6•5
 specifications – 6•1
Front wheel
 bearings – 7•17
 removal and installation – 7•14
Fuel system
 carburettors – 4•6 to 4•12
 check – 1•10
 filter and strainer – 1•19
 hose renewal – 1•24
 pump – 4•16
 tank and tap – 4•3
 warning light and sender – 4•17
Fuses – 9•2, 9•4

G

Gearbox – 2•43, 2•45
Gearchange lever – 6•2
Gearchange mechanism – 2•27

H

Handlebar switches – 9•11, 9•12
Handlebars – 6•4
Headlights
 aim – 1•18
 bulb renewal – 9•6
 check and relay – 9•4
 removal and installation – 9•6
Horn – 9•14

I

Idle speed – 1•9
Ignition system
 check – 5•2
 control unit – 5•5
 HT coils – 5•3
 pick-up coil – 5•3
 specifications – 5•1
 throttle position sensor – 5•4
 timing – 5•5
Ignition (main) switch – 9•11
Inner trim panels (fairing) – 8•4
Instrument cluster – 9•10
Instrument lights – 9•5, 9•11

L

Legal check – 0•15
Levers
 handlebar – 6•5
 gearchange – 6•3
 rear brake – 6•2

Lighting system – 9•4
Lower fairing – 8•3
Lubricants (recommended) – 1•2
Lubricants and fluids – REF•23

M

Maintenance schedule – 1•4
Master cylinders (brake)
 fluid level – 0•14
 overhaul – 7•5, 7•10
Mirrors – 8•6
MOT test checks – REF•27
Mudguard (front) – 8•6

N

Neutral switch – 9•12

O

Oil (engine/transmission)
 change – 1•13
 filter – 1•19
 level check – 0•13
Oil (front forks)
 change – 1•24
 type and quantity – 6•1
Oil cooler – 2•29
Oil level display – 9•10
Oil level sensor and relay – 9•14
Oil pressure check – 1•24
Oil pressure relief valve – 2•30
Oil pump – 2•31
Oil strainer – 2•30
Oil sump – 2•30

P

Pads (brake) – 1•14, 7•2, 7•7
Pick-up coil – 5•3
Pistons and rings – 2•39, 2•40
Pressure relief valve (oil) – 2•30
Pump
 fuel – 4•16
 oil – 2•31
 water – 3•6

R

Radiator – 3•5
Radiator pressure cap – 1•12, 3•2
Rear brake
 caliper – 7•8
 disc – 7•10
 master cylinder – 7•10
 pads – 1•14, 7•7
 pedal – 6•2
Rear suspension
 adjustment – 6•14
 check – 1•16
 linkage – 1•20, 6•13
 shock absorber – 6•12
 specifications – 6•1
 swingarm – 6•15, 6•17

Index

Rear view mirrors – 8•6
Rear wheel
 bearings – 7•17
 removal and installation – 7•15
 sprocket coupling/rubber dampers – 6•19
Regulator/rectifier – 9•21
Relay
 fuel pump – 4•16, 9•14
 headlight – 9•4
 starter – 9•15
 starter circuit cut-out relay – 9•13
 turn signal – 9•8

S

Safety – 0•12, 0•15
Seats and seat cowling – 8•2
Security – REF•20
Selector drum and forks – 2•50
Side panels (fairing) – 8•4
Sidelights
 bulb renewal – 9•6
 check – 9•5
Sidestand – 1•18, 6•3
Sidestand switch – 9•13
Spark plugs – 1•7
Specifications
 brakes – 7•1
 clutch – 2•3
 cooling system – 3•1
 electrical system – 9•1
 engine – 2•1
 fuel system – 4•1
 ignition system – 5•1
 maintenance – 1•2
 suspension – 6•1
 transmission – 2•4
 wheels and tyres – 7•2
Speedometer – 9•10
Sprocket coupling
 bearing – 7•18
 rubber dampers – 6•19

Sprockets – 6•18
Starter motor – 9•16
Starter relay – 9•15
Starter clutch and idler gear – 2•25
Steering
 check – 0•15
 head bearings – 1•16, 1•20, 6•11
 stem – 6•10
Storage – REF•32
Strainer
 fuel – 1•19
 oil – 2•30
Sump – 2•30
Suspension
 adjustment – 6•14
 check – 0•15, 1•15, 1•20, 1•22
 front forks – 6•5, 6•6
 rear linkage – 6•13
 rear shock – 6•12
 specifications – 5•1
 swingarm – 6•15, 6•17
Swingarm
 bearing renewal – 6•17
 check – 1•16, 1•22
 removal and installation – 6•15

T

Tachometer – 9•10
Tail light
 bulb renewal – 9•7
 check – 9•5
 removal and installation – 9•7
Tank and tap (fuel) – 4•3
Temperature display/light and sender – 3•3
Tensioner (cam chain) – 2•10
Thermostat – 3•4
Throttle cables – 1•10, 4•13
Throttle position sensor – 5•4
Timing (ignition) – 5•5

Timing (valve) – 2•13
Tools and workshop Tips – REF•2 et seq
Torque settings – 1•2, 2•4, 3•1, 4•2, 5•1, 6•2, 7•2, 9•2
Transmission
 selector drum and forks – 2•50
 shafts – 2•43, 2•45
 specifications – 2•4
Turn signals
 bulbs and assemblies – 9•8
 check and relay – 9•5, 9•8
Tyres
 general information and fitting – 7•19
 pressures and check – 0•16
 sizes – 7•2

V

Valve clearance check – 1•20
Valve cover – 2•9
Valves/valve seats/valve guides – 2•15, 2•16
VIN (Vehicle Identification Number) – 0•9

W

Warning lights – 9•11
Water pump – 3•6
Weights – 1•10
Wheels
 alignment – 7•14
 bearings – 7•17
 check – 1•15, 7•13
 removal and installation – 7•14, 7•15
 specifications – 7•1
Windshield – 8•6
Wiring diagrams – 9•22

Notes

Haynes Motorcycle Manuals – The Complete List

Title	Book No
BMW 2-valve Twins (70 - 96)	♦ 0249
BMW K100 & 75 2-valve Models (83 - 96)	♦ 1373
BMW R850, 1100 & 1150 4-valve Twins (93 - 04)	♦ 3466
BSA Bantam (48 - 71)	0117
BSA Unit Singles (58 - 72)	0127
BSA Pre-unit Singles (54 - 61)	0326
BSA A7 & A10 Twins (47 - 62)	0121
BSA A50 & A65 Twins (62 - 73)	0155
DUCATI 600, 750 & 900 2-valve V-Twins (91 - 96)	♦ 3290
Ducati MK III & Desmo Singles (69 - 76)	◊ 0445
Ducati 748, 916 & 996 4-valve V-Twins (94 - 01)	♦ 3756
GILERA Runner, DNA, Stalker & Ice (97 - 04)	4163
HARLEY-DAVIDSON Sportsters (70 - 03)	♦ 2534
Harley-Davidson Big Twins (73 - on)	2536
Harley-Davidson Twin Cam 88 (99 - 03)	♦ 2478
HONDA NB, ND, NP & NS50 Melody (81 - 85)	◊ 0622
Honda NE/NB50 Vision & SA50 Vision Met-in (85 - 95)	◊ 1278
Honda MB, MBX, MT & MTX50 (80 - 93)	0731
Honda C50, C70 & C90 (67 - 99)	0324
Honda XR80R & XR100R (85 - 04)	2218
Honda XL/XR 80, 100, 125, 185 & 200 2-valve Models (78 - 87)	0566
Honda H100 & H100S Singles (80 - 92)	◊ 0734
Honda CB/CD125T & CM125C Twins (77 - 88)	◊ 0571
Honda CG125 (76 - 00)	◊ 0433
Honda NS125 (86 - 93)	◊ 3056
Honda MBX/MTX125 & MTX200 (83 - 93)	◊ 1132
Honda CD/CM185 200T & CM250C 2-valve Twins (77 - 85)	0572
Honda XL/XR 250 & 500 (78 - 84)	0567
Honda XR250L, XR250R & XR400R (86 - 03)	2219
Honda CB250 & CB400N Super Dreams (78 - 84)	◊ 0540
Honda CR Motocross Bikes (86 - 01)	2222
Honda CBR400RR Fours (88 - 99)	◊ ♦ 3552
Honda VFR400 (NC30) & RVF400 (NC35) V-Fours (89 - 98)	◊ ♦ 3496
Honda CB500 (93 - 01)	◊ ♦ 3753
Honda CB400 & CB550 Fours (73 - 77)	0262
Honda CX/GL500 & 650 V-Twins (78 - 86)	0442
Honda CBX550 Four (82 - 86)	◊ 0940
Honda XL600R & XR600R (83 - 00)	2183
Honda XL600/650V Transalp & XRV750 Africa Twin (87 - 02)	◊ 3919
Honda CBR600F1 & 1000F Fours (87 - 96)	♦ 1730
Honda CBR600F2 & F3 Fours (91 - 98)	♦ 2070
Honda CBR600F4 (99 - 02)	♦ 3911
Honda CB600F Hornet (98 - 02)	◊ ♦ 3915
Honda CB650 sohc Fours (78 - 84)	0665
Honda NTV600 Revere, NTV650 & NT650V Deauville (88 - 01)	◊ 3243
Honda Shadow VT600 & 750 (USA) (88 - 03)	2312
Honda CB750 sohc Four (69 - 79)	0131
Honda V45/65 Sabre & Magna (82 - 88)	0820
Honda VFR750 & 700 V-Fours (86 - 97)	♦ 2101
Honda VFR800 V-Fours (97 - 01)	♦ 3703
Honda CB750 & CB900 dohc Fours (78 - 84)	0535
Honda VTR1000 (FireStorm, Super Hawk) & XL1000V (Varadero) (97 - 00)	♦ 3744
Honda CBR900RR FireBlade (92 - 99)	♦ 2161
Honda CBR900RR FireBlade (00 - 03)	♦ 4060
Honda CBR1100XX Super Blackbird (97 - 02)	♦ 3901
Honda ST1100 Pan European V-Fours (90 - 01)	♦ 3384
Honda Shadow VT1100 (USA) (85 - 98)	2313
Honda GL1000 Gold Wing (75 - 79)	0309
Honda GL1100 Gold Wing (79 - 81)	0669
Honda Gold Wing 1200 (USA) (84 - 87)	2199

Title	Book No
Honda Gold Wing 1500 (USA) (88 - 00)	2225
KAWASAKI AE/AR 50 & 80 (81 - 95)	1007
Kawasaki KC, KE & KH100 (75 - 99)	1371
Kawasaki KMX125 & 200 (86 - 02)	◊ 3046
Kawasaki 250, 350 & 400 Triples (72 - 79)	0134
Kawasaki 400 & 440 Twins (74 - 81)	0281
Kawasaki 400, 500 & 550 Fours (79 - 91)	0910
Kawasaki EN450 & 500 Twins (Ltd/Vulcan) (85 - 04)	2053
Kawasaki EX & ER500 (GPZ500S & ER-5) Twins (87 - 99)	♦ 2052
Kawasaki ZX600 (Ninja ZX-6, ZZ-R600) Fours (90 - 00)	♦ 2146
Kawasaki ZX-6R Ninja Fours (95 - 02)	♦ 3541
Kawasaki ZX600 (GPZ600R, GPX600R, Ninja 600R & RX) & ZX750 (GPX750R, Ninja 750R) Fours (85 - 97)	♦ 1780
Kawasaki 650 Four (76 - 78)	0373
Kawasaki Vulcan 700/750 & 800 (85 - 01)	♦ 2457
Kawasaki 750 Air-cooled Fours (80 - 91)	0574
Kawasaki ZR550 & 750 Zephyr Fours (90 - 97)	♦ 3382
Kawasaki ZX750 (Ninja ZX-7 & ZXR750) Fours (89 - 96)	♦ 2054
Kawasaki Ninja ZX-7R & ZX-9R (ZX750P, ZX900B/C/D/E) (94 - 00)	♦ 3721
Kawasaki 900 & 1000 Fours (73 - 77)	0222
Kawasaki ZX900, 1000 & 1100 Liquid-cooled Fours (83 - 97)	♦ 1681
MOTO GUZZI 750, 850 & 1000 V-Twins (74 - 78)	0339
MZ ETZ Models (81 - 95)	◊ 1680
NORTON 500, 600, 650 & 750 Twins (57 - 70)	0187
Norton Commando (68 - 77)	0125
PEUGEOT Speedfight, Trekker & Vivacity (96 - 02)	◊ 3920
PIAGGIO (Vespa) Scooters (91 - 03)	◊ 3492
SUZUKI GT, ZR & TS50 (77 - 90)	◊ 0799
Suzuki TS50X (84 - 00)	◊ 1599
Suzuki 100, 125, 185 & 250 Air-cooled Trail bikes (79 - 89)	0797
Suzuki GP100 & 125 Singles (78 - 93)	◊ 0576
Suzuki GS, GN, GZ & DR125 Singles (82 - 99)	◊ 0888
Suzuki 250 & 350 Twins (68 - 78)	0120
Suzuki GT250X7, GT200X5 & SB200 Twins (78 - 83)	◊ 0469
Suzuki GS/GSX250, 400 & 450 Twins (79 - 85)	0736
Suzuki GS500 Twin (89 - 02)	♦ 3238
Suzuki GS550 (77 - 82) & GS750 Fours (76 - 79)	0363
Suzuki GS/GSX550 4-valve Fours (83 - 88)	1133
Suzuki SV650 (99 - 02)	♦ 3912
Suzuki GSX-R600 & 750 (96 - 00)	♦ 3553e
Suzuki GSX-R600 (01 - 02), GSX-R750 (00 - 02) & GSX-R1000 (01 - 02)	♦ 3986e
Suzuki GSF600 & 1200 Bandit Fours (95 - 04)	♦ 3367
Suzuki GS850 Fours (78 - 88)	0536
Suzuki GS1000 Four (77 - 79)	0484
Suzuki GSX-R750, GSX-R1100 (85 - 92), GSX600F, GSX750F, GSX1100F (Katana) Fours (88 - 96)	♦ 2055
Suzuki GSX600/750F & GSX750 (98 - 02)	♦ 3987
Suzuki GS/GSX1000, 1100 & 1150 4-valve Fours (79 - 88)	0737
Suzuki TL1000S/R & DL1000 V-Strom (97 - 04)	♦ 4083
Suzuki GSX1300R Hayabusa (99 - 04)	♦ 4184
TRIUMPH Tiger Cub & Terrier (52 - 68)	0414
Triumph 350 & 500 Unit Twins (58 - 73)	0137
Triumph Pre-Unit Twins (47 - 62)	0251
Triumph 650 & 750 2-valve Unit Twins (63 - 83)	0122
Triumph Trident & BSA Rocket 3 (69 - 75)	0136
Triumph Fuel Injected Triples (97 - 00)	♦ 3755
Triumph Triples & Fours (carburettor engines) (91 - 99)	♦ 2162
VESPA P/PX125, 150 & 200 Scooters (78 - 03)	0707
Vespa Scooters (59 - 78)	0126
YAMAHA DT50 & 80 Trail Bikes (78 - 95)	◊ 0800
Yamaha T50 & 80 Townmate (83 - 95)	◊ 1247
Yamaha YB100 Singles (73 - 91)	◊ 0474

Title	Book No
Yamaha RS/RXS100 & 125 Singles (74 - 95)	0331
Yamaha RD & DT125LC (82 - 87)	◊ 0887
Yamaha TZR125 (87 - 93) & DT125R (88 - 02)	◊ 1655
Yamaha TY50, 80, 125 & 175 (74 - 84)	◊ 0464
Yamaha XT & SR125 (82 - 02)	◊ 1021
Yamaha Trail Bikes (81 - 00)	2350
Yamaha 250 & 350 Twins (70 - 79)	0040
Yamaha XS250, 360 & 400 sohc Twins (75 - 84)	0378
Yamaha RD250 & 350LC Twins (80 - 82)	0803
Yamaha RD350 YPVS Twins (83 - 95)	1158
Yamaha RD400 Twin (75 - 79)	0333
Yamaha XT, TT & SR500 Singles (75 - 83)	0342
Yamaha XZ550 Vision V-Twins (82 - 85)	0821
Yamaha FJ, FZ, XJ & YX600 Radian (84 - 92)	2100
Yamaha XJ600S (Diversion, Seca II) & XJ600N Fours (92 - 03)	♦ 2145
Yamaha YZF600R Thundercat & FZS600 Fazer (96 - 03)	♦ 3702
Yamaha YZF-R6 (98 - 02)	♦ 3900
Yamaha 650 Twins (70 - 83)	0341
Yamaha XJ650 & 750 Fours (80 - 84)	0738
Yamaha XS750 & 850 Triples (76 - 85)	0340
Yamaha TDM850, TRX850 & XTZ750 (89 - 99)	◊ ♦ 3540
Yamaha YZF750R & YZF1000R Thunderace (93 - 00)	♦ 3720
Yamaha FZR600, 750 & 1000 Fours (87 - 96)	♦ 2056
Yamaha XV (Virago) V-Twins (81 - 03)	♦ 0802
Yamaha XVS650 & 1100 Dragstar/V-Star (97 - 04)	♦ 4195
Yamaha XJ900F Fours (83 - 94)	♦ 3239
Yamaha XJ900S Diversion (94 - 01)	♦ 3739
Yamaha YZF-R1 (98 - 01)	♦ 3754
Yamaha FJ1100 & 1200 Fours (84 - 96)	♦ 2057
Yamaha XJR1200 & 1300 (95 - 03)	♦ 3981
Yamaha V-Max (85 - 03)	♦ 4072
ATVs	
Honda ATC70, 90, 110, 185 & 200 (71 - 85)	0565
Honda TRX300 Shaft Drive ATVs (88 - 00)	2125
Honda TRX300EX & TRX400EX ATVs (93 - 04)	2318
Honda Foreman 400 and 450 ATVs (95 - 02)	2465
Kawasaki Bayou 220/250/300 & Prairie 300 ATVs (86 - 03)	2351
Polaris ATVs (85 - 97)	2302
Polaris ATVs (98 - 03)	2508
Yamaha YFS200 Blaster ATV (88 - 98)	2317
Yamaha YFB250 Timberwolf ATVs (92 - 00)	2217
Yamaha YFM350 & YFM400 (ER and Big Bear) ATVs (87 - 03)	2126
Yamaha Banshee and Warrior ATVs (87 - 03)	2314
ATV Basics	10450
TECHBOOK SERIES	
Motorcycle Basics TechBook (2nd Edition)	3515
Motorcycle Electrical TechBook (3rd Edition)	3471
Motorcycle Fuel Systems TechBook	3514
Motorcycle Maintenance TechBook	4071
Motorcycle Workshop Practice TechBook (2nd Edition)	3470
GENERAL MANUALS	
Twist and Go (automatic transmission) Scooters Service and Repair Manual	4082

◊ = not available in the USA   ♦ = Superbike

The manuals on this page are available through good motorcycle dealers and accessory shops.
In case of difficulty, contact: **Haynes Publishing**
(UK) +44 1963 442030   (USA) +1 805 498 6703
(FR) +33 1 47 17 66 29   (SV) +46 18 124016
(Australia/New Zealand) +61 3 9763 8100

MCL17.10/04

Preserving Our Motoring Heritage

The Model J Duesenberg Derham Tourster. Only eight of these magnificent cars were ever built – this is the only example to be found outside the United States of America

Almost every car you've ever loved, loathed or desired is gathered under one roof at the Haynes Motor Museum. Over 300 immaculately presented cars and motorbikes represent every aspect of our motoring heritage, from elegant reminders of bygone days, such as the superb Model J Duesenberg to curiosities like the bug-eyed BMW Isetta. There are also many old friends and flames. Perhaps you remember the 1959 Ford Popular that you did your courting in? The magnificent 'Red Collection' is a spectacle of classic sports cars including AC, Alfa Romeo, Austin Healey, Ferrari, Lamborghini, Maserati, MG, Riley, Porsche and Triumph.

A Perfect Day Out

Each and every vehicle at the Haynes Motor Museum has played its part in the history and culture of Motoring. Today, they make a wonderful spectacle and a great day out for all the family. Bring the kids, bring Mum and Dad, but above all bring your camera to capture those golden memories for ever. You will also find an impressive array of motoring memorabilia, a comfortable 70 seat video cinema and one of the most extensive transport book shops in Britain. The Pit Stop Cafe serves everything from a cup of tea to wholesome, home-made meals or, if you prefer, you can enjoy the large picnic area nestled in the beautiful rural surroundings of Somerset.

John Haynes O.B.E., Founder and Chairman of the museum at the wheel of a Haynes Light 12.

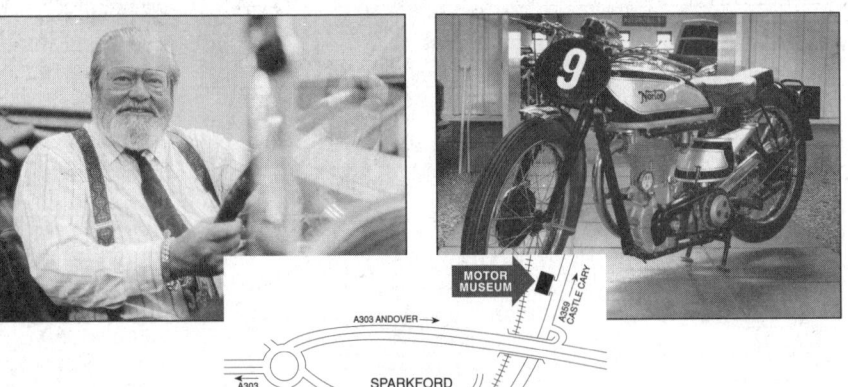

The 1936 490cc sohc-engined International Norton – well known for its racing success

The Museum is situated on the A359 Yeovil to Frome road at Sparkford, just off the A303 in Somerset. It is about 40 miles south of Bristol, and 25 minutes drive from the M5 intersection at Taunton.
Open 9.30am - 5.30pm (10.00am - 4.00pm Winter) 7 days a week, *except Christmas Day, Boxing Day and New Years Day*
Special rates available for schools, coach parties and outings Charitable Trust No. 292048